Advanced Econometrics

Advanced Econometrics

Takeshi Amemiya

Harvard University Press Cambridge, Massachusetts

Printed in the United States of America
10 9 8 7 6 5 4

This book is printed on acid-free paper, and its binding materials have been chosen for strength and durability.

Library of Congress Cataloging in Publication Data
Amemiya, Takeshi.
Advanced econometrics.
Bibliography: p.
Includes index.
1. Econometrics. I. Title.
HB139.A54 1985 330′.028 85-845
ISBN 0-674-00560-0 (alk. paper)

Preface

This book is intended both as a reference book for professional econometricians and as a graduate textbook. If it is used as a textbook, the material contained in the book can be taught in a year-long course, as I have done at Stanford for many years. The prerequisites for such a course should be one year of calculus, one quarter or semester of matrix analysis, one year of intermediate statistical inference (see list of textbooks in note 1 of Chapter 3), and, preferably, knowledge of introductory or intermediate econometrics (say, at the level of Johnston, 1972). This last requirement is not necessary, but I have found in the past that a majority of economics students who take a graduate course in advanced econometrics do have knowledge of introductory or intermediate econometrics.

The main features of the book are the following: a thorough treatment of classical least squares theory (Chapter 1) and generalized least squares theory (Chapter 6); a rigorous discussion of large sample theory (Chapters 3 and 4); a detailed analysis of qualitative response models (Chapter 9), censored or truncated regression models (Chapter 10), and Markov chain and duration models (Chapter 11); and a discussion of nonlinear simultaneous equations models (Chapter 8).

The book presents only the fundamentals of time series analysis (Chapter 5 and a part of Chapter 6) because there are several excellent textbooks on the subject (see the references cited at the beginning of Chapter 5). In contrast, the models I discuss in the last three chapters have been used extensively in recent econometric applications but have not received in any textbook as complete a treatment as I give them here. Some instructors may wish to supplement my book with a textbook in time series analysis.

My discussion of linear simultaneous equations models (Chapter 7) is also brief. Those who wish to study the subject in greater detail should consult the references given in Chapter 7. I chose to devote more space to the discussion of nonlinear simultaneous equations models, which are still at an early stage of development and consequently have received only scant coverage in most textbooks.

In many parts of the book, and in all of Chapters 3 and 4, I have used the theorem-proof format and have attempted to develop all the mathematical results rigorously. However, it has not been my aim to present theorems in full mathematical generality. Because I intended this as a textbook rather than as a monograph, I chose assumptions that are relatively easy to understand and that lead to simple proofs, even in those instances where they could be relaxed. This will enable readers to understand the basic structure of each theorem and to generalize it for themselves depending on their needs and abilities. Many simple applications of theorems are given either in the form of examples in the text or in the form of exercises at the end of each chapter to bring out the essential points of each theorem.

Although this is a textbook in econometrics methodology, I have included discussions of numerous empirical papers to illustrate the practical use of theoretical results. This is especially conspicuous in the last three chapters of the book.

Too many people have contributed to the making of this book through the many revisions it has undergone to mention all their names. I am especially grateful to Trevor Breusch, Hidehiko Ichimura, Tom MaCurdy, Jim Powell, and Gene Savin for giving me valuable comments on the entire manuscript. I am also indebted to Carl Christ, Art Goldberger, Cheng Hsiao, Roger Koenker, Tony Lancaster, Chuck Manski, and Hal White for their valuable comments on parts of the manuscript. I am grateful to Colin Cameron, Tom Downes, Harry Paarsch, Aaron Han, and Choon Moon for proofreading and to the first three for correcting my English. In addition, Tom Downes and Choon Moon helped me with the preparation of the index. Dzung Pham has typed most of the manuscript through several revisions; her unfailing patience and good nature despite many hours of overtime work are much appreciated. David Criswell, Cathy Shimizu, and Bach-Hong Tran have also helped with the typing. The financial support of the National Science Foundation for the research that produced many of the results presented in the book is gratefully acknowledged. Finally, I am indebted to the editors of the *Journal of Economic Literature* for permission to include in Chapter 9 parts of my article entitled "Qualitative Response Models: A Survey" (*Journal of Economic Literature* 19:1483–1536, 1981) and to North-Holland Publishing Company for permission to use in Chapter 10 the revised version of my article entitled "Tobit Models: A Survey" (*Journal of Econometrics* 24:3–61, 1984).

Contents

1 Classical Least Squares Theory 1
2 Recent Developments in Regression Analysis 45
3 Large Sample Theory 81
4 Asymptotic Properties of Extremum Estimators 105
5 Time Series Analysis 159
6 Generalized Least Squares Theory 181
7 Linear Simultaneous Equations Models 228
8 Nonlinear Simultaneous Equations Models 245
9 Qualitative Response Models 267
10 Tobit Models 360
11 Markov Chain and Duration Models 412

Appendix 1 Useful Theorems in Matrix Analysis 459
Appendix 2 Distribution Theory 463
Notes 465
References 475
Name Index 505
Subject Index 511

Advanced Econometrics

1 Classical Least Squares Theory

In this chapter we shall consider the basic results of statistical inference in the classical linear regression model—the model in which the regressors are independent of the error term and the error term is serially uncorrelated and has a constant variance. This model is the starting point of the study; the models to be examined in later chapters are modifications of this one.

1.1 Linear Regression Model

In this section let us look at the reasons for studying the linear regression model and the method of specifying it. We shall start by defining Model 1, to be considered throughout the chapter.

1.1.1 Introduction

Consider a sequence of K random variables $(y_t, x_{2t}, x_{3t}, \ldots, x_{Kt})$, $t = 1, 2, \ldots, T$. Define a T-vector $\mathbf{y} = (y_1, y_2, \ldots, y_T)'$, a $(K-1)$-vector $\mathbf{x}_t^* = (x_{2t}, x_{3t}, \ldots, x_{Kt})'$, and a $[(K-1) \times T]$-vector $\mathbf{x}^* = (\mathbf{x}_1^{*\prime}, \mathbf{x}_2^{*\prime}, \ldots, \mathbf{x}_T^{*\prime})'$. Suppose for the sake of exposition that the joint density of the variables is given by $f(\mathbf{y}, \mathbf{x}^*, \boldsymbol{\theta})$, where $\boldsymbol{\theta}$ is a vector of unknown parameters. We are concerned with inference about the parameter vector $\boldsymbol{\theta}$ on the basis of the observed vectors $\mathbf{y}$ and $\mathbf{x}^*$.

In econometrics we are often interested in the conditional distribution of one set of random variables given another set of random variables; for example, the conditional distribution of consumption given income and the conditional distribution of quantities demanded given prices. Suppose we want to know the conditional distribution of $\mathbf{y}$ given $\mathbf{x}^*$. We can write the joint density as the product of the conditional density and the marginal density as in

$$f(\mathbf{y}, \mathbf{x}^*, \boldsymbol{\theta}) = f(\mathbf{y}|\mathbf{x}^*, \boldsymbol{\theta}_1) f(\mathbf{x}^*, \boldsymbol{\theta}_2). \tag{1.1.1}$$

Regression analysis can be defined as statistical inferences on $\boldsymbol{\theta}_1$. For this purpose we can ignore $f(\mathbf{x}^*, \boldsymbol{\theta}_2)$, provided there is no relationship between $\boldsymbol{\theta}_1$

and $\boldsymbol{\theta}_2$. The vector $\mathbf{y}$ is called the vector of *dependent* or *endogenous* variables, and the vector $\mathbf{x}^*$ is called the vector of *independent* or *exogenous* variables.

In regression analysis we usually want to estimate only the first and second moments of the conditional distribution, rather than the whole parameter vector $\boldsymbol{\theta}_1$. (In certain special cases the first two moments characterize $\boldsymbol{\theta}_1$ completely.) Thus we can define regression analysis as statistical inference on the conditional mean $E(\mathbf{y}|\mathbf{x}^*)$ and the conditional variance-covariance matrix $V(\mathbf{y}|\mathbf{x}^*)$. Generally, these moments are nonlinear functions of $\mathbf{x}^*$. However, in the present chapter we shall consider the special case in which $E(y_t|\mathbf{x}^*)$ is equal to $E(y_t|\mathbf{x}_t^*)$ and is a linear function of $\mathbf{x}_t^*$, and $V(\mathbf{y}|\mathbf{x}^*)$ is a constant times an identity matrix. Such a model is called the *classical* (or *standard*) linear regression model or the *homoscedastic* (meaning constant variance) linear regression model. Because this is the model to be studied in Chapter 1, let us call it simply Model 1.

1.1.2 Model 1

By writing $\mathbf{x}_t = (1, \mathbf{x}_t^{*\prime})'$, we can define Model 1 as follows. Assume

$$y_t = \mathbf{x}_t'\boldsymbol{\beta} + u_t, \qquad t = 1, 2, \ldots, T, \tag{1.1.2}$$

where y_t is a scalar observable random variable, $\boldsymbol{\beta}$ is a K-vector of unknown parameters, $\mathbf{x}_t$ is a K-vector of known constants such that $\Sigma_{t=1}^T \mathbf{x}_t\mathbf{x}_t'$ is nonsingular, and u_t is a scalar, unobservable, random variable (called the error term or the disturbance) such that $Eu_t = 0$, $Vu_t = \sigma^2$ (another unknown parameter) for all t, and $Eu_tu_s = 0$ for $t \neq s$.

Note that we have assumed $\mathbf{x}^*$ to be a vector of known constants. This is essentially equivalent to stating that we are concerned only with estimating the conditional distribution of $\mathbf{y}$ given $\mathbf{x}^*$. The most important assumption of Model 1 is the linearity of $E(y_t|\mathbf{x}_t^*)$; we therefore shall devote the next subsection to a discussion of the implications of that assumption. We have also made the assumption of homoscedasticity ($Vu_t = \sigma^2$ for all t) and the assumption of no serial correlation ($Eu_tu_s = 0$ for $t \neq s$), not because we believe that they are satisfied in most applications, but because they make a convenient starting point. These assumptions will be removed in later chapters.

We shall sometimes impose additional assumptions on Model 1 to obtain certain specific results. Notably, we shall occasionally make the assumption of serial independence of $\{u_t\}$ or the assumption that u_t is normally distributed. In general, independence is a stronger assumption than no correlation, although under normality the two concepts are equivalent. The additional assumptions will be stated whenever they are introduced into Model 1.

1.1.3 Implications of Linearity

Suppose random variables y_t and $\mathbf{x}_t^*$ have finite second moments and their variance-covariance matrix is denoted by

$$V\begin{bmatrix} y_t \\ \mathbf{x}_t^* \end{bmatrix} = \begin{bmatrix} \sigma_1^2 & \boldsymbol{\sigma}_{12}' \\ \boldsymbol{\sigma}_{12} & \boldsymbol{\Sigma}_{22} \end{bmatrix}.$$

Then we can always write

$$y_t = \beta_0 + \mathbf{x}_t^{*\prime}\boldsymbol{\beta}_1 + v_t, \tag{1.1.3}$$

where $\boldsymbol{\beta}_1 = \boldsymbol{\Sigma}_{22}^{-1}\boldsymbol{\sigma}_{12}$, $\beta_0 = Ey_t - \boldsymbol{\sigma}_{12}'\boldsymbol{\Sigma}_{22}^{-1}E\mathbf{x}_t^*$, $Ev_t = 0$, $Vv_t = \sigma_1^2 - \boldsymbol{\sigma}_{12}'\boldsymbol{\Sigma}_{22}^{-1}\boldsymbol{\sigma}_{12}$, and $E\mathbf{x}_t^* v_t = \mathbf{0}$. It is important to realize that Model 1 implies certain assumptions that (1.1.3) does not: (1.1.3) does not generally imply linearity of $E(y_t|\mathbf{x}_t^*)$ because $E(v_t|\mathbf{x}_t^*)$ may not generally be zero.

We call $\beta_0 + \mathbf{x}_t^{*\prime}\boldsymbol{\beta}_1$ in (1.1.3) the *best linear predictor* of y_t given $\mathbf{x}_t^*$ because β_0 and $\boldsymbol{\beta}_1$ can be shown to be the values of b_0 and $\mathbf{b}_1$ that minimize $E(y_t - b_0 - \mathbf{x}_t^{*\prime}\mathbf{b}_1)^2$. In contrast, the conditional mean $E(y_t|\mathbf{x}_t^*)$ is called the *best predictor* of y_t given $\mathbf{x}_t^*$ because $E[y_t - E(y_t|\mathbf{x}_t^*)]^2 \leqq E[y_t - g(\mathbf{x}_t^*)]^2$ for any function g.

The reader might ask why we work with eq. (1.1.2) rather than with (1.1.3). The answer is that (1.1.3) is so general that it does not allow us to obtain interesting results. For example, whereas the natural estimators of β_0 and $\boldsymbol{\beta}_1$ can be defined by replacing the moments of y_t and $\mathbf{x}_t^*$ that characterize β_0 and $\boldsymbol{\beta}_1$ with their corresponding sample moments (they actually coincide with the least squares estimator), the mean of the estimator cannot be evaluated without specifying more about the relationship between $\mathbf{x}_t^*$ and v_t.

How restrictive is the linearity of $E(y_t|\mathbf{x}_t^*)$? It holds if y_t and $\mathbf{x}_t^*$ are jointly normal or if y_t and $\mathbf{x}_t^*$ are both scalar dichotomous (Bernoulli) variables.[1] But the linearity may not hold for many interesting distributions. Nevertheless, the linear assumption is not as restrictive as it may appear at first glance because $\mathbf{x}_t^*$ can be variables obtained by transforming the original independent variables in various ways. For example, if the conditional mean of y_t, the supply of good, is a quadratic function of the price, p_t, we can put $\mathbf{x}_t^* = (p_t, p_t^2)'$, thereby making $E(y_t|\mathbf{x}_t^*)$ linear.

1.1.4 Matrix Notation

To facilitate the subsequent analysis, we shall write (1.1.2) in matrix notation as

$$\mathbf{y} = \mathbf{X}\boldsymbol{\beta} + \mathbf{u}, \tag{1.1.4}$$

where $\mathbf{y} = (y_1, y_2, \ldots, y_T)'$, $\mathbf{u} = (u_1, u_2, \ldots, u_T)'$, and $\mathbf{X} = (\mathbf{x}_1, \mathbf{x}_2, \ldots, \mathbf{x}_T)'$. In other words, $\mathbf{X}$ is the $T \times K$ matrix, the tth row of which is $\mathbf{x}_t'$. The elements of the matrix $\mathbf{X}$ are described as

$$\mathbf{X} = \begin{bmatrix} x_{11} & x_{12} & \cdots & x_{1K} \\ x_{21} & x_{22} & \cdots & x_{2K} \\ \cdot & \cdot & & \cdot \\ \cdot & \cdot & & \cdot \\ \cdot & \cdot & & \cdot \\ x_{T1} & x_{T2} & \cdots & x_{TK} \end{bmatrix}.$$

If we want to focus on the columns of $\mathbf{X}$, we can write $\mathbf{X} = [\mathbf{x}_{(1)}, \mathbf{x}_{(2)}, \ldots, \mathbf{x}_{(K)}]$, where each $\mathbf{x}_{(i)}$ is a T-vector. If there is no danger of confusing $\mathbf{x}_{(i)}$ with $\mathbf{x}_t$, we can drop the parentheses and write simply $\mathbf{x}_i$. In matrix notation the assumptions on $\mathbf{X}$ and $\mathbf{u}$ can be stated as follows: $\mathbf{X}'\mathbf{X}$ is nonsingular, which is equivalent to stating rank $(\mathbf{X}) = K$ if $T \geqq K$; $E\mathbf{u} = \mathbf{0}$; and $E\mathbf{uu}' = \sigma^2 \mathbf{I}_T$, where $\mathbf{I}_T$ is the $T \times T$ identity matrix. (Whenever the size of an identity matrix can be inferred from the context, we write it simply as $\mathbf{I}$.)

In the remainder of this chapter we shall no longer use the partition $\boldsymbol{\beta}' = (\beta_0, \boldsymbol{\beta}_1')$; instead, the elements of $\boldsymbol{\beta}$ will be written as $\boldsymbol{\beta} = (\beta_1, \beta_2, \ldots, \beta_K)'$. Similarly, we shall not necessarily assume that $\mathbf{x}_{(1)}$ is the vector of ones, although in practice this is usually the case. Most of our results will be obtained simply on the assumption that $\mathbf{X}$ is a matrix of constants, without specifying specific values.

1.2 Theory of Least Squares

In this section we shall define the least squares estimator of the parameter $\boldsymbol{\beta}$ in Model 1 and shall show that it is the best linear unbiased estimator. We shall also discuss estimation of the error variance σ^2.

1.2.1 Definition of Least Squares Estimators of $\boldsymbol{\beta}$ and σ^2

The least squares (LS) estimator $\hat{\boldsymbol{\beta}}$ of the regression parameter $\boldsymbol{\beta}$ in Model 1 is defined to be the value of $\boldsymbol{\beta}$ that minimizes the sum of squared residuals[2]

$$S(\boldsymbol{\beta}) = (\mathbf{y} - \mathbf{X}\boldsymbol{\beta})'(\mathbf{y} - \mathbf{X}\boldsymbol{\beta}) \tag{1.2.1}$$
$$= \mathbf{y}'\mathbf{y} - 2\mathbf{y}'\mathbf{X}\boldsymbol{\beta} + \boldsymbol{\beta}'\mathbf{X}'\mathbf{X}\boldsymbol{\beta}.$$

Putting the derivatives of $S(\boldsymbol{\beta})$ with respect to $\boldsymbol{\beta}$ equal to 0, we have

$$\frac{\partial S}{\partial \boldsymbol{\beta}} = -2\mathbf{X}'\mathbf{y} + 2\mathbf{X}'\mathbf{X}\boldsymbol{\beta} = \mathbf{0}, \tag{1.2.2}$$

where $\partial S/\partial \boldsymbol{\beta}$ denotes the K-vector the ith element of which is $\partial S/\partial \beta_i$, β_i being the ith element of $\boldsymbol{\beta}$. Solving (1.2.2) for $\boldsymbol{\beta}$ gives

$$\hat{\boldsymbol{\beta}} = (\mathbf{X}'\mathbf{X})^{-1}\mathbf{X}'\mathbf{y}. \tag{1.2.3}$$

Clearly, $S(\boldsymbol{\beta})$ attains the global minimum at $\hat{\boldsymbol{\beta}}$.

Let us consider the special case $K = 2$ and $\mathbf{x}_t' = (1, x_{2t})$ and represent each of the T-observations (y_t, x_{2t}) by a point on the plane. Then, geometrically, the least squares estimates are the intercept and the slope of a line drawn in such a way that the sum of squares of the deviations between the points and the line is minimized in the direction of the y-axis. Different estimates result if the sum of squares of deviations is minimized in any other direction.

Given the least squares estimator $\hat{\boldsymbol{\beta}}$, we define

$$\hat{\mathbf{u}} = \mathbf{y} - \mathbf{X}\hat{\boldsymbol{\beta}} \tag{1.2.4}$$

and call it the vector of the *least squares residuals*. Using $\hat{\mathbf{u}}$, we can estimate σ^2 by

$$\hat{\sigma}^2 = T^{-1}\hat{\mathbf{u}}'\hat{\mathbf{u}}, \tag{1.2.5}$$

called the least squares estimator of σ^2, although the use of the term *least squares* here is not as compelling as in the estimation of the regression parameters.

Using (1.2.4), we can write

$$\mathbf{y} = \mathbf{X}\hat{\boldsymbol{\beta}} + \hat{\mathbf{u}} = \mathbf{P}\mathbf{y} + \mathbf{M}\mathbf{y}, \tag{1.2.6}$$

where $\mathbf{P} = \mathbf{X}(\mathbf{X}'\mathbf{X})^{-1}\mathbf{X}'$ and $\mathbf{M} = \mathbf{I} - \mathbf{P}$. Because $\hat{\mathbf{u}}$ is orthogonal to $\mathbf{X}$ (that is, $\hat{\mathbf{u}}'\mathbf{X} = \mathbf{0}$), least squares estimation can be regarded as decomposing $\mathbf{y}$ into two orthogonal components: a component that can be written as a linear combination of the column vectors of $\mathbf{X}$ and a component that is orthogonal to $\mathbf{X}$. Alternatively, we can call $\mathbf{P}\mathbf{y}$ the projection of $\mathbf{y}$ onto the space spanned by the column vectors of $\mathbf{X}$ and $\mathbf{M}\mathbf{y}$ the projection of $\mathbf{y}$ onto the space orthogonal to $\mathbf{X}$. Theorem 14 of Appendix 1 gives the properties of a projection matrix such as $\mathbf{P}$ or $\mathbf{M}$. In the special case where both $\mathbf{y}$ and $\mathbf{X}$ are two-dimensional vectors

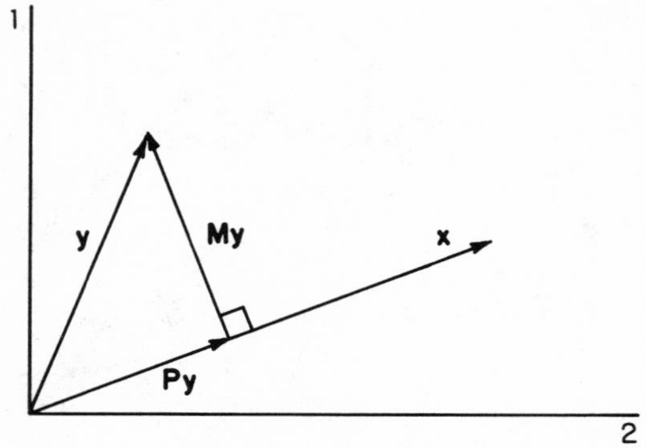

Figure 1.1 Orthogonal decomposition of **y**

(that is, $K = 1$ and $T = 2$), the decomposition (1.2.6) can be illustrated as in Figure 1.1, where the vertical and horizontal axes represent the first and second observations, respectively, and the arrows represent vectors.

From (1.2.6) we obtain

$$\mathbf{y}'\mathbf{y} = \mathbf{y}'\mathbf{P}\mathbf{y} + \mathbf{y}'\mathbf{M}\mathbf{y}. \tag{1.2.7}$$

The goodness of fit of the regression of **y** on **X** can be measured by the ratio $\mathbf{y}'\mathbf{P}\mathbf{y}/\mathbf{y}'\mathbf{y}$, sometimes called R^2. However, it is more common to define R^2 as the square of the sample correlation between **y** and **Py**:

$$R^2 = \frac{(\mathbf{y}'\mathbf{L}\mathbf{P}\mathbf{y})^2}{\mathbf{y}'\mathbf{L}\mathbf{y} \cdot \mathbf{y}'\mathbf{P}\mathbf{L}\mathbf{P}\mathbf{y}}, \tag{1.2.8}$$

where $\mathbf{L} = \mathbf{I}_T - T^{-1}\mathbf{l}\mathbf{l}'$ and $\mathbf{l}$ denotes the T-vector of ones. If we assume one of the columns of **X** is **l** (which is usually the case), we have $\mathbf{LP} = \mathbf{PL}$. Then we can rewrite (1.2.8) as

$$R^2 = \frac{\mathbf{y}'\mathbf{L}\mathbf{P}\mathbf{L}\mathbf{y}}{\mathbf{y}'\mathbf{L}\mathbf{y}} = 1 - \frac{\mathbf{y}'\mathbf{M}\mathbf{y}}{\mathbf{y}'\mathbf{L}\mathbf{y}}. \tag{1.2.9}$$

Thus R^2 can be interpreted as a measure of the goodness of fit of the regression of the deviations of **y** from its mean on the deviations of the columns of **X** from their means. (Section 2.1.4 gives a modification of R^2 suggested by Theil, 1961.)

1.2.2 Least Squares Estimator of a Subset of β

It is sometimes useful to have an explicit formula for a subset of the least squares estimates $\hat{\beta}$. Suppose we partition $\hat{\beta}' = (\hat{\beta}_1', \hat{\beta}_2')$, where $\hat{\beta}_1$ is a K_1-vector and $\hat{\boldsymbol{\beta}}_2$ is a K_2-vector such that $K_1 + K_2 = K$. Partition $\mathbf{X}$ conformably as $\mathbf{X} = (\mathbf{X}_1, \mathbf{X}_2)$. Then we can write $\mathbf{X}'\mathbf{X}\hat{\boldsymbol{\beta}} = \mathbf{X}'\mathbf{y}$ as

$$\mathbf{X}_1'\mathbf{X}_1\hat{\boldsymbol{\beta}}_1 + \mathbf{X}_1'\mathbf{X}_2\hat{\boldsymbol{\beta}}_2 = \mathbf{X}_1'\mathbf{y} \tag{1.2.10}$$

and

$$\mathbf{X}_2'\mathbf{X}_1\hat{\boldsymbol{\beta}}_1 + \mathbf{X}_2'\mathbf{X}_2\hat{\boldsymbol{\beta}}_2 = \mathbf{X}_2'\mathbf{y}. \tag{1.2.11}$$

Solving (1.2.11) for $\hat{\boldsymbol{\beta}}_2$ and inserting it into (1.2.10), we obtain

$$\hat{\boldsymbol{\beta}}_1 = (\mathbf{X}_1'\mathbf{M}_2\mathbf{X}_1)^{-1}\mathbf{X}_1'\mathbf{M}_2\mathbf{y}, \tag{1.2.12}$$

where $\mathbf{M}_2 = \mathbf{I} - \mathbf{X}_2(\mathbf{X}_2'\mathbf{X}_2)^{-1}\mathbf{X}_2'$. Similarly,

$$\hat{\boldsymbol{\beta}}_2 = (\mathbf{X}_2'\mathbf{M}_1\mathbf{X}_2)^{-1}\mathbf{X}_2'\mathbf{M}_1\mathbf{y}, \tag{1.2.13}$$

where $\mathbf{M}_1 = \mathbf{I} - \mathbf{X}_1(\mathbf{X}_1'\mathbf{X}_1)^{-1}\mathbf{X}_1'$.

In Model 1 we assume that $\mathbf{X}$ is of full rank, an assumption that implies that the matrices to be inverted in (1.2.12) and (1.2.13) are both nonsingular. Suppose for a moment that $\mathbf{X}_1$ is of full rank but that $\mathbf{X}_2$ is not. In this case $\boldsymbol{\beta}_2$ cannot be estimated, but $\boldsymbol{\beta}_1$ still can be estimated by modifying (1.2.12) as

$$\hat{\boldsymbol{\beta}}_1 = (\mathbf{X}_1'\mathbf{M}_2^*\mathbf{X}_1)^{-1}\mathbf{X}_1'\mathbf{M}_2^*\mathbf{y}, \tag{1.2.14}$$

where $\mathbf{M}_2^* = \mathbf{I} - \mathbf{X}_2^*(\mathbf{X}_2^{*\prime}\mathbf{X}_2^*)^{-1}\mathbf{X}_2^{*\prime}$, where the columns of $\mathbf{X}_2^*$ consist of a maximal number of linearly independent columns of $\mathbf{X}_2$, provided that $\mathbf{X}_1'\mathbf{M}_2^*\mathbf{X}_1$ is nonsingular. (For the more general problem of estimating a linear combination of the elements of $\boldsymbol{\beta}$, see Section 2.2.3.)

1.2.3 The Mean and Variance of $\hat{\boldsymbol{\beta}}$ and $\hat{\sigma}^2$

Inserting (1.1.4) into (1.2.3), we have

$$\begin{aligned} \hat{\boldsymbol{\beta}} &= (\mathbf{X}'\mathbf{X})^{-1}\mathbf{X}'\mathbf{y} \\ &= \boldsymbol{\beta} + (\mathbf{X}'\mathbf{X})^{-1}\mathbf{X}'\mathbf{u}. \end{aligned} \tag{1.2.15}$$

Clearly, $E\hat{\boldsymbol{\beta}} = \boldsymbol{\beta}$ by the assumptions of Model 1. Using the second line of (1.2.15), we can derive the variance-covariance matrix of $\hat{\boldsymbol{\beta}}$:

$$\begin{aligned} V\hat{\boldsymbol{\beta}} &\equiv E(\hat{\boldsymbol{\beta}} - \boldsymbol{\beta})(\hat{\boldsymbol{\beta}} - \boldsymbol{\beta})' \\ &= E(\mathbf{X}'\mathbf{X})^{-1}\mathbf{X}'\mathbf{u}\mathbf{u}'\mathbf{X}(\mathbf{X}'\mathbf{X})^{-1} \\ &= \sigma^2(\mathbf{X}'\mathbf{X})^{-1}. \end{aligned} \tag{1.2.16}$$

From (1.2.3) and (1.2.4), we have $\hat{\mathbf{u}} = \mathbf{M}\mathbf{u}$, where $\mathbf{M} = \mathbf{I} - \mathbf{X}(\mathbf{X}'\mathbf{X})^{-1}\mathbf{X}'$.

Using the properties of the projection matrix given in Theorem 14 of Appendix 1, we obtain

$$E\hat{\sigma}^2 = T^{-1}E\mathbf{u}'\mathbf{M}\mathbf{u} \tag{1.2.17}$$

$$= T^{-1}E \operatorname{tr} \mathbf{M}\mathbf{u}\mathbf{u}' \quad \text{by Theorem 6 of Appendix 1}$$

$$= T^{-1}\sigma^2 \operatorname{tr} \mathbf{M}$$

$$= T^{-1}(T-K)\sigma^2 \quad \text{by Theorems 7 and 14 of Appendix 1,}$$

which shows that $\hat{\sigma}^2$ is a biased estimator of σ^2. We define the unbiased estimator of σ^2 by

$$\tilde{\sigma}^2 = (T-K)^{-1}\hat{\mathbf{u}}'\hat{\mathbf{u}}. \tag{1.2.18}$$

We shall obtain the variance of $\hat{\sigma}^2$ later, in Section 1.3, under the additional assumption that $\mathbf{u}$ is normal.

The quantity $V\hat{\boldsymbol{\beta}}$ can be estimated by substituting either $\hat{\sigma}^2$ or $\tilde{\sigma}^2$ (defined above) for the σ^2 that appears in the right-hand side of (1.2.16).

1.2.4 Definition of Best

Before we prove that the least squares estimator is best linear unbiased, we must define the term *best.* First we shall define it for scalar estimators, then for vector estimators.

DEFINITION 1.2.1. Let $\hat{\theta}$ and θ^* be scalar estimators of a scalar parameter θ. The estimator $\hat{\theta}$ is said to be *at least as good as* (or *at least as efficient as*) the estimator θ^* if $E(\hat{\theta}-\theta)^2 \leqq E(\theta^*-\theta)^2$ for all parameter values. The estimator $\hat{\theta}$ is said to be *better* (or *more efficient*) than the estimator θ^* if $\hat{\theta}$ is at least as good as θ^* and $E(\hat{\theta}-\theta)^2 < E(\theta^*-\theta)^2$ for at least one parameter value. An estimator is said to be *best* (or *efficient*) in a class if it is better than any other estimator in the class.

The mean squared error is a reasonable criterion in many situations and is mathematically convenient. So, following the convention of the statistical literature, we have defined "better" to mean "having a smaller mean squared error." However, there may be situations in which a researcher wishes to use other criteria, such as the mean absolute error.

DEFINITION 1.2.2. Let $\hat{\boldsymbol{\theta}}$ and $\boldsymbol{\theta}^*$ be estimators of a vector parameter $\boldsymbol{\theta}$. Let $\mathbf{A}$ and $\mathbf{B}$ be their respective mean squared error matrices; that is, $\mathbf{A} = E(\hat{\boldsymbol{\theta}}-\boldsymbol{\theta})(\hat{\boldsymbol{\theta}}-\boldsymbol{\theta})'$ and $\mathbf{B} = E(\boldsymbol{\theta}^*-\boldsymbol{\theta})(\boldsymbol{\theta}^*-\boldsymbol{\theta})'$. Then we say $\hat{\boldsymbol{\theta}}$ is *better* (or *more efficient*) than θ^* if

$$\mathbf{c}'(\mathbf{B}-\mathbf{A})\mathbf{c} \geqq 0 \quad \text{for every vector} \quad \mathbf{c} \quad \text{and every parameter value} \tag{1.2.19}$$

and

$$\mathbf{c}'(\mathbf{B}-\mathbf{A})\mathbf{c} > 0 \quad \text{for at least one value of} \quad \mathbf{c} \quad \text{and at least one value of the parameter.} \tag{1.2.20}$$

This definition of *better* clearly coincides with Definition 1.2.1 if θ is a scalar.

In view of Definition 1.2.1, equivalent forms of statements (1.2.19) and (1.2.20) are statements (1.2.21) and (1.2.22):

$$\mathbf{c}'\hat{\theta} \quad \text{is at least as good as} \quad \mathbf{c}'\theta^* \quad \text{for every vector} \quad \mathbf{c} \tag{1.2.21}$$

and

$$\mathbf{c}'\hat{\theta} \quad \text{is better than} \quad \mathbf{c}'\theta^* \quad \text{for at least one value of} \quad \mathbf{c}. \tag{1.2.22}$$

Using Theorem 4 of Appendix 1, they also can be written as

$$\mathbf{B} \geqq \mathbf{A} \quad \text{for every parameter value} \tag{1.2.23}$$

and

$$\mathbf{B} \neq \mathbf{A} \quad \text{for at least one parameter value.} \tag{1.2.24}$$

(Note that $\mathbf{B} \geqq \mathbf{A}$ means $\mathbf{B}-\mathbf{A}$ is nonnegative definite and $\mathbf{B} > \mathbf{A}$ means $\mathbf{B}-\mathbf{A}$ is positive definite.)

We shall now prove the equivalence of (1.2.20) and (1.2.24). Because the phrase "for at least one parameter value" is common to both statements, we shall ignore it in the following proof. First, suppose (1.2.24) is not true. Then $\mathbf{B}=\mathbf{A}$. Therefore $\mathbf{c}'(\mathbf{B}-\mathbf{A})\mathbf{c}=0$ for every $\mathbf{c}$, a condition that implies that (1.2.20) is not true. Second, suppose (1.2.20) is not true. Then $\mathbf{c}'(\mathbf{B}-\mathbf{A})\mathbf{c}=0$ for every $\mathbf{c}$ and every diagonal element of $\mathbf{B}-\mathbf{A}$ must be 0 (choose $\mathbf{c}$ to be the zero vector, except for 1 in the ith position). Also, the i,jth element of $\mathbf{B}-\mathbf{A}$ is 0 (choose $\mathbf{c}$ to be the zero vector, except for 1 in the ith and jth positions, and note that $\mathbf{B}-\mathbf{A}$ is symmetric). Thus (1.2.24) is not true. This completes the proof.

Note that replacing $\mathbf{B} \neq \mathbf{A}$ in (1.2.24) with $\mathbf{B} > \mathbf{A}$—or making the corresponding change in (1.2.20) or (1.2.22)— is unwise because we could not then rank the estimator with the mean squared error matrix

$$\begin{bmatrix} 1 & 0 \\ 0 & 1 \end{bmatrix}$$

higher than the estimator with the mean squared error matrix

$$\begin{bmatrix} 2 & 0 \\ 0 & 1 \end{bmatrix}.$$

A problem with Definition 1.2.2 (more precisely, a problem inherent in the comparison of vector estimates rather than in this definition) is that often it does not allow us to say one estimator is either better or worse than the other. For example, consider

$$\mathbf{A} = \begin{bmatrix} 1 & 0 \\ 0 & 1 \end{bmatrix} \quad \text{and} \quad \mathbf{B} = \begin{bmatrix} 2 & 0 \\ 0 & \frac{1}{2} \end{bmatrix}. \tag{1.2.25}$$

Clearly, neither $\mathbf{A} \geqq \mathbf{B}$ nor $\mathbf{B} \geqq \mathbf{A}$. In such a case one might compare the trace and conclude that $\hat{\theta}$ is better than θ^* because $\text{tr}\, \mathbf{A} < \text{tr}\, \mathbf{B}$. Another example is

$$\mathbf{A} = \begin{bmatrix} 2 & 1 \\ 1 & 2 \end{bmatrix} \quad \text{and} \quad \mathbf{B} = \begin{bmatrix} 2 & 0 \\ 0 & 2 \end{bmatrix}. \tag{1.2.26}$$

Again, neither $\mathbf{A} \geqq \mathbf{B}$ nor $\mathbf{B} \geqq \mathbf{A}$. If one were using the determinant as the criterion, one would prefer $\hat{\theta}$ over θ^* because $\det \mathbf{A} < \det \mathbf{B}$.

Note that $\mathbf{B} \geqq \mathbf{A}$ implies both $\text{tr}\, \mathbf{B} \geqq \text{tr}\, \mathbf{A}$ and $\det \mathbf{B} \geqq \det \mathbf{A}$. The first follows from Theorem 7 and the second from Theorem 11 of Appendix 1. As these two examples show, neither $\text{tr}\, \mathbf{B} \geqq \text{tr}\, \mathbf{A}$ nor $\det \mathbf{B} \geqq \det \mathbf{A}$ implies $\mathbf{B} \geqq \mathbf{A}$.

Use of the trace as a criterion has an obvious intuitive appeal, inasmuch as it is the sum of the individual variances. Justification for the use of the determinant involves more complicated reasoning. Suppose $\hat{\theta} \sim N(\theta, \mathbf{V})$, where $\mathbf{V}$ is the variance-covariance matrix of $\hat{\theta}$. Then, by Theorem 1 of Appendix 2, $(\hat{\theta} - \theta)'\mathbf{V}^{-1}(\hat{\theta} - \theta) \sim \chi_K^2$, the chi-square distribution with K degrees of freedom, K being the number of elements of θ. Therefore the $(1 - \alpha)\%$ confidence ellipsoid for θ is defined by

$$\{\theta | (\hat{\theta} - \theta)'\mathbf{V}^{-1}(\hat{\theta} - \theta) < \chi_K^2(\alpha)\}, \tag{1.2.27}$$

where $\chi_K^2(\alpha)$ is the number such that $P[\chi_K^2 \geqq \chi_K^2(\alpha)] = \alpha$. Then the volume of the ellipsoid (1.2.27) is proportional to the determinant of $\mathbf{V}$, as shown by Anderson (1958, p. 170).

A more intuitive justification for the determinant criterion is possible for the case in which θ is a two-dimensional vector. Let the mean squared error matrix of an estimator $\hat{\theta} = (\hat{\theta}_1, \hat{\theta}_2)'$ be

$$\begin{bmatrix} a_{11} & a_{12} \\ a_{21} & a_{22} \end{bmatrix}.$$

Suppose that θ_2 is known; define another estimator of θ_1 by $\tilde{\theta}_1 = \hat{\theta}_1 + \alpha(\hat{\theta}_2 - \theta_2)$. Its mean squared error is $a_{11} + \alpha^2 a_{22} + 2\alpha a_{12}$ and attains the minimum value of $a_{11} - (a_{12}^2/a_{22})$ when $\alpha = -a_{12}/a_{22}$. The larger a_{12}, the more efficient can be estimation of θ_1. Because the larger a_{12} implies the smaller determinant, the preceding reasoning provides a justification for the determinant criterion.

Despite these justifications, both criteria inevitably suffer from a certain degree of arbitrariness and therefore should be used with caution. Another useful scalar criterion based on the predictive efficiency of an estimator will be proposed in Section 1.6.

1.2.5 Least Squares as Best Linear Unbiased Estimator (BLUE)

The class of linear estimators of $\boldsymbol{\beta}$ can be defined as those estimators of the form $\mathbf{C}'\mathbf{y}$ for any $T \times K$ constant matrix $\mathbf{C}$. We can further restrict the class by imposing the unbiasedness condition, namely,

$$E\mathbf{C}'\mathbf{y} = \boldsymbol{\beta} \quad \text{for all} \quad \boldsymbol{\beta}. \tag{1.2.28}$$

Inserting (1.1.4) into (1.2.28), we obtain

$$\mathbf{C}'\mathbf{X} = \mathbf{I}. \tag{1.2.29}$$

Clearly, the LS estimator $\hat{\boldsymbol{\beta}}$ is a member of this class. The following theorem proves that LS is best of all the linear unbiased estimators.

THEOREM 1.2.1 (Gauss-Markov). Let $\boldsymbol{\beta}^* = \mathbf{C}'\mathbf{y}$ where $\mathbf{C}$ is a $T \times K$ matrix of constants such that $\mathbf{C}'\mathbf{X} = \mathbf{I}$. Then $\hat{\boldsymbol{\beta}}$ is better than $\boldsymbol{\beta}^*$ if $\hat{\boldsymbol{\beta}} \neq \boldsymbol{\beta}^*$.

Proof. Because $\boldsymbol{\beta}^* = \boldsymbol{\beta} + \mathbf{C}'\mathbf{u}$ because of (1.2.29), we have

$$\begin{aligned} V\boldsymbol{\beta}^* &= E\mathbf{C}'\mathbf{u}\mathbf{u}'\mathbf{C} \\ &= \sigma^2\mathbf{C}'\mathbf{C} \\ &= \sigma^2(\mathbf{X}'\mathbf{X})^{-1} + \sigma^2[\mathbf{C}' - (\mathbf{X}'\mathbf{X})^{-1}\mathbf{X}'][\mathbf{C}' - (\mathbf{X}'\mathbf{X})^{-1}\mathbf{X}']'. \end{aligned} \tag{1.2.30}$$

The theorem follows immediately by noting that the second term of the last line of (1.2.30) is a nonnegative definite matrix.

We shall now give an alternative proof, which contains an interesting point of its own. The class of linear unbiased estimators can be defined alternatively as the class of estimators of the form $(\mathbf{S}'\mathbf{X})^{-1}\mathbf{S}'\mathbf{y}$, where $\mathbf{S}$ is any $T \times K$ matrix of constants such that $\mathbf{S}'\mathbf{X}$ is nonsingular. When it is defined this way, we call it the class of *instrumental variable estimators* (abbreviated as IV) and call the column vectors of $\mathbf{S}$ *instrumental variables.* The variance-covariance matrix of IV easily can be shown to be $\sigma^2(\mathbf{S}'\mathbf{X})^{-1}\mathbf{S}'\mathbf{S}(\mathbf{X}'\mathbf{S})^{-1}$. We get LS when we put $\mathbf{S} = \mathbf{X}$, and the optimality of LS can be proved as follows: Because $\mathbf{I} - \mathbf{S}(\mathbf{S}'\mathbf{S})^{-1}\mathbf{S}'$ is nonnegative definite by Theorem 14(v) of Appendix 1, we have

$$\mathbf{X}'\mathbf{X} \geqq \mathbf{X}'\mathbf{S}(\mathbf{S}'\mathbf{S})^{-1}\mathbf{S}'\mathbf{X}. \tag{1.2.31}$$

Inverting both sides of (1.2.31) and using Theorem 17 of Appendix 1, we obtain the desired result:

$$(\mathbf{X}'\mathbf{X})^{-1} \leqq (\mathbf{S}'\mathbf{X})^{-1}\mathbf{S}'\mathbf{S}(\mathbf{X}'\mathbf{S})^{-1}. \tag{1.2.32}$$

In the preceding analysis we were first given the least squares estimator and then proceeded to prove that it is best of all the linear unbiased estimators. Suppose now that we knew nothing about the least squares estimator and had to find the value of $\mathbf{C}$ that minimizes $\mathbf{C}'\mathbf{C}$ *in the matrix sense* (that is, in terms of a ranking of matrices based on the matrix inequality defined earlier) subject to the condition $\mathbf{C}'\mathbf{X} = \mathbf{I}$. Unlike the problem of scalar minimization, calculus is of no direct use. In such a situation it is often useful to minimize the variance of a linear unbiased estimator of the scalar parameter $\mathbf{p}'\boldsymbol{\beta}$, where $\mathbf{p}$ is an arbitrary K-vector of known constants.

Let $\mathbf{c}'\mathbf{y}$ be a linear estimator of $\mathbf{p}'\boldsymbol{\beta}$. The unbiasedness condition implies $\mathbf{X}'\mathbf{c} = \mathbf{p}$. Because $V\mathbf{c}'\mathbf{y} = \sigma^2\mathbf{c}'\mathbf{c}$, the problem mathematically is

$$\text{Minimize } \mathbf{c}'\mathbf{c} \text{ subject to } \mathbf{X}'\mathbf{c} = \mathbf{p}. \tag{1.2.33}$$

Define

$$S = \mathbf{c}'\mathbf{c} - 2\boldsymbol{\lambda}'(\mathbf{X}'\mathbf{c} - \mathbf{p}), \tag{1.2.34}$$

where $2\boldsymbol{\lambda}$ is a K-vector of Lagrange multipliers. Setting the derivative of S with respect to $\mathbf{c}$ equal to $\mathbf{0}$ yields

$$\mathbf{c} = \mathbf{X}\boldsymbol{\lambda}. \tag{1.2.35}$$

Premultiplying both sides by $\mathbf{X}'$ and using the constraint, we obtain

$$\boldsymbol{\lambda} = (\mathbf{X}'\mathbf{X})^{-1}\mathbf{p}. \tag{1.2.36}$$

Inserting (1.2.36) into (1.2.35), we conclude that the best linear unbiased estimator of $\mathbf{p}'\boldsymbol{\beta}$ is $\mathbf{p}'(\mathbf{X}'\mathbf{X})^{-1}\mathbf{X}'\mathbf{y}$. We therefore have a constructive proof of Theorem 1.2.1.

1.3 Model 1 with Normality

In this section we shall consider Model 1 with the added assumption of the joint normality of $\mathbf{u}$. Because no correlation implies independence under normality, the $\{u_t\}$ are now assumed to be serially independent. We shall show that the maximum likelihood estimator (MLE) of the regression parameter is identical to the least squares estimator and, using the theory of the Cramér-Rao lower bound, shall prove that it is the best unbiased estimator. We shall also discuss maximum likelihood estimation of the variance σ^2.

1.3.1 Maximum Likelihood Estimator

Under Model 1 with normality we have $\mathbf{y} \sim N(\mathbf{X}\boldsymbol{\beta},\sigma^2\mathbf{I})$. Therefore the likelihood function is given by[3]

$$L = (2\pi\sigma^2)^{-T/2} \exp\,[-0.5\sigma^{-2}(\mathbf{y}-\mathbf{X}\boldsymbol{\beta})'(\mathbf{y}-\mathbf{X}\boldsymbol{\beta})]. \tag{1.3.1}$$

Taking the logarithm of this equation and ignoring the terms that do not depend on the unknown parameters, we have

$$\log L = -\frac{T}{2}\log\sigma^2 - \frac{1}{2\sigma^2}(\mathbf{y}-\mathbf{X}\boldsymbol{\beta})'(\mathbf{y}-\mathbf{X}\boldsymbol{\beta}). \tag{1.3.2}$$

Evidently the maximization of log $\mathbf{L}$ is equivalent to the minimization of $(\mathbf{y}-\mathbf{X}\boldsymbol{\beta})'(\mathbf{y}-\mathbf{X}\boldsymbol{\beta})$, so we conclude that the maximum likelihood estimator of $\boldsymbol{\beta}$ is the same as the least squares estimator $\hat{\boldsymbol{\beta}}$ obtained in Section 1.2. Putting $\hat{\boldsymbol{\beta}}$ into (1.3.2) and setting the partial derivative of $\log L$ with respect to σ^2 equal to 0, we obtain the maximum likelihood estimator of σ^2:

$$\hat{\sigma}^2 = T^{-1}\hat{\mathbf{u}}'\hat{\mathbf{u}}, \tag{1.3.3}$$

where $\hat{\mathbf{u}} = \mathbf{y} - \mathbf{X}\hat{\boldsymbol{\beta}}$. This is identical to what in Section 1.2.1 we called the least squares estimator of σ^2.

The mean and the variance-covariance matrix of $\hat{\boldsymbol{\beta}}$ were obtained in Section 1.2.3. Because linear combinations of normal random variables are normal, we have under the present normality assumption

$$\hat{\boldsymbol{\beta}} \sim N[\boldsymbol{\beta},\sigma^2(\mathbf{X}'\mathbf{X})^{-1}]. \tag{1.3.4}$$

The mean of $\hat{\sigma}^2$ is given in Eq. (1.2.17). We shall now derive its variance under the normality assumption. We have

$$
\begin{aligned}
E(\mathbf{u}'\mathbf{M}\mathbf{u})^2 &= E\mathbf{u}'\mathbf{M}\mathbf{u}\mathbf{u}'\mathbf{M}\mathbf{u} \\
&= \text{tr}\,\{\mathbf{M}E[(\mathbf{u}'\mathbf{M}\mathbf{u})\mathbf{u}\mathbf{u}']\} \\
&= \sigma^4\,\text{tr}\,\{\mathbf{M}[2\mathbf{M} + (\text{tr}\,\mathbf{M})\mathbf{I}]\} \\
&= \sigma^4[2\,\text{tr}\,\mathbf{M} + (\text{tr}\,\mathbf{M})^2] \\
&= \sigma^4[2(T-K) + (T-K)^2],
\end{aligned} \tag{1.3.5}
$$

where we have used $Eu_t^3 = 0$ and $Eu_t^4 = 3\sigma^4$ since $u_t \sim N(0, \sigma^2)$. The third equality in (1.3.5) can be shown as follows. If we write the t,sth element of $\mathbf{M}$ as m_{ts}, the i,jth element of the matrix $E(\mathbf{u}'\mathbf{M}\mathbf{u})\mathbf{u}\mathbf{u}'$ is given by $\Sigma_{t=1}^T \Sigma_{s=1}^T m_{ts} E u_t u_s u_i u_j$. Hence it is equal to $2\sigma^4 m_{ij}$ if $i \neq j$ and to $2\sigma^4 m_{ii} + \sigma^4 \Sigma_{t=1}^T m_{tt}$ if $i = j$, from which the third equality follows. Finally, from (1.2.17) and (1.3.5),

$$
V\hat{\sigma}^2 = \frac{2(T-K)\sigma^4}{T^2}. \tag{1.3.6}
$$

Another important result that we shall use later in Section 1.5, where we discuss tests of linear hypotheses, is that

$$
\frac{\mathbf{u}'\mathbf{M}\mathbf{u}}{\sigma^2} \sim \chi^2_{T-K}, \tag{1.3.7}
$$

which readily follows from Theorem 2 of Appendix 2 because $\mathbf{M}$ is indempotent with rank $T-K$. Because the variance of χ^2_{T-K} is $2(T-K)$ by Theorem 1 of Appendix 2, (1.3.6) can be derived alternatively from (1.3.7).

1.3.2 Cramér-Rao Lower Bound

The Cramér-Rao lower bound gives a useful lower bound (in the matrix sense) for the variance-covariance matrix of an unbiased vector estimator.[4] In this section we shall prove a general theorem that will be applied to Model 1 with normality in the next two subsections.

THEOREM 1.3.1 (Cramér-Rao). Let $\mathbf{z}$ be an n-component vector of random variables (not necessarily independent) the joint density of which is given by $L(\mathbf{z}, \boldsymbol{\theta})$, where $\boldsymbol{\theta}$ is a K-component vector of parameters in some parameter space Θ. Let $\tilde{\boldsymbol{\theta}}(\mathbf{z})$ be an unbiased estimator of $\boldsymbol{\theta}$ with a finite variance-covariance matrix. Furthermore, assume that $L(\mathbf{z}, \boldsymbol{\theta})$ and $\tilde{\boldsymbol{\theta}}(\mathbf{z})$ satisfy

(A) $\quad E\dfrac{\partial \log L}{\partial \boldsymbol{\theta}} = \mathbf{0},$

(B) $$E\frac{\partial^2 \log L}{\partial\theta\partial\theta'} = -E\frac{\partial \log L}{\partial\theta}\frac{\partial \log L}{\partial\theta'},$$

(C) $$E\frac{\partial \log L}{\partial\theta}\frac{\partial \log L}{\partial\theta'} > \mathbf{0},$$

(D) $$\int \frac{\partial L}{\partial\theta}\tilde{\theta}'\, d\mathbf{z} = \mathbf{I}.$$

Note: $\partial \log L/\partial\theta$ is a K-vector, so that $\mathbf{0}$ in assumption A is a vector of K zeroes. Assumption C means that the left-hand side is a positive definite matrix. The integral in assumption D is an n-tuple integral over the whole domain of the Euclidean n-space because $\mathbf{z}$ is an n-vector. Finally, $\mathbf{I}$ in assumption D is the identity matrix of size K.

Then we have for $\theta \in \Theta$

$$V(\tilde{\theta}) \geqq \left[-E\frac{\partial^2 \log L}{\partial\theta\partial\theta'}\right]^{-1}. \tag{1.3.8}$$

Proof. Define $\mathbf{P} = E(\tilde{\theta} - \theta)(\tilde{\theta} - \theta)'$, $\mathbf{Q} = E(\tilde{\theta} - \theta)(\partial \log L/\partial\theta')$, and $\mathbf{R} = E(\partial \log L/\partial\theta)(\partial \log L/\partial\theta')$. Then

$$\begin{bmatrix} \mathbf{P} & \mathbf{Q} \\ \mathbf{Q}' & \mathbf{R} \end{bmatrix} \geqq \mathbf{0} \tag{1.3.9}$$

because the left-hand side is a variance-covariance matrix. Premultiply both sides of (1.3.9) by $[\mathbf{I}, -\mathbf{QR}^{-1}]$ and postmultiply by $[\mathbf{I}, -\mathbf{QR}^{-1}]'$. Then we get

$$\mathbf{P} - \mathbf{QR}^{-1}\mathbf{Q}' \geqq \mathbf{0}, \tag{1.3.10}$$

where $\mathbf{R}^{-1}$ can be defined because of assumption C. But we have

$$\mathbf{Q} \equiv E\left[(\tilde{\theta} - \theta)\frac{\partial \log L}{\partial\theta'}\right] \tag{1.3.11}$$

$$= E\left[\tilde{\theta}\frac{\partial \log L}{\partial\theta'}\right] \quad \text{by assumption A}$$

$$= E\left[\tilde{\theta}\frac{1}{L}\frac{\partial L}{\partial\theta'}\right]$$

$$= \int \left[\tilde{\theta}\frac{1}{L}\frac{\partial L}{\partial\theta'}\right] L\, d\mathbf{z}$$

$$= \int \tilde{\theta}\frac{\partial L}{\partial\theta'}\, d\mathbf{z}$$

$$= \mathbf{I} \quad \text{by assumption D.}$$

Therefore (1.3.8) follows from (1.3.10), (1.3.11), and assumption B.

The inverse of the lower bound, namely, $-E\, \partial^2 \log L/\partial\theta\partial\theta'$, is called the *information matrix*. R. A. Fisher first introduced this term as a certain measure of the information contained in the sample (see Rao, 1973, p. 329).

The Cramér-Rao lower bound may not be attained by any unbiased estimator. If it is, we have found the best unbiased estimator. In the next section we shall show that the maximum likelihood estimator of the regression parameter attains the lower bound in Model 1 with normality.

Assumptions A, B, and D seem arbitrary at first glance. We shall now inquire into the significance of these assumptions. Assumptions A and B are equivalent to

(A′) $$\int \frac{\partial L}{\partial \theta}\, d\mathbf{z} = \mathbf{0}$$

(B′) $$\int \frac{\partial^2 L}{\partial \theta \partial \theta'}\, d\mathbf{z} = \mathbf{0},$$

respectively. The equivalence between assumptions A and A′ follows from

$$E\frac{\partial \log L}{\partial \theta} = E\left[\frac{1}{L}\frac{\partial L}{\partial \theta}\right] \tag{1.3.12}$$

$$= \int \left[\frac{1}{L}\frac{\partial L}{\partial \theta}\right] L\, d\mathbf{z}$$

$$= \int \frac{\partial L}{\partial \theta}\, d\mathbf{z}.$$

The equivalence between assumptions B and B′ follows from

$$E\frac{\partial^2 \log L}{\partial \theta \partial \theta'} = E\left\{\frac{\partial}{\partial \theta}\left[\frac{1}{L}\frac{\partial L}{\partial \theta'}\right]\right\} \tag{1.3.13}$$

$$= E\left[-\frac{1}{L^2}\frac{\partial L}{\partial \theta}\frac{\partial L}{\partial \theta'} + \frac{1}{L}\frac{\partial^2 L}{\partial \theta \partial \theta'}\right]$$

$$= -E\left[\frac{\partial \log L}{\partial \theta}\frac{\partial \log L}{\partial \theta'}\right] + \int \frac{\partial^2 L}{\partial \theta \partial \theta'}\, d\mathbf{z}.$$

Furthermore, assumptions A′, B′, and D are equivalent to

(A″) $$\int \frac{\partial L}{\partial \theta}\, d\mathbf{z} = \frac{\partial}{\partial \theta}\int L\, d\mathbf{z}$$

$$\text{(B}''\text{)} \qquad \int \frac{\partial^2 L}{\partial \boldsymbol{\theta} \partial \boldsymbol{\theta}'} d\mathbf{z} = \frac{\partial}{\partial \boldsymbol{\theta}} \int \frac{\partial L}{\partial \boldsymbol{\theta}'} d\mathbf{z}$$

$$\text{(D}'\text{)} \qquad \int \frac{\partial L}{\partial \boldsymbol{\theta}} \tilde{\boldsymbol{\theta}}' \, d\mathbf{z} = \frac{\partial}{\partial \boldsymbol{\theta}} \int L \tilde{\boldsymbol{\theta}}' \, d\mathbf{z},$$

because the right-hand sides of assumptions A″, B″, and D′ are **0**, **0**, and **I**, respectively. Written thus, the three assumptions are all of the form

$$\frac{\partial}{\partial \boldsymbol{\theta}} \int f(\mathbf{z}, \boldsymbol{\theta}) \, d\mathbf{z} = \int \frac{\partial}{\partial \boldsymbol{\theta}} f(\mathbf{z}, \boldsymbol{\theta}) \, d\mathbf{z}; \tag{1.3.14}$$

in other words, the operations of differentiation and integration can be interchanged. In the next theorem we shall give sufficient conditions for (1.3.14) to hold in the case where θ is a scalar. The case for a vector $\boldsymbol{\theta}$ can be treated in essentially the same manner, although the notation gets more complex.

THEOREM 1.3.2. If (i) $\partial f(\mathbf{z}, \theta)/\partial \theta$ is continuous in $\theta \in \Theta$ and $\mathbf{z}$, where Θ is an open set, (ii) $\int f(\mathbf{z}, \theta) \, d\mathbf{z}$ exists, and (iii) $\int |\partial f(\mathbf{z}, \theta)/\partial \theta| d\mathbf{z} < M < \infty$ for all $\theta \in \Theta$, then (1.3.14) holds.

Proof. We have, using assumptions (i) and (ii),

$$\left| \int \left[\frac{f(\mathbf{z}, \theta + h) - f(\mathbf{z}, \theta)}{h} - \frac{\partial f}{\partial \theta}(\mathbf{z}, \theta) \right] d\mathbf{z} \right|$$

$$\leqq \int \left| \frac{f(\mathbf{z}, \theta + h) - f(\mathbf{z}, \theta)}{h} - \frac{\partial f}{\partial \theta}(\mathbf{z}, \theta) \right| d\mathbf{z}$$

$$= \int \left| \frac{\partial f}{\partial \theta}(\mathbf{z}, \theta^*) - \frac{\partial f}{\partial \theta}(\mathbf{z}, \theta) \right| d\mathbf{z},$$

where θ^* is between θ and $\theta + h$. Next, we can write the last integral as $\int = \int_A + \int_{\bar{A}}$, where A is a sufficiently large compact set in the domain of $\mathbf{z}$ and $\bar{A}$ is its complement. But we can make $\int_A$ sufficiently small because of (i) and $\int_{\bar{A}}$ sufficiently small because of (iii).

1.3.3 Least Squares Estimator as Best Unbiased Estimator (BUE)

In this section we shall show that under Model 1 with normality, the least squares estimator of the regression parameters $\boldsymbol{\beta}$ attains the Cramér-Rao lower bound and hence is the best unbiased estimator. Assumptions A, B, and C of Theorem 1.3.1 are easy to verify for our model; as for assumption D, we shall verify it only for the case where β is a scalar and σ^2 is known, assuming that the parameter space of β and σ^2 is compact and does not contain $\sigma^2 = 0$.

Consider $\log L$ given in (1.3.2). In applying Theorem 1.3.1 to our model, we put $\boldsymbol{\theta}' = (\boldsymbol{\beta}', \sigma^2)$. The first- and second-order derivatives of $\log L$ are given by

$$\frac{\partial \log L}{\partial \boldsymbol{\beta}} = \frac{1}{\sigma^2} (\mathbf{X}'\mathbf{y} - \mathbf{X}'\mathbf{X}\boldsymbol{\beta}), \tag{1.3.15}$$

$$\frac{\partial \log L}{\partial (\sigma^2)} = -\frac{T}{2\sigma^2} + \frac{1}{2\sigma^4} (\mathbf{y} - \mathbf{X}\boldsymbol{\beta})'(\mathbf{y} - \mathbf{X}\boldsymbol{\beta}), \tag{1.3.16}$$

$$\frac{\partial^2 \log L}{\partial \boldsymbol{\beta} \partial \boldsymbol{\beta}'} = -\frac{1}{\sigma^2} \mathbf{X}'\mathbf{X}, \tag{1.3.17}$$

$$\frac{\partial^2 \log L}{\partial (\sigma^2)^2} = \frac{T}{2\sigma^4} - \frac{1}{\sigma^6} (\mathbf{y} - \mathbf{X}\boldsymbol{\beta})'(\mathbf{y} - \mathbf{X}\boldsymbol{\beta}), \tag{1.3.18}$$

$$\frac{\partial^2 \log L}{\partial \boldsymbol{\beta} \partial (\sigma^2)} = -\frac{1}{\sigma^4} (\mathbf{X}'\mathbf{y} - \mathbf{X}'\mathbf{X}\boldsymbol{\beta}). \tag{1.3.19}$$

From (1.3.15) and (1.3.16) we can immediately see that assumption A is satisfied. Taking the expectation of (1.3.17), (1.3.18), and (1.3.19), we obtain

$$E \frac{\partial^2 \log L}{\partial \boldsymbol{\theta} \partial \boldsymbol{\theta}'} = -\begin{bmatrix} \frac{1}{\sigma^2} \mathbf{X}'\mathbf{X} & \mathbf{0} \\ \mathbf{0} & \frac{T}{2\sigma^4} \end{bmatrix}. \tag{1.3.20}$$

We have

$$E \frac{\partial \log L}{\partial \boldsymbol{\beta}} \frac{\partial \log L}{\partial \boldsymbol{\beta}'} = \frac{1}{\sigma^4} E\mathbf{X}'\mathbf{u}\mathbf{u}'\mathbf{X} = \frac{1}{\sigma^2} \mathbf{X}'\mathbf{X}, \tag{1.3.21}$$

$$\begin{aligned} E\left[\frac{\partial \log L}{\partial (\sigma^2)}\right]^2 &= \frac{T^2}{4\sigma^4} + \frac{1}{4\sigma^8} E(\mathbf{u}'\mathbf{u})^2 - \frac{T}{2\sigma^6} E\mathbf{u}'\mathbf{u} \\ &= \frac{T}{2\sigma^4}, \end{aligned} \tag{1.3.22}$$

because $E(\mathbf{u}'\mathbf{u})^2 = (T^2 + 2T)\,\sigma^4$, and

$$E \frac{\partial \log L}{\partial \boldsymbol{\beta}} \frac{\partial \log L}{\partial (\sigma^2)} = \mathbf{0}. \tag{1.3.23}$$

Therefore, from (1.3.20) to (1.3.23) we can see that assumptions B and C are both satisfied.

We shall verify assumption D only for the case where β is a scalar and σ^2 is known so that we can use Theorem 1.3.2, which is stated for the case of a scalar parameter. Take $\tilde{\beta}L$ as the f of that theorem. We need to check only the last condition of the theorem. Differentiating (1.3.1) with respect to β, we have

$$\frac{\partial f}{\partial \beta} = \frac{\tilde{\beta}}{\sigma^2}(\mathbf{x}'\mathbf{y} - \beta\mathbf{x}'\mathbf{x})L, \tag{1.3.24}$$

where we have written $\mathbf{X}$ as $\mathbf{x}$, inasmuch as it is a vector. Therefore, by Hölder's inequality (see Royden, 1968, p. 113),

$$\int \left| \frac{\partial f}{\partial \beta} \right| d\mathbf{y} \leqq \frac{1}{\sigma^2} \left(\int \tilde{\beta}^2 L \, d\mathbf{y} \right)^{1/2} \left[\int (\mathbf{x}'\mathbf{y} - \beta\mathbf{x}'\mathbf{x})^2 L \, d\mathbf{y} \right]^{1/2}. \tag{1.3.25}$$

The first integral on the right-hand side is finite because $\tilde{\beta}$ is assumed to have a finite variance. The second integral on the right-hand side is also finite because the moments of the normal distribution are finite. Moreover, both integrals are uniformly bounded in the assumed parameter space. Thus the last condition of Theorem 1.3.2 is satisfied.

Finally, from (1.3.8) and (1.3.20) we have

$$V\tilde{\boldsymbol{\beta}} \geqq \sigma^2(\mathbf{X}'\mathbf{X})^{-1} \tag{1.3.26}$$

for any unbiased $\tilde{\boldsymbol{\beta}}$. The right-hand side of (1.3.26) is the variance-covariance matrix of the least squares estimator of $\boldsymbol{\beta}$, thereby proving that the least squares estimator is the best unbiased estimator under Model 1 with normality. Unlike the result in Section 1.2.5, the result in this section is not constrained by the linearity condition because the normality assumption was added. Nevertheless, even with the normality assumption, there may be a biased estimator that has a smaller average mean squared error than the least squares estimator, as we shall show in Section 2.2. In nonnormal situations, certain nonlinear estimators may be preferred to LS, as we shall see in Section 2.3.

1.3.4 The Cramér-Rao Lower Bound for Unbiased Estimators of σ^2

From (1.3.8) and (1.3.20) the Cramér-Rao lower bound for unbiased estimators of σ^2 in Model 1 with normality is equal to $2\sigma^4 T^{-1}$. We shall examine whether it is attained by the unbiased estimator $\tilde{\sigma}^2$ defined in Eq. (1.2.18). Using (1.2.17) and (1.3.5), we have

$$V\tilde{\sigma}^2 = \frac{2\sigma^4}{T-K}. \tag{1.3.27}$$

Therefore it does not attain the Cramér-Rao lower bound, although the difference is negligible when T is large.

We shall now show that there is a simple biased estimator of σ^2 that has a smaller mean squared error than the Cramér-Rao lower bound. Define the class of estimators

$$\hat{\sigma}_N^2 = \frac{\hat{\mathbf{u}}'\hat{\mathbf{u}}}{N}, \tag{1.3.28}$$

where N is a positive integer. Both $\hat{\sigma}^2$ and $\tilde{\sigma}^2$, defined in (1.2.5) and (1.2.18), respectively, are special cases of (1.3.28). Using (1.2.17) and (1.3.5), we can evaluate the mean squared error of $\hat{\sigma}_N^2$ as

$$E(\hat{\sigma}_N^2 - \sigma^2)^2 = \frac{2(T-K) + (T-K-N)^2}{N^2}\sigma^4. \tag{1.3.29}$$

By differentiating (1.3.29) with respect to N and equating the derivative to zero, we can find the value of N that minimizes (1.3.29) to be

$$N^* = T - K + 2. \tag{1.3.30}$$

Inserting (1.3.30) into (1.3.29), we have

$$E(\hat{\sigma}_{N^*}^2 - \sigma^2)^2 = \frac{2\sigma^4}{T-K+2}, \tag{1.3.31}$$

which is smaller than the Cramér-Rao bound if $K = 1$.

1.4 Model 1 with Linear Constraints

In this section we shall consider estimation of the parameters $\boldsymbol{\beta}$ and σ^2 in Model 1 when there are certain linear constraints on the elements of $\boldsymbol{\beta}$. We shall assume that the constraints are of the form

$$\mathbf{Q}'\boldsymbol{\beta} = \mathbf{c}, \tag{1.4.1}$$

where $\mathbf{Q}$ is a $K \times q$ matrix of known constants and $\mathbf{c}$ is a q-vector of known constants. We shall also assume $q < K$ and rank $(\mathbf{Q}) = q$.

Equation (1.4.1) embodies many of the common constraints that occur in practice. For example, if $\mathbf{Q}' = (\mathbf{I}, \mathbf{0})$ where $\mathbf{I}$ is the identity matrix of size K_1 and $\mathbf{0}$ is the $K_1 \times K_2$ matrix of zeroes such that $K_1 + K_2 = K$, then the constraints mean that the elements of a K_1-component subset of $\boldsymbol{\beta}$ are specified to be equal to certain values and the remaining K_2 elements are allowed to vary freely. As another example, the case in which $\mathbf{Q}'$ is a row vector of ones and $c = 1$ implies the restriction that the sum of the regression parameters is unity.

The study of this subject is useful for its own sake in addition to providing preliminary results for the next section, where we shall discuss tests of the linear hypothesis (1.4.1). We shall define the constrained least squares estimator, present an alternative derivation, show it is BLUE when (1.4.1) is true, and finally consider the case where (1.4.1) is made stochastic by the addition of a random error term to the right-hand side.

1.4.1 Constrained Least Squares Estimator (CLS)

The constrained least squares estimator (CLS) of $\boldsymbol{\beta}$, denoted by $\bar{\boldsymbol{\beta}}$, is defined to be the value of $\boldsymbol{\beta}$ that minimizes the sum of squared residuals

$$S(\boldsymbol{\beta}) = (\mathbf{y} - \mathbf{X}\boldsymbol{\beta})'(\mathbf{y} - \mathbf{X}\boldsymbol{\beta}) \tag{1.4.2}$$

under the constraints (1.4.1). In Section 1.2.1 we showed that (1.4.2) is minimized without constraint at the least squares estimator $\hat{\boldsymbol{\beta}}$. Writing $S(\hat{\boldsymbol{\beta}})$ for the sum of squares of the least squares residuals, we can rewrite (1.4.2) as

$$S(\boldsymbol{\beta}) = S(\hat{\boldsymbol{\beta}}) + (\hat{\boldsymbol{\beta}} - \boldsymbol{\beta})'\mathbf{X}'\mathbf{X}(\hat{\boldsymbol{\beta}} - \boldsymbol{\beta}). \tag{1.4.3}$$

Instead of directly minimizing (1.4.2) under (1.4.1), we minimize (1.4.3) under (1.4.1), which is mathematically simpler.

Put $\hat{\boldsymbol{\beta}} - \boldsymbol{\beta} = \boldsymbol{\delta}$ and $\mathbf{Q}'\hat{\boldsymbol{\beta}} - \mathbf{c} = \boldsymbol{\gamma}$. Then, because $S(\hat{\boldsymbol{\beta}})$ does not depend on $\boldsymbol{\beta}$, the problem is equivalent to the minimization of $\boldsymbol{\delta}'\mathbf{X}'\mathbf{X}\boldsymbol{\delta}$ under $\mathbf{Q}'\boldsymbol{\delta} = \boldsymbol{\gamma}$. Equating the derivatives of $\boldsymbol{\delta}'\mathbf{X}'\mathbf{X}\boldsymbol{\delta} + 2\boldsymbol{\lambda}'(\mathbf{Q}'\boldsymbol{\delta} - \boldsymbol{\gamma})$ with respect to $\boldsymbol{\delta}$ and the q-vector of Lagrange multipliers $\boldsymbol{\lambda}$ to zero, we obtain the solution

$$\boldsymbol{\delta} = (\mathbf{X}'\mathbf{X})^{-1}\mathbf{Q}[\mathbf{Q}'(\mathbf{X}'\mathbf{X})^{-1}\mathbf{Q}]^{-1}\boldsymbol{\gamma}. \tag{1.4.4}$$

Transforming from $\boldsymbol{\delta}$ and $\boldsymbol{\gamma}$ to the original variables, we can write the minimizing value $\bar{\boldsymbol{\beta}}$ of $S(\boldsymbol{\beta})$ as

$$\bar{\boldsymbol{\beta}} = \hat{\boldsymbol{\beta}} - (\mathbf{X}'\mathbf{X})^{-1}\mathbf{Q}[\mathbf{Q}'(\mathbf{X}'\mathbf{X})^{-1}\mathbf{Q}]^{-1}(\mathbf{Q}'\hat{\boldsymbol{\beta}} - \mathbf{c}). \tag{1.4.5}$$

The corresponding estimator of σ^2 can be defined as

$$\bar{\sigma}^2 = T^{-1}(\mathbf{y} - \mathbf{X}\bar{\boldsymbol{\beta}})'(\mathbf{y} - \mathbf{X}\bar{\boldsymbol{\beta}}). \tag{1.4.6}$$

It is easy to show that the $\bar{\boldsymbol{\beta}}$ and $\bar{\sigma}^2$ are the constrained maximum likelihood estimators if we assume normality of $\mathbf{u}$ in Model 1.

1.4.2 An Alternative Derivation of the Constrained Least Squares Estimator

Define a $K \times (K - q)$ matrix $\mathbf{R}$ such that the matrix $(\mathbf{Q}, \mathbf{R})$ is nonsingular and $\mathbf{R}'\mathbf{Q} = \mathbf{0}$. Such a matrix can always be found; it is not unique, and any matrix that satisfies these conditions will do. Then, defining $\mathbf{A} = (\mathbf{Q}, \mathbf{R})'$, $\gamma = \mathbf{A}\boldsymbol{\beta}$, and $\mathbf{Z} = \mathbf{X}\mathbf{A}^{-1}$, we can rewrite the basic model (1.1.4) as

$$\begin{aligned} \mathbf{y} &= \mathbf{X}\boldsymbol{\beta} + \mathbf{u} \qquad (1.4.7) \\ &= \mathbf{X}\mathbf{A}^{-1}\mathbf{A}\boldsymbol{\beta} + \mathbf{u} \\ &= \mathbf{Z}\gamma + \mathbf{u}. \end{aligned}$$

If we partition $\gamma = (\gamma_1', \gamma_2')'$, where $\gamma_1 = \mathbf{Q}'\boldsymbol{\beta}$ and $\gamma_2 = \mathbf{R}'\boldsymbol{\beta}$, we see that the constraints (1.4.1) specify γ_1 and leave γ_2 unspecified. The vector γ_2 has $K - q$ elements; thus we have reduced the problem of estimating K parameters subject to q constraints to the problem of estimating $K - q$ free parameters. Using $\gamma_1 = \mathbf{c}$ and

$$\mathbf{A}^{-1} = [\mathbf{Q}(\mathbf{Q}'\mathbf{Q})^{-1}, \mathbf{R}(\mathbf{R}'\mathbf{R})^{-1}], \qquad (1.4.8)$$

we have from (1.4.7)

$$\mathbf{y} - \mathbf{X}\mathbf{Q}(\mathbf{Q}'\mathbf{Q})^{-1}\mathbf{c} = \mathbf{X}\mathbf{R}(\mathbf{R}'\mathbf{R})^{-1}\gamma_2 + \mathbf{u}. \qquad (1.4.9)$$

Let $\hat{\gamma}_2$ be the least squares estimator of γ_2 in (1.4.9):

$$\hat{\gamma}_2 = \mathbf{R}'\mathbf{R}(\mathbf{R}'\mathbf{X}'\mathbf{X}\mathbf{R})^{-1}\mathbf{R}'\mathbf{X}'[\mathbf{y} - \mathbf{X}\mathbf{Q}(\mathbf{Q}'\mathbf{Q})^{-1}\mathbf{c}]. \qquad (1.4.10)$$

Now, transforming from γ back to $\boldsymbol{\beta}$ by the relationship $\boldsymbol{\beta} = \mathbf{A}^{-1}\gamma$, we obtain the CLS estimator of $\boldsymbol{\beta}$:

$$\begin{aligned} \bar{\boldsymbol{\beta}} &= \mathbf{R}(\mathbf{R}'\mathbf{X}'\mathbf{X}\mathbf{R})^{-1}\mathbf{R}'\mathbf{X}'\mathbf{y} \qquad (1.4.11) \\ &\quad + [\mathbf{I} - \mathbf{R}(\mathbf{R}'\mathbf{X}'\mathbf{X}\mathbf{R})^{-1}\mathbf{R}'\mathbf{X}'\mathbf{X}]\mathbf{Q}(\mathbf{Q}'\mathbf{Q})^{-1}\mathbf{c}. \end{aligned}$$

Note that (1.4.11) is different from (1.4.5). Equation (1.4.5) is valid only if $\mathbf{X}'\mathbf{X}$ is nonsingular, whereas (1.4.11) can be defined even if $\mathbf{X}'\mathbf{X}$ is singular provided that $\mathbf{R}'\mathbf{X}'\mathbf{X}\mathbf{R}$ is nonsingular. We can show that if $\mathbf{X}'\mathbf{X}$ is nonsingular, (1.4.11) is unique and equal to (1.4.5). Denote the right-hand sides of (1.4.5) and (1.4.11) by $\bar{\boldsymbol{\beta}}_1$ and $\bar{\boldsymbol{\beta}}_2$, respectively. Then it is easy to show

$$\begin{bmatrix} \mathbf{R}'\mathbf{X}'\mathbf{X} \\ \mathbf{Q}' \end{bmatrix} (\bar{\boldsymbol{\beta}}_1 - \bar{\boldsymbol{\beta}}_2) = \mathbf{0}. \qquad (1.4.12)$$

Therefore $\bar{\boldsymbol{\beta}}_1 = \bar{\boldsymbol{\beta}}_2$ if the matrix in the square bracket above is nonsingular. But we have

$$\begin{bmatrix} \mathbf{R}'\mathbf{X}'\mathbf{X} \\ \mathbf{Q}' \end{bmatrix} \begin{bmatrix} \mathbf{R}, \mathbf{Q} \end{bmatrix} = \begin{bmatrix} \mathbf{R}'\mathbf{X}'\mathbf{X}\mathbf{R} & \mathbf{R}'\mathbf{X}'\mathbf{X}\mathbf{Q} \\ \mathbf{0} & \mathbf{Q}'\mathbf{Q} \end{bmatrix}, \qquad (1.4.13)$$

where the matrix on the right-hand side is clearly nonsingular because nonsingularity of $\mathbf{X}'\mathbf{X}$ implies nonsingularity of $\mathbf{R}'\mathbf{X}'\mathbf{X}\mathbf{R}$. Because the matrix $[\mathbf{R}, \mathbf{Q}]$ is nonsingular, it follows that the matrix

$$\begin{bmatrix} \mathbf{R}'\mathbf{X}'\mathbf{X} \\ \mathbf{Q}' \end{bmatrix}$$

is nonsingular, as we desired.

1.4.3 Constrained Least Squares Estimator as Best Linear Unbiased Estimator

That $\bar{\boldsymbol{\beta}}$ is the best linear unbiased estimator follows from the fact that $\hat{\gamma}_2$ is the best linear unbiased estimator of γ_2 in (1.4.9); however, we also can prove it directly. Inserting (1.4.9) into (1.4.11) and using (1.4.8), we obtain

$$\bar{\boldsymbol{\beta}} = \boldsymbol{\beta} + \mathbf{R}(\mathbf{R}'\mathbf{X}'\mathbf{X}\mathbf{R})^{-1}\mathbf{R}'\mathbf{X}'\mathbf{u}. \tag{1.4.14}$$

Therefore, $\bar{\boldsymbol{\beta}}$ is unbiased and its variance-covariance matrix is given by

$$V(\bar{\boldsymbol{\beta}}) = \sigma^2\mathbf{R}(\mathbf{R}'\mathbf{X}'\mathbf{X}\mathbf{R})^{-1}\mathbf{R}'. \tag{1.4.15}$$

We shall now define the class of linear estimators by $\boldsymbol{\beta}^* = \mathbf{C}'\mathbf{y} - \mathbf{d}$ where $\mathbf{C}'$ is a $K \times T$ matrix and $\mathbf{d}$ is a K-vector. This class is broader than the class of linear estimators considered in Section 1.2.5 because of the additive constants $\mathbf{d}$. We did not include $\mathbf{d}$ previously because in the unconstrained model the unbiasedness condition would ensure $\mathbf{d} = \mathbf{0}$. Here, the unbiasedness condition $E(\mathbf{C}'\mathbf{y} - \mathbf{d}) = \boldsymbol{\beta}$ implies $\mathbf{C}'\mathbf{X} = \mathbf{I} + \mathbf{G}\mathbf{Q}'$ and $\mathbf{d} = \mathbf{G}\mathbf{c}$ for some arbitrary $K \times q$ matrix $\mathbf{G}$. We have $V(\boldsymbol{\beta}^*) = \sigma^2\mathbf{C}'\mathbf{C}$ as in Eq. (1.2.30) and CLS is BLUE because of the identity

$$\begin{aligned} &\mathbf{C}'\mathbf{C} - \mathbf{R}(\mathbf{R}'\mathbf{X}'\mathbf{X}\mathbf{R})^{-1}\mathbf{R}' \\ &\quad = [\mathbf{C}' - \mathbf{R}(\mathbf{R}'\mathbf{X}'\mathbf{X}\mathbf{R})^{-1}\mathbf{R}'\mathbf{X}'][\mathbf{C}' - \mathbf{R}(\mathbf{R}'\mathbf{X}'\mathbf{X}\mathbf{R})^{-1}\mathbf{R}'\mathbf{X}']', \end{aligned} \tag{1.4.16}$$

where we have used $\mathbf{C}'\mathbf{X} = \mathbf{I} + \mathbf{G}\mathbf{Q}'$ and $\mathbf{R}'\mathbf{Q} = \mathbf{0}$.

1.4.4 Stochastic Constraints

Suppose we add a stochastic error term on the right-hand side of (1.4.1), namely,

$$\mathbf{Q}'\boldsymbol{\beta} = \mathbf{c} + \mathbf{v}, \tag{1.4.17}$$

where $\mathbf{v}$ is a q-vector of random variables such that $E\mathbf{v} = \mathbf{0}$ and $E\mathbf{v}\mathbf{v}' = \tau^2\mathbf{I}$. By making the constraints stochastic we have departed from the domain of classical statistics and entered that of Bayesian statistics, which treats the unknown parameters $\boldsymbol{\beta}$ as random variables. Although we generally adopt the classical viewpoint in this book, we shall occasionally use Bayesian analysis whenever we believe it sheds light on the problem at hand.[5]

In terms of the parameterization of (1.4.7), the constraints (1.4.17) are equivalent to

$$\gamma_1 = \mathbf{c} + \mathbf{v}. \tag{1.4.18}$$

We shall first derive the posterior distribution of γ, using a prior distribution over all the elements of γ, because it is mathematically simpler to do so; and then we shall treat (1.4.18) as what obtains in the limit as the variances of the prior distribution for γ_2 go to infinity. We shall assume σ^2 is known, for this assumption makes the algebra considerably simpler without changing the essentials. For a discussion of the case where a prior distribution is assumed on σ^2 as well, see Zellner (1971, p. 65) or Theil (1971, p. 670).

Let the prior density of γ be

$$f(\gamma) = (2\pi)^{-K/2}|\boldsymbol{\Omega}|^{-1/2} \exp\,[-(1/2)(\gamma - \boldsymbol{\mu})'\boldsymbol{\Omega}^{-1}(\gamma - \boldsymbol{\mu})], \tag{1.4.19}$$

where $\boldsymbol{\Omega}$ is a known variance-covariance matrix. Thus, by Bayes's rule, the posterior density of γ given $\mathbf{y}$ is

$$\begin{aligned} f(\gamma|\mathbf{y}) &= \frac{f(\mathbf{y}|\gamma)f(\gamma)}{\int f(\mathbf{y}|\gamma)f(\gamma)d\gamma} \\ &= c_1 \exp\,\{-(1/2)[\sigma^{-2}(\mathbf{y} - \mathbf{Z}\gamma)'(\mathbf{y} - \mathbf{Z}\gamma) \\ &\quad + (\gamma - \boldsymbol{\mu})'\boldsymbol{\Omega}^{-1}(\gamma - \boldsymbol{\mu})]\}, \end{aligned} \tag{1.4.20}$$

where c_1 does not depend on γ. Rearranging the terms inside the bracket, we have

$$\begin{aligned} &\sigma^{-2}(\mathbf{y} - \mathbf{Z}\gamma)'(\mathbf{y} - \mathbf{Z}\gamma) + (\gamma - \boldsymbol{\mu})'\boldsymbol{\Omega}^{-1}(\gamma - \boldsymbol{\mu}) \\ &= \gamma'(\sigma^{-2}\mathbf{Z}'\mathbf{Z} + \boldsymbol{\Omega}^{-1})\gamma - 2(\sigma^{-2}\mathbf{y}'\mathbf{Z} + \boldsymbol{\mu}'\boldsymbol{\Omega}^{-1})\gamma + \sigma^{-2}\mathbf{y}'\mathbf{y} + \boldsymbol{\mu}'\boldsymbol{\Omega}^{-1}\boldsymbol{\mu} \\ &= (\gamma - \bar{\gamma})'(\sigma^{-2}\mathbf{Z}'\mathbf{Z} + \boldsymbol{\Omega}^{-1})(\gamma - \bar{\gamma}) - \bar{\gamma}'(\sigma^{-2}\mathbf{Z}'\mathbf{Z} + \boldsymbol{\Omega}^{-1})\bar{\gamma} \\ &\quad + \sigma^{-2}\mathbf{y}'\mathbf{y} + \boldsymbol{\mu}'\boldsymbol{\Omega}^{-1}\boldsymbol{\mu}, \end{aligned} \tag{1.4.21}$$

where

$$\bar{\gamma} = (\sigma^{-2}\mathbf{Z}'\mathbf{Z} + \boldsymbol{\Omega}^{-1})^{-1}(\sigma^{-2}\mathbf{Z}'\mathbf{y} + \boldsymbol{\Omega}^{-1}\boldsymbol{\mu}). \tag{1.4.22}$$

Therefore the posterior distribution of γ is

$$\gamma|\mathbf{y} \sim N(\bar{\gamma}, [\sigma^{-2}\mathbf{Z}'\mathbf{Z} + \boldsymbol{\Omega}^{-1}]^{-1}), \tag{1.4.23}$$

and the *Bayes estimator* of γ is the posterior mean $\bar{\gamma}$ given in (1.4.22). Because $\gamma = \mathbf{A}\beta$, the Bayes estimator of β is given by

$$\tilde{\beta} = \mathbf{A}^{-1}[\sigma^{-2}(\mathbf{A}')^{-1}\mathbf{X}'\mathbf{X}\mathbf{A}^{-1} + \mathbf{\Omega}^{-1}]^{-1}[\sigma^{-2}(\mathbf{A}')^{-1}\mathbf{X}'\mathbf{y} + \mathbf{\Omega}^{-1}\mu]$$
$$= (\sigma^{-2}\mathbf{X}'\mathbf{X} + \mathbf{A}'\mathbf{\Omega}^{-1}\mathbf{A})^{-1}(\sigma^{-2}\mathbf{X}'\mathbf{y} + \mathbf{A}'\mathbf{\Omega}^{-1}\mu). \qquad (1.4.24)$$

We shall now specify μ and $\mathbf{\Omega}$ so that they conform to the stochastic constraints (1.4.18). This can be done by putting the first q elements of μ equal to $\mathbf{c}$ (leaving the remaining $K - q$ elements unspecified because their values do not matter in the limit we shall consider later), putting

$$\mathbf{\Omega} = \begin{bmatrix} \tau^2\mathbf{I} & \mathbf{0} \\ \mathbf{0} & \nu^2\mathbf{I} \end{bmatrix}, \qquad (1.4.25)$$

and then taking ν^2 to infinity (which expresses the assumption that nothing is *a priori* known about γ_2). Hence, in the limit we have

$$\lim_{\nu\to\infty} \mathbf{\Omega}^{-1} = \begin{bmatrix} \tau^{-2}\mathbf{I} & \mathbf{0} \\ \mathbf{0} & \mathbf{0} \end{bmatrix}. \qquad (1.4.26)$$

Inserting (1.4.26) into (1.4.24) and writing the first q elements of μ as $\mathbf{c}$, we finally obtain

$$\tilde{\beta} = (\mathbf{X}'\mathbf{X} + \lambda^2\mathbf{Q}\mathbf{Q}')^{-1}(\mathbf{X}'\mathbf{y} + \lambda^2\mathbf{Q}\mathbf{c}), \qquad (1.4.27)$$

where $\lambda^2 = \sigma^2/\tau^2$.

We have obtained the estimator $\tilde{\beta}$ as a special case of the Bayes estimator, but this estimator was originally proposed by Theil and Goldberger (1961) and was called the *mixed estimator* on heuristic grounds. In their heuristic approach, Eqs. (1.1.4) and (1.4.17) are combined to yield a system of equations

$$\begin{bmatrix} \mathbf{y} \\ \lambda\mathbf{c} \end{bmatrix} = \begin{bmatrix} \mathbf{X} \\ \lambda\mathbf{Q}' \end{bmatrix} \beta + \begin{bmatrix} \mathbf{u} \\ -\lambda\mathbf{v} \end{bmatrix}. \qquad (1.4.28)$$

Note that the multiplication of the second part of the equations by λ renders the combined error terms homoscedastic (that is, constant variance) so that (1.4.28) satisfies the assumptions of Model 1. Then Theil and Goldberger proposed the application of the least squares estimator to (1.4.28), an operation that yields the same estimator as $\tilde{\beta}$ given in (1.4.27). An alternative way to interpret this estimator as a Bayes estimator is given in Theil (1971, p. 670).

There is an interesting connection between the Bayes estimator (1.4.27) and the constrained least squares estimator (1.4.11): The latter is obtained as the limit of the former, taking λ^2 to infinity. Note that this result is consistent with our intuition inasmuch as $\lambda^2 \to \infty$ is equivalent to $\tau^2 \to 0$, an equivalency that implies that the stochastic element disappears from the constraints (1.4.17), thereby reducing them to the nonstochastic constraints (1.4.1). We shall demonstrate this below. [Note that the limit of (1.4.27) as $\lambda^2 \to \infty$ is not $(\mathbf{QQ}')^{-1}\mathbf{Qc}$ because $\mathbf{QQ}'$ is singular; rather, the limit is a $K \times K$ matrix with rank $q < K$.]

Define

$$\mathbf{B} \equiv \mathbf{A}(\lambda^{-2}\mathbf{X}'\mathbf{X} + \mathbf{QQ}')\mathbf{A}' \tag{1.4.29}$$
$$= \begin{bmatrix} \lambda^{-2}\mathbf{Q}'\mathbf{X}'\mathbf{XQ} + \mathbf{Q}'\mathbf{QQ}'\mathbf{Q} & \lambda^{-2}\mathbf{Q}'\mathbf{X}'\mathbf{XR} \\ \lambda^{-2}\mathbf{R}'\mathbf{X}'\mathbf{XQ} & \lambda^{-2}\mathbf{R}'\mathbf{X}'\mathbf{XR} \end{bmatrix}.$$

Then, by Theorem 13 of Appendix 1, we have

$$\mathbf{B}^{-1} = \begin{bmatrix} \mathbf{E}^{-1} & -\mathbf{E}^{-1}\mathbf{Q}'\mathbf{X}'\mathbf{XR}(\mathbf{R}'\mathbf{X}'\mathbf{XR})^{-1} \\ -(\mathbf{R}'\mathbf{X}'\mathbf{XR})^{-1}\mathbf{R}'\mathbf{X}'\mathbf{XQE}^{-1} & \mathbf{F}^{-1} \end{bmatrix}, \tag{1.4.30}$$

where

$$\mathbf{E} = \mathbf{Q}'\mathbf{QQ}'\mathbf{Q} + \lambda^{-2}\mathbf{Q}'\mathbf{X}'\mathbf{XQ} - \lambda^{-2}\mathbf{Q}'\mathbf{X}'\mathbf{XR}(\mathbf{R}'\mathbf{X}'\mathbf{XR})^{-1}\mathbf{R}'\mathbf{X}'\mathbf{XQ} \tag{1.4.31}$$

and

$$\mathbf{F} = \lambda^{-2}\mathbf{R}'\mathbf{X}'\mathbf{XR} - \lambda^{-4}\mathbf{R}'\mathbf{X}'\mathbf{XQ}(\lambda^{-2}\mathbf{Q}'\mathbf{X}'\mathbf{XQ} + \mathbf{Q}'\mathbf{QQ}'\mathbf{Q})^{-1}\mathbf{Q}'\mathbf{X}'\mathbf{XR}. \tag{1.4.32}$$

From (1.4.27) and (1.4.29) we have

$$\tilde{\boldsymbol{\beta}} = \mathbf{A}'\mathbf{B}^{-1}\mathbf{A}(\lambda^{-2}\mathbf{X}'\mathbf{y} + \mathbf{Qc}). \tag{1.4.33}$$

Using (1.4.30), we have

$$\lim_{\lambda^2 \to \infty} \mathbf{A}'\mathbf{B}^{-1}\mathbf{A}(\lambda^{-2}\mathbf{X}'\mathbf{y}) = \mathbf{R}(\mathbf{R}'\mathbf{X}'\mathbf{XR})^{-1}\mathbf{R}'\mathbf{X}'\mathbf{y} \tag{1.4.34}$$

and

$$\lim_{\lambda^2 \to \infty} \mathbf{A}'\mathbf{B}^{-1}\mathbf{AQc} = \lim_{\lambda^2 \to \infty} (\mathbf{Q}, \mathbf{R})\mathbf{B}^{-1}\begin{bmatrix} \mathbf{Q}'\mathbf{Qc} \\ \mathbf{0} \end{bmatrix} \tag{1.4.35}$$
$$= \mathbf{Q}(\mathbf{Q}'\mathbf{Q})^{-1}\mathbf{c} - \mathbf{R}(\mathbf{R}'\mathbf{X}'\mathbf{XR})^{-1}\mathbf{R}'\mathbf{X}'\mathbf{XQ}(\mathbf{Q}'\mathbf{Q})^{-1}\mathbf{c}.$$

Thus we have proved

$$\lim_{\lambda^2 \to \infty} \tilde{\boldsymbol{\beta}} = \bar{\boldsymbol{\beta}}, \tag{1.4.36}$$

where $\bar{\boldsymbol{\beta}}$ is given in (1.4.11).

1.5 Test of Linear Hypotheses

In this section we shall regard the linear constraints (1.4.1) as a testable hypothesis, calling it the null hypothesis. Throughout the section we shall assume Model 1 with normality because the distributions of the commonly used test statistics are derived under the assumption of normality. We shall discuss the t test, the F test, and a test of structural change (a special case of the F test).

1.5.1 The t Test

The t test is an ideal test to use when we have a single constraint, that is, $q = 1$. The F test, which will be discussed in the next section, will be used if $q > 1$.

Because $\hat{\boldsymbol{\beta}}$ is normal, as shown in Eq. (1.3.4), we have

$$\mathbf{Q}'\hat{\boldsymbol{\beta}} \sim N[\mathbf{c}, \sigma^2\mathbf{Q}'(\mathbf{X}'\mathbf{X})^{-1}\mathbf{Q}] \tag{1.5.1}$$

under the null hypothesis (that is, if $\mathbf{Q}'\boldsymbol{\beta} = \mathbf{c}$). With $q = 1$, $\mathbf{Q}'$ is a row vector and c is a scalar. Therefore

$$\frac{\mathbf{Q}'\hat{\boldsymbol{\beta}} - c}{[\sigma^2\mathbf{Q}'(\mathbf{X}'\mathbf{X})^{-1}\mathbf{Q}]^{1/2}} \sim N(0, 1). \tag{1.5.2}$$

This is the test statistic one would use if σ were known. As we have shown in Eq. (1.3.7), we have

$$\frac{\hat{\mathbf{u}}'\hat{\mathbf{u}}}{\sigma^2} \sim \chi^2_{T-K}. \tag{1.5.3}$$

The random variables (1.5.2) and (1.5.3) easily can be shown to be independent by using Theorem 6 of Appendix 2 or by noting $E\hat{\mathbf{u}}\hat{\boldsymbol{\beta}}' = \mathbf{0}$, which implies that $\hat{\mathbf{u}}$ and $\hat{\boldsymbol{\beta}}$ are independent because they are normal, which in turn implies that $\hat{\mathbf{u}}'\hat{\mathbf{u}}$ and $\hat{\boldsymbol{\beta}}$ are independent. Hence, by Theorem 3 of Appendix 2 we have

$$\frac{\mathbf{Q}'\hat{\boldsymbol{\beta}} - c}{[\tilde{\sigma}^2\mathbf{Q}'(\mathbf{X}'\mathbf{X})^{-1}\mathbf{Q}]^{1/2}} \sim S_{T-K}, \tag{1.5.4}$$

which is Student's t with $T - K$ degrees of freedom, where $\tilde{\sigma}$ is the square root of the unbiased estimator of σ^2 defined in Eq. (1.2.18). Note that the denominator in (1.5.4) is an estimate of the standard deviation of the numerator. Thus the null hypothesis $\mathbf{Q}'\boldsymbol{\beta} = c$ can be tested by the statistic (1.5.4). We can use a one-tail or two-tail test, depending on the alternative hypothesis.

In Chapter 3 we shall show that even if $\mathbf{u}$ is not normal, (1.5.2) holds asymptotically (that is, approximately when T is large) under general conditions. We shall also show that $\tilde{\sigma}^2$ converges to σ^2 in probability as T goes to infinity (the exact definition will be given there). Therefore under general distributions of **u** the statistic defined in (1.5.4) is asymptotically distributed as $N(0, 1)$ and can be used to test the hypothesis using the standard normal table.[6] In this case $\hat{\sigma}^2$ may be used in place of $\tilde{\sigma}^2$ because $\hat{\sigma}^2$ also converges to σ^2 in probability.

1.5.2 The *F* Test

In this section we shall consider the test of the null hypothesis $\mathbf{Q}'\boldsymbol{\beta} = \mathbf{c}$ against the alternative hypothesis $\mathbf{Q}'\boldsymbol{\beta} \neq \mathbf{c}$ when it involves more than one constraint (that is, $q > 1$).

We shall derive the F test as a simple transformation of the *likelihood ratio test*. Suppose that the likelihood function is in general given by $L(\boldsymbol{\xi}, \boldsymbol{\theta})$, where $\boldsymbol{\xi}$ is a sample and $\boldsymbol{\theta}$ is a vector of parameters. Let the null hypothesis be H_0: $\boldsymbol{\theta} \in S_0$ where S_0 is a subset of the parameter space Θ and let the alternative hypothesis be $H_1: \boldsymbol{\theta} \in S_1$ where S_1 is another subset of Θ. Then the likelihood ratio test is defined by the following procedure:

$$\text{Reject } H_0 \text{ if } \lambda \equiv \frac{\max\limits_{\boldsymbol{\theta} \in S_0} L(\boldsymbol{\xi}, \boldsymbol{\theta})}{\max\limits_{\boldsymbol{\theta} \in S_0 \cup S_1} L(\boldsymbol{\xi}, \boldsymbol{\theta})} < g, \tag{1.5.5}$$

where g is chosen so as to satisfy $P(\lambda < g) = \alpha$ for a given significance level α. The likelihood ratio test may be justified on several grounds: (1) It is intuitively appealing because of its connection with the Neyman-Pearson lemma. (2) It is known to lead to good tests in many cases. (3) It has asymptotically optimal properties, as shown by Wald (1943).

Now let us obtain the likelihood ratio test of $\mathbf{Q}'\boldsymbol{\beta} = \mathbf{c}$ against $\mathbf{Q}'\boldsymbol{\beta} \neq \mathbf{c}$ in Model 1 with normality. When we use the results of Section 1.4.1, the numerator likelihood becomes

$$\begin{aligned} \max_{\mathbf{Q}\boldsymbol{\beta}=\mathbf{c}} L &= (2\pi\bar{\sigma}^2)^{-T/2} \exp\,[-0.5\bar{\sigma}^{-2}(\mathbf{y} - \mathbf{X}\bar{\boldsymbol{\beta}})'(\mathbf{y} - \mathbf{X}\bar{\boldsymbol{\beta}})] \\ &= (2\pi\bar{\sigma}^2)^{-T/2} e^{-T/2}. \end{aligned} \tag{1.5.6}$$

Because in the present case $S_0 \cup S_1$ is the whole parameter space of $\boldsymbol{\beta}$, the maximization in the denominator of (1.5.5) is carried out without constraint. Therefore the denominator likelihood is given by

$$\begin{aligned} \max L &= (2\pi\hat{\sigma}^2)^{-T/2} \exp\,[-0.5\hat{\sigma}^{-2}(\mathbf{y} - \mathbf{X}\hat{\boldsymbol{\beta}})'(\mathbf{y} - \mathbf{X}\hat{\boldsymbol{\beta}})] \\ &= (2\pi\hat{\sigma}^2)^{-T/2} e^{-T/2}. \end{aligned} \tag{1.5.7}$$

Hence, the likelihood ratio test of $\mathbf{Q}'\boldsymbol{\beta} = \mathbf{c}$ is

$$\text{Reject} \quad \mathbf{Q}'\boldsymbol{\beta} = \mathbf{c} \quad \text{if} \quad \lambda = \left[\frac{S(\bar{\boldsymbol{\beta}})}{S(\hat{\boldsymbol{\beta}})}\right]^{-T/2} < g, \tag{1.5.8}$$

where g is chosen as in (1.5.5).

We actually use the equivalent test

$$\text{Reject} \quad \mathbf{Q}'\boldsymbol{\beta} = \mathbf{c} \quad \text{if} \quad \eta \equiv \frac{T-K}{q} \frac{S(\bar{\boldsymbol{\beta}}) - S(\hat{\boldsymbol{\beta}})}{S(\hat{\boldsymbol{\beta}})} > h, \tag{1.5.9}$$

where h is appropriately chosen. Clearly, (1.5.8) and (1.5.9) can be made equivalent by putting $h = [(T-K)/q](g^{-2/T} - 1)$. The test (1.5.9) is called the F test because under the null hypothesis η is distributed as $F(q, T-K)$—the F distribution with q and $T-K$ degrees of freedom—as we shall show next.

From (1.4.3) and (1.4.5) we have

$$S(\bar{\boldsymbol{\beta}}) - S(\hat{\boldsymbol{\beta}}) = (\mathbf{Q}'\hat{\boldsymbol{\beta}} - \mathbf{c})'[\mathbf{Q}'(\mathbf{X}'\mathbf{X})^{-1}\mathbf{Q}]^{-1}(\mathbf{Q}'\hat{\boldsymbol{\beta}} - \mathbf{c}). \tag{1.5.10}$$

But since (1.5.1) holds even if $\mathbf{Q}$ is a matrix, we have by Theorem 1 of Appendix 2

$$\frac{S(\bar{\boldsymbol{\beta}}) - S(\hat{\boldsymbol{\beta}})}{\sigma^2} \sim \chi^2_q. \tag{1.5.11}$$

Because this chi-square variable is independent of the chi-square variable given in (1.5.3) by an application of Theorem 5 of Appendix 2 (or by the independence of $\hat{\mathbf{u}}$ and $\hat{\boldsymbol{\beta}}$), we have by Theorem 4 of Appendix 2

$$\eta = \frac{T-K}{q} \frac{(\mathbf{Q}'\hat{\boldsymbol{\beta}} - \mathbf{c})'[\mathbf{Q}'(\mathbf{X}'\mathbf{X})^{-1}\mathbf{Q}]^{-1}(\mathbf{Q}'\hat{\boldsymbol{\beta}} - \mathbf{c})}{\hat{\mathbf{u}}'\hat{\mathbf{u}}} \sim F(q, T-K). \tag{1.5.12}$$

We shall now give an alternative motivation for the test statistic (1.5.12). For this purpose, consider the general problem of testing the null hypothesis H_0: $\boldsymbol{\theta} = \boldsymbol{\theta}_0$, where $\boldsymbol{\theta} = (\theta_1, \theta_2)'$ is a two-dimensional vector of parameters. Suppose we wish to construct a test statistic on the basis of an estimator $\hat{\boldsymbol{\theta}}$ that is distributed as $N(\boldsymbol{\theta}_0, \mathbf{V})$ under the null hypothesis, where we assume $\mathbf{V}$ to be a known diagonal matrix for simplicity. Consider the following two tests of H_0:

$$\text{Reject} \quad H_0 \quad \text{if} \quad (\hat{\boldsymbol{\theta}} - \boldsymbol{\theta}_0)'(\hat{\boldsymbol{\theta}} - \boldsymbol{\theta}_0) > c \tag{1.5.13}$$

and

$$\text{Reject} \quad H_0 \quad \text{if} \quad (\hat{\boldsymbol{\theta}} - \boldsymbol{\theta}_0)'\mathbf{V}^{-1}(\hat{\boldsymbol{\theta}} - \boldsymbol{\theta}_0) > d, \tag{1.5.14}$$

where c and d are determined so as to make the probability of Type I error equal to the same given value for each test. That (1.5.14) is preferred to (1.5.13) can be argued as follows: Let σ_1^2 and σ_2^2 be the variances of $\hat{\theta}_1$ and $\hat{\theta}_2$, respectively, and suppose $\sigma_1^2 < \sigma_2^2$. Then a deviation of $\hat{\theta}_1$ from θ_{10} provides a greater reason for rejecting H_0 than the same size deviation of $\hat{\theta}_2$ from θ_{20} because the latter could be caused by variability of $\hat{\theta}_2$ rather than by falseness of H_0. The test statistic (1.5.14) precisely incorporates this consideration.

The test (1.5.14) is commonly used for the general case of a q-vector $\boldsymbol{\theta}$ and a general variance-covariance matrix $\mathbf{V}$. Another attractive feature of the test is that

$$(\hat{\boldsymbol{\theta}} - \boldsymbol{\theta}_0)'\mathbf{V}^{-1}(\hat{\boldsymbol{\theta}} - \boldsymbol{\theta}_0) \sim \chi_q^2. \tag{1.5.15}$$

Applying this test to the test of the hypothesis (1.4.1), we readily see that the test should be based on

$$\frac{(\mathbf{Q}'\hat{\boldsymbol{\beta}} - \mathbf{c})'[\mathbf{Q}'(\mathbf{X}'\mathbf{X})^{-1}\mathbf{Q}]^{-1}(\mathbf{Q}'\hat{\boldsymbol{\beta}} - \mathbf{c})}{\sigma^2} \sim \chi_q^2. \tag{1.5.16}$$

This test can be exactly valid only when σ^2 is known and hence is analogous to the standard normal test based on (1.5.2). Thus the F test statistic (1.5.12) may be regarded as a natural adaptation of (1.5.16) to the situation where σ^2 must be estimated. (For a rigorous mathematical discussion of the optimal properties of the F-test, the reader is referred to Scheffé, 1959, p. 46.)

By comparing (1.5.4) and (1.5.12) we immediately note that if $q = 1$ (and therefore $\mathbf{Q}'$ is a row vector) the F statistic is the square of the t statistic. This fact clearly indicates that if $q = 1$ the t test should be used rather than the F test because a one-tail test is possible only with the t test.

As stated earlier, (1.5.1) holds asymptotically even if $\mathbf{u}$ is not normal. Because $\tilde{\sigma}^2 = \hat{\mathbf{u}}'\hat{\mathbf{u}}/(T - K)$ converges to σ^2 in probability, the linear hypothesis can be tested without assuming normality of $\mathbf{u}$ by using the fact that $q\eta$ is asymptotically distributed as χ_q^2. Some people prefer to use the F test in this situation. The remark in note 6 applies to this practice.

The F statistic η given in (1.5.12) takes on a variety of forms as we insert a variety of specific values into $\mathbf{Q}$ and $\mathbf{c}$. As an example, consider the case where $\boldsymbol{\beta}$ is partitioned as $\boldsymbol{\beta}' = (\boldsymbol{\beta}_1', \boldsymbol{\beta}_2')$, where $\boldsymbol{\beta}_1$ is a K_1-vector and $\boldsymbol{\beta}_2$ is a K_2-vector such that $K_1 + K_2 = K$, and the null hypothesis specifies $\boldsymbol{\beta}_2 = \bar{\boldsymbol{\beta}}_2$ and leaves $\boldsymbol{\beta}_1$ unspecified. This hypothesis can be written in the form $\mathbf{Q}'\boldsymbol{\beta} = \mathbf{c}$ by putting $\mathbf{Q}' = (\mathbf{0}, \mathbf{I})$, where $\mathbf{0}$ is the $K_2 \times K_1$ matrix of zeros and $\mathbf{I}$ is the identity matrix of size K_2, and by putting $\mathbf{c} = \bar{\boldsymbol{\beta}}_2$. Inserting these values into (1.5.12) yields

$$\eta = \frac{T-K}{K_2} \frac{(\hat{\boldsymbol{\beta}}_2 - \bar{\boldsymbol{\beta}}_2)'[(\mathbf{0}, \mathbf{I})(\mathbf{X}'\mathbf{X})^{-1}(\mathbf{0}, \mathbf{I})']^{-1}(\hat{\boldsymbol{\beta}}_2 - \bar{\boldsymbol{\beta}}_2)}{\hat{\mathbf{u}}'\hat{\mathbf{u}}} \tag{1.5.17}$$

$$\sim F(K_2, T-K).$$

We can write (1.5.17) in a more suggestive form. Partition $\mathbf{X}$ as $\mathbf{X} = (\mathbf{X}_1, \mathbf{X}_2)$ conformably with the partition of $\boldsymbol{\beta}$ and define $\mathbf{M}_1 = \mathbf{I} - \mathbf{X}_1(\mathbf{X}_1'\mathbf{X}_1)^{-1}\mathbf{X}_1'$. Then by Theorem 13 of Appendix 1 we have

$$[(\mathbf{0}, \mathbf{I})(\mathbf{X}'\mathbf{X})^{-1}(\mathbf{0}, \mathbf{I})']^{-1} = \mathbf{X}_2'\mathbf{M}_1\mathbf{X}_2. \tag{1.5.18}$$

Therefore, using (1.5.18), we can rewrite (1.5.17) as

$$\eta = \frac{T-K}{K_2} \frac{(\hat{\boldsymbol{\beta}}_2 - \bar{\boldsymbol{\beta}}_2)'\mathbf{X}_2'\mathbf{M}_1\mathbf{X}_2(\hat{\boldsymbol{\beta}}_2 - \bar{\boldsymbol{\beta}}_2)}{\hat{\mathbf{u}}'\hat{\mathbf{u}}} \sim F(K_2, T-K). \tag{1.5.19}$$

Of particular interest is the further special case of (1.5.19), where $K_1 = 1$, so that β_1 is a scalar coefficient on the first column of $\mathbf{X}$, which we assume to be the vector of ones (denoted by $\mathbf{l}$), and where $\bar{\boldsymbol{\beta}}_2 = \mathbf{0}$. Then $\mathbf{M}_1$ becomes $\mathbf{L} = \mathbf{I} - T^{-1}\mathbf{l}\mathbf{l}'$. Therefore, using (1.2.13), we have

$$\hat{\boldsymbol{\beta}}_2 = (\mathbf{X}_2'\mathbf{L}\mathbf{X}_2)^{-1}\mathbf{X}_2'\mathbf{L}\mathbf{y}, \tag{1.5.20}$$

so (1.5.19) can now be written as

$$\eta = \frac{T-K}{K-1} \frac{\mathbf{y}'\mathbf{L}\mathbf{X}_2(\mathbf{X}_2'\mathbf{L}\mathbf{X}_2)^{-1}\mathbf{X}_2'\mathbf{L}\mathbf{y}}{\hat{\mathbf{u}}'\hat{\mathbf{u}}} \sim F(K-1, T-K). \tag{1.5.21}$$

Using the definition of R^2 given in (1.2.9), we can rewrite (1.5.21) as

$$\eta = \frac{T-K}{K-1} \frac{R^2}{1-R^2} \sim F(K-1, T-K), \tag{1.5.22}$$

since $\hat{\mathbf{u}}'\hat{\mathbf{u}} = \mathbf{y}'\mathbf{L}\mathbf{y} - \mathbf{y}'\mathbf{L}\mathbf{X}_2(\mathbf{X}_2'\mathbf{L}\mathbf{X}_2)^{-1}\mathbf{X}_2'\mathbf{L}\mathbf{y}$ because of Theorem 15 of Appendix 1. The value of statistic (1.5.22) usually appears in computer printouts and is commonly interpreted as the test statistic for the hypothesis that the population counterpart of R^2 is equal to 0.

1.5.3 A Test of Structural Change when Variances Are Equal

Suppose we have two regression regimes

$$\mathbf{y}_1 = \mathbf{X}_1\boldsymbol{\beta}_1 + \mathbf{u}_1 \tag{1.5.23}$$

and

$$\mathbf{y}_2 = \mathbf{X}_2\boldsymbol{\beta}_2 + \mathbf{u}_2, \tag{1.5.24}$$

where the vectors and matrices in (1.5.23) have T_1 rows and those in (1.5.24) T_2 rows, $\mathbf{X}_1$ is a $T_1 \times K^*$ matrix and $\mathbf{X}_2$ is a $T_2 \times K^*$ matrix, and $\mathbf{u}_1$ and $\mathbf{u}_2$ are normally distributed with zero means and variance-covariance matrix

$$E\begin{bmatrix} \mathbf{u}_1 \\ \mathbf{u}_2 \end{bmatrix}(\mathbf{u}_1', \mathbf{u}_2') = \begin{bmatrix} \sigma_1^2\mathbf{I}_{T_1} & \mathbf{0} \\ \mathbf{0} & \sigma_2^2\mathbf{I}_{T_2} \end{bmatrix}.$$

We assume that both $\mathbf{X}_1$ and $\mathbf{X}_2$ have rank equal to K^*.[7] We want to test the null hypothesis $\boldsymbol{\beta}_1 = \boldsymbol{\beta}_2$ assuming $\sigma_1^2 = \sigma_2^2 (\equiv \sigma^2)$ in the present section and $\sigma_1^2 \neq \sigma_2^2$ in the next section. This test is especially important in econometric time series because the econometrician often suspects the occurrence of a structural change from one era to another (say, from the prewar era to the postwar era), a change that manifests itself in the regression parameters. When $\sigma_1^2 = \sigma_2^2$, this test can be handled as a special case of the standard F test presented in the preceding section.

To apply the F test to the problem, combine Eqs. (1.5.23) and (1.5.24) as

$$\mathbf{y} = \underline{\mathbf{X}}\boldsymbol{\beta} + \mathbf{u}, \tag{1.5.25}$$

where

$$\mathbf{y} = \begin{bmatrix} \mathbf{y}_1 \\ \mathbf{y}_2 \end{bmatrix}, \quad \underline{\mathbf{X}} = \begin{bmatrix} \mathbf{X}_1 & \mathbf{0} \\ \mathbf{0} & \mathbf{X}_2 \end{bmatrix}, \quad \boldsymbol{\beta} = \begin{bmatrix} \boldsymbol{\beta}_1 \\ \boldsymbol{\beta}_2 \end{bmatrix}, \quad \text{and} \quad \mathbf{u} = \begin{bmatrix} \mathbf{u}_1 \\ \mathbf{u}_2 \end{bmatrix}.$$

Then, since $\sigma_1^2 = \sigma_2^2 (\equiv \sigma^2)$, (1.5.25) is the same as Model 1 with normality; hence we can represent our hypothesis $\boldsymbol{\beta}_1 = \boldsymbol{\beta}_2$ as a standard linear hypothesis on Model 1 with normality by putting $T = T_1 + T_2$, $K = 2K^*$, $q = K^*$, $\mathbf{Q}' = (\mathbf{I}, -\mathbf{I})$, and $\mathbf{c} = \mathbf{0}$. Inserting these values into (1.5.12) yields the test statistic

$$\eta = \left(\frac{T_1 + T_2 - 2K^*}{K^*}\right) \frac{(\hat{\boldsymbol{\beta}}_1 - \hat{\boldsymbol{\beta}}_2)'[(\mathbf{X}_1'\mathbf{X}_1)^{-1} + (\mathbf{X}_2'\mathbf{X}_2)^{-1}]^{-1}(\hat{\boldsymbol{\beta}}_1 - \hat{\boldsymbol{\beta}}_2)}{\mathbf{y}'[\mathbf{I} - \underline{\mathbf{X}}(\underline{\mathbf{X}}'\underline{\mathbf{X}})^{-1}\underline{\mathbf{X}}']\mathbf{y}}$$
$$\sim F(K^*, T_1 + T_2 - 2K^*), \tag{1.5.26}$$

where $\hat{\boldsymbol{\beta}}_1 = (\mathbf{X}_1'\mathbf{X}_1)^{-1}\mathbf{X}_1'\mathbf{y}_1$ and $\hat{\boldsymbol{\beta}}_2 = (\mathbf{X}_2'\mathbf{X}_2)^{-1}\mathbf{X}_2'\mathbf{y}_2$.

We shall now give an alternative derivation of (1.5.26). In (1.5.25) we combined Eqs. (1.5.23) and (1.5.24) without making use of the hypothesis $\boldsymbol{\beta}_1 = \boldsymbol{\beta}_2$. If we make use of it, we can combine the two equations as

$$\mathbf{y} = \mathbf{X}\boldsymbol{\beta} + \mathbf{u}, \tag{1.5.27}$$

where we have defined $\mathbf{X} = (\mathbf{X}_1', \mathbf{X}_2')'$ and $\boldsymbol{\beta} = \boldsymbol{\beta}_1 = \boldsymbol{\beta}_2$. Let $S(\hat{\boldsymbol{\beta}})$ be the sum of squared residuals from (1.5.25), that is,

$$S(\hat{\boldsymbol{\beta}}) = \mathbf{y}'[\mathbf{I} - \underline{\mathbf{X}}(\underline{\mathbf{X}}'\underline{\mathbf{X}})^{-1}\underline{\mathbf{X}}']\mathbf{y} \tag{1.5.28}$$

and let $S(\bar{\boldsymbol{\beta}})$ be the sum of squared residuals from (1.5.27), that is,

$$S(\bar{\boldsymbol{\beta}}) = \mathbf{y}'[\mathbf{I} - \mathbf{X}(\mathbf{X}'\mathbf{X})^{-1}\mathbf{X}']\mathbf{y}. \tag{1.5.29}$$

Then using (1.5.9) we have[8]

$$\eta = \frac{T_1 + T_2 - 2K^*}{K^*} \frac{S(\bar{\boldsymbol{\beta}}) - S(\hat{\boldsymbol{\beta}})}{S(\hat{\boldsymbol{\beta}})} \sim F(K^*, T_1 + T_2 - 2K^*). \tag{1.5.30}$$

To show the equivalence of (1.5.26) and (1.5.30), we must show

$$S(\bar{\boldsymbol{\beta}}) - S(\hat{\boldsymbol{\beta}}) = (\hat{\boldsymbol{\beta}}_1 - \hat{\boldsymbol{\beta}}_2)'[(\mathbf{X}_1'\mathbf{X}_1)^{-1} + (\mathbf{X}_2'\mathbf{X}_2)^{-1}]^{-1}(\hat{\boldsymbol{\beta}}_1 - \hat{\boldsymbol{\beta}}_2). \tag{1.5.31}$$

From (1.5.29) we have

$$S(\bar{\boldsymbol{\beta}}) = \mathbf{y}'\left[\mathbf{I} - \begin{bmatrix}\mathbf{X}_1 \\ \mathbf{X}_2\end{bmatrix}(\mathbf{X}_1'\mathbf{X}_1 + \mathbf{X}_2'\mathbf{X}_2)^{-1}(\mathbf{X}_1', \mathbf{X}_2')\right]\mathbf{y} \tag{1.5.32}$$

and from (1.5.28) we have

$$\begin{aligned} S(\hat{\boldsymbol{\beta}}) &= \mathbf{y}'\left[\mathbf{I} - \begin{bmatrix}\mathbf{X}_1(\mathbf{X}_1'\mathbf{X}_1)^{-1}\mathbf{X}_1' & \mathbf{0} \\ \mathbf{0} & \mathbf{X}_2(\mathbf{X}_2'\mathbf{X}_2)^{-1}\mathbf{X}_2'\end{bmatrix}\right]\mathbf{y} \qquad (1.5.33) \\ &= \mathbf{y}_1'[\mathbf{I} - \mathbf{X}_1(\mathbf{X}_1'\mathbf{X}_1)^{-1}\mathbf{X}_1']\mathbf{y}_1 + \mathbf{y}_2'[\mathbf{I} - \mathbf{X}_2(\mathbf{X}_2'\mathbf{X}_2)^{-1}\mathbf{X}_2']\mathbf{y}_2. \end{aligned}$$

Therefore, from (1.5.32) and (1.5.33) we get

$$\begin{aligned} &S(\bar{\boldsymbol{\beta}}) - S(\hat{\boldsymbol{\beta}}) \qquad (1.5.34) \\ &= (\mathbf{y}_1'\mathbf{X}_1, \mathbf{y}_2'\mathbf{X}_2) \\ &\times \begin{bmatrix}(\mathbf{X}_1'\mathbf{X}_1)^{-1} - (\mathbf{X}_1'\mathbf{X}_1 + \mathbf{X}_2'\mathbf{X}_2)^{-1} & -(\mathbf{X}_1'\mathbf{X}_1 + \mathbf{X}_2'\mathbf{X}_2)^{-1} \\ -(\mathbf{X}_1'\mathbf{X}_1 + \mathbf{X}_2'\mathbf{X}_2)^{-1} & (\mathbf{X}_2'\mathbf{X}_2)^{-1} - (\mathbf{X}_1'\mathbf{X}_1 + \mathbf{X}_2'\mathbf{X}_2)^{-1}\end{bmatrix} \\ &\times \begin{bmatrix}\mathbf{X}_1'\mathbf{y}_1 \\ \mathbf{X}_2'\mathbf{y}_2\end{bmatrix} \\ &= (\mathbf{y}_1'\mathbf{X}_1, \mathbf{y}_2'\mathbf{X}_2) \\ &\times \begin{bmatrix}(\mathbf{X}_1'\mathbf{X}_1)^{-1} \\ -(\mathbf{X}_2'\mathbf{X}_2)^{-1}\end{bmatrix}[(\mathbf{X}_1'\mathbf{X}_1)^{-1} + (\mathbf{X}_2'\mathbf{X}_2)^{-1}]^{-1}[(\mathbf{X}_1'\mathbf{X}_1)^{-1}, -(\mathbf{X}_2'\mathbf{X}_2)^{-1}] \\ &\times \begin{bmatrix}\mathbf{X}_1'\mathbf{y}_1 \\ \mathbf{X}_2'\mathbf{y}_2\end{bmatrix}, \end{aligned}$$

the last line of which is equal to the right-hand side of (1.5.31). The last equality of (1.5.34) follows from Theorem 19 of Appendix 1.

The hypothesis $\boldsymbol{\beta}_1 = \boldsymbol{\beta}_2$ is merely one of many linear hypotheses we can impose on the $\boldsymbol{\beta}$ of the model (1.5.25). For instance, we might want to test the equality of a subset of $\boldsymbol{\beta}_1$ with the corresponding subset of $\boldsymbol{\beta}_2$. If the subset consists of the first K_1^* elements of both $\boldsymbol{\beta}_1$ and $\boldsymbol{\beta}_2$, we should put $T = T_1 + T_2$ and $K = 2K^*$ as before, but $q = K_1^*$, $\mathbf{Q}' = (\mathbf{I}, \mathbf{0}, -\mathbf{I}, \mathbf{0})$, and $\mathbf{c} = \mathbf{0}$ in the formula (1.5.12).

If, however, we wish to test the equality of a single element of $\boldsymbol{\beta}_1$ with the corresponding element of $\boldsymbol{\beta}_2$, we should use the t test rather than the F test for the reason given in Section 1.5.2. Suppose the null hypothesis is $\beta_{1i} = \beta_{2i}$ where these are the ith elements of $\boldsymbol{\beta}_1$ and $\boldsymbol{\beta}_2$, respectively. Let the ith columns of $\mathbf{X}_1$ and $\mathbf{X}_2$ be denoted by $\mathbf{x}_{1i}$ and $\mathbf{x}_{2i}$ and let $\mathbf{X}_{1(i)}$ and $\mathbf{X}_{2(i)}$ consist of the remaining $K^* - 1$ columns of $\mathbf{X}_1$ and $\mathbf{X}_2$, respectively. Define $\mathbf{M}_{1(i)} = \mathbf{I} - \mathbf{X}_{1(i)}(\mathbf{X}_{1(i)}'\mathbf{X}_{1(i)})^{-1}\mathbf{X}_{1(i)}'$, $\tilde{\mathbf{x}}_{1i} = \mathbf{M}_{1(i)}\mathbf{x}_{1i}$, and $\tilde{\mathbf{y}}_1 = \mathbf{M}_{1(i)}\mathbf{y}_1$ and similarly define $\mathbf{M}_{2(i)}$, $\tilde{\mathbf{x}}_{2i}$, and $\tilde{\mathbf{y}}_2$. Then using Eqs. (1.2.12) and (1.2.13), we have

$$\hat{\beta}_{1i} = \frac{\tilde{\mathbf{x}}_{1i}'\tilde{\mathbf{y}}_1}{\tilde{\mathbf{x}}_{1i}'\tilde{\mathbf{x}}_{1i}} \sim N\left(\beta_{1i}, \frac{\sigma_1^2}{\tilde{\mathbf{x}}_{1i}'\tilde{\mathbf{x}}_{1i}}\right) \tag{1.5.35}$$

and

$$\hat{\beta}_{2i} = \frac{\tilde{\mathbf{x}}_{2i}'\tilde{\mathbf{y}}_2}{\tilde{\mathbf{x}}_{2i}'\tilde{\mathbf{x}}_{2i}} \sim N\left(\beta_{2i}, \frac{\sigma_2^2}{\tilde{\mathbf{x}}_{2i}'\tilde{\mathbf{x}}_{2i}}\right). \tag{1.5.36}$$

Therefore, under the null hypothesis,

$$\frac{\hat{\beta}_{1i} - \hat{\beta}_{2i}}{\left(\dfrac{\sigma_1^2}{\tilde{\mathbf{x}}_{1i}'\tilde{\mathbf{x}}_{1i}} + \dfrac{\sigma_2^2}{\tilde{\mathbf{x}}_{2i}'\tilde{\mathbf{x}}_{2i}}\right)^{1/2}} \sim N(0, 1). \tag{1.5.37}$$

Also, by Theorem 2 of Appendix 2

$$\frac{\mathbf{y}_1'\mathbf{M}_1\mathbf{y}_1}{\sigma_1^2} + \frac{\mathbf{y}_2'\mathbf{M}_2\mathbf{y}_2}{\sigma_2^2} \sim \chi^2_{T_1+T_2-2K^*}, \tag{1.5.38}$$

where $\mathbf{M}_1 = \mathbf{I} - \mathbf{X}_1(\mathbf{X}_1'\mathbf{X}_1)^{-1}\mathbf{X}_1'$ and $\mathbf{M}_2 = \mathbf{I} - \mathbf{X}_2(\mathbf{X}_2'\mathbf{X}_2)^{-1}\mathbf{X}_2'$. Because (1.5.37) and (1.5.38) are independent, we have by Theorem 3 of Appendix 2

$$\frac{(\hat{\beta}_{1i} - \hat{\beta}_{2i})(T_1 + T_2 - 2K^*)^{1/2}}{\left(\dfrac{\sigma_1^2}{\tilde{\mathbf{x}}_{1i}'\tilde{\mathbf{x}}_{1i}} + \dfrac{\sigma_2^2}{\tilde{\mathbf{x}}_{2i}'\tilde{\mathbf{x}}_{2i}}\right)^{1/2}\left(\dfrac{\mathbf{y}_1'\mathbf{M}_1\mathbf{y}_1}{\sigma_1^2} + \dfrac{\mathbf{y}_2'\mathbf{M}_2\mathbf{y}_2}{\sigma_2^2}\right)^{1/2}} \sim S_{T_1+T_2-2K^*}. \tag{1.5.39}$$

Putting $\sigma_1^2 = \sigma_2^2$ in (1.5.39) simplifies it to

$$\frac{\hat{\beta}_{1i} - \hat{\beta}_{2i}}{\left(\frac{\tilde{\sigma}^2}{\tilde{\mathbf{x}}_{1i}'\tilde{\mathbf{x}}_{1i}} + \frac{\tilde{\sigma}^2}{\tilde{\mathbf{x}}_{2i}'\tilde{\mathbf{x}}_{2i}}\right)^{1/2}} \sim S_{T_1+T_2-2K^*}, \tag{1.5.40}$$

where $\tilde{\sigma}^2$ is the unbiased estimate of σ^2 obtained from the model (1.5.25), that is,

$$\tilde{\sigma}^2 = \frac{1}{T_1 + T_2 - 2K^*} \mathbf{y}'[\mathbf{I} - \underline{\mathbf{X}}(\underline{\mathbf{X}}'\underline{\mathbf{X}})^{-1}\underline{\mathbf{X}}']\mathbf{y}. \tag{1.5.41}$$

1.5.4 A Test of Structural Change when Variances Are Unequal

In this section we shall remove the assumption $\sigma_1^2 = \sigma_2^2$ and shall study how to test the equality of $\boldsymbol{\beta}_1$ and $\boldsymbol{\beta}_2$. The problem is considerably more difficult than the case considered in the previous section; in fact, there is no definitive solution to this problem. Difficulty arises because (1.5.25) is no longer Model 1 because of the heteroscedasticity of u. Another way to pinpoint the difficulty is to note that σ_1^2 and σ_2^2 do not drop out from the formula (1.5.39) for the t statistic.

Before proceeding to discuss tests of the equality of $\boldsymbol{\beta}_1$ and $\boldsymbol{\beta}_2$ when $\sigma_1^2 \neq \sigma_2^2$, we shall first consider a test of the equality of the variances. For, if the hypothesis $\sigma_1^2 = \sigma_2^2$ is accepted, we can use the F test of the previous section. The null hypothesis to be tested is $\sigma_1^2 = \sigma_2^2 (\equiv \sigma^2)$. Under the null hypothesis we have

$$\frac{\mathbf{y}_1'\mathbf{M}_1\mathbf{y}_1}{\sigma^2} \sim \chi^2_{T_1-K^*} \tag{1.5.42}$$

and

$$\frac{\mathbf{y}_2'\mathbf{M}_2\mathbf{y}_2}{\sigma^2} \sim \chi^2_{T_2-K^*}. \tag{1.5.43}$$

Because these two chi-square variables are independent by the assumptions of the model, we have by Theorem 4 of Appendix 2

$$\frac{T_2 - K^*}{T_1 - K^*} \frac{\mathbf{y}_1'\mathbf{M}_1\mathbf{y}_1}{\mathbf{y}_2'\mathbf{M}_2\mathbf{y}_2} \sim F(T_1 - K^*, T_2 - K^*). \tag{1.5.44}$$

Unlike the F test of Section 1.5.2, a two-tailed test should be used here because either a large or a small value of (1.5.44) is a reason for rejecting the null hypothesis.

Regarding the test of the equality of the regression parameters, we shall consider only the special case considered at the end of Section 1.5.3, namely, the test of the equality of single elements, $\beta_{1i} = \beta_{2i}$, where the t test is applicable. The problem is essentially that of testing the equality of two normal means when the variances are unequal; it is well known among statisticians as the *Behrens-Fisher problem.* Many methods have been proposed and others are still being proposed in current journals; yet there is no definitive solution to the problem. Kendall and Stuart (1979, Vol. 2, p. 159) have discussed various methods of coping with the problem. We shall present one of the methods, which is attributable to Welch (1938).

As we noted earlier, the difficulty lies in the fact that one cannot derive (1.5.40) from (1.5.39) unless $\sigma_1^2 = \sigma_2^2$. We shall present a method based on the assumption that a slight modification of (1.5.40), namely,

$$\xi \equiv \frac{\hat{\beta}_{1i} - \hat{\beta}_{2i}}{\left(\dfrac{\tilde{\sigma}_1^2}{\tilde{\mathbf{x}}_{1i}'\tilde{\mathbf{x}}_{1i}} + \dfrac{\tilde{\sigma}_2^2}{\tilde{\mathbf{x}}_{2i}'\tilde{\mathbf{x}}_{2i}} \right)^{1/2}}, \tag{1.5.45}$$

where $\tilde{\sigma}_1^2 = (T_1 - K^*)^{-1}\mathbf{y}_1'\mathbf{M}_1\mathbf{y}_1$ and $\tilde{\sigma}_2^2 = (T_2 - K^*)^{-1}\mathbf{y}_2'\mathbf{M}_2\mathbf{y}_2$, is approximately distributed as Student's t with degrees of freedom to be appropriately determined. Because the statement (1.5.37) is still valid, the assumption that (1.5.45) is approximately Student's t is equivalent to the assumption that w defined by

$$w = \frac{\dfrac{\tilde{\sigma}_1^2}{\tilde{\mathbf{x}}_{1i}'\tilde{\mathbf{x}}_{1i}} + \dfrac{\tilde{\sigma}_2^2}{\tilde{\mathbf{x}}_{2i}'\tilde{\mathbf{x}}_{2i}}}{\dfrac{\sigma_1^2}{\tilde{\mathbf{x}}_{1i}'\tilde{\mathbf{x}}_{1i}} + \dfrac{\sigma_2^2}{\tilde{\mathbf{x}}_{2i}'\tilde{\mathbf{x}}_{2i}}} \cdot \nu \tag{1.5.46}$$

is approximately χ_ν^2 for some ν. Because $Ew = \nu$, w has the same mean as χ_ν^2. We shall determine ν so as to satisfy

$$Vw = 2\nu. \tag{1.5.47}$$

Solving (1.5.47) for ν, we obtain

$$\nu = \frac{\left[\dfrac{\sigma_1^2}{\tilde{\mathbf{x}}_{1i}'\tilde{\mathbf{x}}_{1i}} + \dfrac{\sigma_2^2}{\tilde{\mathbf{x}}_{2i}'\tilde{\mathbf{x}}_{2i}} \right]^2}{\dfrac{\sigma_1^4}{(T_1 - K^*)(\tilde{\mathbf{x}}_{1i}'\tilde{\mathbf{x}}_{1i})^2} + \dfrac{\sigma_2^4}{(T_2 - K^*)(\tilde{\mathbf{x}}_{2i}'\tilde{\mathbf{x}}_{2i})^2}}. \tag{1.5.48}$$

Finally, using the standard normal variable (1.5.37) and the approximate chi-square variable (1.5.46), we have approximately

$$\xi \sim S_{\nu}. \tag{1.5.49}$$

In practice ν will be estimated by inserting $\tilde{\sigma}_1^2$ and $\tilde{\sigma}_2^2$ into the right-hand side of (1.5.48) and then choosing the integer closest to the calculated value.

Unfortunately, Welch's method does not easily generalize to a situation where the equality of vector parameters is involved. Toyoda (1974), like Welch, proposed that both the denominator and the numerator chi-square variables of (1.5.26) be approximated by the moment method; but the resulting test statistic is independent of the unknown parameters only under unrealistic assumptions. Schmidt and Sickles (1977) found Toyoda's approximation to be rather deficient.

In view of the difficulty encountered in generalizing the Welch method, it seems that we should look for other ways to test the equality of the regression parameters in the unequal-variances case. There are two obvious methods that come to mind: They are (1) the asymptotic likelihood ratio test and (2) the asymptotic F test (see Goldfeld and Quandt, 1978).[9]

The likelihood function of the model defined by (1.5.23) and (1.5.24) is

$$\begin{aligned} L = {} & (2\pi)^{-(T_1+T_2)/2}\sigma_1^{-T_1}\sigma_2^{-T_2} \\ & \times \exp\left[-0.5\sigma_1^{-2}(\mathbf{y}_1 - \mathbf{X}_1\boldsymbol{\beta}_1)'(\mathbf{y}_1 - \mathbf{X}_1\boldsymbol{\beta}_1)\right] \\ & \times \exp\left[-0.5\sigma_2^{-2}(\mathbf{y}_2 - \mathbf{X}_2\boldsymbol{\beta}_2)'(\mathbf{y}_2 - \mathbf{X}_2\boldsymbol{\beta}_2)\right]. \end{aligned} \tag{1.5.50}$$

The value of L attained when it is maximized without constraint, denoted by $\hat{L}$, can be obtained by evaluating the parameters of L at $\boldsymbol{\beta}_1 = \hat{\boldsymbol{\beta}}_1$, $\boldsymbol{\beta}_2 = \hat{\boldsymbol{\beta}}_2$, $\sigma_1^2 = \hat{\sigma}_1^2 \equiv T_1^{-1}(\mathbf{y}_1 - \mathbf{X}_1\hat{\boldsymbol{\beta}}_1)'(\mathbf{y}_1 - \mathbf{X}_1\hat{\boldsymbol{\beta}}_1)$, and $\sigma_2^2 = \hat{\sigma}_2^2 \equiv T_2^{-1}(\mathbf{y}_2 - \mathbf{X}_2\hat{\boldsymbol{\beta}}_2)'(\mathbf{y}_2 - \mathbf{X}_2\hat{\boldsymbol{\beta}}_2)$. The value of L attained when it is maximized subject to the constraints $\boldsymbol{\beta}_1 = \boldsymbol{\beta}_2 (\equiv \boldsymbol{\beta})$, denoted by $\bar{L}$, can be obtained by evaluating the parameters of L at the constrained maximum likelihood estimates: $\bar{\boldsymbol{\beta}}_1 = \bar{\boldsymbol{\beta}}_2 (\equiv \bar{\boldsymbol{\beta}})$, $\bar{\sigma}_1^2$, and $\bar{\sigma}_2^2$. These estimates can be iteratively obtained as follows:

Step 1. Calculate $\bar{\boldsymbol{\beta}} = (\hat{\sigma}_1^{-2}\mathbf{X}_1'\mathbf{X}_1 + \hat{\sigma}_2^{-2}\mathbf{X}_2'\mathbf{X}_2)^{-1}(\hat{\sigma}_1^{-2}\mathbf{X}_1'\mathbf{y}_1 + \hat{\sigma}_2^{-2}\mathbf{X}_2'\mathbf{y}_2)$.

Step 2. Calculate $\bar{\sigma}_1^2 = T_1^{-1}(\mathbf{y}_1 - \mathbf{X}_1\bar{\boldsymbol{\beta}})'(\mathbf{y}_1 - \mathbf{X}_1\bar{\boldsymbol{\beta}})$ and $\bar{\sigma}_2^2 = T_2^{-1}(\mathbf{y}_2 - \mathbf{X}_2\bar{\boldsymbol{\beta}})'(\mathbf{y}_2 - \mathbf{X}_2\bar{\boldsymbol{\beta}})$.

Step 3. Repeat Step 1, substituting $\bar{\sigma}_1^2$ and $\bar{\sigma}_2^2$ for $\hat{\sigma}_1^2$ and $\hat{\sigma}_2^2$.

Step 4. Repeat Step 2, substituting the estimates of $\boldsymbol{\beta}$ obtained at Step 3 for $\bar{\boldsymbol{\beta}}$.

Continue this process until the estimates converge. In practice, however, the estimates obtained at the end of Step 1 and Step 2 may be used without changing the asymptotic result (1.5.51).

Using the asymptotic theory of the likelihood ratio test, which will be developed in Section 4.5.1, we have asymptotically (that is, approximately when both T_1 and T_2 are large)

$$-2 \log (\bar{L}/\hat{L}) = T_1 \log (\bar{\sigma}_1^2/\hat{\sigma}_1^2) + T_2 \log (\bar{\sigma}_2^2/\hat{\sigma}_2^2) \sim \chi^2_{K^*}. \tag{1.5.51}$$

The null hypothesis $\boldsymbol{\beta}_1 = \boldsymbol{\beta}_2$ is to be rejected when the statistic (1.5.51) is larger than a certain value.

The asymptotic F test is derived by the following simple procedure: First, estimate σ_1^2 and σ_2^2 by $\hat{\sigma}_1^2$ and $\hat{\sigma}_2^2$, respectively, and define $\hat{\rho} = \hat{\sigma}_1/\hat{\sigma}_2$. Second, multiply both sides of (1.5.24) by $\hat{\rho}$ and define the new equation

$$\mathbf{y}_2^* = \mathbf{X}_2^*\boldsymbol{\beta}_2 + \mathbf{u}_2^*, \tag{1.5.52}$$

where $\mathbf{y}_2^* = \hat{\rho}\mathbf{y}_2$, $\mathbf{X}_2^* = \hat{\rho}\mathbf{X}_2$, and $\mathbf{u}_2^* = \hat{\rho}\mathbf{u}_2$. Third, treat (1.5.23) and (1.5.52) as the given equations and perform the F test (1.5.26) on them. The method works asymptotically because the variance of $\mathbf{u}_2^*$ is approximately the same as that of $\mathbf{u}_1$ when T_1 and T_2 are large, because $\hat{\rho}$ converges to σ_1/σ_2 in probability. Goldfeld and Quandt (1978) conducted a Monte Carlo experiment that showed that, when $\sigma_1^2 \neq \sigma_2^2$, the asymptotic F test performs well, closely followed by the asymptotic likelihood ratio test, whereas the F test based on the assumption of equality of the variances could be considerably inferior.

1.6 Prediction

We shall add to Model 1 the pth period relationship (where $p > T$)

$$y_p = \mathbf{x}_p'\boldsymbol{\beta} + u_p, \tag{1.6.1}$$

where y_p and u_p are scalars and $\mathbf{x}_p$ are the pth period observations on the regressors that we assume to be random variables distributed independently of u_p and $\mathbf{u}$.[10] We shall also assume that u_p is distributed independently of $\mathbf{u}$ with $Eu_p = 0$ and $Vu_p = \sigma^2$. The problem we shall consider in this section is how to predict y_p by a function of $\mathbf{y}$, $\mathbf{X}$, and $\mathbf{x}_p$ when $\boldsymbol{\beta}$ and σ^2 are unknown.

We shall only consider predictors of y_p that can be written in the following form:

$$y_p^* = \mathbf{x}_p'\boldsymbol{\beta}^*, \tag{1.6.2}$$

where $\boldsymbol{\beta}^*$ is an arbitrary estimator of $\boldsymbol{\beta}$ and a function of $\mathbf{y}$ and $\mathbf{X}$. Here, $\boldsymbol{\beta}^*$ may be either linear or nonlinear and unbiased or biased. Although there are more general predictors of the form $f(\mathbf{x}_p, \mathbf{y}, \mathbf{X})$, it is natural to consider (1.6.2) because $\mathbf{x}_p'\boldsymbol{\beta}$ is the best predictor of y_p if $\boldsymbol{\beta}$ is known.

The *mean squared prediction error* of y_p^* conditional on $\mathbf{x}_p$ is given by

$$E[(y_p^* - y_p)^2|\mathbf{x}_p] = \sigma^2 + \mathbf{x}_p' E(\boldsymbol{\beta}^* - \boldsymbol{\beta})(\boldsymbol{\beta}^* - \boldsymbol{\beta})'\mathbf{x}_p, \tag{1.6.3}$$

where the equality follows from the assumption of independence between $\boldsymbol{\beta}^*$ and u_p. Equation (1.6.3) clearly demonstrates that as long as we consider only predictors of the form (1.6.2) and as long as we use the mean squared prediction error as a criterion for ranking predictors, the prediction of y_p is essentially the same problem as the estimation of $\mathbf{x}_p'\boldsymbol{\beta}$. Thus the better the estimator of $\mathbf{x}_p'\boldsymbol{\beta}$ is, the better the predictor of y_p.

In particular, the result of Section 1.2.5 implies that $\mathbf{x}_p'\hat{\boldsymbol{\beta}}$, where $\hat{\boldsymbol{\beta}}$ is the LS estimator, is the best predictor in the class of predictors of the form $\mathbf{x}_p'\mathbf{C}'\mathbf{y}$ such that $\mathbf{C}'\mathbf{X} = \mathbf{I}$, which we shall state as the following theorem:

THEOREM 1.6.1. Let $\hat{\boldsymbol{\beta}}$ be the LS estimator and $\mathbf{C}$ be an arbitrary $T \times K$ matrix of constants such that $\mathbf{C}'\mathbf{X} = \mathbf{I}$. Then

$$E[(\mathbf{x}_p'\hat{\boldsymbol{\beta}} - y_p)^2|\mathbf{x}_p] \leqq E[(\mathbf{x}_p'\mathbf{C}'\mathbf{y} - y_p)^2|\mathbf{x}_p], \tag{1.6.4}$$

where the equality holds if and only if $\mathbf{C} = \mathbf{X}(\mathbf{X}'\mathbf{X})^{-1}$.

Actually we can prove a slightly stronger theorem, which states that the least squares predictor $\mathbf{x}_p'\hat{\boldsymbol{\beta}}$ is the *best linear unbiased predictor.*

THEOREM 1.6.2. Let $\mathbf{d}$ be a T-vector the elements of which are either constants or functions of $\mathbf{x}_p$. Then

$$E[(\mathbf{d}'\mathbf{y} - y_p)^2|\mathbf{x}_p] \geqq E[(\mathbf{x}_p'\hat{\boldsymbol{\beta}} - y_p)^2|\mathbf{x}_p]$$

for any $\mathbf{d}$ such that $E(\mathbf{d}'\mathbf{y}|\mathbf{x}_p) = E(y_p|\mathbf{x}_p)$. The equality holds if and only if $\mathbf{d}' = \mathbf{x}_p'(\mathbf{X}'\mathbf{X})^{-1}\mathbf{X}'$.

Proof. The unbiasedness condition $E(\mathbf{d}'\mathbf{y}|\mathbf{x}_p) = \mathbf{E}(y_p|\mathbf{x}_p)$ implies

$$\mathbf{d}'\mathbf{X} = \mathbf{x}_p'. \tag{1.6.5}$$

Using (1.6.5), we have

$$E[(\mathbf{d}'\mathbf{y} - y_p)^2|\mathbf{x}_p] = E[(\mathbf{d}'\mathbf{u} - u_p)^2|\mathbf{x}_p] \tag{1.6.6}$$

$$= \sigma^2(1 + \mathbf{d}'\mathbf{d}).$$

But from (1.6.3) we obtain

$$E[(\mathbf{x}_p'\hat{\boldsymbol{\beta}} - y_p)^2|\mathbf{x}_p] = \sigma^2[1 + \mathbf{x}_p'(\mathbf{X}'\mathbf{X})^{-1}\mathbf{x}_p]. \tag{1.6.7}$$

Therefore the theorem follows from

$$\mathbf{d}'\mathbf{d} - \mathbf{x}_p'(\mathbf{X}'\mathbf{X})^{-1}\mathbf{x}_p = [\mathbf{d} - \mathbf{X}(\mathbf{X}'\mathbf{X})^{-1}\mathbf{x}_p]'[\mathbf{d} - \mathbf{X}(\mathbf{X}'\mathbf{X})^{-1}\mathbf{x}_p], \qquad (1.6.8)$$

where we have used (1.6.5) again.

Theorem 1.6.2 implies Theorem 1.6.1 because $\mathbf{C}\mathbf{x}_p$ of Theorem 1.6.1 satisfies the condition for $\mathbf{d}$ given by (1.6.5).[11]

In Section 1.2.4 we stated that if we cannot choose between a pair of estimators by the criterion defined by Definition 1.2.2 (that is, if the difference of the mean squared error matrices is neither nonnegative definite nor nonpositive definite), we can use the trace or the determinant as a criterion. The conditional mean squared prediction error defined in (1.6.3) provides an alternative scalar criterion, which may have a more intuitive appeal than the trace or the determinant because it is directly related to an important purpose to which estimation is put—namely, prediction. However, it has one serious weakness: At the time when the choice of estimators is made, $\mathbf{x}_p$ is usually not observed.

A solution to the dilemma is to assume a certain distribution for the random variables $\mathbf{x}_p$ and take the further expectation of (1.6.3) with respect to that distribution. Following Amemiya (1966), let us assume

$$E\mathbf{x}_p\mathbf{x}_p' = T^{-1}\mathbf{X}'\mathbf{X}. \qquad (1.6.9)$$

Then we obtain from (1.6.3) the *unconditional mean squared prediction error*

$$E(y_p^* - y_p)^2 = \sigma^2 + T^{-1}E(\boldsymbol{\beta}^* - \boldsymbol{\beta})'\mathbf{X}'\mathbf{X}(\boldsymbol{\beta}^* - \boldsymbol{\beta}). \qquad (1.6.10)$$

This provides a workable and intuitively appealing criterion for choosing an estimator. The use of this criterion in choosing models will be discussed in Section 2.1.5. The unconditional mean squared prediction error of the least squares predictor $\mathbf{x}_p'\hat{\boldsymbol{\beta}}$ is given by

$$E(\mathbf{x}_p'\hat{\boldsymbol{\beta}} - y_p)^2 = \sigma^2(1 + T^{-1}K). \qquad (1.6.11)$$

Exercises

1. (Section 1.1.2)
   Give an example of a pair of random variables that are noncorrelated but not independent.

2. (Section 1.1.3)
   Let y and x be scalar dichotomous random variables with zero means.

Define $u = y - \mathrm{Cov}(y, x)(Vx)^{-1}x$. Prove $E(u|x) = 0$. Are u and x independent?

3. (Section 1.1.3)
Let y be a scalar random variable and $\mathbf{x}$ be a vector of random variables. Prove $E[y - E(y|\mathbf{x})]^2 \leqq E[y - g(\mathbf{x})]^2$ for any function g.

4. (Section 1.1.3)
A fair die is rolled. Let y be the face number showing and define x by the rule:

$$\begin{aligned} x &= y \quad \text{if} \quad y \quad \text{is even} \\ &= 0 \quad \text{if} \quad y \quad \text{is odd.} \end{aligned}$$

Find the best predictor and the best linear predictor of y based on x and compare the mean squared prediction errors.

5. (Section 1.2.1)
Assume that $\mathbf{y}$ is 3×1 and $\mathbf{X} = (\mathbf{X}_1, \mathbf{X}_2)$ is 3×2 and draw a three-dimensional analog of Figure 1.1.

6. (Section 1.2.5)
Prove that the class of linear unbiased estimators is equivalent to the class of instrumental variables estimators.

7. (Section 1.2.5)
In Model 1 find a member of the class of linear unbiased estimators for which the trace of the mean squared error matrix is the smallest, by minimizing $\mathrm{tr}\, \mathbf{C}'\mathbf{C}$ subject to the constraint $\mathbf{C}'\mathbf{X} = \mathbf{I}$.

8. (Section 1.2.5)
Prove that $\hat{\boldsymbol{\beta}}_1$ defined by (1.2.14) is a best linear unbiased estimator of $\boldsymbol{\beta}_1$.

9. (Section 1.2.5)
In Model 1 further assume $K = 1$ and $\mathbf{X} = \mathbf{l}$, where $\mathbf{l}$ is the vector of ones. Define $\beta^+ = \mathbf{l}'\mathbf{y}/(T + 1)$, obtain its mean squared error, and compare it with that of the least squares estimator $\hat{\beta}$.

10. (Section 1.2.5)
In Model 1 further assume that $T = 3$, $K = 1$, $\mathbf{X} = (1, 1, 1)'$, and that $\{u_t\}$, $t = 1, 2, 3$, are independent with the distribution

$$\begin{aligned} u_t &= \sigma \quad \text{with probability} \quad \tfrac{1}{2} \\ &= -\sigma \quad \text{with probability} \quad \tfrac{1}{2}. \end{aligned}$$

Obtain the mean squared error of $\hat{\beta}_R = \mathbf{y}'\mathbf{y}/\mathbf{x}'\mathbf{y}$ and compare it with that of the least squares estimator $\hat{\beta}$. (Note that $\hat{\beta}_R$, the reverse least squares estimator, is obtained by minimizing the sum of squared errors in the direction of the x-axis.)

11. (Section 1.3.2)
Assume $K = 1$ in Model 1 with normality and furthermore assume $\beta^2 = \sigma^2$. Obtain the maximum likelihood estimator of β and obtain the Cramér-Rao lower bound.

12. (Section 1.4.2)
Suppose

$$\mathbf{Q}' = \begin{bmatrix} 1 & 1 & 1 \\ 1 & 2 & 3 \end{bmatrix}.$$

Find a row vector $\mathbf{R}'$ such that $(\mathbf{Q}, \mathbf{R})$ is nonsingular and $\mathbf{R}'\mathbf{Q} = 0$.

13. (Section 1.4.2)
Somebody has run a least squares regression in the classical regression model (Model 1) and reported

$$\hat{\boldsymbol{\beta}} \equiv \begin{bmatrix} \hat{\beta}_1 \\ \hat{\beta}_2 \\ \hat{\beta}_3 \end{bmatrix} = \begin{bmatrix} 5 \\ -4 \\ 2 \end{bmatrix} \quad \text{and} \quad \hat{\sigma}^2(\mathbf{X}'\mathbf{X})^{-1} = \begin{bmatrix} 3 & 1 & 1 \\ 1 & 2 & 1 \\ 1 & 1 & 2 \end{bmatrix}.$$

On the basis of this information, how would you estimate $\boldsymbol{\beta}$ if you believed $\beta_1 + \beta_2 = \beta_3$?

14. (Section 1.5.3)
We have T observations on the dependent variable y_t and the independent variables x_t and z_t, $t = 1, 2, \ldots, T$. We believe a structural change occurred from the first period consisting of T_1 observations to the second period consisting of T_2 observations ($T_1 + T_2 = T$) in such a way that in the first period Ey_t depends linearly on x_t (with an intercept) but not on z_t whereas in the second period Ey_t depends linearly on z_t (with an intercept) but not on x_t. How do you test this hypothesis? You may assume that $\{y_t\}$ are independent with constant variance σ^2 for $t = 1, 2, \ldots, T$.

15. (Section 1.5.3)
Consider the following two regression equations, each of which satisfies the assumptions of the classical regression model (Model 1):

(1) $\mathbf{y}_1 = \alpha_1 \mathbf{l} + \alpha_2 \mathbf{x}_1 + \mathbf{u}_1$

(2) $\mathbf{y}_2 = \beta_1 \mathbf{l} + \beta_2 \mathbf{x}_2 + \mathbf{u}_2$,

where α's and β's are scalar parameters, $\mathbf{y}_1$, $\mathbf{y}_2$, $\mathbf{x}_1$, $\mathbf{x}_2$, $\mathbf{u}_1$, and $\mathbf{u}_2$ are seven-component vectors, and $\mathbf{l}$ is the seven-component vector of ones. Assume that $\mathbf{u}_1$ and $\mathbf{u}_2$ are normally distributed with the common variance σ^2 and that $\mathbf{u}_1$ and $\mathbf{u}_2$ are independent of each other. Suppose that $\mathbf{l}'\mathbf{x}_1 = \mathbf{l}'\mathbf{x}_2 = 0$ and $\mathbf{l}'\mathbf{y}_1 = \mathbf{l}'\mathbf{y}_2 = 7$. Suppose also that the sample moment matrix of the four observable variables is given as

	$\mathbf{y}_1$	$\mathbf{y}_2$	$\mathbf{x}_1$	$\mathbf{x}_2$
$\mathbf{y}_1$	9.3	7	2	1.5
$\mathbf{y}_2$	7	9	3	1
$\mathbf{x}_1$	2	3	2	1.2
$\mathbf{x}_2$	1.5	1	1.2	1

For example, the table shows $\mathbf{y}_1'\mathbf{y}_1 = 9.3$ and $\mathbf{y}_1'\mathbf{y}_2 = 7$. Should you reject the joint hypothesis "$\alpha_1 = \beta_1$ and $\alpha_1 + 2\alpha_2 = \beta_2$" at the 5% significance level? How about at 1%?

16. (Section 1.5.3)
Consider a classical regression model

$$\mathbf{y}_1 = \alpha_1 \mathbf{x}_1 + \beta_1 \mathbf{z}_1 + \mathbf{u}_1$$

$$\mathbf{y}_2 = \alpha_2 \mathbf{x}_2 + \beta_2 \mathbf{z}_2 + \mathbf{u}_2$$

$$\mathbf{y}_3 = \alpha_3 \mathbf{x}_3 + \beta_3 \mathbf{z}_3 + \mathbf{u}_3,$$

where α's and β's are scalar unknown parameters, the other variables are vectors of ten elements, $\mathbf{x}$'s and $\mathbf{z}$'s are vectors of known constants, and $\mathbf{u}$'s are normal with mean zero and $E\mathbf{u}_i\mathbf{u}_i' = \sigma^2\mathbf{I}$ for every $\mathbf{i}$ and $E\mathbf{u}_i\mathbf{u}_j' = \mathbf{0}$ if $i \neq j$. Suppose the observed vector products are as follow:

$$\mathbf{y}_1'\mathbf{y}_1 = 2, \quad \mathbf{y}_2'\mathbf{y}_2 = 5, \quad \mathbf{y}_3'\mathbf{y}_3 = 2$$

$$\mathbf{y}_1'\mathbf{x}_1 = 1, \quad \mathbf{y}_2'\mathbf{x}_2 = 3, \quad \mathbf{y}_3'\mathbf{x}_3 = 2$$

$$\mathbf{y}_1'\mathbf{z}_1 = 2, \quad \mathbf{y}_2'\mathbf{z}_2 = 3, \quad \mathbf{y}_3'\mathbf{z}_3 = 1$$

$$\mathbf{x}_i'\mathbf{x}_i = \mathbf{z}_i'\mathbf{z}_i = 4 \quad \text{for every} \quad i$$

$$\mathbf{x}_i'\mathbf{z}_i = 0 \quad \text{for every} \quad i.$$

Test the joint hypothesis ($\alpha_1 = \alpha_2$ and $\beta_2 = \beta_3$) at the 5% significance level.

17. (Section 1.6)
Consider Model 1 with the added prediction-period equation (1.6.1). Suppose $\mathbf{Z}$ is a $T \times L$ matrix of known constants and $\mathbf{z}_p$ is an L-vector of known constants. Which of the following predictors of y_p is better? Explain.

$$\hat{y}_p = \mathbf{z}_p'(\mathbf{Z}'\mathbf{Z})^{-1}\mathbf{Z}'\mathbf{y}$$

$$\tilde{y}_p = \mathbf{z}_p'(\mathbf{Z}'\mathbf{Z})^{-1}\mathbf{Z}'\mathbf{X}(\mathbf{X}'\mathbf{X})^{-1}\mathbf{X}'\mathbf{y}.$$

18. (Section 1.6)
Consider the case $K = 2$ in Model 1, where $y_t = \beta_1 + \beta_2 x_t + u_t$. For the prediction period we have $y_p = \beta_1 + \beta_2 x_p + u_p$, where u_p satisfies the assumptions of Section 1.6. Obtain the mean squared prediction error of the predictor $\tilde{y}_p = T^{-1} \Sigma_{t=1}^{T} y_t$ and compare it with the mean squared prediction error of the least squares predictor.

19. (Section 1.6)
Prove that any $\mathbf{d}$ satisfying (1.6.5) can be written as $\mathbf{C}\mathbf{x}_p$ for some $\mathbf{C}$ such that $\mathbf{C}'\mathbf{X} = \mathbf{I}$.

2 Recent Developments in Regression Analysis

In this chapter we shall present three additional topics. They can be discussed in the framework of Model 1 but are grouped here in a separate chapter because they involve developments more recent than the results of the previous chapter.

2.1 Selection of Regressors[1]

2.1.1 Introduction

Most of the discussion in Chapter 1 proceeded on the assumption that a given model (Model 1 with or without normality) is correct. This is the ideal situation that would occur if econometricians could unambiguously answer questions such as which independent variables should be included in the right-hand side of the regression equation; which transformation, if any, should be applied to the independent variables; and what assumptions should be imposed on the distribution of the error terms on the basis of economic theory. In practice this ideal situation seldom occurs, and some aspects of the model specification remain doubtful in the minds of econometricians. Then they must not only estimate the parameters of a given model but also choose a model among many models.

We have already considered a particular type of the problem of model selection, namely, the problem of choosing between Model 1 without constraint and Model 1 with the linear constraints $\mathbf{Q}'\boldsymbol{\beta} = \mathbf{c}$. The model selection of this type (selection among "nested" models), where one model is a special case of the other broader model, is the easiest to handle because the standard technique of hypothesis testing is precisely geared for handling this problem. We shall encounter many instances of this type of problem in later chapters. In Section 2.1, however, we face the more unorthodox problem of choosing between models or hypotheses, neither of which is contained in the other ("nonnested" models).

In particular, we shall study how to choose between the two competing regression equations

$$\mathbf{y} = \mathbf{X}_1\boldsymbol{\beta}_1 + \mathbf{u}_1 \tag{2.1.1}$$

and

$$\mathbf{y} = \mathbf{X}_2\boldsymbol{\beta}_2 + \mathbf{u}_2, \tag{2.1.2}$$

where $\mathbf{X}_1$ is a $T \times K_1$ matrix of constants, $\mathbf{X}_2$ is a $T \times K_2$ matrix of constants, $E\mathbf{u}_1 = E\mathbf{u}_2 = \mathbf{0}$, $E\mathbf{u}_1\mathbf{u}_1' = \sigma_1^2\mathbf{I}$, and $E\mathbf{u}_2\mathbf{u}_2' = \sigma_2^2\mathbf{I}$. Note that this notation differs from that of Chapter 1 in that here there is no explicit connection between $\mathbf{X}_1$ and $\mathbf{X}_2$: $\mathbf{X}_1$ and $\mathbf{X}_2$ may contain some common column vectors or they may not; one of $\mathbf{X}_1$ and $\mathbf{X}_2$ may be completely contained in the other or they may be completely different matrices. Note also that the dependent variable $\mathbf{y}$ is the same for both equations. (Selection among more general models will be discussed briefly in Section 4.5.)

This problem is quite common in econometrics, for econometricians often run several regressions, each of which purports to explain the same dependent variable, and then they choose the equation which satisfies them most according to some criterion. The choice is carried out through an intuitive and unsystematic thought process, as the analysts consider diverse factors such as a goodness of fit, reasonableness of the sign and magnitude of an estimated coefficient, and the value of a t statistic on each regression coefficient. Among these considerations, the degree of fit normally plays an important role, although the others should certainly not be ignored. Therefore, in the present study we shall focus our attention on the problem of finding an appropriate measure of the degree of fit. The multiple correlation coefficient R^2, defined in (1.2.8), has an intuitive appeal and is a useful descriptive statistic; however, it has one obvious weakness, namely, that it attains its maximum of unity when one uses as many independent variables as there are observations (that is, when $K = T$). Much of what we do here may be regarded as a way to rectify that weakness by modifying R^2.

2.1.2 Statistical Decision Theory

We shall briefly explain the terminology used in statistical decision theory. For a more thorough treatment of the subject, the reader should consult Zacks (1971). Statistical decision theory is a branch of game theory that analyzes the game played by statisticians against nature. The goal of the game for statisticians is to make a guess at the value of a parameter (chosen by nature) on the basis of the observed sample, and their gain from the game is a function of how close their guess is to the true value. The major components of the game are Θ, the parameter space; Y, the sample space; and D, the decision space (the totality of functions from Y to Θ). We shall denote a single element of each space by the lowercase letters $\boldsymbol{\theta}$, $\mathbf{y}$, $\mathbf{d}$. Thus, if $\mathbf{y}$ is a particular observed sample (a vector of random variables), $\mathbf{d}$ is a function of $\mathbf{y}$ (called a statistic or an estimator) used to estimate $\boldsymbol{\theta}$. We assume that the loss incurred by choosing $\mathbf{d}$ when the true value of the parameter is $\boldsymbol{\theta}$ is given by the *loss function* $L(\mathbf{d}, \boldsymbol{\theta})$.

We shall define a few standard terms used in statistical decision theory.

Risk. The expected loss $E_y L(\mathbf{d}, \boldsymbol{\theta})$ for which the expectation is taken with respect to $\mathbf{y}$ (which is implicitly in the argument of the function $\mathbf{d}$) is called the *risk* and is denoted by $R(\mathbf{d}|\boldsymbol{\theta})$.

Uniformly smaller risk. The estimator[2] $\mathbf{d}_1$ has a *uniformly smaller risk* than the estimator $\mathbf{d}_2$ if $R(\mathbf{d}_1|\boldsymbol{\theta}) \leqq R(\mathbf{d}_2|\boldsymbol{\theta})$ for all $\boldsymbol{\theta} \in \Theta$ and $R(\mathbf{d}_1|\boldsymbol{\theta}) < R(\mathbf{d}_2|\boldsymbol{\theta})$ for at least one $\boldsymbol{\theta} \in \Theta$.

Admissible. An estimator is *admissible* if there is no $\mathbf{d}$ in D that has a uniformly smaller risk. Otherwise it is called *inadmissible.*

Minimax. The estimator $\mathbf{d}^*$ is called a *minimax* estimator if

$$\max_{\boldsymbol{\theta} \in \Theta} R(\mathbf{d}^*|\boldsymbol{\theta}) = \min_{\mathbf{d} \in D} \max_{\boldsymbol{\theta} \in \Theta} R(\mathbf{d}|\boldsymbol{\theta}).$$

The minimax estimator protects the statistician against the worst possible situation. If $\max_{\boldsymbol{\theta} \in \Theta} R(\mathbf{d}|\boldsymbol{\theta})$ does not exist, it should be replaced with $\sup_{\boldsymbol{\theta} \in \Theta} R(\mathbf{d}|\boldsymbol{\theta})$ in the preceding definition (and min with inf).

Posterior risk. The expected loss $E_{\boldsymbol{\theta}} L(\mathbf{d}, \boldsymbol{\theta})$ for which the expectation is taken with respect to the posterior distribution of $\boldsymbol{\theta}$ given $\mathbf{y}$ is called the *posterior risk* and is denoted by $R(\mathbf{d}|\mathbf{y})$. It obviously depends on the particular prior distribution used in obtaining the posterior distribution.

Bayes estimator. The Bayes estimator, given a particular prior distribution, minimizes the posterior risk $R(\mathbf{d}|\mathbf{y})$. If the loss function is quadratic, namely, $L(\mathbf{d}, \boldsymbol{\theta}) = (\mathbf{d} - \boldsymbol{\theta})' \mathbf{W} (\mathbf{d} - \boldsymbol{\theta})$ where $\mathbf{W}$ is an arbitrary nonsingular matrix, the posterior risk $E_{\boldsymbol{\theta}}(\mathbf{d} - \boldsymbol{\theta})' \mathbf{W} (\mathbf{d} - \boldsymbol{\theta})$ is minimized at $\mathbf{d} = E_{\boldsymbol{\theta}} \boldsymbol{\theta}$, the *posterior mean* of $\boldsymbol{\theta}$. An example of the Bayes estimator was given in Section 1.4.4.

Regret. Let $R(\mathbf{d}|\boldsymbol{\theta})$ be the risk. Then the *regret* $W(\mathbf{d}|\boldsymbol{\theta})$ is defined by

$$W(\mathbf{d}|\boldsymbol{\theta}) = R(\mathbf{d}|\boldsymbol{\theta}) - \min_{\mathbf{d} \in D} R(\mathbf{d}|\boldsymbol{\theta}).$$

Minimax regret. The *minimax regret* strategy minimizes $\max_{\boldsymbol{\theta} \in \Theta} W(\mathbf{d}|\boldsymbol{\theta})$ with respect to $\mathbf{d}$.

Some useful results can be stated informally as remarks rather than stating them formally as theorems.

REMARK 2.1.1. A Bayes estimator is admissible.

REMARK 2.1.2. A minimax estimator is either a Bayes estimator or the limit of a sequence of Bayes estimators. The latter is called a *generalized Bayes estimator.* (In contrast, a Bayes estimator is sometimes called a *proper* Bayes estimator.)

REMARK 2.1.3. A generalized Bayes estimator with a constant risk is minimax.

REMARK 2.1.4. An admissible estimator may or may not be minimax, and a minimax estimator may or may not be admissible.

2.1.3. Bayesian Solution

The Bayesian solution to the selection-of-regressors problem provides a pedagogically useful starting point although it does not necessarily lead to a useful solution in practice. We can obtain the Bayesian solution as a special case of the Bayes estimator (defined in Section 2.1.2) for which both Θ and D consist of two elements. Let the losses be represented as shown in Table 2.1, where L_{12} is the loss incurred by choosing model 1 when model 2 is the true model and L_{21} is the loss incurred by choosing model 2 when model 1 is the true model.[3] Then, by the result of Section 2.1.2, the Bayesian strategy is to choose model 1 if

$$L_{12}P(2|\mathbf{y}) < L_{21}P(1|\mathbf{y}), \tag{2.1.3}$$

where $P(i|\mathbf{y})$, $i = 1$ and 2, is the posterior probability that the model i is true given the sample $\mathbf{y}$. The posterior probabilities are obtained by Bayes's rule as

$$P(1|\mathbf{y}) = \frac{\int f(\mathbf{y}|\boldsymbol{\theta}_1)f(\boldsymbol{\theta}_1|1)P(1)d\boldsymbol{\theta}_1}{\int f(\mathbf{y}|\boldsymbol{\theta}_1)f(\boldsymbol{\theta}_1|1)P(1)d\boldsymbol{\theta}_1 + \int f(\mathbf{y}|\boldsymbol{\theta}_2)f(\boldsymbol{\theta}_2|2)P(2)d\boldsymbol{\theta}_2} \tag{2.1.4}$$

and similarly for $P(2|\mathbf{y})$, where $\boldsymbol{\theta}_i = (\boldsymbol{\beta}_i', \sigma_i^2)'$, $f(\mathbf{y}|\boldsymbol{\theta}_i)$ is the joint density of $\mathbf{y}$ given $\boldsymbol{\theta}_i$, $f(\boldsymbol{\theta}_i|i)$ is the prior density of $\boldsymbol{\theta}_i$ given the model i, and $P(i)$ is the prior probability that the model i is true, for $i = 1$ and 2.

There is an alternative way to characterize the Bayesian strategy. Let S be a subset of the space of $\mathbf{y}$ such that the Bayesian chooses the model 1 if $\mathbf{y} \in S$.

Table 2.1 The loss matrix

Decision \ True model	Model 1	Model 2
Choose model 1	0	L_{12}
Choose model 2	L_{21}	0

Then the Bayesian minimizes the posterior risk

$$L_{12}P(2)P(\mathbf{y} \in S|2) + L_{21}P(1)P(\mathbf{y} \in \overline{S}|1) \tag{2.1.5}$$

with respect to S, where $\overline{S}$ is the complement of S. It is easy to show that the posterior risk (2.1.5) is minimized when S is chosen to be the set of $\mathbf{y}$ that satisfies the inequality (2.1.3).

The actual Bayesian solution is obtained by specifying $f(\mathbf{y}|\boldsymbol{\theta}_i)$, $f(\boldsymbol{\theta}_i|i)$, and $P(i)$ in (2.1.4) and the corresponding expressions for $P(2|\mathbf{y})$. This is not done here because our main purpose is to understand the basic Bayesian thought, in light of which we can perhaps more clearly understand some of the classical strategies to be discussed in subsequent subsections. The interested reader should consult Gaver and Geisel (1974) or Zellner (1971, p. 306). Gaver and Geisel pointed out that if we use the standard specifications, that is, $f(\mathbf{y}|\boldsymbol{\theta}_i)$ normal, $f(\boldsymbol{\theta}_i|i)$ "diffuse" natural conjugate, $P(1) = P(2)$, the Bayesian solution leads to a meaningless result unless $K_1 = K_2$.[4]

2.1.4 Theil's Corrected R^2

Theil (1961, p. 213) proposed a correction of R^2 aimed at eliminating the aforementioned weakness of R^2. Theil's corrected R^2, denoted by $\overline{R}^2$, is defined by

$$1 - \overline{R}^2 = \frac{T}{T-K}(1 - R^2). \tag{2.1.6}$$

Because we have from (1.2.9)

$$1 - R^2 = \frac{\mathbf{y}'\mathbf{M}\mathbf{y}}{\mathbf{y}'\mathbf{L}\mathbf{y}}, \tag{2.1.7}$$

where $\mathbf{M} = \mathbf{I} - \mathbf{X}(\mathbf{X}'\mathbf{X})^{-1}\mathbf{X}'$ and $\mathbf{L} = \mathbf{I} - T^{-1}\mathbf{l}\mathbf{l}'$ as before, choosing the equation with the largest $\overline{R}^2$ is equivalent to choosing the equation with the smallest $\tilde{\sigma}^2 = (T-K)^{-1}\mathbf{y}'\mathbf{M}\mathbf{y}$. Coming back to the choice between Eqs. (2.1.1) and (2.1.2), Theil's strategy based on his $\bar{R}^2$ amounts to choosing Eq. (2.1.1) if

$$\tilde{\sigma}_1^2 < \tilde{\sigma}_2^2, \tag{2.1.8}$$

where
$$\tilde{\sigma}_1^2 = (T-K_1)^{-1}\mathbf{y}'\mathbf{M}_1\mathbf{y},$$
$$\mathbf{M}_1 = \mathbf{I} - \mathbf{X}_1(\mathbf{X}_1'\mathbf{X}_1)^{-1}\mathbf{X}_1',$$
$$\tilde{\sigma}_2^2 = (T-K_2)^{-1}\mathbf{y}'\mathbf{M}_2\mathbf{y}, \quad \text{and}$$
$$\mathbf{M}_2 = \mathbf{I} - \mathbf{X}_2(\mathbf{X}_2'\mathbf{X}_2)^{-1}\mathbf{X}_2'.$$

The inequality (2.1.8) can be regarded as a constraint on $\mathbf{y}$ and hence defines a subset in the space of $\mathbf{y}$. Call it S_0; that is, $S_0 \equiv \{\mathbf{y} | \tilde{\sigma}_1^2 < \tilde{\sigma}_2^2\}$. This choice of S can be evaluated in terms of the Bayesian minimand (2.1.5). Suppose Eq. (2.1.2) is the true model. Then we have

$$\tilde{\sigma}_1^2 - \tilde{\sigma}_2^2 = \frac{\mathbf{y}'\mathbf{M}_1\mathbf{y}}{T-K_1} - \frac{\mathbf{y}'\mathbf{M}_2\mathbf{y}}{T-K_2} \tag{2.1.9}$$
$$= \frac{\boldsymbol{\beta}_2'\mathbf{X}_2'\mathbf{M}_1\mathbf{X}_2\boldsymbol{\beta}_2 + 2\mathbf{u}_2'\mathbf{M}_1\mathbf{X}_2\boldsymbol{\beta}_2 + \mathbf{u}_2'\mathbf{M}_1\mathbf{u}_2}{T-K_1} - \frac{\mathbf{u}_2'\mathbf{M}_2\mathbf{u}_2}{T-K_2}.$$

Therefore

$$E(\tilde{\sigma}_1^2 - \tilde{\sigma}_2^2|2) = \frac{\boldsymbol{\beta}_2'\mathbf{X}_2'\mathbf{M}_1\mathbf{X}_2\boldsymbol{\beta}_2}{T-K_1} > 0. \tag{2.1.10}$$

Therefore, in view of the fact that nothing *a priori* is known about whether $\tilde{\sigma}_1^2 - \tilde{\sigma}_2^2$ is positively or negatively skewed, it seems reasonable to expect that

$$P(\mathbf{y} \in S_0|2) < \tfrac{1}{2}. \tag{2.1.11}$$

For a similar reason it also seems reasonable to expect that

$$P(\mathbf{y} \in \bar{S}_0|1) < \tfrac{1}{2}. \tag{2.1.12}$$

These inequalities indicate that S_0 does offer an intuitive appeal (though a rather mild one) to the classical statistician who, by principle, is reluctant to specify the subjective quantities L_{12}, L_{21}, $P(1)$, and $P(2)$ in the posterior risk (2.1.5).

As we have seen, Theil's corrected R^2 has a certain intuitive appeal and has been widely used by econometricians as a measure of the goodness of fit. However, its theoretical justification is not strong, and the experiences of some researchers have led them to believe that Theil's measure does not correct sufficiently for the degrees of freedom; that is, it still tends to favor the equation with more regressors, although not as much as the uncorrected R^2 (see, for example, Mayer, 1975). In Section 2.1.5 we shall propose a measure that corrects more for the degrees of freedom than Theil's $\bar{R}^2$ does, and in Section 2.1.6 we shall try to justify the proposed measure from a different angle.

2.1.5 Prediction Criterion

A major reason why we would want to consider any measure of the goodness of fit is that the better fit the data have in the sample period, the better prediction we can expect to get for the prediction period. Therefore it makes sense to devise a measure of the goodness of fit that directly reflects the efficiency of prediction. For this purpose we shall compare the mean squared prediction errors of the predictors derived from the two competing equations (2.1.1) and (2.1.2). To evaluate the mean squared prediction error, however, we must know the true model; but, if we knew the true model, we would not have the problem of choosing a model. We get around this dilemma by evaluating the mean squared prediction error of the predictor derived from each model, assuming in turn that each model is the true model. This may be called the *minimini principle* (minimizing the minimum risk)—in contrast to the more standard minimax principle defined in Section 2.1.2—because the performance of each predictor is evaluated under the most favorable condition for it. Although the principle is neither more nor less justifiable than the minimax principle, it is adopted here for mathematical convenience. Using the unconditional mean squared prediction error given in Eq. (1.6.11) after σ^2 is replaced with its unbiased estimator, we define the *Prediction Criterion* (abbreviated PC) by

$$\mathrm{PC}_i = \tilde{\sigma}_i^2(1 + T^{-1}K_i), \qquad i = 1, 2, \tag{2.1.13}$$

for each model, where $\tilde{\sigma}_i^2 = (T - K_i)^{-1}\mathbf{y}'\mathbf{M}_i\mathbf{y}$ is the number of regressors in model i.

If we define the modified R^2, denoted by $\tilde{R}^2$, as

$$1 - \tilde{R}^2 = \frac{T + K}{T - K}(1 - R^2), \tag{2.1.14}$$

choosing the equation with the smallest PC is equivalent to choosing the equation with the largest $\tilde{R}^2$. A comparison of (2.1.6) and (2.1.14) shows that $\tilde{R}^2$ imposes a higher penalty upon increasing the number of regressors than does Theil's $\bar{R}^2$.

Criteria proposed by Mallows (1964) and by Akaike (1973) are similar to the PC, although they are derived from somewhat different principles. To define *Mallows' Criterion* (abbreviated MC), we must first define the matrix $\mathbf{X}$ as that matrix consisting of distinct column vectors contained in the union of $\mathbf{X}_1$ and $\mathbf{X}_2$ and K as the number of the column vectors of $\mathbf{X}$ thus defined. These definitions of $\mathbf{X}$ and K can be generalized to the case where there are more than two competing equations. Then we have

$$\mathrm{MC}_i = \left(\frac{2K_i}{T}\right)\left(\frac{\mathbf{y}'\mathbf{M}\mathbf{y}}{T-K}\right) + \frac{\mathbf{y}'\mathbf{M}_i\mathbf{y}}{T}, \qquad i = 1, 2, \tag{2.1.15}$$

where $\mathbf{M} = \mathbf{I} - \mathbf{X}(\mathbf{X}'\mathbf{X})^{-1}\mathbf{X}'$. Akaike (1973) proposed what he calls the *Akaike Information Criterion* (abbreviated AIC) for the purpose of distinguishing between models more general than regression models (see Section 4.5.2). When the AIC is applied to regression models, it reduces to

$$\mathrm{AIC}_i = \log\left(\frac{\mathbf{y}'\mathbf{M}_i\mathbf{y}}{T}\right) + \frac{2K_i}{T}, \qquad \mathrm{i} = 1, 2. \tag{2.1.16}$$

All three criteria give similar results in common situations (see Amemiya, 1980a). The MC has one unattractive feature: the matrix $\mathbf{X}$ must be specified.

2.1.6 Optimal Significance Level

In the preceding sections we have considered the problem of choosing between equations in which there is no explicit relationship between the competing regressor matrices $\mathbf{X}_1$ and $\mathbf{X}_2$. In a special case where one set of regressors is contained in the other set, the choice of an equation becomes equivalent to the decision of accepting or rejecting a linear hypothesis on the parameters of the broader model. Because the acceptance or rejection of a hypothesis critically depends on the significance level chosen, the problem is that of determining the optimal significance level (or, equivalently, the optimal critical value) of the F test according to some criterion. We shall present the gist of the results obtained in a few representative papers on this topic and then shall explain the connection between these results and the foregoing discussion on modifications of R^2.

Let the broader of the competing models be

$$\mathbf{y} = \mathbf{X}\boldsymbol{\beta} + \mathbf{u} \equiv \mathbf{X}_1\boldsymbol{\beta}_1 + \mathbf{X}_2\boldsymbol{\beta}_2 + \mathbf{u} \tag{2.1.17}$$

where $\mathbf{X}_1$ and $\mathbf{X}_2$ are $T \times K_1$ and $T \times K_2$ matrices, respectively, and for which we assume $\mathbf{u}$ is normal so that model (2.1.17) is the same as Model 1 with normality. Note that the $\mathbf{X}_2$ here has no relationship with the $\mathbf{X}_2$ that appears in Eq. (2.1.2). Suppose we suspect $\boldsymbol{\beta}_2$ might be $\mathbf{0}$ and test the hypothesis $\boldsymbol{\beta}_2 = \mathbf{0}$ by the F test developed in Section 1.5.2. The appropriate test statistic is obtained by putting $\bar{\boldsymbol{\beta}}_2 = \mathbf{0}$ in Eq. (1.5.19) as

$$\eta = \left(\frac{T-K}{K_2}\right)\left(\frac{\mathbf{y}'\mathbf{M}_1\mathbf{y}}{\mathbf{y}'\mathbf{M}\mathbf{y}} - 1\right) \sim F(K_2, T-K). \tag{2.1.18}$$

The researcher first sets the critical value d and then chooses the model (2.1.17) if $\eta \geqq d$ or the constrained model

$$\mathbf{y} = \mathbf{X}_1\boldsymbol{\beta}_1 + \mathbf{u} \tag{2.1.19}$$

if $\eta < d$.

Conventionally, the critical value d is determined rather arbitrarily in such a way that $P(\eta \geqq d)$ evaluated under the null hypothesis equals a preassigned significance level such as 1 or 5 percent. We shall consider a decision-theoretic determination of d. For that we must first specify the risk function. The decision of the researcher who chooses between models (2.1.17) and (2.1.19) on the basis of the F statistic η may be interpreted as a decision to estimate $\boldsymbol{\beta}$ by the estimator $\tilde{\boldsymbol{\beta}}$ defined as

$$\begin{aligned} \tilde{\boldsymbol{\beta}} &= \hat{\boldsymbol{\beta}} && \text{if } \eta \geqq d \\ &= \begin{bmatrix} \hat{\boldsymbol{\beta}}_1 \\ \mathbf{0} \end{bmatrix} && \text{if } \eta < d, \end{aligned} \tag{2.1.20}$$

where $\hat{\boldsymbol{\beta}}$ is the least squares estimator applied to (2.1.17) and $\hat{\boldsymbol{\beta}}_1$ is that applied to (2.1.19). Thus it seems reasonable to adopt the mean squared error matrix $\boldsymbol{\Omega} \equiv E(\tilde{\boldsymbol{\beta}} - \boldsymbol{\beta})(\tilde{\boldsymbol{\beta}} - \boldsymbol{\beta})'$, where the expectation is taken under (2.1.17) as our risk (or expected loss) function. However, $\boldsymbol{\Omega}$ is not easy to work with directly because it depends on many variables and parameters, namely, $\mathbf{X}, \boldsymbol{\beta}, \sigma^2, K, K_1$, and d, in addition to having the fundamental difficulty of being a matrix. (For the derivation of $\boldsymbol{\Omega}$, see Sawa and Hiromatsu, 1973, or Farebrother, 1975.) Thus people have worked with simpler risk functions.

Sawa and Hiromatsu (1973) chose as their risk function the largest characteristic root of

$$[\mathbf{Q}'(\mathbf{X}'\mathbf{X})^{-1}\mathbf{Q}]^{-1/2}\mathbf{Q}'\boldsymbol{\Omega}\mathbf{Q}[\mathbf{Q}'(\mathbf{X}'\mathbf{X})^{-1}\mathbf{Q}]^{-1/2}, \tag{2.1.21}$$

where $\mathbf{Q}' = (\mathbf{0}, \mathbf{I})$ where $\mathbf{0}$ is the $K_2 \times K_1$ matrix of zeros and $\mathbf{I}$ is the identity matrix of size K_2. This transformation of $\boldsymbol{\Omega}$ lacks a strong theoretical justification and is used primarily for mathematical convenience. Sawa and Hiromatsu applied the minimax regret strategy to the risk function (2.1.21) and showed that in the special case $K_2 = 1$, $d \cong 1.88$ is optimal for most reasonable values of $T - K$. Brook (1976) applied the minimax regret strategy to a different transformation of $\mathbf{\Omega}$,

$$\text{tr}\ \mathbf{X}\mathbf{\Omega}\mathbf{X}', \tag{2.1.22}$$

and recommended $d = 2$ on the basis of his results. The risk function (2.1.22) seems more reasonable than (2.1.21) as it is more closely related to the mean squared prediction error (see Section 1.6). At any rate, the conclusions of these two articles are similar.

Now on the basis of these results we can evaluate the criteria discussed in the previous subsections by asking what critical value is implied by each criterion in a situation where a set of the regressors of one model is contained in that of the other model. We must choose between models (2.1.17) and (2.1.19). For each criterion, let ρ denote the ratio of the value of the criterion for model (2.1.19) over that for model (2.1.17). Then, using (2.1.18), we can easily establish a relationship between η and ρ. For Theil's criterion we have from (2.1.6)

$$\eta = \frac{T - K_1}{K - K_1}\rho(\text{Theil}) - \frac{T - K}{K - K_1}. \tag{2.1.23}$$

Therefore we obtain the well-known result—that Theil's criterion selects (2.1.19) over (2.1.17) if and only if $\eta < 1$. Thus, compared with the optimal critical values suggested by Brook or by Sawa and Hiromatsu, Theil's criterion imposes far less of a penalty upon the inclusion of regressors. From the prediction criterion (2.1.13) we get

$$\eta = \frac{(T - K_1)(T + K)}{(K - K_1)(T + K_1)}\rho(\text{PC}) - \frac{T - K}{K - K_1}. \tag{2.1.24}$$

Therefore

$$\rho(\text{PC}) > 1 \quad \text{if and only if} \quad \eta > \frac{2T}{T + K_1}. \tag{2.1.25}$$

Table 2.2 gives the values of $2T/(T + K_1)$ for a few selected values of K_1/T. These values are close to the values recommended by Brook and by Sawa and Hiromatsu. The optimal critical value of the F test implied by the AIC can be easily computed for various values of K_1/T and K/T from (2.1.16) and (2.1.18). The critical value for the AIC is very close to that for the PC, although

Table 2.2 Optimal critical value of the F test implied by PC

$\frac{K_1}{T}$	$\frac{2T}{T+K_1}$
1/10	1.82
1/20	1.90
1/30	1.94

it is slightly smaller. Finally, for the MC we have from (2.1.15)

$$\eta = \frac{T+K}{K-K_1}\rho(\text{MC}) - \frac{T-K+2K_1}{K-K_1}. \tag{2.1.26}$$

Therefore

$$\rho(\text{MC}) > 1 \quad \text{if and only if} \quad \eta > 2. \tag{2.1.27}$$

These results give some credence to the proposition that the modified R^2 proposed here is preferred to Theil's corrected R^2 as a measure of the goodness of fit. However, the reader should take this conclusion with a grain of salt for several reasons: (1) None of the criteria discussed in the previous subsections is derived from completely justifiable assumptions. (2) The results in the literature of the optimal significance level are derived from the somewhat questionable principle of minimizing the maximum regret. (3) The results in the literature on the optimal significance level are relevant to a comparison of the criteria considered in the earlier subsections only to the extent that one set of regressors is contained in the other set. The reader should be reminded again that a measure of the goodness of fit is merely one of the many things to be considered in the whole process of choosing a regression equation.

2.2 Ridge Regression and Stein's Estimator[5]

2.2.1 Introduction

We proved in Section 1.2.5 that the LS estimator is best linear unbiased in Model 1 and proved in Section 1.3.3 that it is best unbiased in Model 1 with normality. In either case a biased estimator may be better than LS (in the sense of having a smaller mean squared error) for some parameter values. In this section we shall consider a variety of biased estimators and compare them to LS in Model 1 with normality.

The biased estimators we shall consider here are either the constrained least squares estimator discussed in Section 1.4.1 or the Bayes estimator discussed in Section 1.4.4 or their variants. If the linear constraints (1.4.1) are true, the constrained least squares estimator is best linear unbiased. Similarly, the Bayes estimator has optimal properties if the regression vector $\boldsymbol{\beta}$ is indeed random and generated according to the prior distribution. In this section, however, we shall investigate the properties of these estimators assuming that the constraints do not necessarily hold. Hence, we have called them biased estimators. Even so, it is not at all surprising that such a biased estimator can beat the least squares estimator over some region of the parameter space. For example, 0 can beat any estimator when the true value of the parameter in question is indeed 0. What *is* surprising is that there exists a biased estimator that dominates the least squares estimates over the whole parameter space when the risk function is the sum of the mean squared errors, as we shall show. Such an estimator was first discovered by Stein (see James and Stein, 1961) and has since attracted the attention of many statisticians, some of whom have extended Stein's results in various directions.

In this section we shall discuss simultaneously two closely related and yet separate ideas: One is the aforementioned idea that a biased estimator can dominate least squares, for which the main result is Stein's, and the other is the idea of *ridge regression* originally developed by Hoerl and Kennard (1970a, b) to cope with the problem of multicollinearity. Although the two ideas were initially developed independently of each other, the resulting estimators are close cousins; in fact, the term *Stein-type estimators* and the term *ridge estimators* are synonymous and may be used to describe the same class of estimators. Nevertheless, it is important to recognize them as separate ideas. We might be tempted to combine the two ideas by asserting that a biased estimator can be good and is especially so if there is multicollinearity. The statement can be proved wrong simply by noting that Stein's original model assumes $\mathbf{X}'\mathbf{X} = \mathbf{I}$, the opposite of multicollinearity. The correct characterization of the two ideas is as follows: (1) Some form of constraint is useful in estimation. (2) Some form of constraint is necessary if there is multicollinearity.

The risk function we shall use throughout this section is the scalar

$$E(\tilde{\boldsymbol{\beta}} - \boldsymbol{\beta})'(\tilde{\boldsymbol{\beta}} - \boldsymbol{\beta}), \tag{2.2.1}$$

where $\tilde{\boldsymbol{\beta}}$ is an estimator in question. This choice of the risk function is as general as

$$E(\tilde{\boldsymbol{\beta}} - \boldsymbol{\beta})'\mathbf{A}(\tilde{\boldsymbol{\beta}} - \boldsymbol{\beta}), \tag{2.2.2}$$

where $\mathbf{A}$ is an arbitrary (known) positive definite matrix, because we can always reduce (2.2.2) to (2.2.1) by transforming Model 1 to

$$\begin{aligned}\mathbf{y} &= \mathbf{X}\boldsymbol{\beta} + \mathbf{u} \\ &= \mathbf{X}\mathbf{A}^{-1/2}\mathbf{A}^{1/2}\boldsymbol{\beta} + \mathbf{u}\end{aligned} \tag{2.2.3}$$

and consider the transformed parameter vector $\mathbf{A}^{1/2}\boldsymbol{\beta}$. Note, however, that (2.2.1) is not as general as the mean squared error matrix $E(\tilde{\boldsymbol{\beta}} - \boldsymbol{\beta})(\tilde{\boldsymbol{\beta}} - \boldsymbol{\beta})'$, which we used in Section 1.2.4, since (2.2.1) is the trace of the mean squared error matrix.

2.2.2 Canonical Model

Let $\mathbf{H}$ be an orthogonal matrix that diagonalizes the matrix $\mathbf{X}'\mathbf{X}$, that is, $\mathbf{H}'\mathbf{H} = \mathbf{I}$ and $\mathbf{H}'\mathbf{X}'\mathbf{X}\mathbf{H} = \boldsymbol{\Lambda}$, where $\boldsymbol{\Lambda}$ is the diagonal matrix consisting of the characteristic roots of $\mathbf{X}'\mathbf{X}$. Defining $\mathbf{X}^* = \mathbf{X}\mathbf{H}$ and $\boldsymbol{\alpha} = \mathbf{H}'\boldsymbol{\beta}$, we can write Eq. (1.1.4) as

$$\mathbf{y} = \mathbf{X}^*\boldsymbol{\alpha} + \mathbf{u}. \tag{2.2.4}$$

If $\hat{\boldsymbol{\alpha}}$ is the least squares estimator of $\boldsymbol{\alpha}$ in model (2.2.4), we have

$$\hat{\boldsymbol{\alpha}} \sim N(\boldsymbol{\alpha}, \sigma^2\boldsymbol{\Lambda}^{-1}). \tag{2.2.5}$$

Because the least squares estimator is a sufficient statistic for the vector of regression coefficients, the estimation of $\boldsymbol{\beta}$ in Model 1 with normality is equivalent to the estimation of $\boldsymbol{\alpha}$ in model (2.2.5). We shall call (2.2.5) the canonical model; it is simpler to analyze than the original model. Because $\mathbf{H}\mathbf{H}' = \mathbf{I}$, the risk function $E(\tilde{\boldsymbol{\beta}} - \boldsymbol{\beta})'(\tilde{\boldsymbol{\beta}} - \boldsymbol{\beta})$ in Model 1 is equivalent to the risk function $E(\tilde{\boldsymbol{\alpha}} - \boldsymbol{\alpha})'(\tilde{\boldsymbol{\alpha}} - \boldsymbol{\alpha})$ in model (2.2.5).

2.2.3 Multicollinearity and Principal Components

In Model 1 we assumed that $\mathbf{X}$ is of full rank [that is, $\text{rank}(\mathbf{X}) = K \leqq T$], or, equivalently, that $\mathbf{X}'\mathbf{X}$ is nonsingular. If it is not, $\mathbf{X}'\mathbf{X}$ cannot be inverted and therefore the least squares estimator cannot be uniquely defined. In other words, there is no unique solution to the normal equation

$$\mathbf{X}'\mathbf{X}\boldsymbol{\beta} = \mathbf{X}'\mathbf{y}. \tag{2.2.6}$$

Even then, however, a subset of the regression parameters still may be estimated by (1.2.14).

We shall now turn to a more general question: Can $\mathbf{F}'\boldsymbol{\beta}$ be estimated by least squares, where $\mathbf{F}$ is an arbitrary $K \times f$ matrix of rank f ($f \leqq K$)? To make sense out of this question, we must first define the least squares estimator of $\mathbf{F}'\boldsymbol{\beta}$. We say that the least squares estimator of $\mathbf{F}'\boldsymbol{\beta}$ is $\mathbf{F}'\hat{\boldsymbol{\beta}}$, where $\hat{\boldsymbol{\beta}}$ is any solution (which may not be unique) of the normal equation (2.2.6), provided $\mathbf{F}'\hat{\boldsymbol{\beta}}$ is unique. If $\mathbf{F}'\hat{\boldsymbol{\beta}}$ is unique, we also say that $\mathbf{F}'\boldsymbol{\beta}$ is *estimable.* Then it is easy to prove that $\mathbf{F}'\boldsymbol{\beta}$ is estimable if and only if we can write $\mathbf{F} = \mathbf{X}'\mathbf{A}$ for some $T \times f$ matrix $\mathbf{A}$, or equivalently, if and only if we can write $\mathbf{F} = \mathbf{X}'\mathbf{X}\mathbf{B}$ for some $K \times f$ matrix $\mathbf{B}$. (See Rao, 1973, pp. 223–224, for the proof.) If $\mathbf{F}'\boldsymbol{\beta}$ is estimable, it can be shown that $\mathbf{F}'\hat{\boldsymbol{\beta}}$ is the best linear unbiased estimator of $\mathbf{F}'\boldsymbol{\beta}$.

The estimability of $\mathbf{F}'\boldsymbol{\beta}$ can be reduced to the estimability of a subset of the regression parameters in the sense of the previous paragraph by the following observation. Let $\mathbf{G}$ be a $K \times (K-f)$ matrix of rank $K-f$ such that $\mathbf{G}'\mathbf{F} = \mathbf{0}$. (We defined a similar matrix in Section 1.4.2.) Then we can write Model 1 as

$$\begin{aligned} \mathbf{y} &= \mathbf{X}\boldsymbol{\beta} + \mathbf{u} \qquad (2.2.7) \\ &= \mathbf{X}[\mathbf{F}(\mathbf{F}'\mathbf{F})^{-1}, \mathbf{G}(\mathbf{G}'\mathbf{G})^{-1}] \begin{bmatrix} \mathbf{F}' \\ \mathbf{G}' \end{bmatrix} \boldsymbol{\beta} + \mathbf{u} \\ &\equiv [\mathbf{Z}_1, \mathbf{Z}_2] \begin{bmatrix} \gamma_1 \\ \gamma_2 \end{bmatrix} + \mathbf{u}, \end{aligned}$$

where the identity defines $\mathbf{Z}_1$, $\mathbf{Z}_2$, γ_1, and γ_2. Then the estimability of $\mathbf{F}'\boldsymbol{\beta}$ is equivalent to the estimability of γ_1.

If $\mathbf{X}'\mathbf{X}$ is singular, $\boldsymbol{\beta}$ is not estimable in the sense defined above (that is, a solution of Eq. 2.2.6 is not unique). This fact does not mean that we should not attempt to estimate $\boldsymbol{\beta}$. We can still meaningfully talk about a class of estimators and study the relative merits of the members of the class. One such class may be the totality of solutions of (2.2.6)—infinite in number. Another class may be the constrained least squares estimator satisfying linear constraints $\mathbf{Q}'\boldsymbol{\beta} = \mathbf{c}$. From Eq. (1.4.11) it is clear that this estimator can be defined even when $\mathbf{X}'\mathbf{X}$ is singular. A third class is the class of Bayes estimators with prior $\mathbf{Q}\boldsymbol{\beta} = \mathbf{c} + \mathbf{v}$ formed by varying $\mathbf{Q}$, $\mathbf{c}$, and the distribution of $\mathbf{v}$. We should mention an important member of the first class that also happens to be a member of the second class. It is called the *principal components* estimator.

Suppose we arrange the diagonal elements of $\boldsymbol{\Lambda}$ defined in Section 2.2.2 in descending order—$\lambda_1 \geqq \lambda_2 \geqq \cdots \geqq \lambda_K$—and let the corresponding characteristic vectors be $\mathbf{h}_1, \mathbf{h}_2, \ldots, \mathbf{h}_K$ so that $\mathbf{H} = (\mathbf{h}_1, \mathbf{h}_2, \ldots, \mathbf{h}_K)$. Then we call $\mathbf{X}\mathbf{h}_i$ the *ith principal component* of $\mathbf{X}$. If $\mathbf{X}'\mathbf{X}$ is singular, some of its characteristic roots are 0. Partition

$$\Lambda = \begin{bmatrix} \Lambda_1 & \mathbf{0} \\ \mathbf{0} & \Lambda_2 \end{bmatrix} \tag{2.2.8}$$

so that the diagonal elements of Λ_1 are positive and those of Λ_2 are all 0, and partition $\mathbf{H} = (\mathbf{H}_1, \mathbf{H}_2)$ conformably. Furthermore, define $\mathbf{X}_1^* = \mathbf{X}\mathbf{H}_1$ and $\mathbf{X}_2^* = \mathbf{X}\mathbf{H}_2$ and partition $\boldsymbol{\alpha}' = (\boldsymbol{\alpha}_1', \boldsymbol{\alpha}_2')$ conformably. Then $\mathbf{X}_2^* = \mathbf{0}$ and hence $\boldsymbol{\alpha}_2$ cannot be estimated. Suppose we estimate $\boldsymbol{\alpha}_1$ by

$$\hat{\boldsymbol{\alpha}}_1 = (\mathbf{X}_1^{*\prime}\mathbf{X}_1^*)^{-1}\mathbf{X}_1^{*\prime}\mathbf{y} \tag{2.2.9}$$

and set $\hat{\boldsymbol{\alpha}}_2 = \mathbf{0}$. (It is arbitrary to choose $\mathbf{0}$ here; any other constant will do.) Transforming $\hat{\boldsymbol{\alpha}}' \equiv (\hat{\boldsymbol{\alpha}}_1', \hat{\boldsymbol{\alpha}}_2')$ into an estimator of $\boldsymbol{\beta}$, we obtain the principal components estimator of $\boldsymbol{\beta}$ by the formula[6]

$$\hat{\boldsymbol{\beta}}_P = \mathbf{H}\hat{\boldsymbol{\alpha}} = \mathbf{H}_1\Lambda_1^{-1}\mathbf{H}_1'\mathbf{X}'\mathbf{y}. \tag{2.2.10}$$

It is easy to show that $\hat{\boldsymbol{\beta}}_P$ satisfies (2.2.6); hence, it is a member of the first class. It is also a member of the second class because it is the constrained least squares subject to $\mathbf{H}_2'\boldsymbol{\beta} = \mathbf{0}$.

It was shown by Fomby, Hill, and Johnson (1978) that the principal components estimator (or constrained least squares subject to $\mathbf{H}_2'\boldsymbol{\beta} = \mathbf{0}$) has a smaller variance-covariance matrix than any constrained least squares estimator obtained subject to the constraints $\mathbf{Q}'\boldsymbol{\beta} = \mathbf{c}$, where $\mathbf{Q}$ and $\mathbf{c}$ can be arbitrary except that $\mathbf{Q}$ has an equal or smaller number of columns than $\mathbf{H}_2$.

We shall now consider a situation where $\mathbf{X}'\mathbf{X}$ is nonsingular but nearly singular. The near singularity of $\mathbf{X}'\mathbf{X}$ is commonly referred to as *multicollinearity.* Another way of characterizing it is to say that the determinant of $\mathbf{X}'\mathbf{X}$ is close to 0 or that the smallest characteristic root of $\mathbf{X}'\mathbf{X}$ is small. (The question of how small is "small" will be better understood later.) We now ask the question, How precisely or imprecisely can we estimate a linear combination of the regression parameters $\mathbf{c}'\boldsymbol{\beta}$ by least squares?[7] Because the matrix $\mathbf{H}$ is nonsingular, we can write $\mathbf{c} = \mathbf{H}\mathbf{d}$ for some vector $\mathbf{d}$. Then we have

$$V(\mathbf{c}'\hat{\boldsymbol{\beta}}) = \sigma^2\mathbf{d}'\Lambda^{-1}\mathbf{d}, \tag{2.2.11}$$

which gives the answer to the question. In other words, the closer $\mathbf{c}$ is to the direction of the first (last) principal component, the more precisely (imprecisely) one can estimate $\mathbf{c}'\boldsymbol{\beta}$. In particular, we note from (2.2.5) that the precision of the estimator of an element of $\boldsymbol{\alpha}$ is directly proportional to the corresponding diagonal element of Λ.

Suppose we partition Λ as in (2.2.8) but this time include all the "large" elements in Λ_1 and "small" elements in Λ_2. The consideration of which roots to include in $\mathbf{\Lambda}_2$ should depend on a subjective evaluation of the statistician regarding the magnitude of the variance to be tolerated. It makes sense to use the principal components estimator (2.2.10) also in the present situation, because $\boldsymbol{\alpha}_2$ can be only imprecisely estimated. (Here, the principal components estimator is not unique because the choice of $\boldsymbol{\alpha}_2$ is a matter of subjective judgment. Therefore it is more precise to call this estimator by a name such as the K_1 principal components estimator specifying the number of elements chosen in $\boldsymbol{\alpha}_1$.)

2.2.4 Ridge Regression

Hoerl and Kennard (1970a, b) proposed the class of estimators defined by

$$\hat{\boldsymbol{\beta}}(\gamma) = (\mathbf{X}'\mathbf{X} + \gamma\mathbf{I})^{-1}\mathbf{X}'\mathbf{y}, \tag{2.2.12}$$

called the *ridge estimators.* Hoerl and Kennard chose these estimators because they hoped to alleviate the instability of the least squares estimator due to the near singularity of $\mathbf{X}'\mathbf{X}$ by adding a positive scalar γ to the characteristic roots of $\mathbf{X}'\mathbf{X}$. They proved that given $\boldsymbol{\beta}$ there exists γ^*, which depends upon $\boldsymbol{\beta}$, such that $E[\hat{\boldsymbol{\beta}}(\gamma^*) - \boldsymbol{\beta}]'[\hat{\boldsymbol{\beta}}(\gamma^*) - \boldsymbol{\beta}] < E(\hat{\boldsymbol{\beta}} - \boldsymbol{\beta})'(\hat{\boldsymbol{\beta}} - \boldsymbol{\beta})$, where $\hat{\boldsymbol{\beta}} = \hat{\boldsymbol{\beta}}(0)$. Because γ^* depends on $\boldsymbol{\beta}$, $\hat{\boldsymbol{\beta}}(\gamma^*)$ is not a practical estimator. But the existence of $\hat{\boldsymbol{\beta}}(\gamma^*)$ gives rise to a hope that one can determine γ, either as a constant or as a function of the sample, in such a way that $\hat{\boldsymbol{\beta}}(\gamma)$ is better than the least squares estimator $\hat{\boldsymbol{\beta}}$ with respect to the risk function (2.2.2) over a wide range of the parameter space.

Hoerl and Kennard proposed the *ridge trace method* to determine the value of γ. The ridge trace is a graph of $\hat{\beta}_i(\gamma)$, the ith element of $\hat{\boldsymbol{\beta}}(\gamma)$, drawn as a function of γ. They proposed that γ be determined as the smallest value at which the ridge trace stabilizes. The method suffers from two weaknesses: (1) The point at which the ridge trace starts to stabilize cannot always be determined objectively. (2) The method lacks theoretical justification inasmuch as its major justification is derived from certain Monte Carlo studies, which, though favorable, are not conclusive. Although several variations of the ridge trace method and many analogous procedures to determine γ have been proposed, we shall discuss only the *empirical Bayes method,* which seems to be the only method based on theoretical grounds. We shall present a variant of it in the next paragraph and more in the next two subsections.

Several authors interpreted the ridge estimator (more precisely, the class of estimators) as the Bayes estimator and proposed the empirical Bayes method of determining γ; we shall follow the discussion of Sclove (1973).[8] Suppose that the prior distribution of $\boldsymbol{\beta}$ is $N(\boldsymbol{\mu}, \sigma_\beta^2\mathbf{I})$, distributed independently of $\mathbf{u}$. Then from (1.4.22) the Bayes estimator of $\boldsymbol{\beta}$ is given by

$$\hat{\boldsymbol{\beta}}^* = (\mathbf{X}'\mathbf{X} + \gamma\mathbf{I})^{-1}(\mathbf{X}'\mathbf{y} + \gamma\boldsymbol{\mu}), \tag{2.2.13}$$

where $\gamma = \sigma^2/\sigma_\beta^2$. Therefore, the ridge estimator (2.2.12) is obtained by putting $\boldsymbol{\mu} = \mathbf{0}$ in (2.2.13). By the empirical Bayes method we mean the estimation of the parameters (in our case, σ_β^2) of the prior distribution using the sample observations. The empirical Bayes method may be regarded as a compromise between the Bayesian and the classical analysis. From the marginal distribution (that is, not conditional on $\boldsymbol{\beta}$) of $\mathbf{y}$, we have

$$E\mathbf{y}'\mathbf{y} = \sigma_\beta^2 \operatorname{tr} \mathbf{X}'\mathbf{X} + T\sigma^2, \tag{2.2.14}$$

which suggests that we can estimate σ_β^2 by

$$\hat{\sigma}_\beta^2 = \frac{\mathbf{y}'\mathbf{y} - T\hat{\sigma}^2}{\operatorname{tr} \mathbf{X}'\mathbf{X}}, \tag{2.2.15}$$

where $\hat{\sigma}^2 = T^{-1}\mathbf{y}'[\mathbf{I} - \mathbf{X}(\mathbf{X}'\mathbf{X})^{-1}\mathbf{X}']\mathbf{y}$ as usual. Finally, we can estimate γ by $\hat{\gamma} = \hat{\sigma}^2/\hat{\sigma}_\beta^2$.

In the next two subsections we shall discuss many more varieties of ridge estimators and what we call *generalized ridge estimators,* some of which involve the empirical Bayes method of determining γ. The canonical model presented in Section 2.2.2 will be considered.

2.2.5 Stein's Estimator: Homoscedastic Case

Let us consider a special case of the canonical model (2.2.5) in which $\boldsymbol{\Lambda} = \mathbf{I}$. James and Stein (1961) showed that $E\|[1 - c(\hat{\boldsymbol{\alpha}}'\hat{\boldsymbol{\alpha}})^{-1}]\hat{\boldsymbol{\alpha}} - \boldsymbol{\alpha}\|^2$ is minimized for all $\boldsymbol{\alpha}$ when $c = (K-2)\sigma^2$ if σ^2 is known and $K \geqq 3$, where $\|\mathbf{x}\|^2$ denotes the vector product $\mathbf{x}'\mathbf{x}$. If we define

$$\text{Stein's estimator } \hat{\boldsymbol{\alpha}}^* = \left[1 - \frac{(K-2)\sigma^2}{\hat{\boldsymbol{\alpha}}'\hat{\boldsymbol{\alpha}}}\right]\hat{\boldsymbol{\alpha}},$$

the result of James and Stein implies in particular that Stein's estimator is uniformly better than the maximum likelihood estimator $\hat{\boldsymbol{\alpha}}$ with respect to the risk function $E(\tilde{\boldsymbol{\alpha}} - \boldsymbol{\alpha})'(\tilde{\boldsymbol{\alpha}} - \boldsymbol{\alpha})$ if $K \geqq 3$. In other words, $\hat{\boldsymbol{\alpha}}$ is inadmissible (see the definition of *inadmissible* in Section 2.1.2). The fact that $\hat{\boldsymbol{\alpha}}$ is minimax with a constant risk (see Hodges and Lehman, 1950) implies that $\hat{\boldsymbol{\alpha}}^*$ is minimax. This surprising result has had a great impact on the theory of statistics.

Translated into the regression model, the result of James and Stein implies two facts: (1) Consider the ridge estimator $(\mathbf{X}'\mathbf{X}+\gamma\mathbf{I})^{-1}\mathbf{X}'\mathbf{y}$ with $\gamma=(K-2)\sigma^2/[\hat{\alpha}'\hat{\alpha}-(K-2)\sigma^2]$. If $\mathbf{X}'\mathbf{X}=\mathbf{I}$, it is reduced precisely to Stein's estimator of $\boldsymbol{\beta}$ since $\mathbf{X}'\mathbf{y} \sim N(\boldsymbol{\beta}, \sigma^2\mathbf{I})$. Therefore this ridge estimator is uniformly better than the least squares estimator if $\mathbf{X}'\mathbf{X}=\mathbf{I}$ (the opposite of multicollinearity). (2) Assume a general $\mathbf{X}'\mathbf{X}$ in Model 1. If we define $\mathbf{A}=(\mathbf{X}'\mathbf{X})^{1/2}$, we have $\mathbf{A}\hat{\boldsymbol{\beta}} \sim N(\mathbf{A}\boldsymbol{\beta}, \sigma^2\mathbf{I})$, where $\hat{\boldsymbol{\beta}}$ is the least squares estimator. Applying Stein's estimator to $\mathbf{A}\hat{\boldsymbol{\beta}}$, we know $E\|(1-B)\mathbf{A}\hat{\boldsymbol{\beta}}-\mathbf{A}\boldsymbol{\beta}\|^2 < E\|\mathbf{A}(\hat{\boldsymbol{\beta}}-\boldsymbol{\beta})\|^2$ for all $\boldsymbol{\beta}$ where $B=(K-2)\sigma^2/\hat{\boldsymbol{\beta}}'\mathbf{X}'\mathbf{X}\hat{\boldsymbol{\beta}}$. Therefore, equivalently, $(1-B)\hat{\boldsymbol{\beta}}$ is uniformly better than $\hat{\boldsymbol{\beta}}$ with respect to the risk function $E(\tilde{\boldsymbol{\beta}}-\boldsymbol{\beta})'\mathbf{X}'\mathbf{X}(\tilde{\boldsymbol{\beta}}-\boldsymbol{\beta})$. Note that this is essentially the risk function we proposed in (1.6.10) in Section 1.6, where we discussed prediction.

So far, we have assumed σ^2 is known. James and Stein showed that even when σ^2 is unknown, if S is distributed independent of $\hat{\boldsymbol{\alpha}}$ and as $\sigma^2\chi_n^2$, then $E\|[1-cS(\hat{\boldsymbol{\alpha}}'\hat{\boldsymbol{\alpha}})^{-1}]\hat{\boldsymbol{\alpha}}-\boldsymbol{\alpha}\|^2$ attains the minimum for all $\boldsymbol{\alpha}$ and σ^2 at $c=(K-2)/(n+2)$ if $K \geqq 3$. They also showed that $[1-cS(\hat{\boldsymbol{\alpha}}'\hat{\boldsymbol{\alpha}})^{-1}]\hat{\boldsymbol{\alpha}}$ is uniformly better than $\hat{\boldsymbol{\alpha}}$ if $0<c<2(K-2)/(n+2)$. In the regression model we can put $S=\mathbf{y}'[\mathbf{I}-\mathbf{X}(\mathbf{X}'\mathbf{X})^{-1}\mathbf{X}']\mathbf{y}$ because it is independent of $\hat{\boldsymbol{\beta}}$ and distributed as $\sigma^2\chi_{T-K}^2$.

Efron and Morris (1972) interpreted Stein's estimator as an empirical Bayes estimator. Suppose $\hat{\boldsymbol{\alpha}} \sim N(\boldsymbol{\alpha}, \sigma^2\mathbf{I})$, where σ^2 is known, and the prior distribution of $\boldsymbol{\alpha}$ is $N(\mathbf{0}, \sigma^2\gamma^{-1}\mathbf{I})$. Then the Bayes estimator is $\hat{\boldsymbol{\alpha}}^*=(1+\gamma)^{-1}\hat{\boldsymbol{\alpha}}=(1-B)\hat{\boldsymbol{\alpha}}$ where $B=\gamma/(1+\gamma)$. The marginal distribution of $\hat{\boldsymbol{\alpha}}$ is $N(\mathbf{0}, \sigma^2B^{-1}\mathbf{I})$. Therefore $B\hat{\boldsymbol{\alpha}}'\hat{\boldsymbol{\alpha}}/\sigma^2 \sim \chi_K^2$. Because $E[(\chi_K^2)^{-1}]=(K-2)^{-1}$ (see Johnson and Kotz, 1970a, vol. 1, p. 166), we have

$$E\left[\frac{(K-2)\sigma^2}{\hat{\boldsymbol{\alpha}}'\hat{\boldsymbol{\alpha}}}\right]=B.$$

Thus we can use the term within the square bracket as an unbiased estimator of B, thereby leading to Stein's estimator.

It is important not to confuse Stein's result with the statement that $E(\hat{\boldsymbol{\alpha}}^*-\boldsymbol{\alpha})(\hat{\boldsymbol{\alpha}}^*-\boldsymbol{\alpha})' < E(\hat{\boldsymbol{\alpha}}-\boldsymbol{\alpha})(\hat{\boldsymbol{\alpha}}-\boldsymbol{\alpha})'$ in the matrix sense. This inequality does not generally hold. Note that Stein's estimator shrinks each component of $\boldsymbol{\alpha}$ by the same factor B. If the amount of shrinkage for a particular component is large, the mean squared error of Stein's estimator for that component may well exceed that of the corresponding component of $\hat{\boldsymbol{\alpha}}$, even though $E\|\hat{\boldsymbol{\alpha}}^*-\boldsymbol{\alpha}\|^2 < E\|\hat{\boldsymbol{\alpha}}-\boldsymbol{\alpha}\|^2$. In view of this possibility, Efron and Morris (1972) proposed a compromise: Limit the amount of shrinkage to a fixed amount for each component. In this way the maximum possible mean squared error for the components of $\boldsymbol{\alpha}$ can be decreased, whereas, with luck, the sum of the mean squared errors will not be increased by very much.

Earlier we stated that the maximum likelihood estimator $\hat{\boldsymbol{\alpha}}$ is inadmissible because it is dominated by Stein's estimator. A curious fact is that Stein's estimator itself is dominated by

$$\text{Stein's positive-rule estimator} \left[1 - \frac{(K-2)\sigma^2}{\hat{\boldsymbol{\alpha}}'\hat{\boldsymbol{\alpha}}}\right]_+ \hat{\boldsymbol{\alpha}},$$

where $[x]_+$ denotes $\max[0, x]$. Hence Stein's estimator is inadmissible, as proved by Baranchik (1970). Efron and Morris (1973) showed that Stein's positive-rule estimator is also inadmissible but cannot be greatly improved upon.

We defined Stein's estimator as the estimator obtained by shrinking $\hat{\boldsymbol{\alpha}}$ toward $\mathbf{0}$. Stein's estimator can easily be modified in such a way that it shrinks $\hat{\boldsymbol{\alpha}}$ toward any other value. It is easy to show that

$$\text{Stein's modified estimator} \left[1 - \frac{(K-2)\sigma^2}{(\hat{\boldsymbol{\alpha}} - \mathbf{c})'(\hat{\boldsymbol{\alpha}} - \mathbf{c})}\right] (\hat{\boldsymbol{\alpha}} - \mathbf{c}) + \mathbf{c}$$

is minimax for any constant vector $\mathbf{c}$. If the stochastic quantity $K^{-1}\mathbf{l}\mathbf{l}'\hat{\boldsymbol{\alpha}}$ is chosen to be $\mathbf{c}$, where $\mathbf{l}$ is the vector of ones, then the resulting estimator can be shown to be minimax for $K \geqq 4$.

2.2.6 Stein's Estimator: Heteroscedastic Case

Assume model (2.2.5), where $\boldsymbol{\Lambda}$ is a general positive definite diagonal matrix. Two estimators for this case can be defined.

Ridge estimator: $\hat{\boldsymbol{\alpha}}^* = (\boldsymbol{\Lambda} + \gamma\mathbf{I})^{-1}\boldsymbol{\Lambda}\hat{\boldsymbol{\alpha}},$

$$\hat{\alpha}_i^* = (1 - B_i)\hat{\alpha}_i \quad \text{where} \quad B_i = \frac{\gamma}{\lambda_i + \gamma}.$$

(Note: The transformation $\boldsymbol{\alpha} = \mathbf{H}'\boldsymbol{\beta}$ translates this estimator into the ridge estimator (2.2.12). γ is either a constant or a function of the sample.)

Generalized ridge estimator: $\hat{\boldsymbol{\alpha}}^* = (\boldsymbol{\Lambda} + \boldsymbol{\Gamma})^{-1}\boldsymbol{\Lambda}\hat{\boldsymbol{\alpha}}$ where $\boldsymbol{\Gamma}$ is diagonal,

$$\hat{\alpha}_i^* = (1 - B_i)\hat{\alpha}_i \quad \text{where}$$

$$B_i = \frac{\gamma_i}{\lambda_i + \gamma_i},$$

$$\hat{\boldsymbol{\beta}}^* = (\mathbf{X}'\mathbf{X} + \mathbf{H}\boldsymbol{\Gamma}\mathbf{H}')^{-1}\mathbf{X}'\mathbf{y}.$$

Other ridge and generalized ridge estimators have been proposed by various authors. In the three following ridge estimators, γ is a positive quantity that does not depend on λ_i; therefore B_i is inversely proportional to λ_i. This is an intuitively appealing property because it seems reasonable to shrink the component with the larger variance more. In the four following generalized ridge estimators, exactly the opposite takes place: The amount of shrinkage B_i is an increasing function of λ_i—an undesirable property. In some of the estimators, σ^2 appears in the formula, and in some, its estimate $\hat{\sigma}^2$, which is assumed to be independent of $\hat{\boldsymbol{\alpha}}$, appears. As pointed out by Efron and Morris (1976), the fundamental properties of Stein's estimators are not changed if σ^2 is independently estimated.

Selected Estimators and Their Properties

Ridge Estimators

Ridge 1 (Sclove, 1973)

$$\gamma = \frac{\sigma^2 \operatorname{tr} \boldsymbol{\Lambda}}{\hat{\boldsymbol{\alpha}}' \boldsymbol{\Lambda} \hat{\boldsymbol{\alpha}}}.$$

Ridge 2 (Hoerl, Kennard, and Baldwin, 1975) and Modified Ridge 2 (Thisted, 1976)

$$\gamma = \frac{K\hat{\sigma}^2}{\hat{\boldsymbol{\alpha}}'\hat{\boldsymbol{\alpha}}}.$$

This estimator is obtained by putting $\boldsymbol{\Lambda} = \mathbf{I}$ in Sclove's estimator. Although the authors claimed its good properties on the basis of a Monte Carlo study, Thisted (1976) showed that it can sometimes be far inferior to the maximum likelihood estimator $\hat{\boldsymbol{\alpha}}$; he proposed a modification, $\gamma = (K-2)\hat{\sigma}^2/\hat{\boldsymbol{\alpha}}'\hat{\boldsymbol{\alpha}}$, and showed that the modified estimator is minimax for some $\boldsymbol{\Lambda}$ if σ^2 is known.

Ridge 3 (Thisted, 1976)

$$\gamma = \frac{\sigma^2}{\sum_{i=1}^{K} d_i \hat{\alpha}_i^2} \qquad \text{if all } d_i < \infty$$

$$= 0 \qquad \text{otherwise,}$$

where

$$d_i = \frac{\lambda_i^{-1}\lambda_{\min}^{-1}}{\left[\left(\sum \lambda_j^{-2}\right) - 2\lambda_i^{-1}\lambda_{\min}^{-1}\right]_+}.$$

This estimator is minimax for all Λ if σ^2 is known. If λ_i are constant, this estimator is reduced to the modified version of Ridge 2. When the λ's are too spread out, however, it becomes indistinguishable from $\hat{\alpha}$ (which *is* minimax).

Generalized Ridge Estimators

Generalized Ridge 1 (Berger, 1975)

$$B_i = \frac{(K-2)\sigma^2\lambda_i}{\hat{\alpha}'\Lambda^2\hat{\alpha}}.$$

This estimator is minimax for all Λ and reduces to Stein's estimator when λ_i are constant.

Generalized Ridge 2 (Berger, 1976)

$$B_i = \frac{f(\hat{\alpha}'\Lambda^2\hat{\alpha})\sigma^2\lambda_i}{\hat{\alpha}'\Lambda^2\hat{\alpha}}.$$

Berger (1976) obtained conditions on f under which it is minimax and admissible for all Λ.

Generalized Ridge 3 (Bhattacharya, 1966). B_i is complicated and therefore is not reproduced here, but it is an increasing function of λ_i and is minimax for all Λ.

Generalized Ridge 4 (Strawderman, 1978)

$$B_i = \frac{a\lambda_i\hat{\sigma}^2}{\hat{\alpha}'\Lambda\hat{\alpha} + g\hat{\sigma}^2 + h + a\hat{\sigma}^2\lambda_i}, \qquad \text{where } \hat{\sigma}^2 \backsim \sigma^2\chi_n^2.$$

This estimator is minimax for all Λ if

$$0 \leqq a \leqq \frac{1}{\lambda_{\max}}\left[\frac{2(K-2)}{n} + 2\right]$$

$$g \geqq \frac{2K}{n+2}$$

$$h \geqq 0.$$

Results

All the generalized ridge estimators are minimax for all Λ and generalized ridge 2 is also admissible, whereas among the ridge estimators only Thisted's (which is strictly not ridge because of a discontinuity) is minimax for all Λ.

Because $\hat{\alpha}$ is minimax with a constant risk, any other minimax estimator dominates $\hat{\alpha}$. However, the mere fact that an estimator dominates $\hat{\alpha}$ does not necessarily make the estimator good in its own right. If the estimator is admissible as well, like Berger's generalized ridge 2, there is no other estimator that dominates it. Even that, however, is no guarantee of excellence because there may be an estimator (which may be neither minimax nor admissible) that has a lower risk over a wide range of the parameter space. It is nice to prove minimaxity and admissibility; however, we should look for other criteria of performance as well, such as whether the amount of shrinkage is proportional to the variance—the criterion in which all the generalized ridge estimators fail.

The exact distributions of Stein's or ridge estimators are generally hard to obtain. However, in many situations they may be well approximated by the jackknife and the bootstrap methods (see Section 4.3.4).

2.2.7 Monte Carlo and Applications

Thisted (1976) compared ridge 2, modified ridge 2, ridge 3, and generalized ridge 1 by the Monte Carlo method and found the somewhat paradoxical result that ridge 2, which is minimax for the smallest subset of $\mathbf{\Lambda}$, performs best in general.

Gunst and Mason (1977) compared by the Monte Carlo method the estimators (1) least squares, (2) principal components, (3) Stein's, and (4) ridge 2. Their conclusion was that although (3) and (4) are frequently better than (1) and (2), the improvement is not large enough to offset the advantages of (1) and (2), namely, the known distribution and the ability to select regressors.

Dempster, Schatzoff, and Wermuth (1977) compared 57 estimators, belonging to groups such as selection of regressors, principal components, Stein's and ridge, in 160 normal linear models with factorial designs using both $E(\tilde{\boldsymbol{\beta}}-\boldsymbol{\beta})'(\tilde{\boldsymbol{\beta}}-\boldsymbol{\beta})$ and $E(\tilde{\boldsymbol{\beta}}-\boldsymbol{\beta})'\mathbf{X}'\mathbf{X}(\tilde{\boldsymbol{\beta}}-\boldsymbol{\beta})$ as the risk function. The winner was their version of ridge based on the empirical Bayes estimation of γ defined by

$$\sum_{i=1}^{K} \frac{\hat{\alpha}_i^2}{\gamma + \lambda_i} = \hat{\sigma}^2 K.$$

The fact that their ridge beat Stein's estimator even with respect to the risk function $E(\tilde{\boldsymbol{\beta}}-\boldsymbol{\beta})'\mathbf{X}'\mathbf{X}(\tilde{\boldsymbol{\beta}}-\boldsymbol{\beta})$ casts some doubt on their design of Monte Carlo experiments, as pointed out by Efron, Morris, and Thisted in the discussion following the article.

For an application of Stein's estimator (pulling toward the overall mean), see Efron and Morris (1975), who considered two problems, one of which is the prediction of the end-of-season batting average from the averages of the first forty at-bats. For applications of ridge estimators to the estimation of production functions, see Brown and Beattie (1975) and Vinod (1976). These authors determined γ by modifications of the Hoerl and Kennard ridge trace analysis. A ridge estimator with a constant γ is used by Brown and Payne (1975) in the study of election night forecasts. Aigner and Judge (1977) used generalized ridge estimators on economic data (see Section 2.2.8).

2.2.8 Stein's Estimator versus Pre-Test Estimators

Let $\hat{\boldsymbol{\alpha}} \sim N(\boldsymbol{\alpha}, \sigma^2\mathbf{I})$ and $S \sim \sigma^2\chi^2_n$ (independent of $\hat{\boldsymbol{\alpha}}$). Consider the strategy: Test the hypothesis $\boldsymbol{\alpha} = \mathbf{0}$ by the F test and estimate $\boldsymbol{\alpha}$ by $\mathbf{0}$ if the hypothesis is accepted (that is, if $S^{-1}\hat{\boldsymbol{\alpha}}'\hat{\boldsymbol{\alpha}} \leqq d$ for an appropriate d) and estimate $\boldsymbol{\alpha}$ by $\hat{\boldsymbol{\alpha}}$ if the hypothesis is rejected. This procedure amounts to estimating $\boldsymbol{\alpha}$ by the estimator $I_d\hat{\boldsymbol{\alpha}}$, where I_d is the indicator function such that $I_d = 1$ if $S^{-1}\hat{\boldsymbol{\alpha}}'\hat{\boldsymbol{\alpha}} > d$ and 0 otherwise. Such an estimator is called a preliminary-test estimator, or a pre-test estimator for short. Sclove, Morris, and Radhakrishnan (1972) proved that $I_d\hat{\boldsymbol{\alpha}}$ is dominated by Stein's positive-rule estimator $[1 - (d_0S/\hat{\boldsymbol{\alpha}}'\hat{\boldsymbol{\alpha}})]_+\hat{\boldsymbol{\alpha}}$ for some d_0 such that $d < d_0 < 2(K-2)/(n+2)$.

A pre-test estimator is commonly used in the regression model. Often the linear hypothesis $\mathbf{Q}'\boldsymbol{\beta} = \mathbf{c}$ is tested, and the constrained least squares estimator (1.4.11) is used if the F statistic (1.5.12) is smaller than a prescribed value and the least squares estimator is used otherwise. An example of this was considered in Eq. (2.1.20). The result of Sclove, Morris, and Radhakrishnan can be extended to this regression situation in the following way.[9]

Let $\mathbf{R}$ be as defined in Section 1.4.2 and let $\mathbf{A} = (\mathbf{Q}, \mathbf{R})'$. Define $\mathbf{Z} = \mathbf{X}\mathbf{A}^{-1}$, $\mathbf{y}^* = \mathbf{y} - \mathbf{X}\mathbf{f}$, and $\boldsymbol{\gamma} = \mathbf{A}(\boldsymbol{\beta} - \mathbf{f})$ where $\mathbf{f}$ is any vector satisfying $\mathbf{c} = \mathbf{Q}'\mathbf{f}$. Then we can write Model 1 as

$$\mathbf{y}^* = \mathbf{Z}\boldsymbol{\gamma} + \mathbf{u}. \tag{2.2.16}$$

Partition $\mathbf{Z}$ and $\boldsymbol{\gamma}$ conformably as $\mathbf{Z} = (\mathbf{Z}_1, \mathbf{Z}_2)$, where $\mathbf{Z}_1 = \mathbf{X}\mathbf{Q}(\mathbf{Q}'\mathbf{Q})^{-1}$ and $\mathbf{Z}_2 = \mathbf{X}\mathbf{R}(\mathbf{R}'\mathbf{R})^{-1}$, and as $\boldsymbol{\gamma}' = (\boldsymbol{\gamma}_1', \boldsymbol{\gamma}_2')$, where $\boldsymbol{\gamma}_1 = \mathbf{Q}'(\boldsymbol{\beta} - \mathbf{f})$ and $\boldsymbol{\gamma}_2 = \mathbf{R}'(\boldsymbol{\beta} - \mathbf{f})$. Then the hypothesis $\mathbf{Q}'\boldsymbol{\beta} = \mathbf{c}$ in the model $\mathbf{y} = \mathbf{X}\boldsymbol{\beta} + \mathbf{u}$ is equivalent to the hypothesis $\boldsymbol{\gamma}_1 = \mathbf{0}$ in the model $\mathbf{y}^* = \mathbf{Z}\boldsymbol{\gamma} + \mathbf{u}$.

Define $\mathbf{W} = (\mathbf{W}_0, \mathbf{W}_1, \mathbf{W}_2)$ as $\mathbf{W}_2 = (\mathbf{Z}_2'\mathbf{Z}_2)^{-1/2}\mathbf{Z}_2'$; $\mathbf{W}_1 = (\bar{\mathbf{Z}}_1'\bar{\mathbf{Z}}_1)^{-1/2}\bar{\mathbf{Z}}_1'$, where $\bar{\mathbf{Z}}_1 = [\mathbf{I} - \mathbf{Z}_2(\mathbf{Z}_2'\mathbf{Z}_2)^{-1}\mathbf{Z}_2']\mathbf{Z}_1$; and $\mathbf{W}_0$ is a matrix satisfying $\mathbf{W}_0'\mathbf{W}_1 = \mathbf{0}$,

$\mathbf{W}_0'\mathbf{W}_2 = \mathbf{0}$, and $\mathbf{W}_0'\mathbf{W}_0 = \mathbf{I}$. Then we have

$$\mathbf{W}'\mathbf{y}^* \sim N(\mathbf{W}'\mathbf{Z}\gamma, \sigma^2\mathbf{I}), \tag{2.2.17}$$

and the hypothesis $\gamma_1 = \mathbf{0}$ in model (2.2.16) is equivalent to the hypothesis $\mathbf{W}_1'\mathbf{Z}\gamma = \mathbf{0}$ in model (2.2.17). Define $I_d = 1$ if $S^{-1}\mathbf{y}^{*\prime}\overline{\mathbf{Z}}_1(\overline{\mathbf{Z}}_1'\overline{\mathbf{Z}}_1)^{-1}\overline{\mathbf{Z}}_1'\mathbf{y}^* > d$ and 0 otherwise and define $D = \{1 - [d_0 S/\mathbf{y}^{*\prime}\overline{\mathbf{Z}}_1(\overline{\mathbf{Z}}_1'\overline{\mathbf{Z}}_1)^{-1}\overline{\mathbf{Z}}_1'\mathbf{y}^*]\}_+$. Then the aforementioned result of Sclove *et al.* implies that

$$D\begin{bmatrix}\mathbf{0}\\ \mathbf{W}_1'\mathbf{y}^*\\ \mathbf{W}_2'\mathbf{y}^*\end{bmatrix} + (1-D)\begin{bmatrix}\mathbf{0}\\ \mathbf{0}\\ \mathbf{W}_2'\mathbf{y}^*\end{bmatrix} \quad \text{dominates}$$

$$I_d\begin{bmatrix}\mathbf{0}\\ \mathbf{W}_1'\mathbf{y}^*\\ \mathbf{W}_2'\mathbf{y}^*\end{bmatrix} + (1-I_d)\begin{bmatrix}\mathbf{0}\\ \mathbf{0}\\ \mathbf{W}_2'\mathbf{y}^*\end{bmatrix}$$

in the estimation of $\mathbf{W}'\mathbf{Z}\gamma$. Therefore, premultiplying by $\mathbf{W}$ (which is the inverse of $\mathbf{W}'$), we see that

$$D\mathbf{Z}(\mathbf{Z}'\mathbf{Z})^{-1}\mathbf{Z}'\mathbf{y}^* + (1-D)\mathbf{Z}_2(\mathbf{Z}_2'\mathbf{Z}_2)^{-1}\mathbf{Z}_2'\mathbf{y}^* \equiv \mathbf{Z}\hat{\gamma} \tag{2.2.18}$$

dominates

$$I_d\mathbf{Z}(\mathbf{Z}'\mathbf{Z})^{-1}\mathbf{Z}'\mathbf{y}^* + (1-I_d)\mathbf{Z}_2(\mathbf{Z}_2'\mathbf{Z}_2)^{-1}\mathbf{Z}_2'\mathbf{y}^* \equiv \mathbf{Z}\tilde{\gamma} \tag{2.2.19}$$

in the estimation of $\mathbf{Z}\gamma$. Finally, we conclude that Stein's positive-rule estimator $\hat{\gamma}$ defined by (2.2.18) dominates the pre-test estimator $\tilde{\gamma}$ defined by (2.2.19) in the sense that $E(\hat{\gamma}-\gamma)'\mathbf{Z}'\mathbf{Z}(\hat{\gamma}-\gamma) \leqq E(\tilde{\gamma}-\gamma)'\mathbf{Z}'\mathbf{Z}(\tilde{\gamma}-\gamma)$ for all γ.

Although the preceding conclusion is the only known result that shows the dominance of a Stein-type estimator over a pre-test estimator (with respect to a particular risk function), any Stein-type or ridge-type estimator presented in the previous subsections can be modified in such a way that "shrinking" or "pulling" is done toward linear constraints $\mathbf{Q}'\boldsymbol{\beta} = \mathbf{c}$.

We can assume $\mathbf{Q}'\mathbf{Q} = \mathbf{I}$ without loss of generality because if $\mathbf{Q}'\mathbf{Q} \neq \mathbf{I}$, we can define $\mathbf{Q}^* = \mathbf{Q}(\mathbf{Q}'\mathbf{Q})^{-1/2}$ and $\mathbf{c}^* = (\mathbf{Q}'\mathbf{Q})^{-1/2}\mathbf{c}$ so that $\mathbf{Q}^{*\prime}\boldsymbol{\beta} = \mathbf{c}^*$ and $\mathbf{Q}^{*\prime}\mathbf{Q}^* = \mathbf{I}$. Denoting the least squares estimator of $\boldsymbol{\beta}$ by $\hat{\boldsymbol{\beta}}$, we have

$$\mathbf{Q}'\hat{\boldsymbol{\beta}} - \mathbf{c} \sim N[\mathbf{Q}'\boldsymbol{\beta} - \mathbf{c}, \sigma^2\mathbf{Q}'(\mathbf{X}'\mathbf{X})^{-1}\mathbf{Q}]. \tag{2.2.20}$$

Defining the matrix $\mathbf{G}$ such that $\mathbf{G}'\mathbf{G} = \mathbf{I}$ and $\mathbf{G}'\mathbf{Q}'(\mathbf{X}'\mathbf{X})^{-1}\mathbf{Q}\mathbf{G} = \boldsymbol{\Sigma}^{-1}$, $\boldsymbol{\Sigma}$ diagonal, we have

$$\mathbf{G}'(\mathbf{Q}'\hat{\boldsymbol{\beta}} - \mathbf{c}) \sim N[\mathbf{G}'(\mathbf{Q}'\boldsymbol{\beta} - \mathbf{c}), \sigma^2\,\boldsymbol{\Sigma}^{-1}]. \tag{2.2.21}$$

Therefore, if $\mathbf{B}$ is the diagonal matrix with the ith diagonal element B_i defined under any of the minimax estimators presented in Section 2.2.6, we have

$$(\mathbf{I}-\mathbf{B})\mathbf{G}'(\mathbf{Q}'\hat{\boldsymbol{\beta}}-\mathbf{c}) \ll \mathbf{G}'(\mathbf{Q}'\hat{\boldsymbol{\beta}}-\mathbf{c}) \quad \text{for} \quad \mathbf{G}'(\mathbf{Q}'\boldsymbol{\beta}-\mathbf{c}), \tag{2.2.22}$$

where "$\hat{\theta}_1 \ll \hat{\theta}_2$ for θ" means that

$$E(\hat{\theta}_1-\theta)'(\hat{\theta}_1-\theta) \leqq E(\hat{\theta}_2-\theta)'(\hat{\theta}_2-\theta)$$

for all $\boldsymbol{\theta}$ with strict inequality holding for at least one value of $\boldsymbol{\theta}$. Therefore we have

$$\mathbf{GDG}'(\mathbf{Q}'\hat{\boldsymbol{\beta}}-\mathbf{c}) \ll \mathbf{Q}'\hat{\boldsymbol{\beta}}-\mathbf{c} \quad \text{for} \quad \mathbf{Q}'\boldsymbol{\beta}-\mathbf{c}, \tag{2.2.23}$$

where $\mathbf{D}=\mathbf{I}-\mathbf{B}$, and consequently

$$\begin{bmatrix} \mathbf{GDG}'(\mathbf{Q}'\hat{\boldsymbol{\beta}}-\mathbf{c})+\mathbf{c} \\ \mathbf{R}'\hat{\boldsymbol{\beta}} \end{bmatrix} \ll \begin{bmatrix} \mathbf{Q}'\hat{\boldsymbol{\beta}} \\ \mathbf{R}'\hat{\boldsymbol{\beta}} \end{bmatrix} \quad \text{for} \quad \begin{bmatrix} \mathbf{Q}'\boldsymbol{\beta} \\ \mathbf{R}'\boldsymbol{\beta} \end{bmatrix}, \tag{2.2.24}$$

where $\mathbf{R}$ is as defined in Section 1.4.2 with the added condition $\mathbf{R}'\mathbf{R}=\mathbf{I}$. Then

$$\begin{bmatrix} \mathbf{Q}' \\ \mathbf{R}' \end{bmatrix}^{-1} \begin{bmatrix} \mathbf{GDG}'(\mathbf{Q}'\hat{\boldsymbol{\beta}}-\mathbf{c})+\mathbf{c} \\ \mathbf{R}'\hat{\boldsymbol{\beta}} \end{bmatrix} \ll \hat{\boldsymbol{\beta}} \quad \text{for} \quad \boldsymbol{\beta}, \tag{2.2.25}$$

which can be simplified as

$$\hat{\boldsymbol{\beta}}-\mathbf{QGBG}'(\mathbf{Q}'\hat{\boldsymbol{\beta}}-\mathbf{c}) \ll \hat{\boldsymbol{\beta}} \quad \text{for} \quad \boldsymbol{\beta}. \tag{2.2.26}$$

Let us consider a concrete example using generalized ridge estimator 1. Putting

$$\mathbf{B}=\frac{(K-2)\sigma^2}{\hat{\boldsymbol{\alpha}}'\,\boldsymbol{\Sigma}^2\,\hat{\boldsymbol{\alpha}}}\,\boldsymbol{\Sigma}$$

in the left-hand side of (2.2.26), we obtain the estimator

$$\hat{\boldsymbol{\beta}}-\frac{(K-2)\sigma^2}{(\mathbf{Q}'\hat{\boldsymbol{\beta}}-\mathbf{c})'[\mathbf{Q}'(\mathbf{X}'\mathbf{X})^{-1}\mathbf{Q}]^{-2}(\mathbf{Q}'\hat{\boldsymbol{\beta}}-\mathbf{c})}\,\mathbf{Q}[\mathbf{Q}'(\mathbf{X}'\mathbf{X})^{-1}\mathbf{Q}]^{-1}(\mathbf{Q}'\hat{\boldsymbol{\beta}}-\mathbf{c}). \tag{2.2.27}$$

Aigner and Judge (1977) applied the estimator (2.2.27) and another estimator attributed to Bock (1975) to the international trade model of Baldwin (1971) and compared these estimates to Baldwin's estimates, which may be regarded as pre-test estimates because Baldwin utilized a certain linear restriction. Aigner and Judge concluded that the conditions under which Bock's estimator is minimax are not satisfied by the trade data and that although Berger's estimator (2.2.27) is always minimax, it gives results very close to the least squares in the trade model.

2.3 Robust Regression

2.3.2 Introduction

In Chapter 1 we established that the least squares estimator is best linear unbiased under Model 1 and best unbiased under Model 1 with normality. The theme of the previous section was essentially that a biased estimator may be better than the least squares estimator under the normality assumption. The theme of this section is that, in the absence of normality, a nonlinear estimator may be better than the least squares estimator. We shall first discuss robust estimation in the i.i.d sample case, and in the next subsection we shall generalize the results to the regression case.

2.3.2 Independent and Identically Distributed Case

Let $y_1, y_2, \ldots, y_T$ be independent observations from a symmetric distribution function $F[(y-\mu)/\sigma]$ such that $F(0)=\frac{1}{2}$. Thus μ is both the population mean and the median. Here σ represents a scale parameter that may not necessarily be the standard deviation. Let the order statistics be $y_{(1)} \leqq y_{(2)} \leqq \cdots \leqq y_{(T)}$. We define the sample median $\tilde{\mu}$ to be $y_{((T+1)/2)}$ if T is odd and any arbitrarily determined point between $y_{(T/2)}$ and $y_{((T/2)+1)}$ if T is even. It has long been known that $\tilde{\mu}$ would be a better estimator of μ than the sample mean $\hat{\mu} = T^{-1}\Sigma_{t=1}^{T} y_t$ if F has heavier tails than the normal distribution. Intuitively speaking, this is because $\tilde{\mu}$ is much less sensitive to the effect of a few wild observations than $\hat{\mu}$ is.

It can be shown that $\tilde{\mu}$ is asymptotically normally distributed with mean μ and variance $[4Tf(0)^2]^{-1}$, where f is the density of F.[10] Using this, we can compare the asymptotic variance of $\tilde{\mu}$ with that of $\hat{\mu}$ for various choices of F. Consider the three densities

$$\text{Normal} \qquad \frac{1}{\sqrt{2\pi}}\, e^{-x^2/2}$$

$$\text{Laplace} \qquad \frac{1}{2}\, e^{-|x|}$$

$$\text{Cauchy} \qquad \frac{1}{\pi}\,\frac{1}{(1+x^2)}.$$

Table 2.3 shows the asymptotic variances of $\hat{\mu}$ and $\tilde{\mu}$ under these three distributions. Clearly, the mean is better than the median under normality but the

Table 2.3 Asymptotic variances (times sample size) of the sample mean and the sample median under selected distributions

	$TV(\hat{\mu})$	$TV(\tilde{\mu})$
Normal	1	1.57
Laplace	2	1
Cauchy	∞	2.47

median outperforms the mean in the case of the other two long-tailed distributions. (Note that the mean is the maximum likelihood estimator under normality and that the median, because it minimizes $\Sigma|y_t - b|$, is the maximum likelihood estimator under the Laplace distribution.) In general, we call an estimator, such as the median, that performs relatively well under distributions heavier-tailed than normal a "robust" estimator. To be precise, therefore, the word *robustness* should be used in reference to the particular class of possible distributions imagined. A comparison of the variances of the mean and the median when the underlying class of distributions is a mixture of two normal distributions can be found in Bickel and Doksum (1977, p. 371), which has an excellent elementary discussion of robust estimation.

Another robust estimator of location that has long been in use is called the *α-trimmed mean,* which is simply the mean of the sample after the proportion α of largest and smallest observations have been removed. These and other similar robust estimators were often used by statisticians in the nineteenth century (see Huber, 1972; Stigler, 1973). However, the popularity of these robust estimators declined at the turn of the century, and in the first half of the present century the sample mean or the least squares estimator became the dominant estimator. This change occurred probably because many sophisticated testing procedures have been developed under the normality assumption (mathematical convenience) and because statisticians have put an undue confidence in the central limit theorem (rationalization). In the last twenty years we have witnessed a resurgence of interest in robust estimation among statisticians who have recognized that the distributions of real data are often significantly different from normal and have heavier tails than the normal in most cases. Tukey and his associates in Princeton have been the leading proponents of this movement. We should also mention Mandelbrot (1963), who has gone so far as to maintain that many economic variables have infinite variance. However, it should be noted that the usefulness of robust estimation is by no means dependent on the unboundedness of the variance; the occurrence of heavier tails than the normal is sufficient to ensure its efficacy. For a survey of recent developments, the reader is referred to Andrews et al. (1972), who reported on Monte Carlo studies of 68 robust estimators, and to Huber (1972, 1977, 1981), Hogg (1974), and Koenker (1981a).

Robust estimators of location can be classified into four groups: M, L_p, L, and R estimators. M, L, and R estimators are the terms used by Huber (1972). L_p estimators constitute a subset of the class M, but we have singled them out because of their particular importance. We shall briefly explain these classes of estimators and then generalize them to the regression case.

M Estimator. The M estimator (stands for "maximum-likelihood-type" estimator) is defined as the value of b that minimizes $\Sigma_{t=1}^{T}\rho[(y_t - b)/s]$ where s is an estimate of the scale parameter σ and ρ is a chosen function. If ρ is twice differentiable and its second derivative is piecewise continuous with $E\rho'[(y_t - \mu)/s_0] = 0$ where s_0 is the probability limit of s,[11] we can use the results of Chapter 4 to show that the M estimator is asymptotically normal with mean μ and variance

$$T^{-1}s_0^2 \frac{E\{\rho'[s_0^{-1}(y_t - \mu)]^2\}}{\{E\rho''[s_0^{-1}(y_t - \mu)]\}^2}. \tag{2.3.1}$$

Note that when $\rho(\lambda) = \lambda^2$, this formula reduces to the familiar formula for variance of the sample mean.

Consider an M estimator proposed by Huber (1964). It is defined by

$$\begin{aligned} \rho(z) &= \tfrac{1}{2}z^2 && \text{if} \quad |z| < c \\ &= c|z| - \tfrac{1}{2}c^2 && \text{if} \quad |z| \geqq c, \end{aligned} \tag{2.3.2}$$

where $z = (y - \mu)/s$ and c is to be chosen by the researcher. (The Monte Carlo studies of Andrews et al. (1972) considered several values of c between 0.7and 2.) Huber (1964) arrived at the ρ function in (2.3.2) as the minimax choice (doing the best against the least favorable distribution) when $F(z) = (1 - \epsilon)\Phi(z) + \epsilon H(z)$, where $z = (y - \mu)/\sigma$, H varies among all the symmetric distributions, Φ is the standard normal distribution function, and ϵ is a given constant between 0 and 1. The value of c depends on ϵ in a certain way. As for s, one may choose any robust estimate of the scale parameter. Huber (1964) proposed the simultaneous solution of

$$\sum_{t=1}^{T} \rho'\left(\frac{y_t - b}{s}\right) = 0 \tag{2.3.3}$$

and

$$\sum_{t=1}^{T} \rho'\left(\frac{y_t - b}{s}\right)^2 = \frac{T}{\sqrt{2\pi}} \int_{-\infty}^{\infty} \rho'(z)^2 e^{-z^2/2} dz \tag{2.3.4}$$

in terms of b and s. Huber's estimate of μ converges to the sample mean or the sample median as c tends to ∞ or 0, respectively.

Another M estimator shown to be robust in the study of Andrews et al. (1972) is the following one proposed by Andrews (1974). Its ρ function is defined by

$$\begin{aligned} -\rho(z) &= 1 + \cos z \qquad \text{if} \quad |z| \leqq \pi \\ &= 0 \qquad\qquad\quad \text{if} \quad |z| > \pi, \end{aligned} \tag{2.3.5}$$

where $z = (y - b)/s$ as before. Andrews' choice of s is (2.1) Median $\{|y_t - \tilde{\mu}|\}$.

L_p Estimator. The L_p estimator is defined as the value of b that minimizes $\Sigma_{t=1}^{T} |y_t - b|^p$. Values of p between 1 and 2 are the ones usually considered. Clearly, $p = 2$ yields the sample mean and $p = 1$ the sample median. For any $p \neq 1$, the asymptotic variance of the estimator is given by (2.3.1). The approximate variance for the case $p = 1$ (the median) was given earlier. Note that an estimate of a scale parameter need not be used in defining the L_p estimator.

L Estimator. The L estimator is defined as a linear combination of order statistics $y_{(1)} \leqq y_{(2)} \leqq \cdots \leqq y_{(T)}$. The sample median and the α-trimmed mean discussed at the beginning of this subsection are members of this class. (As we have seen, the median is a member of L_p and hence of M as well.)

Another member of this class is the *Winsorized mean,* which is similar to a trimmed mean. Whereas a trimmed mean discards largest and smallest observations, a Winsorized mean "accumulates" them at each truncation point. More precisely, it is defined as

$$T^{-1}[(g+1)y_{(g+1)} + y_{(g+2)} + \cdots + y_{(T-g-1)} + (g+1)y_{(T-g)}] \tag{2.3.6}$$

for some integer g.

A generalization of the median is the θth sample quantile, $0 < \theta < 1$; this is defined as $y_{(k)}$, where k is the smallest integer satisfying $k > T\theta$ if $T\theta$ is not an integer, and an arbitrarily determined point between $y_{(T\theta)}$ and $y_{(T\theta+1)}$ if $T\theta$ is an integer. Thus $\theta = \frac{1}{2}$ corresponds to the median. It can be shown that the θth sample quantile, denoted by $\tilde{\mu}(\theta)$, minimizes

$$\sum_{y_t \geqq b} \theta |y_t - b| + \sum_{y_t < b} (1 - \theta)|y_t - b|. \tag{2.3.7}$$

Previously we have written $\tilde{\mu}(\frac{1}{2})$ simply as $\tilde{\mu}$. Gastwirth (1966) proposed a linear combination of quantiles $0.3\tilde{\mu}(\frac{1}{4}) + 0.4\tilde{\mu}(\frac{1}{2}) + 0.3\tilde{\mu}(\frac{3}{4})$ as a robust estimator of location. Its asymptotic distribution can be obtained from the following general result attributed to Mosteller (1946): Suppose $0 < \theta_1 < \theta_2 < \cdots < \theta_n < 1$. Then $\tilde{\mu}(\theta_1), \tilde{\mu}(\theta_2), \ldots, \tilde{\mu}(\theta_n)$ are asymptotically jointly normal with the means equal to their respective population quantiles, $\mu(\theta_1), \mu(\theta_2), \ldots, \mu(\theta_n)$ (that is, $\theta_i = F[\mu(\theta_i)]$), and variances and covariances given by

$$\text{Cov}\,[\tilde{\mu}(\theta_i), \tilde{\mu}(\theta_j)] \equiv \omega_{ij} = \frac{\theta_i(1-\theta_j)}{Tf[\mu(\theta_i)]f[\mu(\theta_j)]}, \qquad i \leqq j. \tag{2.3.8}$$

R Estimator. The *rank* is a mapping from n real numbers to the integers 1 through n in such a way that the smallest number is given rank 1 and the next smallest rank 2 and so on. The rank estimator of μ, denoted by μ^*, is defined as follows: Construct a sequence of $n = 2T$ observations $x_1, x_2, \ldots, x_n$ by defining $x_i = y_i - b$, $i = 1, 2, \ldots, T$, and $x_{T+i} = b - y_i$, $i = 1, 2, \ldots, T$, and let their ranks be $R_1, R_2, \ldots, R_n$. Then μ^* is the value of b that satisfies

$$\sum_{i=1}^{T} J\left(\frac{R_i}{2T+1}\right) = 0,$$

where J is a function with the property $\int_0^1 J(\lambda)\, d\lambda = 0$. Hodges and Lehmann (1963) proposed setting $J(\lambda) = \lambda - \frac{1}{2}$. For this choice of $J(\lambda)$, μ^* can be shown to be equal to Median $\{(y_i + y_j)/2\}$, $1 \leqq i \leqq j \leqq T$. It is asymptotically normal with mean μ and variance

$$\frac{1}{12\,T\left[\int_{-\infty}^{\infty} f^2(y)\, dy\right]^2}. \tag{2.3.9}$$

Remarks

We have covered most of the major robust estimators of location that have been proposed. Of course, we can make numerous variations on these estimators. Note that in some of the estimation methods discussed earlier there are parameters that are left to the discretion of the researcher to determine. One systematic way to determine them is the *adaptive procedure,* in which the values of these parameters are determined on the basis of the information contained in the sample. Hogg (1974) surveyed many such procedures. For example, the α of the α-trimmed mean may be chosen so as to minimize an estimate of the variance of the estimator. Similarly, the weights to be used in the linear combination of order statistics may be determined using the asymptotic variances and covariances of order statistics given in (2.3.8).

Most of the estimators discussed in this subsection were included among the nearly seventy robust estimators considered in the Monte Carlo studies of Andrews et al. (1972). Their studies showed that the performance of the sample mean is clearly inferior. This finding is, however, contested by Stigler (1977), who used real data (eighteenth and nineteenth century observations on physical constants such as the speed of light and the mean density of the earth for which we now know the true values fairly accurately). He found that with his data a slightly trimmed mean did best and the more "drastic" robust estimators did poorly. He believes that the conclusions of Andrews et al. are biased in favor of the drastic robust estimators because they used distributions with significantly heavy tails as the underlying distributions. Andrews et al. did not offer definite advice regarding which robust estimator should be used. This is inevitable because the performance of an estimator depends on the assumed distributions. These observations indicate that it is advisable to perform a preliminary study to narrow the range of distributions that given data are supposed to follow and decide on which robust estimator to use, if any. Adaptive procedures mentioned earlier will give the researcher an added flexibility.

The exact distributions of these robust estimators are generally hard to obtain. However, in many situations they may be well approximated by methods such as the jackknife and the bootstrap (see Section 4.3.4).

2.3.3 Regression Case

Let us generalize some of the estimation methods discussed earlier to the regression situation.

M Estimator. The M estimator is easily generalized to the regression model: It minimizes $\Sigma_{t=1}^{T}\rho[(y_t - \mathbf{x}_t'\mathbf{b})/s]$ with respect to the vector $\mathbf{b}$. Its asymptotic variance-covariance matrix is given by $s_0^2(\mathbf{X}'\mathbf{A}\mathbf{X})^{-1}\mathbf{X}'\mathbf{B}\mathbf{X}(\mathbf{X}'\mathbf{A}\mathbf{X})^{-1}$, where $\mathbf{A}$ and $\mathbf{B}$ are diagonal matrices with the tth diagonal elements equal to $E\rho''[(y_t - \mathbf{x}_t'\beta)/s_0]$ and $E\{\rho'[(y_t - \mathbf{x}_t'\beta)/s_0]^2\}$, respectively.

Hill and Holland (1977) did a Monte Carlo study on the regression generalization of Andrews' M estimator described in (2.3.5). They used $s = (2.1)$ Median {largest $T - K + 1$ of $|y_t - \mathbf{x}_t'\tilde{\beta}|$} as the scale factor in the ρ function, where $\tilde{\boldsymbol{\beta}}$ is the value of $\mathbf{b}$ that minimizes $\Sigma_{t=1}^{T}|y_t - \mathbf{x}_t'\mathbf{b}|$. Actually, their estimator, which they called *one-step sine estimator,* is defined as

$$\hat{\boldsymbol{\beta}}_S = (\mathbf{X}'\mathbf{D}\mathbf{X})^{-1}\mathbf{X}'\mathbf{D}\mathbf{y}, \tag{2.3.10}$$

where $\mathbf{D}$ is the diagonal matrix whose tth diagonal element d_t is defined by

$$\begin{aligned} d_t &= \left[\frac{y_t - \mathbf{x}_t'\tilde{\boldsymbol{\beta}}}{s}\right]^{-1} \sin\left[\frac{y_t - \mathbf{x}_t'\tilde{\boldsymbol{\beta}}}{s}\right] && \text{if} \quad |y_t - \mathbf{x}_t'\tilde{\boldsymbol{\beta}}| \leqq s\pi \\ &= 0 && \text{if} \quad |y_t - \mathbf{x}_t'\tilde{\boldsymbol{\beta}}| > s\pi. \end{aligned} \tag{2.3.11}$$

This is approximately the first step of the so-called Newton-Raphson iteration designed to minimize (2.3.5), as we shall show next.

Put $g(\boldsymbol{\beta}) = \Sigma_{t=1}^{T}\rho(z_t)$ where $z_t = (y_t - \mathbf{x}_t'\boldsymbol{\beta})/s$ and expand $g(\boldsymbol{\beta})$ around $\boldsymbol{\beta} = \tilde{\boldsymbol{\beta}}$ in a Taylor series as

$$g(\boldsymbol{\beta}) \cong g(\tilde{\boldsymbol{\beta}}) + \frac{\partial g}{\partial \boldsymbol{\beta}'}(\boldsymbol{\beta} - \tilde{\boldsymbol{\beta}}) + \tfrac{1}{2}(\boldsymbol{\beta} - \tilde{\boldsymbol{\beta}})' \frac{\partial^2 g}{\partial \boldsymbol{\beta} \partial \boldsymbol{\beta}'}(\boldsymbol{\beta} - \tilde{\boldsymbol{\beta}}), \tag{2.3.12}$$

where the derivatives are evaluated at $\tilde{\boldsymbol{\beta}}$. Let $\hat{\boldsymbol{\beta}}$ be the value of $\boldsymbol{\beta}$ that minimizes the right-hand side of (2.3.12). Thus

$$\hat{\boldsymbol{\beta}} = \tilde{\boldsymbol{\beta}} - \left[\frac{\partial^2 g}{\partial \boldsymbol{\beta} \partial \boldsymbol{\beta}'}\right]^{-1} \frac{\partial g}{\partial \boldsymbol{\beta}}. \tag{2.3.13}$$

This is the first step in the Newton-Raphson iteration (see Section 4.4.1). Inserting

$$\frac{\partial g}{\partial \boldsymbol{\beta}} = -\sum_{t=1}^{T} s^{-1}\rho'\mathbf{x}_t \tag{2.3.14}$$

and

$$\frac{\partial^2 g}{\partial \boldsymbol{\beta} \partial \boldsymbol{\beta}'} = \sum_{t=1}^{T} s^{-2}\rho''\mathbf{x}_t\mathbf{x}_t', \tag{2.3.15}$$

where ρ' and ρ'' are evaluated at $(y_t - \mathbf{x}_t'\tilde{\boldsymbol{\beta}})/s$, into (2.3.13), we obtain

$$\hat{\boldsymbol{\beta}} = \left(\sum_{t=1}^{T} s^{-2}\rho''\mathbf{x}_t\mathbf{x}_t'\right)^{-1} \sum_{t=1}^{T} (s^{-1}\rho'\mathbf{x}_t - s^{-2}\rho''\mathbf{x}_t\mathbf{x}_t'\tilde{\boldsymbol{\beta}}). \tag{2.3.16}$$

Finally, inserting a Taylor approximation

$$\rho' \cong \rho'(0) + s^{-1}(y_t - \mathbf{x}_t'\tilde{\boldsymbol{\beta}})\rho'' \tag{2.3.17}$$

into the right-hand side of (2.3.16), we obtain the estimator (2.3.10).

In their Monte Carlo study, Hill and Holland assumed that the error term is $N(0, 1)$ with probability $1 - \alpha$ and $N(0, c^2)$ with probability α, with various values for c and α. The regressor matrix was artificially generated with various degrees of outlying observations and with the number of regressors ranging from 1 to 6. The sample size was chosen to be 20. The reader should look at the table in their article (Hill and Holland, 1977) to see the striking improvement of $\tilde{\boldsymbol{\beta}}$ or $\hat{\boldsymbol{\beta}}_S$ over the least squares estimator and the minor improvement of $\hat{\boldsymbol{\beta}}_S$ over $\tilde{\boldsymbol{\beta}}$.

L_p Estimator. This class also can easily be generalized to the regression model. It is the value of $\mathbf{b}$ that minimizes $\Sigma_{t=1}^{T} |y_t - \mathbf{x}_t'\mathbf{b}|^p$. A special case in which $p = 1$, which was already defined as $\tilde{\boldsymbol{\beta}}$ in the discussion about the M estimator, will be more fully discussed later as an L estimator. For $p \neq 1$, the asymptotic variance of the L_p estimator can be obtained by the same formula as that used for the asymptotic variance of the M estimator. Forsythe (1972) conducted a Monte Carlo study of L_p estimators for $p = 1.25$, 1.5, 1.75, and 2 (least squares) in a regression model with one fixed regressor and an intercept where the error term is distributed as $GN(0, 1) + (1 - G)N(S, R)$ for several values of G, S, and R. His conclusion: The more "contamination," the smaller p should be.

L Estimator. The θth sample quantile can be generalized to the regression situation by simply replacing b by $\mathbf{x}_t'\mathbf{b}$ in the minimand (2.3.7), as noted by Koenker and Bassett (1978). We shall call the minimizing value the θth sample regression quantile and shall denote it by $\tilde{\boldsymbol{\beta}}(\theta)$. They investigated the conditions for the unique solution of the minimization problem and extended Mosteller's result to the regression case. They established that $\tilde{\boldsymbol{\beta}}(\theta_1), \tilde{\boldsymbol{\beta}}(\theta_2), \ldots, \tilde{\boldsymbol{\beta}}(\theta_n)$ are asymptotically normal with the means equal to $\boldsymbol{\beta} + \boldsymbol{\mu}(\theta_1), \boldsymbol{\beta} + \boldsymbol{\mu}(\theta_2), \ldots, \boldsymbol{\beta} + \boldsymbol{\mu}(\theta_n)$, where $\boldsymbol{\mu}(\theta_i) = [\mu(\theta_i), 0, 0, \ldots, 0]'$, and the variance-covariance matrix is given by

$$\text{Cov}\,[\tilde{\boldsymbol{\beta}}(\theta_i), \tilde{\boldsymbol{\beta}}(\theta_j)] = \omega_{ij}(\mathbf{X}'\mathbf{X})^{-1}, \qquad i \leqq j, \tag{2.3.18}$$

where ω_{ij} is given in (2.3.8). A proof for the special case $\tilde{\boldsymbol{\beta}}(\tfrac{1}{2}) \equiv \tilde{\boldsymbol{\beta}}$ is also given in Bassett and Koenker (1978) (see Section 4.6.2).

Blattberg and Sargent (1971) conducted a Monte Carlo study and compared $\tilde{\boldsymbol{\beta}}$, the least squares estimator, and one other estimator in the model with the regressor and no intercept, assuming the error term has the characteristic function $\exp(-|\sigma\lambda|^\alpha)$ for $\alpha = 1.1$, 1.3, 1.5, 1.7, 1.9, and 2.0. Note that $\alpha = 2$ gives the normal distribution and $\alpha = 1$ the Cauchy distribution. They found that $\tilde{\boldsymbol{\beta}}$ did best in general.

Schlossmacher (1973) proposed the following iterative scheme to obtain $\tilde{\boldsymbol{\beta}}$:

$$\tilde{\boldsymbol{\beta}}_{(i)} = (\mathbf{X}'\mathbf{D}\mathbf{X})^{-1}\mathbf{X}'\mathbf{D}\mathbf{y}, \tag{2.3.19}$$

where $\mathbf{D}$ is the diagonal matrix whose tth diagonal element is given by

$$\begin{aligned} d_t &= |y_t - \mathbf{x}_t'\tilde{\boldsymbol{\beta}}_{(i-1)}|^{-1} \quad &\text{if} \quad |y_t - \mathbf{x}_t'\tilde{\boldsymbol{\beta}}_{(i-1)}| > \epsilon \\ &= 0 &\text{otherwise,} \end{aligned} \tag{2.3.20}$$

where $\tilde{\boldsymbol{\beta}}_{(i)}$ is the estimate obtained at the ith iteration and ϵ is some predefined small number (say, $\epsilon = 10^{-7}$). Schlossmacher offered no theory of convergence but found a good convergence in a particular example.

Fair (1974) proposed the following alternative to (2.3.20):

$$d_t^* = \min\left(|y_t - \mathbf{x}_t'\tilde{\boldsymbol{\beta}}_{(i-1)}|^{-1}, \epsilon^{-1}\right). \tag{2.3.21}$$

Thus Fair bounded the weights from above, whereas Schlossmacher threw out observations that should be getting the greatest weight possible. It is clear that Fair's method is preferable because his weights are continuous and nonincreasing functions of the residuals, whereas Schlossmacher's are not.

A generalization of the trimmed mean to the regression model has been proposed by several authors. We shall consider two such methods. The first, which we shall call $\hat{\boldsymbol{\beta}}(\alpha)$ for $0 < \alpha < \frac{1}{2}$, requires a preliminary estimate, which we shall denote by $\hat{\boldsymbol{\beta}}_0$. The estimation process involves calculating the residuals from $\hat{\boldsymbol{\beta}}_0$, throwing away those observations corresponding to the $[T\alpha]$ smallest and $[T\alpha]$ largest residuals, and then calculating $\hat{\boldsymbol{\beta}}(\alpha)$ by least squares applied to the remaining observations.

The second method uses the θth regression quantile $\tilde{\boldsymbol{\beta}}(\theta)$ of Koenker and Bassett (1978) mentioned earlier. This method involves removing from the sample any observations that have a residual from $\tilde{\boldsymbol{\beta}}(\alpha)$ that is negative or a residual from $\tilde{\boldsymbol{\beta}}(1-\alpha)$ that is positive and then calculating the LS estimator using the remaining observations. This estimator is denoted by $\boldsymbol{\beta}^*(\alpha)$.

Ruppert and Carroll (1980) derived the asymptotic distribution of the two estimators and showed that the properties of $\hat{\boldsymbol{\beta}}(\alpha)$ are sensitive to the choice of the initial estimate $\hat{\boldsymbol{\beta}}_0$ and can be inefficient relative to $\boldsymbol{\beta}^*(\alpha)$. However, if $\hat{\boldsymbol{\beta}}_0 = \frac{1}{2}[\tilde{\boldsymbol{\beta}}(\alpha) + \tilde{\boldsymbol{\beta}}(1-\alpha)]$ and the distribution of the error term is symmetric, $\hat{\boldsymbol{\beta}}(\alpha)$ is asymptotically equivalent to $\boldsymbol{\beta}^*(\alpha)$.

R Estimator. This type of regression estimator was proposed by Jaeckel (1972). He wrote the regression model as $\mathbf{y} = \beta_0\mathbf{l} + \mathbf{X}\boldsymbol{\beta} + \mathbf{u}$, where $\mathbf{X}$ is now the usual regressor matrix except $\mathbf{l}$, the column of ones. Jaeckel's estimator minimizes $D(\mathbf{y} - \mathbf{X}\mathbf{b}) = \Sigma_{t=1}^{T} [R_t - (T+1)/2](y_t - \mathbf{x}_t'\mathbf{b})$, where $R_t = \text{rank}(y_t - \mathbf{x}_t'\mathbf{b})$. Note that R_t is also a function of $\mathbf{b}$. Jaeckel proved that D is a nonnegative, continuous, and convex function of $\mathbf{b}$ and that his estimator is asymptotically normal with mean $\boldsymbol{\beta}$ and variance-covariance matrix

$$\tau^2 \left\{ \mathbf{X}' \left[\mathbf{I} - \frac{\mathbf{l}\mathbf{l}'}{T} \right] \mathbf{X} \right\}^{-1}, \tag{2.3.22}$$

where $\tau^2 = 12^{-1}[\int f^2(u)\, du]^{-2}$. The ratio σ^2/τ^2 is known as the Pitman efficiency of the Wilcoxon rank test and is equal to 0.955 if f is normal and greater than 0.864 for any symmetric distribution, whereas its upper bound is infinity. Because the derivative of D exists almost everywhere, any iterative scheme of minimization that uses only the first derivatives can be used. (Second derivatives are identically zero.) The intercept β_0 may be estimated by the Hodges-Lehmann estimator, Median$\{(\hat{u}_i + \hat{u}_j)/2\}$, $1 \leqq i \leqq j \leqq T$, where $\hat{\mathbf{u}}$ is the vector of the least squares residuals. See the articles by McKean and Hettmansperger (1976) and Hettmansperger and McKean (1977) for tests of linear hypotheses using Jaeckel's estimator.

Exercises

1. (Section 2.1.3)
   Show that the Bayesian minimand (2.1.5) is minimized when S is chosen to be the set of $\mathbf{y}$ that satisfies the inequality (2.1.3).

2. (Section 2.1.5)
   A weakness of PC is that it does not choose the right model with probability 1 when T goes to infinity. (The weakness, however, is not serious.) Suppose we must choose between regressor matrix $\mathbf{X}_1$ and $\mathbf{X}$ such that $\mathbf{X}_1 \subset \mathbf{X}$. Show that

$$\lim_{T\to\infty} P[\text{PC chooses } \mathbf{X}_1 | \mathbf{X}_1 \text{ is true}] = P[\chi^2_{K-K_1} < 2(K - K_1)] < 1.$$

3. (Section 2.1.5)
   Schwartz's (1978) criterion minimizes $T \log \mathbf{y}'\mathbf{M}_i\mathbf{y} + K_i \log T$. Show that this criterion chooses the correct model with probability 1 as T goes to ∞.

4. (Section 2.2.3)
   If $\mathbf{F}'\boldsymbol{\beta}$ is estimable, show that $\mathbf{F}'\hat{\boldsymbol{\beta}}$ is the BLUE of $\mathbf{F}'\boldsymbol{\beta}$, where $\hat{\boldsymbol{\beta}}$ is the LS estimator.

5. (Section 2.2.3)
   Show that $\hat{\boldsymbol{\beta}}_P$ defined in (2.2.10) is a solution of (2.2.6).

6. (Section 2.2.4)
   Show that for any square matrix $\mathbf{A}$ there exists a positive constant γ_0 such that for all $\gamma > \gamma_0$, $\mathbf{A} + \gamma\mathbf{I}$ is nonsingular.

3 Large Sample Theory

Large sample theory plays a major role in the theory of econometrics because econometricians must frequently deal with more complicated models than the classical linear regression model of Chapter 1. Few finite sample results are known for these models, and, therefore, statistical inference must be based on the large sample properties of the estimators. In this chapter we shall present a brief review of random variables and the distribution function, discuss various convergence theorems including laws of large numbers and central limit theorems, and then use these theorems to prove the consistency and the asymptotic normality of the least squares estimator. Additional examples of the application of the convergence theorems will be given.

3.1 A Review of Random Variables and the Distribution Function

This section is not meant to be a complete discussion of the subject; the reader is assumed to know the fundamentals of the theory of probability, random variables, and distribution functions at the level of an intermediate textbook in mathematical statistics.[1] Here we shall introduce a few concepts that are not usually dealt with in intermediate textbooks but are required in the subsequent analysis, in particular, the rigorous definition of a random variable and the definition of the Stieltjes integral.[2]

3.1.1 Random Variables

At the level of an intermediate textbook, a random variable is defined as a real-valued function over a sample space. But a sample space is not defined precisely, and once a random variable is defined the definition is quickly forgotten and a random variable becomes identified with its probability distribution. This treatment is perfectly satisfactory for most practical applications, but certain advanced theorems can be proved more easily by using the fact that a random variable is indeed a function.

We shall first define a *sample space* and a *probability space*. In concrete terms, a sample space may be regarded as the set of all the possible outcomes of an experiment. Thus, in the experiment of throwing a die, the six faces of the die constitute the sample space; and in the experiment of measuring the height of a randomly chosen student, the set of positive real numbers can be chosen as the sample space. As in the first example, a sample space may be a set of objects other than numbers. A subset of a sample space may be called an event. Thus we speak of the event of an ace turning up or the event of an even number showing in the throw of a die. With each event we associate a real number between 0 and 1 called the probability of the event. When we think of a sample space, we often think of the other two concepts as well: the collection of its subsets (events) and the probabilities attached to the events. The term *probability space* refers to all three concepts collectively. We shall develop an abstract definition of a probability space in that collective sense.

Given an abstract sample space Ω, we want to define the collection $\mathcal{A}$ of subsets of Ω that possess certain desired properties.

DEFINITION 3.1.1. The collection $\mathcal{A}$ of subsets of Ω is called a *σ-algebra* if it satisfies the properties:

(i) $\Omega \in \mathcal{A}$.

(ii) $E \in \mathcal{A} \Rightarrow \bar{E} \in \mathcal{A}$. ($\bar{E}$ refers to the complement of E with respect to Ω.)

(iii) $E_j \in \mathcal{A}, \quad j = 1, 2, \ldots \Rightarrow \cup_{j=1}^{\infty} E_j \in \mathcal{A}$.

Given a σ-algebra, we shall define over it a real-valued set function satisfying certain properties.

DEFINITION 3.1.2. A *probability measure*, denoted by $P(\cdot)$, is a real-valued set function that is defined over a σ-algebra $\mathcal{A}$ and satisfies the properties:

(i) $E \in \mathcal{A} \Rightarrow P(E) \geqq 0$.

(ii) $P(\Omega) = 1$.

(iii) If $\{E_j\}$ is a countable collection of disjoint sets in $\mathcal{A}$, then

$$P\left(\bigcup_j E_j\right) = \sum_j P(E_j).$$

A probability space and a random variable are defined as follows:

DEFINITION 3.1.3. Given a sample space Ω, a σ-algebra $\mathcal{A}$ associated with Ω, and a probability measure $P(\cdot)$ defined over $\mathcal{A}$, we call the triplet $(\Omega, \mathcal{A}, P)$ a *probability space*.[3]

DEFINITION 3.1.4. A *random variable* on $(\Omega, \mathcal{A}, P)$ is a real-valued function[4] defined over a sample space Ω, denoted by $X(\omega)$ for $\omega \in \Omega$, such that for any real number x,

$$\{\omega | X(\omega) < x\} \in \mathcal{A}.$$

Let us consider two examples of probability space and random variables defined over them.

EXAMPLE 3.1.1. In the sample space consisting of the six faces of a die, all the possible subsets (including the whole space and the null set) constitute a σ-algebra. A probability measure can be defined, for example, by assiging 1/6 to each face and extending probabilities to the other subsets according to the rules given by Definition 3.1.2. An example of a random variable defined over this space is a mapping of the even-numbered faces to one and the odd-numbered faces to zero.

EXAMPLE 3.1.2. Let a sample space be the closed interval [0, 1]. Consider the smallest σ-algebra containing all the open sets in the interval. Such a σ-algebra is called the collection of *Borel sets* or a *Borel field.* This σ-algebra can be shown to contain all the countable unions and intersections of open and closed sets. A probability measure of a Borel set can be defined, for example, by assigning to every interval (open, closed, or half-open and half-closed) its length and extending the probabilities to the other Borel sets according to the rules set forth in Definition 3.1.2. Such a measure is called *Lebesgue measure.*[5] In Figure 3.1 three random variables, X, Y, and Z, each of which takes the value 1 or 0 with probability $\frac{1}{2}$, are depicted over this probabil-

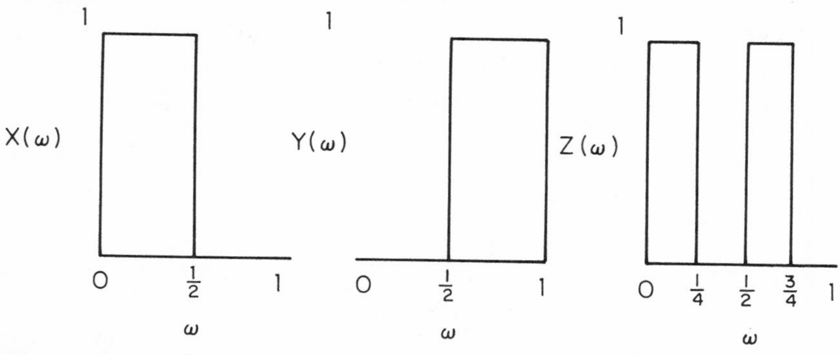

Figure 3.1 Discrete random variables defined over [0, 1] with Lebesgue measure

ity space. Note that Z is independent of either X or Y, whereas X and Y are not independent (in fact $XY = 0$). A continuous random variable $X(\omega)$ with the standard normal distribution can be defined over the same probability space by $X = \Phi^{-1}(\omega)$, where Φ is the standard normal distribution function and "-1" denotes the inverse function.

3.1.2 Distribution Function

DEFINITION 3.1.5. The *distribution function* $F(x)$ of a random variable $X(\omega)$ is defined by

$$F(x) = P\{\omega | X(\omega) < x\}.$$

Note that the distribution function can be defined for any random variable because a probability is assigned to every element of $\mathcal{A}$ and hence to $\{\omega | X(\omega) < x\}$ for any x. We shall write $P\{\omega | X(\omega) < x\}$ more compactly as $P(X < x)$.

A distribution function has the properties:

(i) $F(-\infty) = 0$.

(ii) $F(\infty) = 1$.

(iii) It is nondecreasing and continuous from the left.

[Some authors define the distribution function as $F(x) = P\{\omega | X(\omega) \leqq x\}$. Then it is continuous from the right.]

Using a distribution function, we can define the expected value of a random variable whether it is discrete, continuous, or a mixture of the two. This is done by means of the *Riemann-Stieltjes integral,* which is a simple generalization of the familiar Riemann integral. Let X be a random variable with a distribution function F and let $Y = h(X)$, where $h(\cdot)$ is Borel-measurable.[6] We define the *expected value* of Y, denoted by EY as follows. Divide an interval $[a, b]$ into n intervals with the end points $a = x_0 < x_1 < \ldots < x_{n-1} < x_n = b$ and let x_i^* be an arbitrary point in $[x_i, x_{i+1}]$. Define the partial sum

$$S_n = \sum_{i=0}^{n-1} h(x_i^*)[F(x_{i+1}) - F(x_i)] \tag{3.1.1}$$

associated with this partition of the interval $[a, b]$. If, for any $\epsilon > 0$, there exists a real number A and a partition such that for every finer partition and for any choice of x_i^*, $|S_n - A| < \epsilon$, we call A the *Riemann-Stieltjes integral* and denote it by $\int_a^b h(x)\, dF(x)$. It exists if h is a continuous function except possibly for a countable number of discontinuities, provided that, whenever its discontinuity coincides with that of F, it is continuous from the right.[7] Finally, we define

$$EY = \int_{-\infty}^{\infty} h(x)\, dF(x) = \lim_{\substack{a \to -\infty \\ b \to \infty}} \int_a^b h(x)\, dF(x), \tag{3.1.2}$$

provided the limit (which may be $+\infty$ or $-\infty$) exists regardless of the way $a \to -\infty$ and $b \to \infty$.

If dF/dx exists and is equal to $f(x)$, $F(x_{i+1}) - F(x_i) = f(x_i^*)(x_{i+1} - x_i)$ for some $x_i^* \in [x_{i+1}, x_i]$ by the mean value theorem. Therefore

$$Eh(X) = \int_{-\infty}^{\infty} h(x)f(x)\, dx. \tag{3.1.3}$$

On the other hand, suppose $X = c_i$ with probability p_i, $i = 1, 2, \ldots, K$. Take $a < c_1$ and $c_K < b$; then, for sufficiently large n, each interval contains at most one of the c_i's. Then, of the n terms in the summand of (3.1.1), only K terms containing c_i's are nonzero. Therefore

$$\int_a^b h(x)\, dF(x) = \sum_{i=1}^{K} h(c_i)p_i. \tag{3.1.4}$$

3.2 Various Modes of Convergence

In this section, we shall define four modes of convergence for a sequence of random variables and shall state relationships among them in the form of several theorems.

DEFINITION 3.2.1 (convergence in probability). A sequence of random variables $\{X_n\}$ is said to converge to a random variable X *in probability* if $\lim_{n\to\infty} P(|X_n - X| > \epsilon) = 0$ for any $\epsilon > 0$. We write $X_n \xrightarrow{P} X$ or $\text{plim}\, X_n = X$.

DEFINITION 3.2.2 (convergence in mean square). *A* sequence $\{X_n\}$ is said to converge to X *in mean square* if $\lim_{n\to\infty} E(X_n - X)^2 = 0$. We write $X_n \xrightarrow{M} X$.

DEFINITION 3.2.3 (convergence in distribution). *A* sequence $\{X_n\}$ is said to converge to X *in distribution* if the distribution function F_n of X_n converges to the distribution function F of X at every continuity point of F. We write $X_n \xrightarrow{d} X$, and we call F the *limit distribution* of $\{X_n\}$. If $\{X_n\}$ and $\{Y_n\}$ have the same limit distribution, we write $X_n \overset{LD}{=} Y_n$.

The reason for adding the phrase "at every continuity point of F" can be understood by considering the following example: Consider the sequence

$F_n(\cdot)$ such that

$$F_n(x) = 0, \qquad x < \alpha - \frac{1}{n} \tag{3.2.1}$$

$$= \frac{n}{2}\left(x - \alpha + \frac{1}{n}\right), \qquad \alpha - \frac{1}{n} \leqq x \leqq \alpha + \frac{1}{n}$$

$$= 1, \qquad \alpha + \frac{1}{n} < x.$$

Then $\lim F_n$ is not continuous from the left at α and therefore is not a distribution function. However, we would like to say that the random variable with the distribution (3.2.1) converges in distribution to a degenerate random variable which takes the value α with probability one. The phrase "at every continuity point of F" enables us to do so.

DEFINITION 3.2.4 (almost sure convergence). A sequence $\{X_n\}$ is said to converge to X *almost surely*[8] if

$$P\{\omega \mid \lim_{n\to\infty} X_n(\omega) = X(\omega)\} = 1.$$

We write $X_n \xrightarrow{\text{a.s.}} X$.

The next four theorems establish the logical relationships among the four modes of convergence, depicted in Figure 3.2.[9]

THEOREM 3.2.1 (Chebyshev). $EX_n^2 \to 0 \Rightarrow X_n \xrightarrow{\text{P}} 0$.

Proof. We have

$$EX_n^2 = \int_{-\infty}^{\infty} x^2 \, dF_n(x) \geqq \epsilon^2 \int_S dF_n(x), \tag{3.2.2}$$

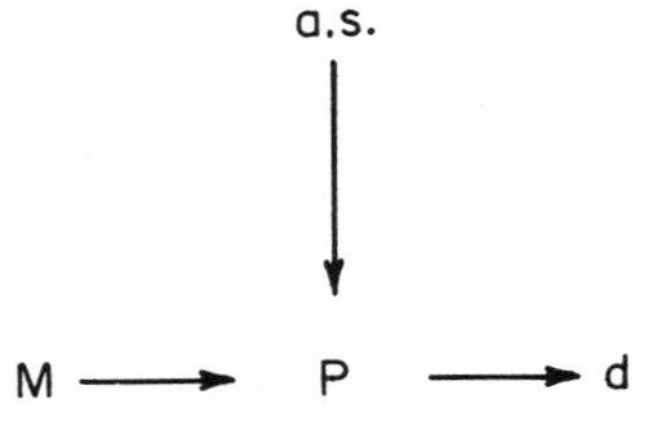

Figure 3.2 Logical relationships among four modes of convergence

where $S = \{x | x^2 \geqq \epsilon^2\}$. But we have

$$\int_S dF_n(x) = \int_{-\infty}^{-\epsilon} dF_n(x) + \int_{\epsilon}^{\infty} dF_n(x) \tag{3.2.3}$$

$$= F_n(-\epsilon) + [1 - F_n(\epsilon)]$$

$$= P(X_n < -\epsilon) + P(X_n \geqq \epsilon)$$

$$\geqq P[X_n^2 > \epsilon^2].$$

Therefore, from (3.2.2) and (3.2.3), we obtain

$$P[X_n^2 > \epsilon^2] \leqq \frac{EX_n^2}{\epsilon^2}. \tag{3.2.4}$$

The theorem immediately follows from (3.2.4).

The inequality (3.2.4) is called *Chebyshev's inequality.* By slightly modifying the proof, we can establish the following generalized form of Chebyshev's inequality:

$$P[g(X_n) > \epsilon^2] \leqq \frac{Eg(X_n)}{\epsilon^2}, \tag{3.2.5}$$

where $g(\cdot)$ is any nonnegative continuous function.

Note that the statement $X_n \xrightarrow{\text{M}} X \Rightarrow X_n \xrightarrow{\text{P}} X$, where X may be either a constant or a random variable, follows from Theorem 3.2.1 if we regard $X_n - X$ as the X_n of the theorem.

We shall state the next two theorems without proof. The proof of Theorem 3.2.2 can be found in Mann and Wald (1943) or Rao (1973, p. 122). The proof of Theorem 3.2.3 is left as an exercise.

THEOREM 3.2.2. $X_n \xrightarrow{\text{P}} X \Rightarrow X_n \xrightarrow{\text{d}} X.$

THEOREM 3.2.3. $X_n \xrightarrow{\text{a.s.}} X \Rightarrow X_n \xrightarrow{\text{P}} X.$

The converse of Theorem 3.2.2 is not generally true, but it holds in the special case where X is equal to a constant α. We shall state it as a theorem, the proof of which is simple and left as an exercise.

THEOREM 3.2.4. $X_n \xrightarrow{\text{d}} \alpha \Rightarrow X_n \xrightarrow{\text{P}} \alpha.$

The converse of Theorem 3.2.3 does not hold either, as we shall show by a well-known example. Define a probability space $(\Omega, \mathcal{A}, P)$ as follows: $\Omega = [0, 1]$, $\mathcal{A}$ = Lebesgue-measurable sets in $[0, 1]$, and P = Lebesgue measure as in Example 3.1.2. Define a sequence of random variables $X_n(\omega)$ as

$$
\begin{aligned}
X_1(\omega) &= 1 \qquad \text{for } 0 \leqq \omega \leqq 1 \\
X_2(\omega) &= 1 \qquad \text{for } 0 \leqq \omega \leqq \frac{1}{2} \\
&= 0 \qquad \text{elsewhere} \\
X_3(\omega) &= 1 \qquad \text{for } \frac{1}{2} \leqq \omega \leqq \frac{1}{2} + \frac{1}{3} \\
&= 0 \qquad \text{elsewhere} \\
X_4(\omega) &= 1 \qquad \text{for } 0 \leqq \omega \leqq \frac{1}{12} \text{ and } \frac{1}{2} + \frac{1}{3} \leqq \omega \leqq 1 \\
&= 0 \qquad \text{elsewhere} \\
X_5(\omega) &= 1 \qquad \text{for } \frac{1}{12} \leqq \omega \leqq \frac{1}{12} + \frac{1}{5} \\
&= 0 \qquad \text{elsewhere} \\
&\vdots
\end{aligned}
$$

In other words, the subset of Ω over which X_n assumes unity has the total length $1/n$ and keeps moving to the right until it reaches the right end point of $[0, 1]$, at which point it moves back to 0 and starts again. For any $1 > \epsilon > 0$, we clearly have

$$P(|X_n| > \epsilon) = \frac{1}{n}$$

and therefore $X_n \xrightarrow{\text{P}} 0$. However, because $\Sigma_{i=1}^{\infty} i^{-1} = \infty$, there is no element in Ω for which $\lim_{n\to\infty} X_n(\omega) = 0$. Therefore $P\{\omega | \lim_{n\to\infty} X_n(\omega) = 0\} = 0$, implying that X_n does not converge to 0 almost surely.

The next three convergence theorems are extremely useful in obtaining the asymptotic properties of estimators.

THEOREM 3.2.5 (Mann and Wald). Let $\mathbf{X}_n$ and $\mathbf{X}$ be K-vectors of random variables and let $g(\cdot)$ be a function from R^K to R such that the set E of discontinuity points of $g(\cdot)$ is closed and $P(\mathbf{X} \in E) = 0$. If $\mathbf{X}_n \xrightarrow{\text{d}} \mathbf{X}$, then $g(\mathbf{X}_n) \xrightarrow{\text{d}} g(\mathbf{X})$.

A slightly more general theorem, in which a continuous function is replaced by a Borel measurable function, was proved by Mann and Wald (1943). The convergence in distribution of the individual elements of the vector $\mathbf{X}_n$ to the corresponding elements of the vector $\mathbf{X}$ is not sufficient for obtaining the above results. However, if the elements of $\mathbf{X}_n$ are independent for every n, the separate convergence is sufficient.

THEOREM 3.2.6. Let $\mathbf{X}_n$ be a vector of random variables with a fixed finite number of elements. Let g be a real-valued function continuous at a constant vector point $\boldsymbol{\alpha}$. Then $\mathbf{X}_n \xrightarrow{P} \boldsymbol{\alpha} \Rightarrow g(\mathbf{X}_n) \xrightarrow{P} g(\boldsymbol{\alpha})$.

Proof. Continuity at $\boldsymbol{\alpha}$ means that for any $\epsilon > 0$ we can find δ such that $\|\mathbf{X}_n - \boldsymbol{\alpha}\| < \delta$ implies $|g(\mathbf{X}_n) - g(\boldsymbol{\alpha})| < \epsilon$. Therefore

$$P[\|\mathbf{X}_n - \boldsymbol{\alpha}\| < \delta] \leqq P[|g(\mathbf{X}_n) - g(\boldsymbol{\alpha})| < \epsilon]. \tag{3.2.6}$$

The theorem follows because the left-hand side of (3.2.6) converges to 1 by the assumption of the theorem.

THEOREM 3.2.7 (Slutsky). If $X_n \xrightarrow{d} X$ and $Y_n \xrightarrow{P} \alpha$, then

(i) $X_n + Y_n \xrightarrow{d} X + \alpha$,

(ii) $X_n Y_n \xrightarrow{d} \alpha X$,

(iii) $(X_n/Y_n) \xrightarrow{d} X/\alpha$, provided $\alpha \neq 0$.

The proof has been given by Rao (1973, p. 122). By repeated applications of Theorem 3.2.7, we can prove the more general theorem that if g is a rational function and $\text{plim } Y_{in} = \alpha_i$, $i = 1, 2, \ldots, J$, and $X_{in} \xrightarrow{d} X_i$ jointly in all $i = 1, 2, \ldots, K$, then the limit distribution of $g(X_{1n}, X_{2n}, \ldots, X_{Kn}, Y_{1n}, Y_{2n}, \ldots, Y_{Jn})$ is the same as the distribution of $g(X_1, X_2, \ldots, X_K, \alpha_1, \alpha_2, \ldots, \alpha_J)$. By using Theorem 3.2.2, this result can also be obtained from Theorem 3.2.5.

The following definition concerning the stochastic order relationship is useful (see Mann and Wald, 1943, for more details).

DEFINITION 3.2.5. Let $\{X_n\}$ be a sequence of random variables and let $\{a_n\}$ be a sequence of positive constants. Then we can write $X_n = o(a_n)$ if $\text{plim}_{n\to\infty} a_n^{-1} X_n = 0$ and $X_n = O(a_n)$ if for any $\epsilon > 0$ there exists an M_ϵ such that

$$P[a_n^{-1}|X_n| \leqq M_\epsilon] \geqq 1 - \epsilon$$

for all values of n.

Sometimes these order relationships are denoted o_p and O_p respectively to distinguish them from the cases where $\{X_n\}$ are nonstochastic. However, we use the same symbols for both stochastic and nonstochastic cases because Definition 3.2.5 applies to the nonstochastic case as well in a trivial way.

3.3 Laws of Large Numbers and Central Limit Theorems

Given a sequence of random variables $\{X_t\}$, define $\bar{X}_n = n^{-1} \Sigma_{t=1}^n X_t$. A law of large numbers (LLN) specifies the conditions under which $\bar{X}_n - E\bar{X}_n$ converges to 0 either almost surely or in probability. The former is called a *strong law of large numbers* and the latter a *weak law.* In many applications the simplest way to show $\bar{X}_n - E\bar{X}_n \xrightarrow{P} 0$ is to show $\bar{X}_n - E\bar{X}_n \xrightarrow{M} 0$ and then apply Theorem 3.2.1 (Chebyshev). We shall state two strong laws of large numbers. For proofs, the reader is referred to Rao (1973, pp. 114–115).

THEOREM 3.3.1 (Kolmogorov LLN 1). Let $\{X_t\}$ be independent with finite variance $VX_t = \sigma_t^2$. If $\Sigma_{t=1}^{\infty} \sigma_t^2/t^2 < \infty$, then $\bar{X}_n - E\bar{X}_n \xrightarrow{\text{a.s.}} 0$.

THEOREM 3.3.2 (Kolmogorov LLN 2). Let $\{X_t\}$ be i.i.d. (independent and identically distributed). Then a necessary and sufficient condition that $\bar{X}_n \xrightarrow{\text{a.s.}} \mu$ is that EX_t exists and is equal to μ.

Theorem 3.3.2 and the result obtained by putting $\bar{X}_n - E\bar{X}_n$ into the X_n of Theorem 3.2.1 are complementary. If we were to use Theorem 3.2.1 to prove $\bar{X}_n - E\bar{X}_n \xrightarrow{P} 0$, we would need the finite variance of X_t, which Theorem 3.3.2 does not require; but Theorem 3.3.2 requires $\{X_t\}$ to be i.i.d., which Theorem 3.2.1 does not.[10]

When all we want is the proof of $\bar{X}_n - E\bar{X}_n \xrightarrow{P} 0$, Theorem 3.3.1 does not add anything to Theorem 3.2.1 because the assumptions of Theorem 3.3.1 imply $\bar{X}_n - E\bar{X}_n \xrightarrow{M} 0$. The proof is left as an exercise.

Now we ask the question, What is an approximate distribution of $\bar{X}_n$ when n is large? Suppose a law of large numbers holds for a sequence $\{X_t\}$ so that $\bar{X}_n - E\bar{X}_n \xrightarrow{P} 0$. It follows from Theorem 3.2.2 that $\bar{X}_n - E\bar{X}_n \xrightarrow{d} 0$. However, it is an uninteresting limit distribution because it is degenerate. It is more meaningful to inquire into the limit distribution of $Z_n = (V\bar{X}_n)^{-1/2} (\bar{X}_n - E\bar{X}_n)$. For, if the limit distribution of Z_n exists, it should be nondegenerate because $VZ_n = 1$ for all n. A central limit theorem (CLT) specifies the conditions under which Z_n converges in distribution to a standard normal random variable [we shall write $Z_n \rightarrow N(0, 1)$].

We shall state three central limit theorems—Lindeberg-Lévy, Liapounov, and Lindeberg-Feller—and shall prove only the first. For proofs of the other two, see Chung (1974) or Gnedenko and Kolmogorov (1954). Lindeberg-

Lévy and Liapounov are special cases of Lindeberg-Feller, in the sense that the assumptions of either one of the first two central limit theorems imply those of Lindeberg-Feller. The assumptions of Lindeberg-Lévy are more restrictive in some respects and less restrictive in other respects than those of Liapounov.

Before we state the central limit theorems, however, we shall define the *characteristic function* of a random variable and study its properties.

DEFINITION 3.3.1. The *characteristic function* of a random variable X is defined by $Ee^{i\lambda X}$.

Thus if the distribution function of X is $F(\cdot)$, the characteristic function is $\int_{-\infty}^{\infty} e^{i\lambda x}\, dF(x)$. The characteristic function is generally a complex number. However, because $e^{i\lambda x} = \cos \lambda x + i \sin \lambda x$, the characteristic function of a random variable with a density function symmetric around 0 is real. The characteristic functon of $N(0, 1)$ can be evaluated as

$$\frac{1}{\sqrt{2\pi}} \int_{-\infty}^{\infty} \exp\left(i\lambda x - \frac{x^2}{2}\right) dx = \exp\left(-\frac{\lambda^2}{2}\right). \tag{3.3.1}$$

Define $g(\lambda) = \text{Log} \int_{-\infty}^{\infty} e^{i\lambda x}\, dF(x)$, where Log denotes the principal logarithm.[11] Then the following Taylor expansion is valid provided EX^r exists:

$$g(\lambda) = \sum_{j=1}^{r} \kappa_j \frac{(i\lambda)^j}{j!} + o(|\lambda|^r), \tag{3.3.2}$$

where $\kappa_j = (\partial^j g/\partial \lambda^j)_{\lambda=0}/i^j$. The coefficients κ_j are called the *cumulants* of X. The first four cumulants are given by $\kappa_1 = EX$, $\kappa_2 = VX$, $\kappa_3 = E(X - EX)^3$, and $\kappa_4 = E(X - EX)^4 - 3(VX)^2$.

The following theorem is essential for proving central limit theorems.

THEOREM 3.3.3. If $E \exp(i\lambda X_n) \rightarrow E \exp(i\lambda X)$ for every λ and if $E \exp(i\lambda X)$ is continuous at $\lambda = 0$, then $X_n \xrightarrow{d} X$.

The proof of Theorem 3.3.3 can be found in Rao (1973, p. 119).

We can now prove the following theorem.

THEOREM 3.3.4 (Lindeberg-Lévy CLT). Let $\{X_t\}$ be i.i.d. with $EX_t = \mu$ and $VX_t = \sigma^2$. Then $Z_n \rightarrow N(0, 1)$.

Proof. We assume $\mu = 0$ without loss of generality, for we can consider $\{X_t - \mu\}$ if $\mu \neq 0$. Define $g(\lambda) = \text{Log}\, E \exp(i\lambda X_t)$. Then from (3.3.2) we have

$$g(\lambda) = -\frac{\sigma^2 \lambda^2}{2} + o(\lambda^2). \tag{3.3.3}$$

We have, using (3.3.3),

$$\operatorname{Log} E \exp (i\lambda Z_n) = \sum_{t=1}^{n} \operatorname{Log} E \exp \left[\frac{i\lambda X_t}{\sigma\sqrt{n}} \right] \tag{3.3.4}$$

$$= ng\left[\frac{\lambda}{\sigma\sqrt{n}}\right]$$

$$= -\frac{\lambda^2}{2} + n \cdot o\left[\frac{\lambda^2}{\sigma^2 n}\right].$$

Therefore the theorem follows from (3.3.1) and Theorem 3.3.3.

THEOREM 3.3.5 (Liapounov CLT). Let $\{X_t\}$ be independent with $EX_t = \mu_t$, $VX_t = \sigma_t^2$, and $E[|X_t - \mu_t|^3] = m_{3t}$. If

$$\lim_{n\to\infty} \left[\sum_{t=1}^{n} \sigma_t^2\right]^{-1/2} \left[\sum_{t=1}^{n} m_{3t}\right]^{1/3} = 0,$$

then $Z_n \to N(0, 1)$.

THEOREM 3.3.6 (Lindeberg-Feller CLT). Let $\{X_t\}$ be independent with distribution functions $\{F_t\}$ and $EX_t = \mu_t$ and $VX_t = \sigma_t^2$. Define $C_n = (\Sigma_{t=1}^n \sigma_t^2)^{1/2}$. If

$$\lim_{n\to\infty} \frac{1}{C_n^2} \sum_{t=1}^{n} \int_{|x-\mu_t|>\epsilon C_n} (x-\mu_t)^2 \, dF_t(x) = 0$$

for every $\epsilon > 0$, then $Z_n \to N(0, 1)$.

In the terminology of Definition 3.2.3, central limit theorems provide conditions under which the *limit distribution* of $Z_n \equiv (V\overline{X}_n)^{-1/2}(\overline{X}_n - E\overline{X}_n)$ is $N(0, 1)$. We now introduce the term *asymptotic distribution.* It simply means the "approximate distribution when n is large." Given the mathematical result $Z_n \xrightarrow{d} N(0, 1)$, we shall make statements such as "the asymptotic distribution of Z_n is $N(0, 1)$" (written as $Z_n \overset{A}{\sim} N(0, 1)$) or "the asymptotic distribution of X_n is $N(EX_n, VX_n)$." These statements should be regarded merely as more intuitive paraphrases of the result $Z_n \xrightarrow{d} N(0, 1)$. Note that it would be meaningless to say "the limit distribution of X_n is $N(EX_n, VX_n)$."

When the asymptotic distribution of X_n is normal, we also say that X_n is *asymptotically normal.*

The following theorem shows the accuracy of a normal approximation to the true distribution (see Bhattacharya and Rao, 1976, p. 110).

THEOREM 3.3.7. Let $\{X_t\}$ be i.i.d. with $EX_t = \mu$, $VX_t = \sigma^2$, and $E|X_t|^3 = m_3$. Let F_n be the distribution function of Z_n and let Φ be that of $N(0, 1)$. Then

$$|F_n(x) - \Phi(x)| \leqq (0.7975) \frac{m_3}{\sigma^3} \frac{1}{\sqrt{n}}$$

for all x.

It is possible to approximate the distribution function F_n of Z_n more accurately by expanding the characteristic function of Z_n in the powers of $n^{-1/2}$. If EX_t^4 exists, we can obtain from (3.3.2)

$$E \exp (i\lambda Z_n) = e^{-\lambda^2/2} \left[1 + \frac{\kappa_3 (i\lambda)^3}{6\sigma^3 \sqrt{n}} + \frac{\kappa_4 (i\lambda)^4}{24\sigma^4 n} + \frac{\kappa_3^2 (i\lambda)^6}{72\sigma^6 n} + O(n^{-3/2}) \right]. \tag{3.3.5}$$

This is called the *Edgeworth expansion* (see Cramér, 1946, p. 228). Because (see Cramér, 1946, p. 106)

$$\int e^{i\lambda x} \phi^{(r)}(x)\, dx = (-i\lambda)^r e^{-\lambda^2/2}, \tag{3.3.6}$$

where $\phi^{(r)}(x)$ is the rth derivative of the density of $N(0, 1)$, we can invert (3.3.5) to obtain

$$F_n(x) = \Phi(x) - \frac{\kappa_3}{6\sigma^3 \sqrt{n}} \Phi^{(3)}(x) + \frac{\kappa_4}{24\sigma^4 n} \Phi^{(4)}(x) + \frac{\kappa_3^2}{72\sigma^6 n} \Phi^{(6)}(x) + O(n^{-3/2}). \tag{3.3.7}$$

We shall conclude this section by stating a multivariate central limit theorem, the proof of which can be found in Rao (1973, p. 128).

THEOREM 3.3.8. Let $\{\mathbf{X}_n\}$ be a sequence of K-dimensional vectors of random variables. If $\mathbf{c}'\mathbf{X}_n$ converges to a normal random variable for every K-dimensional constant vector $\mathbf{c} \neq \mathbf{0}$, then $\mathbf{X}_n$ converges to a multivariate normal random variable. (Note that showing convergence of each element of $\mathbf{X}_n$ separately is not sufficient.)

3.4 Relationships among lim *E*, AE, and plim

Let F_n be the distribution function of X_n and $F_n \rightarrow F$ at continuity points of F. We have defined plim X_n in Definition 3.2.1. We define lim E and AE as follows:

$$\lim EX_n = \lim \int_{-\infty}^{\infty} x \, dF_n(x) \tag{3.4.1}$$

and

$$\text{AE } X_n = \int_{-\infty}^{\infty} x \, dF(x). \tag{3.4.2}$$

In words, AE, which reads *asymptotic expectation* or *asymptotic mean,* is the mean of the limit distribution.

These three limit operators are similar but different; we can construct examples of sequences of random variables such that any two of the three concepts either differ from each other or coincide with each other. We shall state relationships among the operators in the form of examples and theorems. But, first, note the following obvious facts:

(i) Of the three concepts, only plim X_n can be a nondegenerate random variable; therefore, if it is, it must differ from lim EX_n or AE X_n.

(ii) If plim $X_n = \alpha$, a constant, then AE $X_n = \alpha$. This follows immediately from Theorem 3.2.2.

EXAMPLE 3.4.1. Let X_n be defined by

$$X_n = Z \text{ with probability } (n-1)/n$$
$$= n \text{ with probability } 1/n,$$

where $Z \sim N(0, 1)$. Then plim $X_n = Z$, lim $EX_n = 1$, and AE $X_n = EZ = 0$.

EXAMPLE 3.4.2. Let X_n be defined by

$$X_n = 0 \text{ with probability } (n-1)/n$$
$$= n^2 \text{ with probability } 1/n.$$

Then plim $X_n =$ AE $X_n = 0$, and lim $EX_n = \lim n = \infty$.

EXAMPLE 3.4.3. Let $X \sim N(\alpha, 1)$ and $Y_n \sim N(\beta, n^{-1})$, where $\beta \neq 0$. Then X/Y_n is distributed as Cauchy and does not have a mean. Therefore lim $E(X/Y_n)$ cannot be defined either. But, because $Y_n \xrightarrow{P} \beta$, AE$(X/Y_n) = \alpha/\beta$ by Theorem 3.2.7 (iii).

The following theorem, proved in Rao (1973, p. 121), gives the conditions under which lim $E =$ AE.

THEOREM 3.4.1. If $E|X_n|^r < M$ for all n, then $\lim EX_n^s = \text{AE } X_n^s$ for any $s < r$. In particular, if $EX_n^2 < M$, then $\lim EX_n = \text{AE } X_n$. (Note that this condition is violated by all three preceding examples.)

We are now in a position to define two important concepts regarding the asymptotic properties of estimators, namely, asymptotic unbiasedness and consistency.

DEFINITION 3.4.1. The estimator $\hat{\theta}_n$ of θ is said to be *asymptotically unbiased* if AE $\hat{\theta}_n = \theta$. We call AE $\hat{\theta}_n - \theta$ the *asymptotic bias.*

Note that some authors define asymptotic unbiasedness using lim E instead of AE. Then it refers to a different concept.

DEFINITION 3.4.2. The estimator $\hat{\theta}_n$ of θ is said to be a *consistent* estimator if plim $\hat{\theta}_n = \theta$.

Some authors use the term *weakly consistent* in the preceding definition, to distinguish it from the term *strong consistency* used to describe the property $\hat{\theta}_n \xrightarrow{\text{a.s.}} \theta$.[12]

In view of the preceding discussions, it is clear that a consistent estimator is asymptotically unbiased, but not vice versa.

3.5 Consistency and Asymptotic Normality of Least Squares Estimator

The main purpose of this section is to prove the consistency and the asymptotic normality of the least squares estimators of $\boldsymbol{\beta}$ and σ^2 in Model 1 (classical linear regression model) of Chapter 1. The large sample results of the preceding sections will be extensively utilized. At the end of the section we shall give additional examples of the application of the large sample theorems.

THEOREM 3.5.1. In Model 1 the least squares estimator is a consistent estimator of $\boldsymbol{\beta}$ if $\lambda_s(\mathbf{X}'\mathbf{X}) \rightarrow \infty$, where $\lambda_s(\mathbf{X}'\mathbf{X})$ denotes the smallest characteristic root of $\mathbf{X}'\mathbf{X}$.[13]

Proof. The following four statements are equivalent:

(i) $\lambda_s(\mathbf{X}'\mathbf{X}) \rightarrow \infty$.

(ii) $\lambda_l[(\mathbf{X}'\mathbf{X})^{-1}] \rightarrow 0$, where λ_l refers to the largest characteristic root.

(iii) $\text{tr}(\mathbf{X}'\mathbf{X})^{-1} \rightarrow 0$.

(iv) Every diagonal element of $(\mathbf{X}'\mathbf{X})^{-1}$ converges to 0.

Statement (iv) implies the consistency of $\hat{\boldsymbol{\beta}}$ by Theorem 3.2.1.

The reader should verify that it is not sufficient for consistency to assume that all the diagonal elements of $\mathbf{X}'\mathbf{X}$ go to infinity.

THEOREM 3.5.2. If we assume that $\{u_t\}$ are i.i.d. in Model 1, the least squares estimator $\hat{\sigma}^2$ defined in (1.2.5) is a consistent estimator of σ^2.

Proof. We can write

$$\hat{\sigma}^2 = T^{-1}\mathbf{u}'\mathbf{u} - T^{-1}\mathbf{u}'\mathbf{P}\mathbf{u}, \tag{3.5.1}$$

where $\mathbf{P} = \mathbf{X}(\mathbf{X}'\mathbf{X})^{-1}\mathbf{X}'$. By Theorem 3.3.2 (Kolmogorov LLN 2),

$$T^{-1}\mathbf{u}'\mathbf{u} \xrightarrow{P} \sigma^2. \tag{3.5.2}$$

Because $\mathbf{u}'\mathbf{P}\mathbf{u}$ is nonnegative, we can use the generalized Chebyshev inequality (3.2.5) to obtain

$$P(T^{-1}\mathbf{u}'\mathbf{P}\mathbf{u} > \epsilon) \leqq \epsilon^{-1}ET^{-1}\mathbf{u}'\mathbf{P}\mathbf{u} = \sigma^2\epsilon^{-1}T^{-1}K. \tag{3.5.3}$$

Therefore

$$T^{-1}\mathbf{u}'\mathbf{P}\mathbf{u} \xrightarrow{P} 0. \tag{3.5.4}$$

Therefore the theorem follows from (3.5.1), (3.5.2), and (3.5.4) by using Theorem 3.2.6.

We shall prove the asymptotic normality of the least square estimator $\hat{\boldsymbol{\beta}}$ in two steps: first, for the case of one regressor, and, second, for the case of many regressors.

THEOREM 3.5.3. Assume that $\{u_t\}$ are i.i.d. in Model 1. Assume that $K = 1$, and because $\mathbf{X}$ is a vector in this case, write it as $\mathbf{x}$. If

$$\lim_{T\to\infty} (\mathbf{x}'\mathbf{x})^{-1} \max_{1\leq t\leq T} x_t^2 = 0, \tag{3.5.5}$$

then $\sigma^{-1}(\mathbf{x}'\mathbf{x})^{1/2}(\hat{\beta} - \beta) \to N(0, 1)$.

Proof. We prove the theorem using the Lindeberg-Feller CLT (Theorem 3.3.6). Take $x_t u_t$ as the X_t of Theorem 3.3.6. Then $\mu_t = 0$ and $\sigma_t^2 = \sigma^2 x_t^2$. Let F_X and F_Z be the distribution functions of X and Z, respectively, where $X^2 = Z$. Then

$$\int_{x^2>c^2} x^2\, dF_X(x) = \int_{z>c^2} z\, dF_Z(z)$$

for any c. (This can be verified from the definition of the Riemann-Stieltjes integral given in Section 3.1.2.) Therefore we need to prove

$$\lim_{T\to\infty} \frac{1}{\sigma^2 \mathbf{x}'\mathbf{x}} \sum_{t=1}^{T} \int_{\alpha > \epsilon^2\sigma^2\mathbf{x}'\mathbf{x}} \alpha \, dF_t(\alpha) = 0 \tag{3.5.6}$$

for any ϵ, where F_t is the distribution function of $(x_t u_t)^2$. Let G be the distribution function of u_t^2. Then, because $F_t(\alpha) = P(x_t^2 u_t^2 < \alpha) = P(u_t^2 < \alpha/x_t^2) = G(\alpha/x_t^2)$, we have

$$\int_{\alpha > \epsilon^2\sigma^2\mathbf{x}'\mathbf{x}} \alpha \, dF_t(\alpha) = \int_{\alpha > \epsilon^2\sigma^2\mathbf{x}'\mathbf{x}} \alpha \, dG(\alpha/x_t^2)$$

$$= \int_{\lambda > \epsilon^2\sigma^2 x_t^{-2}\mathbf{x}'\mathbf{x}} x_t^2 \lambda \, dG(\lambda).$$

Therefore (3.5.6) follows from the inequality

$$\int_{\lambda > \epsilon^2\sigma^2 x_t^{-2}\mathbf{x}'\mathbf{x}} \lambda \, dG(\lambda) \leqq \int_{\lambda > \epsilon^2\sigma^2(\max_t x_t^2)^{-1}\mathbf{x}'\mathbf{x}} \lambda \, dG(\lambda) \tag{3.5.7}$$

and the assumption (3.5.5).

THEOREM 3.5.4. Assume that $\{u_t\}$ are i.i.d. in Model 1. Assume also

$$\lim_{T\to\infty} (\mathbf{x}_i'\mathbf{x}_i)^{-1} \max_{1 \leqq t \leqq T} x_{ti}^2 = 0 \tag{3.5.8}$$

for every $i = 1, 2, \ldots, K$. Define $\mathbf{Z} = \mathbf{X}\mathbf{S}^{-1}$, where $\mathbf{S}$ is the $K \times K$ diagonal matrix the ith diagonal element of which is $(\mathbf{x}_i'\mathbf{x}_i)^{1/2}$, and assume that $\lim_{T\to\infty} \mathbf{Z}'\mathbf{Z} \equiv \mathbf{R}$ exists and is nonsingular. Then

$$\mathbf{S}(\hat{\boldsymbol{\beta}} - \boldsymbol{\beta}) \to N(\mathbf{0}, \sigma^2\mathbf{R}^{-1}).$$

Proof. We have $\mathbf{S}(\hat{\boldsymbol{\beta}} - \boldsymbol{\beta}) = (\mathbf{Z}'\mathbf{Z})^{-1}\mathbf{Z}'\mathbf{u}$. The limit distribution of $\mathbf{c}'(\mathbf{Z}'\mathbf{Z})^{-1}\mathbf{Z}'\mathbf{u}$ for any constant vector $\mathbf{c}$ is the same as that of $\boldsymbol{\gamma}'\mathbf{Z}'\mathbf{u}$ where $\boldsymbol{\gamma}' = \mathbf{c}'\mathbf{R}^{-1}$. But, because of Theorem 3.5.3, the asymptotic normality of $\boldsymbol{\gamma}'\mathbf{Z}'\mathbf{u}$ holds if

$$\lim_{T\to\infty} (\boldsymbol{\gamma}'\mathbf{Z}'\mathbf{Z}\boldsymbol{\gamma})^{-1} \max_t \left(\sum_{k=1}^{K} \gamma_k z_{tk} \right)^2 = 0, \tag{3.5.9}$$

where γ_k is the kth element of $\boldsymbol{\gamma}$ and z_{tk} is the t,kth element of $\mathbf{Z}$. But, because $\boldsymbol{\gamma}'\mathbf{Z}'\mathbf{Z}\boldsymbol{\gamma} \geqq \lambda_s(\mathbf{Z}'\mathbf{Z})\boldsymbol{\gamma}'\boldsymbol{\gamma}$ by Theorem 10 of Appendix 1, we have

$$(\gamma'\mathbf{Z}'\mathbf{Z}\gamma)^{-1} \max_t \left(\sum_{k=1}^{K} \gamma_k z_{tk} \right)^2 \leqq (\gamma'\mathbf{Z}'\mathbf{Z}\gamma)^{-1}\gamma'\gamma \max_t \sum_{k=1}^{K} z_{tk}^2 \qquad (3.5.10)$$

$$\leqq \frac{\max_t \sum_{k=1}^{K} z_{tk}^2}{\lambda_s(\mathbf{Z}'\mathbf{Z})}$$

$$= \frac{1}{\lambda_s(\mathbf{Z}'\mathbf{Z})} \max_t \sum_{k=1}^{K} \frac{x_{tk}^2}{\mathbf{x}_k'\mathbf{x}_k},$$

where the first inequality above follows from the Cauchy-Schwarz inequality. Therefore (3.5.9) follows from (3.5.10) because the last term of (3.5.10) converges to 0 by our assumptions. Therefore, by Theorem 3.5.3,

$$\frac{\gamma'\mathbf{Z}'\mathbf{u}}{\sigma(\gamma'\mathbf{Z}'\mathbf{Z}\gamma)^{1/2}} \rightarrow N(0, 1)$$

for any constant vector $\gamma \neq \mathbf{0}$. Since $\gamma'\mathbf{Z}'\mathbf{Z}\gamma \rightarrow \mathbf{c}'\mathbf{R}^{-1}\mathbf{c}$, we have

$$\gamma'\mathbf{Z}'\mathbf{u} \rightarrow N(0, \sigma^2\mathbf{c}'\mathbf{R}^{-1}\mathbf{c}).$$

Thus the theorem follows from Theorem 3.3.8.

At this point it seems appropriate to consider the significance of assumption (3.5.5). Note that (3.5.5) implies $\mathbf{x}'\mathbf{x} \rightarrow \infty$. It would be instructive to try to construct a sequence for which $\mathbf{x}'\mathbf{x} \rightarrow \infty$ and yet (3.5.5) does not hold. The following theorem shows, among other things, that (3.5.5) is less restrictive than the commonly used assumption that lim $T^{-1}\mathbf{x}'\mathbf{x}$ exists and is a nonzero constant. It follows that if lim $T^{-1}\mathbf{X}'\mathbf{X}$ exists and is nonsingular, the condition of Theorem 3.5.4. is satisfied.

THEOREM 3.5.5. Given a sequence of constants $\{x_t\}$, consider the statements:

(i) $\lim_{T\rightarrow\infty} T^{-1}c_T = a$, where $a \neq 0$, $a < \infty$, and $c_T = \Sigma_{t=1}^T x_t^2$.
(ii) $\lim_{T\rightarrow\infty} c_T = \infty$.
(iii) $\lim_{T\rightarrow\infty} c_T^{-1}x_T^2 = 0$.
(iv) $\lim_{T\rightarrow\infty} c_T^{-1} \max_{1\leqq t\leqq T} x_t^2 = 0$.

Then, (i) $\Rightarrow$ [(ii) and (iii)] $\Rightarrow$ (iv).

Proof. (i) $\Rightarrow$ (ii) is obvious. We have

$$\frac{Tx_T^2 - c_T}{T(T-1)} = \frac{c_T}{T} - \frac{c_{T-1}}{T-1} \rightarrow 0. \qquad (3.5.11)$$

Therefore $\lim_{T\to\infty}(T-1)^{-1}x_T^2=0$, which implies (i) $\Rightarrow$ (iii). We shall now prove [(ii) and (iii)] $\Rightarrow$ (iv). Given $\epsilon>0$, there exists T_1 such that for any $T \geqq T_1$

$$c_T^{-1}x_T^2<\epsilon \tag{3.5.12}$$

because of (iii). Given this T_1, there exists $T_2>T_1$ such that for any $T>T_2$

$$c_T^{-1}\max_{1\leqq t<T_1} x_t^2<\epsilon \tag{3.5.13}$$

because of (ii). But (3.5.12) implies that for any $T>T_2$

$$c_T^{-1}x_t^2<\epsilon \quad \text{for} \quad t=T_1, T_1+1, \ldots, T. \tag{3.5.14}$$

Finally, (3.5.13) and (3.5.14) imply (iv).

It should be easy to construct a sequence for which (3.5.5) is satisfied but (i) is not.

Next we shall prove the asymptotic normality of the least square estimator of the variance σ^2.

THEOREM 3.5.6. Assume that $\{u_t\}$ are i.i.d. with a finite fourth moment $Eu_t^4\equiv m_4$ in Model 1. Then $\sqrt{T}(\hat{\sigma}^2-\sigma^2)\to N(0, m_4-\sigma^4)$.

Proof. We can write

$$\sqrt{T}(\hat{\sigma}^2-\sigma^2)=\frac{\mathbf{u}'\mathbf{u}-T\sigma^2}{\sqrt{T}}-\frac{1}{\sqrt{T}}\mathbf{u}'\mathbf{P}\mathbf{u}. \tag{3.5.15}$$

The second term of the right-hand side of (3.5.15) converges to 0 in probability by the same reasoning as in the proof of Theorem 3.5.2, and the first term can be dealt with by application of the Lindeberg-Lévy CLT (Theorem 3.3.4). Therefore the theorem follows by Theorem 3.2.7(i).

Let us look at a few more examples of the application of convergence theorems.

EXAMPLE 3.5.1. Consider Model 1 where $K=1$:

$$\mathbf{y}=\beta\mathbf{x}+\mathbf{u}, \tag{3.5.16}$$

where we assume $\lim T^{-1}\mathbf{x}'\mathbf{x}=c\neq 0$ and $\{u_t\}$ are i.i.d. Obtain the probability limit of $\hat{\beta}_R=\mathbf{y}'\mathbf{y}/\mathbf{x}'\mathbf{y}$. (Note that this estimator is obtained by minimizing the sum of squares in the direction of the x-axis.)

We can write

$$\hat{\beta}_R = \frac{\beta^2 + 2\beta \dfrac{\mathbf{x}'\mathbf{u}}{\mathbf{x}'\mathbf{x}} + \dfrac{\mathbf{u}'\mathbf{u}}{\mathbf{x}'\mathbf{x}}}{\beta + \dfrac{\mathbf{x}'\mathbf{u}}{\mathbf{x}'\mathbf{x}}}. \tag{3.5.17}$$

We have $E(\mathbf{x}'\mathbf{u}/\mathbf{x}'\mathbf{x})^2 = \sigma^2(\mathbf{x}'\mathbf{x})^{-1} \rightarrow 0$ as $T \rightarrow \infty$. Therefore, by Theorem 3.2.1,

$$\text{plim} \frac{\mathbf{x}'\mathbf{u}}{\mathbf{x}'\mathbf{x}} = 0. \tag{3.5.18}$$

Also we have

$$\text{plim} \frac{\mathbf{u}'\mathbf{u}}{\mathbf{x}'\mathbf{x}} = \text{plim} \left[\frac{\mathbf{u}'\mathbf{u}}{T} \bigg/ \frac{\mathbf{x}'\mathbf{x}}{T} \right] = \frac{\sigma^2}{c} \tag{3.5.19}$$

because of Theorem 3.2.6 and Theorem 3.3.2 (Kolmogorov LLN 2). Therefore, from (3.5.17), (3.5.18), and (3.5.19) and by using Theorem 3.2.6 again, we obtain

$$\text{plim}\, \hat{\beta}_R = \beta + \frac{\sigma^2}{\beta c}. \tag{3.5.20}$$

Note that c may be allowed to be ∞, in which case $\hat{\beta}_R$ becomes a consistent estimator of β.

EXAMPLE 3.5.2. Consider the same model as in Example 3.5.1 except that we now assume $\lim T^{-2}\mathbf{x}'\mathbf{x} = \infty$. Also assume $\lim_{T\rightarrow\infty} (\mathbf{x}'\mathbf{x})^{-1} \max_{1 \leq t \leq T} x_t^2 = 0$ so that $\hat{\beta}$ is asymptotically normal. (Give an example of a sequence satisfying these two conditions.) Show that $\hat{\beta} = \mathbf{x}'\mathbf{y}/\mathbf{x}'\mathbf{x}$ and $\hat{\beta}_R = \mathbf{y}'\mathbf{y}/\mathbf{x}'\mathbf{y}$ have the same asymptotic distribution.

Clearly, $\text{plim}\, \hat{\beta} = \text{plim}\, \hat{\beta}_R = \beta$. Therefore, by Theorem 3.2.2, both estimators have the same degenerate limit distribution. But the question concerns the asymptotic distribution; therefore we must obtain the limit distribution of each estimator after a suitable normalization. We can write

$$(\mathbf{x}'\mathbf{x})^{1/2}(\hat{\beta}_R - \beta) = \frac{\beta(\mathbf{x}'\mathbf{x})^{1/2}(\hat{\beta} - \beta) + \dfrac{\mathbf{u}'\mathbf{u}}{(\mathbf{x}'\mathbf{x})^{1/2}}}{\beta + \dfrac{\mathbf{x}'\mathbf{u}}{\mathbf{x}'\mathbf{x}}}. \tag{3.5.21}$$

But by our assumptions $\text{plim}\, \mathbf{u}'\mathbf{u}(\mathbf{x}'\mathbf{x})^{-1/2} = 0$ and $\text{plim}\, (\mathbf{x}'\mathbf{u}/\mathbf{x}'\mathbf{x}) = 0$. Therefore $(\mathbf{x}'\mathbf{x})^{1/2}(\hat{\beta}_R - \beta)$ and $(\mathbf{x}'\mathbf{x})^{1/2}(\hat{\beta} - \beta)$ have the same limit distribution by repeated applications of Theorem 3.2.7.

EXAMPLE 3.5.3. Consider Model 1 with $K = 2$:

$$\mathbf{y} = \beta_1 \mathbf{x}_1 + \beta_2 \mathbf{x}_2 + \mathbf{u}, \tag{3.5.22}$$

where we assume that $\{u_t\}$ are i.i.d. Assume also $\lim T^{-1}\mathbf{X}'\mathbf{X} = \mathbf{A}$, where $\mathbf{A}$ is a 2×2 nonsingular matrix. Obtain the asymptotic distribution of $\hat{\beta}_1/\hat{\beta}_2$, where $\hat{\beta}_1$ and $\hat{\beta}_2$ are the least squares estimators of β_1 and β_2, assuming $\beta_2 \neq 0$.

We can write

$$\sqrt{T}\left[\frac{\hat{\beta}_1}{\hat{\beta}_2} - \frac{\beta_1}{\beta_2}\right] = \sqrt{T}\left[\frac{\beta_2(\hat{\beta}_1 - \beta_1) - \beta_1(\hat{\beta}_2 - \beta_2)}{\hat{\beta}_2 \beta_2}\right]. \tag{3.5.23}$$

Because $\text{plim}\, \hat{\beta}_2 = \beta_2$, the right-hand side of (3.5.23) has the same limit distribution as

$$\beta_2^{-1}\sqrt{T}\,(\hat{\beta}_1 - \beta_1) - \beta_1\beta_2^{-2}\sqrt{T}\,(\hat{\beta}_2 - \beta_2).$$

But, because our assumptions imply (3.5.8) by Theorem 3.5.5, $[\sqrt{T}(\hat{\beta}_1 - \beta_1), \sqrt{T}(\hat{\beta}_2 - \beta_2)]$ converges to a bivariate normal variable by Theorem 3.5.4. Therefore, by Theorem 3.2.5, we have

$$\sqrt{T}\left[\frac{\hat{\beta}_1}{\hat{\beta}_2} - \frac{\beta_1}{\beta_2}\right] \rightarrow N(0, \sigma^2 \gamma' \mathbf{A}^{-1} \gamma),$$

where $\gamma' = (\beta_2^{-1}, -\beta_1\beta_2^{-2})$.

Exercises

1. (Section 3.1.2)
   Prove that the distribution function is continuous from the left.

2. (Section 3.2)
   Prove Theorem 3.2.3. HINT: Definition 3.1.2 (iii) implies that if $\Omega_n \subset \Omega_m$ for $n < m$ and $\lim_{n\to\infty} \Omega_n = A$, then $\lim_{n\to\infty} P(\Omega_n) = P(A)$.

3. (Section 3.2)
   Prove Theorem 3.2.4.

4. (Section 3.3)
   Let $\{X_t\}$ be as defined in Theorem 3.3.1. Prove $\lim_{n\to\infty} E(\bar{X}_n - E\bar{X}_n)^2 = 0$.

5. (Section 3.3)
Let $\{a_t\}$, $t = 1, 2, \ldots,$ be a nonnegative sequence such that $(\Sigma_{t=1}^T a_t)/T < M$ for some M and every T. Prove $\lim_{T\to\infty} \Sigma_{t=1}^T (a_t/t^2) < \infty$.

6. (Section 3.3)
Prove that the conditions of Theorem 3.3.6 (Lindeberg-Feller CLT) follow from the conditions of Theorem 3.3.4 (Lindeberg-Lévy CLT) or of Theorem 3.3.5 (Liapounov CLT).

7. (Section 3.3)

Let $\{X_t\}$ be i.i.d. with $EX_t = \mu$. Then $\overline{X}_n \xrightarrow{\text{P}} \mu$. This is a corollary of Theorem 3.3.2 (Kolmogorov LLN 2) and is called *Khinchine's WLLN* (weak law of large numbers). Prove this theorem using characteristic functions.

8. (Section 3.5)
Show that $\lambda_s(\mathbf{X}'\mathbf{X}) \to \infty$ implies $\mathbf{x}_i'\mathbf{x}_i \to \infty$ for every i, where $\mathbf{x}_i$ is the ith column vector of $\mathbf{X}$. Show also that the converse does not hold.

9. (Section 3.5)
Assume $K = 1$ in Model 1 and write $\mathbf{X}$ as $\mathbf{x}$. Assume that $\{u_t\}$ are independent. If there exist L and M such that $0 < L < \mathbf{x}'\mathbf{x}/T < M$ for all T, show $\hat{\beta} \xrightarrow{\text{a.s.}} \beta$.

10. (Section 3.5)
Suppose $\mathbf{y} = \mathbf{y}^* + \mathbf{u}$ and $\mathbf{x} = \mathbf{x}^* + \mathbf{v}$, where each variable is a vector of T components. Assume $\mathbf{y}^*$ and $\mathbf{x}^*$ are nonstochastic and (u_t, v_t) is a bivariate i.i.d. random variable with mean $\mathbf{0}$ and constant variances σ_u^2, σ_v^2, respectively, and covariance σ_{uv}. Assume $\mathbf{y}^* = \beta\mathbf{x}^*$, but $\mathbf{y}^*$ and $\mathbf{x}^*$ are not observable so that we must estimate β on the basis of $\mathbf{y}$ and $\mathbf{x}$. Obtain the probability limit of $\hat{\beta} = \mathbf{x}'\mathbf{y}/\mathbf{x}'\mathbf{x}$ on the assumption that $\lim_{T\to\infty} T^{-1}\mathbf{x}^{*\prime}\mathbf{x}^* = M$.

11. (Section 3.5)
Consider the regression equation $\mathbf{y} = \mathbf{X}_1\boldsymbol{\beta}_1 + \mathbf{X}_2\boldsymbol{\beta}_2 + \mathbf{u}$. Assume all the assumptions of Model 1 except that $\mathbf{X} \equiv (\mathbf{X}_1, \mathbf{X}_2)$ may not be full rank. Let $\mathbf{Z}$ be the matrix consisting of a maximal linearly independent subset of the columns of $\mathbf{X}_2$ and assume that the smallest characteristic root of the matrix $(\mathbf{X}_1, \mathbf{Z})'(\mathbf{X}_1, \mathbf{Z})$ goes to infinity as T goes to infinity. Derive a consistent estimator of $\boldsymbol{\beta}_1$. Prove that it is consistent.

12. (Section 3.5)
Change the assumptions of Theorem 3.5.3 as follows: $\{u_t\}$ are independent with $Eu_t=0$, $Vu_t=\sigma^2$, and $E|u_t|^3=m_3$. Prove $\sigma^{-1}(\mathbf{x}'\mathbf{x})^{1/2}(\hat{\beta}-\beta)\rightarrow N(0, 1)$ using Theorem 3.3.5 (Liapounov CLT).

13. (Section 3.5)
Construct a sequence $\{x_t\}$ such that $\Sigma_{t=1}^{T} x_t^2 \rightarrow \infty$ but the condition (3.5.5) is not satisfied.

14. (Section 3.5)
Construct a sequence $\{x_t\}$ such that the condition (3.5.5) holds but the condition (i) of Theorem 3.5.5. does not.

15. (Section 3.5)
Let $\mathbf{l}$ be the vector of ones. Assuming $\lim T^{-1}\mathbf{l}'\mathbf{x}^* = N \neq 0$ in the model of Exercise 10, prove the consistency of $\tilde{\beta}=\mathbf{l}'\mathbf{y}/\mathbf{l}'\mathbf{x}$ and obtain its asymptotic distribution.

16. (Section 3.5)
Assume that $\{u_t\}$ are i.i.d. in Model 1. Assume $K=1$ and write $\mathbf{X}$ as $\mathbf{x}$. Obtain the asymptotic distribution of $\tilde{\beta}=\mathbf{l}'\mathbf{y}/\mathbf{l}'\mathbf{x}$ assuming $\lim_{T\rightarrow\infty} T^{-1}(\mathbf{l}'\mathbf{x})^2=\infty$ where $\mathbf{l}$ is the vector of ones.

17. (Section 3.5)
Consider the classical regression model $\mathbf{y}=\alpha\mathbf{x}+\beta\mathbf{z}+\mathbf{u}$, where α and β are scalar unknown parameters, $\mathbf{x}$ and $\mathbf{z}$ are T-component vectors of known constants, and $\mathbf{u}$ is a T-component vector of unobservable i.i.d. random variables with zero mean and unit variance. Suppose we are given an estimator $\tilde{\beta}$ that is independent of $\mathbf{u}$ and the limit distribution of $T^{1/2}(\tilde{\beta}-\beta)$ is $N(0, 1)$. Define the estimator $\tilde{\alpha}$ by

$$\tilde{\alpha}=\frac{\mathbf{x}'(\mathbf{y}-\tilde{\beta}\mathbf{z})}{\mathbf{x}'\mathbf{x}}.$$

Assuming $\lim T^{-1}\mathbf{x}'\mathbf{x}=c$ and $\lim T^{-1}\mathbf{x}'\mathbf{z}=d$, obtain the asymptotic distribution of $\tilde{\alpha}$. Assume $c\neq 0$ and $d \neq 0$.

18. (Section 3.5)
Consider the regression model $\mathbf{y}=\beta(\mathbf{x}+\alpha\mathbf{l})+\mathbf{u}$, where $\mathbf{y}$, $\mathbf{x}$, $\mathbf{l}$, and $\mathbf{u}$ are T-vectors and α and β are scalar unknown parameters. Assume that $\mathbf{l}$ is a T-vector of ones, $\lim_{T\rightarrow\infty}\mathbf{x}'\mathbf{l}=0$, and $\lim_{T\rightarrow\infty}T^{-1}\mathbf{x}'\mathbf{x}=c$, where c is a nonzero constant. Also assume that the elements of $\mathbf{u}$ are i.i.d. with zero

mean and constant variance σ^2. Supposing we have an estimate of α denoted by $\hat{\alpha}$ such that it is distributed independently of $\mathbf{u}$ and $\sqrt{T}(\hat{\alpha}-\alpha) \rightarrow N(0, \lambda^2)$, obtain the asymptotic distribution of $\hat{\beta}$ defined by

$$\hat{\beta} = \frac{(\mathbf{x} + \hat{\alpha}\mathbf{l})'\mathbf{y}}{(\mathbf{x} + \hat{\alpha}\mathbf{l})'(\mathbf{x} + \hat{\alpha}\mathbf{l})}.$$

4 Asymptotic Properties of Extremum Estimators

By *extremum estimators* we mean estimators obtained by either maximizing or minimizing a certain function defined over the parameter space. First, we shall establish conditions for the consistency and the asymptotic normality of extremum estimators (Section 4.1), and second, we shall apply the results to important special cases, namely, the maximum likelihood estimator (Section 4.2) and the nonlinear least squares estimator (Section 4.3).

What we call extremum estimators Huber called *M estimators,* meaning maximum-likelihood-like estimators. He developed the asymptotic properties in a series of articles (summarized in Huber, 1981). The emphasis here, however, will be different from his. The treatment in this chapter is more general in the sense that we require neither independent nor identically distributed random variables. Also, the intention here is not to strive for the least stringent set of assumptions but to help the reader understand the fundamental facts by providing an easily comprehensible set of sufficient conditions.

In Sections 4.4 and 4.5 we shall discuss iterative methods for maximization or minimization, the asymptotic properties of the likelihood ratio and asymptotically equivalent tests, and related topics. In Section 4.6 we shall discuss the least absolute deviations estimator, for which the general results of Section 4.1 are only partially applicable.

4.1 General Results

4.1.1 Consistency

Because there is no essential difference between maximization and minimization, we shall consider an estimator that maximizes a certain function of the parameters. Let us denote the function by $Q_T(\mathbf{y}, \theta)$, where $\mathbf{y} = (y_1, y_2, \ldots, y_T)'$ is a T-vector of random variables and θ is a K-vector of parameters. [We shall sometimes write it more compactly as $Q_T(\theta)$.] The vector θ should be understood to be the set of parameters that characterize the distribution of $\mathbf{y}$. Let us denote the domain of $\boldsymbol{\theta}$, or the *parameter space,* by Θ and the "true value" of $\boldsymbol{\theta}$ by $\boldsymbol{\theta}_0$. The parameter space is the set of all the possible values that the true value $\boldsymbol{\theta}_0$ can take. When we take various operations on a function of $\mathbf{y}$, such as expectation or probability limit, we shall use the value $\boldsymbol{\theta}_0$.

As a preliminary to the consistency theorems, we shall define three modes of uniform convergence of a sequence of random variables.

DEFINITION 4.1.1. Let $g_T(\boldsymbol{\theta})$ be a nonnegative sequence of random variables depending on a parameter vector $\boldsymbol{\theta}$. Consider the three modes of uniform convergence of $g_T(\boldsymbol{\theta})$ to 0:

(i) $P[\lim_{T\to\infty} \sup_{\boldsymbol{\theta}\in\Theta} g_T(\boldsymbol{\theta}) = 0] = 1$,

(ii) $\lim_{T\to\infty} P[\sup_{\boldsymbol{\theta}\in\Theta} g_T(\boldsymbol{\theta}) < \epsilon] = 1$ for any $\epsilon > 0$,

(iii) $\lim_{T\to\infty} \inf_{\boldsymbol{\theta}\in\Theta} P[g_T(\boldsymbol{\theta}) < \epsilon] = 1$ for any $\epsilon > 0$.

If (i) holds, we say $g_T(\boldsymbol{\theta})$ converges to 0 *almost surely uniformly* in $\boldsymbol{\theta} \in \Theta$. If (ii) holds, we say $g_T(\boldsymbol{\theta})$ converges to 0 *in probability uniformly* in $\boldsymbol{\theta} \in \Theta$. If (iii) holds, we say $g_T(\boldsymbol{\theta})$ converges to 0 *in probability semiuniformly* in $\boldsymbol{\theta} \in \Theta$.

It is easy to show that (i) implies (ii) and (ii) implies (iii). Consider an example of a sequence for which (iii) holds but (ii) does not. Let the parameter space Θ be [0, 1] and the sample space Ω also be [0, 1] with the probability measure equal to Lebesgue measure. For $\theta \in \Theta$ and $\omega \in \Omega$, define $g_T(\omega, \theta)$ by

$$
\begin{aligned}
g_T(\omega, \theta) &= 1 \quad \text{if} \quad \theta = \frac{i}{T} \quad \text{and} \quad \frac{i}{T} \leqq \omega \leqq \frac{i+1}{T}, \\
&\qquad\qquad i = 0, 1, \ldots, T-1, \\
&= 0 \quad \text{otherwise.}
\end{aligned}
$$

Then, for $0 < \epsilon < 1$,

$$
\begin{aligned}
&\inf_{\theta\in\Theta} P[g_T(\omega, \theta) < \epsilon] = (T-1)/T \quad \text{and} \\
&P[\sup_{\theta\in\Theta} g_T(\omega, \theta) < \epsilon] = 0 \quad \text{for all } T.
\end{aligned}
$$

Now we shall prove the consistency of extremum estimators. Because we need to distinguish between the global maximum and a local maximum, we shall present two theorems to handle the two cases.

THEOREM 4.1.1. Make the assumptions:

(A) The parameter space Θ is a compact subset of the Euclidean K-space (R^K). (Note that $\boldsymbol{\theta}_0$ is in Θ.)

(B) $Q_T(\mathbf{y}, \theta)$ is continuous in $\theta \in \Theta$ for all $\mathbf{y}$ and is a measurable function of $\mathbf{y}$ for all $\theta \in \Theta$.

(C) $T^{-1}Q_T(\theta)$ converges to a nonstochastic function $Q(\theta)$ in probability uniformly in $\theta \in \Theta$ as T goes to ∞, and $Q(\theta)$ attains a unique global maximum at θ_0. (The continuity of $Q(\theta)$ follows from our assumptions.)

Define $\hat{\theta}_T$ as a value that satisfies

$$Q_T(\hat{\theta}_T) = \max_{\theta \in \Theta} Q_T(\theta). \tag{4.1.1}$$

[It is understood that if $\hat{\theta}_T$ is not unique, we appropriately choose one such value in such a way that $\hat{\theta}_T(\mathbf{y})$ is a measurable function of $\mathbf{y}$. This is possible by a theorem of Jennrich (1969, p. 637).] Then $\hat{\theta}_T$ converges to θ_0 in probability.[1]

Proof. Let N be an open neighborhood in R^K containing θ_0. Then $\overline{N} \cap \Theta$, where $\overline{N}$ is the complement of N in R^K, is compact. Therefore $\max_{\theta \in \overline{N} \cap \Theta} Q(\theta)$ exists. Denote

$$\epsilon = Q(\theta_0) - \max_{\theta \in \overline{N} \cap \Theta} Q(\theta). \tag{4.1.2}$$

Let A_T be the event "$|T^{-1}Q_T(\theta) - Q(\theta)| < \epsilon/2$ for all θ." Then

$$A_T \Rightarrow Q(\hat{\theta}_T) > T^{-1}Q_T(\hat{\theta}_T) - \epsilon/2 \tag{4.1.3}$$

and

$$A_T \Rightarrow T^{-1}Q_T(\theta_0) > Q(\theta_0) - \epsilon/2. \tag{4.1.4}$$

But, because $Q_T(\hat{\theta}_T) \geqq Q_T(\theta_0)$ by the definition of $\hat{\theta}_T$, we have from Exp. (4.1.3)

$$A_T \Rightarrow Q(\hat{\theta}_T) > T^{-1}Q_T(\theta_0) - \epsilon/2. \tag{4.1.5}$$

Therefore, adding both sides of the inequalities in (4.1.4) and (4.1.5), we obtain

$$A_T \Rightarrow Q(\hat{\theta}_T) > Q(\theta_0) - \epsilon. \tag{4.1.6}$$

Therefore, from (4.1.2) and (4.1.6) we can conclude $A_T \Rightarrow \hat{\theta}_T \in N$, which implies $P(A_T) \leqq P(\hat{\theta}_T \in N)$. But, since $\lim_{T\to\infty} P(A_T) = 1$ by assumption C, $\hat{\theta}_T$ converges to θ_0 in probability.

Note that $\hat{\theta}_T$ is defined as the value of θ that maximizes $Q_T(\theta)$ within the parameter space Θ. This is a weakness of the theorem in so far as the extremum estimators commonly used in practice are obtained by unconstrained maximization or minimization. This practice prevails because of its relative computational ease, even though constrained maximization or minimization would be more desirable if a researcher believed that the true value lay in a proper subset of R^K. The consistency of the unconstrained maximum $\tilde{\theta}_T$ defined by

$$Q_T(\tilde{\theta}_T) = \sup_{\theta \in R^K} Q_T(\theta) \tag{4.1.7}$$

will follow from the additional assumption

(D) $\lim_{T\to\infty} P[Q_T(\theta_0) > \sup_{\theta \notin \Theta} Q_T(\theta)] = 1$

because of the inequality

$$P[Q_T(\theta_0) > \sup_{\theta \notin \Theta} Q_T(\theta)] \leqq P(\tilde{\theta}_T \in \Theta). \tag{4.1.8}$$

As we shall see in later applications, Q_T is frequently the sum of independent random variables or, at least, of random variables with a limited degree of dependence. Therefore we can usually expect $T^{-1}Q_T(\theta)$ to converge to a constant in probability by using some form of a law of large numbers. However, the theorem can be made more general by replacing $T^{-1}Q_T(\theta)$ with $h(T)^{-1}Q_T(\theta)$, where $h(T)$ is an increasing function of T.

The three major assumptions of Theorem 4.1.1 are (1) the compactness of Θ, (2) the continuity of $Q_T(\theta)$, and (3) the uniform convergence of $T^{-1}Q_T(\theta)$ to $Q(\theta)$. To illustrate the importance of these assumptions, we shall give examples that show what things go wrong when one or more of the three assumptions are removed. In all the examples, Q_T is assumed to be nonstochastic for simplicity.

EXAMPLE 4.1.1. $\Theta = [-1, 1]$, $\theta_0 = -1/2$, $T^{-1}Q_T$ not continuous and not uniformly convergent.

$$\begin{aligned} T^{-1}Q_T(\theta) &= 1 + \theta, \qquad -1 \leqq \theta \leqq \theta_0 \\ &= -\theta, \qquad \theta_0 < \theta \leqq 0 \\ &= \frac{\theta^T}{1-\theta^T}, \qquad 0 < \theta < 1 \\ &= 0, \qquad \theta = 1. \end{aligned}$$

Here the extremum estimator does not exist, although $\lim T^{-1}Q_T$ attains its unique maximum at θ_0.

EXAMPLE 4.1.2. $\Theta = [-1, \infty]$, $\theta_0 = -1/2$, $T^{-1}Q_T$ continuous but not uniformly convergent.

$$
\begin{aligned}
Q(\theta) &= 1 + \theta, \qquad && -1 \leqq \theta \leqq \theta_0 \\
&= -\theta, && \theta_0 < \theta \leqq 0 \\
&= 0, && \text{elsewhere.}
\end{aligned}
$$

$$T^{-1}Q_T(\theta) = Q(\theta) + h_T(\theta),$$

where

$$
\begin{aligned}
h_T(\theta) &= \theta - T, \qquad && T \leqq \theta \leqq T + 1 \\
&= T + 2 - \theta, && T + 1 < \theta \leqq T + 2 \\
&= 0, && \text{elsewhere.}
\end{aligned}
$$

Here we have plim $\hat{\theta}_T =$ plim $(T + 1) = \infty$, although lim $T^{-1}Q_T = Q$ attains its unique maximum at θ_0.

EXAMPLE 4.1.3. $\Theta = [0, 2]$, $\theta_0 = 1.5$, $T^{-1}Q_T$ continuous but not uniformly convergent.

$$
\begin{aligned}
T^{-1}Q_T(\theta) &= T\theta, \qquad && 0 \leqq \theta \leqq \frac{1}{2T} \\
&= 1 - T\theta, && \frac{1}{2T} < \theta \leqq \frac{1}{T} \\
&= 0, && \frac{1}{T} < \theta \leqq 1 \\
&= \frac{T}{T+1}(\theta - 1), && 1 < \theta \leqq \theta_0 \\
&= \frac{T}{T+1}(2 - \theta), && \theta_0 < \theta \leqq 2.
\end{aligned}
$$

Here we have plim $\hat{\theta}_T =$ plim $(2T)^{-1} = 0$, although lim $T^{-1}Q_T$ attains its unique maximum at θ_0.

EXAMPLE 4.1.4. $\Theta = [-2, 1]$, $\theta_0 = -1$, $T^{-1}Q_T$ not continuous but uniformly convergent.

$$
\begin{aligned}
T^{-1}Q_T(\theta) &= (1-2^{1-T})\theta + 2 - 2^{2-T}, \qquad -2 \leqq \theta \leqq -1 \\
&= -(1-2^{1-T})\theta, \qquad -1 < \theta \leqq 0 \\
&= \frac{2^{T+1}-2}{2^{T+1}-1}\theta, \qquad 0 < \theta \leqq 1 - 2^{-(T+1)} \\
&= \frac{2^{T+1}-2}{2^{T+1}-1}\theta + 2 - 2^{1-T}, \qquad 1 - 2^{-(T+1)} < \theta < 1 \\
&= 0, \qquad \theta = 1.
\end{aligned}
$$

Here we have plim $\hat{\theta}_T = \text{plim}\, [1 - 2^{-(T+1)}] = 1$, although lim $T^{-1}Q_T$ attains its unique maximum at θ_0. (If we change this example so that $\Theta = [-2, 1)$, $T^{-1}Q_T$ becomes continuous and only the compactness assumption is violated.)

The estimator $\hat{\theta}_T$ of Theorem 4.1.1 maximizes the function $Q_T(\boldsymbol{\theta})$ globally. However, in practice it is often difficult to locate a global maximum of $Q_T(\boldsymbol{\theta})$, for it means that we must look through the whole parameter space except in the fortunate situation where we can prove that $Q_T(\boldsymbol{\theta})$ is globally concave.

Another weakness of the theorem is that it is often difficult to prove that $Q(\boldsymbol{\theta})$ attains its unique global maximum at $\boldsymbol{\theta}_0$. Therefore we would also like to have a theorem regarding the consistency of a local maximum.

Still another reason for having such a theorem is that we can generally prove asymptotic normality only for the local maximum, as we shall show in Section 4.1.2. Theorem 4.1.2 is such a theorem.

THEOREM 4.1.2. Make the assumptions:

(A) Let Θ be an open subset of the Euclidean K-space. (Thus the true value $\boldsymbol{\theta}_0$ is an interior point of Θ.)

(B) $Q_T(\mathbf{y}, \boldsymbol{\theta})$ is a measurable function of $\mathbf{y}$ for all $\boldsymbol{\theta} \in \Theta$, and $\partial Q_T/\partial\boldsymbol{\theta}$ exists and is continuous in an open neighborhood $N_1(\boldsymbol{\theta}_0)$ of $\boldsymbol{\theta}_0$. (Note that this implies Q_T is continuous for $\boldsymbol{\theta} \in N_1$.)

(C) There exists an open neighborhood $N_2(\boldsymbol{\theta}_0)$ of $\boldsymbol{\theta}_0$ such that $T^{-1}Q_T(\boldsymbol{\theta})$ converges to a nonstochastic function $Q(\boldsymbol{\theta})$ in probability uniformly in $\boldsymbol{\theta}$ in $N_2(\boldsymbol{\theta}_0)$, and $Q(\boldsymbol{\theta})$ attains a strict local maximum at $\boldsymbol{\theta}_0$.

Let Θ_T be the set of roots of the equation

$$\frac{\partial Q_T}{\partial \boldsymbol{\theta}} = \mathbf{0} \tag{4.1.9}$$

corresponding to the local maxima. If that set is empty, set Θ_T equal to $\{\mathbf{0}\}$.

Then, for any $\epsilon > 0$,

$$\lim_{T\to\infty} P[\inf_{\theta\in\Theta_T} (\theta-\theta_0)'(\theta-\theta_0) > \epsilon] = 0.$$

Proof. Choose a compact set $S \subset N_1 \cap N_2$. Then the value of θ, say θ_T^*, that globally maximizes $Q_T(\theta)$ in S is consistent by Theorem 4.1.1. But because the probability that $T^{-1}Q_T(\theta)$ attains a local maximum at θ_T^* approaches 1 as T goes to ∞, $\lim_{T\to\infty} P(\theta_T^* \in \Theta_T) = 1$.

We sometimes state the conclusion of Theorem 4.1.2 simply as "there is a consistent root of the Eq. (4.1.9)."

The usefulness of Theorem 4.1.2 is limited by the fact that it merely states that one of the local maxima is consistent and does not give any guide as to how to choose a consistent maximum. There are two ways we can gain some degree of confidence that a local maximum is a consistent root: (1) if the solution gives a reasonable value from an economic-theoretic viewpoint and (2) if the iteration by which the local maximum was obtained started from a consistent estimator. We shall discuss the second point more fully in Section 4.4.2.

4.1.2 Asymptotic Normality

In this subsection we shall show that under certain conditions a consistent root of Eq. (4.1.9) is asymptotically normal. The precise meaning of this statement will be made clear in Theorem 4.1.3.

THEOREM 4.1.3. Make the following assumptions in addition to the assumptions of Theorem 4.1.2:

(A) $\partial^2 Q_T/\partial\theta\partial\theta'$ exists and is continuous in an open, convex neighborhood of θ_0.

(B) $T^{-1}(\partial^2 Q_T/\partial\theta\partial\theta')_{\theta_T^*}$ converges to a finite nonsingular matrix $\mathbf{A}(\theta_0) = \lim ET^{-1}(\partial^2 Q_T/\partial\theta\partial\theta')_{\theta_0}$ in probability for any sequence θ_T^* such that plim $\theta_T^* = \theta_0$.

(C) $T^{-1/2}(\partial Q_T/\partial\theta)_{\theta_0} \to N[\mathbf{0}, \mathbf{B}(\theta_0)]$, where $\mathbf{B}(\theta_0) = \lim ET^{-1}(\partial Q_T/\partial\theta)_{\theta_0} \times (\partial Q_T/\partial\theta')_{\theta_0}$.

Let $\{\hat{\theta}_T\}$ be a sequence obtained by choosing one element from Θ_T defined in Theorem 4.1.2 such that plim $\hat{\theta}_T = \theta_0$. (We call $\hat{\theta}_T$ a consistent root.) Then

$$\sqrt{T}(\hat{\theta}_T - \theta_0) \to N[\mathbf{0}, \mathbf{A}(\theta_0)^{-1}\mathbf{B}(\theta_0)\mathbf{A}(\theta_0)^{-1}].$$

Proof. By a Taylor expansion we have

$$\left.\frac{\partial Q_T}{\partial \theta}\right|_{\hat{\theta}_T} = \left.\frac{\partial Q_T}{\partial \theta}\right|_{\theta_0} + \left.\frac{\partial^2 Q_T}{\partial \theta \partial \theta'}\right|_{\theta^*} (\hat{\theta}_T - \theta_0), \tag{4.1.10}$$

where θ^* lies between $\hat{\theta}_T$ and θ_0.[2] Noting that the left-hand side of (4.1.10) is $\mathbf{0}$ by the definition of $\hat{\theta}_T$, we obtain

$$\sqrt{T}(\hat{\theta}_T - \theta_0) = -\left[\frac{1}{T}\left.\frac{\partial^2 Q_T}{\partial \theta \partial \theta'}\right|_{\theta^*}\right]^+ \frac{1}{\sqrt{T}}\left.\frac{\partial Q_T}{\partial \theta}\right|_{\theta_0}, \tag{4.1.11}$$

where + denotes the Moore-Penrose generalized inverse (see note 6 of Chapter 2). Because plim $\theta^* = \theta_0$, assumption B implies

$$\operatorname{plim} \frac{1}{T}\left.\frac{\partial^2 Q_T}{\partial \theta \partial \theta'}\right|_{\theta^*} = \mathbf{A}(\theta_0). \tag{4.1.12}$$

Finally, the conclusion of the theorem follows from assumption C and Eqs. (4.1.11) and (4.1.12) by repeated applications of Theorem 3.2.7.

As we noted earlier, Q_T is frequently the sum of independent random variables (or, at least, of random variables with a limited degree of dependence). Therefore it is not unreasonable to assume the conclusions of a law of large numbers and a central limit theorem in assumptions B and C, respectively. However, as we also noted earlier, the following more general normalization may be necessary in certain cases: In assumption B, change $T^{-1}\partial^2 Q_T/\partial\theta\partial\theta'$ to $\mathbf{H}(T)\partial^2 Q_T/\partial\theta\partial\theta'\mathbf{H}(T)$, where $\mathbf{H}(T)$ is a diagonal matrix such that $\lim_{T\to\infty} \mathbf{H}(T) = \mathbf{0}$; in assumption C, change $T^{-1/2}\partial Q_T/\partial\theta$ to $\mathbf{H}(T)\partial Q_T/\partial\theta$; and in the conclusion of the theorem, state the limit distribution in terms of $\mathbf{H}(T)^{-1}(\hat{\theta}_T - \theta_0)$.

Because assumption B is often not easily verifiable, we shall give two alternative assumptions, each of which implies assumption B. Let $g_T(\theta) \equiv g(\mathbf{y}, \theta)$ be a function of a T-vector of random variables $\mathbf{y} = (y_1, y_2, \ldots, y_T)'$ and a continuous function of a K-vector of parameters θ in Θ, an open subset of the Euclidean K-space, almost surely. We assume that $g(\mathbf{y}, \theta)$ is a random variable (that is, g is a measurable function of $\mathbf{y}$). We seek conditions that ensure plim $[g_T(\hat{\theta}_T) - g_T(\theta_0)] = 0$ whenever plim $\hat{\theta}_T = \theta_0$. Note that Theorem 3.2.6 does not apply here because in that theorem $g(\cdot)$ is a fixed function not varying with T.

THEOREM 4.1.4. Assume that $\partial g_T/\partial\theta$ exists for $\theta \in \Theta$, an open convex set, and that for any $\epsilon > 0$ there exists M_ϵ such that

$$P(\sup_{\theta\in\Theta}|\partial g_T/\partial\theta^i| < M_\epsilon) \geqq 1 - \epsilon$$

for all T and for all i, where θ^i is the ith element of the vector $\boldsymbol{\theta}$. Then plim $g_T(\hat{\boldsymbol{\theta}}_T) =$ plim $g_T(\boldsymbol{\theta}_0)$ if $\boldsymbol{\theta}_0 \equiv$ plim $\hat{\boldsymbol{\theta}}_T$ is in Θ.

Proof. The proof of Theorem 4.1.4 follows from the Taylor expansion

$$g_T(\hat{\boldsymbol{\theta}}_T) = g_T(\boldsymbol{\theta}_0) + \left.\frac{\partial g_T}{\partial \boldsymbol{\theta}'}\right|_{\boldsymbol{\theta}^*} (\hat{\boldsymbol{\theta}}_T - \boldsymbol{\theta}_0),$$

where $\boldsymbol{\theta}^*$ lies between $\hat{\boldsymbol{\theta}}_T$ and $\boldsymbol{\theta}_0$.

THEOREM 4.1.5. Suppose $g_T(\boldsymbol{\theta})$ converges in probability to a nonstochastic function $g(\boldsymbol{\theta})$ uniformly in $\boldsymbol{\theta}$ in an open neighborhood $N(\boldsymbol{\theta}_0)$ of $\boldsymbol{\theta}_0$. Then plim $g_T(\hat{\boldsymbol{\theta}}_T) = g(\boldsymbol{\theta}_0)$ if plim $\hat{\boldsymbol{\theta}}_T = \boldsymbol{\theta}_0$ and $g(\boldsymbol{\theta})$ is continuous at $\boldsymbol{\theta}_0$.

Proof. Because the convergence of $g_T(\boldsymbol{\theta})$ is uniform in $\boldsymbol{\theta}$ and because $\hat{\boldsymbol{\theta}}_T \in N(\boldsymbol{\theta}_0)$ for sufficiently large T with a probability as close to one as desired, we can show that for any $\epsilon > 0$ and $\delta > 0$, there exists T_1 such that for $T > T_1$

$$P\left[|g_T(\hat{\boldsymbol{\theta}}_T) - g(\hat{\boldsymbol{\theta}}_T)| \geqq \frac{\epsilon}{2}\right] < \frac{\delta}{2}. \tag{4.1.13}$$

Because g is continuous at $\boldsymbol{\theta}_0$ by our assumption, $g(\hat{\boldsymbol{\theta}}_T)$ converges to $g(\boldsymbol{\theta}_0)$ in probability by Theorem 3.2.6. Therefore, for any $\epsilon > 0$ and $\delta > 0$, there exists T_2 such that for $T > T_2$

$$P\left[|g(\hat{\boldsymbol{\theta}}_T) - g(\boldsymbol{\theta}_0)| \geqq \frac{\epsilon}{2}\right] < \frac{\delta}{2}. \tag{4.1.14}$$

Therefore, from the inequalities (4.1.13) and (4.1.14) we have for $T > \max[T_1, T_2]$

$$P[|g_T(\hat{\boldsymbol{\theta}}_T) - g(\boldsymbol{\theta}_0)| \leqq \epsilon] \geqq 1 - \delta. \tag{4.1.15}$$

The inequality (4.1.13) requires that uniform convergence be defined by either (i) or (ii) of Definition 4.1.1. Definition 4.1.1(iii) is not sufficient, as shown in the following example attributed to A. Ronald Gallant. Let $\phi_T(\theta)$ be a continuous function with support on $[-T^{-1}, T^{-1}]$ and $\phi_T(0) = 1$. Define $g_T(\omega, \theta) = \phi_T(\omega - T\theta)$ if $0 \leqq \omega, \theta \leqq 1$, and $g_T(\omega, \theta) = 0$ otherwise. Assume that the probability measure over $0 \leqq \omega \leqq 1$ is Lebesgue measure and $\hat{\theta}_T = \omega/T$. Then

$$\inf_{0 \leqq \theta \leqq 1} P[g_T(\omega, \theta) < \epsilon] \geqq 1 - \frac{2}{T} \rightarrow 1,$$

meaning that $g_T(\omega, \theta)$ converges to 0 semiuniformly in θ. But $g_T(\omega, \hat{\theta}_T) = 1$

for all T. Note that in this example

$$P[\sup_{0 \leqq \theta \leqq 1} g_T(\omega, \theta) < \epsilon] = 0.$$

Hence, $g_T(\omega, \theta)$ does not converge uniformly in θ in the sense of definition 4.1.1(ii).

The following theorem is useful because it gives the combined conditions for the consistency and asymptotic normality of a local extremum estimator. In this way we can do away with the condition that $Q(\theta)$ attains a strict local maximum at θ_0.

THEOREM 4.1.6. In addition to assumptions A–C of Theorem 4.1.3, assume

(A) $T^{-1}Q_T(\theta)$ converges to a nonstochastic function $Q(\theta)$ in probability uniformly in θ in an open neighborhood of θ_0.

(B) $\mathbf{A}(\theta_0)$ as defined in assumption B of Theorem 4.1.3 is a negative definite matrix.

(C) plim $T^{-1}\partial^2 Q_T/\partial\theta\partial\theta'$ exists and is continuous in a neighborhood of θ_0.

Then the conclusions of Theorems 4.1.2 and 4.1.3 follow.

Proof. By a Taylor expansion we have in an open neighborhood of θ_0

$$\frac{1}{T} Q_T(\theta) = \frac{1}{T} Q_T(\theta_0) + \frac{1}{T} \left.\frac{\partial Q_T}{\partial \theta'}\right|_{\theta_0} (\theta - \theta_0) + \frac{1}{2}(\theta - \theta_0)' \frac{1}{T} \left.\frac{\partial^2 Q_T}{\partial\theta\partial\theta'}\right|_{\theta^*} (\theta - \theta_0), \tag{4.1.16}$$

where θ^* lies between θ and θ_0. Taking the probability limit of both sides of (4.1.16) and using assumptions B and C of Theorem 4.1.3 and A of this theorem, we have

$$Q(\theta) = Q(\theta_0) + \tfrac{1}{2}(\theta - \theta_0)'\mathbf{A}^*(\theta - \theta_0), \tag{4.1.17}$$

where

$$\mathbf{A}^* = \text{plim} \frac{1}{T} \left.\frac{\partial^2 Q_T}{\partial\theta\partial\theta'}\right|_{\theta^*}.$$

But $\mathbf{A}^*$ is a negative definite matrix because of assumption B of Theorem 4.1.3 and assumptions B and C of this theorem. Therefore

$$Q(\theta) < Q(\theta_0) \quad \text{for} \quad \theta \neq \theta_0. \tag{4.1.18}$$

Thus all the assumptions of Theorem 4.1.2 are satisfied.

4.2 Maximum Likelihood Estimator

4.2.1 Definition

Let $L_T(\theta) = L(\mathbf{y}, \theta)$ be the joint density of a T-vector of random variables $\mathbf{y} = (y_1, y_2, \ldots, y_T)'$ characterized by a K-vector of parameters θ. When we regard it as a function of θ, we call it the likelihood function. The term *maximum likelihood estimator* (MLE) is often used to mean two different concepts: (1) the value of θ that globally maximizes the likelihood function $L(\mathbf{y}, \theta)$ over the parameter space Θ; or (2) any root of the likelihood equation

$$\frac{\partial L_T(\theta)}{\partial \theta} = \mathbf{0} \tag{4.2.1}$$

that corresponds to a local maximum. We use it only in the second sense and use the term *global maximum likelihood estimator* to refer to the first concept. We sometimes use the term *local maximum likelihood estimator* to refer to the second concept.

4.2.2 Consistency

The conditions for the consistency of the global MLE or the local MLE can be immediately obtained from Theorem 4.1.1 or Theorem 4.1.2 by putting $Q_T(\theta) = \log L_T(\theta)$. We consider the logarithm of the likelihood function because $T^{-1} \log L_T(\theta)$ usually converges to a finite constant. Clearly, taking the logarithm does not change the location of either global or local maxima.

So far we have not made any assumption about the distribution of $\mathbf{y}$. If we assume that $\{y_t\}$ are i.i.d. with common density function $f(\cdot, \theta)$, we can write

$$\log L(\mathbf{y}, \theta) = \sum_{t=1}^{T} \log f(y_t, \theta). \tag{4.2.2}$$

In this case we can replace assumption C of either Theorem 4.1.1 or Theorem 4.1.2 by the following two assumptions:

$$E \sup_{\theta \in \Theta} |\log f(y_t, \theta)| < \infty, \tag{4.2.3}$$

and

$$\log f(y_t, \theta) \quad \text{is a continuous function of} \quad \theta \quad \text{for each} \quad y_t. \tag{4.2.4}$$

In Theorem 4.2.1 we shall show that assumptions (4.2.3) and (4.2.4) imply

$$\operatorname{plim} \frac{1}{T} \sum_{t=1}^{T} \log f(y_t, \theta) = E \log f(y_t, \theta) \quad \text{uniformly in} \quad \theta \in \Theta. \tag{4.2.5}$$

Furthermore, we have by Jensen's inequality (see Rao, 1973, p. 58, for the proof)

$$E \log \frac{f(y_t, \theta)}{f(y_t, \theta_0)} < \log E \frac{f(y_t, \theta)}{f(y_t, \theta_0)} = 0 \quad \text{for} \quad \theta \neq \theta_0, \tag{4.2.6}$$

where the expectation is taken using the true value θ_0, and, therefore

$$E \log f(y_t, \theta) < E \log f(y_t, \theta_0) \quad \text{for} \quad \theta \neq \theta_0. \tag{4.2.7}$$

As in (4.2.7), we have $T^{-1}E \log L_T(\theta) < T^{-1}E \log L_T(\theta_0)$ for $\theta \neq \theta_0$ and for all T. However, when we take the limit of both sides of the inequality (4.2.7) as T goes to infinity, we have

$$\lim_{T \to \infty} T^{-1}E \log L_T(\theta) \leqq \lim_{T \to \infty} T^{-1}E \log L_T(\theta_0).$$

Hence, one generally needs to assume that $\lim_{T \to \infty} T^{-1}E \log L_T(\theta)$ is uniquely maximized at $\theta = \theta_0$.

That (4.2.3) and (4.2.4) imply (4.2.5) follows from the following theorem when we put $g_t(\theta) = \log f(y_t, \theta) - E \log f(y_t, \theta)$.

THEOREM 4.2.1. Let $g(\mathbf{y}, \theta)$ be a measurable function of $\mathbf{y}$ in Euclidean space for each $\theta \in \Theta$, a compact subset of R^K (Euclidean K-space), and a continuous function of $\theta \in \Theta$ for each $\mathbf{y}$. Assume $E\, g(\mathbf{y}, \theta) = 0$. Let $\{\mathbf{y}_t\}$ be a sequence of i.i.d. random vectors such that $E \sup_{\theta \in \Theta} |g(\mathbf{y}_t, \theta)| < \infty$. Then $T^{-1}\Sigma_{t=1}^{T} g(\mathbf{y}_t, \theta)$ converges to 0 in probability uniformly in $\theta \in \Theta$.

Proof.[3] Partition Θ into n nonoverlapping regions $\Theta_1^n, \Theta_2^n, \ldots, \Theta_n^n$ in such a way that the distance between any two points within each Θ_i^n goes to 0 as n goes to ∞. Let $\theta_1, \theta_2, \ldots, \theta_n$ be an arbitrary sequence of K-vectors such that $\theta_i \in \Theta_i^n$, $i = 1, 2, \ldots, n$. Then writing $g_t(\theta)$ for $g(\mathbf{y}_t, \theta)$, we have for any $\epsilon > 0$

$$P\left[\sup_{\theta \in \Theta} \left| T^{-1} \sum_{t=1}^{T} g_t(\theta) \right| > \epsilon \right] \tag{4.2.8}$$

$$\leqq P\left[\bigcup_{i=1}^{n} \left\{ \sup_{\theta \in \Theta_i^n} \left| T^{-1} \sum_{t=1}^{T} g_t(\theta) \right| > \epsilon \right\}\right]$$

$$\leqq \sum_{i=1}^{n} P\left[\sup_{\theta \in \Theta_i^n} \left| T^{-1} \sum_{t=1}^{T} g_t(\theta) \right| > \epsilon\right]$$

$$\leqq \sum_{i=1}^{n} P\left[\left| T^{-1} \sum_{t=1}^{T} g_t(\theta_i) \right| > \frac{\epsilon}{2}\right] + \sum_{i=1}^{n} P\left[T^{-1} \sum_{t=1}^{T} \sup_{\theta \in \Theta_i^n} |g_t(\theta) - g_t(\theta_i)| > \frac{\epsilon}{2}\right],$$

where the first inequality follows from the fact that if A implies B then $P(\text{A}) \leqq P(\text{B})$ and the last inequality follows from the triangle inequality. Because $g_t(\theta)$ is uniformly continuous in $\theta \in \Theta$, we have for every i

$$\lim_{n \to \infty} \sup_{\theta \in \Theta_i^n} |g_t(\theta) - g_t(\theta_i)| = 0. \tag{4.2.9}$$

But, because

$$\sup_{\theta \in \Theta_i^n} |g_t(\theta) - g_t(\theta_i)| \leqq 2 \sup_{\theta \in \Theta} |g_t(\theta)| \tag{4.2.10}$$

and the right-hand side of the inequality (4.2.10) is integrable by our assumptions, (4.2.9) implies by the Lebesgue convergence theorem (Royden, 1968, p. 88)

$$\lim_{n \to \infty} E \sup_{\theta \in \Theta_i^n} |g_t(\theta) - g_t(\theta_i)| = 0 \tag{4.2.11}$$

uniformly for i. Take n so large that the expected value in (4.2.11) is smaller than $\epsilon/2$. Finally, the conclusion of the theorem follows from Theorem 3.3.2 (Kolmogorov LLN 2) by taking T to infinity.

This theorem can be generalized to the extent that $T^{-1}\Sigma_{t=1}^{T} g_t(\theta_i)$ and $T^{-1}\Sigma_{t=1}^{T} \sup_{\theta \in \Theta_i^n} |g_t(\theta) - g_t(\theta_i)|$ can be subjected to a law of large numbers. The following theorem, which is a special case of a theorem attributed to Hoadley (1971) (see also White, 1980b), can be proved by making a slight modification of the proof of Theorem 4.2.1 and using Markov's law of large numbers (Chapter 3, note 10).

THEOREM 4.2.2. Let $g_t(\mathbf{y}, \theta)$ be a measurable function of $\mathbf{y}$ in Euclidean space for each t and for each $\theta \in \Theta$, a compact subset of R^K (Euclidean K-space), and a continuous function of θ uniformly in $\mathbf{y}$ and t. Assume $E\, g_t(\mathbf{y}, \theta) = 0$. Let $\{\mathbf{y}_t\}$ be a sequence of independent and not necessarily identically distributed random vectors such that $E \sup_{\theta \in \Theta} |g_t(\mathbf{y}_t, \theta)|^{1+\delta} \leqq M < \infty$ for some $\delta > 0$. Then $T^{-1}\Sigma_{t=1}^{T} g_t(\mathbf{y}_t, \theta)$ converges to 0 in probability uniformly in $\theta \in \Theta$.

We will need a similar theorem (Jennrich, 1969, p. 636) for the case where $\mathbf{y}_t$ is a vector of constants rather than of random variables.

THEOREM 4.2.3. Let $\mathbf{y}_1, \mathbf{y}_2, \ldots, \mathbf{y}_T$ be vectors of constants. We define the *empirical distribution function* of $(\mathbf{y}_1, \mathbf{y}_2, \ldots, \mathbf{y}_T)$ by $F_T(\boldsymbol{\alpha}) = T^{-1}\Sigma_{t=1}^{T} \chi(\mathbf{y}_t < \boldsymbol{\alpha})$, where χ takes the value 1 or 0 depending on whether the event in its argument occurs or not. Note that $\mathbf{y}_t < \boldsymbol{\alpha}$ means every element of the vector $\mathbf{y}_t$ is smaller than the corresponding element of $\boldsymbol{\alpha}$. Assume that $g(\mathbf{y}, \boldsymbol{\theta})$ is a bounded and continuous function of $\mathbf{y}$ in Euclidean space and $\boldsymbol{\theta}$ in a compact set Θ. Also assume that F_T converges to a distribution function F. Then $\lim_{T\to\infty} T^{-1}\Sigma_{t=1}^{T} g(\mathbf{y}_t, \boldsymbol{\theta}) = \int g(\mathbf{y}, \boldsymbol{\theta})\, dF(\mathbf{y})$ uniformly in $\boldsymbol{\theta}$.

There are many results in the literature concerning the consistency of the maximum likelihood estimator in the i.i.d. case. Rao (1973, p. 364) has presented the consistency of the local MLE, which was originally proved by Cramér (1946). Wald (1949) proved the consistency of the global MLE without assuming compactness of the parameter space, but his conditions are difficult to verify in practice. Many other references concerning the asymptotic properties of the MLE can be found in survey articles by Norden (1972, 1973).

As an example of the application of Theorem 4.1.1, we shall prove the consistency of the maximum likelihood estimators of $\boldsymbol{\beta}$ and σ^2 in Model 1. Because in this case the maximum likelihood estimators can be written as explicit functions of the sample, it is easier to prove consistency by a direct method, as we have already done in Section 3.5. We are considering this more complicated proof strictly for the purpose of illustration.

EXAMPLE 4.2.1. Prove the consistency of the maximum likelihood estimators of the parameters of Model 1 with normality using Theorem 4.1.1, assuming that $\lim T^{-1}\mathbf{X}'\mathbf{X}$ is a finite positive definite matrix.

In Section 1.1 we used the symbols $\boldsymbol{\beta}$ and σ^2 to denote the true values because we did not need to distinguish them from the domain of the likelihood function. But now we shall put the subscript 0 to denote the true value; therefore we can write Eq. (1.1.4) as

$$\mathbf{y} = \mathbf{X}\boldsymbol{\beta}_0 + \mathbf{u}, \tag{4.2.12}$$

where $Vu_t = \sigma_0^2$. From (1.3.1) we have

$$\begin{aligned} \log L_T &= -\frac{T}{2}\log 2\pi - \frac{T}{2}\log \sigma^2 - \frac{1}{2\sigma^2}(\mathbf{y} - \mathbf{X}\boldsymbol{\beta})'(\mathbf{y} - \mathbf{X}\boldsymbol{\beta}) \qquad (4.2.13) \\ &= -\frac{T}{2}\log 2\pi - \frac{T}{2}\log \sigma^2 \\ &\quad - \frac{1}{2\sigma^2}[\mathbf{X}(\boldsymbol{\beta}_0 - \boldsymbol{\beta}) + \mathbf{u}]'[\mathbf{X}(\boldsymbol{\beta}_0 - \boldsymbol{\beta}) + \mathbf{u}], \end{aligned}$$

where the second equality is obtained by using (4.2.12). Therefore

$$\text{plim}\ \frac{1}{T}\log L_T = -\frac{1}{2}\log 2\pi - \frac{1}{2}\log \sigma^2 \qquad (4.2.14)$$

$$-\frac{1}{2\sigma^2}(\boldsymbol{\beta}_0-\boldsymbol{\beta})'\lim \frac{\mathbf{X}'\mathbf{X}}{T}(\boldsymbol{\beta}_0-\boldsymbol{\beta}) - \frac{1}{2}\frac{\sigma_0^2}{\sigma^2}.$$

Define a compact parameter space Θ by

$$c_1 \leqq \sigma^2 \leqq c_2, \qquad \boldsymbol{\beta}'\boldsymbol{\beta} \leqq c_3, \qquad (4.2.15)$$

where c_1 is a small positive constant and c_2 and c_3 are large positive constants, and assume that $(\boldsymbol{\beta}_0', \sigma_0^2)$ is an interior point of Θ. Then, clearly, the convergence in (4.2.14) is uniform in Θ and the right-hand side of (4.2.14) is uniquely maximized at $(\boldsymbol{\beta}_0', \sigma_0^2)$. Put $\boldsymbol{\theta} = (\boldsymbol{\beta}', \sigma^2)'$ and define $\hat{\boldsymbol{\theta}}_T$ by

$$\log L_T(\hat{\boldsymbol{\theta}}_T) = \max_{\boldsymbol{\theta}\in\Theta} \log L_T(\boldsymbol{\theta}). \qquad (4.2.16)$$

Then $\hat{\boldsymbol{\theta}}_T$ is clearly consistent by Theorem 4.1.1. Now define $\tilde{\boldsymbol{\theta}}_T$ by

$$\log L_T(\tilde{\boldsymbol{\theta}}_T) = \max \log L_T(\boldsymbol{\theta}), \qquad (4.2.17)$$

where the maximization in (4.2.17) is over the whole Euclidean $(K+1)$-space. Then the consistency of $\tilde{\boldsymbol{\theta}}_T$, which we set out to prove, would follow from

$$\lim_{T\to\infty} P(\tilde{\boldsymbol{\theta}}_T = \hat{\boldsymbol{\theta}}_T) = 1. \qquad (4.2.18)$$

The proof of (4.2.18) would be simple if we used our knowledge of the explicit formulae for $\tilde{\boldsymbol{\theta}}_T$ in this example. But that would be cheating. The proof of (4.2.18) using condition D given after the proof of Theorem 4.1.1 is left as an exercise.

There are cases where the global maximum likelihood estimator is inconsistent, whereas a root of the likelihood equation (4.2.1) can be consistent, as in the following example.

EXAMPLE 4.2.2. Let $y_t, t = 1, 2, \ldots, T$, be independent with the common distribution defined by

$$f(y_t) = N(\mu_1, \sigma_1^2) \quad \text{with probability} \quad \lambda \qquad (4.2.19)$$

$$= N(\mu_2, \sigma_2^2) \quad \text{with probability} \quad 1-\lambda.$$

This distribution is called a mixture of normal distributions. The likelihood function is given by

$$L = \prod_{t=1}^{T} \left[\frac{\lambda}{\sqrt{2\pi}\sigma_1} \exp\,[-(y_t - \mu_1)^2/(2\sigma_1^2)] + \frac{1-\lambda}{\sqrt{2\pi}\sigma_2} \exp\,[-(y_t - \mu_2)^2/(2\sigma_2^2)] \right]. \tag{4.2.20}$$

If we put $\mu_1 = y_1$ and let σ_1 approach 0, the term of the product that corresponds to $t = 1$ goes to infinity, and, consequently, L goes to infinity. Hence, the global MLE canot be consistent. Note that this example violates assumption C of Theorem 4.1.1 because $Q(\theta)$ does not attain a global maximum at θ_0. However, the conditions of Theorem 4.1.2 are generally satisfied by this model. An extension of this model to the regression case is called the switching regression model (see Quandt and Ramsey, 1978).

It is hard to construct examples in which the maximum likelihood estimator (assuming the likelihood function is correctly specified) is not consistent and another estimator is. Neyman and Scott (1948) have presented an interesting example of this type. In their example MLE is not consistent because the number of incidental (or nuisance) parameters goes to infinity as the sample size goes to infinity.

4.2.3 Asymptotic Normality

The asymptotic normality of the maximum likelihood estimator or, more precisely, a consistent root of the likelihood equation (4.2.1), can be analyzed by putting $Q_T = \log L_T$ in Theorem 4.1.3. If $\{y_t\}$ are independent, we can write

$$\log L_T = \sum_{t=1}^{T} \log f_t(y_t, \theta), \tag{4.2.21}$$

where f_t is the marginal density of y_t. Thus, under general conditions on f_t, we can apply a law of large numbers to $\partial^2 \log L_T/\partial\theta\partial\theta'$ and a central limit theorem to $\partial \log L_T/\partial\theta$. Even if $\{y_t\}$ are not independent, a law of large numbers and a central limit theorem may still be applicable as long as the degree of dependence is limited in a certain manner, as we shall show in later chapters. Thus we see that assumptions B and C of Theorem 4.1.3 are expected to hold generally in the case of the maximum likelihood estimator.

Moreover, when we use the characteristics of L_T as a joint density function, we can get more specific results than Theorem 4.1.3, namely as we have shown in Section 1.3.2, the regularity conditions on the likelihood function given in assumptions A′ and B′ of Section 1.3.2 imply

$$\mathbf{A}(\theta_0) = -\mathbf{B}(\theta_0). \tag{4.2.22}$$

Therefore, we shall make (4.2.22) an additional assumption and state it formally as a theorem.

THEOREM 4.2.4. Under the assumptions of Theorem 4.1.3 and assumption (4.2.22), the maximum likelihood estimator $\hat{\theta}_T$ satisfies

$$\sqrt{T}(\hat{\theta}_T - \theta_0) \rightarrow N\left\{\mathbf{0}, -\left[\lim E \frac{1}{T} \frac{\partial^2 \log L_T}{\partial\theta\partial\theta'}\bigg|_{\theta_0}\right]^{-1}\right\}. \tag{4.2.23}$$

If $\{y_t\}$ are i.i.d. with the common density function $f(\cdot, \theta)$, we can replace assumptions B and C of Theorem 4.1.3 as well as the additional assumption (4.2.22) with the following conditions on $f(\cdot, \theta)$ itself:

$$\int \frac{\partial f}{\partial \theta} dy = \mathbf{0}, \tag{4.2.24}$$

$$\int \frac{\partial^2 f}{\partial\theta\partial\theta'} dy = \mathbf{0}, \tag{4.2.25}$$

$$\operatorname{plim} \frac{1}{T} \sum_{t=1}^{T} \frac{\partial^2 \log f}{\partial\theta\partial\theta'} = E \frac{\partial^2 \log f}{\partial\theta\partial\theta'} \quad \text{uniformly in } \theta \text{ in an open neighborhood of } \theta_0. \tag{4.2.26}$$

A sufficient set of conditions for (4.2.26) can be found by putting $g_t(\theta) = \partial^2 \log f_t/\partial\theta_i\partial\theta_j$ in Theorem 4.2.1. Because $\log L_T = \Sigma_{t=1}^T \log f(y_t, \theta)$ in this case, (4.2.26) implies assumption B of Theorem 4.1.3 because of Theorem 4.1.5. Assumption C of Theorem 4.1.3 follows from (4.2.24) and (4.2.26) on account of Theorem 3.3.4 (Lindeberg-Lévy CLT) since (4.2.24) implies $E(\partial \log f/\partial\theta)_{\theta_0} = \mathbf{0}$. Finally, it is easy to show that assumptions (4.2.24)–(4.2.26) imply (4.2.22).

We shall use the same model as that used in Example 4.2.1 and shall illustrate how the assumptions of Theorem 4.1.3 and the additional assumption (4.2.22) are satisfied. As for Example 4.2.1, the sole purpose of Example 4.2.3 is as an illustration, as the same results have already been obtained by a direct method in Chapter 3.

EXAMPLE 4.2.3. Under the same assumptions made in Example 4.2.1, prove the asymptotic normality of the maximum likelihood estimator $\hat{\theta} = (\hat{\beta}', \hat{\sigma}^2)'$.

We first obtain the first and second derivatives of log L:

$$\frac{\partial \log L}{\partial \boldsymbol{\beta}} = -\frac{1}{\sigma^2}(\mathbf{X}'\mathbf{X}\boldsymbol{\beta} - \mathbf{X}'\mathbf{y}), \tag{4.2.27}$$

$$\frac{\partial \log L}{\partial \sigma^2} = -\frac{T}{2\sigma^2} + \frac{1}{2\sigma^4}(\mathbf{y} - \mathbf{X}\boldsymbol{\beta})'(\mathbf{y} - \mathbf{X}\boldsymbol{\beta}), \tag{4.2.28}$$

$$\frac{\partial^2 \log L}{\partial \boldsymbol{\beta}\partial \boldsymbol{\beta}'} = -\frac{1}{\sigma^2}\mathbf{X}'\mathbf{X}, \tag{4.2.29}$$

$$\frac{\partial^2 \log L}{\partial (\sigma^2)^2} = \frac{T}{2\sigma^4} - \frac{1}{\sigma^6}(\mathbf{y} - \mathbf{X}\boldsymbol{\beta})'(\mathbf{y} - \mathbf{X}\boldsymbol{\beta}), \tag{4.2.30}$$

$$\frac{\partial^2 \log L}{\partial \sigma^2 \partial \boldsymbol{\beta}} = \frac{1}{\sigma^4}(\mathbf{X}'\mathbf{X}\boldsymbol{\beta} - \mathbf{X}'\mathbf{y}). \tag{4.2.31}$$

From (4.2.29), (4.2.30), and (4.2.31) we can clearly see that assumptions A and B of Theorem 4.1.3 are satisfied. Also from these equations we can evaluate the elements of $\mathbf{A}(\boldsymbol{\theta}_0)$:

$$\operatorname{plim} \frac{1}{T} \frac{\partial^2 \log L}{\partial \boldsymbol{\beta}\partial \boldsymbol{\beta}'}\bigg|_{\boldsymbol{\theta}_0} = -\frac{1}{\sigma_0^2} \lim \frac{\mathbf{X}'\mathbf{X}}{T}, \tag{4.2.32}$$

$$\operatorname{plim} \frac{1}{T} \frac{\partial^2 \log L}{\partial (\sigma^2)^2}\bigg|_{\boldsymbol{\theta}_0} = -\frac{1}{2\sigma_0^4}, \tag{4.2.33}$$

$$\operatorname{plim} \frac{1}{T} \frac{\partial^2 \log L}{\partial \sigma^2 \partial \boldsymbol{\beta}}\bigg|_{\boldsymbol{\theta}_0} = \mathbf{0}. \tag{4.2.34}$$

From (4.2.27) and (4.2.28) we obtain

$$\frac{1}{\sqrt{T}} \frac{\partial \log L}{\partial \boldsymbol{\beta}}\bigg|_{\boldsymbol{\theta}_0} = \frac{1}{\sigma_0^2} \frac{\mathbf{X}'\mathbf{u}}{\sqrt{T}} \quad \text{and} \quad \frac{1}{\sqrt{T}} \frac{\partial \log L}{\partial \sigma^2}\bigg|_{\boldsymbol{\theta}_0} = \frac{1}{2\sigma_0^4} \frac{\mathbf{u}'\mathbf{u} - T\sigma_0^2}{\sqrt{T}}.$$

Thus, by applying either the Lindeberg-Feller or Liapounov CLT to a sequence of an arbitrary linear combination of a $(K+1)$-vector $(x_{1t}u_t, x_{2t}u_t, \ldots, x_{Kt}u_t, u_t^2 - \sigma_0^2)$, we can show

$$\frac{1}{\sqrt{T}} \frac{\partial \log L}{\partial \boldsymbol{\beta}}\bigg|_{\boldsymbol{\theta}_0} \to N\left(0, \frac{1}{\sigma_0^2} \lim \frac{\mathbf{X}'\mathbf{X}}{T}\right) \tag{4.2.35}$$

and

$$\frac{1}{\sqrt{T}} \frac{\partial \log L}{\partial \sigma^2}\bigg|_{\boldsymbol{\theta}_0} \to N\left(0, \frac{1}{2\sigma_0^4}\right) \tag{4.2.36}$$

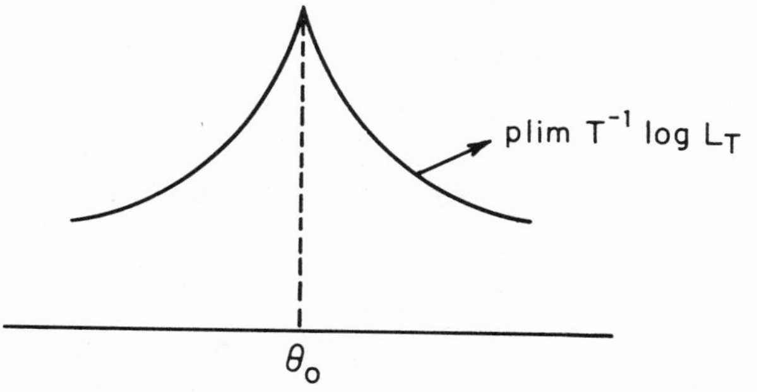

Figure 4.1 The log likelihood function in a nonregular case

with zero asymptotic covariance between (4.2.35) and (4.2.36). Thus assumption C of Theorem 4.1.3 has been shown to hold. Finally, results (4.2.32) through (4.2.36) show that assumption (4.2.22) is satisfied. We write the conclusion (4.2.23) specifically for the present example as

$$\sqrt{T}\begin{bmatrix}\hat{\beta}-\beta_0\\ \hat{\sigma}^2-\sigma_0^2\end{bmatrix} \to N\left\{\mathbf{0}, \begin{bmatrix}\sigma_0^2(\lim T^{-1}\mathbf{X}'\mathbf{X})^{-1} & \mathbf{0}\\ \mathbf{0} & 2\sigma_0^4\end{bmatrix}\right\}. \tag{4.2.37}$$

There are cases where the global maximum likelihood estimator exists but does not satisfy the likelihood equation (4.2.1). Then Theorem 4.1.3 cannot be used to prove the asymptotic normality of MLE. The model of Aigner, Amemiya, and Poirier (1976) is such an example. In their model, plim T^{-1} log L_T exists and is maximized at the true parameter value θ_0 so that MLE is consistent. However, problems arise because plim T^{-1} log L_T is not smooth at θ_0; it looks like Figure 4.1. In such a case, it is generally difficult to prove asymptotic normality.

4.2.4 Asymptotic Efficiency

The asymptotic normality (4.2.23) means that if T is large the variance-covariance matrix of a maximum likelihood estimator may be approximated by

$$-\left[E\left.\frac{\partial^2 \log L_T}{\partial\theta\partial\theta'}\right|_{\theta_0}\right]^{-1}, \tag{4.2.38}$$

But (4.2.38) is precisely the Cramér-Rao lower bound of an unbiased estimator derived in Section 1.3.2. At one time statisticians believed that a consistent and asymptotically normal estimator with the asymptotic covariance matrix

(4.2.38) was asymptotically minimum variance among all consistent and asymptotically normal estimators. But this was proved wrong by the following counterexample, attributed to Hodges and reported in LeCam (1953).

EXAMPLE 4.2.4. Let $\hat{\theta}_T$ be an estimator of a scalar parameter such that plim $\hat{\theta}_T = \theta$ and $\sqrt{T}(\hat{\theta}_T - \theta) \rightarrow N[0, v(\theta)]$. Define the estimator $\theta_T^* = w_T\hat{\theta}_T$, where

$$\begin{aligned} w_T &= 0 \quad \text{if} \quad |\hat{\theta}_T| < T^{-1/4} \\ &= 1 \quad \text{if} \quad |\hat{\theta}_T| \geqq T^{-1/4}. \end{aligned}$$

It can be shown (the proof is left as an exercise) that $\sqrt{T}(\theta_T^* - \theta) \rightarrow N[0, v^*(\theta)]$, where $v^*(0) = 0$ and $v^*(\theta) = v(\theta)$ if $\theta \neq 0$.

The estimator θ_T^* of Example 4.2.4 is said to be *superefficient.* Despite the existence of superefficient estimators, we can still say something good about an estimator with the asymptotic variance-covariance matrix (4.2.38). We shall state two such results without proof. One is the result of LeCam (1953), which states that the set of $\boldsymbol{\theta}$ points on which a superefficient estimator has an asymptotic variance smaller than the Cramér-Rao lower bound is of Lebesgue measure zero. The other is the result of Rao (1973, p. 350) that the matrix (4.2.38) is the lower bound for the asymptotic variance-covariance matrix of all the consistent and asymptotically normal estimators for which the convergence to a normal distribution is uniform over compact intervals of $\boldsymbol{\theta}$. These results seem to justify our use of the term *asymptotically efficient* in the following sense:

DEFINITION 4.2.1. A consistent estimator is said to be *asymptotically efficient* if it satisfies statement (4.2.23).

Thus the maximum likelihood estimator under the appropriate assumptions is asymptotically efficient by definition. An asymptotically efficient estimator is also referred to as *best asymptotically normal* (BAN for short). There are BAN estimators other than MLE. Many examples of these will be discussed in subsequent chapters, for example, the weighted least squares estimator will be discussed Section 6.5.3, the two-stage and three-stage least squares estimators in Sections 7.3.3 and 7.4, and the minimum chi-square estimators in Section 9.2.5. Barankin and Gurland (1951) have presented a general method of generating BAN estimators. Because their results are mathematically too abstract to present here, we shall state only a simple corollary of their results: Let $\{\mathbf{y}_t\}$ be an i.i.d. sequence of random vectors with $E\,\mathbf{y}_t = \boldsymbol{\mu}(\boldsymbol{\theta})$, $E(\mathbf{y}_t - \boldsymbol{\mu})(\mathbf{y}_t - \boldsymbol{\mu})' = \boldsymbol{\Sigma}(\boldsymbol{\theta})$, and with exponential family density

$$f(\mathbf{y}, \theta) = \exp\,[\alpha_0(\theta) + \beta_0(\mathbf{y}) + \sum_{i=1}^{K} \alpha_i(\theta)\beta_i(\mathbf{y})]$$

and define $\mathbf{z}_T = T^{-1}\Sigma_{t=1}^T \mathbf{y}_t$. Then the minimization of $[\mathbf{z}_T - \mu(\theta)]' \Sigma(\theta)^{-1}[\mathbf{z}_T - \mu(\theta)]$ yields a BAN estimator of θ (see also Taylor, 1953; Ferguson, 1958).[4]

Different BAN estimators may have different finite sample distributions. Recently many interesting articles in the statistical literature have compared the approximate distribution (with a higher degree of accuracy than the asymptotic distribution) of MLE with those of other BAN estimators. For example, Ghosh and Subramanyam (1974) have shown that in the exponential family the mean squared error up to $O(T^{-2})$ of MLE after correcting its bias up to $O(T^{-1})$ is smaller than that of any other BAN estimator with similarly corrected bias. This result is referred to as the *second-order efficiency* of MLE,[5] and examples of it will be given in Sections 7.3.5 and 9.2.6.

4.2.5 Concentrated Likelihood Function

We often encounter in practice the situation where the parameter vector θ_0 can be naturally partitioned into two subvectors $\boldsymbol{\alpha}_0$ and $\boldsymbol{\beta}_0$ as $\theta_0 = (\boldsymbol{\alpha}_0', \boldsymbol{\beta}_0')'$. The regression model is one such example; in this model the parameters consist of the regression coefficients and the error variance. First, partition the maximum likelihood estimator as $\hat{\theta} = (\hat{\boldsymbol{\alpha}}', \hat{\boldsymbol{\beta}}')'$. Then, the limit distribution of $\sqrt{T}(\hat{\boldsymbol{\alpha}} - \boldsymbol{\alpha}_0)$ can easily be derived from statement (4.2.23). Partition the inverse of the asymptotic variance-covariance matrix of statement (4.2.23) conformably with the partition of the parameter vector as

$$-\lim E \frac{1}{T} \frac{\partial^2 \log L_T}{\partial\theta\partial\theta'}\bigg|_{\theta_0} = \begin{bmatrix} \mathbf{A} & \mathbf{B} \\ \mathbf{B}' & \mathbf{C} \end{bmatrix}. \tag{4.2.39}$$

Then, by Theorem 13 of Appendix 1, we have

$$\sqrt{T}(\hat{\boldsymbol{\alpha}} - \boldsymbol{\alpha}_0) \to N[\mathbf{0}, (\mathbf{A} - \mathbf{B}\mathbf{C}^{-1}\mathbf{B}')^{-1}]. \tag{4.2.40}$$

Let the likelihood function be $L(\boldsymbol{\alpha}, \boldsymbol{\beta})$. Sometimes it is easier to maximize L in two steps (first, maximize it with respect to $\boldsymbol{\beta}$, insert the maximizing value of $\boldsymbol{\beta}$ back into L; second, maximize L with respect to $\boldsymbol{\alpha}$) than to maximize L simultaneously for $\boldsymbol{\alpha}$ and $\boldsymbol{\beta}$. More precisely, define

$$L^*(\boldsymbol{\alpha}) = L[\boldsymbol{\alpha}, \hat{\boldsymbol{\beta}}(\boldsymbol{\alpha})], \tag{4.2.41}$$

where $\hat{\boldsymbol{\beta}}(\boldsymbol{\alpha})$ is defined as a root of

$$\left.\frac{\partial \log L}{\partial \boldsymbol{\beta}}\right|_{\hat{\boldsymbol{\beta}}} = \mathbf{0}, \tag{4.2.42}$$

and define $\hat{\boldsymbol{\alpha}}$ as a root of

$$\left.\frac{\partial \log L^*}{\partial \boldsymbol{\alpha}}\right|_{\hat{\boldsymbol{\alpha}}} = \mathbf{0}. \tag{4.2.43}$$

We call $L^*(\boldsymbol{\alpha})$ the *concentrated likelihood function* of $\boldsymbol{\alpha}$. In this subsection we shall pose and answer affirmatively the question: If we treat $L^*(\boldsymbol{\alpha})$ as if it were a proper likelihood function and obtain the limit distribution by (4.2.23), do we get the same result as (4.2.40)?

From Theorem 4.1.3 and its proof we have

$$\sqrt{T}(\hat{\boldsymbol{\alpha}} - \boldsymbol{\alpha}_0) \overset{\text{LD}}{=} -\left[\operatorname{plim} \frac{1}{T} \left.\frac{\partial^2 \log L^*}{\partial \boldsymbol{\alpha} \partial \boldsymbol{\alpha}'}\right|_{\boldsymbol{\alpha}_0}\right]^{-1} \frac{1}{\sqrt{T}} \left.\frac{\partial \log L^*}{\partial \boldsymbol{\alpha}}\right|_{\boldsymbol{\alpha}_0}, \tag{4.2.44}$$

where $\overset{\text{LD}}{=}$ means that both sides of the equation have the same limit distribution. Differentiating both sides of (4.2.41) and evaluating the derivative at $\boldsymbol{\alpha}_0$ yields

$$\begin{aligned} \left.\frac{\partial \log L^*}{\partial \boldsymbol{\alpha}}\right|_{\boldsymbol{\alpha}_0} &= \left.\frac{\partial \log L}{\partial \boldsymbol{\alpha}}\right|_{\boldsymbol{\alpha}_0, \hat{\boldsymbol{\beta}}(\boldsymbol{\alpha}_0)} + \left.\frac{\partial \hat{\boldsymbol{\beta}}'}{\partial \boldsymbol{\alpha}}\right|_{\boldsymbol{\alpha}_0} \left.\frac{\partial \log L}{\partial \boldsymbol{\beta}}\right|_{\boldsymbol{\alpha}_0, \hat{\boldsymbol{\beta}}(\boldsymbol{\alpha}_0)} \\ &= \left.\frac{\partial \log L}{\partial \boldsymbol{\alpha}}\right|_{\boldsymbol{\alpha}_0, \hat{\boldsymbol{\beta}}(\boldsymbol{\alpha}_0)}, \end{aligned} \tag{4.2.45}$$

where the second equality follows from (4.2.42). By a Taylor expansion we have

$$\left.\frac{\partial \log L}{\partial \boldsymbol{\alpha}}\right|_{\boldsymbol{\alpha}_0, \hat{\boldsymbol{\beta}}(\boldsymbol{\alpha}_0)} = \left.\frac{\partial \log L}{\partial \boldsymbol{\alpha}}\right|_{\boldsymbol{\theta}_0} + \left.\frac{\partial^2 \log L}{\partial \boldsymbol{\alpha} \partial \boldsymbol{\beta}'}\right|_{\boldsymbol{\theta}^+} [\hat{\boldsymbol{\beta}}(\boldsymbol{\alpha}_0) - \boldsymbol{\beta}_0], \tag{4.2.46}$$

where $\boldsymbol{\theta}^+$ lies between $[\boldsymbol{\alpha}_0', \hat{\boldsymbol{\beta}}(\boldsymbol{\alpha}_0)']$ and $\boldsymbol{\theta}_0$. But we have

$$\sqrt{T}[\hat{\boldsymbol{\beta}}(\boldsymbol{\alpha}_0) - \boldsymbol{\beta}_0] \overset{\text{LD}}{=} -\left[\lim E \frac{1}{T} \left.\frac{\partial^2 \log L}{\partial \boldsymbol{\beta} \partial \boldsymbol{\beta}'}\right|_{\boldsymbol{\theta}_0}\right]^{-1} \frac{1}{\sqrt{T}} \left.\frac{\partial \log L}{\partial \boldsymbol{\beta}}\right|_{\boldsymbol{\theta}_0}. \tag{4.2.47}$$

Therefore, from (4.2.45), (4.2.46), and (4.2.47), we obtain

$$\frac{1}{\sqrt{T}} \left.\frac{\partial \log L^*}{\partial \boldsymbol{\alpha}}\right|_{\boldsymbol{\alpha}_0} \overset{\text{LD}}{=} (\mathbf{I}, -\mathbf{B}\mathbf{C}^{-1}) \frac{1}{\sqrt{T}} \left.\frac{\partial \log L}{\partial \boldsymbol{\theta}}\right|_{\boldsymbol{\theta}_0}. \tag{4.2.48}$$

Finally, using (4.2.22), we obtain from (4.2.48)

$$\frac{1}{\sqrt{T}} \left.\frac{\partial \log L^*}{\partial \boldsymbol{\alpha}}\right|_{\boldsymbol{\alpha}_0} \to N(\mathbf{0}, \mathbf{A} - \mathbf{B}\mathbf{C}^{-1}\mathbf{B}'). \tag{4.2.49}$$

Next, differentiating both sides of the identity

$$\frac{\partial \log L^*(\boldsymbol{\alpha})}{\partial \boldsymbol{\alpha}} = \frac{\partial \log L[\boldsymbol{\alpha}, \hat{\boldsymbol{\beta}}(\boldsymbol{\alpha})]}{\partial \boldsymbol{\alpha}} \tag{4.2.50}$$

with respect to $\boldsymbol{\alpha}$ yields

$$\left.\frac{\partial^2 \log L^*}{\partial \boldsymbol{\alpha} \partial \boldsymbol{\alpha}'}\right|_{\alpha_0} = \left.\frac{\partial^2 \log L}{\partial \boldsymbol{\alpha} \partial \boldsymbol{\alpha}'}\right|_{\alpha_0, \hat{\beta}(\alpha_0)} + \left.\frac{\partial \hat{\boldsymbol{\beta}}'}{\partial \boldsymbol{\alpha}}\right|_{\alpha_0} \left.\frac{\partial^2 \log L}{\partial \boldsymbol{\beta} \partial \boldsymbol{\alpha}'}\right|_{\alpha_0, \hat{\beta}(\alpha_0)}. \tag{4.2.51}$$

Differentiating both sides of (4.2.42) with respect to $\boldsymbol{\alpha}$ yields

$$\left.\frac{\partial^2 \log L}{\partial \boldsymbol{\alpha} \partial \boldsymbol{\beta}'}\right|_{\alpha_0, \hat{\beta}(\alpha_0)} + \left.\frac{\partial \hat{\boldsymbol{\beta}}'}{\partial \boldsymbol{\alpha}}\right|_{\alpha_0} \left.\frac{\partial^2 \log L}{\partial \boldsymbol{\beta} \partial \boldsymbol{\beta}'}\right|_{\alpha_0, \hat{\beta}(\alpha_0)} = \mathbf{0}. \tag{4.2.52}$$

Combining (4.2.51) and (4.2.52) yields

$$\left.\frac{\partial^2 \log L^*}{\partial \boldsymbol{\alpha} \partial \boldsymbol{\alpha}'}\right|_{\alpha_0} = \left.\frac{\partial^2 \log L}{\partial \boldsymbol{\alpha} \partial \boldsymbol{\alpha}'}\right|_{\alpha_0, \hat{\beta}(\alpha_0)} - \left.\frac{\partial^2 \log L}{\partial \boldsymbol{\alpha} \partial \boldsymbol{\beta}'}\right|_{\alpha_0, \hat{\beta}(\alpha_0)} \left[\left.\frac{\partial^2 \log L}{\partial \boldsymbol{\beta} \partial \boldsymbol{\beta}'}\right|_{\alpha_0, \hat{\beta}(\alpha_0)}\right]^{-1} \left.\frac{\partial^2 \log L}{\partial \boldsymbol{\beta} \partial \boldsymbol{\alpha}'}\right|_{\alpha_0, \hat{\beta}(\alpha_0)}, \tag{4.2.53}$$

which implies

$$\operatorname{plim} \frac{1}{T} \left.\frac{\partial^2 \log L^*}{\partial \boldsymbol{\alpha} \partial \boldsymbol{\alpha}'}\right|_{\alpha_0} = -(\mathbf{A} - \mathbf{B}\mathbf{C}^{-1}\mathbf{B}'). \tag{4.2.54}$$

Finally, we have proved that (4.2.44), (4.2.49), and (4.2.54) lead precisely to the conclusion (4.2.40) as desired.

4.3 Nonlinear Least Squares Estimator

4.3.1 Definition

We shall first present the *nonlinear regression model,* which is a nonlinear generalization of Model 1 of Chapter 1. The assumptions we shall make are also similar to those of Model 1. As in Chapter 1 we first shall state only the fundamental assumptions and later shall add a few more assumptions as needed for obtaining particular results.

We assume

$$y_t = f_t(\boldsymbol{\beta}_0) + u_t, \qquad t = 1, 2, \ldots, T, \tag{4.3.1}$$

where y_t is a scalar observable random variable, $\boldsymbol{\beta}_0$ is a K-vector of unknown parameters, and $\{u_t\}$ are i.i.d. unobservable random variables such that $Eu_t = 0$ and $Vu_t = \sigma_0^2$ (another unknown parameter) for all t.

The assumptions on the function f_t will be specified later. Often in practice we can write $f_t(\boldsymbol{\beta}_0) = f(\mathbf{x}_t, \boldsymbol{\beta}_0)$, where $\mathbf{x}_t$ is a vector of exogenous variables (known constants), which, unlike the linear regression model, may not necessarily be of the same dimension as $\boldsymbol{\beta}_0$.

As in Chapter 1, we sometimes write (4.3.1) in vector form as

$$\mathbf{y} = \mathbf{f}(\boldsymbol{\beta}_0) + \mathbf{u}, \tag{4.3.2}$$

where $\mathbf{y}$, $\mathbf{f}$, and $\mathbf{u}$ are all T-vectors, for which the tth element is defined in (4.3.1).

Nonlinearity arises in many diverse ways in econometric applications. For example, it arises when the observed variables in a linear regression model are transformed to take account of serial correlation of the error terms (cf. Section 6.3). Another example is the distributed-lag model (see Section 5.6), in which the coefficients on the lagged exogenous variables are specified to decrease with lags in a certain nonlinear fashion. In both of these examples, nonlinearity exists only in parameters and not in variables.

More general nonlinear models, in which nonlinearity is present both in parameters and variables, are used in the estimation of production functions and demand functions. The Cobb-Douglas production function with an additive error term is given by

$$Q_t = \beta_1 K_t^{\beta_2} L_t^{\beta_3} + u_t, \tag{4.3.3}$$

where Q, K, and L denote output, capital input, and labor input, respectively.[6] The CES production function (see Arrow et al., 1961) may be written as

$$Q_t = \beta_1[\beta_2 K_t^{-\beta_3} + (1-\beta_2)L_t^{-\beta_3}]^{-\beta_4/\beta_3} + u_t. \tag{4.3.4}$$

See Mizon (1977) for several other nonlinear production functions. In the estimation of demand functions, a number of highly nonlinear functions have been proposed (some of these are also used for supply functions), for example, translog (Christensen, Jorgenson, and Lau, 1975), generalized Leontief (Diewert, 1974), S-branch (Brown and Heien, 1972), and quadratic (Howe, Pollak, and Wales, 1979).

As in the case of the maximum likelihood estimator, we can define the *nonlinear least squares estimator* (abbreviated as NLLS) of $\boldsymbol{\beta}_0$ in two ways, depending on whether we consider the global minimum or a local minimum. In the global case we define it as the value of $\boldsymbol{\beta}$ that minimizes

$$S_T = \sum_{t=1}^{T} [y_t - f_t(\boldsymbol{\beta})]^2 \tag{4.3.5}$$

over some parameter space B. In the local case we define it as a root of the normal equation

$$\frac{\partial S_T}{\partial \boldsymbol{\beta}} = \mathbf{0}. \tag{4.3.6}$$

We shall consider only the latter case because (4.3.6) is needed to prove asymptotic normality, as we have seen in Section 4.1.2. Given the NLLS estimator $\hat{\boldsymbol{\beta}}$ of $\boldsymbol{\beta}_0$, we define the NLLS estimator of σ_0^2, denoted as $\hat{\sigma}^2$, by

$$\hat{\sigma}^2 = T^{-1}S_T(\hat{\boldsymbol{\beta}}). \tag{4.3.7}$$

Note that $\hat{\boldsymbol{\beta}}$ and $\hat{\sigma}^2$ defined above are also the maximum likelihood estimators if the $\{u_t\}$ are normally distributed.

4.3.2 Consistency[7]

We shall make additional assumptions in the nonlinear regression model so that the assumptions of Theorem 4.1.2 are satisfied.

THEOREM 4.3.1. In the nonlinear regression model (4.3.1), make the additional assumptions: There exists an open neighborhood N of $\boldsymbol{\beta}_0$ such that

(A) $\partial f_t/\partial \boldsymbol{\beta}$ exists and is continuous on N.

(B) $f_t(\boldsymbol{\beta})$ is continuous in $\boldsymbol{\beta} \in N$ uniformly in t; that is, given $\epsilon > 0$ there exists $\delta > 0$ such that $|f_t(\boldsymbol{\beta}_1) - f_t(\boldsymbol{\beta}_2)| < \epsilon$ whenever $(\boldsymbol{\beta}_1 - \boldsymbol{\beta}_2)'(\boldsymbol{\beta}_1 - \boldsymbol{\beta}_2) < \delta$ for all $\boldsymbol{\beta}_1, \boldsymbol{\beta}_2 \in N$ and for all t.[8]

(C) $T^{-1}\Sigma_{t=1}^{T} f_t(\boldsymbol{\beta}_1)f_t(\boldsymbol{\beta}_2)$ converges uniformly in $\boldsymbol{\beta}_1, \boldsymbol{\beta}_2 \in N$.

(D) $\lim T^{-1}\Sigma_{t=1}^{T}[f_t(\boldsymbol{\beta}_0) - f_t(\boldsymbol{\beta})]^2 \neq 0$ if $\boldsymbol{\beta} \neq \boldsymbol{\beta}_0$.

Then a root of (4.3.6) is consistent in the sense of Theorem 4.1.2.

Proof. Inserting (4.3.1) into (4.3.5), we can rewrite T^{-1} times (4.3.5) as

$$\begin{aligned} \frac{1}{T}S_T &= \frac{1}{T}\sum_{t=1}^{T} u_t^2 + \frac{1}{T}\sum_{t=1}^{T}[f_t(\boldsymbol{\beta}_0) - f_t(\boldsymbol{\beta})]^2 \\ &\quad + \frac{2}{T}\sum_{t=1}^{T}[f_t(\boldsymbol{\beta}_0) - f_t(\boldsymbol{\beta})]u_t \\ &\equiv A_1 + A_2 + A_3. \end{aligned} \tag{4.3.8}$$

The term A_1 converges to σ_0^2 in probability by Theorem 3.3.2 (Kolmogorov LLN 2). The term A_2 converges to a function that has a local minimum at $\boldsymbol{\beta}_0$ uniformly in $\boldsymbol{\beta}$ because of assumptions C and D. We shall show that A_3 converges to 0 in probability uniformly in $\boldsymbol{\beta} \in N$ by an argument similar to the proof of Theorem 4.2.1. First, $\operatorname{plim}_{T\to\infty} T^{-1}\Sigma_{t=1}^{T} f_t(\boldsymbol{\beta}_0)u_t = 0$ because of assumption C and Theorem 3.2.1. Next, consider $\sup_{\boldsymbol{\beta}\in N} T^{-1}|\Sigma_{t=1}^{T} f_t(\boldsymbol{\beta})u_t|$. Partition N into n nonoverlapping regions $N_1, N_2, \ldots, N_n$. Because of assumption B, for any $\epsilon > 0$ we can find a sufficiently large n such that for each $i = 1, 2, \ldots, n$

$$|f_t(\boldsymbol{\beta}_1) - f_t(\boldsymbol{\beta}_2)| < \frac{\epsilon}{2(\sigma_0^2+1)^{1/2}} \quad \text{for} \quad \boldsymbol{\beta}_1, \boldsymbol{\beta}_2 \in N_i \quad \text{and for all} \quad t. \tag{4.3.9}$$

Therefore, using the Cauchy-Schwartz inequality, we have

$$\sup_{\boldsymbol{\beta}\in N_i}\left|\frac{1}{T}\sum_{t=1}^{T} f_t(\boldsymbol{\beta})u_t\right| \leqq \frac{1}{T}\left|\sum_{t=1}^{T} f_t(\boldsymbol{\beta}_i)u_t\right| + \left(\frac{1}{T}\sum_{t=1}^{T} u_t^2\right)^{1/2} \frac{\epsilon}{2(\sigma_0^2+1)^{1/2}}, \tag{4.3.10}$$

where $\boldsymbol{\beta}_i$ is an arbitrary fixed point in N_i. Therefore

$$\begin{aligned} P\left[\sup_{\boldsymbol{\beta}\in N}\left|\frac{1}{T}\sum_{t=1}^{T} f_t(\boldsymbol{\beta})u_t\right| > \epsilon\right] &\leqq \sum_{i=1}^{n} P\left[\sup_{\boldsymbol{\beta}\in N_i}\left|\frac{1}{T}\sum_{t=1}^{T} f_t(\boldsymbol{\beta})u_t\right| > \epsilon\right] \\ &\leqq \sum_{i=1}^{n} P\left[\left|\frac{1}{T}\sum_{t=1}^{T} f_t(\boldsymbol{\beta}_i)u_t\right| > \frac{\epsilon}{2}\right] \\ &\quad + nP\left[\frac{1}{T}\sum_{t=1}^{T} u_t^2 > \sigma_0^2 + 1\right]. \end{aligned} \tag{4.3.11}$$

Finally, we obtain the desired result by taking the limit of both sides of the inequality (4.3.11) as T goes to ∞. Thus we have shown that assumption C of Theorem 4.1.2 is satisfied. Assumptions A and B of Theorem 4.1.2 are clearly satisfied.

Assumption C of Theorem 4.3.1 is not easily verifiable in practice; therefore it is desirable to find a sufficient set of conditions that imply assumption C and are more easily verifiable. One such set is provided by Theorem 4.2.3. To apply the theorem to the present problem, we should assume $f_t(\boldsymbol{\beta}) = f(\mathbf{x}_t, \boldsymbol{\beta})$ and take $\mathbf{x}_t$ and $f_t(\boldsymbol{\beta}_1)f_t(\boldsymbol{\beta}_2)$ as the $\mathbf{y}_t$ and $g(\mathbf{y}_t, \theta)$ of Theorem 4.2.3, respectively. Alternatively, one could assume that $\{\mathbf{x}_t\}$ are i.i.d. random variables and use Theorem 4.2.1.

In the next example the conditions of Theorem 4.3.1 will be verified for a simple nonlinear regression model.

EXAMPLE 4.3.1. Consider the nonlinear regression model (4.3.1) with $f_t(\beta_0) = \log(\beta_0 + x_t)$, where β_0 and x_t are scalars. Assume (i) the parameter space B is a bounded open interval (c, d), (ii) $x_t + \beta > \delta > 0$ for every t and for every $\beta \in$ B, and (iii) $\{x_t\}$ are i.i.d. random variables such that $E\{[\log(d + x_t)]^2\} < \infty$. Prove that a root of (4.3.6) is consistent.

First, note that $\log(\beta_0 + x_t)$ is well defined because of assumptions (i) and (ii). Let us verify the conditions of Theorem 4.3.1. Condition A is clearly satisfied because of assumptions (i) and (ii). Condition B is satisfied because

$$|\log(\beta_1 + x_t) - \log(\beta_2 + x_t)| \leqq |\beta_t^* + x_t|^{-1}|\beta_1 - \beta_2|$$

by the mean value theorem, where β_t^* (depending on x_t) is between β_1 and β_2, and because $|\beta_t^* + x_t|^{-1}$ is uniformly bounded on account of assumptions (i) and (ii). Condition C follows from assumption (iii) because of Theorem 4.2.1. To verify condition D, use the mean value theorem to obtain

$$\frac{1}{T}\sum_{t=1}^{T}[\log(\beta + x_t) - \log(\beta_0 + x_t)]^2$$

$$= \frac{1}{T}\left[\sum_{t=1}^{T}(\beta_t^+ + x_t)^{-2}\right](\beta - \beta_0)^2,$$

where β_t^+ (depending on x_t) is between β and β_0. But

$$\frac{1}{T}\sum_{t=1}^{T}(\beta_t^+ + x_t)^{-2} \geqq \frac{1}{T}\sum_{t=1}^{T}(d + x_t)^{-2}$$

and

$$\underset{T\to\infty}{\text{plim}}\ \frac{1}{T}\sum_{t=1}^{T}(d + x_t)^{-2} = E(d + x_t)^{-2} > 0$$

because of assumptions (i), (ii), and (iii) and Theorem 3.3.2 (Kolmogorov LLN 2). Therefore condition D holds.

When $f_t(\beta_0)$ has a very simple form, consistency can be proved more simply and with fewer assumptions by using Theorem 4.1.1 or Theorem 4.1.2 directly rather than Theorem 4.3.1, as we shall show in the following example.

EXAMPLE 4.3.2. Consider the nonlinear regression model (4.3.1) with $f_t(\beta_0) = (\beta_0 + x_t)^2$ and assume (i) $a \leqq \beta_0 \leqq b$ where a and b are real numbers such that $a < b$, (ii) $\lim_{T\to\infty} T^{-1}\Sigma_{t=1}^{T} x_t = q$, and (iii) $\lim_{T\to\infty} T^{-1}\Sigma_{t=1}^{T} x_t^2 = p > q^2$. Prove that the value of β that minimizes $\Sigma_{t=1}^{T}[y_t - (\beta + x_t)^2]^2$ in the domain $[a, b]$ is a consistent estimator of β_0.

We have

$$\underset{T\to\infty}{\text{plim}}\ \frac{1}{T}\sum_{t=1}^{T}[y_t-(\beta+x_t)^2]^2$$
$$=\sigma_0^2+(\beta_0^2-\beta^2)^2+4(\beta_0-\beta)^2p+4(\beta_0^2-\beta^2)(\beta_0-\beta)q$$
$$\equiv Q(\beta),$$

where the convergence is clearly uniform in $\beta\in[a,b]$. But, because

$$Q(\beta)\geqq\sigma_0^2+(\beta_0-\beta)^2(\beta_0+\beta+2q)^2,$$

$Q(\beta)$ is uniquely minimized at $\beta=\beta_0$. Therefore the estimator in question is consistent by Theorem 4.1.1.

4.3.3 Asymptotic Normality

We shall now prove the asymptotic normality of the NLLS estimator of $\boldsymbol{\beta}$ by making assumptions on f_t to satisfy the assumptions of Theorem 4.1.3.

First, consider assumption C of Theorem 4.1.3. We have

$$\frac{\partial S_T}{\partial\boldsymbol{\beta}}=-2\sum_{t=1}^{T}[y_t-f_t(\boldsymbol{\beta})]\frac{\partial f_t}{\partial\boldsymbol{\beta}}. \tag{4.3.12}$$

Therefore we have

$$\frac{1}{\sqrt{T}}\left.\frac{\partial S_T}{\partial\boldsymbol{\beta}}\right|_{\boldsymbol{\beta}_0}=-\frac{2}{\sqrt{T}}\sum_{t=1}^{T}u_t\left.\frac{\partial f_t}{\partial\boldsymbol{\beta}}\right|_{\boldsymbol{\beta}_0}. \tag{4.3.13}$$

The results of Section 3.5 show that if we assume in the nonlinear regression model that

$$\lim_{T\to\infty}\frac{1}{T}\sum_{t=1}^{T}\left.\frac{\partial f_t}{\partial\boldsymbol{\beta}}\right|_{\boldsymbol{\beta}_0}\left.\frac{\partial f_t}{\partial\boldsymbol{\beta}'}\right|_{\boldsymbol{\beta}_0}\quad(\equiv\mathbf{C}) \tag{4.3.14}$$

is a finite nonsingular matrix,[9]

then the limit distribution of (4.3.13) is $N(\mathbf{0},4\sigma_0^2\mathbf{C})$.

Second, consider the assumption of Theorem 4.1.5 that implies assumption B of Theorem 4.1.3, except for nonsingularity. From (4.3.12) we have

$$\frac{1}{T}\frac{\partial^2 S_T}{\partial\boldsymbol{\beta}\partial\boldsymbol{\beta}'}=\frac{2}{T}\sum_{t=1}^{T}\frac{\partial f_t}{\partial\boldsymbol{\beta}}\frac{\partial f_t}{\partial\boldsymbol{\beta}'}-\frac{2}{T}\sum_{t=1}^{T}u_t\frac{\partial^2 f_t}{\partial\boldsymbol{\beta}\partial\boldsymbol{\beta}'} \tag{4.3.15}$$

$$-\frac{2}{T}\sum_{t=1}^{T}[f_t(\beta_0)-f_t(\beta)]\frac{\partial^2 f_t}{\partial\beta\partial\beta'}$$

$$\equiv \mathbf{A}_1+\mathbf{A}_2+\mathbf{A}_3.$$

We must make the assumption of Theorem 4.1.5 hold for each of the three terms in (4.3.15). First, for $\mathbf{A}_1$ to satisfy the assumption of Theorem 4.1.5, we must assume

$$\frac{1}{T}\sum_{t=1}^{T}\frac{\partial f_t}{\partial\beta}\frac{\partial f_t}{\partial\beta'} \text{ converges to a finite matrix uniformly} \tag{4.3.16}$$

for all β in an open neighborhood of β_0.

For $\mathbf{A}_2$ to converge to $\mathbf{0}$ in probability uniformly in a neighborhood of β_0, we require (as we can infer from the proof of the convergence of A_3 in Theorem 4.3.1) that

$$\frac{\partial^2 f_t}{\partial\beta_i\partial\beta_j} \text{ is continuous in } \beta \text{ in an open} \tag{4.3.17}$$

neighborhood of β_0 uniformly in t

and

$$\lim_{T\to\infty}\frac{1}{T^2}\sum_{t=1}^{T}\left[\frac{\partial^2 f_t}{\partial\beta_i\partial\beta_j}\right]^2=0 \quad \text{for all } \beta \tag{4.3.18}$$

in an open neighborhood of β_0.

Finally, the uniform convergence of $\mathbf{A}_3$ requires

$$\frac{1}{T}\sum_{t=1}^{T}f_t(\beta_1)\left.\frac{\partial^2 f_t}{\partial\beta\partial\beta'}\right|_{\beta_2} \text{ converges to a finite matrix uniformly}$$

for all β_1 and β_2 in an open neighborhood of β_0. (4.3.19)

Thus under these assumptions we have

$$\operatorname{plim}\frac{1}{T}\left.\frac{\partial^2 S_T}{\partial\beta\partial\beta'}\right|_{\beta_T^*}=2\lim\frac{1}{T}\sum_{t=1}^{T}\left.\frac{\partial f_t}{\partial\beta}\right|_{\beta_0}\left.\frac{\partial f_t}{\partial\beta'}\right|_{\beta_0} \tag{4.3.20}$$

whenever $\operatorname{plim}\beta_T^*=\beta_0$.

These results can be summarized as a theorem.

THEOREM 4.3.2. In addition to the assumptions of the nonlinear regression model and the assumptions of Theorem 4.3.1, assume conditions (4.3.14), and (4.3.16)–(4.3.19). Then, if $\hat{\boldsymbol{\beta}}_T$ is a consistent root of the normal equation (4.3.6), we have

$$\sqrt{T}(\hat{\boldsymbol{\beta}}_T - \boldsymbol{\beta}_0) \rightarrow N(\mathbf{0}, \sigma_0^2 \mathbf{C}^{-1}). \tag{4.3.21}$$

As in condition C of Theorem 4.3.1, a simple way to verify conditions (4.3.16) and (4.3.19) is to assume that $\mathbf{x}_t$ are i.i.d. and use Theorem 4.2.1. Condition (4.3.18) follows from the uniform convergence of $T^{-1}\Sigma_{t=1}^T (\partial^2 f_t/\partial\beta_i\partial\beta_j)^2$, which in turn can be verified by using Theorem 4.2.1. It would be instructive for the reader to verify these conditions for Example 4.3.1 and to prove the asymptotic normality of the estimator in question.

When $f_t(\boldsymbol{\beta}_0)$ has a simple form, the convergence of $T^{-1}\partial^2 S_T/\partial\boldsymbol{\beta}\partial\boldsymbol{\beta}'$ can be easily established and, therefore, a cumbersome verification of conditions (4.3.16)–(4.3.19) can be avoided. To illustrate this point, we shall consider the model of Example 4.3.2 again.

EXAMPLE 4.3.3. Consider the model of Example 4.3.2 and, in addition to conditions (i), (ii), and (iii) given there, also assume (iv) $a < \beta_0 < b$ and (v) $\lim_{T\rightarrow\infty} T^{-1}\Sigma_{t=1}^T x_t^4 = r$. Obtain the asymptotic distribution of the value of β that minimizes $\Sigma_{t=1}^T [y_t - (\beta + x_t)^2]^2$ in the domain $(-\infty, \infty)$.

Note that here the minimization is carried out over the whole real line whereas in Example 4.3.2 it was done in the interval $[a, b]$. We denote the unconstrained minimum by $\hat{\beta}$ and the constrained minimum by $\tilde{\beta}$. In Example 4.3.2 we proved plim $\tilde{\beta} = \beta_0$. But, because β_0 is an interior point of $[a, b]$ by assumption (iv), $\lim P[\hat{\beta} = \tilde{\beta}] = 1$; therefore we also have plim $\hat{\beta} = \beta_0$.

Using (4.1.11), we have

$$\sqrt{T}(\hat{\beta} - \beta_0) = -\left[\frac{1}{T}\left.\frac{\partial^2 S_T}{\partial\beta^2}\right|_{\beta^*}\right]^{-1} \frac{1}{\sqrt{T}}\left.\frac{\partial S_T}{\partial\beta}\right|_{\beta_0} \tag{4.3.22}$$

where β^* lies between $\hat{\beta}$ and β_0. We have

$$\frac{1}{\sqrt{T}}\left.\frac{\partial S_T}{\partial\beta}\right|_{\beta_0} = -\frac{4}{\sqrt{T}}\sum_{t=1}^T u_t(\beta_0 + x_t). \tag{4.3.23}$$

Therefore, using assumptions (ii) and (iii) and Theorems 3.5.3 and 3.5.5, we obtain

$$\frac{1}{\sqrt{T}}\left.\frac{\partial S_T}{\partial\beta}\right|_{\beta_0} \rightarrow N[0, 16\sigma_0^2(\beta_0^2 + p + 2\beta_0 q)]. \tag{4.3.24}$$

We also have

$$\frac{1}{T}\left.\frac{\partial^2 S_T}{\partial\beta^2}\right|_{\beta^*} = \frac{8}{T}\sum_{t=1}^T (\beta^* + x_t)^2 - \frac{4}{T}\sum_{t=1}^T [y_t - (\beta^* + x_t)^2]. \tag{4.3.25}$$

Because the right-hand side of (4.3.25) is a continuous function of a finite fixed number of sequences of random variables, we can use Theorem 3.2.6 to evaluate its probability limit. Thus, because plim $\beta^* = \beta_0$, we obtain

$$\text{plim}\,\frac{1}{T}\frac{\partial^2 S_T}{\partial \beta^2}\bigg|_{\beta^*} = 8(\beta_0^2 + p + 2\beta_0 q). \tag{4.3.26}$$

Finally, (4.3.22), (4.3.24), and (4.3.26) imply by Theorem 3.2.7 (iii) that

$$\sqrt{T}(\hat{\beta} - \beta_0) \rightarrow N\left[0, \frac{\sigma_0^2}{4(\beta_0^2 + p + 2\beta_0 q)}\right]. \tag{4.3.27}$$

The distribution of the NLLS estimator may be approximated more accurately by using the Edgeworth expansion (see Pfanzagl, 1973).

4.3.4 Bootstrap and Jacknife Methods

In this subsection, we shall consider briefly two methods of approximating the distribution of the nonlinear least squares estimator; these methods are called the *bootstrap* and the *jackknife* methods (see Efron, 1982, for the details). As the reader will see from the following discussion, they can be applied to many situations other than the nonlinear regression model.

The bootstrap method is carried out in the following steps:

1. Calculate $\hat{u}_t = y_t - f_t(\hat{\boldsymbol{\beta}})$, where $\hat{\boldsymbol{\beta}}$ is the NLLS estimator.
2. Calculate the empirical distribution function F of $\{\hat{u}_t\}$.
3. Generate NT random variables $\{u_{it}^*\}$, $i = 1, 2, \ldots, N$ and $t = 1, 2, \ldots, T$, according to F, and calculate $y_{it}^* = f_t(\hat{\boldsymbol{\beta}}) + u_{it}^*$.
4. Calculate the NLLS estimator $\boldsymbol{\beta}_i^*$ that minimizes

$$\sum_{t=1}^{T} [y_{it}^* - f_t(\boldsymbol{\beta})]^2 \text{ for } i = 1, 2, \ldots, N.$$

5. Approximate the distribution of $\hat{\boldsymbol{\beta}}$ by the empirical distribution function of $\{\boldsymbol{\beta}_i^*\}$.

The jackknife method works as follows: Partition $\mathbf{y}$ as $\mathbf{y}' = (\mathbf{y}_1', \mathbf{y}_2', \ldots, \mathbf{y}_N')$, where each $\mathbf{y}_i$ is an m-vector such that $mN = T$. Let $\hat{\boldsymbol{\beta}}$ be the NLLS estimator using all data and let $\hat{\boldsymbol{\beta}}_{-i}$ be the NLLS estimator obtained by omitting $\mathbf{y}_i$. Then "pseudovalues" $\boldsymbol{\beta}_i^* = N\hat{\boldsymbol{\beta}} - (N-1)\hat{\boldsymbol{\beta}}_{-i}$, $i = 1, 2, \ldots, N$, can be treated like N observations (though not independent) on $\hat{\boldsymbol{\beta}}$. Thus, for example, $V\hat{\boldsymbol{\beta}}$ may be estimated by $(N-1)^{-1} \Sigma_{i=1}^N (\boldsymbol{\beta}_i^* - \bar{\boldsymbol{\beta}}^*)(\boldsymbol{\beta}_i^* - \bar{\boldsymbol{\beta}}^*)'$, where $\bar{\boldsymbol{\beta}}^* = N^{-1}\Sigma_{i=1}^N \boldsymbol{\beta}_i^*$.

It is interesting to note that $\bar{\beta}^*$ may be regarded as an estimator of β in its own right and is called the jackknife estimator. Akahira (1983) showed that in the i.i.d. sample case the jackknife estimator is asymptotically equivalent to the bias-corrected maximum likelihood estimator (see Section 4.2.4) to the order T^{-1}.

4.3.5 Tests of Hypotheses

In the process of proving Theorem 4.3.2, we have in effect shown that asymptotically

$$\hat{\beta}_T - \beta_0 \cong (\mathbf{G}'\mathbf{G})^{-1}\mathbf{G}'\mathbf{u}, \tag{4.3.28}$$

where we have put $\mathbf{G} = (\partial \mathbf{f}/\partial \beta')_{\beta_0}$. Note that (4.3.28) exactly holds in the linear case because then $\mathbf{G} = \mathbf{X}$. The practical consequence of the approximation (4.3.28) is that all the results for the linear regression model (Model 1) are asymptotically valid for the nonlinear regression model if we treat $\mathbf{G}$ as the regressor matrix. (In practice we must use $\hat{\mathbf{G}} \equiv (\partial \mathbf{f}/\partial \beta')_{\hat{\beta}}$, where $\hat{\beta}$ is the NLLS estimator.)

Let us generalize the t and F statistics of the linear model by this principle. If the linear hypothesis $\mathbf{Q}'\beta = c$ consists of a single equation, we can use the following generalization of (1.5.4):

$$\frac{\mathbf{Q}'\hat{\beta} - c}{\tilde{\sigma}[\mathbf{Q}'(\hat{\mathbf{G}}'\hat{\mathbf{G}})^{-1}\mathbf{Q}]^{1/2}} \overset{A}{\sim} t_{T-k}, \tag{4.3.29}$$

where $\overset{A}{\sim}$ means "asymptotically distributed as" and $\tilde{\sigma}^2 = (T-K)^{-1}S_T(\hat{\beta})$. Gallant (1975a) examined the accuracy of the approximation (4.3.29) by a Monte Carlo experiment using the model

$$f_t(\beta) = \beta_1 x_{1t} + \beta_2 x_{2t} + \beta_4 \exp(\beta_3 x_{3t}). \tag{4.3.30}$$

For each of the four parameters, the empirical distribution of the left-hand side of (4.3.29) matched the distribution of t_{T-k} reasonably well, although, as we would suspect, the performance was the poorest for $\hat{\beta}_3$.

If $\mathbf{Q}'\beta = \mathbf{c}$ consists of $q(>1)$ equations, we obtain two different approximate F statistics depending on whether we generalize the formula (1.5.9) or the formula (1.5.12). Generalizing (1.5.9), we obtain

$$\frac{T-K}{q}\,\frac{S_T(\bar{\beta}) - S_T(\hat{\beta})}{S_T(\hat{\beta})} \overset{A}{\sim} F(q, T-k), \tag{4.3.31}$$

where $\bar{\beta}$ is the constrained NLLS estimator obtained by minimizing $S_T(\beta)$

subject to $\mathbf{Q}'\boldsymbol{\beta} = \mathbf{c}$. Generalizing the formula (1.5.12), we obtain

$$\frac{T-K}{q}\frac{(\mathbf{Q}'\hat{\boldsymbol{\beta}}-\mathbf{c})'[\mathbf{Q}'(\hat{\mathbf{G}}'\hat{\mathbf{G}})^{-1}\mathbf{Q}]^{-1}(\mathbf{Q}'\hat{\boldsymbol{\beta}}-\mathbf{c})}{S_T(\hat{\boldsymbol{\beta}})} \overset{A}{\sim} F(q, T-k). \quad (4.3.32)$$

These two formulae were shown to be identical in the linear model, but they are different in the nonlinear model. A Monte Carlo study by Gallant (1975b), using the model (4.3.30), indicated that the test based on (4.3.31) has higher power than the test based on (4.3.32).

4.4 Methods of Iteration

Be it for the maximum likelihood or the nonlinear least squares estimator, we cannot generally solve the equation of the form (4.1.9) explicitly for $\boldsymbol{\theta}$. Instead, we must solve it iteratively: Start from an initial estimate of $\boldsymbol{\theta}$ (say $\hat{\boldsymbol{\theta}}_1$) and obtain a sequence of estimates $\{\hat{\boldsymbol{\theta}}_n\}$ by iteration, which we hope will converge to the global maximum (or minimum) of Q_T or at least a root of Eq. (4.1.9). Numerous iterative methods have been proposed and used. In this section we shall discuss several well-known methods that are especially suitable for obtaining the maximum likelihood and the nonlinear least squares estimator. Many of the results of this section can be found in Goldfeld and Quandt (1972), Draper and Smith (1981), or, more extensively, in Quandt (1983).

4.4.1 Newton-Raphson Method

The Newton-Raphson method is based on the following quadratic approximation of the maximand (or minimand, as the case may be):

$$Q(\theta) \cong Q(\hat{\theta}_1) + \mathbf{g}_1'(\theta - \hat{\theta}_1) + \tfrac{1}{2}(\theta - \hat{\theta}_1)'\mathbf{H}_1(\theta - \hat{\theta}_1), \quad (4.4.1)$$

where $\hat{\theta}_1$ is an initial estimate and

$$\mathbf{g}_1 = \left.\frac{\partial Q}{\partial \theta}\right|_{\hat{\theta}_1} \quad \text{and} \quad \mathbf{H}_1 = \left.\frac{\partial^2 Q}{\partial \theta \partial \theta'}\right|_{\hat{\theta}_1}.$$

The second-round estimator $\hat{\theta}_2$ of the Newton-Raphson iteration is obtained by maximizing the right-hand side of the approximation (4.4.1). Therefore

$$\hat{\theta}_2 = \hat{\theta}_1 - \mathbf{H}_1^{-1}\mathbf{g}_1. \quad (4.4.2)$$

The iteration (4.4.2) is to be repeated until the sequence $\{\hat{\theta}_n\}$ thus obtained converges.

Inserting iteration (4.4.2) back into approximation (4.4.1) yields

$$Q(\hat{\theta}_2) \cong Q(\hat{\theta}_1) - \tfrac{1}{2}(\hat{\theta}_2 - \hat{\theta}_1)'\mathbf{H}_1(\hat{\theta}_2 - \hat{\theta}_1). \tag{4.4.3}$$

Equation (4.4.3) shows a weakness of this method: Even if (4.4.3) holds exactly, $Q(\hat{\theta}_2) > Q(\hat{\theta}_1)$ is not guaranteed unless $\mathbf{H}_1$ is a negative definite matrix. Another weakness is that even if $\mathbf{H}_1$ is negative definite, $\hat{\theta}_2 - \hat{\theta}_1$ may be too large or too small: If it is too large, it overshoots the target; if it is too small, the speed of convergence is slow.

The first weakness may be alleviated if we modify (4.4.2) as

$$\hat{\theta}_2 = \hat{\theta}_1 - (\mathbf{H}_1 - \alpha_1 \mathbf{I})^{-1}\mathbf{g}_1, \tag{4.4.4}$$

where $\mathbf{I}$ is the identity matrix and α_1 is a scalar to be appropriately chosen by the researcher subject to the condition that $\mathbf{H}_1 - \alpha_1\mathbf{I}$ is negative definite. This modification was proposed by Goldfeld, Quandt, and Trotter (1966) and is called *quadratic hill-climbing.* [Goldfeld, Quandt, and Trotter (1966) and Goldfeld and Quandt (1972, Chapter 1) have discussed how to choose α_1 and the convergence properties of the method.]

The second weakness may be remedied by the modification

$$\hat{\theta}_2 = \hat{\theta}_1 - \lambda_1 \mathbf{H}_1^{-1}\mathbf{g}_1, \tag{4.4.5}$$

where the scalar λ_1 is to be appropriately determined. Fletcher and Powell (1963) have presented a method to determined λ_1 by cubic interpolation of $Q(\theta)$ along the current search direction. [This method is called the DFP iteration because Fletcher and Powell refined the method originally proposed by Davidson (1959).] Also, Berndt et al. (1974) have presented another method for choosing λ_1.

The Newton-Raphson method can be used to obtain either the maximum likelihood or the nonlinear least squares estimator by choosing the appropriate Q. In the case of the MLE, $E(\partial^2 \log L/\partial\theta\partial\theta')$ may be substituted for $\partial^2 \log L/\partial\theta\partial\theta'$ in defining $\mathbf{H}$. If this is done, the iteration is called the *method of scoring* (see Rao, 1973, p. 366, or Zacks, 1971, p. 232). In view of Eq. (4.2.22), $-E(\partial \log L/\partial\theta)(\partial \log L/\partial\theta')$ may be used instead; then we need not calculate the second derivatives of log L.

4.4.2 The Asymptotic Properties of the Second-Round Estimator in the Newton-Raphson Method

Ordinarily, iteration (4.4.2) is to be repeated until convergence takes place. However, if $\hat{\theta}_1$ is a consistent estimator of θ_0 such that $\sqrt{T}(\hat{\theta}_1 - \theta_0)$ has a proper limit distribution, the second-round estimator $\hat{\theta}_2$ has the same asymptotic distribution as a consistent root of Eq. (4.1.9). In this case further iteration does not bring any improvement, at least asymptotically. To show this, consider

$$\mathbf{g}_1 = \left.\frac{\partial Q}{\partial \theta}\right|_{\theta_0} + \left.\frac{\partial^2 Q}{\partial \theta \partial \theta'}\right|_{\theta^*} (\hat{\theta}_1 - \theta_0), \tag{4.4.6}$$

where θ^* lies between $\hat{\theta}_1$ and θ_0. Inserting (4.4.6) into (4.4.2) yields

$$\sqrt{T}(\hat{\theta}_2 - \theta_0) = \left\{ \mathbf{I} - \left[\left.\frac{\partial^2 Q}{\partial \theta \partial \theta'}\right|_{\hat{\theta}_1} \right]^{-1} \left[\left.\frac{\partial^2 Q}{\partial \theta \partial \theta'}\right|_{\theta^*} \right] \right\} \sqrt{T}(\hat{\theta}_1 - \theta_0) \tag{4.4.7}$$
$$- \left[\frac{1}{T} \left.\frac{\partial^2 Q}{\partial \theta \partial \theta'}\right|_{\hat{\theta}_1} \right]^{-1} \frac{1}{\sqrt{T}} \left.\frac{\partial Q}{\partial \theta}\right|_{\theta_0}.$$

But, because under the condition of Theorem 4.1.3

$$\operatorname{plim} \frac{1}{T} \left.\frac{\partial^2 Q}{\partial \theta \partial \theta'}\right|_{\hat{\theta}_1} = \operatorname{plim} \frac{1}{T} \left.\frac{\partial^2 Q}{\partial \theta \partial \theta'}\right|_{\theta^*} = \operatorname{plim} \frac{1}{T} \left.\frac{\partial^2 Q}{\partial \theta \partial \theta'}\right|_{\theta_0}, \tag{4.4.8}$$

we have

$$\sqrt{T}(\hat{\theta}_2 - \theta_0) \overset{\text{LD}}{=} - \left[\operatorname{plim} \frac{1}{T} \left.\frac{\partial^2 Q}{\partial \theta \partial \theta'}\right|_{\theta_0} \right]^{-1} \frac{1}{\sqrt{T}} \left.\frac{\partial Q}{\partial \theta}\right|_{\theta_0}, \tag{4.4.9}$$

which proves the desired result.

4.4.3 Gauss-Newton Method

The Gauss-Newton method was specifically designed to calculate the nonlinear least square estimator. Expanding $f_t(\boldsymbol{\beta})$ of Eq. (4.3.5) in a Taylor series around the initial estimate $\hat{\boldsymbol{\beta}}_1$, we obtain

$$f_t(\boldsymbol{\beta}) \cong f_t(\hat{\boldsymbol{\beta}}_1) + \left.\frac{\partial f_t}{\partial \boldsymbol{\beta}'}\right|_{\hat{\boldsymbol{\beta}}_1} (\boldsymbol{\beta} - \hat{\boldsymbol{\beta}}_1). \tag{4.4.10}$$

Substituting the right-hand side of (4.4.10) for $f_t(\boldsymbol{\beta})$ in (4.3.5) yields

$$S \cong \sum_{t=1}^{T} \left[y_t - f_t(\hat{\boldsymbol{\beta}}_1) - \left.\frac{\partial f_t}{\partial \boldsymbol{\beta}'}\right|_{\hat{\boldsymbol{\beta}}_1} (\boldsymbol{\beta} - \hat{\boldsymbol{\beta}}_1) \right]^2. \tag{4.4.11}$$

The second-round estimator $\hat{\boldsymbol{\beta}}_2$ of the Gauss-Newton iteration is obtained by minimizing the right-hand side of approximation (4.4.11) with respect to $\boldsymbol{\beta}$ as

$$\hat{\boldsymbol{\beta}}_2 = \hat{\boldsymbol{\beta}}_1 - \frac{1}{2}\left[\sum_{t=1}^{T} \frac{\partial f_t}{\partial \boldsymbol{\beta}}\bigg|_{\hat{\boldsymbol{\beta}}_1} \frac{\partial f_t}{\partial \boldsymbol{\beta}'}\bigg|_{\hat{\boldsymbol{\beta}}_1}\right]^{-1} \frac{\partial S}{\partial \boldsymbol{\beta}}\bigg|_{\hat{\boldsymbol{\beta}}_1}, \tag{4.4.12}$$

where

$$\frac{\partial S}{\partial \boldsymbol{\beta}}\bigg|_{\hat{\boldsymbol{\beta}}_1} = -2 \sum_{t=1}^{T} [y_t - f_t(\hat{\boldsymbol{\beta}}_1)] \frac{\partial f_t}{\partial \boldsymbol{\beta}}\bigg|_{\hat{\boldsymbol{\beta}}_1}. \tag{4.4.13}$$

The iteration (4.4.12) is to be repeated until convergence is obtained. This method involves only the first derivatives of f_t, whereas the Newton-Raphson iteration applied to nonlinear least squares estimation involves the second derivatives of f_t as well.

The Gauss-Newton iteration may be alternatively motivated as follows: Evaluating the approximation (4.4.10) at $\boldsymbol{\beta}_0$ and inserting it into Eq. (4.3.1), we obtain

$$y_t - f_t(\hat{\boldsymbol{\beta}}_1) + \frac{\partial f_t}{\partial \boldsymbol{\beta}'}\bigg|_{\hat{\boldsymbol{\beta}}_1} \hat{\boldsymbol{\beta}}_1 \cong \frac{\partial f_t}{\partial \boldsymbol{\beta}'}\bigg|_{\hat{\boldsymbol{\beta}}_1} \boldsymbol{\beta}_0 + u_t. \tag{4.4.14}$$

Then the second-round estimator $\hat{\boldsymbol{\beta}}_2$ can be interpreted as the least squares estimate of $\boldsymbol{\beta}_0$ applied to the linear regression equation (4.4.14), treating the whole left-hand side as the dependent variable and $(\partial f_t/\partial \boldsymbol{\beta}')_{\hat{\boldsymbol{\beta}}_1}$ as the vector of independent variables. Equation (4.4.14) reminds us of the point raised at the beginning of Section 4.3.5, namely, the nonlinear regression model asymptotically behaves like a linear regression model if we treat $\partial \mathbf{f}/\partial \boldsymbol{\beta}'$ evaluated at a good estimate of $\boldsymbol{\beta}$ as the regressor matrix.

The Gauss-Newton iteration suffers from weaknesses similar to those of the Newton-Raphson iteration, namely, the possibility of an exact or near singularity of the matrix to be inverted in (4.4.12) and the possibility of too much or too little change from $\hat{\boldsymbol{\beta}}_1$ to $\hat{\boldsymbol{\beta}}_2$.

To deal with the first weakness, Marquardt (1963) proposed a modification

$$\hat{\boldsymbol{\beta}}_2 = \hat{\boldsymbol{\beta}}_1 - \frac{1}{2}\left[\sum_{t=1}^{T} \frac{\partial f_t}{\partial \boldsymbol{\beta}}\bigg|_{\hat{\boldsymbol{\beta}}_1} \frac{\partial f_t}{\partial \boldsymbol{\beta}'}\bigg|_{\hat{\boldsymbol{\beta}}_1} + \alpha_1 \mathbf{I}\right]^{-1} \frac{\partial S}{\partial \boldsymbol{\beta}}\bigg|_{\hat{\boldsymbol{\beta}}_1}, \tag{4.4.15}$$

where α_1 is a positive scalar to be appropriately chosen.

To deal with the second weakness, Hartley (1961) proposed the following modification: First, calculate

$$\Delta_1 = -\frac{1}{2}\left[\sum_{t=1}^{T} \frac{\partial f_t}{\partial \boldsymbol{\beta}}\bigg|_{\hat{\boldsymbol{\beta}}_1} \frac{\partial f_t}{\partial \boldsymbol{\beta}'}\bigg|_{\hat{\boldsymbol{\beta}}_1}\right]^{-1} \frac{\partial S}{\partial \boldsymbol{\beta}}\bigg|_{\hat{\boldsymbol{\beta}}_1} \tag{4.4.16}$$

and, second, choose λ_1 to minimize

$$S(\hat{\boldsymbol{\beta}}_1 + \lambda_1 \boldsymbol{\Delta}_1), \qquad 0 \leqq \lambda_1 \leqq 1. \tag{4.4.17}$$

Hartley proved that under general conditions his iteration converges to a root of Eq. (4.3.6). (Gallant, 1975a, has made useful comments on Marquardt's and Hartley's algorithms.)

As in the Newton-Raphson method, it can be shown that the second-round estimator of the Gauss-Newton iteration is asymptotically as efficient as NLLS if the iteration is started from an estimator $\hat{\boldsymbol{\beta}}_1$ such that $\sqrt{T}(\hat{\boldsymbol{\beta}}_1 - \boldsymbol{\beta}_0)$ converges to a nondegenerate random variable.

Finally, we want to mention several empirical papers in which the Gauss-Newton iteration and related iterative methods have been used. Bodkin and Klein (1967) estimated Cobb-Douglas and CES production functions by the Newton-Raphson method. Charatsis (1971) estimated the CES production function by a modification of the Gauss-Newton method similar to that of Hartley (1961) and found that in 64 out of 74 samples it converged within six iterations. Mizon (1977), in a paper whose major aim was to choose among nine production functions including Cobb-Douglas and CES, used the conjugate gradient method of Powell (1964) (see Quandt, 1983). Mizon's article also contained interesting econometric applications of various statistical techniques we shall discuss in Section 4.5, namely, a comparison of the likelihood ratio and related tests, Akaike information criterion, tests of separate families of hypotheses, and the Box-Cox transformation (Section 8.1.2). Sargent (1978) estimated a rational expectations model (which gives rise to nonlinear constraints among parameters) by the DFP algorithm.

4.5 Asymptotic Tests and Related Topics

4.5.1 Likelihood Ratio and Related Tests

Let $L(\mathbf{x}, \boldsymbol{\theta})$ be the joint density of a T-vector of random variables $\mathbf{x} = (x_1, x_2, \ldots, x_T)'$ characterized by a K-vector of parameters $\boldsymbol{\theta}$. We assume all the conditions used to prove the asymptotic normality (4.2.23) of the maximum likelihood estimator $\hat{\boldsymbol{\theta}}$. In this section we shall discuss the asymptotic tests of the hypothesis

$$\mathbf{h}(\boldsymbol{\theta}) = \mathbf{0}, \tag{4.5.1}$$

where $\mathbf{h}$ is a q-vector valued differentiable function with $q < K$. We assume that (4.5.1) can be equivalently written as

$$\boldsymbol{\theta} = \mathbf{r}(\boldsymbol{\alpha}), \tag{4.5.2}$$

where $\boldsymbol{\alpha}$ is a p-vector of parameters such that $p = K - q$. We denote the constrained maximum likelihood estimator subject to (4.5.1) or (4.5.2) as $\bar{\boldsymbol{\theta}} = \mathbf{r}(\hat{\boldsymbol{\alpha}})$.

Three asymptotic tests of (4.5.1) are well known; they are the *likelihood ratio test* (LRT), *Wald's test* (Wald, 1943), and *Rao's score test* (Rao, 1947). The definitions of their respective test statistics are

$$\text{LRT} = -2 \log \frac{\max\limits_{\mathbf{h}(\boldsymbol{\theta})=\mathbf{0}} L(\boldsymbol{\theta})}{\max L(\boldsymbol{\theta})} = 2[\log L(\hat{\boldsymbol{\theta}}) - \log L(\bar{\boldsymbol{\theta}})], \tag{4.5.3}$$

$$\text{Wald} = -\mathbf{h}(\hat{\boldsymbol{\theta}})' \left\{ \left.\frac{\partial \mathbf{h}}{\partial \boldsymbol{\theta}'}\right|_{\hat{\boldsymbol{\theta}}} \left[\left.\frac{\partial^2 \log L}{\partial \boldsymbol{\theta} \partial \boldsymbol{\theta}'}\right|_{\hat{\boldsymbol{\theta}}} \right]^{-1} \left.\frac{\partial \mathbf{h}'}{\partial \boldsymbol{\theta}}\right|_{\hat{\boldsymbol{\theta}}} \right\}^{-1} \mathbf{h}(\hat{\boldsymbol{\theta}}), \tag{4.5.4}$$

$$\text{Rao} = -\left.\frac{\partial \log L}{\partial \boldsymbol{\theta}'}\right|_{\bar{\boldsymbol{\theta}}} \left[\left.\frac{\partial^2 \log L}{\partial \boldsymbol{\theta} \partial \boldsymbol{\theta}'}\right|_{\bar{\boldsymbol{\theta}}} \right]^{-1} \left.\frac{\partial \log L}{\partial \boldsymbol{\theta}}\right|_{\bar{\boldsymbol{\theta}}}. \tag{4.5.5}$$

Maximization of $\log L$ subject to the constraint (4.5.1) is accomplished by setting the derivative of $\log L - \boldsymbol{\lambda}'\mathbf{h}(\boldsymbol{\theta})$ with respect to $\boldsymbol{\theta}$ and $\boldsymbol{\lambda}$ to $\mathbf{0}$, where $\boldsymbol{\lambda}$ is the vector of Lagrange multipliers. Let the solutions be $\bar{\boldsymbol{\theta}}$ and $\bar{\boldsymbol{\lambda}}$. Then they satisfy

$$\left.\frac{\partial \log L}{\partial \boldsymbol{\theta}}\right|_{\bar{\boldsymbol{\theta}}} = \left.\frac{\partial \mathbf{h}'}{\partial \boldsymbol{\theta}}\right|_{\bar{\boldsymbol{\theta}}} \bar{\boldsymbol{\lambda}}.$$

Inserting this equation into the right-hand side of (4.5.5) yields $\text{Rao} = -\bar{\boldsymbol{\lambda}}'\mathbf{B}\bar{\boldsymbol{\lambda}}$ where

$$\mathbf{B} = \left.\frac{\partial \mathbf{h}}{\partial \boldsymbol{\theta}'}\right|_{\bar{\boldsymbol{\theta}}} \left[\left.\frac{\partial^2 \log L}{\partial \boldsymbol{\theta} \partial \boldsymbol{\theta}'}\right|_{\bar{\boldsymbol{\theta}}} \right]^{-1} \left.\frac{\partial \mathbf{h}'}{\partial \boldsymbol{\theta}}\right|_{\bar{\boldsymbol{\theta}}}.$$

Silvey (1959) showed that $\mathbf{B}^{-1}$ is the asymptotic variance-covariance matrix of $\bar{\boldsymbol{\lambda}}$ and hence called Rao's test the *Lagrange multiplier test.* For a more thorough discussion of the three tests, see Engle (1984).

All three test statistics can be shown to have the same limit distribution, $\chi^2(q)$, under the null hypothesis. In Wald and Rao, $\partial^2 \log L/\partial\boldsymbol{\theta}\partial\boldsymbol{\theta}'$ can be replaced with $T \operatorname{plim} T^{-1}\partial^2 \log L/\partial\boldsymbol{\theta}\partial\boldsymbol{\theta}'$ without affecting the limit distribution. In each test the hypothesis (4.5.1) is to be rejected when the value of the test statistic is large.

We shall prove $\text{LRT} \rightarrow \chi^2(q)$. By a Taylor expansion we have

$$\log L(\boldsymbol{\theta}_0) = \log L(\hat{\boldsymbol{\theta}}) + \left.\frac{\partial \log L}{\partial \boldsymbol{\theta}'}\right|_{\hat{\boldsymbol{\theta}}} (\boldsymbol{\theta}_0 - \hat{\boldsymbol{\theta}}) \tag{4.5.6}$$

$$+ \frac{1}{2} (\boldsymbol{\theta}_0 - \hat{\boldsymbol{\theta}})' \left.\frac{\partial^2 \log L}{\partial \boldsymbol{\theta} \partial \boldsymbol{\theta}'}\right|_{\boldsymbol{\theta}^*} (\boldsymbol{\theta}_0 - \hat{\boldsymbol{\theta}}),$$

where θ^* lies between θ_0 and $\hat{\theta}$. Noting that the second term of the right-hand side of (4.5.6) is $\mathbf{0}$ by the definition of $\hat{\theta}$, we have

$$\log L(\hat{\theta}) - \log L(\theta_0) \overset{\text{LD}}{=} \tfrac{1}{2}T(\hat{\theta} - \theta_0)' \mathcal{I}_\theta (\hat{\theta} - \theta_0), \tag{4.5.7}$$

where we have defined

$$\mathcal{I}_\theta = -\lim E \frac{1}{T} \frac{\partial^2 \log L}{\partial \theta \partial \theta'}\bigg|_{\theta_0}. \tag{4.5.8}$$

Treating $L[\mathbf{r}(\boldsymbol{\alpha})] \equiv L(\boldsymbol{\alpha})$ as a function of $\boldsymbol{\alpha}$, we similarly obtain

$$\log L(\hat{\boldsymbol{\alpha}}) - \log L(\boldsymbol{\alpha}_0) \overset{\text{LD}}{=} \tfrac{1}{2}T(\hat{\boldsymbol{\alpha}} - \boldsymbol{\alpha}_0)' \mathcal{I}_\alpha (\hat{\boldsymbol{\alpha}} - \boldsymbol{\alpha}_0), \tag{4.5.9}$$

where

$$\mathcal{I}_\alpha = -\lim E \frac{1}{T} \frac{\partial^2 \log L}{\partial \boldsymbol{\alpha} \partial \boldsymbol{\alpha}'}\bigg|_{\boldsymbol{\alpha}_0}. \tag{4.5.10}$$

Noting $L(\theta_0) = L(\boldsymbol{\alpha}_0)$, we have from (4.5.3), (4.5.7), and (4.5.9)

$$\text{LRT} \overset{\text{LD}}{=} T(\hat{\theta} - \theta_0)' \mathcal{I}_\theta (\hat{\theta} - \theta_0) - T(\hat{\boldsymbol{\alpha}} - \boldsymbol{\alpha}_0)' \mathcal{I}_\alpha (\hat{\boldsymbol{\alpha}} - \boldsymbol{\alpha}_0). \tag{4.5.11}$$

But from Theorem 4.1.3 and its proof we have

$$\sqrt{T}(\hat{\theta} - \theta_0) \overset{\text{LD}}{=} \mathcal{I}_\theta^{-1} \frac{1}{\sqrt{T}} \frac{\partial \log L}{\partial \theta}\bigg|_{\theta_0} \tag{4.5.12}$$

and

$$\sqrt{T}(\hat{\boldsymbol{\alpha}} - \boldsymbol{\alpha}_0) \overset{\text{LD}}{=} \mathcal{I}_\alpha^{-1} \frac{1}{\sqrt{T}} \frac{\partial \log L}{\partial \boldsymbol{\alpha}}\bigg|_{\boldsymbol{\alpha}_0}. \tag{4.5.13}$$

Since

$$\frac{1}{\sqrt{T}} \frac{\partial \log L}{\partial \boldsymbol{\alpha}}\bigg|_{\boldsymbol{\alpha}_0} = \mathbf{R}' \frac{1}{\sqrt{T}} \frac{\partial \log L}{\partial \theta}\bigg|_{\theta_0}, \tag{4.5.14}$$

where $\mathbf{R} = (\partial \mathbf{r}/\partial \boldsymbol{\alpha}')_{\boldsymbol{\alpha}_0}$, and

$$\frac{1}{\sqrt{T}} \frac{\partial \log L}{\partial \theta}\bigg|_{\theta_0} \rightarrow N(\mathbf{0}, \mathcal{I}_\theta), \tag{4.5.15}$$

we have from (4.5.11)–(4.5.15)

$$\text{LRT} \overset{\text{LD}}{=} \mathbf{u}'(\mathcal{I}_\theta^{-1} - \mathbf{R}\mathcal{I}_\alpha^{-1}\mathbf{R}')\mathbf{u}, \tag{4.5.16}$$

where $\mathbf{u} \sim N(\mathbf{0}, \mathcal{I}_\theta)$. Finally, defining

$$\boldsymbol{\epsilon} = \mathcal{I}_\theta^{-1/2}\mathbf{u} \sim N(\mathbf{0}, \mathbf{I}), \tag{4.5.17}$$

we obtain

$$\text{LRT} \stackrel{\text{LD}}{=} \boldsymbol{\epsilon}'(\mathbf{I} - \mathcal{I}_\theta^{1/2}\mathbf{R}\mathcal{I}_\alpha^{-1}\mathbf{R}'\mathcal{I}_\theta^{1/2})\boldsymbol{\epsilon}. \tag{4.5.18}$$

But, because

$$\mathcal{I}_\alpha = \mathbf{R}'\mathcal{I}_\theta\mathbf{R}, \tag{4.5.19}$$

$\mathbf{I} - \mathcal{I}_\theta^{1/2}\mathbf{R}\mathcal{I}_\alpha^{-1}\mathbf{R}'\mathcal{I}_\theta^{1/2}$ can be easily shown to be an idempotent matrix of rank q. Therefore, by Theorem 2 of Appendix 2, LRT $\rightarrow \chi^2(q)$.

The proof of Wald $\rightarrow \chi^2(q)$ and Rao $\rightarrow \chi^2(q)$ are omitted; the former is very easy and the latter is as involved as the preceding proof.

Next we shall find explicit formulae for the three tests (4.5.3), (4.5.4), and (4.5.5) for the nonlinear regression model (4.3.1) when the error $\mathbf{u}$ is normal. Let $\hat{\boldsymbol{\beta}}$ be the NLLS estimator of $\boldsymbol{\beta}_0$ and let $\bar{\boldsymbol{\beta}}$ be the constrained NLLS, that is, the value of $\boldsymbol{\beta}$ that minimizes (4.3.5) subject to the constraint $\mathbf{h}(\boldsymbol{\beta}) = \mathbf{0}$. Also, define $\hat{\mathbf{G}} = (\partial\mathbf{f}/\partial\boldsymbol{\beta}')_{\hat{\boldsymbol{\beta}}}$ and $\bar{\mathbf{G}} = (\partial\mathbf{f}/\partial\boldsymbol{\beta}')_{\bar{\boldsymbol{\beta}}}$. Then the three test statistics are defined as

$$\text{LRT} = T[\log T^{-1}S_T(\bar{\boldsymbol{\beta}}) - \log T^{-1}S_T(\hat{\boldsymbol{\beta}})], \tag{4.5.20}$$

$$\text{Wald} = \frac{T\mathbf{h}(\hat{\boldsymbol{\beta}})'\left[\left.\frac{\partial\mathbf{h}}{\partial\boldsymbol{\beta}'}\right|_{\hat{\boldsymbol{\beta}}}(\hat{\mathbf{G}}'\hat{\mathbf{G}})^{-1}\left.\frac{\partial\mathbf{h}'}{\partial\boldsymbol{\beta}}\right|_{\hat{\boldsymbol{\beta}}}\right]^{-1}\mathbf{h}(\hat{\boldsymbol{\beta}})}{S_T(\hat{\boldsymbol{\beta}})}, \tag{4.5.21}$$

and

$$\text{Rao} = \frac{T[\mathbf{y} - \mathbf{f}(\bar{\boldsymbol{\beta}})]'\bar{\mathbf{G}}(\bar{\mathbf{G}}'\bar{\mathbf{G}})^{-1}\bar{\mathbf{G}}'[\mathbf{y} - \mathbf{f}(\bar{\boldsymbol{\beta}})]}{S_T(\bar{\boldsymbol{\beta}})}. \tag{4.5.22}$$

Because (4.5.20), (4.5.21), and (4.5.22) are special cases of (4.5.3), (4.5.4), and (4.5.5), all three statistics are asymptotically distributed as $\chi^2(q)$ under the null hypothesis if $\mathbf{u}$ is normal.[10] Furthermore, we can show that statistics (4.5.20), (4.5.21), and (4.5.22) are asymptotically distributed as $\chi^2(q)$ under the null even if $\mathbf{u}$ is not normal. Thus these statistics can be used to test a nonlinear hypothesis under a nonnormal situation.

In the linear model with linear hypothesis $\mathbf{Q}'\boldsymbol{\beta} = \mathbf{0}$, statistics (4.5.20)–(4.5.22) are further reduced to

$$\text{LRT} = T\log[S_T(\bar{\boldsymbol{\beta}})/S_T(\hat{\boldsymbol{\beta}})], \tag{4.5.23}$$

$$\text{Wald} = T[S_T(\bar{\boldsymbol{\beta}}) - S_T(\hat{\boldsymbol{\beta}})]/S_T(\hat{\boldsymbol{\beta}}), \tag{4.5.24}$$

and

$$\text{Rao} = T[S_T(\bar{\boldsymbol{\beta}}) - S_T(\hat{\boldsymbol{\beta}})]/S_T(\bar{\boldsymbol{\beta}}). \tag{4.5.25}$$

Thus we can easily show Wald $\geqq$ LRT $\geqq$ Rao. The inequalities hold also in the multiequation linear model, as shown by Berndt and Savin (1977). Although the inequalities do not always hold for the nonlinear model, Mizon (1977) found Wald $\geqq$ LRT most of the time in his samples.

Gallant and Holly (1980) obtained the asymptotic distribution of the three statistics under local alternative hypotheses in a nonlinear simultaneous equations model. Translated into the nonlinear regression model, their results can be stated as follows: If there exists a sequence of true values $\{\boldsymbol{\beta}_0^T\}$ such that $\lim \boldsymbol{\beta}_0^T = \boldsymbol{\beta}_0$ and $\boldsymbol{\delta} \equiv \lim T^{1/2}(\boldsymbol{\beta}_0^T - \text{plim}\, \bar{\boldsymbol{\beta}})$ is finite, statistics (4.5.20), (4.5.21), and (4.5.22) converge to chi-square with q degrees of freedom and noncentrality parameter λ, where

$$\lambda = \sigma_0^{-2}\boldsymbol{\delta}' \left.\frac{\partial \mathbf{h}'}{\partial \boldsymbol{\beta}}\right|_{\boldsymbol{\beta}_0} \left[\left.\frac{\partial \mathbf{h}}{\partial \boldsymbol{\beta}'}\right|_{\boldsymbol{\beta}_0} (\mathbf{G}'\mathbf{G})^{-1} \left.\frac{\partial \mathbf{h}'}{\partial \boldsymbol{\beta}}\right|_{\boldsymbol{\beta}_0} \right]^{-1} \left.\frac{\partial \mathbf{h}}{\partial \boldsymbol{\beta}'}\right|_{\boldsymbol{\beta}_0} \boldsymbol{\delta}. \tag{4.5.26}$$

Note that if $\boldsymbol{\xi}$ is distributed as a q-vector $N(\mathbf{0}, \mathbf{V})$, then $(\boldsymbol{\xi} + \boldsymbol{\mu})'\mathbf{V}^{-1}(\boldsymbol{\xi} + \boldsymbol{\mu})$ is distributed as chi-square with q degrees of freedom and noncentrality parameter $\boldsymbol{\mu}'\mathbf{V}^{-1}\boldsymbol{\mu}$. In other words, the asymptotic local power of the tests based on the three statistics is the same.

There appear to be only a few studies of the small sample properties of the three tests, some of which are quoted in Breusch and Pagan (1980). No clear-cut ranking of the tests emerged from these studies.

A generalization of the Wald statistic can be used to test the hypothesis (4.5.1), even in a situation where the likelihood function is unspecified, as long as an asymptotically normal estimator $\tilde{\boldsymbol{\beta}}$ of $\boldsymbol{\beta}$ is available. Suppose $\tilde{\boldsymbol{\beta}}$ is asymptotically distributed as $N(\boldsymbol{\beta}, \mathbf{V})$ under the null hypothesis, with $\mathbf{V}$ estimated consistently by $\hat{\mathbf{V}}$. Then the generalized Wald statistic is defined by

$$\text{G.W.} = \mathbf{h}(\tilde{\boldsymbol{\beta}})' \left[\left.\frac{\partial \mathbf{h}}{\partial \boldsymbol{\beta}'}\right|_{\tilde{\boldsymbol{\beta}}} \hat{\mathbf{V}} \left.\frac{\partial \mathbf{h}'}{\partial \boldsymbol{\beta}}\right|_{\tilde{\boldsymbol{\beta}}} \right]^{-1} \mathbf{h}(\tilde{\boldsymbol{\beta}}) \tag{4.5.27}$$

and is asymptotically distributed as $\chi^2(q)$ under the null hypothesis. Note that (4.5.21) is a special case of (4.5.27).

Another related asymptotic test is the specification test of Hausman (1978). It can be used to test a more general hypothesis than (4.5.1). The only requirement of the test is that we have an estimator, usually a maximum likelihood estimator, that is asymptotically efficient under the null hypothesis but loses consistency under an alternative hypothesis and another estimator that is asymptotically less efficient than the first under the null hypothesis but remains consistent under an alternative hypothesis. If we denote the first estimator by $\hat{\theta}$ and the second by $\tilde{\theta}$, the Hausman test statistic is defined by $(\hat{\theta}-\tilde{\theta})'\hat{\mathbf{V}}^{-1}(\hat{\theta}-\tilde{\theta})$, where $\hat{\mathbf{V}}$ is a consistent estimator of the asymptotic variance-covariance matrix of $(\hat{\theta}-\tilde{\theta})$. Under the null hypothesis it is asymptotically distributed as chi-square with degrees of freedom equal to the dimension of the vector θ.

If we denote the asymptotic variance-covariance matrix by $\mathbf{V}$, it is well known that $\mathbf{V}(\hat{\theta}-\tilde{\theta})=\mathbf{V}(\tilde{\theta})-\mathbf{V}(\hat{\theta})$. This equality follows from $\mathbf{V}(\hat{\theta})=\mathbf{V}_{12}$, where $\mathbf{V}_{12}$ is the asymptotic covariance between $\hat{\theta}$ and $\tilde{\theta}$. To verify this equality, note that if it did not hold, we could define a new estimator $\hat{\theta}+[\mathbf{V}(\hat{\theta})-\mathbf{V}_{12}][\mathbf{V}(\hat{\theta}-\tilde{\theta})]^{-1}(\tilde{\theta}-\hat{\theta})$, the asymptotic variance-covariance matrix of which is $\mathbf{V}(\hat{\theta})-[\mathbf{V}(\hat{\theta})-\mathbf{V}_{12}][\mathbf{V}(\hat{\theta}-\tilde{\theta})]^{-1}[\mathbf{V}(\hat{\theta})-\mathbf{V}_{12}]'$, which is smaller (in the matrix sense) than $\mathbf{V}(\hat{\theta})$. But this is a contradiction because $\hat{\theta}$ is asymptotically efficient by assumption.

4.5.2 Akaike Information Criterion

The Akaike information criterion in the context of the linear regression model was mentioned in Section 2.1.5. Here we shall consider it in a more general setting. Suppose we want to test the hypothesis (4.5.2) on the basis of the likelihood ratio test (4.5.3). It means that we choose $L(\theta)$ over $L(\alpha)$ if

$$\text{LRT} > d, \tag{4.5.28}$$

where d is determined so that $P[\text{LRT} > d|L(\alpha)] = c$, a certain prescribed constant such as 5%. However, if we must choose one model out of many competing models $L(\alpha_1)$, $L(\alpha_2)$, . . . , this classical testing procedure is at best time consuming and at worst inconclusive. Akaike (1973) proposed a simple procedure that enables us to solve this kind of model-selection problem. Here we shall give only a brief account; for the full details the reader is referred to Akaike's original article or to Amemiya (1980a).

We can write a typical member of the many competing models $L(\alpha_1)$, $L(\alpha_2)$, . . . as $L(\alpha)$. Akaike proposed the loss function

$$W(\theta_0, \hat{\alpha}) = -\frac{2}{T}\int \left[\log \frac{L(\hat{\alpha})}{L(\theta_0)}\right] L(\theta_0)\, d\mathbf{x}, \tag{4.5.29}$$

where $\hat{\alpha}$ is treated as a constant in the integration. Because $W(\theta_0, \hat{\alpha}) \geqq W(\theta_0, \theta_0) = 0$, (4.5.29) can serve as a reasonable loss function that is to be minimized among the competing models. However, because W depends on the unknown parameters θ_0, a predictor of W must be used instead. After rather complicated algebraic manipulation, Akaike arrived at the following simple predictor of W, which he called the *Akaike Information Criterion* (AIC):

$$\text{AIC} = -\frac{2}{T} \log L(\hat{\boldsymbol{\alpha}}) + \frac{2p}{T}, \tag{4.5.30}$$

where p is the dimension of the vector $\boldsymbol{\alpha}$. The idea is to choose the model for which AIC is smallest. Akaike's explanation regarding why AIC (plus a certain omitted term that does not depend on $\hat{\boldsymbol{\alpha}}$ or p) may be regarded as a good predictor of W is not entirely convincing. Nevertheless, many empirical researchers think that AIC serves as a satisfactory guideline for selecting a model.

4.5.3 Tests of Separate Families of Hypotheses

So far we have considered testing or choosing hypotheses on parameters within one family of models or likelihood functions. The procedures discussed in the preceding sections cannot be used to choose between two entirely different likelihood functions, say $L_f(\theta)$ and $L_g(\gamma)$. For example, this case arises when we must decide whether a particular sample comes from a lognormal or a gamma population. Such models, which do not belong to a single parametric family of models, are called *nonnested models.*

Suppose we want to test the null hypothesis L_f against the alternative L_g. Cox (1961, 1962) proposed the test statistic

$$\begin{aligned} R_f = \log L_f(\hat{\theta}) - [E_\theta \log L_f(\theta)]_{\hat{\theta}} - \log L_g(\hat{\gamma}) \\ + [E_\theta \log L_g(\gamma_\theta)]_{\hat{\theta}}, \end{aligned} \tag{4.5.31}$$

where $\gamma_\theta = \text{plim}_\theta \, \hat{\gamma}$ (meaning the probability limit is taken assuming $L_f(\theta)$ is the true model) and ^ indicates maximum likelihood estimates. We are to accept L_f if R_f is larger than a critical value determined by the asymptotic distribution of R_f. Cox proved that R_f is asymptotically normal with zero mean and variance equal to $E(v_f^2) - E(v_f \mathbf{w}_f')(E\mathbf{w}_f\mathbf{w}_f')^{-1}E(v_f\mathbf{w}_f)$, where $v_f = \log L_f(\theta) - \log L_g(\gamma_\theta) - E_\theta[\log L_f(\theta) - \log L_g(\gamma_\theta)]$ and $\mathbf{w}_f = \partial \log L_f(\theta)/\partial\theta$. Amemiya (1973b) has presented a more rigorous derivation of the asymptotic distribution of R_f.

A weakness of Cox's test is its inherent asymmetry; the test of L_f against L_g based on R_f may contradict the test of L_g against L_f based on the analogous test statistic R_g. For example, L_f may be rejected by R_f and at the same time L_g may be rejected by R_g.

Pesaran (1982) compared the power of the Cox test and other related tests. For other recent references on the subject of nonnested models in general, see White (1983).

4.6 Least Absolute Deviations Estimator

The practical importance of the least absolute deviations (LAD) estimator as a robust estimator was noted in Section 2.3. Besides its practical importance, the LAD estimator poses an interesting theoretical problem because the general results of Section 4.1 can be used to prove only the consistency of the LAD estimator but not its asymptotic normality, even though the LAD estimator is an extremum estimator. In Section 4.6.1 we shall prove the asymptotic normality of the median, which is the LAD estimator in the i.i.d. sample case, using a method different from the method of Section 4.1.2 and shall point out why the latter method fails in this case. In Section 4.6.2 we shall use the general results of Section 4.1.1 to prove the consistency of the LAD estimator in a regression model. Finally, in Section 4.6.3 we shall indicate what lines of proof of asymptotic normality may be used for the LAD estimator in a regression model.

The cases where the general asymptotic results of Section 4.1 cannot be wholly used may be referred to as nonregular cases. Besides the LAD estimator, we have already noted some nonregular cases in Section 4.2.3 and will encounter more in Sections 9.5 and 9.6. It is hoped that the methods outlined in the present section may prove useful for dealing with unsolved problems in other nonregular cases.

4.6.1 Asymptotic Normality of the Median

Let $\{Y_t\}$, $t = 1, 2, \ldots, T$, be a sequence of i.i.d. random variables with common distribution function F and density function f. The *population median* M is defined by

$$F(M) = \frac{1}{2}. \tag{4.6.1}$$

We assume F to be such that M is uniquely determined by (4.6.1), which follows from assuming $f(y) > 0$ in the neighborhood of $y = M$. We also assume that $f'(y)$ exists for $y > M$ in a neighborhood of M. Define the binary random variable $W_t(\alpha)$ by

$$W_t(\alpha) = 1 \quad \text{if} \quad Y_t \geqq \alpha \tag{4.6.2}$$
$$\quad = 0 \quad \text{if} \quad Y_t < \alpha$$

for every real number α. Using (4.6.2), we define the *sample median* m_T by

$$m_T = \inf \left\{ \alpha \,\middle|\, \sum_{t=1}^{T} W_t(\alpha) \leqq \frac{T}{2} \right\}. \tag{4.6.3}$$

The median as defined above is clearly unique.[11]

The asymptotic normality of m_T can be proved in the following manner: Using (4.6.3), we have for any y

$$P(m_T < M + T^{-1/2}y) = P\left[\sum_{t=1}^{T} W_t(M + T^{-1/2}y) \leqq \frac{T}{2} \right]. \tag{4.6.4}$$

Define

$$P_t = 1 - P(Y_t < M + T^{-1/2}y).$$

Then, because by a Taylor expansion

$$P_t = \frac{1}{2} - T^{-1/2}f(M)y - O(T^{-1}), \tag{4.6.5}$$

we have

$$P\left(\sum_{t=1}^{T} W_t^* \leqq \frac{T}{2} \right) = P[Z_T + O(T^{-1/2}) \leqq f(M)y], \tag{4.6.6}$$

where $W_t^* = W_t(M + T^{-1/2}y)$ and $Z_T = T^{-1/2}\Sigma_{t=1}^{T}(W_t^* - P_t)$. We now derive the limit distribution of Z_T using the characteristic function (Definition 3.3.1). We have

$$\begin{aligned} E \exp(i\lambda Z_T) &= \prod_{t=1}^{T} E \exp[i\lambda T^{-1/2}(W_t^* - P_t)] \\ &= \prod_{t=1}^{T} \{P_t \exp[i\lambda T^{-1/2}(1 - P_t)] \\ &\quad + (1 - P_t) \exp(-i\lambda T^{-1/2}P_t)\} \\ &= \left[1 - \frac{\lambda^2}{8T} + o(T^{-1}) \right]^T \\ &\to \exp(-\lambda^2/8), \end{aligned} \tag{4.6.7}$$

where the third equality above is based on (4.6.5) and the expansion of the exponent: $e^x = 1 + x + 2^{-1}x^2 + \ldots$. Therefore $Z_T \to N(0, 4^{-1})$, which implies by Theorem 3.2.7

$$Z_T + O(T^{-1/2}) \to N(0, 4^{-1}). \tag{4.6.8}$$

Finally, from (4.6.4), (4.6.6), and (4.6.8), we have proved

$$\sqrt{T}(m_T - M) \to N[0, 4^{-1}f(M)^{-2}]. \tag{4.6.9}$$

The consistency of m_T follows from statement (4.6.9). However, it also can be proved by a direct application of Theorem 4.1.1. Let $\overline{m}_T$ be the set of the θ points that minimize[12]

$$S_T = \sum_{t=1}^{T} |Y_t - \theta| - \sum_{t=1}^{T} |Y_t - M|. \tag{4.6.10}$$

Then, clearly, $m_T \in \overline{m}_T$. We have

$$Q \equiv \text{plim } T^{-1}S_T = \theta + 2 \int_{\theta}^{M} \lambda f(\lambda)\, d\lambda - 2\theta \int_{\theta}^{\infty} f(\lambda)\, d\lambda, \tag{4.6.11}$$

where the convergence can be shown to be uniform in θ. The derivation of (4.6.11) and the uniform convergence will be shown for a regression model, for which the present i.i.d. model is a special case, in the next subsection. Because

$$\frac{\partial Q}{\partial \theta} = -1 + 2F(\theta) \tag{4.6.12}$$

and

$$\frac{\partial^2 Q}{\partial \theta^2} = 2f(\theta), \tag{4.6.13}$$

we conclude that Q is uniquely minimized at $\theta = M$ and hence m_T is consistent by Theorem 4.1.1.

Next, we shall consider two complications that prevent us from proving the asymptotic normality of the median by using Theorem 4.1.3: One is that $\partial S_T/\partial\theta = 0$ may have no roots and the other is that $\partial^2 S_T/\partial\theta^2 = 0$ except for a finite number of points. These statements are illustrated in Figure 4.2, which depicts two typical shapes of S_T.

Despite these complications, assumption C of Theorem 4.1.3 is still valid if we interpret the derivative to mean the left derivative. That is to say, define for $\Delta > 0$

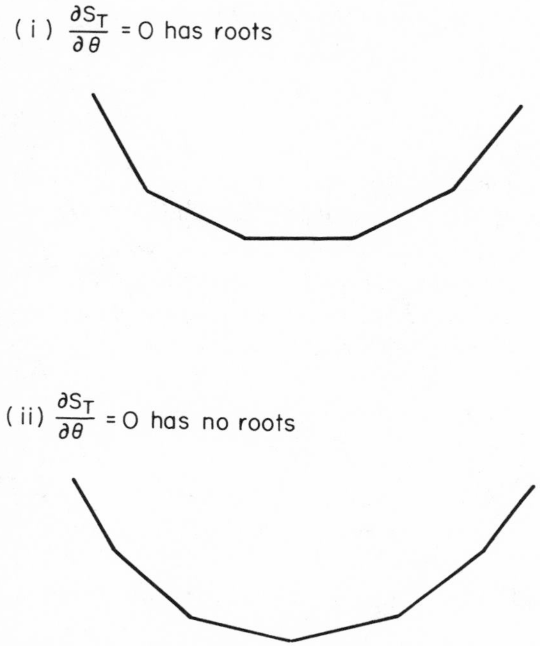

Figure 4.2 Complications proving the asymptotic normality of the median

$$\frac{\partial S_T}{\partial \theta} = \lim_{\Delta \to 0} \frac{S_T(\theta) - S_T(\theta - \Delta)}{\Delta}. \tag{4.6.14}$$

Then, from (4.6.10), we obtain

$$\left.\frac{\partial S_T}{\partial \theta}\right|_M = \sum_{t=1}^{T} [1 - 2W_t(M)]. \tag{4.6.15}$$

Because $\{W_t(M)\}$ are i.i.d. with mean $\frac{1}{2}$ and variance $\frac{1}{4}$, we have by Theorem 3.3.4 (Lindeberg-Lévy CLT)

$$\frac{1}{\sqrt{T}} \left.\frac{\partial S_T}{\partial \theta}\right|_M \rightarrow N(0, 1). \tag{4.6.16}$$

Assumption B of Theorem 4.1.3 does not hold because $\partial^2 S_T/\partial \theta^2 = 0$ for almost every θ. But, if we substitute $[\partial^2 Q/\partial \theta^2]_M$ for plim $T^{-1}[\partial^2 S_T/\partial \theta^2]_M$ in assumption B of Theorem 4.1.3, the conclusion of the theorem yields exactly the right result (4.6.9) because of (4.6.13) and (4.6.16).

4.6.2 Consistency of Least Absolute Deviations Estimator

Consider a classical regression model

$$\mathbf{y} = \mathbf{X}\boldsymbol{\beta}_0 + \mathbf{u}, \tag{4.6.17}$$

where $\mathbf{X}$ is a $T \times K$ matrix of bounded constants such that $\lim_{T\to\infty} T^{-1}\mathbf{X}'\mathbf{X}$ is a finite positive-definite matrix and $\mathbf{u}$ is a T-vector of i.i.d. random variables with continuous density function $f(\cdot)$ such that $\int_0^\infty f(\lambda)\, d\lambda = \frac{1}{2}$ and $f(x) > 0$ for all x in a neighborhood of 0. It is assumed that the parameter space B is compact. We also assume that the empirical distribution function of the rows of $\mathbf{X}$, $\{\mathbf{x}_t'\}$, converges to a distribution function. The LAD estimator $\hat{\boldsymbol{\beta}}$ is defined to be a value of $\boldsymbol{\beta}$ that minimizes

$$S_T = \sum_{t=1}^{T} |y_t - \mathbf{x}_t'\boldsymbol{\beta}| - \sum_{t=1}^{T} |u_t|. \tag{4.6.18}$$

This is a generalization of (4.6.10). Like the median, the LAD estimator may not be unique.

We shall now prove the consistency of the LAD estimator using Theorem 4.1.1. From (4.6.18) we have

$$S_T = \sum_{t=1}^{T} h(u_t|\mathbf{x}_t'\boldsymbol{\delta}), \tag{4.6.19}$$

where $\boldsymbol{\delta} = \boldsymbol{\beta} - \boldsymbol{\beta}_0$ and $h(z|\alpha)$ is defined as

$$\begin{aligned}
\text{If } \alpha \geqq 0, \quad h(z|\alpha) &= \alpha && \text{if } z \leqq 0 \\
&= \alpha - 2z && \text{if } 0 < z < \alpha \\
&= -\alpha && \text{if } z \geqq \alpha. \\
\text{If } \alpha < 0, \quad h(z|\alpha) &= \alpha && \text{if } z \leqq \alpha \\
&= -\alpha + 2z && \text{if } \alpha < z < 0 \\
&= -\alpha && \text{if } z \geqq 0.
\end{aligned} \tag{4.6.20}$$

Then $h(z|\mathbf{x}_t'\boldsymbol{\delta})$ is a continuous function of $\boldsymbol{\delta}$ uniformly in t and is uniformly bounded in t and $\boldsymbol{\delta}$ by our assumptions. Therefore $h(u_t|\mathbf{x}_t'\boldsymbol{\delta}) - Eh(u_t|\mathbf{x}_t'\boldsymbol{\delta})$ satisfies the conditions for $g_t(\mathbf{y}, \boldsymbol{\theta})$ in Theorem 4.2.2. Moreover, $\lim_{T=\infty} T^{-1} \Sigma_{t=1}^{T} Eh(u_t|\mathbf{x}_t'\boldsymbol{\delta})$ can be shown to exist by Theorem 4.2.3. Therefore

$$
\begin{aligned}
Q &\equiv \text{plim } T^{-1}S_T \qquad (4.6.21)\\
&= 2 \lim_{T\to\infty} \frac{1}{T} \sum_{t=1}^{T} \int_{\mathbf{x}_t'\boldsymbol{\delta}}^{0} \lambda f(\lambda)\, d\lambda \\
&\quad - 2 \lim_{T\to\infty} \frac{1}{T} \sum_{t=1}^{T} \left[\int_{\mathbf{x}_t'\boldsymbol{\delta}}^{\infty} f(\lambda)\, d\lambda \cdot \mathbf{x}_t'\boldsymbol{\delta} \right] + \lim_{T\to\infty} \frac{1}{T} \sum_{t=1}^{T} \mathbf{x}_t'\boldsymbol{\delta},
\end{aligned}
$$

where the convergence of each term is uniform in $\boldsymbol{\delta}$ by Theorem 4.2.3.

Thus it only remains to show that Q attains a global minimum at $\boldsymbol{\delta} = \mathbf{0}$. Differentiating (4.6.21) with respect to $\boldsymbol{\delta}$ yields

$$
\frac{\partial Q}{\partial \boldsymbol{\delta}} = -2 \lim \sum_{t=1}^{T} \frac{1}{T} \left[\int_{\mathbf{x}_t'\boldsymbol{\delta}}^{\infty} f(\lambda)\, d\lambda \cdot \mathbf{x}_t \right] + \lim \frac{1}{T} \sum_{t=1}^{T} \mathbf{x}_t, \qquad (4.6.22)
$$

which is equal to $\mathbf{0}$ at $\boldsymbol{\delta} = \mathbf{0}$ because $\int_0^\infty f(\lambda)\, d\lambda = \frac{1}{2}$ by our assumption. Moreover, because

$$
\frac{\partial^2 Q}{\partial \boldsymbol{\delta} \partial \boldsymbol{\delta}'} = 2 \lim \frac{1}{T} \sum_{t=1}^{T} f(\mathbf{x}_t'\boldsymbol{\delta})\mathbf{x}_t\mathbf{x}_t' \qquad (4.6.23)
$$

is positive definite at $\boldsymbol{\delta} = \mathbf{0}$ because of our assumptions, Q attains a local minimum at $\boldsymbol{\delta} = \mathbf{0}$. Next we shall show that this local minimum is indeed the global minimum by showing that $\partial Q/\partial \boldsymbol{\delta} \neq \mathbf{0}$ if $\boldsymbol{\delta} \neq \mathbf{0}$. Suppose $\partial Q/\partial \boldsymbol{\delta} = \mathbf{0}$ at $\boldsymbol{\delta}_1 \neq \mathbf{0}$. Then, evaluating (4.6.22) at $\boldsymbol{\delta}_1$ and premultiplying it by $\boldsymbol{\delta}_1'$, we obtain

$$
\lim \frac{1}{T} \sum_{t=1}^{T} \left[\frac{1}{2} - \int_{\mathbf{x}_t'\boldsymbol{\delta}_1}^{\infty} f(\lambda)\, d\lambda \right] \mathbf{x}_t'\boldsymbol{\delta}_1 = 0. \qquad (4.6.24)
$$

To show (4.6.24) is a contradiction, let a_1, a_2, and M be positive real numbers such that $|\mathbf{x}_t'\boldsymbol{\delta}_1| < M$ for all t and $f(\lambda) \geqq a_1$ whenever $|\lambda| \leqq a_2$. Such numbers exist because of our assumptions. Then we have

$$
\begin{aligned}
\sum_{t=1}^{T} \left[\frac{1}{2} - \int_{\mathbf{x}_t'\boldsymbol{\delta}_1}^{\infty} f(\lambda)\, d\lambda \right] \mathbf{x}_t'\boldsymbol{\delta}_1 &= \sum_{t=1}^{T} \left| \frac{1}{2} - \int_{\mathbf{x}_t'\boldsymbol{\delta}_1}^{\infty} f(\lambda)\, d\lambda \right| |\mathbf{x}_t'\boldsymbol{\delta}_1| \qquad (4.6.25)\\
&\geqq \frac{a_1 a_2}{M} \boldsymbol{\delta}_1'\mathbf{X}'\mathbf{X}\boldsymbol{\delta}_1 .
\end{aligned}
$$

Therefore (4.6.24) is a contradiction because of our assumption that $\lim T^{-1}\mathbf{X}'\mathbf{X}$ is positive definite. This completes the proof of the consistency of the LAD estimator by means of Theorem 4.1.1.

4.6.3 Asymptotic Normality of Least Absolute Deviations Estimator

As noted in Section 4.6.1, the asymptotic normality of LAD cannot be proved by means of Theorem 4.1.3; nor is the proof of Section 4.6.1 easily generalizable to the regression case. We shall give a brief outline of a proof of asymptotic normality. The interested reader should refer to Koenker and Bassett (1982) and the references of that article.[13]

The asymptotic normality of the LAD estimator $\hat{\boldsymbol{\beta}}$ is based on the following three fundamental results:

$$\frac{1}{\sqrt{T}} \sum_{t=1}^{T} \mathbf{x}_t \psi(y_t - \mathbf{x}_t'\hat{\boldsymbol{\beta}}) \xrightarrow{\text{a.s.}} \mathbf{0}, \tag{4.6.26}$$

where $\psi(x) = \text{sgn}\,(x)$,

$$\frac{1}{\sqrt{T}} \sum_{t=1}^{T} \mathbf{x}_t \psi(y_t - \mathbf{x}_t'\hat{\boldsymbol{\beta}}) - \frac{1}{\sqrt{T}} \sum_{t=1}^{T} \mathbf{x}_t \psi(u_t) - \left\{ \frac{1}{\sqrt{T}} \sum_{t=1}^{T} \mathbf{x}_t [E\psi(y_t - \mathbf{x}_t'\boldsymbol{\beta})]_{\hat{\boldsymbol{\beta}}} - \frac{1}{\sqrt{T}} \sum_{t=1}^{T} \mathbf{x}_t E\psi(y_t - \mathbf{x}_t'\boldsymbol{\beta}_0) \right\} \xrightarrow{\text{P}} \mathbf{0}, \tag{4.6.27}$$

and

$$\frac{1}{\sqrt{T}} \sum_{t=1}^{T} \mathbf{x}_t [E\psi(y_t - \mathbf{x}_t'\boldsymbol{\beta})]_{\hat{\boldsymbol{\beta}}} \overset{\text{LD}}{=} \frac{1}{\sqrt{T}} \sum_{t=1}^{T} \mathbf{x}_t E\psi(y_t - \mathbf{x}_t'\boldsymbol{\beta}_0) + \operatorname{plim} \frac{1}{T} \sum_{t=1}^{T} \mathbf{x}_t \left[\frac{\partial}{\partial \boldsymbol{\beta}'} E\psi(y_t - \mathbf{x}_t'\boldsymbol{\beta}) \right]_{\boldsymbol{\beta}_0} \cdot \sqrt{T}(\hat{\boldsymbol{\beta}} - \boldsymbol{\beta}_0). \tag{4.6.28}$$

These results imply

$$\sqrt{T}(\hat{\boldsymbol{\beta}} - \boldsymbol{\beta}_0) \overset{\text{LD}}{=} \left\{ \operatorname{plim} \frac{1}{T} \sum_{t=1}^{T} \mathbf{x}_t \left[\frac{\partial}{\partial \boldsymbol{\beta}'} E\psi(y_t - \mathbf{x}_t'\boldsymbol{\beta}) \right]_{\boldsymbol{\beta}_0} \right\}^{-1} \cdot \frac{1}{\sqrt{T}} \sum_{t=1}^{T} \mathbf{x}_t \psi(u_t). \tag{4.6.29}$$

Noting $E\psi(y_t - \mathbf{x}_t'\boldsymbol{\beta}) = 1 - 2F(\mathbf{x}_t'\boldsymbol{\delta})$, $E\psi(u_t) = 0$, and $V\psi(u_t) = 1$, we obtain

$$\sqrt{T}(\hat{\boldsymbol{\beta}} - \boldsymbol{\beta}_0) \rightarrow N(\mathbf{0}, 4^{-1}f(0)^{-2}[\lim_{T\to\infty} T^{-1}\mathbf{X}'\mathbf{X}]^{-1}). \tag{4.6.30}$$

The proof of (4.6.26) is straightforward and is given in Ruppert and Carroll (1980, Lemma A2, p. 836). The proof of (4.6.27) is complicated; it follows from Lemma 1 (p. 831) and Lemma A3 (p. 836) of Ruppert and Carroll, who in turn used results of Bickel (1975). Equation (4.6.28) is a Taylor series approximation.

Exercises

1. (Section 4.1.1)
Prove (i) $\Rightarrow$ (ii) $\Rightarrow$ (iii) in Definition 4.1.1.

2. (Section 4.1.1)
In the model of Exercise 11 in Chapter 1, obtain the probability limits of the two roots of the likelihood equation, assuming $\lim_{T\to\infty} T^{-1}\mathbf{x}'\mathbf{x} = c$, where c is a finite, positive constant.

3. (Section 4.1.1)
In the model of Exercise 2 (this chapter), prove the existence of a consistent root, using Theorem 4.1.2.

4. (Section 4.1.2)
Suppose that $\{X_T\}$ are essentially bounded; that is, for any $\epsilon > 0$, there exists M_ϵ such that $P(|X_T| < M_\epsilon) \geqq 1 - \epsilon$ for all T. Show that if $\text{plim}_{T\to\infty} Y_T = 0$, then $\text{plim}_{T\to\infty} X_T Y_T = 0$. (This is needed in the proof of Theorem 4.1.4.)

5. (Section 4.2.2)
Prove (4.2.18) by verifying Condition D given after (4.1.7). Assume for simplicity that σ^2 is known. (Proof for the case of unknown σ^2 is similar but more complicated.)

6. (Section 4.2.2)
Let X_{it}, $i = 1, 2, \ldots, n$, $t = 1, 2, \ldots, T$, be independent with the distribution $N(\mu_t, \sigma^2)$. Obtain the probability limit of the maximum likelihood estimator of σ^2 assuming that n is fixed and T goes to infinity (cf. Neyman and Scott, 1948).

7. (Section 4.2.3)
Let $\{X_t\}$, $t = 1, 2, \ldots, T$, be i.i.d. with the probability distribution

$$X_t = 1 \quad \text{with probability} \quad p$$
$$= 0 \quad \text{with probability} \quad 1 - p.$$

Prove the consistency and asymptotic normality of the maximum likelihood estimator using Theorems 4.1.1 and 4.2.4. (The direct method is much simpler but not to be used here for the sake of an exercise.)

8. (Section 4.2.3)
Prove the asymptotic normality of the consistent root in the model of Exercise 2 (this chapter).

9. (Section 4.2.3)
Let $\{X_t\}$ be i.i.d. with uniform distribution over $(0, \theta)$. Show that if $\hat{\theta}$ is defined by $T^{-1}(T+1) \max (X_1, X_2, \ldots, X_T)$, $\lim_{T\to\infty} P[T(\hat{\theta}-\theta) < x] = \exp(\theta^{-1}x - 1)$ for $x \leqq \theta$.

10. (Section 4.2.3)
Consider the model

$$y_t = \beta_0 + u_t, \qquad t = 1, 2, \ldots, T,$$

where y_t and u_t are scalar random variables and β_0 is a scalar unknown parameter. If $\{u_t\}$ are i.i.d. with $Eu_t = 0$, $Eu_t^2 = \beta_0^2$, $Eu_t^3 = 0$, and $Eu_t^4 = m_4$ (note that we do not assume the normality of u_t), which of the following three estimators do you prefer most and why?
(1) $\hat{\beta}_1 = T^{-1}\Sigma_{t=1}^T y_t$,
(2) $\hat{\beta}_2$, which maximizes $S = -(T/2)\log \beta^2 - (1/2\beta^2)\Sigma_{t=1}^T (y_t - \beta)^2$,
(3) $\hat{\beta}_3$ defined as 0.5 times the value of β that minimizes

$$W = \sum_{t=1}^{T} \left[\frac{y_t - \beta}{\beta}\right]^2.$$

11. (Section 4.2.3)
Derive the asymptotic variance of the estimator of β obtained by minimizing $\Sigma_{t=1}^T (y_t - \beta x_t)^4$, where y_t is independent with the distribution $N(\beta_0 x_t, \sigma_0^2)$ and $\lim_{T\to\infty} T^{-1}\Sigma_{t=1}^T x_t^2$ is a finite, positive constant. You may assume consistency and asymptotic normality. Indicate the additional assumptions on x_t one needs. Note if $Z \sim N(0, \sigma^2)$, $EZ^{2k} = \sigma^{2k}(2k)!/(2^k k!)$.

12. (Section 4.2.4)
Complete the proof of Example 4.2.4—the derivation of the asymptotic normality of the superefficient estimator.

13. (Section 4.2.5)
In the model of Example 4.2.3, obtain the asymptotic variance-covariance matrix of $\hat{\boldsymbol{\beta}}$ using the concentrated likelihood function in $\boldsymbol{\beta}$.

14. (Section 4.3.2)
What assumptions are needed to prove consistency in Example 4.3.2 using Theorem 4.3.1?

15. (Section 4.3.3)
Prove the asymptotic normality of the NLLS estimator in Example 4.3.1.

16. (Section 4.3.3)
Consider a nonlinear regression model

$$y_t = (\beta_0 + x_t)^2 + u_t,$$

where we assume
(A) $\{u_t\}$ are i.i.d. with $Eu_t = 0$ and $Vu_t = \sigma_0^2$.
(B) Parameter space $B = [-\frac{1}{2}, \frac{1}{2}]$.
(C) $\{x_t\}$ are i.i.d. with the uniform distribution over [1, 2], distributed independently of $\{u_t\}$. [$EX^r = (r+1)^{-1}(2^{r+1} - 1)$ for every positive or negative integer r except $r = -1$. $EX^{-1} = \log 2$.]
Define two estimators of β_0:
(1) $\hat{\beta}$ minimizes $S_T(\beta) = \Sigma_{t=1}^T [y_t - (\beta + x_t)^2]^2$ over B.
(2) $\tilde{\beta}$ minimizes $W_T(\beta) = \Sigma_{t=1}^T \{y_t/(\beta + x_t)^2 + \log [(\beta + x_t)^2]\}$ over B.
If $\beta_0 = 0$, which of the two estimators do you prefer? Explain your preference on the basis of asymptotic results.

17. (Section 4.3.5)
Your client wants to test the hypothesis $\alpha + \beta = 1$ in the nonlinear regression model

$$Q_t = L_t^\alpha K_t^\beta + u_t, \qquad t = 1, 2, \ldots, T,$$

where L_t and K_t are assumed exogenous and $\{u_t\}$ are i.i.d. with $Eu_t = 0$ and $Vu_t = \sigma^2$. Write your answer in such a way that your client can perform the test by reading your answer without reading anything else, except that you may assume he can compute linear least squares estimates and has access to all the statistical tables and knows how to use them. Assume that your client understands high-school algebra but not calculus or matrix analysis.

18. (Section 4.4.3)
Prove the asymptotic efficiency of the second-round estimator of the Gauss-Newton iteration.

19. (Section 4.5.1)
Prove Wald $\rightarrow \chi^2(q)$, where Wald is defined in Eq. (4.5.4).

20. (Section 4.5.1)
Prove Rao $\rightarrow \chi^2(q)$, where Rao is defined in Eq. (4.5.5).

21. (Section 4.5.1)
Show Wald $\geqq$ LRT $\geqq$ Rao, where these statistics are defined by (4.5.23), (4.5.24), and (4.5.25).

22. (Section 4.6.1)
Consider the regression model $y_t = \beta_0 x_t + u_t$, where $\{x_t\}$ are known constants such that $\lim_{T\to\infty} T^{-1}\Sigma_{t=1}^{T} x_t^2$ is a finite positive constant and $\{u_t\}$ satisfy the conditions for $\{Y_t\}$ given in Section 4.6.1. By modifying the proof of the asymptotic normality of the median given in Section 4.6.1, prove the asymptotic normality of the estimator of β obtained by minimizing $\Sigma_{t=1}^{T}|y_t - \beta x_t|$.

23. (Section 4.6.1)
Let $\{X_t\}$ be i.i.d. with a uniform density over $(-\frac{1}{2}, \frac{1}{2})$ and let Y be the binary variable taking values $T^{-1/2}$ and $-T^{-1/2}$ with equal probability and distributed independently of $\{X_t\}$. Define $W_t = 1$ if $X_t + Y \geqq 0$ and $W_t = 0$ if $X_t + Y < 0$. Prove that $T^{-1/2}\Sigma_{t=1}^{T}(W_t - \frac{1}{2})$ converges to a mixture of $N(1, \frac{1}{4})$ and $N(-1, \frac{1}{4})$ with equal probability.

5 Time Series Analysis

Because there are many books concerned solely with time series analysis, this chapter is brief; only the most essential topics are considered. The reader who wishes to study this topic further should consult Doob (1953) for a rigorous probabilistic foundation of time series analysis; Anderson (1971) or Fuller (1976) for estimation and large sample theory; Nerlove, Grether, and Carvalho (1979) and Harvey (1981a, b), for practical aspects of fitting time series by autoregressive and moving-average models; Whittle (1983) for the theory of prediction; Granger and Newbold (1977) for the more practical aspects of prediction; and Brillinger (1975) for the estimation of the spectral density.

In Section 5.1 we shall define stationary time series and the autocovariance function and spectral density of stationary time series. In Section 5.2 autoregressive models will be defined and their estimation problems discussed. In Section 5.3 autoregressive models with moving-average residuals will be defined. In Section 5.4 we shall discuss the asymptotic properties of the LS and ML estimators in the autoregressive model, and in Section 5.5 we shall discuss prediction briefly. Finally, in Section 5.6 we shall discuss distributed-lag models.

5.1 Introduction

5.1.1 Stationary Time Series

A time series is a sequence of random variables $\{y_t\}$, $t = 0, \pm 1, \pm 2, \ldots$. We assume $Ey_t = 0$ for every t. (If $Ey_t \neq 0$, we must subtract the mean before we subject it to the analysis of this chapter.) We say a sequence $\{y_t\}$ is *strictly stationary* if the joint distribution of any finite subset $y_{t_1}, y_{t_2}, \ldots, y_{t_K}$ depends only on $t_2 - t_1, t_3 - t_1, \ldots, t_K - t_1$ and not on t_1. We say a sequence is *weakly stationary* if $Ey_t y_s$ depends only on $|t - s|$ and not on t. If a process is strictly stationary and if the autocovariances exist, the process is weakly stationary.

In Section 5.2 through 5.4 we shall be concerned only with strictly stationary time series. The distributed-lag models discussed in Section 5.6 are generally not stationary in either sense. Time series with trends are not stationary, and economic time series often exhibit trends. However, this fact does not diminish the usefulness of Section 5.2 through 5.4 because a time series may be analyzed after a trend is removed. A trend may be removed either by direct subtraction or by differencing. The latter means considering first differences $\{y_t - y_{t-1}\}$, second differences $\{(y_t - y_{t-1}) - (y_{t-1} - y_{t-2})\}$, and so forth.

There are three fundamental ways to analyze a stationary time series. First, we can specify a model for it, such as an autoregressive model (which we shall study in Section 5.2) or a combined autoregressive, moving-average model (which we shall study in Section 5.3). Second, we can examine *autocovariances* $Ey_t y_{t+h}$, $h = 0, 1, 2, \ldots$. Third, we can examine the Fourier transform of autocovariances called *spectral density*. In Sections 5.1.2 and 5.1.3 we shall study autocovariances and spectral density.

5.1.2 Autocovariances

Define $\gamma_h = Ey_t y_{t+h}$, $h = 0, 1, 2, \ldots$. A sequence $\{\gamma_h\}$ contains important information about the characteristics of a time series $\{y_t\}$. It is useful to arrange $\{\gamma_h\}$ as an *autocovariance matrix*

$$\boldsymbol{\Sigma} = \begin{bmatrix} \gamma_0 & \gamma_1 & \gamma_2 & \cdot & \cdot & \gamma_{T-1} \\ \gamma_1 & \gamma_0 & \gamma_1 & \cdot & \cdot & \gamma_{T-2} \\ \gamma_2 & \gamma_1 & \cdot & & & \cdot \\ \cdot & \cdot & & \cdot & & \cdot \\ \cdot & \cdot & & & \cdot & \gamma_1 \\ \gamma_{T-1} & \gamma_{T-2} & \cdot & \cdot & \gamma_1 & \gamma_0 \end{bmatrix}. \tag{5.1.1}$$

This matrix is symmetric, its main diagonal line consists only of γ_0, the next diagonal lines have only γ_1, and so on. Such a matrix is called a *Toeplitz form.*

5.1.3 Spectral Density

Spectral density is the Fourier transform of autocovariances defined by

$$f(\omega) = \sum_{h=-\infty}^{\infty} \gamma_h e^{-ih\omega}, \qquad -\pi \leqq \omega \leqq \pi, \tag{5.1.2}$$

provided the right-hand side converges.

Substituting $e^{i\lambda} = \cos \lambda + i \sin \lambda$, we obtain

$$f(\omega) = \sum_{h=-\infty}^{\infty} \gamma_h [\cos (h\omega) - i \sin (h\omega)] \tag{5.1.3}$$

$$= \sum_{h=-\infty}^{\infty} \gamma_h \cos (h\omega),$$

where the second equality follows from $\gamma_h = \gamma_{-h}$ and $\sin \lambda = -\sin(-\lambda)$. Therefore spectral density is real and symmetric around $\omega = 0$.

Inverting (5.1.2), we obtain

$$\gamma_h = (2\pi)^{-1} \int_{-\pi}^{\pi} e^{ih\omega} f(\omega)\, d\omega \tag{5.1.4}$$

$$= \pi^{-1} \int_{0}^{\pi} \cos (h\omega) f(\omega)\, d\omega.$$

An interesting interpretation of (5.1.4) is possible. Suppose y_t is a linear combination of cosine and sine waves with random coefficients:

$$y_t = \sum_{k=1}^{n} [\xi_k \cos (\omega_k t) + \zeta_k \sin (\omega_k t)], \tag{5.1.5}$$

where $\omega_k = k\pi/n$ and $\{\xi_k\}$ and $\{\zeta_k\}$ are independent of each other and independent across k with $E\xi_k = E\zeta_k = 0$ and $V\xi_k = V\zeta_k = \sigma_k^2$. Then we have

$$\gamma_h = \sum_{k=1}^{n} \sigma_k^2 \cos (\omega_k h), \tag{5.1.6}$$

which is analogous to (5.1.4). Thus a stationary time series can be interpreted as an infinite sum (actually an integral) of cycles with random coefficients, and a spectral density as a decomposition of the total variance of y_t into the variances of the component cycles with various frequencies.

There is a relationship between the characteristic roots of the covariance matrix (5.1.1) and the spectral density (5.1.2). The values of the spectral density $f(\omega)$ evaluated at T equidistant points of ω in $[-\pi, \pi]$ are approximately the characteristic roots of $\mathbf{\Sigma}_T$ (see Grenander and Szego, 1958, p. 65, or Amemiya and Fuller, 1967, p. 527).

5.2 Autoregressive Models

5.2.1 First-Order Autoregressive Model

Consider a sequence of random variables $\{y_t\}$, $t = 0, \pm 1, \pm 2, \ldots$, which follows

$$y_t = \rho y_{t-1} + \epsilon_t, \tag{5.2.1}$$

where we assume

ASSUMPTION A. $\{\epsilon_t\}$, $t = 0, \pm 1, \pm 2, \ldots$, are i.i.d. with $E\epsilon_t = 0$ and $E\epsilon_t^2 = \sigma^2$ and independent of $y_{t-1}, y_{t-2}, \ldots$.

ASSUMPTION B. $|\rho| < 1$.

ASSUMPTION C. $Ey_t = 0$ and $Ey_t y_{t+h} = \gamma_h$ for all t. (That is, $\{y_t\}$ are weakly stationary.)

Model (5.2.1) with Assumptions A, B, and C is called a *stationary first-order autoregressive model,* abbreviated as AR(1).

From (5.2.1) we have

$$y_t = \rho^s y_{t-s} + \sum_{j=0}^{s-1} \rho^j \epsilon_{t-j}. \tag{5.2.2}$$

But $\lim_{s\to\infty} E(\rho^s y_{t-s})^2 = 0$ because of Assumptions B and C. Therefore we have

$$y_t = \sum_{j=0}^{\infty} \rho^j \epsilon_{t-j}, \tag{5.2.3}$$

which means that the partial summation of the right-hand side converges to y_t in the mean square. The model (5.2.1) with Assumptions A, B, and C is equivalent to the model (5.2.3) with Assumptions A and B. The latter is called the *moving-average* representation of the former.

A quick mechanical way to obtain the moving-average representation (5.2.3) of (5.2.1) and vice-versa is to define the lag operator L such that $Ly_t = y_{t-1}$, $L^2 y_t = y_{t-2}, \ldots$. Then (5.2.1) can be written as

$$(1 - \rho L) y_t = \epsilon_t, \tag{5.2.4}$$

where 1 is the identity operator such that $1 y_t = y_t$. Therefore

$$y_t = (1 - \rho L)^{-1} \epsilon_t = \left(\sum_{j=0}^{\infty} \rho^j L^j \right) \epsilon_t, \tag{5.2.5}$$

which is (5.2.3).

An AR(1) process can be generated as follows: Define y_0 as a random variable independent of $\epsilon_1, \epsilon_2, \ldots$, with $Ey_0 = 0$ and $Ey_0^2 = \sigma^2/(1-\rho^2)$. Then define y_t by (5.2.2) after putting $s = t$.

The autocovariances $\{\gamma_h\}$ can be expressed as functions of ρ and σ^2 as follows: Multiplying (5.2.1) with y_{t-h} and taking the expectation yields

$$\gamma_h = \rho\gamma_{h-1}, \qquad h = 1, 2, \ldots . \tag{5.2.6}$$

From (5.2.1), $E(y_t - \rho y_{t-1})^2 = E\epsilon_t^2$, so that we have

$$(1+\rho^2)\gamma_0 - 2\rho\gamma_1 = \sigma^2. \tag{5.2.7}$$

Solving (5.2.6) and (5.2.7), we obtain

$$\gamma_h = \frac{\sigma^2\rho^h}{1-\rho^2}, \qquad h = 0, 1, 2, \ldots . \tag{5.2.8}$$

Note that Assumption C implies $\gamma_{-h} = \gamma_h$.

Arranging the autocovariances in the form of a matrix as in (5.1.1), we obtain the autocovariance matrix of AR(1),

$$\boldsymbol{\Sigma}_1 = \frac{\sigma^2}{1-\rho^2}\begin{bmatrix} 1 & \rho & \cdot & \cdot & \rho^{T-1} \\ \rho & 1 & \rho & \cdot & \rho^{T-2} \\ \cdot & & & & \\ \cdot & & & & \\ \rho^{T-1} & & & & 1 \end{bmatrix}. \tag{5.2.9}$$

Now let us examine an alternative derivation of $\boldsymbol{\Sigma}_1$ that is useful for deriving the determinant and the inverse of $\boldsymbol{\Sigma}_1$ and is easily generalizable to higher-order processes. Define T-vectors $\mathbf{y} = (y_1, y_2, \ldots, y_T)'$ and $\boldsymbol{\epsilon}_{(1)}^* = [(1-\rho^2)^{1/2}y_1, \epsilon_2, \epsilon_3, \ldots, \epsilon_T]'$ and a $T \times T$ matrix

$$\mathbf{R}_1 = \begin{bmatrix} (1-\rho^2)^{1/2} & 0 & 0 & \cdot & \cdot & 0 \\ -\rho & 1 & 0 & & & \\ 0 & -\rho & 1 & & & \\ \cdot & & & & & \\ \cdot & \cdot & 0 & -\rho & 1 & 0 \\ 0 & \cdot & \cdot & 0 & -\rho & 1 \end{bmatrix}. \tag{5.2.10}$$

Then we have

$$\mathbf{R}_1\mathbf{y} = \boldsymbol{\epsilon}_{(1)}^*. \tag{5.2.11}$$

But, because $E\boldsymbol{\epsilon}_{(1)}^*\boldsymbol{\epsilon}_{(1)}^{*\prime} = \sigma^2\mathbf{I}$, we obtain

$$\boldsymbol{\Sigma}_1 = \sigma^2\mathbf{R}_1^{-1}(\mathbf{R}_1')^{-1}, \tag{5.2.12}$$

which can be shown to be identical with (5.2.9). Taking the determinant of both sides of (5.2.12) yields

$$|\mathbf{\Sigma}_1| = \frac{\sigma^{2T}}{1-\rho^2}. \tag{5.2.13}$$

Inverting both sides of (5.2.12) yields

$$\mathbf{\Sigma}_1^{-1} = \frac{1}{\sigma^2}\mathbf{R}_1'\mathbf{R}_1 \tag{5.2.14}$$

$$= \frac{1}{\sigma^2}\begin{bmatrix} 1 & -\rho & 0 & 0 & \cdot & 0 \\ -\rho & 1+\rho^2 & -\rho & 0 & \cdot & 0 \\ 0 & -\rho & 1+\rho^2 & \cdot & \cdot & \cdot \\ \cdot & \cdot & \cdot & \cdot & \cdot & \cdot \\ \cdot & \cdot & \cdot & -\rho & 1+\rho^2 & -\rho \\ \cdot & \cdot & \cdot & 0 & -\rho & 1 \end{bmatrix}.$$

By inserting (5.2.8) into (5.1.2), we can derive the spectral density of AR(1):

$$f_1(\omega) = \frac{\sigma^2}{1-\rho^2}\sum_{h=-\infty}^{\infty} \rho^{|h|}e^{-ih\omega} \tag{5.2.15}$$

$$= \frac{\sigma^2}{1-\rho^2}\left[1 + \sum_{h=1}^{\infty}(\rho e^{i\omega})^h + \sum_{h=1}^{\infty}(\rho e^{-i\omega})^h\right]$$

$$= \frac{\sigma^2}{1-\rho^2}\left[1 + \frac{\rho e^{i\omega}}{1-\rho e^{i\omega}} + \frac{\rho e^{-i\omega}}{1-\rho e^{-i\omega}}\right]$$

$$= \frac{\sigma^2}{1-2\rho\cos\omega+\rho^2}, \qquad -\pi \leqq \omega \leqq \pi.$$

5.2.2 Second-Order Autoregressive Model

A stationary second-order autoregressive model, abbreviated as AR(2), is defined by

$$y_t = \rho_1 y_{t-1} + \rho_2 y_{t-2} + \epsilon_t, \qquad t = 0, \pm 1, \pm 2, \ldots, \tag{5.2.16}$$

where we assume Assumptions A, C, and

ASSUMPTION B′. The roots of $z^2 - \rho_1 z - \rho_2 = 0$ lie inside the unit circle.

Using the lag operator defined in Section 5.2.1, we can write (5.2.16) as

$$(1 - \rho_1 L - \rho_2 L^2)y_t = \epsilon_t. \tag{5.2.17}$$

Hence,

$$(1-\mu_1 L)(1-\mu_2 L)y_t = \epsilon_t, \tag{5.2.18}$$

where μ_1 and μ_2 are the roots of $z^2 - \rho_1 z - \rho_2 = 0$. Premultiplying (5.2.18) by $(1-\mu_1 L)^{-1}(1-\mu_2 L)^{-1}$, we obtain

$$y_t = \left(\sum_{j=0}^{\infty} \mu_1^j L^j \sum_{k=0}^{\infty} \mu_2^k L^k\right) \epsilon_t \tag{5.2.19}$$

$$= \sum_{s=0}^{\infty} \left(\sum_{\substack{j+k=s \\ j,k \geqq 0}} \mu_1^j \mu_2^k\right) \epsilon_{t-s}.$$

Convergence in the mean-square sense of (5.2.19) is ensured by Assumption B′. Note that even if μ_1 and μ_2 are complex, the coefficients on the ϵ_{t-s} are always real.

The values of ρ_1 and ρ_2 for which the condition $|\mu_1|, |\mu_2| < 1$ is satisfied correspond to the inner region of the largest triangle in Figure 5.1. In the region above the parabola, the roots are real, whereas in the region below it, they are complex.

The autocovariances may be obtained as follows: Multiplying (5.2.16) by y_{t-1} and taking the expectation, we obtain

$$\gamma_1 = \rho_1 \gamma_0 + \rho_2 \gamma_1. \tag{5.2.20}$$

Squaring each side of (5.2.16) and taking the expectation, we obtain

$$\gamma_0 = (\rho_1^2 + \rho_2^2)\gamma_0 + 2\rho_1\rho_2\gamma_1 + \sigma^2. \tag{5.2.21}$$

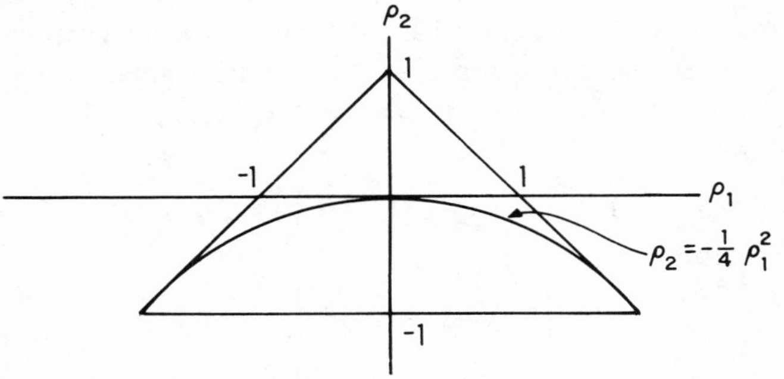

Figure 5.1 Regions of the coefficients in AR(2)

Solving (5.2.20) and (5.2.21) for γ_0 and γ_1, we obtain

$$\gamma_0 = \frac{\sigma^2(\rho_2 - 1)}{(1+\rho_2)[\rho_1^2 - (1-\rho_2)^2]} \tag{5.2.22}$$

and

$$\gamma_1 = \frac{-\sigma^2\rho_1}{(1+\rho_2)[\rho_1^2 - (1-\rho_2)^2]}. \tag{5.2.23}$$

Next, multiplying (5.2.16) by y_{t-h} and taking the expectation, we obtain

$$\gamma_h = \rho_1\gamma_{h-1} + \rho_2\gamma_{h-2}, \qquad h \geqq 2. \tag{5.2.24}$$

Note that $\{\gamma_h\}$ satisfy the same difference equation as $\{y_t\}$ except for the random part. This is also true for a higher-order autoregressive process. Thus, given the initial conditions (5.2.22) and (5.2.23), the second-order difference equation (5.2.24) can be solved (see Goldberg, 1958) as

$$\begin{aligned}\gamma_h &= \frac{\mu_1^h}{\mu_1 - \mu_2}(\gamma_1 - \mu_2\gamma_0) \\ &\quad - \frac{\mu_2^h}{\mu_1 - \mu_2}(\gamma_1 - \mu_1\gamma_0) \quad \text{if} \quad \mu_1 \neq \mu_2 \\ &= \mu^{h-1}[h(\gamma_1 - \mu\gamma_0) + \mu\gamma_0] \quad \text{if} \quad \mu_1 = \mu_2 = \mu.\end{aligned} \tag{5.2.25}$$

If μ_1 and μ_2 are complex, (5.2.25) may be rewritten as

$$\gamma_h = \frac{r^{h-1}[\gamma_1 \sin h\theta - \gamma_0 r \sin (h-1)\theta]}{\sin\theta}, \tag{5.2.26}$$

where $\mu_1 = re^{i\theta}$ and $\mu_2 = re^{-i\theta}$.

Arranging the autocovariances given in (5.2.25) in the form of (5.1.1) yields the autocovariance matrix of AR(2), denoted $\mathbf{\Sigma}_2$. We shall not write it explicitly; instead, we shall express it as a function of a transformation analogous to (5.2.10). If we define a T-vector $\boldsymbol{\epsilon}_{(2)}^* = (a_1y_1, a_2y_1 + a_3y_2, \epsilon_3, \epsilon_4, \ldots, \epsilon_T)$ and a $T \times T$ matrix

$$\mathbf{R}_2 = \begin{bmatrix} a_1 & 0 & 0 & \cdot & \cdot & \cdot & 0 \\ a_2 & a_3 & 0 & & & & \\ -\rho_2 & -\rho_1 & 1 & 0 & & & \\ 0 & -\rho_2 & -\rho_1 & 1 & 0 & & \\ \cdot & & & & & & \\ \cdot & & & & & 1 & 0 \\ 0 & \cdot & \cdot & 0 & -\rho_2 & -\rho_1 & 1 \end{bmatrix}, \tag{5.2.27}$$

we have

$$\mathbf{R}_2\mathbf{y} = \boldsymbol{\epsilon}^*_{(2)}. \tag{5.2.28}$$

Now, if we determine a_1, a_2, and a_3 by solving $V(a_1y_1) = \sigma^2$, $V(a_2y_1 + a_3y_2) = \sigma^2$, and $E[a_1y_1(a_2y_1 + a_3y_2)] = 0$, we have $E\boldsymbol{\epsilon}^*_{(2)}\boldsymbol{\epsilon}^{*\prime}_{(2)} = \sigma^2\mathbf{I}$. Therefore we obtain from (5.2.28)

$$\boldsymbol{\Sigma}_2 = \sigma^2\mathbf{R}_2^{-1}(\mathbf{R}_2')^{-1}. \tag{5.2.29}$$

Higher-order autoregressive processes can be similarly handled.

5.2.3 *p*th-Order Autogressive Model

A stationary pth-order autoregressive process, abbreviated as AR(p), is defined by

$$y_t = \sum_{j=1}^{p} \rho_j y_{t-j} + \epsilon_t, \qquad t = 0, \pm 1, \pm 2, \ldots, \tag{5.2.30}$$

where we assume Assumptions A and C and

ASSUMPTION B″. The roots of $\Sigma_{j=0}^{p} \rho_j z^{p-j} = 0$, $\rho_0 = -1$, lie inside the unit circle.

A representation of the $T \times T$ autocovariance matrix $\boldsymbol{\Sigma}_p$ of AR(p) analogous to (5.2.12) or (5.2.29) is possible. The j, kth element ($j, k = 0, 1, \ldots, T-1$) of $\boldsymbol{\Sigma}_p^{-1}$ can be shown to be the coefficient on $\xi^j\zeta^k$ in

$$\sum_{t=0}^{T-1} \xi^t\zeta^t \sum_{j=0}^{p} \rho_j \xi^j \sum_{j=0}^{p} \rho_j \zeta^j - \sum_{j=0}^{p-1} \xi^j\zeta^j \sum_{j=0}^{p} \rho_j \xi^{T-j} \sum_{j=0}^{p} \rho_j \zeta^{T-j},$$

where $\rho_0 = -1$ (see Whittle, 1983, p. 73).

We shall prove a series of theorems concerning the properties of a general autoregressive process. Each theorem except Theorem 5.2.4 is stated in such a way that its premise is the conclusion of the previous theorem.

THEOREM 5.2.1. $\{y_t\}$ defined in (5.2.30) with Assumptions A, B″, and C can be written as a moving-average process of the form

$$y_t = \sum_{j=0}^{\infty} \phi_j \epsilon_{t-j}, \qquad \sum_{j=0}^{\infty} |\phi_j| < \infty, \tag{5.2.31}$$

where $\{\epsilon_t\}$ are i.i.d. with $E\epsilon_t = 0$ and $E\epsilon_t^2 = \sigma^2$.

Proof. From (5.2.30) we have

$$\left[\prod_{j=1}^{p} (1 - \mu_j L)\right] y_t = \epsilon_t, \tag{5.2.32}$$

where $\mu_1, \mu_2, \ldots, \mu_p$ are the roots of $\Sigma_{j=0}^{p} \rho_j z^{p-j}$. Therefore we have

$$y_t = \left[\prod_{j=1}^{p} \left(\sum_{k=0}^{\infty} \mu_j^k L^k\right)\right] \epsilon_t. \tag{5.2.33}$$

Equating the coefficients of (5.2.31) and (5.2.33), we obtain

$$\phi_0 = 1 \tag{5.2.34}$$

$$\phi_1 = \mu_1 + \mu_2 + \ldots + \mu_p$$

$$\phi_2 = \sum_{p \geqq i \geqq j \geqq 1} \mu_i \mu_j$$

$$\vdots$$

$$\phi_n = \sum_{p \geqq i_1 \geqq i_2 \geqq \ldots \geqq i_n \geqq 1} \mu_{i_1} \mu_{i_2} \ldots \mu_{i_n}.$$

Therefore

$$\sum_{j=0}^{\infty} |\phi_j| \leqq (1 + \mu_M + \mu_M^2 + \ldots)^p = \left(\frac{1}{1 - \mu_M}\right)^p < \infty, \tag{5.2.35}$$

where $\mu_M = \max[|\mu_1|, |\mu_2|, \ldots, |\mu_p|]$.

THEOREM 5.2.2. Let $\{y_t\}$ be any sequence of random variables satisfying (5.2.31). Then

$$\sum_{h=0}^{\infty} |\gamma_h| < \infty, \tag{5.2.36}$$

where $\gamma_h = Ey_t y_{t+h}$.

Proof. We have

$$\gamma_0 = \sigma^2(\phi_0^2 + \phi_1^2 + \ldots)$$

$$\gamma_1 = \sigma^2(\phi_0\phi_1 + \phi_1\phi_2 + \ldots)$$

$$\gamma_2 = \sigma^2(\phi_0\phi_2 + \phi_1\phi_3 + \ldots), \qquad \text{and so on.}$$

Therefore

$$\sum_{h=0}^{\infty} |\gamma_h| \leqq \sigma^2 \left(\sum_{j=0}^{\infty} |\phi_j| \right)^2, \tag{5.2.37}$$

from which the theorem follows.

THEOREM 5.2.3. Let $\{y_t\}$ be any stationary sequence satisfying (5.2.36). Then the characteristic roots of the $T \times T$ autocovariance matrix $\mathbf{\Sigma}$ of $\{y_t\}$ are bounded from above.

Proof. Let $\mathbf{x} = (x_0, x_1, \ldots, x_{T-1})'$ be the characteristic vector of $\mathbf{\Sigma}$ corresponding to a root λ. That is,

$$\mathbf{\Sigma x} = \lambda \mathbf{x}. \tag{5.2.38}$$

Suppose $|x_t| = \max [|x_0|, |x_1|, \ldots, |x_{T-1}|]$. The $(t+1)$st equation of (5.2.38) can be written as

$$\gamma_t x_0 + \gamma_{t-1} x_1 + \ldots + \gamma_0 x_t + \ldots + \gamma_{T-1-t} x_{T-1} = \lambda x_t. \tag{5.2.39}$$

Therefore, because $\lambda \geqq 0$,

$$|\gamma_t| + |\gamma_{t-1}| + \ldots + |\gamma_0| + \ldots + |\gamma_{T-1-t}| \geqq \lambda. \tag{5.2.40}$$

Therefore

$$2 \sum_{h=0}^{T} |\gamma_h| \geqq \lambda, \tag{5.2.41}$$

from which the theorem follows.

The premise of the next theorem is weaker than the conclusion of the preceding theorem. In terms of the spectral density, the premise of Theorem 5.2.4 is equivalent to its existence, and the conclusion of Theorem 5.2.3 to its continuity.

THEOREM 5.2.4. Let $\{y_t\}$ be any sequence of random variables satisfying

$$y_t = \sum_{j=0}^{\infty} \phi_j \epsilon_{t-j}, \qquad \sum_{j=0}^{\infty} \phi_j^2 < \infty, \tag{5.2.42}$$

where $\{\epsilon_t\}$ are i.i.d with $E\epsilon_t = 0$ and $E\epsilon_t^2 = \sigma^2$. Then

$$\lim_{h \to \infty} \gamma_h = 0. \tag{5.2.43}$$

Note that (5.2.31) implies (5.2.42).

Proof. The theorem follows from the Cauchy-Schwartz inequality, namely,

$$\gamma_h^2 = \sigma^4(\phi_0\phi_h + \phi_1\phi_{h+1} + \ldots)^2 \tag{5.2.44}$$

$$\leqq \sigma^4 \sum_{j=0}^{\infty} \phi_j^2 \sum_{j=h}^{\infty} \phi_j^2.$$

5.3 Autogressive Models with Moving-Average Residuals

A *stationary autoregressive, moving-average model* is defined by

$$\sum_{j=0}^{p} \rho_j y_{t-j} = \sum_{j=0}^{q} \beta_j \epsilon_{t-j}, \qquad \rho_0 = \beta_0 = -1, \quad t = 0, \pm 1, \pm 2, \ldots, \tag{5.3.1}$$

where we assume Assumptions A, B″, C, and

Assumption D. The roots of $\Sigma_{j=0}^{q} \beta_j z^{q-j} = 0$ lie inside the unit circle.

Such a model will be called ARMA(p, q) for short.

We can write (5.3.1) as

$$\rho(L)y_t = \beta(L)\epsilon_t, \tag{5.3.2}$$

where $\rho(L) = \Sigma_{j=0}^{p} \rho_j L^j$ and $\beta(L) = \Sigma_{j=0}^{q} \beta_j L^j$. Because of Assumptions B″ and C, we can express y_t as an infinite moving average

$$y_t = \rho^{-1}(L)\beta(L)\epsilon_t \equiv \phi(L)\epsilon_t, \tag{5.3.3}$$

where $\phi(L) = \Sigma_{j=0}^{\infty} \phi_j L^j$. Similarly, because of Assumption D, we can express y_t as an infinite autoregressive process

$$\psi(L)y_t \equiv \beta^{-1}(L)\rho(L)y_t = \epsilon_t, \tag{5.3.4}$$

where $\psi(L) = \Sigma_{j=0}^{\infty} \psi_j L^j$.

The spectral density of ARMA(p, q) is given by

$$f(\omega) = \sigma^2 \frac{\left| \sum_{j=0}^{q} \beta_j e^{-ij\omega} \right|^2}{\left| \sum_{j=0}^{p} \rho_j e^{-ij\omega} \right|^2}, \qquad -\pi \leqq \omega \leqq \pi, \tag{5.3.5}$$

where $|z|^2 = z\bar{z}$ for a complex number z with $\bar{z}$ being its complex conjugate. Note that (5.3.5) is reduced to (5.2.15) in the special case of AR(1). We also see from (5.3.5) that the spectral density of a moving-average model is, except for σ^2, the inverse of the spectral density of an autoregressive model with the same order and the same coefficients. Because the spectral density of a stationary process approximately corresponds to the set of the characteristic roots of the autocovariance matrix, as was noted earlier, we can show that the autocovariance matrix of a moving-average model is approximately equal to the inverse of the autocovariance matrix of the corresponding autoregressive model. We shall demonstrate this for the case of MA(1).

Consider an MA(1) model defined by

$$y_t = \epsilon_t - \rho\epsilon_{t-1}, \tag{5.3.6}$$

where $|\rho| < 1$ and $\{\epsilon_t\}$ are i.i.d. with $E\epsilon_t = 0$ and $V\epsilon_t = \sigma^2$. The $T \times T$ autocovariance matrix is given by

$$\mathbf{\Sigma}_{(1)} = \sigma^2 \begin{bmatrix} 1+\rho^2 & -\rho & 0 & \cdot & 0 & 0 \\ -\rho & 1+\rho^2 & & & & \\ 0 & & \cdot & & & \\ \cdot & & & \cdot & & \\ \cdot & & & & 1+\rho^2 & -\rho \\ 0 & & & & -\rho & 1+\rho^2 \end{bmatrix}. \tag{5.3.7}$$

We wish to approximate the inverse of $\mathbf{\Sigma}_{(1)}$. If we define a T-vector $\boldsymbol{\eta}$ such that its first element is $\epsilon_1 - \rho\epsilon_0 - (1-\rho^2)^{1/2}\epsilon_1$ and the other $T-1$ elements are zeroes, we have

$$\mathbf{y} = \mathbf{R}_1\boldsymbol{\epsilon} + \boldsymbol{\eta}, \tag{5.3.8}$$

where $\mathbf{R}_1$ is given by (5.2.10). Therefore[1]

$$\mathbf{\Sigma}_{(1)} \cong \sigma^2\mathbf{R}_1\mathbf{R}_1'. \tag{5.3.9}$$

But we can directly verify

$$\mathbf{R}_1\mathbf{R}_1' \cong \mathbf{R}_1'\mathbf{R}_1. \tag{5.3.10}$$

From (5.2.12), (5.3.9), and (5.3.10), we conclude

$$\begin{aligned} \sigma^2\mathbf{\Sigma}_{(1)}^{-1} &\cong \mathbf{R}_1^{-1}(\mathbf{R}_1')^{-1} \\ &= \frac{1}{\sigma^2}\mathbf{\Sigma}_1. \end{aligned} \tag{5.3.11}$$

Whittle (1983, p. 75) has presented the exact inverse of $\mathbf{\Sigma}_{(1)}$. The j, kth element ($j, k = 0, 1, \ldots, T-1$) of $\mathbf{\Sigma}_{(1)}^{-1}$, denoted $\Sigma_{(1)}^{jk}$, is given by

$$\Sigma_{(1)}^{jk} = \frac{(\rho^{-(j+1)} - \rho^{j+1})(\rho^{-(T-k)} - \rho^{T-k})}{\rho(\rho^{-1} - \rho)(\rho^{-(T+1)} - \rho^{T+1})}. \tag{5.3.12}$$

However, the exact inverse is complicated for higher-order moving-average models, and the approximation (5.3.11) is attractive because the same inverse relationship is also valid for higher-order processes.

Anderson (1971, p. 223) has considered the estimation of the parameters of ARMA(p, q) without the normality assumption on $\{\epsilon_t\}$, and Box and Jenkins (1976) have derived the maximum likelihood estimator assuming normality in the *autoregressive integrated moving-average process.* This is the model in which the sequence obtained by repeatedly first-differencing the original series follows ARMA(p, q). The computation of MLE can be time-consuming because the inverse of the covariance matrix of the process, even if we use the approximation mentioned in the preceding paragraph, is a complicated nonlinear function of the parameters (see Harvey, 1981b, for various computational methods).

5.4 Asymptotic Properties of Least Squares and Maximum Likelihood Estimator in the Autoregressive Model

We shall first consider the least squares (LS) estimation of the parameters ρ's and σ^2 of an AR(p) model (5.2.30) using T observations $y_1, y_2, \ldots, y_T$. In vector notation we can write model (5.2.30) as

$$\mathbf{y} = \mathbf{Y}\boldsymbol{\rho} + \boldsymbol{\epsilon}, \tag{5.4.1}$$

where $\mathbf{y} = (y_{p+1}, y_{p+2}, \ldots, y_T)'$, $\boldsymbol{\epsilon} = (\epsilon_{p+1}, \epsilon_{p+2}, \ldots, \epsilon_T)'$, $\boldsymbol{\rho} = (\rho_1, \rho_2, \ldots, \rho_p)'$, and

$$\mathbf{Y} = \begin{bmatrix} y_p & y_{p-1} & \cdots & y_1 \\ y_{p+1} & y_p & \cdots & y_2 \\ \vdots & \vdots & & \vdots \\ y_{T-1} & y_{T-2} & \cdots & y_{T-p} \end{bmatrix}.$$

The LS estimator $\hat{\boldsymbol{\rho}}$ of $\boldsymbol{\rho}$ is defined as $\hat{\boldsymbol{\rho}} = (\mathbf{Y}'\mathbf{Y})^{-1}\mathbf{Y}'\mathbf{y}$. In the special case of $p = 1$, it becomes

$$\hat{\rho} = \frac{\sum_{t=2}^{T} y_{t-1} y_t}{\sum_{t=2}^{T} y_{t-1}^2}. \tag{5.4.2}$$

Model (5.4.1) superficially looks like the classical regression model (1.1.4), but it is not because the regressors $\mathbf{Y}$ cannot be regarded as constants. This makes it difficult to derive the mean and variance of $\hat{\boldsymbol{\rho}}$ for general p. However, in the case of $p = 1$, the exact distribution of $\hat{\rho}$ can be calculated by direct integration using the method of Imhof (1961). The distribution is negatively skewed and downward biased. Phillips (1977) derived the Edgeworth expansion [up to the order of $O(T^{-1})$] of the distribution of $\hat{\rho}$ in the case of $p = 1$ assuming the normality of $\{\epsilon_t\}$ and compared it with the exact distribution. He found that the approximation is satisfactory for $\rho = 0.4$ but not for $\rho = 0.8$.

In the general AR(p) model we must rely on the asymptotic properties of the LS estimator. For model (5.4.1) with Assumptions A, B″, and C, Anderson (1971, p. 193) proved

$$\sqrt{T}(\hat{\boldsymbol{\rho}} - \boldsymbol{\rho}) \rightarrow N(\mathbf{0}, \sigma^2 \boldsymbol{\Sigma}_p^{-1}), \tag{5.4.3}$$

where $\boldsymbol{\Sigma}_p$ is the $p \times p$ autovariance matrix of AR(p).[2] We can estimate σ^2 consistently by

$$\hat{\sigma}^2 = T^{-1}(\mathbf{y} - \mathbf{Y}\hat{\boldsymbol{\rho}})'(\mathbf{y} - \mathbf{Y}\hat{\boldsymbol{\rho}}). \tag{5.4.4}$$

Because $\text{plim}_{T\rightarrow\infty} T^{-1}\mathbf{Y}'\mathbf{Y} = \boldsymbol{\Sigma}_p$, the distribution of $\hat{\boldsymbol{\rho}}$ may be approximated by $N[\boldsymbol{\rho}, \sigma^2(\mathbf{Y}'\mathbf{Y})^{-1}]$. Note that this conclusion is identical to the conclusion we derived for the classical regression model in Theorem 3.5.4. Thus the asymptotic theory of estimation and hypothesis testing developed in Chapters 3 and 4 for the classical regression model (1.1.4) can be applied to the autoregressive model (5.4.1). There is one difference: In testing a null hypothesis that specifies the values of all the elements of $\boldsymbol{\rho}$, $\sigma^2\boldsymbol{\Sigma}_p^{-1}$ need not be estimated because it depends only on $\boldsymbol{\rho}$ [see (5.4.16) for the case of $p = 1$].

We shall consider the simplest case of AR(1) and give a detailed proof of the consistency and a sketch of the proof of the asymptotic normality. These are based on the proof of Anderson (1971).

From (5.4.2) we have

$$\hat{\rho} - \rho = \frac{\sum_{t=2}^{T} y_{t-1}\epsilon_t}{\sum_{t=2}^{T} y_{t-1}^2}. \tag{5.4.5}$$

We shall prove consistency by showing that T^{-1} times the numerator converges to 0 in probability and that T^{-1} times the denominator converges to a positive constant in probability.

The cross product terms in $(\Sigma_{t=2}^{T} y_{t-1}\epsilon_t)^2$ are of the form $y_t y_{t+s}\epsilon_{t+1}\epsilon_{t+1+s}$.

But their expectation is 0 because ϵ_{t+1+s} is independent of $y_t y_{t+s} \epsilon_{t+1}$. Thus

$$E\left(\frac{1}{T}\sum_{t=2}^{T} y_{t-1}\epsilon_t\right)^2 = \frac{T-1}{T^2}\frac{\sigma^4}{1-\rho^2}. \tag{5.4.6}$$

Therefore, by Theorem 3.2.1 (Chebyshev), we have

$$\operatorname*{plim}_{T\to\infty} \frac{1}{T}\sum_{t=2}^{T} y_{t-1}\epsilon_t = 0. \tag{5.4.7}$$

Putting $\epsilon_t = y_t - \rho y_{t-1}$ in (5.4.7), we have

$$\operatorname*{plim}_{T\to\infty} \frac{1}{T}\sum_{t=2}^{T} y_{t-1}(y_t - \rho y_{t-1}) = 0. \tag{5.4.8}$$

By Theorem 3.3.2 (Kolmogorov LLN 2), we have

$$\operatorname*{plim}_{T\to\infty} \frac{1}{T}\sum_{t=2}^{T} (y_t - \rho y_{t-1})^2 = \sigma^2. \tag{5.4.9}$$

By adding (5.4.9) and 2ρ times (5.4.8), we have

$$\operatorname*{plim}_{T\to\infty} \left(\frac{1}{T}\sum_{t=2}^{T} y_t^2 - \rho^2 \frac{1}{T}\sum_{t=2}^{T} y_{t-1}^2\right) = \sigma^2. \tag{5.4.10}$$

Therefore

$$\operatorname*{plim}_{T\to\infty} \frac{1}{T}\sum_{t=2}^{T} y_t^2 = \frac{\sigma^2}{1-\rho^2} + \frac{\rho^2}{1-\rho^2}\operatorname*{plim}_{T\to\infty}\frac{1}{T}(y_1^2 - y_T^2). \tag{5.4.11}$$

But the last term of (5.4.11) is 0 because of (3.2.5)—generalized Chebyshev's inequality. Therefore

$$\operatorname*{plim}_{T\to\infty} \frac{1}{T}\sum_{t=2}^{T} y_t^2 = \frac{\sigma^2}{1-\rho^2}. \tag{5.4.12}$$

The consistency of $\hat{\rho}$ follows from (5.4.5), (5.4.7), and (5.4.12) because of Theorem 3.2.6.

Next consider asymptotic normality. For this purpose we need the following definition: A sequence $\{v_t\}$ is said to be *K-dependent* if $(v_{t_1}, v_{t_2}, \ldots, v_{t_n})$ are independent of $(v_{s_1}, v_{s_2}, \ldots, v_{s_m})$ for any set of integers satisfying

$$t_1 < t_2 \ldots < t_n < s_1 < s_2 < \ldots < s_m \quad \text{and} \quad t_n + K < s_1.$$

To apply a central limit theorem to $\Sigma_{t=1}^{T} v_t$, split the T observations into S successive groups with $M + K$ observations [so that $S(M + K) = T$] and then in each group retain the first M observations and eliminate the remaining K

observations. If we choose S and M in such a way that $S \rightarrow \infty$, $M \rightarrow \infty$, and $S/T \rightarrow 0$ as $T \rightarrow \infty$, the elimination of K observations from each of the S groups does not matter asymptotically.

We can write

$$\frac{1}{\sqrt{T}} \sum_{t=2}^{T} y_{t-1}\epsilon_t = \frac{1}{\sqrt{T}} \sum_{t=2}^{T} v_{Nt} + \Delta_{NT}, \tag{5.4.13}$$

where $v_{Nt} = \epsilon_t \sum_{s=0}^{N} \rho^s \epsilon_{t-1-s}$ and $\Delta_{NT} = \frac{1}{\sqrt{T}} \sum_{t=2}^{T} (\epsilon_t \sum_{s=N+1}^{\infty} \rho^s \epsilon_{t-1-s})$. But we have

$$E\Delta_{NT}^2 = \frac{1}{T} \sum_{t=2}^{T} \sum_{\tau=2}^{T} \sum_{s=N+1}^{\infty} \sum_{w=N+1}^{\infty} \rho^s \rho^w E\epsilon_t \epsilon_\tau \epsilon_{t-1-s} \epsilon_{t-1-w} \tag{5.4.14}$$

$$= \frac{\sigma^4(T-1)}{T} \sum_{s=N+1}^{\infty} \rho^{2s}.$$

Therefore Δ_{NT} can be ignored for large enough N. (Anderson, 1971, Theorem 7.7.1, has given an exact statement of this.) We can show that for a fixed N,

$$Ev_{Nt} = 0, \qquad Ev_{Nt}^2 = \sigma^4 \sum_{s=0}^{N} \rho^{2s}, \quad \text{and} \quad Ev_{Nt}v_{N\tau} = 0 \quad \text{for} \quad t \neq \tau.$$

Moreover, v_{Nt} and $v_{N,t+N+2}$ are independent for all t. Therefore $\{v_{Nt}\}$ for each N are $(N+1)$-dependent and can be subjected to a central limit theorem (see Anderson, 1971, Theorem 7.7.5). Therefore

$$\frac{1}{\sqrt{T}} \sum_{t=2}^{T} y_{t-1}\epsilon_t \rightarrow N\left(0, \frac{\sigma^4}{1-\rho^2}\right). \tag{5.4.15}$$

Combining (5.4.12) and (5.4.15), we have

$$\sqrt{T}(\hat{\rho} - \rho) \rightarrow N(0, 1-\rho^2). \tag{5.4.16}$$

Now we consider the MLE in AR(1) under the normality of $\{\epsilon_t\}$. The likelihood function is given by

$$L = (2\pi)^{-T/2}|\mathbf{\Sigma}_1|^{-1/2} \exp\left[-(1/2)\mathbf{y}'\mathbf{\Sigma}_1^{-1}\mathbf{y}\right], \tag{5.4.17}$$

where $|\mathbf{\Sigma}_1|$ and $\mathbf{\Sigma}_1^{-1}$ are given in (5.2.13) and (5.2.14), respectively. Therefore

$$\log L = -\frac{T}{2}\log(2\pi) - \frac{T}{2}\log\sigma^2 \tag{5.4.18}$$

$$+ \frac{1}{2}\log(1-\rho^2) - \frac{1}{2\sigma^2}Q,$$

where $Q = (1 + \rho^2) \Sigma_{t=1}^{T} y_t^2 - \rho^2(y_1^2 + y_T^2) - 2\rho \Sigma_{t=2}^{T} y_{t-1} y_t$. Putting $\partial \log L/\partial\sigma^2 = 0$, we obtain

$$\sigma^2 = \frac{1}{T} Q. \tag{5.4.19}$$

Inserting (5.4.19) into (5.4.18) yields the concentrated log likelihood function (aside from terms not depending on the unknown parameters)

$$\log L^* = -\frac{T}{2} \log (2\pi) - \frac{T}{2} \log Q + \frac{1}{2} \log (1 - \rho^2). \tag{5.4.20}$$

Setting $\partial \log L^*/\partial\rho = 0$ results in a cubic equation in ρ with a unique real root in the range $[-1, 1]$. Beach and Mackinnon (1978) have reported a method of deriving this root.

However, by setting $\partial Q/\partial\rho = 0$, we obtain a much simpler estimator:

$$\hat{\rho}_A = \frac{\sum_{t=2}^{T} y_{t-1} y_t}{\sum_{t=2}^{T-1} y_t^2}. \tag{5.4.21}$$

We call it the approximate MLE. Note that it is similar to the least square estimator $\hat{\rho}$, given in (5.4.2), for which the range of the summation in the denominator is from $t = 2$ to T. If we denote the true MLE by $\hat{\rho}_M$, we can easily show that $\sqrt{T}(\hat{\rho}_A - \rho)$ and $\sqrt{T}(\hat{\rho}_M - \rho)$ have the same limit distribution by using the result of Section 4.2.5.

5.5 Prediction

In the classical regression model with nonstochastic regressors, the problem of predicting a future value of the dependent variable and the problem of estimating the regression parameters can be solved in a unified way. For example, the least squares predictor is the best linear unbiased predictor, as shown in Section 1.6. But, in time series models such as AR or MA, in which the regressors are stochastic, the problem of optimal prediction is not a simple corollary of the problem of optimal estimation because (1.6.3) no longer holds. In view of this difficulty, what we usually do in practice is to obtain the optimal predictor on the assumption that the parameters are known and then insert the estimates obtained by the best known method, such as maximum likelihood, mechanically into the formula for the optimal predictor.

There is an extensive literature on the theory concerning the optimal prediction of a stationary time series when the parameters of the process are assumed known (see Whittle, 1983, and the references in it).

In the simplest case of AR(1), the optimal predictor of y_{t+n} given $y_t, y_{t-1}, \ldots$ is obtained as follows: From (5.2.2) we obtain

$$y_{t+n} = \rho^n y_t + \sum_{j=0}^{n-1} \rho^j \epsilon_{t+n-j}. \tag{5.5.1}$$

Taking the conditional expectation of both sides given $y_t, y_{t-1}, \ldots$, we obtain

$$\hat{y}_{t+n} \equiv E(y_{t+n}|y_t, y_{t-1}, \ldots) = \rho^n y_t. \tag{5.5.2}$$

In the mixed autoregressive, moving-average model (5.3.1), the optimal predictor of y_{t+n} given $y_t, y_{t-1}, \ldots$ is obtained as follows: From (5.3.3) we obtain

$$y_{t+n} = \sum_{k=0}^{\infty} \phi_k \epsilon_{t+n-k}. \tag{5.5.3}$$

Putting $\epsilon_{t+n} = \epsilon_{t+n-1} = \ldots = \epsilon_{t+1} = 0$ in (5.5.3), we obtain the optimal predictor

$$\hat{y}_{t+n} = \sum_{j=0}^{\infty} \phi_{j+n} \epsilon_{t-j}. \tag{5.5.4}$$

Finally, putting $\epsilon_{t-j} = \phi^{-1}(L) y_{t-j}$ in (5.5.4), we obtain

$$\hat{y}_{t+n} = \phi^{-1}(L) \sum_{j=0}^{\infty} \phi_{j+n} L^j y_t. \tag{5.5.5}$$

(See Whittle, 1983, p. 32.)

5.6 Distributed-Lag Models

5.6.1 The General Lag

If we add an exogenous variable to the right-hand side of Eq. (5.3.2), we obtain

$$\rho(L) y_t = \alpha x_t + \beta(L) \epsilon_t. \tag{5.6.1}$$

Such a model is called a *distributed-lag model* by econometricians because solving (5.6.1) for y_t yields

$$y_t = \alpha \rho^{-1}(L) x_t + \rho^{-1}(L) \beta(L) \epsilon_t, \tag{5.6.2}$$

where $\rho^{-1}(L)$ describes a distribution of the effects of the lagged values of x_t (that is, $x_t, x_{t-1}, x_{t-2}, \ldots$) on y_t. There is a vast amount of econometric literature on *distributed-lag models.* The interested reader is referred to the aforementioned works by Fuller (1976); Nerlove, Grether, and Carvalho (1979); and Dhrymes (1971). A model of the form (5.6.2) also arises as a solution of the rational expectations model (see Shiller, 1978; Wallis, 1980). We shall discuss briefly two of the most common types of distributed-lag models: the geometric lag and the Almon lag.

5.6.2 The Geometric Lag

The geometric lag model is defined by

$$y_t = \alpha \sum_{j=0}^{\infty} \lambda^j x_{t-j} + v_t. \tag{5.6.3}$$

This model was first used in econometric applications by Koyck (1954) (hence, it is sometimes referred to as the *Koyck lag*) and by Nerlove (1958). Griliches's survey article (1967) contains a discussion of this model and other types of distributed-lag models. This model has the desirable property of having only two parameters, but it cannot deal with more general types of lag distribution where the effect of x on y attains its peak after a certain number of lags and then diminishes.

By inverting the lag operator $\Sigma_{j=0}^{\infty} \lambda^j L^j$, we can write (5.6.3) equivalently as

$$y_t = \lambda y_{t-1} + \alpha x_t + u_t, \tag{5.6.4}$$

where $u_t = v_t - \lambda v_{t-1}$. If $\{u_t\}$ are i.i.d., the estimation of λ and α is not much more difficult than the estimation in the purely autoregressive model discussed in Section 5.4. Under general conditions the least squares estimator can be shown to be consistent and asymptotically normal (see Crowder, 1980). For a discussion of the estimation of λ and α when $\{v_t\}$, rather than $\{u_t\}$, are i.i.d., see Amemiya and Fuller (1967) and Hatanaka (1974) (also see Section 6.3.7 for further discussion of this model).

5.6.3 The Almon Lag

Almon (1965) proposed a distributed-lag model

$$y_t = \sum_{j=1}^{N} \beta_j x_{t+1-j} + v_t, \tag{5.6.5}$$

in which $\beta_1, \beta_2, \ldots, \beta_N$ lie on the curve of a qth-order polynomial; that is,

$$\beta_j = \delta_0 + \delta_1 j + \delta_2 j^2 + \ldots + \delta_q j^q, \qquad j = 1, 2, \ldots, N. \tag{5.6.6}$$

By defining vectors $\boldsymbol{\beta} = (\beta_1, \beta_2, \ldots, \beta_N)'$ and $\boldsymbol{\delta} = (\delta_0, \delta_1, \ldots, \delta_q)'$, we can write (5.6.6) in vector notation as

$$\boldsymbol{\beta} = \mathbf{J}\boldsymbol{\delta}, \tag{5.6.7}$$

where

$$\mathbf{J} = \begin{bmatrix} 1 & 1 & 1 & \cdot & \cdot & 1 \\ 1 & 2 & 2^2 & & & 2^q \\ \cdot & \cdot & \cdot & & & \cdot \\ \cdot & \cdot & \cdot & & & \cdot \\ \cdot & \cdot & \cdot & & & \cdot \\ 1 & N & N^2 & \cdot & \cdot & N^q \end{bmatrix}.$$

The estimation of $\boldsymbol{\delta}$ can be done by the least squares method. Let $\mathbf{X}$ be a $T \times N$ matrix, the t, jth element of which is x_{t-1-j}. Then $\hat{\boldsymbol{\delta}} = (\mathbf{J}'\mathbf{X}'\mathbf{X}\mathbf{J})^{-1}\mathbf{J}'\mathbf{X}'\mathbf{y}$ and $\hat{\boldsymbol{\beta}} = \mathbf{J}\hat{\boldsymbol{\delta}}$.[3] Note that $\hat{\boldsymbol{\beta}}$ is a special case of the constrained least squares estimator (1.4.11) where $\mathbf{R} = \mathbf{J}$ and $\mathbf{c} = \mathbf{0}$.

By choosing N and q judiciously, a researcher can hope to attain both a reasonably flexible distribution of lags and parsimony in the number of parameters to estimate. Amemiya and Morimune (1974) showed that a small order of polynomials ($q = 2$ or 3) works surprisingly well for many economic time series.

Some researchers prefer to constrain the value of the polynomial to be 0 at $j = N + 1$. This amounts to imposing another equation

$$\delta_0 + \delta_1(N+1) + \delta_2(N+1)^2 + \ldots + \delta_q(N+1)^q = 0 \tag{5.6.8}$$

in addition to (5.6.6). Solving (5.6.8) for δ_0 and inserting it into the right-hand side of (5.6.7) yields the vector equation

$$\boldsymbol{\beta} = \mathbf{J}^*\boldsymbol{\delta}^*, \tag{5.6.9}$$

where $\boldsymbol{\delta}^* = (\delta_1, \delta_2, \ldots, \delta_q)'$ and $\mathbf{J}^*$ should be appropriately defined.

Exercises

1. (Section 5.2.1)
Prove that model (5.2.1) with Assumptions A, B, and C is equivalent to model (5.2.3) with Assumptions A and B.

2. (Section 5.2.1)
Show that the process defined in the paragraph following Eq. (5.2.5) is AR(1).

3. (Section 5.3)
Find the exact inverse of the variance-covariance matrix of MA(1) using (5.3.12) and compare it with the variance-covariance matrix of AR(1).

4. (Section 5.3)
In the MA(1) process defined by (5.3.6), define $y_t^* = \epsilon_t^* - \rho^{-1}\epsilon_{t-1}^*$, where $\{\epsilon_t^*\}$ are i.i.d. with $E\epsilon_t^* = 0$, $V\epsilon_t^* = \rho^2\sigma^2$. Show that the autocovariances of y_t and y_t^* are the same.

5. (Section 5.4)
If X, Y, and Z are jointly normal and if X is independent of either Y or Z, then $EXYZ = EXEYZ$ (Anderson, 1958, p. 22). Show by a counterexample that the equality does not in general hold without the normality assumption.

6. (Section 5.4)
Show that $\sqrt{T}(\hat{\rho}_A - \rho)$ and $\sqrt{T}(\hat{\rho}_M - \rho)$ have the same limit distribution.

7. (Section 5.4)
In the AR(1) process defined by (5.2.1), define the first differences $y_t^* = y_t - y_{t-1}$ and derive $\text{plim}_{T\to\infty} \Sigma_{t=3}^T y_{t-1}^* y_t^* / \Sigma_{t=3}^T y_{t-1}^{*2}$.

8. (Section 5.4)
In the AR(2) process defined by (5.2.16), derive $\text{plim}_{T\to\infty} \Sigma_{t=2}^T y_{t-1}y_t / \Sigma_{t=2}^T y_{t-1}^2$.

9. (Section 5.5)
Derive (5.5.2) from the general formula of (5.5.5).

10. (Section 5.5)
In the MA(1) process defined by (5.3.6), obtain the optimal predictor of y_{t+n} given $y_t, y_{t-1}, \ldots$.

11. (Section 5.6)
Show that (5.6.7) can be written in the equivalent form $\mathbf{Q}'\boldsymbol{\beta} = \mathbf{0}$, where $\mathbf{Q}$ is an $N \times (N - q - 1)$ matrix such that $[\mathbf{Q}, \mathbf{J}]$ is nonsingular and $\mathbf{Q}'\mathbf{J} = \mathbf{0}$. Find such a $\mathbf{Q}$ when $N = 4$ and $q = 2$.

6 Generalized Least Squares Theory

One of the important assumptions of the standard regression model (Model 1) is the assumption that the covariance matrix of the error terms is a scalar times the identity matrix. In this chapter we shall relax this assumption. In Section 6.1 the case in which the covariance matrix is known will be considered. It is pedagogically useful to consider this case before we consider, in Section 6.2, a more realistic case of an unknown covariance matrix. Then in Sections 6.3 through 6.7 various ways of specifying the covariance matrix will be considered.

6.1 The Case of a Known Covariance Matrix

6.1.1 Model 6

The linear regression model we shall consider in this chapter, called Model 6, is defined by

$$\mathbf{y} = \mathbf{X}\boldsymbol{\beta} + \mathbf{u}, \tag{6.1.1}$$

where $\mathbf{X}$ is a $T \times K$ matrix of known constants with rank $K(\leqq T)$, $\boldsymbol{\beta}$ is a K-vector of unknown parameters, and $\mathbf{u}$ is a T-vector of random variables with $E\mathbf{u} = \mathbf{0}$ and $E\mathbf{u}\mathbf{u}' = \boldsymbol{\Sigma}$, a known $T \times T$ positive-definite covariance matrix. (In Section 6.1.5 we shall consider briefly the case of a singular covariance matrix.) We shall write the t,sth element of $\boldsymbol{\Sigma}$ as σ_{ts}.

6.1.2 Generalized Least Squares Estimator

Because $\boldsymbol{\Sigma}$ is positive definite, we can define $\boldsymbol{\Sigma}^{-1/2}$ as $\mathbf{H}\mathbf{D}^{-1/2}\mathbf{H}'$, where $\mathbf{H}$ is an orthogonal matrix consisting of the characteristic vectors of $\boldsymbol{\Sigma}$, $\mathbf{D}$ is the diagonal matrix consisting of the characteristic roots of $\boldsymbol{\Sigma}$, and $\mathbf{D}^{-1/2}$ is obtained by taking the $(-\frac{1}{2})$th power of every diagonal element of $\mathbf{D}$ (see Theorem 3 of Appendix 1). Premultiplying (6.1.1) by $\boldsymbol{\Sigma}^{-1/2}$ yields

$$\mathbf{y}^* = \mathbf{X}^*\boldsymbol{\beta} + \mathbf{u}^*, \tag{6.1.2}$$

where $\mathbf{y}^* = \mathbf{\Sigma}^{-1/2}\mathbf{y}$, $\mathbf{X}^* = \mathbf{\Sigma}^{-1/2}\mathbf{X}$, and $\mathbf{u}^* = \mathbf{\Sigma}^{-1/2}\mathbf{u}$. Note that $E\mathbf{u}^* = \mathbf{0}$ and $E\mathbf{u}^*\mathbf{u}^{*\prime} = \mathbf{I}$, so (6.1.2) is Model 1 except that we do not assume the elements of $\mathbf{u}^*$ are i.i.d. here. The *generalized least squares* (GLS) estimator of $\boldsymbol{\beta}$ in model (6.1.1), denoted $\hat{\boldsymbol{\beta}}_G$, is defined as the least squares estimator of $\boldsymbol{\beta}$ in model (6.1.2); namely,

$$\hat{\boldsymbol{\beta}}_G = (\mathbf{X}^{*\prime}\mathbf{X}^*)^{-1}\mathbf{X}^{*\prime}\mathbf{y}^* \tag{6.1.3}$$
$$= (\mathbf{X}'\mathbf{\Sigma}^{-1}\mathbf{X})^{-1}\mathbf{X}'\mathbf{\Sigma}^{-1}\mathbf{y}.$$

Using the results of Section 1.2, we obtain that $E\hat{\boldsymbol{\beta}}_G = \boldsymbol{\beta}$ and

$$V\hat{\boldsymbol{\beta}}_G = (\mathbf{X}'\mathbf{\Sigma}^{-1}\mathbf{X})^{-1}. \tag{6.1.4}$$

Furthermore, GLS is the best linear unbiased estimator of Model 6. (Note that in Section 1.2.5 we did not require the independence of the error terms to prove that LS is BLUE.)

6.1.3 Efficiency of Least Squares Estimator

It is easy to show that in Model 6 the least squares estimator $\hat{\boldsymbol{\beta}}$ is unbiased with its covariance matrix given by

$$V\hat{\boldsymbol{\beta}} = (\mathbf{X}'\mathbf{X})^{-1}\mathbf{X}'\mathbf{\Sigma}\mathbf{X}(\mathbf{X}'\mathbf{X})^{-1}. \tag{6.1.5}$$

Because GLS is BLUE, it follows that

$$(\mathbf{X}'\mathbf{X})^{-1}\mathbf{X}'\mathbf{\Sigma}\mathbf{X}(\mathbf{X}'\mathbf{X})^{-1} \geqq (\mathbf{X}'\mathbf{\Sigma}^{-1}\mathbf{X})^{-1}, \tag{6.1.6}$$

which can also be directly proved. There are cases where the equality holds in (6.1.6), as shown in the following theorem.

THEOREM 6.1.1. Let $\mathbf{X}'\mathbf{X}$ and $\mathbf{\Sigma}$ both be positive definite. Then the following statements are equivalent.

(A) $(\mathbf{X}'\mathbf{X})^{-1}\mathbf{X}'\mathbf{\Sigma}\mathbf{X}(\mathbf{X}'\mathbf{X})^{-1} = (\mathbf{X}'\mathbf{\Sigma}^{-1}\mathbf{X})^{-1}$.

(B) $\mathbf{\Sigma}\mathbf{X} = \mathbf{X}\mathbf{B}$ for some nonsingular $\mathbf{B}$.

(C) $(\mathbf{X}'\mathbf{X})^{-1}\mathbf{X}' = (\mathbf{X}'\mathbf{\Sigma}^{-1}\mathbf{X})^{-1}\mathbf{X}'\mathbf{\Sigma}^{-1}$.

(D) $\mathbf{X} = \mathbf{H}\mathbf{A}$ for some nonsingular $\mathbf{A}$ where the columns of $\mathbf{H}$ are K characteristic vectors of $\mathbf{\Sigma}$.

(E) $\mathbf{X}'\mathbf{\Sigma}\mathbf{Z} = \mathbf{0}$ for any $\mathbf{Z}$ such that $\mathbf{Z}'\mathbf{X} = \mathbf{0}$.

(F) $\mathbf{\Sigma} = \mathbf{X}\mathbf{\Gamma}\mathbf{X}' + \mathbf{Z}\mathbf{\Theta}\mathbf{Z}' + \sigma^2\mathbf{I}$ for some $\mathbf{\Gamma}$ and $\mathbf{\Theta}$ and $\mathbf{Z}$ such that $\mathbf{Z}'\mathbf{X} = \mathbf{0}$.

Proof. We show that statement A $\Rightarrow$ statement B $\Rightarrow$ statement C:

$$
\begin{aligned}
\text{Statement A} &\Rightarrow \mathbf{X}'\boldsymbol{\Sigma}\mathbf{X} = \mathbf{X}'\mathbf{X}(\mathbf{X}'\boldsymbol{\Sigma}^{-1}\mathbf{X})^{-1}\mathbf{X}'\mathbf{X} \\
&\Rightarrow \mathbf{X}'\boldsymbol{\Sigma}^{1/2}[\mathbf{I} - \boldsymbol{\Sigma}^{-1/2}\mathbf{X}(\mathbf{X}'\boldsymbol{\Sigma}^{-1}\mathbf{X})^{-1}\mathbf{X}'\boldsymbol{\Sigma}^{-1/2}]\boldsymbol{\Sigma}^{1/2}\mathbf{X} = \mathbf{0} \\
&\Rightarrow \boldsymbol{\Sigma}^{1/2}\mathbf{X} = \boldsymbol{\Sigma}^{-1/2}\mathbf{X}\mathbf{B} \text{ for some } \mathbf{B} \text{ using Theorem 14 of Appendix 1} \\
&\Rightarrow \boldsymbol{\Sigma}\mathbf{X} = \mathbf{X}\mathbf{B} \text{ for some } \mathbf{B} \\
&\Rightarrow (\mathbf{X}'\mathbf{X})^{-1}\mathbf{X}'\boldsymbol{\Sigma}\mathbf{X} = \mathbf{B} \\
&\Rightarrow \mathbf{B} \text{ is nonsingular because } \mathbf{X}'\boldsymbol{\Sigma}\mathbf{X} \text{ is nonsingular} \\
&\Rightarrow \text{statement B} \\
&\Rightarrow \mathbf{X}'\boldsymbol{\Sigma}^{-1}\mathbf{X} = (\mathbf{B}')^{-1}\mathbf{X}'\mathbf{X} \text{ and } \mathbf{X}'\boldsymbol{\Sigma}^{-1} = (\mathbf{B}')^{-1}\mathbf{X}' \\
&\Rightarrow \text{statement C.}
\end{aligned}
$$

Statement C $\Rightarrow$ statement D can be easily proved using Theorem 16 of Appendix 1. (Anderson, 1971, p. 561, has given the proof.) Statement D $\Rightarrow$ statement A and statement B $\Rightarrow$ statement E are straightforward. To prove statement E $\Rightarrow$ statement B, note

$$
\begin{aligned}
\text{statement E} &\Rightarrow \mathbf{X}'\boldsymbol{\Sigma}(\mathbf{Z}, \mathbf{X}) = (\mathbf{0}, \mathbf{X}'\boldsymbol{\Sigma}\mathbf{X}) \\
&\Rightarrow \mathbf{X}'\boldsymbol{\Sigma} = (\mathbf{0}, \mathbf{X}'\boldsymbol{\Sigma}\mathbf{X})[\mathbf{Z}(\mathbf{Z}'\mathbf{Z})^{-1}, \mathbf{X}(\mathbf{X}'\mathbf{X})^{-1}]' \\
&\qquad = \mathbf{X}'\boldsymbol{\Sigma}\mathbf{X}(\mathbf{X}'\mathbf{X})^{-1}\mathbf{X}' \text{ using Theorem 15 of Appendix 1} \\
&\Rightarrow \text{statement B because } \mathbf{X}'\boldsymbol{\Sigma}\mathbf{X}(\mathbf{X}'\mathbf{X})^{-1} \text{ is nonsingular.}
\end{aligned}
$$

For a proof of the equivalence of statement F and the other five statements, see Rao (1965).

There are situations in which LS is equal to GLS. For example, consider

$$\mathbf{y} = \mathbf{X}(\boldsymbol{\beta} + \mathbf{v}) + \mathbf{u}, \tag{6.1.7}$$

where $\boldsymbol{\beta}$ is a vector of unknown parameters and $\mathbf{u}$ and $\mathbf{v}$ are random variables with $E\mathbf{u} = \mathbf{0}$, $E\mathbf{v} = \mathbf{0}$, $E\mathbf{u}\mathbf{u}' = \sigma^2\mathbf{I}$, $E\mathbf{v}\mathbf{v}' = \boldsymbol{\Gamma}$, and $E\mathbf{u}\mathbf{v}' = \mathbf{0}$. In this model, statement F of Theorem 6.1.1 is satisfied because $E(\mathbf{X}\mathbf{v} + \mathbf{u})(\mathbf{X}\mathbf{v} + \mathbf{u})' = \mathbf{X}\boldsymbol{\Gamma}\mathbf{X}' + \sigma^2\mathbf{I}$. Therefore LS = GLS in the estimation of $\boldsymbol{\beta}$.

There are situations in which the conditions of Theorem 6.1.1 are asymptotically satisfied so that LS and GLS have the same asymptotic distribution. Anderson (1971, p. 581) has presented two such examples:

$$y_t = \beta_1 + \beta_2 t + \beta_3 t^2 + \ldots + \beta_K t^{K-1} + u_t \tag{6.1.8}$$

and

$$y_t = \beta_1 \cos \lambda_1 t + \beta_2 \cos \lambda_2 t + \ldots + \beta_K \cos \lambda_K t + u_t, \tag{6.1.9}$$

where in each case $\{u_t\}$ follow a general stationary process defined by (5.2.42). [That is, take the y_t of (5.2.42) as the present u_t.]

We shall verify that condition B of Theorem 6.1.1 is approximately satisfied for the polynomial regression (6.1.8) with $K = 3$ when $\{u_t\}$ follow the stationary first-order autoregressive model (5.2.1). Define $\mathbf{X} = (\mathbf{x}_1, \mathbf{x}_2, \mathbf{x}_3)$, where the tth elements of the vectors $\mathbf{x}_1$, $\mathbf{x}_2$, and $\mathbf{x}_3$ are $x_{1t} = 1$, $x_{2t} = t$, and $x_{3t} = t^2$, respectively. Then it is easy to show $\mathbf{\Sigma}^{-1}\mathbf{X} \cong \mathbf{XA}$, where $\mathbf{\Sigma}$ is given in (5.2.9) and

$$\mathbf{A} = \frac{1}{\sigma^2}\begin{bmatrix} (1-\rho)^2 & 0 & -2\rho \\ 0 & (1-\rho)^2 & 0 \\ 0 & 0 & (1-\rho)^2 \end{bmatrix}.$$

The approximate equality is exact except for the first and the last rows.

We have seen in the preceding discussion that in Model 6 LS is generaly not efficient. Use of LS in Model 6 has another possible drawback: The covariance matrix given in (6.1.5) may not be estimated consistently using the usual formula $\hat{\sigma}^2(\mathbf{X}'\mathbf{X})^{-1}$. Under appropriate assumptions we have $\text{plim}\ \hat{\sigma}^2 = \lim T^{-1}\ \text{tr}\ \mathbf{M\Sigma}$, where $\mathbf{M} = \mathbf{I} - \mathbf{X}(\mathbf{X}'\mathbf{X})^{-1}\mathbf{X}'$. Therefore $\text{plim}\ \hat{\sigma}^2(\mathbf{X}'\mathbf{X})^{-1}$ is generally different from (6.1.5). Furthermore, we cannot unequivocally determine the direction of the bias. Consequently, the standard t and F tests of linear hypotheses developed in Chapter 1 are no longer valid.

6.1.4 Consistency of the Least Squares Estimator

We shall obtain a useful set of conditions on $\mathbf{X}$ and $\mathbf{\Sigma}$ for the consistency of LS in Model 6. We shall use the following lemma in matrix analysis.

LEMMA 6.1.1. Let $\mathbf{A}$ and $\mathbf{B}$ be nonnegative definite matrices of size n. Then $\text{tr}\ (\mathbf{AB}) \leq \lambda_l(\mathbf{A})\ \text{tr}\ \mathbf{B}$, where $\lambda_l(\mathbf{A})$ denotes the largest characteristic root of $\mathbf{A}$.

Proof. Let $\mathbf{H}$ be a matrix such that $\mathbf{H}'\mathbf{AH} = \mathbf{D}$, diagonal, and $\mathbf{H}'\mathbf{H} = \mathbf{I}$. Then, $\text{tr}\ (\mathbf{AB}) = \text{tr}\ (\mathbf{H}'\mathbf{AHH}'\mathbf{BH}) = \text{tr}\ \mathbf{DQ}$, where $\mathbf{Q} = \mathbf{H}'\mathbf{BH}$. Let d_i be the ith diagonal element of $\mathbf{D}$ and q_{ii} be of $\mathbf{Q}$. Then

$$\text{tr}\ (\mathbf{DQ}) = \sum_{i=1}^{n} d_i q_{ii} \leq \max_i d_i \cdot \sum_{i=1}^{n} q_{ii} = \lambda_l(\mathbf{A})\ \text{tr}\ \mathbf{B}.$$

Now we can prove the following theorem.

THEOREM 6.1.2. In Model 6 assume
(A) $\lambda_l(\mathbf{\Sigma})$ bounded for all T,
(B) $\lambda_s(\mathbf{X}'\mathbf{X}) \to \infty$.
Then $\text{plim}_{T\to\infty} \hat{\boldsymbol{\beta}} = \boldsymbol{\beta}$.

Proof. We have

$$\begin{aligned} \operatorname{tr} V\hat{\boldsymbol{\beta}} &= \operatorname{tr} [(\mathbf{X}'\mathbf{X})^{-1}\mathbf{X}'\boldsymbol{\Sigma}\mathbf{X}(\mathbf{X}'\mathbf{X})^{-1}] \\ &= \operatorname{tr} [\boldsymbol{\Sigma}\mathbf{X}(\mathbf{X}'\mathbf{X})^{-2}\mathbf{X}'] \\ &\leqq \lambda_l(\boldsymbol{\Sigma}) \operatorname{tr} [\mathbf{X}(\mathbf{X}'\mathbf{X})^{-2}\mathbf{X}'] \text{ by Lemma 6.1.1} \\ &= \lambda_l(\boldsymbol{\Sigma}) \operatorname{tr} (\mathbf{X}'\mathbf{X})^{-1} \\ &\leqq K \frac{\lambda_l(\boldsymbol{\Sigma})}{\lambda_s(\mathbf{X}'\mathbf{X})}. \end{aligned}$$

But the last term converges to 0 because of assumptions A and B.

Note that Theorem 3.5.1 is a special case of Theorem 6.1.2. One interesting implication of Theorems 6.1.2 and 5.2.3 is that LS is consistent if $\mathbf{u}$ follows a stationary time series satisfying (5.2.36).

We have not proved the asymptotic normality of LS or GLS in this section because the proof would require additional specific assumptions about the generation of $\mathbf{u}$.

6.1.5 A Singular Covariance Matrix

If the covariance matrix $\boldsymbol{\Sigma}$ is singular, we obviously cannot define GLS by (6.1.3). Suppose that the rank of $\boldsymbol{\Sigma}$ is $S < T$. Then, by Theorem 3 of Appendix 1, we can find an orthogonal matrix $\mathbf{H} = (\mathbf{H}_1, \mathbf{H}_2)$, where $\mathbf{H}_1$ is $T \times S$ and $\mathbf{H}_2$ is $T \times (T - S)$, such that $\mathbf{H}_1'\boldsymbol{\Sigma}\mathbf{H}_1 = \boldsymbol{\Lambda}$, a diagonal matrix consisting of the S positive characteristic roots of $\boldsymbol{\Sigma}$, $\mathbf{H}_1'\boldsymbol{\Sigma}\mathbf{H}_2 = \mathbf{0}$, and $\mathbf{H}_2'\boldsymbol{\Sigma}\mathbf{H}_2 = \mathbf{0}$. The premultiplication of (6.1.1) by $\mathbf{H}'$ yields two vector equations:

$$\mathbf{H}_1'\mathbf{y} = \mathbf{H}_1'\mathbf{X}\boldsymbol{\beta} + \mathbf{H}_1'\mathbf{u} \tag{6.1.11}$$

and

$$\mathbf{H}_2'\mathbf{y} = \mathbf{H}_2'\mathbf{X}\boldsymbol{\beta}. \tag{6.1.12}$$

Note that there is no error term in (6.1.12) because $E\mathbf{H}_2'\mathbf{u}\mathbf{u}'\mathbf{H}_2 = \mathbf{H}_2'\boldsymbol{\Sigma}\mathbf{H}_2 = \mathbf{0}$ and therefore $\mathbf{H}_2'\mathbf{u}$ is identically equal to a zero vector. Then the best linear unbiased estimator of $\boldsymbol{\beta}$ is GLS applied to (6.1.11) subject to linear constraints (6.1.12).[1] Or, equivalently, it is LS applied to

$$\boldsymbol{\Lambda}^{-1/2}\mathbf{H}_1'\mathbf{y} = \boldsymbol{\Lambda}^{-1/2}\mathbf{H}_1'\mathbf{X}\boldsymbol{\beta} + \boldsymbol{\Lambda}^{-1/2}\mathbf{H}_1'\mathbf{u} \tag{6.1.13}$$

subject to the same constraints. Thus it can be calculated by appropriately redefining the symbols $\mathbf{X}$, $\mathbf{Q}$, and $\mathbf{c}$ in formula (1.4.5).

6.2 The Case of an Unknown Covariance Matrix

In the remainder of this chapter, we shall consider Model 6 assuming that $\mathbf{\Sigma}$ is unknown and therefore must be estimated. Suppose we somehow obtain an estimator $\hat{\mathbf{\Sigma}}$. Then we define the *feasible generalized least squares* (FGLS) estimator by

$$\hat{\boldsymbol{\beta}}_F = (\mathbf{X}'\hat{\mathbf{\Sigma}}^{-1}\mathbf{X})^{-1}\mathbf{X}'\hat{\mathbf{\Sigma}}^{-1}\mathbf{y}, \tag{6.2.1}$$

assuming $\hat{\mathbf{\Sigma}}$ is nonsingular.

For $\hat{\boldsymbol{\beta}}_F$ to be a reasonably good estimator, we should at least require it to be consistent. This means that the number of the free parameters that characterize $\mathbf{\Sigma}$ should be either bounded or allowed to go to infinity at a slower rate than T. Thus one must impose particular structure on $\mathbf{\Sigma}$, specifying how it depends on a set of free parameters that are fewer than T in number. In this section we shall consider five types of models in succession. For each we shall impose a particular structure on $\mathbf{\Sigma}$ and then study the properties of LS and FGLS and other estimators of $\boldsymbol{\beta}$. We shall also discuss the estimation of $\mathbf{\Sigma}$. The five models we shall consider are (1) serial correlation, (2) seemingly unrelated regression models, (3) heteroscedasticity, (4) error components models, and (5) random coefficients models.

In each of the models mentioned in the preceding paragraph, $\hat{\mathbf{\Sigma}}$ is obtained from the least squares residuals $\hat{\mathbf{u}} \equiv \mathbf{y} - \mathbf{X}\hat{\boldsymbol{\beta}}$, where $\hat{\boldsymbol{\beta}}$ is the LS estimator. Under general conditions we shall show that $\hat{\boldsymbol{\beta}}$ is consistent in these models and hence that $\hat{\mathbf{\Sigma}}$ is consistent. Using this result, we shall show that $\hat{\boldsymbol{\beta}}_F$ has the same asymptotic distribution as $\hat{\boldsymbol{\beta}}_G$.

In some situations we may wish to use (6.2.1) as an iterative procedure; that is, given $\hat{\boldsymbol{\beta}}_F$ we can calculate the new residuals $\mathbf{y} - \mathbf{X}\hat{\boldsymbol{\beta}}_F$, reestimate $\mathbf{\Sigma}$, and insert it into the right-hand side of (6.2.1). The asymptotic distribution is unchanged by iterating, but in certain cases (for example, if $\mathbf{y}$ is normal) iterating will allow convergence to the maximum likelihood estimator (see Oberhofer and Kmenta, 1974).

6.3 Serial Correlation

In this section we shall consider mainly Model 6 where $\mathbf{u}$ follows AR(1) defined in (5.2.1). Most of our results hold also for more general stationary processes, as will be indicated. The covariance matrix of $\mathbf{u}$, denoted $\mathbf{\Sigma}_1$, is as given in (5.2.9), and its inverse is given in (5.2.14).

6.3.1 Asymptotic Normality of the Least Squares Estimator

As was noted earlier, the first step in obtaining FGLS is calculating LS. Therefore the properties of FGLS depend on the properties of LS. The least squares estimator is consistent in this model if assumption B of Theorem 6.1.2 is satisfied because in this case assumption A is satisfied because of Theorem 5.2.3. In fact, Theorem 5.2.3 states that assumption A is satisfied even when $\mathbf{u}$ follows a more general process than AR(1). So in this subsection we shall prove only the asymptotic normality of LS, and we shall do so for a process of $\mathbf{u}$ more general than AR(1) but only for the case of one regressor (that is, $K = 1$) in Model 6. (Anderson, 1971, p. 585, has given the proof in the case of K regressors. He assumed an even more general process for $\mathbf{u}$ than the one we assume in the following proof.)

THEOREM 6.3.1. Assume $K = 1$ in Model 6. Because $\mathbf{X}$ is a T-vector in this case, we shall denote it by $\mathbf{x}$ and its tth element by x_t. Assume

(A) $\lim_{T\to\infty} \dfrac{\mathbf{x}'\mathbf{x}}{T} = c_1 \neq 0.$

(B) $u_t = \Sigma_{j=0}^{\infty} \phi_j \epsilon_{t-j}$, $\Sigma_{j=0}^{\infty} |\phi_j| < \infty$, where $\{\epsilon_t\}$ are i.i.d. with $E\epsilon_t = 0$ and $E\epsilon_t^2 = \sigma^2$.

Then $\sqrt{T}(\hat{\beta} - \beta) \to N(0, c_1^{-2}c_2)$, where $c_2 = \lim_{T\to\infty} T^{-1}\mathbf{x}'E\mathbf{u}\mathbf{u}'\mathbf{x}$.

Proof. We need only prove $T^{-1/2}\mathbf{x}'\mathbf{u} \to N(0, c_2)$ because then the theorem follows from assumption A and Theorem 3.2.7 (iii) (Slutsky). We can write

$$\frac{1}{\sqrt{T}} \sum_{t=1}^{T} x_t u_t = \frac{1}{\sqrt{T}} \sum_{t=1}^{T} x_t \sum_{j=0}^{N} \phi_j \epsilon_{t-j} + \frac{1}{\sqrt{T}} \sum_{t=1}^{T} x_t \sum_{j=N+1}^{\infty} \phi_j \epsilon_{t-j} \tag{6.3.1}$$

$$\equiv A_1 + A_2.$$

But $V(A_2) \leq T^{-1}\mathbf{x}'\mathbf{x}\sigma^2(\Sigma_{j=N+1}^{\infty}|\phi_j|)^2$. Therefore A_2 can be ignored if one takes N large enough. We have

$$A_1 = \frac{1}{\sqrt{T}} \sum_{t=1}^{T-N} \epsilon_t \sum_{j=0}^{N} \phi_j x_{t+j} + \frac{1}{\sqrt{T}} \sum_{t=1-N}^{0} \epsilon_t \sum_{j=1-t}^{N} \phi_j x_{t+j} \tag{6.3.2}$$

$$+ \frac{1}{\sqrt{T}} \sum_{t=T-N+1}^{T} \epsilon_t \sum_{j=0}^{T-t} \phi_j x_{t-j}$$

$$\equiv A_{11} + A_{12} + A_{13}.$$

But $V(A_{12}) \leqq T^{-1}\sigma^2 NM^2(\Sigma_{j=1}^{N}|\phi_j|)^2$, which goes to 0 as $T \rightarrow \infty$ for a fixed N. The same is true for A_{13}. The theorem follows by noting that $\Sigma_{j=0}^{N}\phi_j x_{t+j}$ satisfies the condition for x_t in Theorem 3.5.3.

6.3.2 Estimation of ρ

Because $\mathbf{\Sigma}$ defined in (5.2.9) depends on σ^2 only through a scalar multiplication, $\hat{\boldsymbol{\beta}}_G$ defined in (6.1.3) does not depend on σ^2. Therefore, in obtaining FGLS (6.2.1), we need to estimate only ρ. The most natural estimator of ρ is

$$\hat{\rho} = \frac{\sum_{t=2}^{T} \hat{u}_{t-1}\hat{u}_t}{\sum_{t=2}^{T} \hat{u}_{t-1}^2}, \tag{6.3.3}$$

where $\hat{u}_t = y_t - \mathbf{x}_t'\hat{\boldsymbol{\beta}}$. The consistency of $\hat{\rho}$ is straightforward. We shall prove its asymptotic normality.

Using $u_t = \rho u_{t-1} + \epsilon_t$, we have

$$\sqrt{T}(\hat{\rho} - \rho) = \frac{\frac{1}{\sqrt{T}} \sum_{t=2}^{T} u_{t-1}\epsilon_t + \Delta_1}{\frac{1}{T} \sum_{t=2}^{T} u_{t-1}^2 + \Delta_2}, \tag{6.3.4}$$

where

$$\begin{aligned} \Delta_1 = {} & \frac{1}{\sqrt{T}} \sum_{t=2}^{T} (\boldsymbol{\beta} - \hat{\boldsymbol{\beta}})'\mathbf{x}_{t-1}\mathbf{x}_t'(\boldsymbol{\beta} - \hat{\boldsymbol{\beta}}) + \frac{1}{\sqrt{T}} \sum_{t=2}^{T} (\boldsymbol{\beta} - \hat{\boldsymbol{\beta}})'\mathbf{x}_{t-1}u_t \\ & + \frac{1}{\sqrt{T}} \sum_{t=2}^{T} (\boldsymbol{\beta} - \hat{\boldsymbol{\beta}})'\mathbf{x}_t u_{t-1} - \frac{\rho}{\sqrt{T}} \sum_{t=2}^{T} [(\boldsymbol{\beta} - \hat{\boldsymbol{\beta}})'\mathbf{x}_{t-1}]^2 \\ & - \frac{2\rho}{\sqrt{T}} \sum_{t=2}^{T} (\boldsymbol{\beta} - \hat{\boldsymbol{\beta}})'\mathbf{x}_{t-1}u_{t-1} \end{aligned} \tag{6.3.5}$$

and

$$\Delta_2 = \frac{1}{T} \sum_{t=2}^{T} [(\boldsymbol{\beta} - \hat{\boldsymbol{\beta}})'\mathbf{x}_{t-1}]^2 + \frac{2}{T} \sum_{t=2}^{T} (\boldsymbol{\beta} - \hat{\boldsymbol{\beta}})'\mathbf{x}_{t-1}u_{t-1}. \tag{6.3.6}$$

If we assume that $\lim_{T\rightarrow\infty} T^{-1}\mathbf{X}'\mathbf{X}$ is a finite nonsingular matrix, it is easy to show that both Δ_1 and Δ_2 converge to 0 in probability. For this, we need only the consistency of the LS estimator $\hat{\boldsymbol{\beta}}$ and $\sqrt{T}(\hat{\boldsymbol{\beta}} - \boldsymbol{\beta}) = O(1)$ but not the asymptotic normality. Therefore, by repeated applications of Theorem 3.2.7 (Slutsky), we conclude that $\sqrt{T}(\hat{\rho}-\rho)$ has the same limit distribution as

$$\sqrt{T}\left[\frac{\sum_{t=2}^{T} u_{t-1}u_t}{\sum_{t=2}^{T} u_{t-1}^2}-\rho\right].$$

Hence the asymptotic normality of $\hat{\rho}$ follows from the result of Section 5.4.

6.3.3 Feasible Generalized Least Squares Estimator

Inserting $\hat{\rho}$ defined in (6.3.3) into $\mathbf{\Sigma}_1^{-1}$ defined in (5.2.14) and then inserting the estimate of $\mathbf{\Sigma}^{-1}$ into (6.2.1), we obtain the FGLS estimator $\hat{\boldsymbol{\beta}}_F$. As noted earlier, σ^2 drops out of the formula (6.2.1) and therefore need not be estimated in the calculation of $\hat{\boldsymbol{\beta}}_F$. (However, σ^2 needs to be estimated in order to estimate the covariance matrix of $\hat{\boldsymbol{\beta}}_F$.) The consistency of $\hat{\boldsymbol{\beta}}_F$ can be proved easily under general conditions, but the proof of the asymptotic normality is rather involved. The reader is referred to Amemiya (1973a), where it has been proved that $\hat{\boldsymbol{\beta}}_F$ has the same asymptotic distribution as $\hat{\boldsymbol{\beta}}_G$ under general assumptions on $\mathbf{X}$ when $\{u_t\}$ follow an autoregressive process with moving-average errors. More specifically,

$$\sqrt{T}(\hat{\boldsymbol{\beta}}_F-\boldsymbol{\beta}) \rightarrow N[\mathbf{0}, \lim_{T\rightarrow\infty} T(\mathbf{X}'\mathbf{\Sigma}^{-1}\mathbf{X})^{-1}]. \tag{6.3.7}$$

In a finite sample, $\hat{\boldsymbol{\beta}}_F$ may not be as efficient as $\hat{\boldsymbol{\beta}}_G$. In fact, there is no assurance that $\hat{\boldsymbol{\beta}}_F$ is better than the LS estimator $\hat{\boldsymbol{\beta}}$. Harvey (1981a, p. 191) presented a summary of several Monte Carlo studies comparing $\hat{\boldsymbol{\beta}}_F$ with $\hat{\boldsymbol{\beta}}$. Taylor (1981) argued on the basis of analytic approximations of the moments of the estimators that the relative efficiency of $\hat{\boldsymbol{\beta}}_F$ vis-à-vis $\hat{\boldsymbol{\beta}}$ crucially depends on the process of the independent variables.

6.3.4 A Useful Transformation for the Calculation of the Feasible Generalized Least Squares Estimator

Let $\hat{\mathbf{R}}_1$ be the matrix obtained by inserting $\hat{\rho}$ into the right-hand side of (5.2.10). Then we have by (5.2.14) $\hat{\boldsymbol{\beta}}_F=(\mathbf{X}'\hat{\mathbf{R}}_1'\hat{\mathbf{R}}_1\mathbf{X})^{-1}\mathbf{X}'\hat{\mathbf{R}}_1'\hat{\mathbf{R}}_1\mathbf{y}$. Thus $\hat{\boldsymbol{\beta}}_F$ can be obtained by least squares after transforming all the variables by $\hat{\mathbf{R}}_1$. Another, somewhat simpler transformation is defined by eliminating the first row of $\hat{\mathbf{R}}_1$. This is called the *Cochrane-Orcutt transformation* (Cochrane and

Orcutt, 1949). The resulting estimator is slightly different from FGLS but has the same asymptotic distribution.

If $\{u_t\}$ follow AR(2) defined by (5.2.16), the relevant transformation is given by (5.2.27), where a's are determined by solving $V(a_1u_1) = \sigma^2$, $V(a_2u_1 + a_3u_2) = \sigma^2$, and $E[a_1u_1(a_2u_1 + a_3u_2)] = 0$. A generalization of the Cochrane-Orcutt transformation is obtained by eliminating the first two rows of $\hat{\mathbf{R}}_2$. Higher-order autoregressive processes can be similarly handled.

6.3.5 Maximum Likelihood Estimator

Let us derive the MLE of $\boldsymbol{\beta}$, ρ, and σ^2 in Model 6, assuming that $\{u_t\}$ are normal and follow AR(1). The log likelihood function of the model has the same appearance as (5.4.18) and is given by

$$\log L = -\frac{T}{2}\log 2\pi - \frac{T}{2}\log \sigma^2 + \frac{1}{2}\log(1-\rho^2) - \frac{1}{2\sigma^2}Q, \tag{6.3.8}$$

where $Q = (1+\rho^2)\Sigma_{t=1}^{T}u_t^2 - \rho^2(u_1^2 + u_T^2) - 2\rho\Sigma_{t=2}^{T}u_{t-1}u_t$ where we have written $u_t = y_t - \mathbf{x}_t'\boldsymbol{\beta}$ for short. Putting $\partial \log L/\partial\sigma^2 = 0$, we obtain

$$\sigma^2 = \frac{1}{T}Q. \tag{6.3.9}$$

Inserting (6.3.9) into (6.3.8), we obtain the concentrated log likelihood function (aside from terms not depending on the unknown parameters)

$$\log L^* = -\frac{T}{2}\log Q + \frac{1}{2}\log(1-\rho^2). \tag{6.3.10}$$

For a given value of $\boldsymbol{\beta}$, ρ may be estimated either by the true MLE, which maximizes $\log L^*$ using the method of Beach and MacKinnon (1978), or by the approximate MLE, which minimizes $\log Q$, as was noted earlier in Section 5.4. Both have the same asymptotic distribution. The formula for the approximate MLE is

$$\rho = \frac{\sum_{t=2}^{T}(y_{t-1} - \mathbf{x}_{t-1}'\boldsymbol{\beta})(y_t - \mathbf{x}_t'\boldsymbol{\beta})}{\sum_{t=2}^{T-1}(y_{t-1} - \mathbf{x}_{t-1}'\boldsymbol{\beta})^2}. \tag{6.3.11}$$

Given ρ, the value of $\boldsymbol{\beta}$ that maximizes $\log L^*$ is clearly

$$\boldsymbol{\beta} = (\mathbf{X}'\boldsymbol{\Sigma}^{-1}\mathbf{X})^{-1}\mathbf{X}'\boldsymbol{\Sigma}^{-1}\mathbf{y}, \tag{6.3.12}$$

where $\boldsymbol{\Sigma}$ is as given in (5.2.9). The approximate MLE of $\boldsymbol{\beta}$, ρ, and σ^2 are obtained by solving (6.3.9), (6.3.11), and (6.3.12) simultaneously.

These equations defining the approximate MLE are highly nonlinear, so that the MLE must be obtained either by a search method or by an iteration. We have already described the common iterative procedure of going back and forth between (6.3.11) and (6.3.12), starting from the LS $\hat{\boldsymbol{\beta}}$.

For the asymptotic normality of MLE in Model 6 where $\{u_t\}$ follow a stationary autoregressive, moving-average process, see Pierce (1971).

6.3.6 Durbin-Watson Test

In this subsection we shall consider the test of the hypothesis $\rho = 0$ in Model 6 with $\{u_t\}$ following AR(1). The Durbin-Watson test statistic, proposed by Durbin and Watson (1950, 1951), is defined by

$$d = \frac{\sum_{t=2}^{T} (\hat{u}_t - \hat{u}_{t-1})^2}{\sum_{t=1}^{T} \hat{u}_t^2}, \tag{6.3.13}$$

where $\{\hat{u}_t\}$ are the least squares residuals. By comparing (6.3.13) with (6.3.3), we can show that

$$d = 2 - 2\hat{\rho} + o(T^{-1}). \tag{6.3.14}$$

From this we know that $\text{plim } d = 2 - 2\rho$, and the asymptotic distribution of d follows easily from the asymptotic distribution of $\hat{\rho}$ derived in Section 6.3.2.

To derive the exact distribution of d under the null hypothesis, it is useful to rewrite (6.3.13) as

$$d = \frac{\mathbf{u}'\mathbf{MAMu}}{\mathbf{u}'\mathbf{Mu}}, \tag{6.3.15}$$

where $\mathbf{M} = \mathbf{I} - \mathbf{X}(\mathbf{X}'\mathbf{X})^{-1}\mathbf{X}'$ and $\mathbf{A}$ is a $T \times T$ symmetric matrix defined by

$$\mathbf{A} = \begin{bmatrix} 1 & -1 & 0 & \cdot & \cdot & 0 \\ -1 & 2 & -1 & 0 & \cdot & 0 \\ \cdot & & & & & \\ \cdot & & & & & \\ 0 & \cdot & 0 & -1 & 2 & -1 \\ 0 & \cdot & \cdot & 0 & -1 & 1 \end{bmatrix}. \tag{6.3.16}$$

Because **MAM** commutes with **M**, there exists an orthogonal matrix **H** that diagonalizes both (see Theorem 8 of Appendix 1). Let $\nu_1, \nu_2, \ldots, \nu_{T-K}$ be the nonzero characteristic roots of **MAM**. Then we can rewrite (6.3.15) as

$$d = \frac{\sum_{i=1}^{T-K} \nu_i \zeta_i^2}{\sum_{i=1}^{T-K} \zeta_i^2}, \tag{6.3.17}$$

where $\{\zeta_i\}$ are i.i.d. $N(0, 1)$. In the form of (6.3.17), the density of d can be represented as a definite integral (Plackett, 1960, p. 26). The significance points of d can be computed either by the direct evaluation of the integral (Imhof, 1961) or by approximating the density on the basis of the first few moments. Durbin and Watson (1950, 1951) chose the latter method and suggested two variants: the Beta approximation based on the first two moments and the Jacobi approximation based on the first four moments. For a good discussion of many other methods for evaluating the significance points of d, see Durbin and Watson (1971).

The problem of finding the moments of d is simplified because of the independence of d and the denominator of d (see Theorem 7 of Appendix 2), which implies

$$E(d^s) = \frac{E\left(\sum_{i=1}^{T-K} \nu_i \zeta_i^2\right)^s}{E\left(\sum_{i=1}^{T-K} \zeta_i^2\right)^s}, \tag{6.3.18}$$

for any positive integer s. Thus, for example,

$$Ed = \frac{1}{T-K} \sum_{i=1}^{T-K} \nu_i \tag{6.3.19}$$

and

$$Vd = \frac{2 \sum_{i=1}^{T-K} (\nu_i - Ed)^2}{(T-K)(T-K+2)}, \tag{6.3.20}$$

where the term involving ν_i can be evaluated using

$$\sum_{i=1}^{T-K} \nu_i^s = \text{tr}\,(\mathbf{MA})^s. \tag{6.3.21}$$

The Beta approximation assumes that $x = d/4$ has a density given by

$$\frac{1}{B(p, q)} x^{p-1}(1-x)^{q-1}, \qquad 0 \leqq x \leqq 1; \qquad 0 \quad \text{otherwise}, \tag{6.3.22}$$

so that $Ed = 4p/(p+q)$ and $Vd = 16pq/[(p+q)^2(p+q+1)]$. The Jacobi approximation assumes that $x = d/4$ has a density given by

$$\frac{x^{q-1}(1-x)^{p-q}}{B(q, p-q+1)}[1 + a_3G_3(x) + a_4G_4(x)], \tag{6.3.23}$$

where G_3 and G_4 are the third- and fourth-order Jacobi polynomials as defined by Abramowitz and Segun (1965, Definition 22.2.2). The parameters p and q are determined so that the first two moments of (6.3.23) are equated to those of d, and a_3 and a_4 are determined so that the third and fourth moments match. In either approximation method the significance points can be computed by a straightforward computer program for integration.

The distribution of d depends upon $\mathbf{X}$. That means investigators must calculate the significance points for each of their problems by any of the approximation methods discussed in the previous section. Such computations are often expensive. To make such a computation unnecessary in certain cases, Durbin and Watson (1950, 1951) obtained upper and lower bounds of d that do not depend on $\mathbf{X}$ and tabulated the significance points for these. The bounds for d are given by

$$d_{\mathrm{L}} = \frac{\sum_{i=1}^{T-K} \lambda_i \zeta_i^2}{\sum_{i=1}^{T-K} \zeta_i^2} \quad \text{and} \quad d_{\mathrm{U}} = \frac{\sum_{i=1}^{T-K} \lambda_{i+K-1} \zeta_i^2}{\sum_{i=1}^{T-K} \zeta_i^2}, \tag{6.3.24}$$

where $\lambda_i \equiv 2(1 - \cos i\pi T^{-1})$ are the positive characteristic roots of $\mathbf{A}$. (The remaining characteristic root of $\mathbf{A}$ is $\lambda_0 \equiv 0$.) These bounds were obtained under the assumption that $\mathbf{X}$ contains a vector of ones and that no other column of $\mathbf{X}$ is a characteristic vector of $\mathbf{A}$.[2] Durbin and Watson (1951) calculated the significance points (at the 1, 2.5, and 5% levels) of d_{L} and d_{U} for $K = 1, 2, \ldots, 6$ and $T = 15, 16, \ldots, 100$ by the Jacobi approximation. Let $d_{\mathrm{L}\alpha}$ and $d_{\mathrm{U}\alpha}$ be the critical values of these bounds at the α% significance level. Then test $H_0: \rho = 0$ against $H_1: \rho > 0$ by the procedure:

$$\text{Reject} \quad H_0 \quad \text{if} \quad d \leqq d_{\mathrm{L}\alpha} \tag{6.3.25}$$

$$\text{Accept} \quad H_0 \quad \text{if} \quad d \geqq d_{\mathrm{U}\alpha}.$$

If $d_{L\alpha} < d < d_{U\alpha}$, the test is inconclusive. To test $H_0: \rho = 0$ against $H_1: \rho < 0$, Durbin and Watson suggested the following procedure:

$$\text{Reject } H_0 \text{ if } d \geqq 4 - d_{L\alpha} \tag{6.3.26}$$
$$\text{Accept } H_0 \text{ if } d \leqq 4 - d_{U\alpha}.$$

If these tests are inconclusive, the significance points of (6.3.17) must be evaluated directly.

6.3.7 Joint Presence of Lagged Endogenous Variables and Serial Correlation

In this last subsection we shall depart from Model 6 and consider briefly a problem that arises when $\mathbf{X}$ in (6.1.1) contains lagged values of $\mathbf{y}$. An example of such a model is the geometric distributed-lag model (5.6.4), where the errors are serially correlated. This is an important problem because this situation often occurs in practice and many of the results that have been obtained up to this point in Section 6.3 are invalidated in the presence of lagged endogenous variables.

Consider model (5.6.4) and suppose $\{u_t\}$ follow AR(1), $u_t = \rho u_{t-1} + \epsilon_t$, where $\{\epsilon_t\}$ are i.i.d. with $E\epsilon_t = 0$ and $V\epsilon_t = \sigma^2$. The LS estimators of λ and α are clearly inconsistent because $\text{plim}_{T\to\infty} T^{-1}\Sigma_{t=1}^T y_{t-1}u_t \neq 0$. The GLS estimators of λ and α based on the true value of ρ possess not only consistency but also all the good asymptotic properties because the transformation $\mathbf{R}_1$ defined in (5.2.10) essentially reduces the model to the one with independent errors. However, it is interesting to note that FGLS, although still consistent, does not have the same asymptotic distribution as GLS, as we shall show.

Write (5.6.4) in vector notation as

$$\mathbf{y} = \lambda \mathbf{y}_{-1} + \alpha \mathbf{x} + \mathbf{u} \equiv \mathbf{Z}\gamma + \mathbf{u}, \tag{6.3.27}$$

where $\mathbf{y}_{-1} = (y_0, y_1, \ldots, y_{T-1})'$. Suppose, in defining FGLS, we use a consistent estimator of ρ, denoted $\hat{\rho}$, such that $\sqrt{T}(\hat{\rho} - \rho)$ converges to a nondegenerate normal variable. Then the FGLS estimator of γ, denoted $\hat{\gamma}_F$, is given by

$$\hat{\gamma}_F = (\mathbf{Z}'\hat{\mathbf{R}}_1'\hat{\mathbf{R}}_1\mathbf{Z})^{-1}\mathbf{Z}'\hat{\mathbf{R}}_1'\hat{\mathbf{R}}_1\mathbf{y}, \tag{6.3.28}$$

where $\hat{\mathbf{R}}_1$ is derived from $\mathbf{R}_1$ by replacing ρ with $\hat{\rho}$. The asymptotic distribution of $\hat{\gamma}_F$ can be derived from the following equations:

$$\sqrt{T}(\hat{\gamma}_F - \gamma) = (T^{-1}\mathbf{Z}'\hat{\mathbf{R}}_1'\hat{\mathbf{R}}_1\mathbf{Z})^{-1}T^{-1/2}\mathbf{Z}'\hat{\mathbf{R}}_1'\hat{\mathbf{R}}_1\mathbf{u} \tag{6.3.29}$$
$$\overset{\text{LD}}{=} (\text{plim } T^{-1}\mathbf{Z}'\mathbf{R}_1'\mathbf{R}_1\mathbf{Z})^{-1}$$
$$\times [T^{-1/2}\mathbf{Z}'\mathbf{R}_1'\mathbf{R}_1\mathbf{u} + (T^{-1/2}\mathbf{Z}'\hat{\mathbf{R}}_1'\hat{\mathbf{R}}_1\mathbf{u}$$
$$- T^{-1/2}\mathbf{Z}'\mathbf{R}_1'\mathbf{R}_1\mathbf{u})].$$

Let w_T be the first element of the two-dimensional vector $(T^{-1/2}\mathbf{Z}'\hat{\mathbf{R}}_1'\hat{\mathbf{R}}_1\mathbf{u} - T^{-1/2}\mathbf{Z}'\mathbf{R}_1'\mathbf{R}_1\mathbf{u})$. Then we have

$$w_T = \sqrt{T}(\hat{\rho}^2 - \rho^2)\frac{1}{T}\sum_{t=1}^{T-2} y_t u_{t+1} \tag{6.3.30}$$
$$-\sqrt{T}(\hat{\rho} - \rho)\frac{1}{T}\left(\sum_{t=1}^{T-1} y_t u_t + \sum_{t=0}^{T-2} y_t u_{t+2}\right)$$
$$\overset{\text{LD}}{=} \frac{\sigma^2}{\lambda\rho - 1}\sqrt{T}(\hat{\rho} - \rho).$$

Thus we conclude that the asymptotic distribution of FGLS differs from that of GLS and depends on the asymptotic distribution of $\hat{\rho}$ (see Amemiya and Fuller, 1967, for further discussion). Amemiya and Fuller showed how to obtain an asymptotically efficient *feasible* estimator. Such an estimator is not as efficient as GLS.

The theory of the test of independence discussed in the preceding subsection must also be modified under the present model. If **X** contained lagged dependent variables, $y_{t-1}, y_{t-2}, \ldots$, we will still have Eq. (6.3.17) formally, but $\{\zeta_i\}$ will no longer be independent normal because **H** will be a random matrix correlated with **u**. Therefore the Durbin-Watson bounds will no longer be valid.

Even the asymptotic distribution of d under the null hypothesis of independence is different in this case from the case in which **X** is purely nonstochastic. The asymptotic distribution of d is determined by the asymptotic distribution of $\hat{\rho}$ because of (6.3.14). When **X** is nonstochastic, we have $\sqrt{T}(\hat{\rho} - \rho) \rightarrow N(0, 1 - \rho^2)$ by the results of Section 6.3.2. But, if **X** contains the lagged dependent variables, the asymptotic distribution of $\hat{\rho}$ will be different. This can be seen by looking at the formula for $\sqrt{T}(\hat{\rho} - \rho)$ in Eq. (6.3.4). The third term, for example, of the right-hand side of (6.3.5), which is $T^{-1/2}\Sigma_{t=2}^{T}(\boldsymbol{\beta} - \hat{\boldsymbol{\beta}})'\mathbf{x}_t u_{t-1}$ does not converge to 0 in probability because $\mathbf{x}_t$ and u_{t-1} are correlated. Therefore the conclusion obtained there does not hold.

We consider the asymptotic distribution of $\hat{\rho}$ in the simplest case

$$y_t = \alpha y_{t-1} + u_t, \qquad u_t = \rho u_{t-1} + \epsilon_t, \tag{6.3.31}$$

where $|\alpha|, |\rho| < 1$, $\{\epsilon_t\}$ are i.i.d. with $E\epsilon_t = 0$ and $E\epsilon_t^2 = \sigma^2$, and both $\{y_t\}$ and $\{u_t\}$ are stationary. Define

$$\hat{\rho} = \frac{\sum_{t=2}^{T} \hat{u}_{t-1}\hat{u}_t}{\sum_{t=2}^{T} \hat{u}_{t-1}^2}, \tag{6.3.32}$$

where $\hat{u}_t = y_t - \hat{\alpha} y_{t-1}$ and $\hat{\alpha}$ is the least squares estimator. Consider the limit distribution of $\sqrt{T}\hat{\rho}$ under the assumption $\rho = 0$. Because the denominator times T^{-1} converges to σ^2 in probability, we have asymptotically

$$\sqrt{T}\hat{\rho} \overset{\text{LD}}{=} \frac{1}{\sigma^2} \frac{1}{\sqrt{T}} \sum_{t=2}^{T} \hat{u}_{t-1}\hat{u}_t \tag{6.3.33}$$

$$\overset{\text{LD}}{=} \frac{1}{\sigma^2} \frac{1}{\sqrt{T}} \sum_{t=2}^{T} [u_{t-1}u_t - (1-\alpha^2) y_{t-1}u_t].$$

Therefore the asymptotic variance (denoted AV) of $\sqrt{T}\hat{\rho}$ is given by

$$\text{AV}(\sqrt{T}\hat{\rho}) = \frac{1}{\sigma^4} \frac{1}{T} V\left\{\sum_{t=2}^{T} [u_{t-1}u_t - (1-\alpha^2) y_{t-1}u_t]\right\} \tag{6.3.34}$$

$$= \frac{1}{\sigma^4} \frac{1}{T} \left[E\left(\sum_{t=2}^{T} u_{t-1}u_t\right)^2 + (1-\alpha^2)^2 E\left(\sum_{t=2}^{T} y_{t-1}u_t\right)^2 \right.$$

$$\left. - 2(1-\alpha^2) E\left(\sum_{t=2}^{T} u_{t-1}u_t \sum_{t=2}^{T} y_{t-1}u_t\right)\right]$$

$$= \alpha^2(1 - T^{-1}).$$

Hence, assuming that the asymptotic normality holds, we have

$$\sqrt{T}\hat{\rho} \rightarrow N(0, \alpha^2). \tag{6.3.35}$$

Durbin (1970) obtained the following more general result: Even if higher-order lagged values of y_t and purely exogenous variables are contained among the regressors, we have under the assumption $\rho = 0$

$$\sqrt{T}\hat{\rho} \rightarrow N[0, 1 - \text{AV}(\sqrt{T}\hat{\alpha}_1)], \tag{6.3.36}$$

where $\hat{\alpha}_1$ is the least squares estimate of the coefficient on y_{t-1}. He proposed that the test of the independence be based on the asymptotic normality above.[3]

6.4 Seemingly Unrelated Regression Model

The seemingly unrelated regression (SUR) model proposed by Zellner (1962) consists of the following N regression equations, each of which satisfies the assumptions of the standard regression model (Model 1):

$$\mathbf{y}_i = \mathbf{X}_i \boldsymbol{\beta}_i + \mathbf{u}_i, \qquad i = 1, 2, \ldots, N, \tag{6.4.1}$$

where $\mathbf{y}_i$ and $\mathbf{u}_i$ are T-vectors, $\mathbf{X}_i$ is a $T \times K_i$ matrix, and $\boldsymbol{\beta}_i$ is a K_i-vector. Let u_{it} be the tth element of the vector $\mathbf{u}_i$. Then we assume that $(u_{1t}, u_{2t}, \ldots, u_{Nt})$ is an i.i.d. random vector with $Eu_{it} = 0$ and $\text{Cov}\,(u_{it}, u_{jt}) = \sigma_{ij}$. Defining $\mathbf{y} = (\mathbf{y}_1', \mathbf{y}_2', \ldots, \mathbf{y}_N')'$, $\boldsymbol{\beta} = (\boldsymbol{\beta}_1', \boldsymbol{\beta}_2', \ldots, \boldsymbol{\beta}_N')'$, $\mathbf{u} = (\mathbf{u}_1', \mathbf{u}_2', \ldots, \mathbf{u}_N')'$, and $\underline{\mathbf{X}} = \text{diag}\,(\mathbf{X}_1, \mathbf{X}_2, \ldots, \mathbf{X}_N)$, we can write (6.4.1) as

$$\mathbf{y} = \underline{\mathbf{X}} \boldsymbol{\beta} + \mathbf{u}. \tag{6.4.2}$$

This is clearly a special case of Model 6, where the covariance matrix of $\mathbf{u}$ is given by

$$E\mathbf{u}\mathbf{u}' \equiv \boldsymbol{\Omega} = \boldsymbol{\Sigma} \otimes \mathbf{I}_T, \tag{6.4.3}$$

where $\boldsymbol{\Sigma} = \{\sigma_{ij}\}$ and $\otimes$ denotes the Kronecker product (see Theorem 22 of Appendix 1).

This model is useful not only for its own sake but also because it reduces to a certain kind of heteroscedastic model if $\boldsymbol{\Sigma}$ is diagonal (a model that will be discussed in Section 6.5) and because it can be shown to be equivalent to a certain error components model (which will be discussed in Section 6.6).

The GLS estimator of $\boldsymbol{\beta}$ is defined by $\hat{\boldsymbol{\beta}}_G = (\underline{\mathbf{X}}'\boldsymbol{\Omega}^{-1}\underline{\mathbf{X}})^{-1}\underline{\mathbf{X}}'\boldsymbol{\Omega}^{-1}\mathbf{y}$. Because of (6.4.3) we have $\boldsymbol{\Omega}^{-1} = \boldsymbol{\Sigma}^{-1} \otimes \mathbf{I}$, using Theorem 22 (i) of Appendix 1. In the special case in which $\mathbf{X}_1 = \mathbf{X}_2 = \ldots = \mathbf{X}_N$, we can show $\hat{\boldsymbol{\beta}}_G = \hat{\boldsymbol{\beta}}$ as follows: Denoting the common value of $\mathbf{X}_i$ by $\mathbf{X}$ and using Theorem 22 (i) of Appendix 1 repeatedly, we have

$$\begin{aligned} \hat{\boldsymbol{\beta}}_G &= [\underline{\mathbf{X}}'(\boldsymbol{\Sigma}^{-1} \otimes \mathbf{I})\underline{\mathbf{X}}]^{-1}\underline{\mathbf{X}}'(\boldsymbol{\Sigma}^{-1} \otimes \mathbf{I})\mathbf{y} \qquad (6.4.4) \\ &= [(\mathbf{I} \otimes \mathbf{X}')(\boldsymbol{\Sigma}^{-1} \otimes \mathbf{I})(\mathbf{I} \otimes \mathbf{X})]^{-1}(\mathbf{I} \otimes \mathbf{X}')(\boldsymbol{\Sigma}^{-1} \otimes \mathbf{I})\mathbf{y} \\ &= (\boldsymbol{\Sigma}^{-1} \otimes \mathbf{X}'\mathbf{X})^{-1}(\boldsymbol{\Sigma}^{-1} \otimes \mathbf{X}')\mathbf{y} \\ &= [\mathbf{I} \otimes (\mathbf{X}'\mathbf{X})^{-1}\mathbf{X}']\mathbf{y} \\ &= (\underline{\mathbf{X}}'\underline{\mathbf{X}})^{-1}\underline{\mathbf{X}}'\mathbf{y}. \end{aligned}$$

The same result can be also obtained by using Theorem 6.1.1. Statement E is especially easy to verify for the present problem.

To define FGLS, we must first estimate $\mathbf{\Sigma}$. A natural consistent estimator of its i,jth element is provided by $\hat{\sigma}_{ij} = T^{-1}\hat{\mathbf{u}}_i'\hat{\mathbf{u}}_j$, where $\hat{\mathbf{u}}_i \equiv \mathbf{y}_i - \mathbf{X}_i\hat{\boldsymbol{\beta}}_i$ are the least squares residuals from the ith equation. These estimates are clearly consistent as T goes to ∞ while N is fixed. Because of the special form of $\mathbf{\Omega}^{-1}$ given in the preceding paragraph, it is quite straightforward to prove that FGLS and GLS have the same asymptotic distribution (as $T \rightarrow \infty$) under general assumptions on $\mathbf{u}$ and $\underline{\mathbf{X}}$. The limit distribution of $\sqrt{T}(\hat{\boldsymbol{\beta}}_G - \boldsymbol{\beta})$ or $\sqrt{T}(\hat{\boldsymbol{\beta}}_F - \boldsymbol{\beta})$ is $N[\mathbf{0}, (\lim T^{-1}\underline{\mathbf{X}}'\mathbf{\Omega}^{-1}\underline{\mathbf{X}})^{-1}]$. Suitable assumptions on $\mathbf{u}$ and $\underline{\mathbf{X}}$ can easily be inferred from Theorem 3.5.4.

FGLS is generally unbiased provided that it possesses a mean, as proved in a simple, elegant theorem by Kakwani (1967). The exact covariance matrix of FGLS in simple situations has been obtained by several authors and compared with that of GLS or LS (surveyed by Srivastava and Dwivedi, 1979). A particularly interesting result is attributable to Kariya (1981), who obtained the following inequalities concerning the covariance matrices of GLS and FGLS in a two-equation model with normal errors:

$$V\hat{\boldsymbol{\beta}}_{\mathrm{G}} \leqq V\hat{\boldsymbol{\beta}}_{\mathrm{F}} \leqq \left[1 + \frac{2}{T-r-3}\right] V\hat{\boldsymbol{\beta}}_{\mathrm{G}}, \tag{6.4.5}$$

where $r = \text{rank}[\mathbf{X}_1, \mathbf{X}_2]$.

6.5 Heteroscedasticity

A heteroscedastic regression model is Model 6 where $\mathbf{\Sigma}$ is a diagonal matrix, the diagonal elements of which assume at least two different values. Heteroscedasticity is a common occurrence in econometric applications and can often be detected by plotting the least squares residuals against time, the dependent variable, the regression mean, or any other linear combination of the independent variables. For example, Prais and Houthakker (1955) found that a variability of the residuals from a regression of food expenditure on income increases with income. In the subsequent subsections we shall consider various ways to parameterize the heteroscedasticity. We shall consider the estimation of the heteroscedasticity parameters as well as the regression coefficients. We shall also discuss tests for heteroscedasticity.

6.5.1 Unrestricted Heteroscedasticity

When heteroscedasticity is unrestricted, the heteroscedasticity is not parameterized. So we shall treat each of the T variances $\{\sigma_t^2\}$ as an unknown parameter. Clearly, we cannot consistently estimate these variances because we have but one observation per variance. Nevertheless, it is possible to estimate the regression coefficients $\boldsymbol{\beta}$ consistently and more efficiently than by LS and to test for heteroscedasticity.

The idea of obtaining estimates of the regression coefficients that are more efficient than LS in an unrestricted heteroscedastic regression model has been developed independently by White (1982) and by Chamberlain (1982), following the idea of Eicker (1963), who suggested an estimator of $V\hat{\boldsymbol{\beta}}$ (6.1.5) that does not require the consistent estimation of $\boldsymbol{\Sigma}$. The following discussion follows Amemiya (1983c).

Let $\mathbf{W}$ be a $T \times (T-K)$ matrix of constants such that $[\mathbf{X}, \mathbf{W}]$ is nonsingular and $\mathbf{W}'\mathbf{X} = \mathbf{0}$. Then, premultiplying (6.1.1) by $[\mathbf{X}, \mathbf{W}]'$, GLS estimation of $\boldsymbol{\beta}$ can be interpreted as GLS applied simultaneously to

$$\mathbf{X}'\mathbf{y} = \mathbf{X}'\mathbf{X}\boldsymbol{\beta} + \mathbf{X}'\mathbf{u} \tag{6.5.1}$$

and

$$\mathbf{W}'\mathbf{y} = \mathbf{W}'\mathbf{u}. \tag{6.5.2}$$

Thus, applying Theorem 13 of Appendix 1 to

$$\begin{bmatrix} \mathbf{X}'\boldsymbol{\Sigma}\mathbf{X} & \mathbf{X}'\boldsymbol{\Sigma}\mathbf{W} \\ \mathbf{W}'\boldsymbol{\Sigma}\mathbf{X} & \mathbf{W}'\boldsymbol{\Sigma}\mathbf{W} \end{bmatrix}^{-1},$$

we obtain

$$\hat{\boldsymbol{\beta}}_G = \hat{\boldsymbol{\beta}} - (\mathbf{X}'\mathbf{X})^{-1}\mathbf{X}'\boldsymbol{\Sigma}\mathbf{W}(\mathbf{W}'\boldsymbol{\Sigma}\mathbf{W})^{-1}\mathbf{W}'\mathbf{y}. \tag{6.5.3}$$

Of course, it is also possible to derive (6.5.3) directly from (6.1.3) without regard to the interpretation given above. An advantage of (6.5.3) over (6.1.3) is that the former does not depend on $\boldsymbol{\Sigma}^{-1}$. Note that one cannot estimate $T^{-1}\mathbf{X}'\boldsymbol{\Sigma}^{-1}\mathbf{X}$ consistently unless $\boldsymbol{\Sigma}$ can be consistently estimated. To transform (6.5.3) into a feasible estimator, one is tempted to replace $\boldsymbol{\Sigma}$ by a diagonal matrix $\mathbf{D}$ whose tth element is $(y_t - \mathbf{x}_t'\hat{\boldsymbol{\beta}})^2$. Then it is easy to prove that under general assumptions plim $T^{-1}\mathbf{X}'\mathbf{D}\mathbf{W} =$ plim $T^{-1}\mathbf{X}'\boldsymbol{\Sigma}\mathbf{W}$ and plim $T^{-1}\mathbf{W}'\mathbf{D}\mathbf{W} =$ plim $T^{-1}\mathbf{W}'\boldsymbol{\Sigma}\mathbf{W}$ element by element. However, one difficulty remains: Because the size of these matrices increases with T, the resulting feasible estimator is not asymptotically equivalent to GLS.

We can solve this problem partially by replacing (6.5.2) with

$$\mathbf{W}_1'\mathbf{y} = \mathbf{W}_1'\mathbf{u}, \tag{6.5.4}$$

where $\mathbf{W}_1$ consists of N columns of $\mathbf{W}$, N being a fixed number. When GLS is applied to (6.5.1) and (6.5.4), it is called the *partially generalized least squares* (PGLS) and the estimator is given by

$$\hat{\beta}_P = \hat{\beta} - (\mathbf{X}'\mathbf{X})^{-1}\mathbf{X}'\mathbf{\Sigma}\mathbf{W}_1(\mathbf{W}_1'\mathbf{\Sigma}\mathbf{W}_1)^{-1}\mathbf{W}_1'\mathbf{y}. \tag{6.5.5}$$

PGLS is more efficient than LS because

$$V\hat{\beta} - V\hat{\beta}_P = (\mathbf{X}'\mathbf{X})^{-1}\mathbf{X}'\mathbf{\Sigma}\mathbf{W}_1(\mathbf{W}_1'\mathbf{\Sigma}\mathbf{W}_1)^{-1}\mathbf{W}_1'\mathbf{\Sigma}\mathbf{X}(\mathbf{X}'\mathbf{X})^{-1}, \tag{6.5.6}$$

which is clearly nonnegative definite, but it is less efficient than GLS. An asymptotically equivalent feasible version of $\hat{\beta}_P$ is obtained by replacing the $\mathbf{\Sigma}$ in (6.5.5) by the $\mathbf{D}$ defined in the preceding paragraph.

White (1980a) proposed testing the hypothesis $\sigma_t^2 = \sigma^2$ for all t by comparing $(\mathbf{X}'\mathbf{X})^{-1}\mathbf{X}'\mathbf{D}\mathbf{X}(\mathbf{X}'\mathbf{X})^{-1}$ with $\hat{\sigma}^2(\mathbf{X}'\mathbf{X})^{-1}$, where $\mathbf{D}$ is as defined earlier and $\hat{\sigma}^2$ is the least squares estimator of σ^2 defined in (1.2.5). Equivalently, White considered elements of $\mathbf{X}'\mathbf{D}\mathbf{X} - \hat{\sigma}^2\mathbf{X}'\mathbf{X}$. If we stack the elements of the upper triangular part of this matrix, we obtain a vector of $(K^2 + K)/2$ dimension defined by $\mathbf{S}'(\hat{\mathbf{u}}^2 - \hat{\sigma}^2\mathbf{l})$, where $\hat{\mathbf{u}}^2$ is a T-vector the tth element of which is $\hat{u}_t^2$, $\mathbf{l}$ is a T-vector of ones, and $\mathbf{S}$ is a $T \times (K^2 + K)/2$ matrix, the columns of which are $(x_{i1}x_{j1}, x_{i2}x_{j2}, \ldots, x_{iT}x_{jT})'$ for $1 \leqq i, j \leqq K$, and $i \leqq j$. It is easy to show that $T^{-1/2}\mathbf{S}'(\hat{\mathbf{u}}^2 - \hat{\sigma}^2\mathbf{l}) \rightarrow N(\mathbf{0}, \mathbf{A})$, where $\mathbf{A} = \lim\,(T^{-1}\mathbf{S}'\mathbf{\Lambda}\mathbf{S} + T^{-2}\mathbf{l}'\mathbf{\Lambda}\mathbf{l} \cdot \mathbf{S}'\mathbf{l}\mathbf{l}'\mathbf{S} - T^{-2}\mathbf{S}'\mathbf{\Lambda}\mathbf{l} \cdot \mathbf{l}'\mathbf{S} - T^{-2}\mathbf{S}'\mathbf{l} \cdot \mathbf{l}'\mathbf{\Lambda}\mathbf{S})$ and $\mathbf{\Lambda} = E(\mathbf{u}^2 - \sigma^2\mathbf{l}) \cdot (\mathbf{u}^2 - \sigma^2\mathbf{l})'$. The test statistic proposed by White is

$$(\hat{\mathbf{u}}^2 - \hat{\sigma}^2\mathbf{l})'\mathbf{S}(T\hat{\mathbf{A}})^{-1}\mathbf{S}'(\hat{\mathbf{u}}^2 - \hat{\sigma}^2\mathbf{l}),$$

where $\hat{\mathbf{A}}$ is obtained from $\mathbf{A}$ by eliminating lim and replacing $\mathbf{\Lambda}$ with $\mathbf{D}\{(\hat{u}_t^2 - \hat{\sigma}^2)^2\}$. This statistic is asymptotically distributed as chi-square with $(K^2 + K)/2$ degrees of freedom under the null hypothesis. It can be simply computed as TR^2 from the regression of $\hat{u}_t^2$ on the products and cross products of $\mathbf{x}_t$.

6.5.2 Constant Variance in a Subset of the Sample

The heteroscedastic model we shall consider in this subsection represents the simplest way to restrict the number of estimable parameters to a finite and manageable size. We assume that the error vector $\mathbf{u}$ is partitioned into N nonoverlapping subvectors as $\mathbf{u} = (\mathbf{u}_1', \mathbf{u}_2', \ldots, \mathbf{u}_N')'$ such that $E\mathbf{u}_i\mathbf{u}_i' = \sigma_i^2\mathbf{I}_{T_i}$. We can estimate each σ_i^2 consistently from the least squares residuals provided that each T_i goes to infinity with T. Note that this model is a special case of Zellner's SUR model discussed in Section 6.4, so that the asymptotic results given there also hold here. We shall consider a test of homoscedasticity and the exact moments of FGLS.

If we assume the normality of $\mathbf{u}$, the hypothesis $\sigma_i^2 = \sigma^2$ for all i can be tested by the likelihood ratio test in a straightforward manner. Partitioning $\mathbf{y}$ and $\mathbf{X}$ into N subsets that conform to the partition of $\mathbf{u}$, we can write the constrained and unconstrained log likelihood functions respectively as

$$\text{CLL} = -\frac{T}{2} \log \sigma^2 - \frac{1}{2\sigma^2} \sum_{i=1}^{N} (\mathbf{y}_i - \mathbf{x}_i\boldsymbol{\beta})'(\mathbf{y}_i - \mathbf{X}_i\boldsymbol{\beta}) \tag{6.5.7}$$

and

$$\text{ULL} = -\frac{1}{2} \sum_{i=1}^{N} T_i \log \sigma_i^2 - \frac{1}{2} \sum_{i=1}^{N} \frac{1}{\sigma_i^2} (\mathbf{y}_i - \mathbf{X}_i\boldsymbol{\beta})'(\mathbf{y}_i - \mathbf{X}_i\boldsymbol{\beta}). \tag{6.5.8}$$

Therefore -2 times the log likelihood ratio is given by

$$-2 \log \text{LRT} = \sum_{i=1}^{N} T_i \log (\hat{\sigma}^2/\hat{\sigma}_i^2), \tag{6.5.9}$$

where $\hat{\sigma}^2$ and $\hat{\sigma}_i^2$ are the constrained and unconstrained MLE, respectively. The statistic is asymptotically distributed as chi-square with $N-1$ degrees of freedom.[4]

Taylor (1978) has considered a special case in which $N = 2$ in a model with normal errors and has derived the formulae for the moments of FGLS. By evaluating the covariance matrix of FGLS at various parameter values, Taylor has shown that FGLS is usually far more efficient than LS and is only slightly less efficient than GLS.

We shall sketch briefly the derivation of the moments of FGLS. Let $\mathbf{C}$ be a $K \times K$ matrix such that

$$\mathbf{C}'\mathbf{X}_1'\mathbf{X}_1\mathbf{C} = \sigma_1^2\mathbf{I} \tag{6.5.10}$$

and

$$\mathbf{C}'\mathbf{X}_2'\mathbf{X}_2\mathbf{C} = \sigma_2^2\boldsymbol{\Lambda}, \tag{6.5.11}$$

where $\boldsymbol{\Lambda}$ is a diagonal matrix, the elements $\lambda_1, \lambda_2, \ldots, \lambda_K$ of which are the roots of the equation

$$|\sigma_2^{-2}\mathbf{X}_2'\mathbf{X}_2 - \lambda\sigma_1^{-2}\mathbf{X}_1'\mathbf{X}_1| = 0. \tag{6.5.12}$$

The existence of such a matrix is guaranteed by Theorem 16 of Appendix 1. With $\mathbf{S} = \mathbf{C}(\mathbf{I} + \boldsymbol{\Lambda})^{-1/2}$, transform the original equation $\mathbf{y} = \mathbf{X}\boldsymbol{\beta} + \mathbf{u}$ to

$$\mathbf{y} = \mathbf{X}^*\gamma + \mathbf{u}, \tag{6.5.13}$$

where $\mathbf{X}^* = \mathbf{X}\mathbf{S}$ and $\gamma = \mathbf{S}^{-1}\boldsymbol{\beta}$. The FGLS estimator of γ, denoted $\hat{\gamma}$, is given by

$$\hat{\gamma} = (\tilde{\sigma}_1^{-2}\mathbf{X}_1^{*\prime}\mathbf{X}_1^* + \tilde{\sigma}_2^{-2}\mathbf{X}_2^{*\prime}\mathbf{X}_2^*)^{-1}(\tilde{\sigma}_1^{-2}\mathbf{X}_1^{*\prime}\mathbf{y}_1 + \tilde{\sigma}_2^{-2}\mathbf{X}_2^{*\prime}\mathbf{y}_2), \quad (6.5.14)$$

where $\tilde{\sigma}_i^2 = (T_i - K)^{-1}(\mathbf{y}_i - \mathbf{X}_i\hat{\beta})'(\mathbf{y}_i - \mathbf{X}_i\hat{\beta})$.[5]

Using $\sigma_1^{-2}\mathbf{X}_1^{*\prime}\mathbf{X}_1^* = (\mathbf{I} + \mathbf{\Lambda})^{-1}$ and $\sigma_2^{-2}\mathbf{X}_2^{*\prime}\mathbf{X}_2^* = \mathbf{\Lambda}(\mathbf{I} + \mathbf{\Lambda})^{-1}$, we obtain

$$\hat{\gamma} - \gamma = (\mathbf{I} + \mathbf{\Lambda})[\sigma_1^{-2}\mathbf{D}\mathbf{X}_1^{*\prime}\mathbf{u}_1 + \sigma_2^{-2}\mathbf{\Lambda}^{-1}(\mathbf{I} - \mathbf{D})\mathbf{X}_2^{*\prime}\mathbf{u}_2], \quad (6.5.15)$$

where $\mathbf{D}$ is a diagonal matrix the ith diagonal element of which is equal to $\sigma_1^2\tilde{\sigma}_2^2/(\sigma_1^2\tilde{\sigma}_2^2 + \lambda_i\sigma_2^2\tilde{\sigma}_1^2)$. Finally, the moments of $\hat{\gamma} - \gamma$ can be obtained by making use of the independence of $\mathbf{D}$ with $\mathbf{X}_1^{*\prime}\mathbf{u}_1$ and $\mathbf{X}_2^{*\prime}\mathbf{u}_2$ and of known formulae for the moments of $\mathbf{D}$ that involve a hypergeometric function.

Kariya (1981) has derived the following inequalities concerning the covariance matrices of GLS and FGLS in a two-equation model:

$$V\hat{\beta}_G \leq V\hat{\beta}_F \leq \left[1 + \frac{1}{2(T_1 - K - 2)} + \frac{1}{2(T_2 - K - 2)}\right] V\hat{\beta}_G. \quad (6.5.16)$$

6.5.3 General Parametric Heteroscedasticity

In this subsection we shall assume $\sigma_t^2 = g_t(\alpha, \beta_1)$ without specifying g, where β_1 is a subset (possibly whole) of the regression parameters β and α is another vector of parameters unrelated to β. In applications it is often assumed that $g_t(\alpha, \beta_1) = g(\alpha, \mathbf{x}_t'\beta)$. The estimation of α and β can be done in several steps. In the first step, we obtain the LS estimator of β, denoted $\hat{\beta}$. In the second step, α and β_1 can be estimated by minimizing $\Sigma_{t=1}^T[\hat{u}_t^2 - g_t(\alpha, \beta_1)]^2$, where $\hat{u}_t = y_t - \mathbf{x}_t'\hat{\beta}$. The consistency and the asymptotic normality of the resulting estimators, denoted $\tilde{\alpha}$ and $\tilde{\beta}_1$, have been proved by Jobson and Fuller (1980). In the third step we have two main options: FGLS using $g_t(\tilde{\alpha}, \hat{\beta}_1)$ or MLE under normality using $\tilde{\alpha}$ and $\hat{\beta}$ as the initial estimates in some iterative algorithm.[6] Carroll and Ruppert (1982a) proved that under general assumptions FGLS has the same asymptotic distribution as GLS. Jobson and Fuller derived simple formulae for the method of scoring and proved that the estimator of β obtained at the second iteration is asymptotically efficient (and is asymptotically more efficient than GLS or FGLS). Carroll and Ruppert (1982b) have pointed out, however, that GLS or FGLS is more robust against a misspecification in the g function. Carroll and Ruppert (1982a) have proposed a robust version of FGLS (cf. Section 2.3) in an attempt to make it robust also against nonnormality.

There are situations where FGLS has the same asymptotic distribution as MLE. Amemiya (1973b), whose major goal lay in another area, compared the asymptotic efficiency of FGLS vis-à-vis MLE in cases where y_t has mean $\mathbf{x}_t'\beta$

and variance $\eta^2(\mathbf{x}_t'\boldsymbol{\beta})^2$ and follows one of the three distributions: (1) normal, (2) lognormal, and (3) gamma. This is the form of heteroscedasticity suggested by Prais and Houthakker (1955). It was shown that FGLS is asymptotically efficient if y_t has a gamma distribution. Thus this is an example of the BAN estimators mentioned in Section 4.2.4.

This last result is a special case of the following more general result attributable to Nelder and Wedderburn (1972). Let $\{y_t\}$ be independently distributed with the density

$$f(y_t) = \exp\{\alpha(\boldsymbol{\lambda})[g(\theta_t)y_t - h(\theta_t) + k(\boldsymbol{\lambda}, y_t)]\}, \tag{6.5.17}$$

where α and $\theta_t \equiv q(\mathbf{x}_t, \boldsymbol{\beta})$ are scalars and $\boldsymbol{\lambda}$, $\mathbf{x}_t$, and $\boldsymbol{\beta}$ are vectors. It is assumed that $h'(\theta_t) = \theta_t g'(\theta_t)$ for every t, which implies that $Ey_t = \theta_t$ and $Vy_t = [\alpha(\boldsymbol{\lambda})g'(\theta_t)]^{-1}$. Then, in the estimation of $\boldsymbol{\beta}$, the method of scoring is identical to the Gauss-Newton nonlinear weighted least squares iteration (cf. Section 4.4.3). The binomial distribution is a special case of (6.5.17). To see this, define the binary variable y_t that takes unity with probability θ_t and zero with probability $1-\theta_t$ and put $\alpha(\lambda) = 1$, $g(\theta_t) = \log\theta_t - \log(1-\theta_t)$, $h(\theta_t) = -\log(1-\theta_t)$, and $k(\lambda, y_t) = 0$. The normal distribution is also a special case: Take $y_t \sim N(\theta_t, \lambda^2)$, $\alpha(\lambda) = \lambda^{-2}$, $g(\theta_t) = \theta_t$, $h(\theta_t) = \theta_t^2/2$, and $k(\lambda, y_t) = -2^{-1}\lambda^2 \log(2\pi\lambda^2) - y_t^2/2$. The special case of Amemiya (1973b) is obtained by putting $\alpha(\lambda) = -\lambda$, $g(\theta_t) = \theta_t^{-1}$, $h(\theta_t) = -\log\theta_t$, and $k(\lambda, y_t) = \lambda^{-1}\log\Gamma(\lambda) - \log\lambda + \lambda^{-1}(1-\lambda)\log y_t$.

There are series of articles that discuss tests of homoscedasticity against heteroscedasticity of the form $\sigma_t^2 = g(\alpha, \mathbf{x}_t'\boldsymbol{\beta})$, where α is a scalar such that $g(0, \mathbf{x}_t'\boldsymbol{\beta})$ does not depend on t. Thus the null hypothesis is stated as $\alpha = 0$. Anscombe (1961) was the first to propose such a test, which was later modified by Bickel (1978). Hammerstrom (1981) proved that Bickel's test is locally uniformly most powerful under normality.

6.5.4 Variance as a Linear Function of Regressors

In this subsection we shall consider the model $\sigma_t^2 = \mathbf{z}_t'\boldsymbol{\alpha}$, where $\mathbf{z}_t$ is a G-vector of known constants and $\boldsymbol{\alpha}$ is a G-vector of unknown parameters unrelated to the regression coefficients $\boldsymbol{\beta}$. Such a parametric heteroscedastic regression model has been frequently discussed in the literature. This is not surprising, for this specification is as simple as a linear regression model and is more general than it appears because the elements of $\mathbf{z}_t$ may be nonlinear transformations of independent variables. The elements of $\mathbf{z}_t$ can also be related to $\mathbf{x}_t$ without affecting the results obtained in the following discussion. We shall consider the estimation of $\boldsymbol{\alpha}$ and the test of the hypothesis $\sigma_t^2 = \sigma^2$ under this model.

Hildreth and Houck (1968) and Goldfeld and Quandt (1972) were among the first to study the estimation of $\boldsymbol{\alpha}$. We shall call these estimators HH and GQ for short. We shall follow the discussion of Amemiya (1977b), who proposed an estimator of $\boldsymbol{\alpha}$ asymptotically more efficient under normality than the HH and GQ estimators.

Hildreth and Houck presented their model as a random coefficients model (cf. Section 6.7) defined by

$$y_t = \mathbf{x}_t'(\boldsymbol{\beta} + \boldsymbol{\xi}_t), \tag{6.5.18}$$

where $\{\boldsymbol{\xi}_t\}$ are K-dimensional i.i.d. vectors with $E\boldsymbol{\xi}_t = \mathbf{0}$ and $E\boldsymbol{\xi}_t\boldsymbol{\xi}_t' = \mathbf{D}\{\alpha_t\}$. The last matrix denotes a $K \times K$ diagonal matrix, the tth element of which is α_t. Thus the Hildreth and Houck model is shown to be a special case of the model where the variance is a linear function of regressors by putting $\mathbf{z}_t = (x_{1t}^2, x_{2t}^2, \ldots, x_{Kt}^2)'$.

We shall compare the HH, GQ, and Amemiya estimators under the assumption of the normality of $\mathbf{u}$. All three estimators are derived from a regression model in which $\hat{u}_t^2$ serves as the dependent variable. Noting $\hat{u}_t = u_t - \mathbf{x}_t'(\mathbf{X}'\mathbf{X})^{-1}\mathbf{X}'\mathbf{u}$, we can write

$$\hat{u}_t^2 = \mathbf{z}_t'\boldsymbol{\alpha} + v_{1t} - 2v_{2t} + v_{3t}, \tag{6.5.19}$$

where $v_{1t} = u_t^2 - \sigma_t^2$, $v_{2t} = u_t\mathbf{x}_t'(\mathbf{X}'\mathbf{X})^{-1}\mathbf{X}'\mathbf{u}$, and $v_{3t} = [\mathbf{x}_t'(\mathbf{X}'\mathbf{X})^{-1}\mathbf{X}'\mathbf{u}]^2$. We can write (6.5.19) in vector notation as

$$\hat{\mathbf{u}}^2 = \mathbf{Z}\boldsymbol{\alpha} + \mathbf{v}_1 - 2\mathbf{v}_2 + \mathbf{v}_3. \tag{6.5.20}$$

We assume that $\mathbf{X}$ fulfills the assumptions of Theorem 3.5.4 and that $\lim_{T\to\infty} T^{-1}\mathbf{Z}'\mathbf{Z}$ is a nonsingular finite matrix. (Amemiya, 1977b, has presented more specific assumptions.)

Equation (6.5.20) is not strictly a regression equation because $E\mathbf{v}_2 \neq \mathbf{0}$ and $E\mathbf{v}_3 \neq \mathbf{0}$. However, they can be ignored asymptotically because they are $O(T^{-1/2})$ and $O(T^{-1})$, respectively. Therefore the asymptotic properties of LS, GLS, and FGLS derived from (6.5.20) can be analyzed as if $\mathbf{v}_1$ were the only error term. (Of course, this statement must be rigorously proved, as has been done by Amemiya, 1977b.)

The GQ estimator, denoted $\hat{\boldsymbol{\alpha}}_1$, is LS applied to (6.5.20). Thus

$$\hat{\boldsymbol{\alpha}}_1 = (\mathbf{Z}'\mathbf{Z})^{-1}\mathbf{Z}'\hat{\mathbf{u}}^2. \tag{6.5.21}$$

It can be shown that $\sqrt{T}(\hat{\boldsymbol{\alpha}}_1 - \boldsymbol{\alpha})$ has the same limit distribution as

$\sqrt{T}(\mathbf{Z}'\mathbf{Z})^{-1}\mathbf{Z}'\mathbf{v}_1$. Consequently, $\hat{\alpha}_1$ is consistent and asymptotically normal with the asymptotic covariance matrix given by

$$\mathbf{V}_1 = 2(\mathbf{Z}'\mathbf{Z})^{-1}\mathbf{Z}'\mathbf{D}^2\mathbf{Z}(\mathbf{Z}'\mathbf{Z})^{-1}, \tag{6.5.22}$$

where $\mathbf{D} \equiv E\mathbf{u}\mathbf{u}' = \mathbf{D}\{\mathbf{z}_t'\boldsymbol{\alpha}\}$.

The HH estimator $\hat{\alpha}_2$ is LS applied to a regression equation that defines $E\hat{u}_t^2$:

$$\hat{\mathbf{u}}^2 = \dot{\mathbf{M}}\mathbf{Z}\boldsymbol{\alpha} + \mathbf{w}, \tag{6.5.23}$$

where $\dot{\mathbf{M}}$ is obtained by squaring every element of $\mathbf{M} = \mathbf{I} - \mathbf{X}(\mathbf{X}'\mathbf{X})^{-1}\mathbf{X}'$ and $E\mathbf{w} = \mathbf{0}$. Thus

$$\hat{\alpha}_2 = (\mathbf{Z}'\dot{\mathbf{M}}\dot{\mathbf{M}}\mathbf{Z})^{-1}\mathbf{Z}'\dot{\mathbf{M}}\hat{\mathbf{u}}^2. \tag{6.5.24}$$

It can be shown that

$$E\mathbf{w}\mathbf{w}' = 2\mathbf{Q}, \tag{6.5.25}$$

where $\mathbf{Q} = \mathbf{MDM} * \mathbf{MDM}$. The symbol $*$ denotes the Hadamard product defined in Theorem 23 of Appendix 1. (Thus we could have written $\dot{\mathbf{M}}$ as $\mathbf{M} * \mathbf{M}$.) Therefore the exact covariance matrix of $\hat{\alpha}_2$ is given by

$$\mathbf{V}_2 = 2(\mathbf{Z}'\dot{\mathbf{M}}\dot{\mathbf{M}}\mathbf{Z})^{-1}\mathbf{Z}'\dot{\mathbf{M}}\mathbf{Q}\dot{\mathbf{M}}\mathbf{Z}(\mathbf{Z}'\dot{\mathbf{M}}\dot{\mathbf{M}}\mathbf{Z})^{-1}. \tag{6.5.26}$$

To compare the GQ and the HH estimators we shall consider a modification of the HH estimator, called MHH, which is defined as

$$\hat{\alpha}_2^* = (\mathbf{Z}'\dot{\mathbf{M}}\dot{\mathbf{M}}\mathbf{Z})^{-1}\mathbf{Z}'\dot{\mathbf{M}}\dot{\mathbf{M}}\hat{\mathbf{u}}^2. \tag{6.5.27}$$

Because $\mathbf{v}_2$ and $\mathbf{v}_3$ in (6.5.20) are of $O(T^{-1/2})$ and $O(T^{-1})$, respectively, this estimator is consistent and asymptotically normal with the asymptotic covariance matrix given by

$$\mathbf{V}_2^* = 2(\mathbf{Z}'\dot{\mathbf{M}}\dot{\mathbf{M}}\mathbf{Z})^{-1}\mathbf{Z}'\dot{\mathbf{M}}\dot{\mathbf{M}}\mathbf{D}^2\dot{\mathbf{M}}\dot{\mathbf{M}}\mathbf{Z}(\mathbf{Z}'\dot{\mathbf{M}}\dot{\mathbf{M}}\mathbf{Z})^{-1}. \tag{6.5.28}$$

Amemiya (1978a) showed that

$$\mathbf{Q} \geqq \dot{\mathbf{M}}\mathbf{D}^2\dot{\mathbf{M}}, \tag{6.5.29}$$

or that $\mathbf{Q} - \dot{\mathbf{M}}\mathbf{D}^2\dot{\mathbf{M}}$ is nonnegative definite, by showing $\mathbf{A}'\mathbf{A} * \mathbf{A}'\mathbf{A} \geqq (\mathbf{A} * \mathbf{A})'(\mathbf{A} * \mathbf{A})$ for any square matrix $\mathbf{A}$ (take $\mathbf{A} = \mathbf{D}^{1/2}\mathbf{M}$). The latter inequality follows from Theorem 23 (i) of Appendix 1. Therefore $\mathbf{V}_2 \geqq \mathbf{V}_2^*$, thereby implying that MHH is asymptotically more efficient than HH.

Now, from (6.5.27) we note that MHH is a "wrong" GLS applied to (6.5.20), assuming $E\mathbf{v}_1\mathbf{v}_1'$ were $(\dot{\mathbf{M}}\dot{\mathbf{M}})^{-1}$ when, in fact, it is $2\mathbf{D}^2$. Therefore we cannot make a definite comparison between GQ and MHH, nor between GQ and HH. However, this consideration does suggest an estimator that is asymptotically more efficient than either GQ or MHH, namely, FGLS applied to Eq. (6.5.20),

$$\hat{\boldsymbol{\alpha}}_3 = (\mathbf{Z}'\hat{\mathbf{D}}_1^{-2}\mathbf{Z})^{-1}\mathbf{Z}'\hat{\mathbf{D}}_1^{-2}\hat{\mathbf{u}}^2, \tag{6.5.30}$$

where $\hat{\mathbf{D}}_1 = \mathbf{D}\{\mathbf{z}_t'\hat{\boldsymbol{\alpha}}_1\}$. Amemiya (1977b) showed that the estimator is consistent and asymptotically normal with the asymptotic covariance matrix given by

$$\mathbf{V}_3 = 2(\mathbf{Z}'\mathbf{D}^{-2}\mathbf{Z})^{-1}. \tag{6.5.31}$$

Amemiya (1977) has also shown that the estimator has the same asymptotic distribution as MLE.[7]

It should be noted that all four estimators defined earlier are consistent even if $\mathbf{u}$ is not normal, provided that the fourth moment of u_t is finite. All the formulae for the asymptotic covariance matrices in this subsection have been obtained under the normality assumption, and, therefore, the ranking of estimators is not preserved in the absence of normality.

So far we have concentrated on the estimation of $\boldsymbol{\alpha}$. Given any one of the estimators of $\boldsymbol{\alpha}$ defined in this subsection, say $\hat{\boldsymbol{\alpha}}_3$, we can estimate $\boldsymbol{\beta}$ by FGLS

$$\hat{\boldsymbol{\beta}}_F = (\mathbf{X}'\hat{\mathbf{D}}_3^{-1}\mathbf{X})^{-1}\mathbf{X}'\hat{\mathbf{D}}_3^{-1}\mathbf{y}. \tag{6.5.32}$$

We can iterate back and forth between (6.5.30) and (6.5.32). That is, in the next round of the iteration, we can redefine $\hat{\mathbf{u}}$ as $\mathbf{y} - \mathbf{X}\hat{\boldsymbol{\beta}}_F$ and obtain a new estimate of $\hat{\boldsymbol{\alpha}}_3$, which in turn can be used to redefine $\hat{\mathbf{D}}_3$, and so on. Buse (1982) showed that this iteration is equivalent under normality to the method of scoring. Goldfeld and Quandt (1972) presented a Monte Carlo study of the performance of LS, FGLS, and MLE in the estimation of $\boldsymbol{\beta}$ in the model where $y_t = \beta_1 + \beta_2 x_t + u_t$ and $Vu_t = \alpha_1 + \alpha_2 x_t + \alpha_3 x_t^2$.

We shall conclude this subsection with a brief account of tests of homoscedasticity in the model where the variance is a linear function of regressors. Assuming that the first column of $\mathbf{Z}$ is a vector of ones, the null hypothesis of homoscedasticity can be set up as H_0: $\boldsymbol{\alpha} = (\sigma^2, 0, 0, \ldots, 0)'$ in this model. Breusch and Pagan (1979) derived Rao's score test (cf. Section 4.5.1) of H_0 as

$$\text{Rao} = \frac{1}{2\hat{\sigma}^4}(\hat{\mathbf{u}}^2 - \hat{\sigma}^2\mathbf{l})'\mathbf{Z}(\mathbf{Z}'\mathbf{Z})^{-1}\mathbf{Z}'(\hat{\mathbf{u}}^2 - \hat{\sigma}^2\mathbf{l}), \tag{6.5.33}$$

where $\mathbf{l}$ is the T-vector of ones. It is asymptotically distributed as χ^2_{G-1}. Because the asymptotic distribution may not be accurate in small sample, Breusch and

Pagan suggested estimating $P(\text{Rao} > c)$ by simulation. They pointed out that since Rao's score test depends only on $\hat{\mathbf{u}}$, the simulation is relatively simple. For a simple way to make (6.5.33) robust to nonnormality, see Koenker (1981b).

Goldfeld and Quandt (1965) proposed the following nonparametric test of homoscedasticity, which they called the peak test: First, order the residuals $\hat{u}_t$ in the order of $\mathbf{z}_t'\hat{\boldsymbol{\alpha}}$ for a given estimator $\hat{\boldsymbol{\alpha}}$. This defines a sequence $\{\hat{u}_{(i)}\}$ where $j \leqq k$ if and only if $\mathbf{z}_j'\hat{\boldsymbol{\alpha}} \leqq \mathbf{z}_k'\hat{\boldsymbol{\alpha}}$. (Instead of $\mathbf{z}_t'\hat{\boldsymbol{\alpha}}$, we can use any variable that we suspect influences σ_t^2 most significantly.) Second, define that a peak occurs at $j > 1$ if and only if $|\hat{u}_j| > |\hat{u}_k|$ for all $k < j$. Third, if the number of peaks exceeds the critical value, reject homoscedasticity. Goldfeld and Quandt (1965, 1972) presented tables of critical values.

6.5.5 Variance as an Exponential Function of Regressors

As we mentioned before, the linear specification, however simple, is more general than it appears. However, a researcher may explicitly specify the variance to be a certain nonlinear function of the regressors. The most natural choice is an exponential function because, unlike a linear specification, it has the attractive feature of ensuring positive variances. Harvey (1976), who assumed $y_t \sim N[\mathbf{x}_t'\boldsymbol{\beta}, \exp(\mathbf{z}_t'\boldsymbol{\alpha})]$, proposed estimating $\boldsymbol{\alpha}$ by LS applied to the regression of $\log \hat{u}_t^2$ on $\mathbf{z}_t$ and showed that the estimator is consistent if 1.2704 is subtracted from the estimate of the constant term. Furthermore, the estimator has an asymptotic covariance matrix equal to $4.9348(\mathbf{Z}'\mathbf{Z})^{-1}$, more than double the asymptotic covariance matrix of MLE, which is $2(\mathbf{Z}'\mathbf{Z})^{-1}$.

6.6 Error Components Models

Error components models are frequently used by econometricians in analyzing panel data—observations from a cross-section of the population (such as consumers, firms, and states, and hereafter referred to as individuals) at various points in time. Depending on whether the error term consists of three components (a cross-section-specific component, a time-specific component, and a component that depends both on individuals and on time) or two components (excluding the time-specific component), these models are called *three error components models* (3ECM) and *two error components models* (2ECM), respectively. Two error components models are more frequently used in econometrics than 3ECM because it is usually more important to include a cross-section-specific component than a time-specific component.

For example, in studies explaining earnings, to which error components models have often been applied, the cross-section-specific component may be regarded as the error term arising from permanent earnings and is more important than the time-specific component.

We shall discuss first 3ECM and then various generalizations of 2ECM. These generalizations are (1) the Balestra-Nerlove model (2ECM with lagged endogenous variables), (2) 2ECM with a serially correlated error, and (3) 2ECM with endogenous regressors.

6.6.1 Three Error Components Models

Three error components models are defined by

$$y_{it} = \mathbf{x}_{it}'\boldsymbol{\beta} + u_{it}, \qquad i = 1, 2, \ldots, N, \quad t = 1, 2, \ldots, T, \tag{6.6.1}$$

and

$$u_{it} = \mu_i + \lambda_t + \epsilon_{it}, \tag{6.6.2}$$

where μ_i and λ_t are the cross-section-specific and time-specific components mentioned earlier. Assume that the sequence $\{\mu_i\}$, $\{\lambda_t\}$, and $\{\epsilon_{it}\}$ are i.i.d. random variables with zero mean and are mutually independent with the variances σ_μ^2, σ_λ^2, and σ_ϵ^2, respectively. In addition, assume that $\mathbf{x}_{it}$ is a K-vector of known constants, the first element of which is 1 for all i and t.

We shall write (6.6.1) and (6.6.2) in matrix notation by defining several symbols. Define $\mathbf{y}$, $\mathbf{u}$, $\boldsymbol{\epsilon}$, and $\mathbf{X}$ as matrices of size $NT \times 1$, $NT \times 1$, $NT \times 1$, and $NT \times K$, respectively, such that their $[(i-1)T + t]$th rows are y_{it}, u_{it}, ϵ_{it}, and $\mathbf{x}_{it}'$, respectively. Also define $\boldsymbol{\mu} = (\mu_1, \mu_2, \ldots, \mu_N)'$, $\boldsymbol{\lambda} = (\lambda_1, \lambda_2, \ldots, \lambda_T)'$, $\mathbf{L} = \mathbf{I}_N \otimes \mathbf{l}_T$, where $\mathbf{l}_T$ is a T-vector of ones, and $\underline{\mathbf{I}} = \mathbf{l}_N \otimes \mathbf{I}_T$. Then we can write (6.6.1) and (6.6.2) as

$$\mathbf{y} = \mathbf{X}\boldsymbol{\beta} + \mathbf{u} \tag{6.6.3}$$

and

$$\mathbf{u} = \mathbf{L}\boldsymbol{\mu} + \underline{\mathbf{I}}\boldsymbol{\lambda} + \boldsymbol{\epsilon}. \tag{6.6.4}$$

The covariance matrix $\boldsymbol{\Omega} \equiv E\mathbf{u}\mathbf{u}'$ can be written as

$$\boldsymbol{\Omega} = \sigma_\mu^2 \mathbf{A} + \sigma_\lambda^2 \mathbf{B} + \sigma_\epsilon^2 \mathbf{I}_{NT}, \tag{6.6.5}$$

where $\mathbf{A} = \mathbf{LL}'$ and $\mathbf{B} = \underline{\mathbf{I}}\underline{\mathbf{I}}'$. Its inverse is given by

$$\mathbf{\Omega}^{-1} = \frac{1}{\sigma_\epsilon^2} (\mathbf{I}_{NT} - \gamma_1 \mathbf{A} - \gamma_2 \mathbf{B} + \gamma_3 \mathbf{J}), \tag{6.6.6}$$

where
$$\gamma_1 = \sigma_\mu^2(\sigma_\epsilon^2 + T\sigma_\mu^2)^{-1},$$
$$\gamma_2 = \sigma_\lambda^2(\sigma_\epsilon^2 + N\sigma_\lambda^2)^{-1},$$
$$\gamma_3 = \gamma_1\gamma_2(2\sigma_\epsilon^2 + T\sigma_\mu^2 + N\sigma_\lambda^2)(\sigma_\epsilon^2 + T\sigma_\mu^2 + N\sigma_\lambda^2)^{-1},$$
and $\mathbf{J}$ is an $NT \times NT$ matrix consisting entirely of ones.

In this model the LS estimator of $\boldsymbol{\beta}$ is unbiased and generally consistent if both N and T go to ∞, but if $\mathbf{\Omega}$ is known, GLS provides a more efficient estimator. Later we shall consider FGLS using certain estimates of the variances, but first we shall show that we can obtain an estimator of $\boldsymbol{\beta}$ that has the same asymptotic distribution as GLS (as both N and T go to ∞) but that does not require the estimation of the variances.

To define this estimator, it is useful to separate the first element of $\boldsymbol{\beta}$ (the intercept) from its remaining elements. We shall partition $\boldsymbol{\beta} = (\beta_0, \boldsymbol{\beta}_1')'$ and $\mathbf{X} = (\mathbf{l}, \mathbf{X}_1)$.[8] We shall call this estimator the *transformation estimator* because it is based on the following transformation, which eliminates the cross-section- and time-specific components from the errors. Define the $NT \times NT$ matrix

$$\mathbf{Q} = \mathbf{I} - \frac{1}{T}\mathbf{A} - \frac{1}{N}\mathbf{B} + \frac{1}{NT}\mathbf{J}. \tag{6.6.7}$$

It is easy to show that $\mathbf{Q}$ is a projection matrix of rank $NT - N - T + 1$ that is orthogonal to $\mathbf{l}$, $\mathbf{L}$, and $\underline{\mathbf{I}}$. Let $\mathbf{H}$ be an $NT \times (NT - N - T + 1)$ matrix, the columns of which are the characteristic vectors of $\mathbf{Q}$ corresponding to the unit roots. Premultiplying (6.6.3) by $\mathbf{H}'$ yields

$$\mathbf{H}'\mathbf{y} = \mathbf{H}'\mathbf{X}_1\boldsymbol{\beta}_1 + \mathbf{H}'\boldsymbol{\epsilon}, \tag{6.6.8}$$

which is Model 1 because $E\mathbf{H}'\boldsymbol{\epsilon\epsilon}'\mathbf{H} = \sigma_\epsilon^2\mathbf{I}$. The transformation estimator of $\boldsymbol{\beta}_1$, denoted $\hat{\boldsymbol{\beta}}_{Q1}$, is defined as LS applied to (6.6.8):

$$\hat{\boldsymbol{\beta}}_{Q1} = (\mathbf{X}_1'\mathbf{Q}\mathbf{X}_1)^{-1}\mathbf{X}_1'\mathbf{Q}\mathbf{y}. \tag{6.6.9}$$

The transformation estimator can be interpreted as the LS estimator of $\boldsymbol{\beta}_1$, treating $\mu_1, \mu_2, \ldots, \mu_N$ and $\lambda_1, \lambda_2, \ldots, \lambda_T$ as if they were unknown regression parameters. Then formula (6.6.9) is merely a special case of the general formula for expressing a subset of the LS estimates given in (1.2.14). This interpretation explains why the estimator is sometimes called the *fixed-*

effects estimator (since μ's and λ's are treated as fixed effects rather than as random variables) or the *dummy-variable regression*. Still another name for the estimator is the *covariance estimator*.

To compare (6.6.9) with the corresponding GLS estimator, we need to derive the corresponding subset of GLS $\hat{\boldsymbol{\beta}}_G$. We have

$$\hat{\boldsymbol{\beta}}_{G1} = [\mathbf{X}_1'\boldsymbol{\Omega}^{-1}\mathbf{X}_1 - \mathbf{X}_1'\boldsymbol{\Omega}^{-1}\mathbf{l}(\mathbf{l}'\boldsymbol{\Omega}^{-1}\mathbf{l})^{-1}\mathbf{l}'\boldsymbol{\Omega}^{-1}\mathbf{X}_1]^{-1} \times [\mathbf{X}_1'\boldsymbol{\Omega}^{-1}\mathbf{y} - \mathbf{X}_1'\boldsymbol{\Omega}^{-1}\mathbf{l}(\mathbf{l}'\boldsymbol{\Omega}^{-1}\mathbf{l})^{-1}\mathbf{l}'\boldsymbol{\Omega}^{-1}\mathbf{y}] = [\mathbf{X}_1'(\mathbf{I} - \gamma_1\mathbf{A} - \gamma_2\mathbf{B} + \gamma_4\mathbf{J})\mathbf{X}_1]^{-1}\mathbf{X}_1'(\mathbf{I} - \gamma_1\mathbf{A} - \gamma_2\mathbf{B} + \gamma_4\mathbf{J})\mathbf{y}, \tag{6.6.10}$$

where $\gamma_4 = (NT\sigma_\mu^2\sigma_\lambda^2 - \sigma_\epsilon^4)/NT(\sigma_\epsilon^2 + T\sigma_\mu^2)(\sigma_\epsilon^2 + N\sigma_\lambda^2)$. Note the similarity between $\mathbf{Q}$ and $\mathbf{I} - \gamma_1\mathbf{A} - \gamma_2\mathbf{B} + \gamma_4\mathbf{J}$. The asymptotic equivalence between $\hat{\boldsymbol{\beta}}_{Q1}$ and $\hat{\boldsymbol{\beta}}_{G1}$ essentially follows from this similarity. If both N and T go to ∞ (it does not matter how they go to ∞), it is straightforward to prove that under reasonable assumptions on $\mathbf{X}$ and $\mathbf{u}$, $\sqrt{NT}(\hat{\boldsymbol{\beta}}_{Q1} - \boldsymbol{\beta}_1)$ and $\sqrt{NT}(\hat{\boldsymbol{\beta}}_{G1} - \boldsymbol{\beta}_1)$ converge to $N[\mathbf{0}, \lim NT(\mathbf{X}_1'\mathbf{Q}\mathbf{X}_1)^{-1}]$. A proof of the special case of $\mathbf{l}'\mathbf{X}_1 = \mathbf{0}$ has been given by Wallace and Hussain (1969).

The GLS estimator of β_0 is given by

$$\hat{\beta}_{G0} = \frac{\mathbf{l}'\mathbf{y} - \mathbf{l}'\mathbf{X}_1\hat{\boldsymbol{\beta}}_{G1}}{NT}. \tag{6.6.11}$$

Similarly, we can define the transformation estimator of β_0 by

$$\hat{\beta}_{Q0} = \frac{\mathbf{l}'\mathbf{y} - \mathbf{l}'\mathbf{X}_1\hat{\boldsymbol{\beta}}_{Q1}}{NT}. \tag{6.6.12}$$

We have

$$\hat{\beta}_{G0} - \beta_0 = \frac{\mathbf{l}'\mathbf{u} - \mathbf{l}'\mathbf{X}_1(\hat{\boldsymbol{\beta}}_{G1} - \boldsymbol{\beta}_1)}{NT} \tag{6.6.13}$$

and similarly for $\hat{\beta}_{Q0} - \beta_0$. Note that

$$\mathbf{l}'\mathbf{u} = T\sum_{i=1}^{N}\mu_i + N\sum_{t=1}^{T}\lambda_t + \sum_{i=1}^{N}\sum_{t=1}^{T}\epsilon_{it}, \tag{6.6.14}$$

where the probabilistic orders of the three terms in the right-hand side of (6.6.14) are $T\sqrt{N}$, $N\sqrt{T}$, and $\sqrt{NT}$, respectively. Because the probabilistic order of $\mathbf{l}'\mathbf{X}_1(\hat{\boldsymbol{\beta}}_{G1} - \boldsymbol{\beta}_1)$ or $\mathbf{l}'\mathbf{X}_1(\hat{\boldsymbol{\beta}}_{Q1} - \boldsymbol{\beta}_1)$ is $\sqrt{NT}$, it does not affect the asymptotic distribution of $\hat{\beta}_{G0}$ or $\hat{\beta}_{Q0}$. Hence, these two estimators have the same asymptotic distribution. To derive their asymptotic distribution, we must specify whether N or T goes to ∞ faster. If N grows faster than T, $\sqrt{T}(\hat{\beta}_{G0} - \beta_0)$ and $\sqrt{T}(\hat{\beta}_{Q0} - \beta_0)$ have the same limit distribution as $\Sigma_{t=1}^{T} \lambda_t / \sqrt{T}$, whereas if T grows faster than N, $\sqrt{N}(\hat{\beta}_{G0} - \beta_0)$ and $\sqrt{N}(\hat{\beta}_{Q0} - \beta_0)$ have the same limit distribution as $\Sigma_{i=1}^{N} \mu_i / \sqrt{N}$.

Because of the form of $\mathbf{\Omega}^{-1}$ given in (6.6.6), FGLS can be calculated if we can estimate the three variances σ_ϵ^2, σ_μ^2, and σ_λ^2. Several estimators of the variances have been suggested in the literature. (A Monte Carlo comparison of several estimators of the variances and the resulting FGLS has been done by Baltagi, 1981.) Amemiya (1971) proved the asymptotic normality of the following so-called analysis-of-variance estimators of the variances:

$$\hat{\sigma}_\epsilon^2 = \frac{\hat{\mathbf{u}}'\mathbf{Q}\hat{\mathbf{u}}}{(N-1)(T-1)}, \tag{6.6.15}$$

$$\hat{\sigma}_\mu^2 = \frac{\hat{\mathbf{u}}'\left[\frac{T-1}{T}\mathbf{A} - \frac{T-1}{NT}\mathbf{J} - \mathbf{Q}\right]\hat{\mathbf{u}}}{T(N-1)(T-1)}, \tag{6.6.16}$$

and

$$\hat{\sigma}_\lambda^2 = \frac{\hat{\mathbf{u}}'\left[\frac{N-1}{N}\mathbf{B} - \frac{N-1}{NT}\mathbf{J} - \mathbf{Q}\right]\hat{\mathbf{u}}}{N(N-1)(T-1)}, \tag{6.6.17}$$

where $\hat{\mathbf{u}} = \mathbf{y} - \mathbf{X}\hat{\boldsymbol{\beta}}_Q$. Amemiya also proved that they are asymptotically more efficient than the estimates obtained by using $\mathbf{y} - \mathbf{X}\hat{\boldsymbol{\beta}}$ for $\hat{\mathbf{u}}$, where $\hat{\boldsymbol{\beta}}$ is the LS estimator.

These estimates of the variances, or any other estimates with the respective probabilistic order of $(NT)^{-1/2}$, $N^{-1/2}$, and $T^{-1/2}$, can be inserted into the right-hand side of (6.6.6) for calculating FGLS. Fuller and Battese (1974) proved that under general conditions FGLS and GLS have the same asymptotic distribution.

6.6.2 Two Error Components Model

In 2ECM there is no time-specific error component. Thus the model is a special case of 3ECM obtained by putting $\sigma_\lambda^2 = 0$. This model was first used in econometric applications by Balestra and Nerlove (1966). However, because in the Balestra-Nerlove model a lagged endogenous variable is included among regressors, which causes certain additional statistical problems, we shall discuss it separately in Section 6.6.3.

In matrix notation, 2ECM is defined by

$$\mathbf{y} = \mathbf{X}\boldsymbol{\beta} + \mathbf{u} \tag{6.6.18}$$

and

$$\mathbf{u} = \mathbf{L}\boldsymbol{\mu} + \boldsymbol{\epsilon}. \tag{6.6.19}$$

The covariance matrix $\boldsymbol{\Omega} \equiv E\mathbf{u}\mathbf{u}'$ is given by

$$\boldsymbol{\Omega} = \sigma_\mu^2 \mathbf{A} + \sigma_\epsilon^2 \mathbf{I}_{NT}, \tag{6.6.20}$$

and its inverse by

$$\boldsymbol{\Omega}^{-1} = \frac{1}{\sigma_\epsilon^2}(\mathbf{I}_{NT} - \gamma_1 \mathbf{A}), \tag{6.6.21}$$

where $\gamma_1 = \sigma_\mu^2/(\sigma_\epsilon^2 + T\sigma_\mu^2)$ as before.

We can define GLS and FGLS as in Section 6.6.1. We shall discuss the estimation of γ_1 required for FGLS later. The asymptotic equivalence of GLS and FGLS follows from Fuller and Battese (1974) because they allowed for the possibility of $\sigma_\lambda^2 = 0$ in their proof. The transformation estimator of $\boldsymbol{\beta}$ can be defined as in (6.6.9) and (6.6.12) except that here the transformation matrix $\mathbf{Q}$ is given by

$$\mathbf{Q} = \mathbf{I} - T^{-1}\mathbf{A}. \tag{6.6.22}$$

The asymptotic equivalence between GLS and the transformation estimator can be similarly proved, except that in the 2ECM model $\sqrt{N}(\hat{\beta}_{G0} - \beta_0)$ and $\sqrt{N}(\hat{\beta}_{Q0} - \beta_0)$ have the same limit distribution as $\Sigma_{i=1}^N \mu_i/\sqrt{N}$ regardless of the way N and T go to ∞.

Following Maddala (1971), we can give an interesting interpretation of GLS in comparison to the transformation estimator. Let $\mathbf{L}$ be as defined in Section 6.6.1 and let $\mathbf{F}$ be an $NT \times N(T-1)$ matrix satisfying $\mathbf{F}'\mathbf{L} = \mathbf{0}$ and $\mathbf{F}'\mathbf{F} = \mathbf{I}$. Then (6.6.18) can be equivalently written as the following two sets of regression equations:

$$T^{-1/2}\mathbf{L}'\mathbf{y} = T^{-1/2}\mathbf{L}'\mathbf{X}\boldsymbol{\beta} + \boldsymbol{\eta}_1 \tag{6.6.23}$$

and

$$\mathbf{F}'\mathbf{y} = \mathbf{F}'\mathbf{X}\boldsymbol{\beta} + \boldsymbol{\eta}_2, \tag{6.6.24}$$

where $E\boldsymbol{\eta}_1\boldsymbol{\eta}_1' = (\sigma_\epsilon^2 + T\sigma_\mu^2)\mathbf{I}_N$, $E\boldsymbol{\eta}_2\boldsymbol{\eta}_2' = \sigma_\epsilon^2\mathbf{I}_{N(T-1)}$, and $E\boldsymbol{\eta}_1\boldsymbol{\eta}_2' = \mathbf{0}$. Maddala calls (6.6.23) the between-group regression and (6.6.24) the within-group regression. The transformation estimator $\hat{\boldsymbol{\beta}}_{Q1}$ can be interpreted as LS applied to (6.6.24). (Note that since the premultiplication by $\mathbf{F}'$ eliminates the vector of ones, β_0 cannot be estimated from this equation.) GLS $\hat{\beta}_G$ can be interpreted as GLS applied to (6.6.23) and (6.6.24) simultaneously. Because these equations constitute the heteroscedastic regression model analyzed in Section 6.5.2, GLS has the following simple form:

$$\hat{\beta}_G = (\mathbf{X}'\mathbf{P}\mathbf{X} + c\mathbf{X}'\mathbf{M}\mathbf{X})^{-1}(\mathbf{X}'\mathbf{P}\mathbf{y} + c\mathbf{X}'\mathbf{M}\mathbf{y}), \tag{6.6.25}$$

where $c = (\sigma_\epsilon^2 + T\sigma_\mu^2)/\sigma_\epsilon^2$, $\mathbf{P} = T^{-1}\mathbf{L}\mathbf{L}'$, and $\mathbf{M} = \mathbf{I} - \mathbf{P}$. To define FGLS, c may be estimated as follows: Estimate $\sigma_\epsilon^2 + T\sigma_\mu^2$ by the LS estimator of the variance obtained from regression (6.6.23), estimate σ_ϵ^2 by the LS estimator of the variance obtained from regression (6.6.24), and then take the ratio.

As we noted earlier, (6.6.23) and (6.6.24) constitute the heteroscedastic regression model analyzed in Section 6.5.2. Therefore the finite-sample study of Taylor (1978) applied to this model, but Taylor (1980) dealt with this model specifically.

Next, following Balestra and Nerlove (1966), we derive MLE of the model assuming the normality of $\mathbf{u}$. For this purpose it is convenient to adopt the following re-parameterization used by Balestra and Nerlove: Define $\sigma^2 = \sigma_\epsilon^2 + \sigma_\mu^2$, $\rho = \sigma_\mu^2/\sigma^2$, and $\mathbf{R} = (1-\rho)\mathbf{I}_T + \rho\mathbf{l}_T\mathbf{l}_T'$. Then we have

$$\mathbf{\Omega} = \sigma^2(\mathbf{I}_N \otimes \mathbf{R}),$$

$$\mathbf{\Omega}^{-1} = \sigma^{-2}(\mathbf{I}_N \otimes \mathbf{R}^{-1}),$$

$$\mathbf{R}^{-1} = (1-\rho)^{-1}\{\mathbf{I}_T - [\rho/(1-\rho+\rho T)]\mathbf{l}_T\mathbf{l}_T'\},$$

and

$$|\mathbf{R}| = (1-\rho)^T[1 + \rho T/(1-\rho)].$$

Using these results, we can write the log likelihood function as

$$\begin{aligned} L &= -\frac{1}{2}\log|\mathbf{\Omega}| - \frac{1}{2}\mathbf{u}'\mathbf{\Omega}^{-1}\mathbf{u} \qquad (6.6.26) \\ &= -\frac{NT}{2}\log\sigma^2 - \frac{NT}{2}\log(1-\rho) - \frac{N}{2}\log\left(1 + \frac{\rho T}{1-\rho}\right) \\ &\quad - \frac{1}{2\sigma^2}\mathbf{u}'(\mathbf{I}\otimes\mathbf{R}^{-1})\mathbf{u}, \end{aligned}$$

where we have written $\mathbf{u}$ for $\mathbf{y} - \mathbf{X}\boldsymbol{\beta}$. From (6.6.26) it is clear that the MLE of $\boldsymbol{\beta}$ given ρ is the same as GLS and that the MLE of σ^2 must satisfy

$$\sigma^2 = \frac{\mathbf{u}'(\mathbf{I}\otimes\mathbf{R}^{-1})\mathbf{u}}{NT}. \tag{6.6.27}$$

Inserting (6.6.27) into (6.6.26) yields the concentrated log likelihood function

$$L^* = -\frac{NT}{2}\log\left[\sum_i\sum_t u_{it}^2 - \frac{\rho}{1-\rho+\rho T}\sum_i\left(\sum_t u_{it}\right)^2\right] \tag{6.6.28}$$

$$-\frac{N}{2}\log\left[1+\frac{\rho T}{1-\rho}\right].$$

Putting $\partial L^*/\partial\rho = 0$ yields

$$\sum_i\sum_t u_{it}^2 - \frac{\rho}{1-\rho+\rho T}\sum_i\left(\sum_t u_{it}\right)^2 = \frac{1-\rho}{1-\rho+\rho T}\sum_i\left(\sum_t u_{it}\right)^2, \tag{6.6.29}$$

from which we obtain

$$\rho = \frac{\sum_i\left(\sum_t u_{it}\right)^2 - \sum_i\sum_t u_{it}^2}{(T-1)\sum_i\sum_t u_{it}^2}. \tag{6.6.30}$$

Also, using (6.6.29,) we can simplify (6.6.27) as

$$\sigma^2 = \frac{\sum_i\sum_t u_{it}^2}{NT}. \tag{6.6.31}$$

The MLE of $\boldsymbol{\beta}$, ρ, and σ^2 can be obtained by simultaneously solving the formula for GLS, (6.6.30), and (6.6.31).

Both Balestra and Nerlove (1966) and Maddala (1971) pointed out that the right-hand side of (6.6.30) can be negative. To ensure a positive estimate of ρ, Balestra and Nerlove suggested the following alternative formula for ρ:

$$\rho = \frac{N\sum_i\left(\sum_t u_{it}\right)^2 - \left(\sum_i\sum_t u_{it}\right)^2}{NT\sum_i\sum_t u_{it}^2}. \tag{6.6.32}$$

It is easy to show that the right-hand of (6.6.32) is always positive.

Maddala (1971) showed that the ρ given in (6.6.30) is less than 1. Berzeg (1979) showed that if we allow for a nonzero covariance $\sigma_{\mu\epsilon}$ between μ_i and ϵ_{it}, the formulae for MLE are the same as those given in (6.6.30) and (6.6.31) by redefining $\sigma^2 = \sigma_\mu^2 + 2\sigma_{\mu\epsilon} + \sigma_\epsilon^2$ and $\rho = (\sigma_\mu^2 + 2\sigma_{\mu\epsilon})/\sigma^2$ and in this model the MLE of ρ lies between 0 and 1.

One possible way to calculate FGLS consists of the following steps: (1) Obtain the transformation estimator $\hat{\boldsymbol{\beta}}_Q$. (2) Define $\hat{\mathbf{u}}_Q = \mathbf{y} - \mathbf{X}\hat{\boldsymbol{\beta}}_Q$; (3) Insert $\hat{\mathbf{u}}_Q$ into the right-hand side of Eq. (6.6.32). (4) Use the resulting estimator of ρ to construct FGLS. In the third step the numerator of (6.6.32) divided by N^2T^2 can be interpreted as the sample variance of the LS estimator of $\mu_i + \beta_0$ obtained from the regression $\mathbf{y} = \mathbf{X}_1\boldsymbol{\beta}_1 + \mathbf{L}(\boldsymbol{\mu} + \beta_0\mathbf{l}) + \boldsymbol{\epsilon}$.

6.6.3 Balestra-Nerlove Model

As we mentioned earlier, this is a generalization of 2ECM in the sense that a lagged endogenous variable $y_{i,t-1}$ is included among the regressors. Balestra and Nerlove (1966) used this model to analyze the demand for natural gas in 36 states in the period 1950–1962.

All the asymptotic results stated earlier for 2ECM hold also for the Balestra-Nerlove model provided that both N and T go to ∞, as shown by Amemiya (1967). However, there are certain additional statistical problems caused by the presence of a lagged endogenous variable; we shall delineate these problems in the following discussion.

First, the LS estimator of $\boldsymbol{\beta}$ obtained from (6.6.18) is always unbiased and is consistent if N goes to ∞. However, if $\mathbf{x}_{it}$ contain $y_{i,t-1}$, LS is inconsistent even when both N and T go to ∞. To see this, consider the simplest case

$$y_{it} = \beta y_{i,t-1} + \mu_i + \epsilon_{it}, \tag{6.6.33}$$

where we assume $|\beta| < 1$ for stationarity and $y_{i0} = 0$ for simplicity. Solving the difference equation (6.6.33) and omitting i, we obtain

$$y_{t-1} = \frac{1-\beta^{t-1}}{1-\beta}\mu + \epsilon_{t-1} + \beta\epsilon_{t-2} + \ldots + \beta^{t-2}\epsilon_1. \tag{6.6.34}$$

Therefore, putting back the subscript i,

$$\operatorname*{plim}_{T\to\infty} \frac{1}{T}\sum_{t=1}^{T} y_{i,t-1} = \frac{\mu_i}{1-\beta}. \tag{6.6.35}$$

Therefore

$$\operatorname*{plim}_{\substack{N\to\infty \\ T\to\infty}} \frac{1}{NT}\sum_{i=1}^{N}\sum_{t=1}^{T} \mu_i y_{i,t-1} = \frac{\sigma_\mu^2}{1-\beta}, \tag{6.6.36}$$

which implies the inconsistency of LS.

Second, we show that the transformation estimator $\hat{\beta}_{Q1}$ is consistent if and only if T goes to ∞.[9] We have

$$\hat{\beta}_{Q1} - \beta_1 = (\mathbf{X}_1'\mathbf{Q}\mathbf{X}_1)^{-1}\mathbf{X}_1'\mathbf{Q}\boldsymbol{\epsilon}, \tag{6.6.37}$$

where $\mathbf{Q}$ is given by (6.6.22). We need to consider only the column of $\mathbf{X}_1$, which corresponds to the lagged endogenous variable, denoted $\mathbf{y}_{-1}$, and only the $T^{-1}\mathbf{A}$ part of $\mathbf{Q}$. Thus the consistency (as $T \rightarrow \infty$) of $\hat{\beta}_{Q1}$ follows from

$$\frac{1}{NT^2}\mathbf{y}_{-1}'\mathbf{A}\boldsymbol{\epsilon} = \frac{1}{NT^2}\sum_{i=1}^{N}\left(\sum_{t=1}^{T} y_{i,t-1}\sum_{t=1}^{T}\epsilon_{it}\right). \tag{6.6.38}$$

Third, if y_{i0} (the value of $y_{i,t-1}$ at time $t = 1$) is assumed to be an unknown parameter for each i, the MLE of $\boldsymbol{\beta}$ is inconsistent unless T goes to ∞ (Anderson and Hsiao, 1981, 1982). The problem of how to specify the initial values is important in a panel data study, where typically N is large but T is not.

Fourth, the possibility of a negative MLE of ρ is enhanced by the presence of a lagged endogenous variable, as shown analytically by Maddala (1971) and confirmed by a Monte Carlo study of Nerlove (1971). In his Monte Carlo study, Nerlove compared various estimators of $\boldsymbol{\beta}$ and concluded that the FGLS described at the end of Section 6.6.2 performs best. He found that the transformation estimator of the coefficient on $y_{i,t-1}$ has a tendency of downward bias.

6.6.4 Two Error Components Model with a Serially Correlated Error

In the subsection we shall discuss the 2ECM defined by Eqs. (6.6.18) and (6.6.19) in which $\boldsymbol{\epsilon}$ follows an AR(1) process, that is,

$$\epsilon_{it} = \gamma\epsilon_{i,t-1} + \xi_{it}, \tag{6.6.39}$$

where $\{\xi_{it}\}$ are i.i.d. with zero mean and variance σ_ξ^2. As in the Balestra-Nerlove model, the specification of ϵ_{i0} will be important if T is small. Lillard and Willis (1978) used model (6.6.39) to explain the log of earnings by the independent variables such as race, education, and labor force experience. They assumed stationarity for $\{\epsilon_{it}\}$, which is equivalent to assuming $E\epsilon_{i0} = 0$, $V\epsilon_{i0} = \sigma_\xi^2/(1-\gamma^2)$, and the independence of ϵ_{i0} from $\xi_{i1}, \xi_{i2}, \ldots$. Thus, in the Lillard-Willis model, $E\mathbf{u}\mathbf{u}' = (\sigma_\mu^2\mathbf{l}_T\mathbf{l}_T' + \boldsymbol{\Gamma}) \otimes \mathbf{I}_N$, where $\boldsymbol{\Gamma}$ is like (5.2.9) with $\sigma^2 = \sigma_\xi^2$ and $\rho = \gamma$. Lillard and Willis estimated $\boldsymbol{\beta}$ and $\boldsymbol{\mu}$ by LS and σ_μ^2, σ_ξ^2, and γ by inserting the LS residuals into the formulae for the normal MLE. Anderson and Hsiao (1982) have presented the properties of the full MLE in this model.

The model of Lillard and Weiss (1979) is essentially the same as model

(6.6.39) except that in the Lillard-Weiss model there is an additional error component, so that $\mathbf{u} = \mathbf{L}\mu + [\mathbf{I} - \mathbf{L}(\mathbf{L}'\mathbf{L})^{-1}\mathbf{L}'](\mathbf{I} \otimes \mathbf{f})\zeta + \epsilon$, where $\mathbf{f} = (1, 2, \ldots, T)'$ and ζ is independent of μ and ϵ. The authors used LS, FGLS, and MLE to estimate the parameters of their model.[10] The MLE was calculated using the LISREL program developed by Joreskog and Sorbom (1976). Hause (1980) has presented a similar model.

Finally, MaCurdy (1982) generalized the Lillard-Willis model to a more general time series process for ϵ_{it}. He eliminated μ_i by first differencing and treating $y_{it} - y_{i,t-1}$ as the dependent variable. Then he tried to model the LS predictor for $\epsilon_{it} - \epsilon_{i,t-1}$ by a standard Box-Jenkins-type procedure. MaCurdy argued that in a typical panel data model with small T and large N the assumption of stationarity is unnecessary, and he assumed that the initial values $\epsilon_{i0}, \epsilon_{i,-1}, \ldots$ are i.i.d. random variables across i with zero mean and unknown variances.

6.6.5 Two Error Components Model with Endogenous Regressors

The two error components model with endogenous regressors is defined by

$$\begin{aligned} \mathbf{y}_1 &= \mathbf{X}_1\beta + \mathbf{Z}\gamma + \mathbf{Y}_1\delta + \mu + \epsilon_1 \\ \mathbf{y}_2 &= \mathbf{X}_2\beta + \mathbf{Z}\gamma + \mathbf{Y}_2\delta + \mu + \epsilon_2 \\ &\ \ \vdots \\ \mathbf{y}_T &= \mathbf{X}_T\beta + \mathbf{Z}\gamma + \mathbf{Y}_T\delta + \mu + \epsilon_T, \end{aligned} \tag{6.6.40}$$

where $\mathbf{y}_t$, $t = 1, 2, \ldots, T$, is an N-vector, $\mathbf{X}_t$ is an $N \times K$ matrix of known constants, $\mathbf{Z}$ is an $N \times G$ matrix of endogenous variables, $\mathbf{Y}_t$ is an $N \times F$ matrix of endogenous variables, and μ and ϵ_t are N-vectors of random variables with the same characteristics as in 2ECM. The variable $\mathbf{Z}$ is always assumed to be correlated with both μ and ϵ_t, whereas $\mathbf{Y}_t$ is sometimes assumed to be correlated with both μ and ϵ_t and sometimes only with μ. The two error components model with endogenous regressors was analyzed by Chamberlain and Griliches (1975) and Hausman and Taylor (1981). Chamberlain and Griliches discussed maximum likelihood estimation assuming normality, whereas Hausman and Taylor considered the application of instrumental variable procedures.

Amemiya and MaCurdy (1983) proposed two instrumental variables estimators: one is optimal if $\mathbf{Y}_t$ is correlated with ϵ_t and the other is optimal if $\mathbf{Y}_t$ is uncorrelated with $\boldsymbol{\epsilon}_t$. When we write model (6.6.40) simply as $\mathbf{y} = \mathbf{W}\boldsymbol{\alpha} + \mathbf{u}$, the first estimator is defined by

$$\hat{\alpha}_1 = (\mathbf{W}'\boldsymbol{\Omega}^{-1/2}\mathbf{P}_1\boldsymbol{\Omega}^{-1/2}\mathbf{W})^{-1}\mathbf{W}'\boldsymbol{\Omega}^{-1/2}\mathbf{P}_1\boldsymbol{\Omega}^{-1/2}\mathbf{y}, \qquad (6.6.41)$$

where $\mathbf{P}_1$ is the projection matrix onto the space spanned by the column vectors of the $NT \times KT^2$ matrix $\boldsymbol{\Omega}^{-1/2}(\mathbf{I}_T \otimes \mathbf{S})$, where $\mathbf{S} = (\mathbf{X}_1, \mathbf{X}_2, \ldots, \mathbf{X}_T)$. Amemiya and MaCurdy have shown that it is asymptotically optimal among all the instrumental variables estimators if $\mathbf{Y}_t$ is correlated with $\boldsymbol{\epsilon}_t$. The second estimator is defined by

$$\hat{\alpha}_2 = (\mathbf{W}'\boldsymbol{\Omega}^{-1/2}\mathbf{P}_2\boldsymbol{\Omega}^{-1/2}\mathbf{W})^{-1}\mathbf{W}'\boldsymbol{\Omega}^{-1/2}\mathbf{P}_2\boldsymbol{\Omega}^{-1/2}\mathbf{y}, \qquad (6.6.42)$$

where $\mathbf{P}_2 = \mathbf{I} - T^{-1}\mathbf{1}_T\mathbf{1}_T' \otimes [\mathbf{I}_N - \mathbf{S}(\mathbf{S}'\mathbf{S})^{-1}\mathbf{S}']$. It is asymptotically optimal among all the instrumental variables estimators if $\mathbf{Y}_t$ is uncorrelated with $\boldsymbol{\epsilon}_t$. The second estimator is a modification of the one proposed by Hausman and Taylor (1981). In both of these estimators, $\boldsymbol{\Omega}$ must be estimated. If a standard consistent estimator is used, however, the asymptotic distribution is not affected.

6.7 Random Coefficients Models

Random coefficients models (RCM) are models in which the regression coefficients are random variables, the means, variances, and covariances of which are unknown parameters to estimate. The Hildreth and Houck model, which we discussed in Section 6.5.4, is a special case of RCM. The error components models, which we discussed in Section 6.6, are also special cases of RCM. We shall discuss models for panel data in which the regression coefficients contain individual-specific and time-specific components that are independent across individuals and over time periods. We shall discuss in succession models proposed by Kelejian and Stephan (1983), Hsiao (1974, 1975), Swamy (1970), and Swamy and Mehta (1977). In the last subsection we shall mention several other related models, including so-called varying parameter regression models in which the time-specific component evolves with time according to some dynamic process. As RCM have not been applied as extensively as ECM, we shall devote less space to this section than to the last.

6.7.1 The Kelejian and Stephan Model

The RCM analyzed by Kelejian and Stephan (1983) is a slight generalization of Hsiao's model, which we shall discuss in the next subsection. Their model is defined by

$$y_{it} = \mathbf{x}'_{it}\boldsymbol{\beta} + \mathbf{x}'_{it}(\boldsymbol{\mu}_i + \boldsymbol{\lambda}_t) + \epsilon_{it}, \tag{6.7.1}$$

$i = 1, 2, \ldots, N$ and $t = 1, 2, \ldots, T$. Note that we have separated out the nonstochastic part $\boldsymbol{\beta}$ and the random part $\boldsymbol{\mu}_i + \boldsymbol{\lambda}_t$ of the regression coefficients. Using the symbols defined in Section 6.6.1 and two additional symbols, we can write (6.7.1) in vector notation as

$$\mathbf{y} = \mathbf{X}\boldsymbol{\beta} + \underline{\mathbf{X}}\boldsymbol{\mu} + \mathbf{X}^*\boldsymbol{\lambda} + \boldsymbol{\epsilon}, \tag{6.7.2}$$

where we have defined $\underline{\mathbf{X}} = \text{diag}\,(\mathbf{X}_1, \mathbf{X}_2, \ldots, \mathbf{X}_N)$, $\mathbf{X}^* = (\mathbf{X}_1^{*\prime}, \mathbf{X}_2^{*\prime}, \ldots, \mathbf{X}_N^{*\prime})'$, where $\mathbf{X}_i^* = \text{diag}\,(\mathbf{x}'_{i1}, \mathbf{x}'_{i2}, \ldots, \mathbf{x}'_{iT})$. It is assumed that $\boldsymbol{\mu}$, $\boldsymbol{\lambda}$, and $\boldsymbol{\epsilon}$ have zero means, are uncorrelated with each other, and have covariance matrices given by $E\boldsymbol{\mu}\boldsymbol{\mu}' = \mathbf{I}_N \otimes \boldsymbol{\Sigma}_\mu$, $E\boldsymbol{\lambda}\boldsymbol{\lambda}' = \mathbf{I}_T \otimes \boldsymbol{\Sigma}_\lambda$, and $E\boldsymbol{\epsilon}\boldsymbol{\epsilon}' = \boldsymbol{\Sigma}_\epsilon$, where $\boldsymbol{\Sigma}_\mu$, $\boldsymbol{\Sigma}_\lambda$, and $\boldsymbol{\Sigma}_\epsilon$ are all nonsingular.

Kelejian and Stephan were concerned only with the probabilistic order of the GLS estimator of $\boldsymbol{\beta}$—an important and interesting topic previously overlooked in the literature. For this purpose we can assume that $\boldsymbol{\Sigma}_\mu$, $\boldsymbol{\Sigma}_\lambda$, and $\boldsymbol{\Sigma}_\epsilon$ are known. We shall discuss the estimation of these parameters in Sections 6.7.2 and 6.7.3, where we shall consider models more specific than model (6.7.1). In these models $\boldsymbol{\Sigma}_\epsilon$ is specified to depend on a fixed finite number of parameters: most typically, $\boldsymbol{\Sigma}_\epsilon = \sigma^2\mathbf{I}_{NT}$.

The probabilistic order of $\hat{\boldsymbol{\beta}}_G$ can be determined by deriving the order of the inverse of its covariance matrix, denoted simply as $\mathbf{V}$. We have

$$\mathbf{V}^{-1} = \mathbf{X}'[\underline{\mathbf{X}}(\mathbf{I} \otimes \boldsymbol{\Sigma}_\mu)\underline{\mathbf{X}}' + \boldsymbol{\Lambda}]^{-1}\mathbf{X}, \tag{6.7.3}$$

where $\boldsymbol{\Lambda} = \mathbf{X}^*(\mathbf{I}_T \otimes \boldsymbol{\Sigma}_\lambda)\mathbf{X}^{*\prime} + \boldsymbol{\Sigma}_\epsilon$. Using Theorem 20 of Appendix 1, we obtain

$$\begin{aligned}[\underline{\mathbf{X}}(\mathbf{I}_N \otimes \boldsymbol{\Sigma}_\mu)\underline{\mathbf{X}}' + \boldsymbol{\Lambda}]^{-1} \\ = \boldsymbol{\Lambda}^{-1} - \boldsymbol{\Lambda}^{-1}\underline{\mathbf{X}}[(\mathbf{I}_N \otimes \boldsymbol{\Sigma}_\mu^{-1}) + \underline{\mathbf{X}}'\boldsymbol{\Lambda}^{-1}\underline{\mathbf{X}}]^{-1}\underline{\mathbf{X}}'\boldsymbol{\Lambda}^{-1}.\end{aligned} \tag{6.7.4}$$

Therefore, noting $\mathbf{X} = \underline{\mathbf{X}}(\mathbf{l}_N \otimes \mathbf{I}_K)$ and defining $\mathbf{A} = \underline{\mathbf{X}}'\boldsymbol{\Lambda}^{-1}\underline{\mathbf{X}}$, we have

$$\mathbf{V}^{-1} = (\mathbf{l}_N \otimes \mathbf{I}_K)'\{\mathbf{A} - \mathbf{A}[(\mathbf{I}_N \otimes \boldsymbol{\Sigma}_\mu^{-1}) + \mathbf{A}]^{-1}\mathbf{A}\}(\mathbf{l}_N \otimes \mathbf{I}_K). \tag{6.7.5}$$

Finally, using Theorem 19 (ii) of Appendix 1, we can simplify the (6.7.5) as

$$\mathbf{V}^{-1} = (\mathbf{l}_N \otimes \mathbf{I}_K)'[(\mathbf{I}_N \otimes \boldsymbol{\Sigma}_\mu) + \mathbf{A}^{-1}]^{-1}(\mathbf{l}_N \otimes \mathbf{I}_K) \tag{6.7.6}$$

or as

$$\mathbf{V}^{-1} = N\boldsymbol{\Sigma}_\mu^{-1} - (\mathbf{l}_N \otimes \boldsymbol{\Sigma}_\mu^{-1})'[(\mathbf{I}_N \otimes \boldsymbol{\Sigma}_\mu^{-1}) + \mathbf{A}]^{-1}(\mathbf{l}_N \otimes \boldsymbol{\Sigma}_\mu^{-1}). \tag{6.7.7}$$

Equation (6.7.7) is identical with Eq. (11) of Kelejian and Stephan (1983, p. 252).

Now we can determine the order of $\mathbf{V}^{-1}$. If we write the i, jth block submatrix of $[(\mathbf{I}_N \otimes \mathbf{\Sigma}_\mu^{-1}) + \mathbf{A}]^{-1}$, $i, j = 1, 2, \ldots, N$, as $\mathbf{G}^{ij}$, the second term of the right-hand side of (6.7.7) can be written as $\mathbf{\Sigma}_\mu^{-1}(\Sigma_{i=1}^N \Sigma_{j=1}^N \mathbf{G}^{ij})\mathbf{\Sigma}_\mu^{-1}$. Therefore the order of this term is N^2/T. Therefore, if T goes to ∞ at a rate equal to or faster than N, the order of $\mathbf{V}^{-1}$ is N. But, because our model is symmetric in i and t, we can conclude that if N goes to ∞ at a rate equal to or faster than T, the order of $\mathbf{V}^{-1}$ is T. Combining the two, we can state the order of $\mathbf{V}^{-1}$ is min (N, T) or that the probabilistic order of $\hat{\boldsymbol{\beta}}_G$ is max $(N^{-1/2}, T^{-1/2})$.

6.7.2 Hsiao's Model

Hsiao's model (1974, 1975) is obtained as a special case of the model of the preceding subsection by assuming $\mathbf{\Sigma}_\mu$ and $\mathbf{\Sigma}_\lambda$ are diagonal and putting $\mathbf{\Sigma}_\epsilon = \sigma^2\mathbf{I}_{NT}$.

Hsiao (1975) proposed the following method of estimating $\mathbf{\Sigma}_\mu$, $\mathbf{\Sigma}_\lambda$, and σ^2: For simplicity assume that $\mathbf{X}$ does not contain a constant term. A simple modification of the subsequent discussion necessary for the case in which $\mathbf{X}$ contains the constant term is given in the appendix of Hsiao (1975). Consider the time series equation for the ith individual:

$$\mathbf{y}_i = \mathbf{X}_i(\boldsymbol{\beta} + \boldsymbol{\mu}_i) + \mathbf{X}_i^*\boldsymbol{\lambda} + \boldsymbol{\epsilon}_i. \tag{6.7.8}$$

If we treat $\boldsymbol{\mu}_i$ as if it were a vector of unknown constants (which is permissible so far as the estimation of $\mathbf{\Sigma}_\lambda$ and σ^2 is concerned), model (6.7.8) is the heteroscedastic regression model considered in Section 6.5.4. Hsiao suggested estimating $\mathbf{\Sigma}_\lambda$ and σ^2 either by the Hildreth-Houck estimator (6.5.24) or their alternative estimator described in note 7 (this chapter). In this way we obtain N independent estimates of $\mathbf{\Sigma}_\lambda$ and σ^2. Hsiao suggested averaging these N estimates. (Of course, these estimates can be more efficiently combined, but that may not be worth the effort.) By applying one of the Hildreth-Houck estimators to the cross-section equations for T time periods, $\mathbf{\Sigma}_\mu$ can be similarly estimated. (In the process we get another estimate of σ^2.)

Hsiao also discussed three methods of estimating $\boldsymbol{\beta}$. The first method is FGLS using the estimates of the variances described in the preceding paragraph. The second method is an analog of the transformation estimator defined for ECM in Section 6.6.1. It is defined as the LS estimator of $\boldsymbol{\beta}$ obtained from (6.7.2) treating $\boldsymbol{\mu}$ and $\boldsymbol{\lambda}$ as if they were unknown constants. The third method is MLE derived under the normality of $\mathbf{y}$, by which $\boldsymbol{\beta}$, $\mathbf{\Sigma}_\mu$, $\mathbf{\Sigma}_\lambda$, and σ^2

are obtained simultaneously. Hsiao applied to his model the method of scoring that Anderson (1969) derived for a very general random coefficients model, where the covariance matrix of the error term can be expressed as a linear combination of known matrices with unknown weights. (Note that Anderson's model is so general that it encompasses all the models considered in this chapter.) Hsiao essentially proved that the three estimators have the same asymptotic distribution, although his proof is somewhat marred by his assumption that these estimators are of the probabilistic order of $(NT)^{-1/2}$.

6.7.3 Swamy's Model

Swamy's model (1970) is a special case of the Kelejian-Stephan model obtained by putting

$$\mathbf{\Sigma}_\lambda = \mathbf{0} \quad \text{and} \quad \mathbf{\Sigma}_\epsilon = \mathbf{\Sigma} \otimes \mathbf{I}_T,$$

where $\mathbf{\Sigma} = \text{diag}\,(\sigma_1^2, \sigma_2^2, \ldots, \sigma_N^2)$. It is more restrictive than Hsiao's model in the sense that there is no time-specific component in Swamy's model, but it is more general in the sense that Swamy assumes neither the diagonality of $\mathbf{\Sigma}_\mu$ nor the homoscedasticity of $\boldsymbol{\epsilon}$ like Hsiao.

Swamy proposed estimating $\mathbf{\Sigma}_\mu$ and $\mathbf{\Sigma}$ in the following steps:

Step 1. Estimate σ_i^2 by $\hat{\sigma}_i^2 = \mathbf{y}_i'[\mathbf{I} - \mathbf{X}_i(\mathbf{X}_i'\mathbf{X}_i)^{-1}\mathbf{X}_i']\mathbf{y}_i/(T-K)$.

Step 2. Define $\mathbf{b}_i = (\mathbf{X}_i'\mathbf{X}_i)^{-1}\mathbf{X}_i'\mathbf{y}_i$.

Step 3. Estimate $\mathbf{\Sigma}_\mu$ by $\hat{\mathbf{\Sigma}}_\mu = (N-1)^{-1}\Sigma_{i=1}^N(\mathbf{b}_i - N^{-1}\Sigma_{i=1}^N\mathbf{b}_i) \times (\mathbf{b}_i - N^{-1}\Sigma_{i=1}^N\mathbf{b}_i)' - N^{-1}\Sigma_{i=1}^N\hat{\sigma}_i^2(\mathbf{X}_i'\mathbf{X}_i)^{-1}$.

It is easy to show that $\hat{\sigma}_i^2$ and $\hat{\mathbf{\Sigma}}_\mu$ are unbiased estimators of σ_i^2 and $\mathbf{\Sigma}_\mu$, respectively.

Swamy proved that the FGLS estimator of $\boldsymbol{\beta}$ using $\hat{\sigma}_i^2$ and $\hat{\mathbf{\Sigma}}_\mu$ is asymptotically normal with the order $N^{-1/2}$ and asymptotically efficient under the normality assumption. Note that GLS is of the order of $N^{-1/2}$ in Swamy's model because, using (6.7.7), we have in Swamy's model

$$\mathbf{V}^{-1} = N\mathbf{\Sigma}_\mu^{-1} - \mathbf{\Sigma}_\mu^{-1}\left[\sum_{i=1}^N (\mathbf{\Sigma}_\mu^{-1} + \sigma_i^{-2}\mathbf{X}_i'\mathbf{X}_i)^{-1}\right]\mathbf{\Sigma}_\mu^{-1} \tag{6.7.9}$$

$$= O(N) - O(N/T).$$

6.7.4 The Swamy-Mehta Model

The Swamy-Mehta model (1977) is obtained from the Kelejian-Stephan model by putting $\sigma^2 = 0$ but making the time-specific component more general as $[\text{diag}\,(\mathbf{X}_1^*, \mathbf{X}_2^*, \ldots, \mathbf{X}_N^*)]\lambda^*$, where $E\lambda^* = \mathbf{0}$ and $E\lambda^*\lambda^{*\prime} = \text{diag}\,(\mathbf{I}_T \otimes \mathbf{\Sigma}_1, \mathbf{I}_T \otimes \mathbf{\Sigma}_2, \ldots, \mathbf{I}_T \otimes \mathbf{\Sigma}_N)$. In their model, (6.7.7) is reduced to

$$\mathbf{V}^{-1} = N\mathbf{\Sigma}_\mu^{-1} - \mathbf{\Sigma}_\mu^{-1}\left(\sum_{i=1}^{N} \{\mathbf{\Sigma}_\mu^{-1} + \mathbf{X}_i'[\mathbf{X}_i^*(\mathbf{I}_T \otimes \mathbf{\Sigma}_i)\mathbf{X}_i^{*\prime}]^{-1}\mathbf{X}_i\}^{-1}\right)\mathbf{\Sigma}_\mu^{-1}$$

$$= O(N) - O(N/T), \tag{6.7.10}$$

as in Swamy's model.

6.7.5 Other Models

In the preceding subsections we have discussed models in which cross-section-specific components are independent across individuals and time-specific components are independent over time periods. We shall cite a few references for each of the other types of random coefficients models. They are classified into three types on the basis of the type of regression coefficients: (1) Regression coefficients are nonstochastic, and they either continuously or discretely change over cross-section units or time periods. (2) Regression coefficients follow a stochastic, dynamic process over time. (3) Regression coefficients are themselves dependent variables of separate regression models. Note that type 1 is strictly not a RCM, but we have mentioned it here because of its similarity to RCM. Types 1 and 2 together constitute the *varying parameter regression models.*

References for type 1 are Quandt (1958), Hinkley (1971), and Brown, Durbin, and Evans (1975). References for type 2 are Rosenberg (1973), Cooley and Prescott (1976), and Harvey (1978). A reference for type 3 is Amemiya (1978b).

Exercises

1. (Section 6.1.2)
   Consider a classic regression model

   $$\mathbf{y} = \alpha\mathbf{x} + \beta\mathbf{z} + \mathbf{u},$$

   where α and β are scalar unknown parameters; $\mathbf{x}$ and $\mathbf{z}$ are T-component vectors of known constants such that $\mathbf{x}'\mathbf{l} = \mathbf{z}'\mathbf{l} = 0$, where $\mathbf{l}$ is a T-component vector of ones; and $\mathbf{u}$ is a T-component vector of unobservable i.i.d. random variables with zero mean and unit variance. Suppose we are given an estimator $\tilde{\beta}$ such that $E\tilde{\beta} = \beta$, $V\tilde{\beta} = T^{-1}$, and $E\mathbf{u}\tilde{\beta} = T^{-1/2}\rho\mathbf{l}$, where ρ is a known constant with $0 \leqq |\rho| < 1$. Write down the expression for the best estimator of α you can think of. Justify your choice.

2. (Section 6.1.2)
In the model of Exercise 17 of Chapter 3, assume that the exact distribution of $\tilde{\beta}$ is known to be $N(\beta, T^{-1})$.
   a. Obtain the mean squared error of $\tilde{\alpha}$.
   b. Find an estimator of α whose mean squared error is smaller than that of $\tilde{\alpha}$.

3. (Section 6.1.3)
Prove that statement D $\Rightarrow$ statement C in Theorem 6.1.1.

4. (Section 6.1.3)
If $K = 1$ in Model 6, the efficiency of LS relative to GLS can be defined by

$$\text{Eff} = \frac{(\mathbf{x}'\mathbf{x})^2}{(\mathbf{x}'\mathbf{\Sigma}^{-1}\mathbf{x})(\mathbf{x}'\mathbf{\Sigma}\mathbf{x})}.$$

Watson (1955) showed $\text{Eff} \geqq 4\lambda_l\lambda_s/(\lambda_l + \lambda_s)^2$, where λ_l and λ_s are the largest and smallest characteristic roots of $\mathbf{\Sigma}$, respectively. Evaluate this lower bound for the case where $\mathbf{\Sigma}$ is given by (5.2.9), using the approximation of the characteristic roots by the spectral density (cf. Section 5.1.3).

5. (Section 6.1.3)
In Model 6 assume $K = 1$ and $\mathbf{X} = \mathbf{l}$, a vector of ones. Also assume $\mathbf{\Sigma}$ is equal to $\mathbf{\Sigma}_1$ given in (5.2.9). Calculate the limit of the efficiency of LS as $T \rightarrow \infty$. (Efficiency is defined in Exercise 4.)

6. (Section 6.1.3)
Prove (6.1.6) directly, without using the fact that GLS is BLUE.

7. (Section 6.1.5)
Consider a regression model

$$\mathbf{y} = \mathbf{X}\boldsymbol{\beta} + \mathbf{u},$$

where $E\mathbf{u} = 0$ and $E\mathbf{u}\mathbf{u}' = \mathbf{P} = \mathbf{Z}(\mathbf{Z}'\mathbf{Z})^{-1}\mathbf{Z}'$. We assume that $\mathbf{X}$ and $\mathbf{Z}$ are $T \times K$ and $T \times G$ matrices of constants, respectively, such that $\text{rank}(\mathbf{X}) = K$, $\text{rank}(\mathbf{Z}) = G < T$, and $\mathbf{P}\mathbf{X} = \mathbf{X}$. Find a linear unbiased estimator of $\boldsymbol{\beta}$ the variance-covariance matrix of which is smaller than or equal to that of any other linear unbiased estimator. Is such an estimator unique?

8. (Section 6.2)
Suppose $\mathbf{y} \sim N(\mathbf{X}\boldsymbol{\beta}, \boldsymbol{\Sigma})$, where there is no restriction on $\boldsymbol{\Sigma}$ except that it is positive definite. Can you obtain the MLE of $\boldsymbol{\Sigma}$ by setting the derivative of the log likelihood function with respect to $\boldsymbol{\Sigma}$ equal to $\mathbf{0}$?

9. (Section 6.3.2)
Show that Δ_1 and Δ_2 given in (6.3.5) and (6.3.6) converge to 0 in probability under the assumption of the text.

10. (Section 6.3.2)
Combining $y_t = \mathbf{x}_t'\boldsymbol{\beta} + u_t$ and $u_t = \rho u_{t-1} + \epsilon_t$, we can write

$$y_t = \rho y_{t-1} + \mathbf{x}_t'\boldsymbol{\beta} - \rho \mathbf{x}_{t-1}'\boldsymbol{\beta} + \epsilon_t.$$

Durbin (1960) proposed estimating ρ by the least squares coefficient on y_{t-1} in the regression of y_t on y_{t-1}, x_t, and x_{t-1}. In vector notation

$$\hat{\rho}_{\mathrm{D}} = \frac{\mathbf{y}_{-1}'[\mathbf{I} - \mathbf{Z}(\mathbf{Z}'\mathbf{Z})^{-1}\mathbf{Z}']\mathbf{y}}{\mathbf{y}_{-1}'[\mathbf{I} - \mathbf{Z}(\mathbf{Z}'\mathbf{Z})^{-1}\mathbf{Z}']\mathbf{y}_{-1}},$$

where $\mathbf{y} = (y_1, y_2, \ldots, y_T)'$, $\mathbf{y}_{-1} = (y_0, y_1, \ldots, y_{T-1})'$, $\mathbf{Z} = (\mathbf{X}, \mathbf{X}_{-1})$, $\mathbf{X} = (\mathbf{x}_1, \mathbf{x}_2, \ldots, \mathbf{x}_T)'$, $\mathbf{X}_{-1} = (\mathbf{x}_0, \mathbf{x}_1, \ldots, \mathbf{x}_{T-1})'$. Show that $\hat{\rho}_{\mathrm{D}}$ has the same asymptotic distribution as $\Sigma_{t=1}^T u_{t-1}u_t / \Sigma_{t=1}^T u_{t-1}^2$ if $\lim_{T\to\infty} T^{-1}\mathbf{Z}'\mathbf{Z}$ is a finite nonsingular matrix.

11. (Section 6.3.3)
In Model 6 suppose $K = 1$ and $\{u_t\}$ follow AR(1), $u_t = \rho u_{t-1} + \epsilon_t$. If we thought $\{u_t\}$ were i.i.d., we would estimate the variance of LS $\hat{\beta}_L$ by $\hat{V} = \hat{\sigma}^2/\mathbf{x}'\mathbf{x}$, where $\hat{\sigma}^2 = T^{-1}[\mathbf{y}'\mathbf{y} - (\mathbf{x}'\mathbf{x})^{-1}(\mathbf{y}'\mathbf{x})^2]$. But the true variance is $V = \mathbf{x}'\boldsymbol{\Sigma}\mathbf{x}/(\mathbf{x}'\mathbf{x})^2$, where $\boldsymbol{\Sigma}$ is as given in (5.2.9). What can you say about the sign of $\hat{V} - V$?

12. (Section 6.3.3)
Consider $y_t = \beta x_t + u_t$, $u_t = \rho u_{t-1} + \epsilon_t$, where x_t is nonstochastic, $|\rho| < 1$, $\{\epsilon_t\}$ are i.i.d. with $E\epsilon_t = 0$, $V\epsilon_t = \sigma^2$, $\{u_t\}$ are stationary, and β, ρ, and σ^2 are unknown parameters. Given a sample (y_t, x_t), $t = 1, 2, \ldots, T$, and given x_{T+1}, what do you think is the best predictor of y_{T+1}?

13. (Section 6.3.3)
Let $y_t = \beta t + u_t$, where $\{u_t\}$ follow AR(1), $u_t = \rho u_{t-1} + \epsilon_t$. Define the following two predictors of y_{T+1}: $\hat{y}_{T+1} = (T+1)\hat{\beta}$ and $\tilde{y}_{T+1} = (T+1)\tilde{\beta}$, where $\hat{\beta}$ and $\tilde{\beta}$ are the LS and GLS estimators of β based on y_1,

$y_2, \ldots, y_T$, respectively. In defining GLS, ρ is assumed known. Assuming $\rho > 0$, compare the two mean squared prediction errors.

14. (Section 6.3.5)
Suppose $E\mathbf{y} = \mathbf{X}\boldsymbol{\beta}$ and $V\mathbf{y} = \boldsymbol{\Sigma}(\boldsymbol{\beta})$, meaning that the covariance matrix of $\mathbf{y}$ is a function of $\boldsymbol{\beta}$. The true distribution of $\mathbf{y}$ is unspecified. Show that minimizing $(\mathbf{y} - \mathbf{X}\boldsymbol{\beta})'\boldsymbol{\Sigma}(\boldsymbol{\beta})^{-1}(\mathbf{y} - \mathbf{X}\boldsymbol{\beta})$ with respect to $\boldsymbol{\beta}$ yields an inconsistent estimator, whereas minimizing $(\mathbf{y} - \mathbf{X}\boldsymbol{\beta})'\boldsymbol{\Sigma}(\boldsymbol{\beta})^{-1}(\mathbf{y} - \mathbf{X}\boldsymbol{\beta}) + \log|\boldsymbol{\Sigma}(\boldsymbol{\beta})|$ yields a consistent estimator. Note that the latter estimator would be MLE if $\mathbf{y}$ were normal.

15. (Section 6.3.6)
Show $\lim_{T\to\infty} (Ed_{\text{L}} - 2)^2 = 0$, where d_{L} is defined in (6.3.24). Use that to show $\text{plim}_{T\to\infty}\, d_{\text{L}} = 2$.

16. (Section 6.3.6)
In the table of significance points given by Durbin and Watson (1951), $d_{\text{U}} - d_{\text{L}}$ gets smaller as the sample size increases. Explain this phenomenon.

17. (Section 6.3.7)
Verify (6.3.30).

18. (Section 6.3.7)
Prove (6.3.33).

19. (Section 6.3.7)
In the model (6.3.31), show $\text{plim}\, \hat{\rho} = \alpha\rho(\alpha + \rho)/(1 + \alpha\rho)$ (cf. Malinvaud, 1961).

20. (Section 6.3.7)
Consider model (6.3.27). Define the T-vector $\mathbf{x}_{-1} = (x_0, x_1, \ldots, x_{T-1})'$ and the $T \times 2$ matrix $\mathbf{S} = (\mathbf{x}, \mathbf{x}_{-1})$. Show that the instrumental variables estimator $\hat{\gamma} \equiv (\mathbf{S}'\mathbf{Z})^{-1}\mathbf{S}'\mathbf{y}$ is consistent and obtain its asymptotic distribution. Show that the estimator $\hat{\rho}$ of ρ obtained by using the residuals $\mathbf{y} - \mathbf{Z}\hat{\gamma}$ is consistent and obtain its asymptotic distribution.

21. (Section 6.4)
In the SUR model show that FGLS and GLS have the same asymptotic distribution as T goes to infinity under appropriate assumptions on $\mathbf{u}$ and $\underline{\mathbf{X}}$. Specify the assumptions.

22. (Section 6.5.1)
Consider a regression model

$$y_t = \mathbf{x}_t'\boldsymbol{\beta} + u_t, \qquad u_t = \rho u_{t-1} + \epsilon_t, \qquad t = 1, 2, \ldots, T.$$

Assume
(A) $\mathbf{x}_t$ is a vector of known constants such that $\Sigma_{t=1}^T \mathbf{x}_t\mathbf{x}_t'$ is a nonsingular matrix.
(B) $u_0 = 0$.
(C) $\{\epsilon_t\}$ are independent with $E\epsilon_t = 0$ and $V\epsilon_t = \sigma_t^2$.
(D) $\{\sigma_t^2\}$ are known and bounded both from above and away from 0.
(E) $\boldsymbol{\beta}$ and ρ are unknown parameters.
Explain how you would estimate $\boldsymbol{\beta}$. Justify your choice of the estimator.

23. (Section 6.5.3)
Show that the density of a multinomial model with more than two responses or the density of a normal model where the variance is proportional to the square of the mean cannot be written in the form of (6.5.17).

24. (Section 6.5.4)
Show that $\sqrt{T}(\hat{\boldsymbol{\alpha}}_1 - \boldsymbol{\alpha})$, where $\hat{\boldsymbol{\alpha}}_1$ is defined in (6.5.21), has the same limit distribution as $\sqrt{T}(\mathbf{Z}'\mathbf{Z})^{-1}\mathbf{Z}'\mathbf{v}_1$.

25. (Section 6.5.4)
Show (6.5.25).

26. (Section 6.5.4)
Consider a heteroscedastic nonlinear regression model

$$y_t = f_t(\beta_0) + u_t,$$

where $\{u_t\}$ are independent and distributed as $N(0, \mathbf{z}_t'\boldsymbol{\alpha}_0)$, β_0 is a scalar unknown parameter, and $\boldsymbol{\alpha}_0$ is a vector of unknown parameters.
Assume
(A) If $\hat{\beta}$ is the NLLS estimator of β_0, $\sqrt{T}(\hat{\beta} - \beta_0) \rightarrow N(0, c)$, where $0 < c < \infty$.
(B) $\{z_t\}$ are vectors of known constants such that $|\mathbf{z}_t| < \mathbf{h}$ for some finite vector $\mathbf{h}$ (meaning that every element of $|\mathbf{z}_t|$ is smaller than the corresponding element of $\mathbf{h}$), $\mathbf{z}_t'\boldsymbol{\alpha}_0$ is positive and bounded away from 0, and $T^{-1}\Sigma_{t=1}^T \mathbf{z}_t\mathbf{z}_t'$ is nonsingular for every T and converges to a finite nonsingular matrix.
(C) $|\partial f_t/\partial\beta| < M$ for some finite M for every t and every β.
Generalize the Goldfeld-Quandt estimator of $\boldsymbol{\alpha}_0$ to the nonlinear case and derive its asymptotic distribution.

27. (Section 6.6.2)
Consider an error components model

$$y_{it} = \mathbf{x}_{it}'\boldsymbol{\beta} + \mu_i + \epsilon_{it}, \qquad i = 1, 2, \ldots, N \text{ and}$$
$$t = 1, 2, \ldots, T,$$

where $\mathbf{x}_{it}$ is a K-vector of constants and μ_i and ϵ_{it} are scalar random variables with zero means. Define $\boldsymbol{\mu} = (\mu_1, \mu_2, \ldots, \mu_N)'$, $\boldsymbol{\epsilon}_i = (\epsilon_{i1}, \epsilon_{i2}, \ldots, \epsilon_{iT})'$, and $\boldsymbol{\epsilon} = (\boldsymbol{\epsilon}_1', \boldsymbol{\epsilon}_2', \ldots, \boldsymbol{\epsilon}_N')'$. Then we assume $E\boldsymbol{\mu\mu}' = \sigma_\mu^2 \mathbf{I}_N$, $E\boldsymbol{\epsilon\epsilon}' = \mathbf{I}_N \otimes \boldsymbol{\Sigma}$, and $E\boldsymbol{\mu\epsilon}' = \mathbf{0}$, where $\boldsymbol{\Sigma}$ is a T-dimensional diagonal matrix the tth diagonal element of which is $\sigma_t^2 > 0$.Assume σ_μ^2 and $\boldsymbol{\Sigma}$ are known. Obtain the formulae for the following two estimators of $\boldsymbol{\beta}$:

1. The generalized least squares estimator $\hat{\boldsymbol{\beta}}_{\text{G}}$;
2. The fixed-effects estimator $\tilde{\boldsymbol{\beta}}$ (it is defined here as the generalized least squares estimator of $\boldsymbol{\beta}$ treating μ_i as if they were unknown parameters rather than random variables).

28. (Section 6.6.2)
Consider the model $\mathbf{y} = \mathbf{X}\boldsymbol{\beta} + v\mathbf{z} + \mathbf{u}$, where

$\mathbf{y}$: $T+1$, observable
$\mathbf{X}$: $T \times K$, known constants
$\mathbf{z}$: $T \times 1$, known constants
$\boldsymbol{\beta}$: $K \times 1$, unknown constants
v: scalar, unobservable, $Ev = 0$, $Vv = \sigma^2$
$\mathbf{u}$: $T \times 1$, unobservable, $E\mathbf{u} = \mathbf{0}$, $E\mathbf{uu}' = \mathbf{I}$.

Assume v and $\mathbf{u}$ are independent and σ^2 is a known constant. Also assume $\mathbf{X}'\mathbf{z} \neq \mathbf{0}$ and rank$[\mathbf{X}, \mathbf{z}] = K + 1$. Rank the following three estimators in terms of the mean squared error matrix:

$$\text{LS}(\hat{\boldsymbol{\beta}}_{\text{L}}): \quad (\mathbf{X}'\mathbf{X})^{-1}\mathbf{X}'\mathbf{y}$$

$$\text{GLS}(\hat{\boldsymbol{\beta}}_{\text{G}}): \quad (\mathbf{X}'\boldsymbol{\Sigma}^{-1}\mathbf{X})^{-1}\mathbf{X}'\boldsymbol{\Sigma}^{-1}\mathbf{y}, \quad \text{where} \quad \boldsymbol{\Sigma} = E(v\mathbf{z} + \mathbf{u})(v\mathbf{z} + \mathbf{u})'$$

$$\text{QLS}(\hat{\boldsymbol{\beta}}_{\text{Q}}): \quad (\mathbf{X}'\mathbf{J}\mathbf{X})^{-1}\mathbf{X}'\mathbf{J}\mathbf{y}, \quad \text{where} \quad \mathbf{J} = \mathbf{I} - \frac{\mathbf{zz}'}{\mathbf{z}'\mathbf{z}}$$

7 Linear Simultaneous Equations Models

In this chapter we shall give only the basic facts concerning the estimation of the parameters in linear simultaneous equations. A major purpose of the chapter is to provide a basis for the discussion of nonlinear simultaneous equations to be given in the next chapter. Another purpose is to provide a rigorous derivation of the asymptotic properties of several commonly used estimators. For more detailed discussion of linear simultaneous equations, the reader is referred to textbooks by Christ (1966) and Malinvaud (1980).

7.1 Model and Identification

We can write the simultaneous equations model as

$$\mathbf{Y}\boldsymbol{\Gamma} = \mathbf{X}\mathbf{B} + \mathbf{U} \tag{7.1.1}$$

where $\mathbf{Y}$ is a $T \times N$ matrix of observable random variables (endogenous variables), $\mathbf{X}$ is a $T \times K$ matrix of known constants (exogenous variables), $\mathbf{U}$ is a $T \times N$ matrix of unobservable random variables, and $\boldsymbol{\Gamma}$ and $\mathbf{B}$ are $N \times N$ and $K \times N$ matrices of unknown parameters. We denote the t, ith element of $\mathbf{Y}$ by y_{ti}, the ith column of $\mathbf{Y}$ by $\mathbf{y}_i$, and the tth row of $\mathbf{Y}$ by $\mathbf{y}'_{(t)}$, and similarly for $\mathbf{X}$ and $\mathbf{U}$. This notation is consistent with that of Chapter 1.

As an example of the simultaneous equations model, consider the following demand and supply equations:

$$\text{Demand:}\quad p_t = \gamma_1 q_t + \mathbf{x}'_{t1}\boldsymbol{\beta}_1 + u_{t1}.$$
$$\text{Supply:}\quad q_t = \gamma_2 p_t + \mathbf{x}'_{t2}\boldsymbol{\beta}_2 + u_{t2}.$$

The demand equation specifies the price the consumer is willing to pay for given values of the quantity and the independent variables plus the error term, and the supply equation specifies the quantity the producer is willing to supply for given values of the price and the independent variables plus the error term. The observed price and quantity are assumed to be the equilibrium values that satisfy both equations. This is the classic explanation of how a simultaneous equations model arises. For an interesting alternative explanation in which the simultaneous equations model is regarded as the limit of a multivariate time series model as the length of the time lag goes to 0, see articles by Strotz (1960) and Fisher (1970).

We impose the following assumptions:

ASSUMPTION 7.1.1. The sequence of N-vectors $\{\mathbf{u}_{(t)}\}$ is i.i.d. with zero mean and an unknown covariance matrix $\mathbf{\Sigma}$. (Thus $E\mathbf{U} = \mathbf{0}$ and $ET^{-1}\mathbf{U}'\mathbf{U} = \mathbf{\Sigma}$.) We do not assume normality of $\{\mathbf{u}_{(t)}\}$, although some estimators considered in this chapter are obtained by maximizing a normal density.

ASSUMPTION 7.1.2. Rank of $\mathbf{X}$ is K, and $\lim T^{-1}\mathbf{X}'\mathbf{X}$ exists and is nonsingular.

ASSUMPTION 7.1.3. $\mathbf{\Gamma}$ is nonsingular.

Solving (7.1.1) for $\mathbf{Y}$, we obtain

$$\mathbf{Y} = \mathbf{X\Pi} + \mathbf{V}, \tag{7.1.2}$$

where

$$\mathbf{\Pi} = \mathbf{B\Gamma}^{-1} \tag{7.1.3}$$

and $\mathbf{V} = \mathbf{U\Gamma}^{-1}$. We define $\mathbf{\Lambda} \equiv \mathbf{\Gamma}^{-1\prime}\mathbf{\Sigma\Gamma}^{-1}$. We shall call (7.1.2) the *reduced form equations,* in contrast to (7.1.1), which are called the *structural equations.*

We assume that the diagonal elements of $\mathbf{\Gamma}$ are ones. This is merely a normalization and involves no loss of generality. In addition, we assume that certain elements of $\mathbf{\Gamma}$ and $\mathbf{B}$ are zeros.[1] Let $-\boldsymbol{\gamma}_i$ be the column vector consisting of those elements of the ith column of $\mathbf{\Gamma}$ that are specified to be neither 1 nor 0, and let $\boldsymbol{\beta}_i$ be the column vector consisting of those elements of the ith column of $\mathbf{B}$ that are not specified to be 0. Also, let $\mathbf{Y}_i$ and $\mathbf{X}_i$ be the subsets of the columns of $\mathbf{Y}$ and $\mathbf{X}$ that are postmultiplied by $-\boldsymbol{\gamma}_i$ and $\boldsymbol{\beta}_i$, respectively. Then we can write the ith structural equation as

$$\begin{aligned} \mathbf{y}_i &= \mathbf{Y}_i\boldsymbol{\gamma}_i + \mathbf{X}_i\boldsymbol{\beta}_i + \mathbf{u}_i \\ &\equiv \mathbf{Z}_i\boldsymbol{\alpha}_i + \mathbf{u}_i. \end{aligned} \tag{7.1.4}$$

We denote the number of columns of $\mathbf{Y}_i$ and $\mathbf{X}_i$ by N_i and K_i, respectively. Combining N such equations, we can write (7.1.1) alternatively as

$$\mathbf{y} = \underline{\mathbf{Z}}\boldsymbol{\alpha} + \mathbf{u}, \tag{7.1.5}$$

where $\mathbf{y} = (\mathbf{y}_1', \mathbf{y}_2', \ldots, \mathbf{y}_N')'$,
$\boldsymbol{\alpha} = (\boldsymbol{\alpha}_1', \boldsymbol{\alpha}_2', \ldots, \boldsymbol{\alpha}_N')'$,
$\mathbf{u} = (\mathbf{u}_1', \mathbf{u}_2', \ldots, \mathbf{u}_N')'$,
and $\underline{\mathbf{Z}} = \text{diag}(\mathbf{Z}_1, \mathbf{Z}_2, \ldots, \mathbf{Z}_N)$.

We define $\boldsymbol{\Omega} \equiv E\mathbf{u}\mathbf{u}' = \boldsymbol{\Sigma} \otimes \mathbf{I}_T$. Note that (7.1.5) is analogous to the multivariate regression model (6.4.2), except that $\underline{\mathbf{Z}}$ in (7.1.5) includes endogenous variables.

We now ask, Is $\boldsymbol{\alpha}_i$ identified? The precise definition of *identification* differs among authors and can be very complicated. In this book we shall take a simple approach and use the word synonymously with "existence of a consistent estimator."[2] Thus our question is, Is there a consistent estimator of $\boldsymbol{\alpha}_i$? Because there is a consistent estimator of $\boldsymbol{\Pi}$ under our assumptions (for example, the least squares estimator $\hat{\boldsymbol{\Pi}} = (\mathbf{X}'\mathbf{X})^{-1}\mathbf{X}'\mathbf{Y}$ will do), our question can be paraphrased as, Does (7.1.3) uniquely determine $\boldsymbol{\alpha}_i$ when $\boldsymbol{\Pi}$ is determined?

To answer this question, we write that part of (7.1.3) that involves $\boldsymbol{\gamma}_i$ and $\boldsymbol{\beta}_i$ as

$$\boldsymbol{\pi}_{i1} - \boldsymbol{\Pi}_{i1}\boldsymbol{\gamma}_i = \boldsymbol{\beta}_i \tag{7.1.6}$$

and

$$\boldsymbol{\pi}_{i0} - \boldsymbol{\Pi}_{i0}\boldsymbol{\gamma}_i = \mathbf{0}. \tag{7.1.7}$$

Here, $(\boldsymbol{\pi}_{i1}', \boldsymbol{\pi}_{i0}')'$ is the ith column of $\boldsymbol{\Pi}$, and $(\boldsymbol{\Pi}_{i1}', \boldsymbol{\Pi}_{i0}')'$ is the subset of the columns of $\boldsymbol{\Pi}$ that are postmultiplied by $\boldsymbol{\gamma}_i$. The second subscript 0 or 1 indicates the rows corresponding to the zero or nonzero elements of the ith column of $\mathbf{B}$. Note that $\boldsymbol{\Pi}_{i0}$ is a $K_{(i)} \times N_i$ matrix, where $K_{(i)} = K - K_i$. From (7.1.7) it is clear that $\boldsymbol{\gamma}_i$ is uniquely determined if and only if

$$\text{rank}(\boldsymbol{\Pi}_{i0}) = N_i. \tag{7.1.8}$$

This is called the *rank condition* of identifiability. It is clear from (7.1.6) that once $\boldsymbol{\gamma}_i$ is uniquely determined, $\boldsymbol{\beta}_i$ is uniquely determined. For (7.1.8) to hold, it is necessary to assume

$$K_{(i)} \geqq N_i, \tag{7.1.9}$$

which means that the number of excluded exogenous variables is greater than or equal to the number of included endogenous variables. The condition (7.1.9) is called the *order condition* of identifiability.[3]

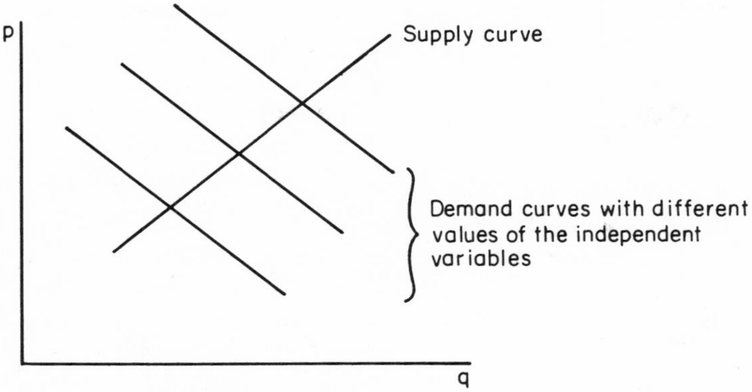

Figure 7.1 Demand and supply curves

If (7.1.8) does not hold, we say $\boldsymbol{\alpha}_i$ is *not identified* or is *underidentified.* If (7.1.8) holds, and moreover, if $K_{(i)} = N_i$, we say $\boldsymbol{\alpha}_i$ is *exactly identified* or is *just-identified.* If (7.1.8) holds and $K_{(i)} > N_i$, we say $\boldsymbol{\alpha}_i$ is *overidentified.*

If $\boldsymbol{\beta}_1 \neq \mathbf{0}$ and $\boldsymbol{\beta}_2 = \mathbf{0}$ in the demand and supply model given in the beginning of this section, γ_2 is identified but γ_1 is not. This fact is illustrated in Figure 7.1, where the equilibrium values of the quantity and the price will be scattered along the supply curve as the demand curve shifts with the values of the independent variables. Under the same assumption on the $\boldsymbol{\beta}$'s, we have

$$\boldsymbol{\Pi}_1 = \frac{1}{1-\gamma_1\gamma_2}\boldsymbol{\beta}_1 \quad \text{and} \quad \boldsymbol{\Pi}_2 = \frac{\gamma_2}{1-\gamma_1\gamma_2}\boldsymbol{\beta}_1, \tag{7.1.10}$$

where $\boldsymbol{\Pi}_1$ and $\boldsymbol{\Pi}_2$ are the coefficients on $\mathbf{x}_1$ in the reduced form equations for p and q, respectively. From (7.1.10) it is clear that if β_1 consists of a single element, γ_2 is exactly identified, whereas if $\boldsymbol{\beta}_1$ is a vector of more than one element, γ_2 is overidentified.

7.2 Full Information Maximum Likelihood Estimator

In this section we shall define the maximum likelihood estimator of the parameters of model (7.1.1) obtained by assuming the normality of $\mathbf{U}$, and we shall derive its asymptotic properties without assuming normality. We attach the term *full information* (FIML) to distinguish it from the *limited information* maximum likelihood (LIML) estimator, which we shall discuss later.

The logarithmic likelihood function under the normality assumption is given by

$$\log L = -\frac{NT}{2}\log(2\pi) + T\log\|\boldsymbol{\Gamma}\| - \frac{T}{2}\log|\boldsymbol{\Sigma}| \qquad (7.2.1)$$

$$-\frac{1}{2}\operatorname{tr}\boldsymbol{\Sigma}^{-1}(\mathbf{Y}\boldsymbol{\Gamma} - \mathbf{XB})'(\mathbf{Y}\boldsymbol{\Gamma} - \mathbf{XB}),$$

where $\|\boldsymbol{\Gamma}\|$ denotes the absolute value of the determinant of $\boldsymbol{\Gamma}$. We define the FIML estimators as the values of $\boldsymbol{\Sigma}$, $\boldsymbol{\Gamma}$, and $\mathbf{B}$ that maximize $\log L$ subject to the normalization on $\boldsymbol{\Gamma}$ and the zero restrictions on $\boldsymbol{\Gamma}$ and $\mathbf{B}$. We shall derive its properties without assuming normality; once we have defined FIML, we shall treat it simply as an extremum estimator that maximizes the function given in (7.2.1). We shall prove the consistency and asymptotic normality of FIML under Assumptions 7.1.1, 7.1.2, and 7.1.3; in addition we shall assume the identifiability condition (7.1.8) and $T \geqq N + K$.

Differentiating $\log L$ with respect to $\boldsymbol{\Sigma}$ using the rules of matrix differentiation given in Theorem 21 of Appendix 1 and equating the derivative to $\mathbf{0}$, we obtain

$$\boldsymbol{\Sigma} = T^{-1}(\mathbf{Y}\boldsymbol{\Gamma} - \mathbf{XB})'(\mathbf{Y}\boldsymbol{\Gamma} - \mathbf{XB}). \qquad (7.2.2)$$

Inserting (7.2.2) into (7.2.1) yields the concentrated log likelihood function

$$\log L^* = -\frac{T}{2}\log|(\mathbf{Y} - \mathbf{XB}\boldsymbol{\Gamma}^{-1})'(\mathbf{Y} - \mathbf{XB}\boldsymbol{\Gamma}^{-1})|, \qquad (7.2.3)$$

where we have omitted terms that do not depend on the unknown parameters. The condition $T \geqq N + K$ is needed because without it the determinant can be made equal to 0 for some choice of $\mathbf{B}$ and $\boldsymbol{\Gamma}$. Thus the FIML estimators of the unspecified elements of $\mathbf{B}$ and $\boldsymbol{\Gamma}$ can be defined as those values that minimize

$$S_T = |T^{-1}(\mathbf{Y} - \mathbf{XB}\boldsymbol{\Gamma}^{-1})'(\mathbf{Y} - \mathbf{XB}\boldsymbol{\Gamma}^{-1})|. \qquad (7.2.4)$$

Inserting $\mathbf{Y} = \mathbf{XB}_0\boldsymbol{\Gamma}_0^{-1} + \mathbf{V}$, where $\mathbf{B}_0$ and $\boldsymbol{\Gamma}_0$ denote the true values, into (7.2.4) and taking the probability limit, we obtain

$$\operatorname{plim} S_T = |\boldsymbol{\Lambda}_0 + (\mathbf{B}_0\boldsymbol{\Gamma}_0^{-1} - \mathbf{B}\boldsymbol{\Gamma}^{-1})'\mathbf{A}(\mathbf{B}_0\boldsymbol{\Gamma}_0^{-1} - \mathbf{B}\boldsymbol{\Gamma}^{-1})|, \qquad (7.2.5)$$

where $\mathbf{A} = \lim T^{-1}\mathbf{X}'\mathbf{X}$. Moreover, the convergence is clearly uniform in $\mathbf{B}$ and $\boldsymbol{\Gamma}$ in the neighborhood of $\mathbf{B}_0$ and $\boldsymbol{\Gamma}_0$ in the sense defined in Chapter 4. Inasmuch as $\operatorname{plim} S_T$ is minimized uniquely at $\mathbf{B} = \mathbf{B}_0$ and $\boldsymbol{\Gamma} = \boldsymbol{\Gamma}_0$ because of the identifiability condition, the FIML estimators of the unspecified elements of $\mathbf{\Gamma}$ and $\mathbf{B}$ are consistent by Theorem 4.1.2. It follows from (7.2.2) that the FIML estimator of $\mathbf{\Sigma}$ is also consistent.

The asymptotic normality of the FIML estimators of $\mathbf{\Gamma}$ and $\mathbf{B}$ can be proved by using Theorem 4.1.3, which gives the conditions for the asymptotic normality of a general extremum estimator. However, here we shall prove it by representing FIML in the form of an instrumental variables estimator. The instrumental variables interpretation of FIML is originally attributable to Durbin (1963) and is discussed by Hausman (1975).

Differentiating (7.2.1) with respect to the unspecified elements of $\mathbf{B}$ (cf. Theorem 21, Appendix 1) and equating the derivatives to $\mathbf{0}$, we obtain

$$\mathbf{X}'(\mathbf{Y\Gamma} - \mathbf{XB})\mathbf{\Sigma}^{-1} \overset{*}{=} \mathbf{0}, \tag{7.2.6}$$

where $\overset{*}{=}$ means that only those elements of the left-hand side of (7.2.6) that correspond to the unspecified elements of $\mathbf{B}$ are set equal to $\mathbf{0}$. The ith column of the left-hand side of (7.2.6) is $\mathbf{X}'(\mathbf{Y\Gamma} - \mathbf{XB})\boldsymbol{\sigma}^i$, where $\boldsymbol{\sigma}^i$ is the ith column of $\mathbf{\Sigma}^{-1}$. Note that this is the derivative of $\log L$ with respect to the ith column of $\mathbf{B}$. But, because only the K_i elements of the ith column of $\mathbf{B}$ are nonzero, (7.2.6) is equivalent to

$$\mathbf{X}_i'(\mathbf{Y\Gamma} - \mathbf{XB})\boldsymbol{\sigma}^i = \mathbf{0}, \qquad i = 1, 2, \ldots, N. \tag{7.2.7}$$

We can combine the N equations of (7.2.7) as

$$\begin{bmatrix} \mathbf{X}_1' & \mathbf{0} & \cdot & \cdot & \mathbf{0} \\ \mathbf{0} & \mathbf{X}_2' & & & \\ \cdot & & \cdot & & \\ \cdot & & & \cdot & \\ \mathbf{0} & & & & \mathbf{X}_N' \end{bmatrix} (\mathbf{\Sigma}^{-1} \otimes \mathbf{I}) \begin{bmatrix} \mathbf{y}_1 - \mathbf{Z}_1\boldsymbol{\alpha}_1 \\ \mathbf{y}_2 - \mathbf{Z}_2\boldsymbol{\alpha}_2 \\ \cdot \\ \cdot \\ \mathbf{y}_N - \mathbf{Z}_N\boldsymbol{\alpha}_N \end{bmatrix} = \mathbf{0}. \tag{7.2.8}$$

Differentiating (7.2.1) with respect to the unspecified elements of $\mathbf{\Gamma}$ and equating the derivatives to $\mathbf{0}$, we obtain

$$T(\mathbf{\Gamma}')^{-1} - \mathbf{Y}'(\mathbf{Y\Gamma} - \mathbf{XB})\mathbf{\Sigma}^{-1} \overset{+}{=} \mathbf{0}, \tag{7.2.9}$$

where $\overset{+}{=}$ means that only those elements of the left-hand side of (7.2.9) that correspond to the unspecified elements of $\mathbf{\Gamma}$ are set equal to $\mathbf{0}$. Solving (7.2.2) for $T\mathbf{I}$ and inserting it into (7.2.9) yield

$$\overline{\mathbf{Y}}'(\mathbf{Y\Gamma} - \mathbf{XB})\mathbf{\Sigma}^{-1} \overset{+}{=} \mathbf{0}, \tag{7.2.10}$$

where $\overline{\mathbf{Y}} = \mathbf{XB\Gamma}^{-1}$. In exactly the same way that we rewrote (7.2.6) as (7.2.8), we can rewrite (7.2.10) as

$$\begin{bmatrix} \bar{\mathbf{Y}}_1' & \mathbf{0} & \cdot & \cdot & \mathbf{0} \\ \mathbf{0} & \bar{\mathbf{Y}}_2' & & & \\ \cdot & & \cdot & & \\ \cdot & & & \cdot & \\ \mathbf{0} & & & & \bar{\mathbf{Y}}_N' \end{bmatrix} (\boldsymbol{\Sigma}^{-1} \otimes \mathbf{I}) \begin{bmatrix} \mathbf{y}_1 - \mathbf{Z}_1\boldsymbol{\alpha}_1 \\ \mathbf{y}_2 - \mathbf{Z}_2\boldsymbol{\alpha}_2 \\ \cdot \\ \cdot \\ \mathbf{y}_N - \mathbf{Z}_N\boldsymbol{\alpha}_N \end{bmatrix} = \mathbf{0}, \tag{7.2.11}$$

where $\bar{\mathbf{Y}}_i$ consists of the nonstochastic part of those vectors of $\mathbf{Y}$ that appear in the right-hand side of the ith structural equation.

Defining $\bar{\mathbf{Z}}_i = (\bar{\mathbf{Y}}_i, \mathbf{X}_i)$ and $\underline{\bar{\mathbf{Z}}} = \text{diag}(\bar{\mathbf{Z}}_1, \bar{\mathbf{Z}}_2, \ldots, \bar{\mathbf{Z}}_N)$, we can combine (7.2.8) and (7.2.11) into a single equation

$$\boldsymbol{\alpha} = [\underline{\bar{\mathbf{Z}}}'(\boldsymbol{\Sigma}^{-1} \otimes \mathbf{I})\underline{\mathbf{Z}}]^{-1}\underline{\bar{\mathbf{Z}}}'(\boldsymbol{\Sigma}^{-1} \otimes \mathbf{I})\mathbf{y}. \tag{7.2.12}$$

The FIML estimator of $\boldsymbol{\alpha}$, denoted $\hat{\boldsymbol{\alpha}}$, is a solution of (7.2.12), where $\boldsymbol{\Sigma}$ is replaced by the right-hand side of (7.2.2). Because both $\underline{\bar{\mathbf{Z}}}$ and $\boldsymbol{\Sigma}$ in the right-hand side of (7.2.12) depend on $\boldsymbol{\alpha}$, (7.2.12) defines $\hat{\boldsymbol{\alpha}}$ implicitly. Nevertheless, this representation is useful for deriving the asymptotic distribution of FIML as well as for comparing it with the 3SLS estimator (see Section 7.4).

Equation (7.2.12), with $\boldsymbol{\Sigma}$ replaced by the right-hand side of (7.2.2), can be used as an iterative algorithm for calculating $\hat{\boldsymbol{\alpha}}$. Evaluate $\underline{\bar{\mathbf{Z}}}$ and $\boldsymbol{\Sigma}$ in the right-hand side of (7.2.12) using an initial estimate of $\boldsymbol{\alpha}$, thus obtaining a new estimate of $\boldsymbol{\alpha}$ by (7.2.12). Insert the new estimate into the right-hand side, and so on. However, Chow (1968) found a similar algorithm inferior to the more standard Newton-Raphson iteration (cf. Section 4.4.1).

The asymptotic normality of $\hat{\boldsymbol{\alpha}}$, follows easily from (7.2.12). Let $\hat{\underline{\bar{\mathbf{Z}}}}$ and $\hat{\boldsymbol{\Sigma}}$ be $\underline{\bar{\mathbf{Z}}}$ and $\boldsymbol{\Sigma}$ evaluated at $\hat{\boldsymbol{\alpha}}$, respectively. Then we have from (7.2.12)

$$\sqrt{T}(\hat{\boldsymbol{\alpha}} - \boldsymbol{\alpha}) = [T^{-1}\hat{\underline{\bar{\mathbf{Z}}}}'(\hat{\boldsymbol{\Sigma}}^{-1} \otimes \mathbf{I})\underline{\mathbf{Z}}]^{-1}T^{-1/2}\hat{\underline{\bar{\mathbf{Z}}}}'(\hat{\boldsymbol{\Sigma}}^{-1} \otimes \mathbf{I})\mathbf{u}. \tag{7.2.13}$$

Because $\hat{\boldsymbol{\alpha}}$ and $\hat{\boldsymbol{\Sigma}}$ are consistent estimators, we can prove, by a straightforward application of Theorems 3.2.7, 3.5.4, and 3.5.5, that under Assumptions 7.1.1, 7.1.2, and 7.1.3

$$\sqrt{T}(\hat{\boldsymbol{\alpha}} - \boldsymbol{\alpha}) \rightarrow N\{\mathbf{0}, [\lim T^{-1}\underline{\bar{\mathbf{Z}}}'(\boldsymbol{\Sigma}^{-1}\otimes\mathbf{I})\underline{\bar{\mathbf{Z}}}]^{-1}\}. \tag{7.2.14}$$

7.3 Limited Information Model

7.3.1 Introduction

In this section we shall consider situations in which a researcher wishes to estimate only the parameters of one structural equation. Although these parameters can, of course, be estimated simultaneously with the parameters of the remaining equations by FIML, we shall consider simpler estimators that do not require the estimation of the parameters of the other structural equations.

We shall assume for simplicity that a researcher wishes to estimate the parameters of the first structural equation

$$\mathbf{y}_1 = \mathbf{Y}_1\gamma + \mathbf{X}_1\boldsymbol{\beta} + \mathbf{u}_1 (\equiv \mathbf{Z}_1\boldsymbol{\alpha} + \mathbf{u}_1), \tag{7.3.1}$$

where we have omitted the subscript 1 from γ, $\boldsymbol{\beta}$, and $\boldsymbol{\alpha}$. We shall not specify the remaining structural equations; instead, we shall merely specify the reduced form equations for $\mathbf{Y}_1$,

$$\mathbf{Y}_1 = \mathbf{X}\boldsymbol{\Pi}_1 + \mathbf{V}_1, \tag{7.3.2}$$

which is a subset of (7.1.2). The model defined by (7.3.1) and (7.3.2) can be regarded as a simplified simultaneous equations model in which simultaneity appears only in the first equation. We call this the *limited information model.* In contrast, we call model (7.1.1) the *full information model.*

Assumptions 7.1.1 and 7.1.2 are still maintained. However, Assumption 7.1.3 need not be assumed if we assume (7.3.2). Assumption 7.1.1 implies that the rows of $(\mathbf{u}_1, \mathbf{V}_1)$ are i.i.d. with zero mean. Throughout this section we shall denote the variance-covariance matrix of each row of $(\mathbf{u}_1, \mathbf{V}_1)$ by $\boldsymbol{\Sigma}$. Partition $\boldsymbol{\Sigma}$ as

$$\boldsymbol{\Sigma} = \begin{bmatrix} \sigma_1^2 & \boldsymbol{\Sigma}_{12} \\ \boldsymbol{\Sigma}_{21} & \boldsymbol{\Sigma}_{22} \end{bmatrix},$$

where σ_1^2 is the variance of each element of $\mathbf{u}_1$. We assume that $\boldsymbol{\alpha}$ is identifiable. It means that, if we partition $\boldsymbol{\Pi}_1$ as $\boldsymbol{\Pi}_1 = (\boldsymbol{\Pi}_{11}', \boldsymbol{\Pi}_{10}')'$ in such a way that $\mathbf{X}_1$ is postmultiplied by $\boldsymbol{\Pi}_{11}$, then the rank of $\boldsymbol{\Pi}_{10}$ is equal to N_1, the number of elements of γ.

7.3.2 Limited Information Maximum Likelihood Estimator

The LIML estimator is obtained by maximizing the joint density of $\mathbf{y}_1$ and $\mathbf{Y}_1$ under the normality assumption with respect to $\boldsymbol{\alpha}$, $\boldsymbol{\Pi}$, and $\boldsymbol{\Sigma}$ without any constraint. Anderson and Rubin (1949) proposed this estimator (without the particular normalization on $\boldsymbol{\Gamma}$ we have adopted here) and obtained an explicit formula for the LIML estimator:[4]

$$\hat{\boldsymbol{\alpha}}_{\mathrm{L}} = [\mathbf{Z}_1'(\mathbf{I} - \lambda\mathbf{M})\mathbf{Z}_1]^{-1}\mathbf{Z}_1'(\mathbf{I} - \lambda\mathbf{M})\mathbf{y}_1, \tag{7.3.3}$$

where λ is the smallest characteristic root of $\mathbf{W}_1\mathbf{W}^{-1}$, $\mathbf{W} = [\mathbf{y}_1, \mathbf{Y}_1]'\mathbf{M}[\mathbf{y}_1, \mathbf{Y}_1]$, $\mathbf{W}_1 = [\mathbf{y}_1, \mathbf{Y}_1]'\mathbf{M}_1[\mathbf{y}_1, \mathbf{Y}_1]$, $\mathbf{M} = \mathbf{I} - \mathbf{X}(\mathbf{X}'\mathbf{X})^{-1}\mathbf{X}'$, and $\mathbf{M}_1 = \mathbf{I} - \mathbf{X}_1(\mathbf{X}_1'\mathbf{X}_1)^{-1}\mathbf{X}_1'$.

7.3.3 Two-Stage Least Squares Estimator

The two-stage least squares (2SLS) estimator of $\boldsymbol{\alpha}$, proposed by Theil (1953),[5] is defined by

$$\hat{\boldsymbol{\alpha}}_{2S} = (\mathbf{Z}_1'\mathbf{P}\mathbf{Z}_1)^{-1}\mathbf{Z}_1'\mathbf{P}\mathbf{y}_1, \tag{7.3.4}$$

where $\mathbf{P} = \mathbf{X}(\mathbf{X}'\mathbf{X})^{-1}\mathbf{X}$.

7.3.4 Asymptotic Distribution of the Limited Information Maximum Likelihood Estimator and the Two-Stage Least Squares Estimator

The LIML and 2SLS estimators of $\boldsymbol{\alpha}$ have the same asymptotic distribution. In this subsection we shall derive it without assuming the normality of the observations.

We shall derive the asymptotic distribution of 2SLS. From (7.3.4) we have

$$\sqrt{T}(\hat{\boldsymbol{\alpha}}_{2S} - \boldsymbol{\alpha}) = (T^{-1}\mathbf{Z}_1'\mathbf{P}\mathbf{Z}_1)^{-1}T^{-1/2}\mathbf{Z}_1'\mathbf{P}\mathbf{u}_1. \tag{7.3.5}$$

The limit distribution of $\sqrt{T}(\hat{\boldsymbol{\alpha}}_{2S} - \boldsymbol{\alpha})$ is derived by showing that plim $T^{-1}\mathbf{Z}_1'\mathbf{P}\mathbf{Z}_1$ exists and is nonsingular and that the limit distribution of $T^{-1/2}\mathbf{Z}_1'\mathbf{P}\mathbf{u}_1$ is normal.

First, consider the probability limit of $T^{-1}\mathbf{Z}_1'\mathbf{P}\mathbf{Z}_1$. Substitute $(\mathbf{X}\boldsymbol{\Pi}_1 + \mathbf{V}_1, \mathbf{X}_1)$ for $\mathbf{Z}_1$ in $T^{-1}\mathbf{Z}_1'\mathbf{P}\mathbf{Z}_1$. Then any term involving $\mathbf{V}_1$ converges to $\mathbf{0}$ in probability. For example,

$$\begin{aligned}\operatorname{plim} T^{-1}\mathbf{X}_1'\mathbf{X}(\mathbf{X}'\mathbf{X})^{-1}\mathbf{X}'\mathbf{V}_1 &= \operatorname{plim} T^{-1}\mathbf{X}_1'\mathbf{X}(T^{-1}\mathbf{X}'\mathbf{X})^{-1}T^{-1}\mathbf{X}'\mathbf{V}_1\\ &= \operatorname{plim} T^{-1}\mathbf{X}_1'\mathbf{X}(\operatorname{plim} T^{-1}\mathbf{X}'\mathbf{X})^{-1}\operatorname{plim} T^{-1}\mathbf{X}'\mathbf{V}_1 = \mathbf{0}.\end{aligned}$$

The second equality follows from Theorem 3.2.6, and the third equality follows from plim $T^{-1}\mathbf{X}'\mathbf{V}_1 = \mathbf{0}$, which can be proved using Theorem 3.2.1. Therefore

$$\begin{aligned}\operatorname{plim} T^{-1}\mathbf{Z}_1'\mathbf{P}\mathbf{Z}_1 &= \begin{bmatrix}\boldsymbol{\Pi}_{11}' & \boldsymbol{\Pi}_{10}'\\ \mathbf{I} & \mathbf{0}\end{bmatrix}(\operatorname{plim} T^{-1}\mathbf{X}'\mathbf{X})\begin{bmatrix}\boldsymbol{\Pi}_{11} & \mathbf{I}\\ \boldsymbol{\Pi}_{10} & \mathbf{0}\end{bmatrix}\\ &\equiv \mathbf{A}.\end{aligned} \tag{7.3.6}$$

Furthermore, $\mathbf{A}$ is nonsingular because rank $(\Pi_{10}) = N_1$, which is assumed for identifiability.

Next, consider the limit distribution of $T^{-1/2}\mathbf{Z}_1'\mathbf{P}\mathbf{u}_1$. From Theorem 3.2.7 we have

$$\frac{1}{\sqrt{T}}\mathbf{Z}_1'\mathbf{P}\mathbf{u}_1 \overset{\text{LD}}{=} \frac{1}{\sqrt{T}}\begin{bmatrix}\mathbf{\Pi}_1'\mathbf{X}' \\ \mathbf{X}_1'\end{bmatrix}\mathbf{u}_1, \tag{7.3.7}$$

where $\overset{\text{LD}}{=}$ means that both sides of it have the same limit distribution. But, using Theorem 3.5.4, we can show

$$\frac{1}{\sqrt{T}}\begin{bmatrix}\mathbf{\Pi}_1'\mathbf{X}' \\ \mathbf{X}_1'\end{bmatrix}\mathbf{u}_1 \rightarrow N(\mathbf{0}, \sigma_1^2\mathbf{A}). \tag{7.3.8}$$

Thus, from Eqs. (7.3.5) through (7.3.8) and by using Theorem 3.2.7 again, we conclude

$$\sqrt{T}(\hat{\boldsymbol{\alpha}}_{2S} - \boldsymbol{\alpha}) \rightarrow N(\mathbf{0}, \sigma_1^2\mathbf{A}^{-1}). \tag{7.3.9}$$

To prove that the LIML estimator of $\boldsymbol{\alpha}$ has the same asymptotic distribution as 2SLS, we shall first prove

$$\operatorname{plim} \sqrt{T}(\lambda - 1) = 0. \tag{7.3.10}$$

We note

$$\lambda = \min_{\boldsymbol{\delta}} \frac{\boldsymbol{\delta}'\mathbf{W}_1\boldsymbol{\delta}}{\boldsymbol{\delta}'\mathbf{W}\boldsymbol{\delta}}, \tag{7.3.11}$$

which follows from the identity

$$\frac{\boldsymbol{\delta}'\mathbf{W}_1\boldsymbol{\delta}}{\boldsymbol{\delta}'\mathbf{W}\boldsymbol{\delta}} = \frac{\boldsymbol{\eta}'\mathbf{W}^{-1/2}\mathbf{W}_1\mathbf{W}^{-1/2}\boldsymbol{\eta}}{\boldsymbol{\eta}'\boldsymbol{\eta}},$$

where $\boldsymbol{\eta} = \mathbf{W}^{1/2}\boldsymbol{\delta}$, and from Theorems 5 and 10 of Appendix 1. Because

$$1 \leqq \min_{\boldsymbol{\delta}} \frac{\boldsymbol{\delta}'\mathbf{W}_1\boldsymbol{\delta}}{\boldsymbol{\delta}'\mathbf{W}\boldsymbol{\delta}} \leqq \frac{(1, -\boldsymbol{\gamma}')\mathbf{W}_1(1, -\boldsymbol{\gamma}')'}{(1, -\boldsymbol{\gamma}')\mathbf{W}(1, -\boldsymbol{\gamma}')'},$$

we have

$$\lambda - 1 \leqq \frac{\mathbf{u}_1'\mathbf{M}_1\mathbf{u}_1}{\mathbf{u}_1'\mathbf{M}\mathbf{u}_1} - 1 \tag{7.3.12}$$

$$= \frac{\mathbf{u}_1'[\mathbf{X}(\mathbf{X}'\mathbf{X})^{-1}\mathbf{X}' - \mathbf{X}_1(\mathbf{X}_1'\mathbf{X}_1)^{-1}\mathbf{X}_1']\mathbf{u}_1}{\mathbf{u}_1'\mathbf{M}\mathbf{u}_1}.$$

Therefore the desired result (7.3.10) follows from noting, for example, $\operatorname{plim} T^{-1/2}\mathbf{u}_1'\mathbf{X}(\mathbf{X}'\mathbf{X})^{-1}\mathbf{X}'\mathbf{u}_1 = 0$. From (7.3.3) we have

$$\sqrt{T}(\hat{\boldsymbol{\alpha}}_{\mathrm{L}}-\boldsymbol{\alpha})=[T^{-1}\mathbf{Z}_1'\mathbf{P}\mathbf{Z}_1-(\lambda-1)T^{-1}\mathbf{Z}_1'\mathbf{M}\mathbf{Z}_1]^{-1} \times [T^{-1/2}\mathbf{Z}_1'\mathbf{P}\mathbf{u}_1-(\lambda-1)T^{-1/2}\mathbf{Z}_1'\mathbf{M}\mathbf{u}_1]. \quad (7.3.13)$$

But (7.3.10) implies that both $(\lambda-1)T^{-1}\mathbf{Z}_1'\mathbf{M}\mathbf{Z}_1$ and $(\lambda-1)T^{-1/2}\mathbf{Z}_1'\mathbf{M}\mathbf{u}_1$ converge to $\mathbf{0}$ in probability. Therefore, by Theorem 3.2.7,

$$\sqrt{T}(\hat{\boldsymbol{\alpha}}_{\mathrm{L}}-\boldsymbol{\alpha})\overset{\mathrm{LD}}{=}\sqrt{T}(\mathbf{Z}_1'\mathbf{P}\mathbf{Z}_1)^{-1}\mathbf{Z}_1'\mathbf{P}\mathbf{u}_1, \quad (7.3.14)$$

which implies that the LIML estimator of $\boldsymbol{\alpha}$ has the same asymptotic distribution as 2SLS.

7.3.5 Exact Distributions of the Limited Information Maximum Likelihood Estimator and the Two-Stage Least Squares Estimator

The exact finite sample distributions of the two estimators differ. We shall discuss briefly the main results about these distributions as well as their approximations. The discussion is very brief because there are several excellent survey articles on this topic by Mariano (1982), Anderson (1982), Taylor (1982), and Phillips (1983).

In the early years (say, until the 1960s) most of the results were obtained by Monte Carlo studies; a summary of these results has been given by Johnston (1972). The conclusions of these Monte Carlo studies concerning the choice between LIML and 2SLS were inconclusive, although they gave a slight edge to 2SLS in terms of the mean squared error or similar moment criteria. However, most of these studies did not realize that the moment criteria may not be appropriate in view of the later established fact that LIML does not have a moment of any order and 2SLS has moments of the order up to and including the degree of overidentifiability ($K_{(i)}-N_i$ in our notation).

The exact distributions of the two estimators and their approximations have since been obtained, mostly for a simple two-equation model.[6] Anderson (1982) summarized these results and showed that 2SLS exhibits a greater median-bias than LIML, especially when the degree of simultaneity and the degree of overidentifiability are large, and that the convergence to normality of 2SLS is slower than that of LIML.

Another recent result favors LIML over 2SLS; Fuller (1977) proposed the modified LIML that is obtained by substituting $\lambda - c/(T-K_2)$, where c is any constant, for λ in (7.3.3). He showed that it has finite moments and dominates 2SLS in terms of the mean squared error to $O(T^{-2})$. Fuller's estimator can be interpreted as another example of the second-order efficiency of the bias-corrected MLE (see Section 4.2.4).

However, we must treat these results with caution. First, both Anderson's and Fuller's results were obtained under the assumption of normality, whereas the asymptotic distribution can be obtained without normality. Second, Anderson's results were obtained only for a simple model; and, moreover, it is difficult to verify in practice exactly how large the degrees of simultaneity and overidentifiability should be for LIML to dominate 2SLS. Third, we should also compare the performance of estimators under misspecified models. Monte Carlo studies indicate that the simpler the estimator the more robust it tends to be against misspecification. (See Taylor, 1983, for a critical appraisal of the finite sample results.)

7.3.6 Interpretations of the Two-Stage Least Squares Estimator

There are many interpretations of 2SLS. They are useful when we attempt to generalize 2SLS to situations in which some of the standard assumptions of the model are violated. Different interpretations often lead to different generalizations. Here we shall give four that we consider most useful.

Theil's interpretation is most famous, and from it the name 2SLS is derived. In the first stage, the least squares method is applied to Eq. (7.3.2) and the least squares predictor $\hat{\mathbf{Y}}_1 \equiv \mathbf{P}\mathbf{Y}_1$ is obtained. In the second stage, $\hat{\mathbf{Y}}_1$ is substituted for $\mathbf{Y}_1$ in the right-hand side of (7.3.1) and $\mathbf{y}_1$ is regressed on $\hat{\mathbf{Y}}_1$ and $\mathbf{X}_1$. The least squares estimates of γ_1 and $\boldsymbol{\beta}_1$ thus obtained are 2SLS.

The two-stage least squares estimator can be interpreted as the asymptotically best instrumental variables estimator. This is the way Basmann (1957) motivated his estimator, which is equivalent to 2SLS. The instrumental variables estimator applied to (7.3.1) is commonly defined as $(\mathbf{S}'\mathbf{Z}_1)^{-1}\mathbf{S}'\mathbf{y}_1$ for some matrix $\mathbf{S}$ of the same size as $\mathbf{Z}_1$. But, here, we shall define it more generally as

$$\hat{\boldsymbol{\alpha}}_{\mathrm{I}} = (\mathbf{Z}_1'\mathbf{P}_S\mathbf{Z}_1)^{-1}\mathbf{Z}_1'\mathbf{P}_S\mathbf{y}_1, \tag{7.3.15}$$

where $\mathbf{P}_S = \mathbf{S}(\mathbf{S}'\mathbf{S})^{-1}\mathbf{S}'$. The matrix $\mathbf{S}$ should have T rows, but the number of columns need not be the same as that of $\mathbf{Z}_1$. In addition, we assume that $\mathbf{S}$ satisfies the following three conditions:

(i) plim $T^{-1}\mathbf{S}'\mathbf{S}$ exists and is nonsingular,
(ii) plim $T^{-1}\mathbf{S}'\mathbf{u}_1 = \mathbf{0}$, and
(iii) plim $T^{-1}\mathbf{S}'\mathbf{V}_1 = \mathbf{0}$.

Under these assumptions we obtain, in a manner analogous to the derivation of (7.3.9),

$$\sqrt{T}(\hat{\boldsymbol{\alpha}}_{\mathrm{I}} - \boldsymbol{\alpha}) \rightarrow N(\mathbf{0}, \sigma_1^2\mathbf{C}^{-1}), \tag{7.3.16}$$

where

$$\mathbf{C} = \begin{bmatrix} \mathbf{\Pi}_{11}' & \mathbf{\Pi}_{10}' \\ \mathbf{I} & \mathbf{0} \end{bmatrix} \text{plim } T^{-1}\mathbf{X}'\mathbf{P}_S\mathbf{X} \begin{bmatrix} \mathbf{\Pi}_{11} & \mathbf{I} \\ \mathbf{\Pi}_{10} & \mathbf{0} \end{bmatrix}. \tag{7.3.17}$$

Because $\mathbf{A} \geqq \mathbf{C}$, we conclude by Theorem 17 of Appendix 1 that 2SLS is the asymptotically best in the class of the instrumental variables estimators defined above.[7]

For a third interpretation, we note that the projection matrix $\mathbf{P}$ used to define 2SLS in (7.3.4) purports to eliminate the stochastic part of $\mathbf{Y}_1$. If $\mathbf{V}_1$ were observable, the elimination of the stochastic part of $\mathbf{Y}_1$ could be more directly accomplished by another projection matrix $\mathbf{M}_{V_1} \equiv \mathbf{I} - \mathbf{V}_1(\mathbf{V}_1'\mathbf{V}_1)^{-1}\mathbf{V}_1'$. The asymptotic variance-covariance matrix of the resulting estimator is $(\sigma_1^2 - \mathbf{\Sigma}_{12}\mathbf{\Sigma}_{22}^{-1}\mathbf{\Sigma}_{21})\mathbf{A}^{-1}$ and hence smaller than that of 2SLS. When we predict $\mathbf{V}_1$ by $\mathbf{MY}_1$, where $\mathbf{M} = \mathbf{I} - \mathbf{X}(\mathbf{X}'\mathbf{X})^{-1}\mathbf{X}'$, and use it in place of $\mathbf{M}_{V_1}$, we obtain 2SLS.

The last interpretation we shall give originates in the article by Anderson and Sawa (1973). Let the reduced form for $\mathbf{y}_1$ be

$$\mathbf{y}_1 = \mathbf{X}\boldsymbol{\pi}_1 + \mathbf{v}_1. \tag{7.3.18}$$

Then (7.3.1), (7.3.2), and (7.3.18) imply

$$\boldsymbol{\pi}_1 = \mathbf{\Pi}_1\boldsymbol{\gamma} + \mathbf{J}_1\boldsymbol{\beta}, \tag{7.3.19}$$

where $\mathbf{J}_1 = (\mathbf{X}'\mathbf{X})^{-1}\mathbf{X}'\mathbf{X}_1$. From (7.3.19) we obtain

$$\hat{\boldsymbol{\pi}}_1 = \hat{\mathbf{\Pi}}_1\boldsymbol{\gamma} + \mathbf{J}_1\boldsymbol{\beta} + (\hat{\boldsymbol{\pi}}_1 - \boldsymbol{\pi}_1) - (\hat{\mathbf{\Pi}}_1 - \mathbf{\Pi}_1)\boldsymbol{\gamma}, \tag{7.3.20}$$

where $\hat{\boldsymbol{\pi}}_1$ and $\hat{\mathbf{\Pi}}_1$ are the least squares estimators of $\boldsymbol{\pi}_1$ and $\mathbf{\Pi}_1$, respectively. Then 2SLS can be interpreted as generalized least squares applied to (7.3.20). To see this, merely note that (7.3.20) is obtained by premultiplying (7.3.1) by $(\mathbf{X}'\mathbf{X})^{-1}\mathbf{X}'$.

7.3.7 Generalized Two-Stage Least Squares Estimator

Consider regression equations

$$\mathbf{y} = \mathbf{Z}\boldsymbol{\alpha} + \mathbf{u} \tag{7.3.21}$$

and

$$\mathbf{Z} = \mathbf{X}\mathbf{\Pi} + \mathbf{V}, \tag{7.3.22}$$

where $E\mathbf{u} = \mathbf{0}$, $E\mathbf{V} = \mathbf{0}$, $E\mathbf{uu}' = \mathbf{\Psi}$, and $\mathbf{u}$ and $\mathbf{V}$ are possibly correlated. We assume that $\mathbf{\Psi}$ is a known nonsingular matrix. Although the limited information model can be written in this way by assuming that certain elements of **V** are identically equal to 0, the reader may regard these two equations in a more abstract sense and not necessarily as arising from the limited information model considered in Section 7.3.1.

Premultiplying (7.3.21) and (7.3.22) by $\mathbf{\Psi}^{-1/2}$, we obtain

$$\mathbf{\Psi}^{-1/2}\mathbf{y} = \mathbf{\Psi}^{-1/2}\mathbf{Z}\boldsymbol{\alpha} + \mathbf{\Psi}^{-1/2}\mathbf{u} \tag{7.3.23}$$

and

$$\mathbf{\Psi}^{-1/2}\mathbf{Z} = \mathbf{\Psi}^{-1/2}\mathbf{X}\mathbf{\Pi} + \mathbf{\Psi}^{-1/2}\mathbf{V}. \tag{7.3.24}$$

We define the G2SLS estimator of $\boldsymbol{\alpha}$ as the 2SLS estimator of $\boldsymbol{\alpha}$ applied to (7.3.23) and (7.3.24); that is,

$$\hat{\boldsymbol{\alpha}}_{G2S} = [\mathbf{Z}'\mathbf{\Psi}^{-1}\mathbf{X}(\mathbf{X}'\mathbf{\Psi}^{-1}\mathbf{X})^{-1}\mathbf{X}'\mathbf{\Psi}^{-1}\mathbf{Z}]^{-1}\mathbf{Z}'\mathbf{\Psi}^{-1}\mathbf{X}(\mathbf{X}'\mathbf{\Psi}^{-1}\mathbf{X})^{-1}\mathbf{X}'\mathbf{\Psi}^{-1}\mathbf{y}. \tag{7.3.25}$$

Given appropriate assumptions on $\mathbf{\Psi}^{-1/2}\mathbf{X}$, $\mathbf{\Psi}^{-1/2}\mathbf{u}$, and $\mathbf{\Psi}^{-1/2}\mathbf{V}$, we can show

$$\sqrt{T}(\hat{\boldsymbol{\alpha}}_{G2S} - \boldsymbol{\alpha}) \rightarrow N[\mathbf{0}, (\lim T^{-1}\mathbf{\Pi}'\mathbf{X}'\mathbf{\Psi}^{-1}\mathbf{X}\mathbf{\Pi})^{-1}]. \tag{7.3.26}$$

As in Section 7.3.6, we can show that G2SLS is asymptotically the best instrumental variables estimator in the model defined by (7.3.21) and (7.3.22). The limit distribution is unchanged if a regular consistent estimator of $\mathbf{\Psi}$ is substituted.

The idea of G2SLS is attributable to Theil (1961), who defined it in another asymptotically equivalent way: $(\mathbf{Z}'\mathbf{P}\mathbf{\Psi}^{-1}\mathbf{Z})^{-1}\mathbf{Z}'\mathbf{P}\mathbf{\Psi}^{-1}\mathbf{y}$. It has the same asymptotic distribution as $\hat{\boldsymbol{\alpha}}_{G2S}$.

7.4 Three-Stage Least Squares Estimator

In this section we shall again consider the full information model defined by (7.1.1). The 3SLS estimator of $\boldsymbol{\alpha}$ in (7.1.5) can be defined as a special case of G2SLS applied to the same equation. The reduced form equation comparable to (7.3.22) is provided by

$$\underline{\mathbf{Z}} = \underline{\mathbf{X}}\underline{\mathbf{\Pi}} + \underline{\mathbf{V}}, \tag{7.4.1}$$

where $\underline{\mathbf{X}} = \mathbf{I} \otimes \mathbf{X}$, $\underline{\mathbf{\Pi}} = \text{diag}[(\mathbf{\Pi}_1, \mathbf{J}_1),(\mathbf{\Pi}_2, \mathbf{J}_2), \ldots, (\mathbf{\Pi}_N, \mathbf{J}_N)]$, $\underline{\mathbf{V}} = \text{diag}[(\mathbf{V}_1, \mathbf{0}),(\mathbf{V}_2, \mathbf{0}), \ldots, (\mathbf{V}_N, \mathbf{0})]$, and $\mathbf{J}_i = (\mathbf{X}'\mathbf{X})^{-1}\mathbf{X}'\mathbf{X}_i$.

To define 3SLS (proposed by Zellner and Theil, 1962), we need a consistent estimator of $\mathbf{\Sigma}$, which can be obtained as follows:

Step 1. Obtain the 2SLS estimator of $\boldsymbol{\alpha}_i$, $i = 1, 2, \ldots, N$.
Step 2. Calculate $\hat{\mathbf{u}}_i = \mathbf{y}_i - \mathbf{Z}_i\hat{\boldsymbol{\alpha}}_{i,2S}$, $i = 1, 2, \ldots, N$.
Step 3. Estimate σ_{ij} by $\hat{\sigma}_{ij} \equiv T^{-1}\hat{\mathbf{u}}_i'\hat{\mathbf{u}}_j$.
Next, inserting $\mathbf{Z} = \underline{\mathbf{Z}}$, $\mathbf{X} = \underline{\mathbf{X}}$, and $\boldsymbol{\Psi} = \hat{\boldsymbol{\Sigma}} \otimes \mathbf{I}$ into (7.3.25), we have after some manipulation of Kronecker products (see Theorem 22 of Appendix 1).

$$\hat{\boldsymbol{\alpha}}_{3S} = [\underline{\mathbf{Z}}'(\hat{\boldsymbol{\Sigma}}^{-1} \otimes \mathbf{P})\underline{\mathbf{Z}}]^{-1}\underline{\mathbf{Z}}'(\hat{\boldsymbol{\Sigma}}^{-1} \otimes \mathbf{P})\mathbf{y} \tag{7.4.2}$$
$$= [\hat{\underline{\mathbf{Z}}}'(\hat{\boldsymbol{\Sigma}}^{-1} \otimes \mathbf{I})\hat{\underline{\mathbf{Z}}}]^{-1}\hat{\underline{\mathbf{Z}}}'(\hat{\boldsymbol{\Sigma}}^{-1} \otimes \mathbf{I})\mathbf{y},$$

where $\hat{\underline{\mathbf{Z}}} = \text{diag}(\hat{\mathbf{Z}}_1, \hat{\mathbf{Z}}_2, \ldots, \hat{\mathbf{Z}}_N)$ and $\hat{\mathbf{Z}}_i = \mathbf{P}\mathbf{Z}_i$. The second formula of (7.4.2) is similar to the instrumental variables representation of FIML given in (7.2.12). We can make use of this similarity and prove that 3SLS has the same asymptotic distribution as FIML. For exact distributions of 3SLS and FIML, see the survey articles mentioned in Section 7.3.5.

7.5 Further Topics

The following topics have not been discussed in this chapter but many important results in these areas have appeared in the literature over the past several years: (1) lagged endogenous variables included in $\mathbf{X}$; (2) serially correlated errors; (3) prediction; and (4) undersized samples (that is, $\mathbf{X}$ having more columns than rows). Harvey (1981a) has given a detailed discussion of the first two topics. Recent results concerning the third topic can be found in articles by Sant (1978) and by Nagar and Sahay (1978). For a discussion of the fourth topic, consult the articles by Brundy and Jorgenson (1974) and by Swamy (1980).

Exercises

1. (Section 7.3.1)
In the limited information model defined by (7.3.1) and (7.3.2), let $\mathbf{X} = (\mathbf{X}_1, \mathbf{X}_2)$ where $\mathbf{X}_1$ and $\mathbf{X}_2$ have K_1 and K_2 columns, respectively. Suppose we define a class of instrumental variables estimators of $\boldsymbol{\alpha}$ by $(\mathbf{S}'\mathbf{Z}_1)^{-1}\mathbf{S}'\mathbf{y}$, where $\mathbf{S} = (\mathbf{X}_2\mathbf{A}, \mathbf{X}_1)$ with $\mathbf{A}$ being a $K_2 \times N_1$ $(K_2 \geqq N_1)$ matrix of constants. Show that there exists some $\mathbf{A}$ for which the instrumental variables estimator is consistent if and only if the rank condition of identifiability is satisfied for Eq. (7.3.1).

2. (Section 7.3.3)
Show that the LIML estimator of γ is obtained by minimizing $\boldsymbol{\delta}'\mathbf{W}_1\boldsymbol{\delta}/\boldsymbol{\delta}'\mathbf{W}\boldsymbol{\delta}$, where $\boldsymbol{\delta} = (1, -\gamma')'$, with respect to γ. Hence the estimator

is sometimes referred to as the *least variance ratio estimator.* Also, show that the minimization of $\boldsymbol{\delta}'\mathbf{W}_1\boldsymbol{\delta} - \boldsymbol{\delta}'\mathbf{W}\boldsymbol{\delta}$ yields the 2SLS estimator of γ.

3. (Section 7.3.3)
Consider the model

$$\mathbf{y} = \mathbf{Y}\boldsymbol{\gamma} + \mathbf{X}_1\boldsymbol{\beta} + \mathbf{u} \equiv \mathbf{Z}\boldsymbol{\alpha} + \mathbf{u}$$

$$\mathbf{Y} = \mathbf{X}\boldsymbol{\Pi} + \mathbf{V} \equiv \overline{\mathbf{Y}} + \mathbf{V},$$

where

$$\frac{1}{T} E(\mathbf{u}, \mathbf{V})'(\mathbf{u}, \mathbf{V}) = \boldsymbol{\Sigma} = \begin{bmatrix} \boldsymbol{\Sigma}_{11} & \boldsymbol{\Sigma}_{12} \\ \boldsymbol{\Sigma}_{21} & \boldsymbol{\Sigma}_{22} \end{bmatrix}.$$

Obtain the asymptotic variance-covariance matrix of $\tilde{\boldsymbol{\alpha}} \equiv (\overline{\mathbf{Y}}'\overline{\mathbf{Y}})^{-1}\overline{\mathbf{Y}}'\mathbf{y}$ and compare it with that of the 2SLS estimator of $\boldsymbol{\alpha}$.

4. (Section 7.3.3)
In a two-equation model

$$\mathbf{y}_1 = \gamma_1 \mathbf{y}_2 + \mathbf{u}_1$$

$$\mathbf{y}_2 = \gamma_2 \mathbf{y}_1 + \beta_1 \mathbf{x}_1 + \beta_2 \mathbf{x}_2 + \mathbf{u}_2,$$

compute the LIML and 2SLS estimates of γ_1, given the following moment matrices

$$\mathbf{X}'\mathbf{X} = \begin{bmatrix} 1 & 0 \\ 0 & 1 \end{bmatrix}, \quad \mathbf{Y}'\mathbf{Y} = \begin{bmatrix} \frac{7}{2} & 2 \\ 2 & \frac{3}{2} \end{bmatrix}, \quad \mathbf{X}'\mathbf{Y} = \begin{bmatrix} 1 & 1 \\ \frac{3}{2} & \frac{1}{2} \end{bmatrix},$$

where $\mathbf{X} = (\mathbf{x}_1, \mathbf{x}_2)$ and $\mathbf{Y} = (\mathbf{y}_1, \mathbf{y}_2)$.

5. (Section 7.3.7)
Show that Theil's G2SLS defined at the end of Section 7.3.7 is asymptotically equivalent to the definition (7.3.25).

6. (Section 7.3.7)
Define $\tilde{\boldsymbol{\alpha}} = [\mathbf{Z}'\mathbf{X}(\mathbf{X}'\boldsymbol{\Psi}\mathbf{X})^{-1}\mathbf{X}'\mathbf{Z}]^{-1}\mathbf{Z}'\mathbf{X}(\mathbf{X}'\boldsymbol{\Psi}\mathbf{X})^{-1}\mathbf{X}'\mathbf{y}$. Show that this is a consistent estimator of $\boldsymbol{\alpha}$ in model (7.3.21) but not as asymptotically as efficient as $\hat{\boldsymbol{\alpha}}_{G2S}$ defined in (7.3.25).

7. (Section 7.4)
Suppose that a simultaneous equations model is defined by (7.1.5) and the reduced form $\underline{\mathbf{Z}} = [\mathbf{I} \otimes \mathbf{X}]\boldsymbol{\Pi} + \mathbf{V}$. Show that $\hat{\boldsymbol{\alpha}}_{G2S}$ defined in (7.3.25) and Theil's G2SLS defined at the end of Section 7.3.7 will lead to the same 3SLS when applied to this model.

8. (Section 7.4)
Consider the following model:
(1) $\mathbf{y}_1 = \gamma \mathbf{y}_2 + \mathbf{u}_1$
(2) $\mathbf{y}_2 = \beta_1 \mathbf{x}_1 + \beta_2 \mathbf{x}_2 + \mathbf{u}_2 = \mathbf{X}\boldsymbol{\beta} + \mathbf{u}_2$,
where γ, β_1, and β_2 are scalar unknown parameters, $\mathbf{x}_1$ and $\mathbf{x}_2$ are T-component vectors of constants such that $T^{-1}\mathbf{X}'\mathbf{X}$ is nonsingular for every T and also in the limit, $\mathbf{y}_1$ and $\mathbf{y}_2$ are T-component vectors of observable random variables, and $\mathbf{u}_1$ and $\mathbf{u}_2$ are T-component vectors of unobservable random variables that are independently and identically distributed with zero mean and contemporaneous variance-covariance matrix

$$\boldsymbol{\Sigma} = \begin{bmatrix} \sigma_1^2 & \sigma_{12} \\ \sigma_{12} & \sigma_2^2 \end{bmatrix}.$$

a. Prove that the 3SLS estimator of γ is identical with the 2SLS estimator of γ.

b. Transform Eqs. (1) and (2) to obtain the following equivalent model:
(3) $\mathbf{y}_2 = \frac{1}{\gamma} \mathbf{y}_1 - \frac{1}{\gamma} \mathbf{u}_1$
(4) $\mathbf{y}_1 = \gamma\beta_1 \mathbf{x}_1 + \gamma\beta_2 \mathbf{x}_2 + \gamma \mathbf{u}_2 + \mathbf{u}_1$.
Define the reverse 2SLS estimator of γ as the reciprocal of the 2SLS estimator of $1/\gamma$ obtained from Eqs. (3) and (4). Prove that the reverse 2SLS estimator of γ has the same asymptotic distribution as the 2SLS estimator of γ.

c. Assume that at period p outside the sample the following relationship holds:
(5) $y_{1p} = \gamma y_{2p} + u_{1p}$
(6) $y_{2p} = \beta_1 x_{1p} + \beta_2 x_{2p} + u_{2p} = \mathbf{x}_p'\boldsymbol{\beta} + u_{2p}$,
where u_{1p} and u_{2p} are independent of $\mathbf{u}_1$ and $\mathbf{u}_2$ with zero mean and variance-covariance matrix $\boldsymbol{\Sigma}$. We want to predict y_{1p} when x_{1p} and x_{2p} are given. Compare the mean squared prediction error of the indirect least squares predictor, defined by
(7) $\hat{y}_{1p} = \mathbf{x}_p'(\mathbf{X}'\mathbf{X})^{-1}\mathbf{X}'\mathbf{y}_1$
with the mean squared prediction error of the 2SLS predictor defined by
(8) $\tilde{y}_{1p} = \tilde{\gamma}\mathbf{x}_p'(\mathbf{X}'\mathbf{X})^{-1}\mathbf{X}'\mathbf{y}_2$,
where $\tilde{\gamma}$ is the 2SLS estimator of γ. Can we say one is uniformly smaller than the other?

8 Nonlinear Simultaneous Equations Models

In this chapter we shall develop the theory of statistical inference for nonlinear simultaneous equations models. The main results are taken from the author's recent contributions (especially, Amemiya, 1974c, 1975a, 1976a, 1977a). Some additional results can be found in Amemiya (1983a). Section 8.1 deals with the estimation of the parameters of a single equation and Section 8.2 with that of simultaneous equations. Section 8.3 deals with tests of hypotheses, prediction, and computation.

8.1 Estimation in a Single Equation

8.1.1 Nonlinear Two-Stage Least Squares Estimator

In this section we shall consider the nonlinear regression equation

$$y_t = f_t(\mathbf{Y}_t, \mathbf{X}_{1t}, \boldsymbol{\alpha}_0) + u_t, \qquad t = 1, 2, \ldots, T, \tag{8.1.1}$$

where y_t is a scalar endogeneous variable, $\mathbf{Y}_t$ is a vector of endogenous variables, $\mathbf{X}_{1t}$ is a vector of exogenous variables, $\boldsymbol{\alpha}_0$ is a K-vector of unknown parameters, and $\{u_t\}$ are scalar i.i.d. random variables with $Eu_t = 0$ and $Vu_t = \sigma^2$. This model does not specify the distribution of $\mathbf{Y}_t$. Equation (8.1.1) may be one of many structural equations that simultaneously define the distribution of y_t and $\mathbf{Y}_t$, but here we are not concerned with the other equations. Sometimes we shall write $f(\mathbf{Y}_t, \mathbf{X}_{1t}, \boldsymbol{\alpha}_0)$ simply as $f_t(\boldsymbol{\alpha}_0)$ or as f_t. We define T-vectors $\mathbf{y}$, $\mathbf{f}$, and $\mathbf{u}$, the tth elements of which are y_t, f_t, and u_t, respectively, and matrices $\mathbf{Y}$ and $\mathbf{X}_1$, the tth rows of which are $\mathbf{Y}_t'$ and $\mathbf{X}_{1t}'$, respectively.[1]

The nonlinear least squares estimator of $\boldsymbol{\alpha}_0$ in this model is generally inconsistent for the same reason that the least squares estimator is inconsistent in a linear simultaneous equations model. We can see this by considering (4.3.8) and noting that plim $A_3 \neq 0$ in general because f_t may be correlated with u_t in the model (8.1.1) because of the possible dependence of $\mathbf{Y}_t$ on y_t. In this section we shall consider how we can generalize the two-stage least squares

(2SLS) method to the nonlinear model (8.1.1) so that we can obtain a consistent estimator.

Following the article by Amemiya (1974c), we define the class of nonlinear two-stage least squares (NL2S) estimators of $\boldsymbol{\alpha}_0$ in the model (8.1.1) as the value of $\boldsymbol{\alpha}$ that minimizes

$$S_T(\boldsymbol{\alpha}|\mathbf{W}) = (\mathbf{y} - \mathbf{f})'\mathbf{W}(\mathbf{W}'\mathbf{W})^{-1}\mathbf{W}'(\mathbf{y} - \mathbf{f}), \tag{8.1.2}$$

where $\mathbf{W}$ is some matrix of constants with rank at least equal to K.

In the literature prior to the article by Amemiya (1974c), a generalization of 2SLS was considered only in special cases of the fully nonlinear model (8.1.1), namely, (1) the case of nonlinearity only in parameters and (2) the case of nonlinearity only in variables. See, for example, the article by Zellner, Huang, and Chau (1965) for the first case and the article by Kelejian (1971) for the second case.[2] The definition in the preceding paragraph contains as special cases the Zellner-Huang-Chau definition and the Kelejian definition, as well as Theil's 2SLS. By defining the estimator as a solution of a minimization problem, it is possible to prove its consistency and asymptotic normality by the techniques discussed in Chapter 4.

First, we shall prove the consistency of NL2S using the general result for an extremum estimator given in Theorem 4.1.2. The proof is analogous to but slightly different from a proof given by Amemiya (1974c). The proof differs from the proof of the consistency of NLLS (Theorem 4.3.1) in that the derivative of $\mathbf{f}$ is used more extensively here.

THEOREM 8.1.1. Consider the nonlinear regression model (8.1.1) with the additional assumptions:

(A) $\lim T^{-1}\mathbf{W}'\mathbf{W}$ exists and is nonsingular.

(B) $\partial f_t/\partial\boldsymbol{\alpha}$ exists and is continuous in $N(\boldsymbol{\alpha}_0)$, an open neighborhood of $\boldsymbol{\alpha}_0$.

(C) $T^{-1}\mathbf{W}'(\partial\mathbf{f}/\partial\boldsymbol{\alpha}')$ converges in probability uniformly in $\boldsymbol{\alpha} \in N(\boldsymbol{\alpha}_0)$.

(D) $\text{plim}\, T^{-1}\mathbf{W}'(\partial\mathbf{f}/\partial\boldsymbol{\alpha}')_{\boldsymbol{\alpha}_0}$ is full rank.

Then a solution of the minimization of (8.1.2) is consistent in the sense of Theorem 4.1.2.

Proof. Inserting (8.1.1) into (8.1.2), we can rewrite T^{-1} times (8.1.2) as

$$\begin{aligned} T^{-1}S_T &= T^{-1}\mathbf{u}'\mathbf{P}_W\mathbf{u} + T^{-1}(\mathbf{f}_0 - \mathbf{f})'\mathbf{P}_W(\mathbf{f}_0 - \mathbf{f}) \\ &\quad + T^{-1}2(\mathbf{f}_0 - \mathbf{f})'\mathbf{P}_W\mathbf{u} \\ &\equiv A_1 + A_2 + A_3, \end{aligned} \tag{8.1.3}$$

where $\mathbf{P}_W = \mathbf{W}(\mathbf{W}'\mathbf{W})^{-1}\mathbf{W}'$, $\mathbf{f} = \mathbf{f}(\boldsymbol{\alpha})$, and $\mathbf{f}_0 = \mathbf{f}(\boldsymbol{\alpha}_0)$. Note that (8.1.3) is similar to (4.3.8). First, A_1 converges to 0 in probability because of assumption A and the assumptions on $\{u_t\}$. Second, consider A_2. Assumption B enables us to write

$$\mathbf{f} = \mathbf{f}_0 + \mathbf{G}_*(\boldsymbol{\alpha} - \boldsymbol{\alpha}_0), \tag{8.1.4}$$

where $\mathbf{G}_*$ is the matrix the tth row of which is $\partial f_t/\partial \boldsymbol{\alpha}^*$ evaluated at $\boldsymbol{\alpha}_t^*$ between $\boldsymbol{\alpha}$ and $\boldsymbol{\alpha}_0$. Therefore we have

$$A_2 = T^{-1}(\boldsymbol{\alpha}_0 - \boldsymbol{\alpha})'\mathbf{G}_*'\mathbf{P}_W\mathbf{G}_*(\boldsymbol{\alpha}_0 - \boldsymbol{\alpha}). \tag{8.1.5}$$

Therefore, because of assumptions C and D, A_2 converges in probability uniformly in $\boldsymbol{\alpha} \in N(\boldsymbol{\alpha}_0)$ to a function that is uniquely minimized at $\boldsymbol{\alpha}_0$. Finally, consider A_3. We have by the Cauchy-Schwartz inequality

$$\begin{aligned} T^{-1}|(\mathbf{f}_0 - \mathbf{f})'\mathbf{P}_W\mathbf{u}| &= T^{-1}|(\boldsymbol{\alpha}_0 - \boldsymbol{\alpha})'\mathbf{G}_*'\mathbf{P}_W\mathbf{u}| \\ &\leqq [T^{-1}(\boldsymbol{\alpha}_0 - \boldsymbol{\alpha})'\mathbf{G}_*'\mathbf{P}_W\mathbf{G}_*(\boldsymbol{\alpha}_0 - \boldsymbol{\alpha})]^{1/2} \\ &\quad \times [T^{-1}\mathbf{u}'\mathbf{P}_W\mathbf{u}]^{1/2}. \end{aligned} \tag{8.1.6}$$

Therefore the results obtained above regarding A_1 and A_2 imply that A_3 converges to 0 in probability uniformly in $\boldsymbol{\alpha} \in N(\boldsymbol{\alpha}_0)$. Thus we have verified all the conditions of Theorem 4.1.2.

Next, we shall prove the asymptotic normality of NL2S by verifying the conditions of Theorem 4.1.3.

THEOREM 8.1.2. In addition to the assumptions of the nonlinear regression model (8.1.1) and those of Theorem 8.1.1, make the following assumptions:

(A) $\partial^2 f_t/\partial\boldsymbol{\alpha}\partial\boldsymbol{\alpha}'$ exists and is continuous in $\boldsymbol{\alpha} \in N(\boldsymbol{\alpha}_0)$.

(B) $T^{-1}\mathbf{W}'(\partial^2\mathbf{f}/\partial\alpha_i\partial\boldsymbol{\alpha}')$ converges in probability to a finite matrix uniformly in $\boldsymbol{\alpha} \in N(\boldsymbol{\alpha}_0)$, where α_i is the ith element of the vector $\boldsymbol{\alpha}$.

Then, if we denote a consistent solution of the minimization of (8.1.2) by $\hat{\boldsymbol{\alpha}}$, we have

$$\sqrt{T}(\hat{\boldsymbol{\alpha}} - \boldsymbol{\alpha}_0) \rightarrow N\{\mathbf{0}, \sigma^2[\text{plim } T^{-1}\mathbf{G}_0'\mathbf{P}_W\mathbf{G}_0]^{-1}\},$$

where $\mathbf{G}_0$ is $\partial\mathbf{f}/\partial\boldsymbol{\alpha}'$ evaluated at $\boldsymbol{\alpha}_0$.

Proof. First, consider condition C of Theorem 4.1.3. We have

$$\frac{1}{\sqrt{T}}\frac{\partial S_T}{\partial \boldsymbol{\alpha}}\bigg|_{\boldsymbol{\alpha}_0} = -\frac{2}{T}\mathbf{G}_0'\mathbf{W} \cdot \sqrt{T}(\mathbf{W}'\mathbf{W})^{-1}\mathbf{W}'\mathbf{u}. \tag{8.1.7}$$

But, using Theorems 3.5.4 and 3.5.5, $\sqrt{T}(\mathbf{W}'\mathbf{W})^{-1}\mathbf{W}'\mathbf{u} \rightarrow N[\mathbf{0}, \sigma^2$

$\lim T(\mathbf{W}'\mathbf{W})^{-1}]$ because of assumption A of Theorem 8.1.1 and the assumptions on $\{u_t\}$. Therefore, because of assumption D of Theorem 8.1.1 and because of Theorem 3.2.7, we have

$$\frac{1}{\sqrt{T}} \frac{\partial S_T}{\partial \boldsymbol{\alpha}}\bigg|_{\boldsymbol{\alpha}_0} \rightarrow N(\mathbf{0}, 4\sigma^2 \operatorname{plim} \frac{1}{T} \mathbf{G}_0'\mathbf{P}_W\mathbf{G}_0). \tag{8.1.8}$$

Second, consider assumption B of Theorem 4.1.3. We have, for any $\tilde{\boldsymbol{\alpha}}$ such that $\operatorname{plim} \tilde{\boldsymbol{\alpha}} = \boldsymbol{\alpha}_0$,

$$\frac{1}{T} \frac{\partial S_T}{\partial \boldsymbol{\alpha}\partial \boldsymbol{\alpha}'}\bigg|_{\tilde{\boldsymbol{\alpha}}} = \frac{2}{T} \tilde{\mathbf{G}}'\mathbf{P}_W\tilde{\mathbf{G}} - 2\left\{\left[\frac{1}{T}\mathbf{u}'\mathbf{W} - \frac{1}{T}(\tilde{\boldsymbol{\alpha}} - \boldsymbol{\alpha}_0)'\mathbf{G}_+\mathbf{W}\right]\left[\frac{\mathbf{W}'\mathbf{W}}{T}\right]^{-1} \times \left[\frac{1}{T}\mathbf{W}' \frac{\partial^2 f}{\partial \alpha_i \partial \boldsymbol{\alpha}'}\bigg|_{\tilde{\boldsymbol{\alpha}}}\right]\right\}, \tag{8.1.9}$$

where { } in the second term of the right-hand side is the matrix the ith row of which is given inside { }, $\tilde{\mathbf{G}}$ is $\partial \mathbf{f}/\partial \boldsymbol{\alpha}'$ evaluated at $\tilde{\boldsymbol{\alpha}}$, and $\mathbf{G}_+$ is the matrix the tth row of which is $\partial f_t/\partial \boldsymbol{\alpha}'$ evaluated at $\boldsymbol{\alpha}_t^+$ between $\tilde{\boldsymbol{\alpha}}$ and $\boldsymbol{\alpha}_0$. But the term inside { } converges to $\mathbf{0}$ in probability because of assumptions A and C of Theorem 8.1.1 and assumption B of this theorem. Therefore assumptions A and C of Theorem 8.1.1 imply

$$\operatorname{plim} \frac{1}{T} \frac{\partial^2 S_T}{\partial \boldsymbol{\alpha}\partial \boldsymbol{\alpha}'}\bigg|_{\tilde{\boldsymbol{\alpha}}} = \operatorname{plim} \frac{2}{T} \mathbf{G}_0'\mathbf{P}_W\mathbf{G}_0. \tag{8.1.10}$$

Finally, because assumption A of this theorem implies assumption A of Theorem 4.1.3, we have verified all the conditions of Theorem 4.1.3. Hence, the conclusion of the theorem follows from (8.1.8) and (8.1.10).

Amemiya (1975a) considered, among other things, the optimal choice of $\mathbf{W}$. It is easy to show that $\operatorname{plim} T(\mathbf{G}_0'\mathbf{P}_W\mathbf{G}_0)^{-1}$ is minimized in the matrix sense (that is, $\mathbf{A} > \mathbf{B}$ means $\mathbf{A} - \mathbf{B}$ is a positive definite matrix) when we choose $\mathbf{W} = \overline{\mathbf{G}} \equiv E\mathbf{G}_0$. We call the resulting estimator the *best nonlinear two-stage least squares* (BNL2S) estimator. The asymptotic covariance matrix of $\sqrt{T}$ times the estimator is given by

$$\mathbf{V}_B = \sigma^2 \operatorname{plim} T(\overline{\mathbf{G}}'\overline{\mathbf{G}})^{-1}. \tag{8.1.11}$$

However, BNL2S is not a practical estimator because (1) it is often difficult to find an explicit expression for $\overline{\mathbf{G}}$, and (2) $\overline{\mathbf{G}}$ generally depends on the unknown parameter vector α_0. The second problem is less serious because α_0 may be replaced by any consistent member of the NL2S class using some $\mathbf{W}$.

Given the first problem, the following procedure recommended by Amemiya (1976a) seems the best practical way to approximate BNL2S:

Step 1. Compute $\hat{\alpha}$, a member of the NL2S class.

Step 2. Evaluate $\mathbf{G} \equiv \partial \mathbf{f}/\partial \alpha'$ at $\hat{\alpha}$—call it $\hat{\mathbf{G}}$.

Step 3. Treat $\hat{\mathbf{G}}$ as the dependent variables of regressions and search for the optimal set of independent variables, denoted $\mathbf{W}_0$, that best predict $\hat{\mathbf{G}}$.

Step 4. Set $\mathbf{W} = \mathbf{W}_0$.

If we wanted to be more elaborate, we could search for a different set of independent variables for each column of $\hat{\mathbf{G}}$ (say, $\mathbf{W}_i$ for the ith column $\hat{\mathbf{g}}_i$) and set $\mathbf{W} = [\mathbf{P}_{W_1}\hat{\mathbf{g}}_1, \mathbf{P}_{W_2}\hat{\mathbf{g}}_2, \ldots, \mathbf{P}_{W_K}\hat{\mathbf{g}}_K]$.

Kelejian (1974) proposed another way to approximate $\overline{\mathbf{G}}$. He proposed this method for the model that is nonlinear only in variables, but it could also work for certain fully nonlinear cases. Let the tth row of $\mathbf{G}_0$ be $\mathbf{G}_{0t}'$, that is, $\mathbf{G}_{0t}' = (\partial f_t/\partial \alpha')_{\alpha_0}$. Then, because $\mathbf{G}_{0t}$ is a function of $\mathbf{Y}_t$ and α_0, it is also a function of u_t and α_0; therefore write $\mathbf{G}_t(u_t, \alpha_0)$. Kelejian's suggestion was to generate u_t independently n times by simulation and approximate $E\mathbf{G}_{0t}$ by $n^{-1} \Sigma_{i=1}^{n} \mathbf{G}_t(u_{ti}, \hat{\alpha})$, where $\hat{\alpha}$ is some consistent estimator of α_0. Kelejian also pointed out that $\mathbf{G}_t(0, \hat{\alpha})$ is also a possible approximation for $E\mathbf{G}_t$; although it is computationally simpler, it is likely to be a worse approximation than that given earlier.

8.1.2 Box-Cox Transformation

Box and Cox (1964) proposed the model[3]

$$z_t(\lambda) = \mathbf{x}_t'\beta + u_t, \tag{8.1.12}$$

where, for $y_t > 0$,

$$\begin{aligned} z_t(\lambda) &= \frac{y_t^\lambda - 1}{\lambda} \quad &\text{if} \quad \lambda \neq 0 \\ &= \log y_t \quad &\text{if} \quad \lambda = 0. \end{aligned} \tag{8.1.13}$$

Note that because $\lim_{\lambda \to 0}(y_t^\lambda - 1)/\lambda = \log y_t$, $z_t(\lambda)$ is continuous at $\lambda = 0$. It is assumed that $\{u_t\}$ are i.i.d. with $Eu_t = 0$ and $Vu_t = \sigma^2$.

The transformation $z_t(\lambda)$ is attractive because it contains y_t and $\log y_t$ as special cases, and therefore the choice between y_t and $\log y_t$ can be made within the framework of classical statistical inference.

Box and Cox proposed estimating λ, $\boldsymbol{\beta}$, and σ^2 by the method of maximum likelihood assuming the normality of u_t. However, u_t cannot be normally distributed unless $\lambda = 0$ because $z_t(\lambda)$ is subject to the following bounds:

$$z_t(\lambda) \geqq -\frac{1}{\lambda} \quad \text{if} \quad \lambda > 0 \tag{8.1.14}$$

$$\leqq -\frac{1}{\lambda} \quad \text{if} \quad \lambda < 0.$$

Later we shall discuss their implications on the properties of the Box-Cox MLE.

This topic is relevant here because we can apply NL2S to this model with only a slight modification. To accommodate a model such as (8.1.12), we generalize (8.1.1) as

$$f(y_t, \mathbf{Y}_t, \mathbf{X}_{1t}, \boldsymbol{\alpha}) = u_t. \tag{8.1.15}$$

Then all the results of the previous section are valid with only an apparent modification. The minimand (8.1.2), which defines the class of NL2S estimators, should now be written as

$$\mathbf{f}'\mathbf{W}(\mathbf{W}'\mathbf{W})^{-1}\mathbf{W}'\mathbf{f}, \tag{8.1.16}$$

and the conclusions of Theorem 8.1.1 and 8.1.2 remain intact.

Define the NL2S estimator (actually, a class of estimators) of $\boldsymbol{\alpha} = (\lambda, \boldsymbol{\beta}')'$, denoted $\hat{\boldsymbol{\alpha}}$, in the model (8.1.12) as the value of $\boldsymbol{\alpha}$ that minimizes

$$[\mathbf{z}(\lambda) - \mathbf{X}\boldsymbol{\beta}]'\mathbf{W}(\mathbf{W}'\mathbf{W})^{-1}\mathbf{W}'[\mathbf{z}(\lambda) - \mathbf{X}\boldsymbol{\beta}], \tag{8.1.17}$$

where $\mathbf{z}(\lambda)$ is the vector the tth element of which is $z_t(\lambda)$. The discussion about the choice of $\mathbf{W}$ given in the preceding section applies here as well. One practical choice of $\mathbf{W}$ would be to use the $\mathbf{x}$'s and their powers and cross products. Using arguments similar to the ones given in the preceding section, we can prove the consistency and the asymptotic normality of the estimator. The asymptotic covariance matrix of $\sqrt{T}(\hat{\boldsymbol{\alpha}} - \boldsymbol{\alpha})$ is given by

$$V(\hat{\boldsymbol{\alpha}}) = \sigma^2 \operatorname{plim} T \left[\begin{bmatrix} \dfrac{\partial \mathbf{z}'}{\partial \lambda} \\ -\mathbf{X}' \end{bmatrix} \mathbf{W}(\mathbf{W}'\mathbf{W})^{-1}\mathbf{W}' \left[\frac{\partial \mathbf{z}}{\partial \lambda}, -\mathbf{X} \right] \right]^{-1}. \tag{8.1.18}$$

The Box-Cox maximum likelihood estimator is defined as the pseudo MLE obtained under the assumption that $\{u_t\}$ are normally distributed. In other words, the Box-Cox MLE $\tilde{\boldsymbol{\theta}}$ of $\boldsymbol{\theta} = (\lambda, \boldsymbol{\beta}', \sigma^2)'$ maximizes

$$\log L = -\frac{T}{2} \log \sigma^2 - \frac{1}{2\sigma^2} \sum_{t=1}^{T} (z_t - \beta' \mathbf{x}_t)^2 + (\lambda - 1) \sum_{t=1}^{T} \log y_t. \tag{8.1.19}$$

Because u_t cannot in reality be normally distributed, (8.1.19) should be regarded simply as a maximand that defines an extremum estimator rather than a proper logarithmic likelihood function. This fact has two implications:

1. We cannot appeal to the theorem about the consistency of the maximum likelihood estimator; instead, we must evaluate the probability limit as the value of the parameter at which $\lim T^{-1} E \log L$ is maximized.

2. The asymptotic covariance matrix of $\sqrt{T}(\tilde{\theta} - \theta)$ is not equal to the usual expression $-\lim T[E\partial^2 \log L/\partial\theta\partial\theta']^{-1}$ but is given by

$$V(\tilde{\theta}) = \lim T \left[E \frac{\partial^2 \log L}{\partial\theta\partial\theta'} \right]^{-1} E \frac{\partial \log L}{\partial\theta} \frac{\partial \log L}{\partial\theta'} \left[E \frac{\partial^2 \log L}{\partial\theta\partial\theta'} \right]^{-1}, \tag{8.1.20}$$

where the derivatives are evaluated at plim $\tilde{\theta}$.

Thus, to derive the probability limit and the asymptotic covariance matrix of $\tilde{\theta}$, we must evaluate $E \log L$ and the expectations that appear in (8.1.20) by using the true distribution of u_t.

Various authors have studied the properties of the Box-Cox MLE under various assumptions about the true distribution of u_t. Draper and Cox (1969) derived an asymptotic expansion for $E\, \partial \log L/\partial\lambda$ in the model without regressors and showed that it is nearly equal to 0 (indicating the approximate consistency of the Box-Cox MLE $\tilde{\lambda}$) if the skewness of $z_t(\lambda)$ is small. Zarembka (1974) used a similar analysis and showed $E\, \partial \log L/\partial\lambda \neq 0$ if $\{u_t\}$ are heteroscedastic. Hinkley (1975) proposed for the model without regressors an interesting simple estimator of λ, which does not require the normality assumption; he compared it with the Box-Cox MLE $\tilde{\lambda}$ under the assumption that y_t is truncated normal (this assumption was also suggested by Poirier, 1978). Hinkley showed by a Monte Carlo study that the Box-Cox MLE $\tilde{\lambda}$ and $\tilde{\beta}$ perform generally well under this assumption. Amemiya and Powell (1981) showed analytically that if y_t is truncated normal, plim $\tilde{\lambda} < \lambda$ if $\lambda > 0$ and plim $\tilde{\lambda} > \lambda$ if $\lambda < 0$.

Amemiya and Powell (1981) also considered the case where y_t follows a two-parameter gamma distribution. This assumption actually alters the model as it introduces a natural heteroscedasticity in $\{u_t\}$. In this case, the formula (8.1.18) is no longer valid and the correct formula is given by

$$V(\hat{\alpha}) = \text{plim}\; T(\mathbf{Z}'\mathbf{P}_W\mathbf{Z})^{-1}\mathbf{Z}'\mathbf{P}_W\mathbf{D}\mathbf{P}_W\mathbf{Z}(\mathbf{Z}'\mathbf{P}_W\mathbf{Z})^{-1}, \tag{8.1.21}$$

where $\mathbf{Z} = (\partial \mathbf{z}/\partial\lambda, -\mathbf{X})$ and $\mathbf{D} = E\mathbf{uu}'$. Amemiya and Powell considered a simple regression model with one independent variable and showed that NL2S dominates the Box-Cox MLE for most of the plausible parameter values considered not only because the inconsistency of the Box-Cox MLE is significant but also because its asymptotic variance is much larger.

There have been numerous econometric applications of the Box-Cox MLE. In the first of such studies, Zarembka (1968) applied the transformation to the study of demand for money. Zarembka's work was followed up by studies by White (1972) and Spitzer (1976). For applications in other areas of economics, see articles by Heckman and Polachek (1974) (earnings–schooling relationship); by Benus, Kmenta, and Shapiro (1976) (food expenditure analysis); and by Ehrlich (1977) (crime rate).

All of these studies use the Box-Cox MLE and none uses NL2S. In most of these studies, the asymptotic covariance matrix for $\tilde{\boldsymbol{\beta}}$ is obtained as if $z_t(\tilde{\lambda})$ were the dependent variable of the regression—a practice that can lead to gross errors. In many of the preceding studies, independent variables as well as the dependent variable are transformed by the Box-Cox transformation but possibly with different parameters.

8.1.3 Nonlinear Limited Information Maximum Likelihood Estimator

In the preceding section we assumed the model (8.1.1) without specifying the model for $\mathbf{Y}_t$ or assuming the normality of u_t and derived the asymptotic distribution of the class of NL2S estimators and the optimal member of the class—BNL2S. In this section we shall specify the model for $\mathbf{Y}_t$ and shall assume that all the error terms are normally distributed; under these assumptions we shall derive the nonlinear limited information maximum likelihood (NLLI) estimator, which is asymptotically more efficient than BNL2S. The NLLI estimator takes advantage of the added assumptions, and consequently its asymptotic properties depend crucially on the validity of the assumptions. Thus we are aiming at a higher efficiency at the possible sacrifice of robustness.

Assume, in addition to (8.1.1),

$$\mathbf{Y}_t' = \mathbf{X}_t'\mathbf{\Pi} + \mathbf{V}_t', \tag{8.1.22}$$

where $\mathbf{V}_t$ is a vector of random variables, $\mathbf{X}_t$ is a vector of known constants, and $\mathbf{\Pi}$ is a matrix of unknown parameters. We assume that $(u_t, \mathbf{V}_t')$ are independent drawings from a multivariate normal distribution with zero mean and variance-covariance matrix

$$\mathbf{\Sigma} = \begin{bmatrix} \sigma^2 & \boldsymbol{\sigma}_{12}' \\ \boldsymbol{\sigma}_{12} & \mathbf{\Sigma}_{22} \end{bmatrix}. \tag{8.1.23}$$

We define $\mathbf{X}$ and $\mathbf{V}$ as matrices the tth rows of which are $\mathbf{X}_t'$ and $\mathbf{V}_t'$, respectively. Because $\mathbf{u}$ and $\mathbf{V}$ are jointly normal, we can write

$$\mathbf{u} = \mathbf{V}\mathbf{\Sigma}_{22}^{-1}\boldsymbol{\sigma}_{12} + \boldsymbol{\epsilon}, \tag{8.1.24}$$

where $\boldsymbol{\epsilon}$ is independent of $\mathbf{V}$ and distributed as $N(\mathbf{0}, \sigma^{*2}\mathbf{I})$, where $\sigma^{*2} = \sigma^2 - \boldsymbol{\sigma}_{12}'\mathbf{\Sigma}_{22}^{-1}\boldsymbol{\sigma}_{12}$.

The model defined in (8.1.24) may be regarded either as a simplified nonlinear simultaneous equations model in which both the nonlinearity and the simultaneity appear only in the first equation or as the model that represents the "limited information" of the investigator. In the latter interpretation, $\mathbf{X}_t$ are not necessarily the original exogenous variables of the system, some of which appear in the arguments of $\mathbf{f}$, but, rather, are the variables a linear combination of which the investigator believes will explain $\mathbf{Y}_t$ effectively.

Because the Jacobian of the transformation from $(\mathbf{u}, \mathbf{V})$ to $(\mathbf{y}, \mathbf{Y})$ is unity in our model, the log likelihood function assuming normality can be written, apart from a constant, as

$$L^{**} = -\frac{T}{2}\log|\mathbf{\Sigma}| - \frac{1}{2}\operatorname{tr}\mathbf{\Sigma}^{-1}\mathbf{Q}, \tag{8.1.25}$$

where

$$\mathbf{Q} = \begin{bmatrix} \mathbf{u}'\mathbf{u} & \mathbf{u}'\mathbf{V} \\ \mathbf{V}'\mathbf{u} & \mathbf{V}'\mathbf{V} \end{bmatrix},$$

$\mathbf{u}$ and $\mathbf{V}$ representing $\mathbf{y} - \mathbf{f}$ and $\mathbf{Y} - \mathbf{X}\mathbf{\Pi}$, respectively. Solving $\partial L^{**}/\partial\mathbf{\Sigma} = \mathbf{0}$ for $\mathbf{\Sigma}$ yields

$$\mathbf{\Sigma} = T^{-1}\mathbf{Q}. \tag{8.1.26}$$

Substituting (8.1.26) into (8.1.25), we obtain a concentrated log likelihood function

$$L^* = -\frac{T}{2}(\log \mathbf{u}'\mathbf{u} + \log|\mathbf{V}'\mathbf{M}_u\mathbf{V}|). \tag{8.1.27}$$

Solving $\partial L^*/\partial\mathbf{\Pi} = \mathbf{0}$ for $\mathbf{\Pi}$, we obtain

$$\mathbf{\Pi} = (\mathbf{X}'\mathbf{M}_u\mathbf{X})^{-1}\mathbf{X}'\mathbf{M}_u\mathbf{Y}, \tag{8.1.28}$$

where $\mathbf{M}_u = \mathbf{I} - (\mathbf{u}'\mathbf{u})^{-1}\mathbf{u}\mathbf{u}'$. Substituting (8.1.28) into (8.1.27) yields a further concentrated log likelihood function

$$L = -\frac{T}{2}(\log \mathbf{u}'\mathbf{u} + \log|\mathbf{Y}'\mathbf{M}_u\mathbf{Y} - \mathbf{Y}'\mathbf{M}_u\mathbf{X}(\mathbf{X}'\mathbf{M}_u\mathbf{X})^{-1}\mathbf{X}'\mathbf{M}_u\mathbf{Y}|), \tag{8.1.29}$$

which depends only on $\boldsymbol{\alpha}$. Interpreting our model as that which represents the limited information of the researcher, we call the value of $\boldsymbol{\alpha}$ that minimizes (8.1.29) the NLLI estimator. The asymptotic covariance matrix of $\sqrt{T}$ times the estimator is given by

$$\mathbf{V}_{\mathrm{L}} = \operatorname{plim} T\left[\frac{1}{\sigma^{*2}}\mathbf{G}'\mathbf{M}_V\mathbf{G} - \left(\frac{1}{\sigma^{*2}} - \frac{1}{\sigma^2}\right)\mathbf{G}'\mathbf{M}_X\mathbf{G}\right]^{-1}, \tag{8.1.30}$$

where $\mathbf{M}_V = \mathbf{I} - \mathbf{V}(\mathbf{V}'\mathbf{V})^{-1}\mathbf{V}'$ and $\mathbf{M}_X = \mathbf{I} - \mathbf{X}(\mathbf{X}'\mathbf{X})^{-1}\mathbf{X}'$.

The maximization of (8.1.29) may be done by the iterative procedures discussed in Section 4.4. Another iterative method may be defined as follows: Rewrite (8.1.27) equivalently as

$$L^* = -\frac{T}{2}(\log \mathbf{u}'\mathbf{M}_V\mathbf{u} + \log|\mathbf{V}'\mathbf{V}|) \tag{8.1.31}$$

and iterate back and forth between (8.1.28) and (8.1.31). That is, obtain $\hat{\mathbf{\Pi}} = (\mathbf{X}'\mathbf{X})^{-1}\mathbf{X}'\mathbf{Y}$ and $\hat{\mathbf{V}} = \mathbf{Y} - \mathbf{X}\hat{\mathbf{\Pi}}$, maximize (8.1.31) with respect to $\boldsymbol{\alpha}$ after replacing $\mathbf{V}$ with $\hat{\mathbf{V}}$, call this estimator $\hat{\boldsymbol{\alpha}}$ and define $\hat{\mathbf{u}} = \mathbf{y} - \mathbf{f}(\hat{\boldsymbol{\alpha}})$, insert it into (8.1.28) to obtain another estimator of $\mathbf{\Pi}$, and repeat the procedure until convergence.

The estimator $\hat{\boldsymbol{\alpha}}$ defined in the preceding paragraph is interesting in its own right. It is the value of $\boldsymbol{\alpha}$ that minimizes

$$(\mathbf{y} - \mathbf{f})'[\mathbf{I} - \mathbf{M}_X\mathbf{Y}(\mathbf{Y}'\mathbf{M}_X\mathbf{Y})^{-1}\mathbf{Y}'\mathbf{M}_X](\mathbf{y} - \mathbf{f}). \tag{8.1.32}$$

Amemiya (1975a) called this estimator the *modified nonlinear two-stage least squares* (MNL2S) estimator. The asymptotic covariance matrix of $\sqrt{T}(\hat{\boldsymbol{\alpha}} - \boldsymbol{\alpha})$ is given by

$$\begin{aligned}\mathbf{V}_{\mathrm{M}} = \operatorname{plim} T(\mathbf{G}'\mathbf{M}_V\mathbf{G})^{-1}[\sigma^{*2}\mathbf{G}'\mathbf{M}_V\mathbf{G} \\ + (\sigma^2 - \sigma^{*2})\mathbf{G}'\mathbf{P}_X\mathbf{G}](\mathbf{G}'\mathbf{M}_V\mathbf{G})^{-1}.\end{aligned} \tag{8.1.33}$$

Amemiya (1975a) proved $\mathbf{V}_{\mathrm{L}} < \mathbf{V}_{\mathrm{M}} < \mathbf{V}_{\mathrm{B}}$. It is interesting to note that if $\mathbf{f}$ is linear in $\boldsymbol{\alpha}$ and $\mathbf{Y}$, MNL2S is reduced to the usual 2SLS (see Section 7.3.6).

In Sections 8.1.1 and 8.1.3, we discussed four estimators: (1) NL2S (as a class); (2) BNL2S; (3) MNL2S; (4) NLLI. If we denote NL2S($\mathbf{W} = \mathbf{X}$) by SNL2S (the first S stands for standard), we have in the linear case

$$\text{SNL2S} \equiv \text{BNL2S} \equiv \text{MNL2S} \cong \text{NLLI}, \tag{8.1.34}$$

where $\equiv$ means exact identity and $\cong$ means asymptotic equivalence. In the nonlinear model defined by (8.1.1) and (8.1.22) with the normality assumption, we can establish the following ranking in terms of the asymptotic covariance matrix:

$$\text{SNL2S} \ll \text{BNL2S} \ll \text{MNL2S} \ll \text{NLLI}, \tag{8.1.35}$$

where $\ll$ means "is worse than." However, it is important to remember that the first two estimators are consistent under more general assumptions than those under which the last two estimators are consistent, as we shall show in the following simple example.

Consider a very simple case of (8.1.1) and (8.1.22) given by

$$y_t = \alpha z_t^2 + u_t \tag{8.1.36}$$

and

$$z_t = \pi x_t + v_t, \tag{8.1.37}$$

where we assume the vector (u_t, v_t) is i.i.d. with zero mean and a finite nonsingular covariance matrix. Inserting (8.1.37) into (8.1.36) yields

$$y_t = \alpha\pi^2 x_t^2 + \alpha\sigma_v^2 + (u_t + 2\alpha\pi x_t v_t + \alpha v_t^2 - \alpha\sigma_v^2), \tag{8.1.38}$$

where the composite error term (contained within the parantheses) has zero mean. In this model, SNL2S is 2SLS with z_t^2 regressed on x_t in the first stage, and BNL2S is 2SLS with z_t^2 regressed on the constant term and x_t^2 in the first stage. Clearly, both estimators are consistent under general conditions without further assumptions on u_t and v_t. On the other hand, it is not difficult to show that the consistency of MNL2S and NLLI requires the additional assumption

$$Ev_t^2 Ev_t^2 u_t = Ev_t^3 Ev_t u_t, \tag{8.1.39}$$

which is satisfied if u_t and v_t are jointly normal.

8.2 Estimation in a System of Equations

8.2.1 Introduction

Define a system of N nonlinear simultaneous equations by

$$f_{it}(\mathbf{y}_t, \mathbf{x}_t, \boldsymbol{\alpha}_i) = u_{it}, \qquad i = 1, 2, \ldots, N, \qquad t = 1, 2, \ldots, T, \tag{8.2.1}$$

where $\mathbf{y}_t$ is an N-vector of endogenous variables, $\mathbf{x}_t$ is a vector of exogenous variables, and $\boldsymbol{\alpha}_i$ is a K_i-vector of unknown parameters. We assume that the

N-vector $\mathbf{u}_t = (u_{1t}, u_{2t}, \ldots, u_{Nt})'$ is an i.i.d. vector random variable with zero mean and variance-covariance matrix $\mathbf{\Sigma}$. Not all of the elements of vectors $\mathbf{y}_t$ and $\mathbf{x}_t$ may actually appear in the arguments of each f_{it}. We assume that each equation has its own vector of parameters $\boldsymbol{\alpha}_i$ and that there are no constraints among $\boldsymbol{\alpha}_i$'s, but the subsequent results can easily be modified if each $\boldsymbol{\alpha}_i$ can be parametrically expressed as $\boldsymbol{\alpha}_i(\boldsymbol{\theta})$, where the number of elements in $\boldsymbol{\theta}$ is less than $\Sigma_{i=1}^N K_i$.

Strictly speaking, (8.2.1) is not a complete model by itself because there is no guarantee that a unique solution for $\mathbf{y}_t$ exists for every possible value of u_{it} unless some stringent assumptions are made on the form of f_{it}. Therefore we assume either that f_{it} satisfies such assumptions or that if there is more than one solution for $\mathbf{y}_t$, there is some additional mechanism by which a unique solution is chosen.[4]

We shall not discuss the problem of identification in the model (8.2.1). There are not many useful results in the literature beyond the basic discussion of Fisher (1966), as summarized by Goldfeld and Quandt (1972, p. 221), and a recent extension by Brown (1983). Nevertheless, we want to point out that nonlinearity generally helps rather than hampers identification, so that, for example, in a nonlinear model the number of excluded exogenous variables in a given equation need not be greater than or equal to the number of parameters of the same equation. We should also point out that we have actually given one sufficient condition for identifiability—that plim $T^{-1}(\mathbf{G}_0'\mathbf{P}_W\mathbf{G}_0)$ in the conclusion of Theorem 8.1.2 is nonsingular.

Definition of the symbols used in the following sections may facilitate the discussion.

$\boldsymbol{\alpha} = (\boldsymbol{\alpha}_1', \boldsymbol{\alpha}_2', \ldots, \boldsymbol{\alpha}_N')'$

$\mathbf{\Lambda} = \mathbf{\Sigma} \otimes \mathbf{I}$, where $\otimes$ is the Kronecker product

$f_{it} = f_{it}(\mathbf{y}_t, \mathbf{x}_t, \boldsymbol{\alpha}_i)$

$\mathbf{f}_t =$ an N-vector, the ith element of which is f_{it}

$\mathbf{f}_{(i)} =$ a T-vector, the tth element is f_{it}.

$\underline{\mathbf{f}} = (\mathbf{f}_{(1)}', \mathbf{f}_{(2)}', \ldots, \mathbf{f}_{(N)}')'$, an NT-vector

$\mathbf{F} = (\mathbf{f}_{(1)}, \mathbf{f}_{(2)}, \ldots, \mathbf{f}_{(N)})$, a $T \times N$ matrix

$\mathbf{g}_{it} = \dfrac{\partial f_{it}}{\partial \boldsymbol{\alpha}_i}$, a K_i-vector

$\mathbf{G}_i = \dfrac{\partial \mathbf{f}_{(i)}}{\partial \boldsymbol{\alpha}_i'}$, a $T \times K_i$ matrix, the tth row is $\mathbf{g}_{it}'$

$\underline{\mathbf{G}} = \text{diag}\{\mathbf{G}_1, \mathbf{G}_2, \ldots, \mathbf{G}_N\}$, an $NT \times (\Sigma_{i=1}^N K_i)$ block diagonal matrix

8.2.2 Nonlinear Three-Stage Least Squares Estimator

As a natural extension of the class of the NL2S estimators—the version that minimizes (8.1.22), Jorgenson and Laffont (1974) defined the class of nonlinear three-stage least squares (NL3S) estimators as the value of $\boldsymbol{\alpha}$ that minimizes

$$\underline{\mathbf{f}}'[\hat{\boldsymbol{\Sigma}}^{-1} \otimes \mathbf{W}(\mathbf{W}'\mathbf{W})^{-1}\mathbf{W}']\underline{\mathbf{f}}, \tag{8.2.2}$$

where $\hat{\boldsymbol{\Sigma}}$ is a consistent estimate of $\boldsymbol{\Sigma}$. For example,

$$\hat{\boldsymbol{\Sigma}} = \frac{1}{T}\sum_{t=1}^{T} \mathbf{f}_t(\hat{\boldsymbol{\alpha}})\mathbf{f}_t(\hat{\boldsymbol{\alpha}})', \tag{8.2.3}$$

where $\hat{\boldsymbol{\alpha}}$ is the NL2S estimator obtained from each equation. This definiton of the NL3S estimators is analogous to the definition of the linear 3SLS as a generalization of the linear 2SLS. The consistency and the asymptotic normality of the NL3S estimators defined in (8.2.2) and (8.2.3) have been proved by Jorgenson and Laffont (1974) and Gallant (1977).

The consistency of the NL2S and NL3S estimators of the parameters of model (8.2.1) can be proved with minimal assumptions on u_{it}—namely, those stated after (8.2.1). This robustness makes the estimators attractive. Another important strength of the estimators is that they retain their consistency regardless of whether or not (8.2.1) yields a unique solution for $\mathbf{y}_t$ and, in the case of multiple solutions, regardless of what additional mechanism chooses a unique solution. (MaCurdy, 1980, has discussed this point further.) However, in predicting the future value of the dependent variable, we must know the mechanism that yields a unique solution.

Amemiya (1977a) defined the class of the NL3S estimators more generally as the value of $\boldsymbol{\alpha}$ that minimizes

$$\underline{\mathbf{f}}'\hat{\boldsymbol{\Lambda}}^{-1}\mathbf{S}(\mathbf{S}'\hat{\boldsymbol{\Lambda}}^{-1}\mathbf{S})^{-1}\mathbf{S}'\hat{\boldsymbol{\Lambda}}^{-1}\underline{\mathbf{f}}, \tag{8.2.4}$$

where $\hat{\boldsymbol{\Lambda}}$ is a consistent estimate of $\boldsymbol{\Lambda}$ and $\mathbf{S}$ is a matrix of constants with NT rows and with the rank of at least $\Sigma_{i=1}^{N} K_i$. This definition is reduced to the Jorgenson-Laffont definition if $\mathbf{S} = \text{diag}(\mathbf{W}, \mathbf{W}, \ldots, \mathbf{W})$. The asymptotic variance-covariance matrix of $\sqrt{T}$ times the estimator is given by

$$\mathbf{V}_3 = \text{plim } T[\underline{\mathbf{G}}'\boldsymbol{\Lambda}^{-1}\mathbf{S}(\mathbf{S}'\boldsymbol{\Lambda}^{-1}\mathbf{S})^{-1}\mathbf{S}'\boldsymbol{\Lambda}^{-1}\underline{\mathbf{G}}]^{-1}. \tag{8.2.5}$$

Its lower bound is equal to

$$\mathbf{V}_{\mathrm{B3}} = \lim T[E\underline{\mathbf{G}}'\boldsymbol{\Lambda}^{-1}E\underline{\mathbf{G}}]^{-1} \tag{8.2.6}$$

which is attained when we choose $\mathbf{S} = E\underline{\mathbf{G}}$. We call this estimator the *BNL3S* estimator (B for "best").

We can also attain the lower bound (8.2.6) using the Jorgenson-Laffont definition, but that is possible if and only if the space spanned by the column vectors of $\mathbf{W}$ contains the union of the spaces spanned by the column vectors of $E\mathbf{G}_i$ for $i = 1, 2, \ldots, N$. This necessitates including many columns in $\mathbf{W}$, which is likely to increase the finite sample variance of the estimator although it has no effect asymptotically. This is a disadvantage of the Jorgenson-Laffont definition compared to the Amemiya definition.

Noting that BNL3S is not practical, as was the case with BNL2S, Amemiya (1976a) suggested the following approximation:

Step 1. Compute $\hat{\boldsymbol{\alpha}}_i$, an SNL2S estimator of $\boldsymbol{\alpha}_i$, $i = 1, 2, \ldots, N$.

Step 2. Evaluate $\mathbf{G}_i$ at $\hat{\boldsymbol{\alpha}}_i$—call it $\hat{\mathbf{G}}_i$.

Step 3. Treat $\hat{\mathbf{G}}_i$ as the dependent variables of a regression and search for the optimal set of independent variables $\mathbf{W}_i$ that best predict $\hat{\mathbf{G}}_i$.

Step 4. Choose $\mathbf{S} = \text{diag}\{\mathbf{P}_1\hat{\mathbf{G}}_1, \mathbf{P}_2\hat{\mathbf{G}}_2, \ldots, \mathbf{P}_N\hat{\mathbf{G}}_N\}$, where $\mathbf{P}_i = \mathbf{W}_i(\mathbf{W}_i'\mathbf{W}_i)^{-1}\mathbf{W}_i'$.

Applications of NL3S can be found in articles by Jorgenson and Lau (1975), who estimated a three-equation translog expenditure model; by Jorgenson and Lau (1978), who estimated a two-equation translog expenditure model; and by Haessel (1976), who estimated a system of demand equations, nonlinear only in parameters, by both NL2S and NL3S estimators.

8.2.3 Nonlinear Full Information Maximum Likelihood Estimator

In this subsection we shall consider the maximum likelihood estimator of model (8.2.1) under the normality assumption of u_{it}. To do so we must assume that (8.2.1) defines a one-to-one correspondence between $\mathbf{y}_t$ and $\mathbf{u}_t$. This assumption enables us to write down the likelihood function in the usual way as the product of the density of $\mathbf{u}_t$ and the Jacobian. Unfortunately, this is a rather stringent assumption, which considerably limits the usefulness of the nonlinear full information maximum likelihood (NLFI) estimator in practice. There are two types of problems: (1) There may be no solution for $\mathbf{y}$ for some values of $\mathbf{u}$. (2) There may be more than one solution for $\mathbf{y}$ for some values of $\mathbf{u}$. In the first case the domain of $\mathbf{u}$ must be restricted, a condition that implies that the normality assumption cannot hold. In the second case we must specify a mechanism by which a unique solution is chosen, a condition that would complicate the likelihood function. We should note that the NL2S and NL3S estimators are free from both of these problems.

Assuming $\mathbf{u}_t \sim N(\mathbf{0}, \mathbf{\Sigma})$, we can write the log likelihood function of model (8.2.1) as

$$L^* = -\frac{T}{2} \log |\mathbf{\Sigma}| + \sum_{t=1}^{T} \log \|\partial \mathbf{f}_t / \partial \mathbf{y}_t'\| - \frac{1}{2} \sum_{t=1}^{T} \mathbf{f}_t' \mathbf{\Sigma}^{-1} \mathbf{f}_t. \tag{8.2.7}$$

Solving $\partial L^*/\partial \mathbf{\Sigma} = \mathbf{0}$ for $\mathbf{\Sigma}$, we get

$$\mathbf{\Sigma} = \frac{1}{T} \sum_{t=1}^{T} \mathbf{f}_t \mathbf{f}_t'. \tag{8.2.8}$$

Inserting (8.2.8) into (8.2.7) yields the concentrated log likelihood function

$$L = \sum_{t=1}^{T} \log \|\partial \mathbf{f}_t / \partial \mathbf{y}_t'\| - \frac{T}{2} \log \left| \frac{1}{T} \sum_{t=1}^{T} \mathbf{f}_t \mathbf{f}_t' \right|. \tag{8.2.9}$$

The NLFI maximum likelihood estimator of $\boldsymbol{\alpha}$ is defined as the value of $\boldsymbol{\alpha}$ that maximizes (8.2.9).

Amemiya (1977a) proved that if the true distribution of $\mathbf{u}_t$ is normal, NLFI is consistent, asymptotically normal, and in general has a smaller asymptotic covariance matrix than BNL3S. It is well known that in the linear model the full information maximum likelihood estimator has the same asymptotic distribution as the three-stage least squares estimator. Amemiya showed that the asymptotic equivalence occurs if and only if f_{it} can be written in the form

$$f_{it}(\mathbf{y}_t, \mathbf{x}_t, \boldsymbol{\alpha}_i) = A_i(\boldsymbol{\alpha}_i)' \mathbf{z}(\mathbf{y}_t, \mathbf{x}_t) + B_i(\boldsymbol{\alpha}_i, \mathbf{x}_t), \tag{8.2.10}$$

where $\mathbf{z}$ is an N-vector of surrogate variables.

If the true distribution of $\mathbf{u}_t$ is not normal, on the other hand, Amemiya proved that NLFI is generally not consistent, whereas NL3S is known to be consistent even then. This, again, is contrary to the linear case in which the full information maximum likelihood estimator obtained under the assumption of normality is consistent even if the true distribution is not normal. Note that this result is completely separate from and in no way contradicts the quite likely fact that the maximum likelihood estimator of a nonlinear model derived under the assumption of a certain regular nonnormal distribution is consistent if the true distribution is the same as the assumed distribution.

We shall see how the consistency of NLFI crucially depends on the normality assumption. Differentiating (8.2.9) with respect to $\boldsymbol{\alpha}_i$, we obtain

$$\frac{\partial L}{\partial \boldsymbol{\alpha}_i} = \sum_{t=1}^{T} \frac{\partial \mathbf{g}_{it}}{\partial u_{it}} - T \sum_{t=1}^{T} \mathbf{g}_{it} \mathbf{f}_t' \left(\sum_{t=1}^{T} \mathbf{f}_t \mathbf{f}_t' \right)_i^{-1}, \tag{8.2.11}$$

where $(\quad)_i^{-1}$ denotes the ith column of the inverse of the matrix within the parentheses. The consistency of NLFI is equivalent to the condition

$$\lim E \frac{1}{T} \frac{\partial L}{\partial \boldsymbol{\alpha}_i}\bigg|_{\boldsymbol{\alpha}_0} = \mathbf{0} \tag{8.2.12}$$

and hence to the condition

$$\lim \frac{1}{T} \sum_{t=1}^{T} E \frac{\partial \mathbf{g}_{it}}{\partial u_{it}} = \lim \frac{1}{T} \sum_{t=1}^{T} E\mathbf{g}_{it}\mathbf{u}_t'\boldsymbol{\sigma}^i, \tag{8.2.13}$$

where $\boldsymbol{\sigma}^i$ is the ith column of $\boldsymbol{\Sigma}^{-1}$. Now (8.2.13) could hold even if each term of a summation is different from the corresponding term of the other, but that event is extremely unlikely. Therefore we can say that the consistency of NLFI is essentially equivalent to the condition

$$E \frac{\partial \mathbf{g}_{it}}{\partial u_{it}} = E\mathbf{g}_{it}\mathbf{u}_t'\boldsymbol{\sigma}^i. \tag{8.2.14}$$

It is interesting to note that the condition (8.2.14) holds if $\mathbf{u}_t$ is normal because of the following lemma.[5]

LEMMA. Suppose $\mathbf{u} = (u_1, u_2, \ldots, u_N)'$ is distributed as $N(\mathbf{0}, \boldsymbol{\Sigma})$, where $\boldsymbol{\Sigma}$ is positive definite. If $\partial h(\mathbf{u})/\partial u_i$ is continuous, $E|\partial h/\partial u_i| < \infty$, and $E|hu_i| < \infty$, then

$$E \frac{\partial h}{\partial u_i} = Eh\mathbf{u}'\boldsymbol{\sigma}^i, \tag{8.2.15}$$

where $\boldsymbol{\sigma}^i$ is the ith column of $\boldsymbol{\Sigma}^{-1}$.

In simple models the condition (8.2.14) may hold without normality. In the model defined by (8.1.36) and (8.1.37), we have $g_{1t} = -z_t^2$ and $g_{2t} = -x_t$. Therefore (8.2.14) clearly holds for $i = 2$ for any distribution of $\mathbf{u}_t$ provided that the mean is $\mathbf{0}$. The equation for $i = 1$ gives (8.1.39), which is satisfied by a class of distributions including the normal distribution. (Phillips, 1982, has presented another simple example.) However, if $\mathbf{g}_{it}$ is a more complicated nonlinear function of the exogenous variables and the parameters $\{\boldsymbol{\alpha}_i\}$ as well as of $\mathbf{u}$, (8.2.14) can be made to hold only when we specify a density that depends on the exogenous variables and the parameters of the model. In such a case, normality can be regarded, for all practical purposes, as a necessary and sufficient condition for the consistency of NLFI.

It is interesting to compare certain iterative formulae for calculating NLFI and BNL3S. By equating the right-hand side of (8.2.11) to $\mathbf{0}$ and rearranging terms, we can obtain the following iteration to obtain NLFI:

$$\hat{\alpha}_{(2)} = \hat{\alpha}_{(1)} - (\underline{\tilde{\mathbf{G}}}'\hat{\Lambda}^{-1}\underline{\mathbf{G}})^{-1}\underline{\tilde{\mathbf{G}}}'\hat{\Lambda}^{-1}\underline{\mathbf{f}}, \tag{8.2.16}$$

where

$$\tilde{\mathbf{G}}_i' = \mathbf{G}_i' - \frac{1}{T}\sum_{t=1}^{T}\frac{\partial \mathbf{g}_{it}}{\partial \mathbf{u}_t'}\mathbf{F}' \tag{8.2.17}$$

and $\underline{\tilde{\mathbf{G}}} = \text{diag}(\tilde{\mathbf{G}}_1, \tilde{\mathbf{G}}_2, \ldots, \tilde{\mathbf{G}}_N)$ and all the variables that appear in the second term of the right-hand side of (8.2.16) are evaluated at $\hat{\alpha}_{(1)}$.

The Gauss-Newton iteration for BNL3S is defined by

$$\hat{\alpha}_{(2)} = \hat{\alpha}_{(1)} - (\underline{\bar{\mathbf{G}}}'\hat{\Lambda}^{-1}\underline{\mathbf{G}})^{-1}\underline{\bar{\mathbf{G}}}'\hat{\Lambda}^{-1}\underline{\mathbf{f}}, \tag{8.2.18}$$

where $\bar{\mathbf{G}}_i' = E\mathbf{G}_i'$ and $\underline{\bar{\mathbf{G}}} = \text{diag}(\bar{\mathbf{G}}_1, \bar{\mathbf{G}}_2, \ldots, \bar{\mathbf{G}}_N)$ as before.

Thus we see that the only difference between (8.2.16) and (8.2.18) is in the respective "instrumental variables" used in the formulae. Note that $\tilde{\mathbf{G}}_i$ defined in (8.2.17) can work as a proper set of "instrumental variables" (that is, variables uncorrelated with $\mathbf{u}_t$) only if $\mathbf{u}_t$ satisfies the condition of the aforementioned lemma, whereas $\bar{\mathbf{G}}_i$ is always a proper set of instrumental variables, a fact that implies that BNL3S is more robust than NLFI. If $\mathbf{u}_t$ is normal, however, $\tilde{\mathbf{G}}_i$ contains more of the part of $\mathbf{G}_i$ uncorrelated with $\mathbf{u}_t$ than $\bar{\mathbf{G}}_i$ does, which implies that NLFI is more efficient than BNL3S under normality.

Note that (8.2.16) is a generalization of the formula (7.2.12) for the linear case. Unlike the iteration of the linear case, however, the iteration defined by (8.2.16) does not have the property that $\hat{\alpha}_{(2)}$ is asymptotically equivalent to NLFI when $\hat{\alpha}_{(1)}$ is consistent. Therefore its main value may be pedagogical, and it may not be useful in practice.

8.3 Tests of Hypotheses, Prediction, and Computation

8.3.1 Tests of Hypotheses

Suppose we want to test a hypothesis of the form $\mathbf{h}(\alpha) = \mathbf{0}$ in model (8.1.1), where $\mathbf{h}$ is a q-vector of nonlinear functions. Because we have not specified the distribution of $\mathbf{Y}_t$, we could not use the three tests defined in (4.5.3), (4.5.4), and (4.5.5) even if we assumed the normality of $\mathbf{u}$. But we can use two test statistics: (1) the generalized Wald test statistic analogous to (4.5.21), and (2) the difference between the constrained and the unconstrained sums of squared residuals (denoted SSRD). Let $\hat{\alpha}$ and $\tilde{\alpha}$ be the solutions of the unconstrained and the constrained minimization of (8.1.2), respectively. Then the generalized Wald statistic is given by

$$\text{Wald} = \frac{T}{S_T(\hat{\boldsymbol{\alpha}})} \mathbf{h}(\hat{\boldsymbol{\alpha}})'[\hat{\mathbf{H}}(\hat{\mathbf{G}}'\mathbf{P}_W\hat{\mathbf{G}})^{-1}\hat{\mathbf{H}}']^{-1}\mathbf{h}(\hat{\boldsymbol{\alpha}}), \tag{8.3.1}$$

where $\hat{\mathbf{H}} = [\partial\mathbf{h}/\partial\boldsymbol{\alpha}']_{\hat{\alpha}}$ and $\hat{\mathbf{G}} = [\partial\mathbf{f}/\partial\boldsymbol{\alpha}']_{\hat{\alpha}}$, and the SSRD statistic is given by

$$\text{SSRD} = \frac{T}{S_T(\hat{\boldsymbol{\alpha}})} [S_T(\tilde{\boldsymbol{\alpha}}) - S_T(\hat{\boldsymbol{\alpha}})]. \tag{8.3.2}$$

Both test statistics are asymptotically distributed as chi-square with q degrees of freedom.

Gallant and Jorgenson (1979) derived the asymptotic distribution (a noncentral chi-square) of the two test statistics under the assumption that $\boldsymbol{\alpha}$ deviates from the hypothesized constraints in the order of $T^{-1/2}$.

As an application of the SSRD test, Gallant and Jorgenson tested the hypothesis of homogeneity of degree zero of an equation for durables in the two-equation translog expenditure model of Jorgenson and Lau (1978).

The Wald and SSRD tests can be straightforwardly extended to the system of equations (8.2.1) by using NL3S in lieu of NL2S. As an application of the SSRD test using NL3S, Gallant and Jorgenson tested the hypothesis of symmetry of the matrix of parameters in the three-equation translog expenditure model of Jorgenson and Lau (1975).

If we assume (8.1.22) in addition to (8.1.1) and assume normality, the model is specified (although it is a limited information model); therefore the three tests of Section 4.5.1 can be used with NLLI. The same is true of NLFI in model (8.1.22) under normality. The asymptotic results of Gallant and Holly (1980) given in Section 4.5.1 are also applicable if we replace $\sigma^2(\mathbf{G}'\mathbf{G})^{-1}$ in the right-hand side of (4.5.26) by the asymptotic covariance matrix of the NLFI estimator.

8.3.2 Prediction

Bianchi and Calzolari (1980) proposed a method by which we can calculate the mean squared prediction error matrix of a vector predictor based on any estimator of the nonlinear simultaneous equations model. Suppose the structural equations can be written as $\mathbf{f}(\mathbf{y}_p, \mathbf{x}_p, \boldsymbol{\alpha}) = \mathbf{u}_p$ at the prediction period p and we can solve for $\mathbf{y}_p$ as $\mathbf{y}_p = \mathbf{g}(\mathbf{x}_p, \boldsymbol{\alpha}, \mathbf{u}_p)$. Define the predictor $\hat{\mathbf{y}}_p$ based on the estimator $\hat{\boldsymbol{\alpha}}$ by $\hat{\mathbf{y}}_p = \mathbf{g}(\mathbf{x}_p, \hat{\boldsymbol{\alpha}}, \mathbf{0})$. (Note that $\mathbf{y}_p$ is an N-vector.) We call this the deterministic predictor. Then we have

$$\begin{aligned} E(\mathbf{y}_p - \hat{\mathbf{y}}_p)(\mathbf{y}_p - \hat{\mathbf{y}}_p)' &\qquad (8.3.3) \\ = E[\mathbf{g}(\mathbf{x}_p, \boldsymbol{\alpha}, \mathbf{u}_p) - \mathbf{g}(\mathbf{x}_p, \boldsymbol{\alpha}, \mathbf{0})]\,[\mathbf{g}(\mathbf{x}_p, \boldsymbol{\alpha}, \mathbf{u}_p) - \mathbf{g}(\mathbf{x}_p, \boldsymbol{\alpha}, \mathbf{0})]' \\ + E[\mathbf{g}(\mathbf{x}_p, \boldsymbol{\alpha}, \mathbf{0}) - \mathbf{g}(\mathbf{x}_p, \hat{\boldsymbol{\alpha}}, \mathbf{0})]\,[\mathbf{g}(\mathbf{x}_p, \boldsymbol{\alpha}, \mathbf{0}) - \mathbf{g}(\mathbf{x}_p, \hat{\boldsymbol{\alpha}}, \mathbf{0})]' \\ \equiv \mathbf{A}_1 + \mathbf{A}_2. \end{aligned}$$

Bianchi and Calzolari suggested that $\mathbf{A}_1$ be evaluated by simulation. As for $\mathbf{A}_2$, we can easily obtain its asymptotic value from the knowledge of the asymptotic distribution of $\hat{\boldsymbol{\alpha}}$.

Mariano and Brown (1983) and Brown and Mariano (1982) compared the deterministic predictor $\hat{\mathbf{y}}_p$ defined in the preceding paragraph with two other predictors called the Monte Carlo predictor $\bar{\mathbf{y}}_p$ and the residual-based predictor $\tilde{\mathbf{y}}_p$ defined as

$$\bar{\mathbf{y}}_p = \frac{1}{S}\sum_{s=1}^{S} \mathbf{g}(\mathbf{x}_p, \hat{\boldsymbol{\alpha}}, \mathbf{v}_s), \qquad (8.3.4)$$

where $\{\mathbf{v}_s\}$ are i.i.d. with the same distribution as $\mathbf{u}_p$, and

$$\tilde{\mathbf{y}}_p = \frac{1}{T}\sum_{t=1}^{T} \mathbf{g}(\mathbf{x}_p, \hat{\boldsymbol{\alpha}}, \hat{\mathbf{u}}_t), \qquad (8.3.5)$$

where $\hat{\mathbf{u}}_t = \mathbf{f}(\mathbf{y}_t, \mathbf{x}_t, \hat{\boldsymbol{\alpha}})$.

Because $\mathbf{y}_p - \hat{\mathbf{y}}_p = (\mathbf{y}_p - E\mathbf{y}_p) + (E\mathbf{y}_p - \hat{\mathbf{y}}_p)$ for any predictor $\hat{\mathbf{y}}_p$, we should compare predictors on the basis of how well $E\mathbf{y}_p = E\mathbf{g}(\mathbf{x}_p, \boldsymbol{\alpha}, \mathbf{u}_p)$ is estimated by each predictor. Moreover, because $\hat{\boldsymbol{\alpha}}$ is common for the three predictors, we can essentially consider the situation where $\hat{\boldsymbol{\alpha}}$ in the predictor is replaced by the parameter $\boldsymbol{\alpha}$. Thus the authors' problem is essentially equivalent to that of comparing the following three estimators of $E\mathbf{g}(\mathbf{u}_p)$:

Deterministic: $\mathbf{g}(\mathbf{0})$

Monte Carlo: $\frac{1}{S}\sum_{s=1}^{S} \mathbf{g}(\mathbf{v}_s)$

Residual-based: $\frac{1}{T}\sum_{t=1}^{T} \mathbf{g}(\mathbf{u}_t)$

Clearly, the deterministic predictor is the worst, as Mariano and Brown (1983) concluded. According to their other article (Brown and Mariano, 1982), the choice between the Monte Carlo and residual-based predictors depends on the consideration that the former can be more efficient if S is large and the assumed distribution of $\mathbf{u}_p$ is true, whereas the latter is simpler to compute and more robust in the sense that the distribution of $\mathbf{u}_p$ need not be specified.

8.3.3 Computation

The discussion of the computation of NLFI preceded the theoretical discussion of the statistical properties of NLFI by more than ten years. The first article on computation was by Eisenpress and Greenstadt (1966), who proposed a modified Newton-Raphson iteration. Their modification combined both (4.4.4) and (4.4.5). Chow (1973) differed from Eisenpress and Greenstadt in that he obtained simpler formulae by assuming that different parameters appear in different equations, as in (8.2.1). We have already mentioned the algorithm considered by Amemiya (1977a), mainly for a pedagogical purpose. Dagenais (1978) modified this algorithm to speed up the convergence and compared it with a Newton-Raphson method proposed by Chow and Fair (1973) and with the DFP algorithm mentioned in Section 4.4.1 in certain examples of nonlinear models. The results are inconclusive. Belsley (1979) compared the computational speed of the DFP algorithm in computing NLFI and NL3S in five models of various degrees of complexity and found that NL3S was three to ten times faster. Nevertheless, Belsley showed that the computation of NLFI is quite feasible and can be improved by using a more suitable algorithm and by using the approximation of the Jacobian proposed by Fair—see Eq. (8.3.6).

Fair and Parke (1980) estimated Fair's (1976) macro model (97 equations, 29 of which are stochastic, with 182 parameters including 12 first-order autoregressive coefficients), which is nonlinear in variables as well as in parameters (this latter nonlinearity is caused by the transformation to take account of the first-order autoregression of the errors), by OLS, SNL2S, the Jorgenson-Laffont NL3S, and NLFI. The latter two estimators are calculated by a derivative-free algorithm proposed by Parke (1982).

Parke noted that the largest model for which NLFI and NL3S had been calculated before Parke's study was the one Belsley calculated, a model that contained 19 equations and 61 unknown coefficients. Parke also noted that Newton's method is best for linear models and that the DFP method is preferred for small nonlinear models; however, Parke's method is the only feasible one for large nonlinear models.

Fair and Parke used the approximation of the Jacobian

$$\sum_{t=1}^{T} \log |\mathbf{J}_t| = \frac{T}{n} (\log |\mathbf{J}_{t_1}| + \log |\mathbf{J}_{t_2}| + \ldots + \log |\mathbf{J}_{t_n}|), \tag{8.3.6}$$

where $\mathbf{J}_t = \partial \mathbf{f}_t / \partial \mathbf{y}_t'$, n is a small integer, and $t_1, t_2, \ldots, t_n$ are equally spaced between 1 and T.

The hypothesis (8.2.14) can be tested by Hausman's test (Section 4.5.1) using either NLFI versus NL3S or NLFI versus NL2S. By this test, Fair found little difference among the estimators. Fair also found that in terms of predictive accuracy there is not much difference among the different estimators, but, in terms of policy response, OLS is set apart from the rest.

Hatanaka (1978) considered a simultaneous equations model nonlinear only in variables. Such a model can be written as $\mathbf{F}(\mathbf{Y}, \mathbf{X})\mathbf{\Gamma} + \mathbf{X}\mathbf{B} = \mathbf{U}$. Define $\hat{\mathbf{Y}}$ by $\mathbf{F}(\hat{\mathbf{Y}}, \mathbf{X})\hat{\mathbf{\Gamma}} + \mathbf{X}\hat{\mathbf{B}} = \mathbf{0}$, where $\hat{\mathbf{\Gamma}}$ and $\hat{\mathbf{B}}$ are the OLS estimates. Then Hatanaka proposed using $\mathbf{F}(\hat{\mathbf{Y}}, \mathbf{X})$ as the instruments to calculate 3SLS. He proposed the method-of-scoring iteration to calculate NLFI, where the iteration is started at the aforementioned 3SLS.

Exercises

1. (Section 8.1.2)
   Define what you consider to be the best estimators of α and β in the model $(y_t + \alpha)^2 = \beta x_t + u_t$, $t = 1, 2, \ldots, T$, where $\{x_t\}$ are known constants and $\{u_t\}$ are i.i.d. with $Eu_t = 0$ and $Vu_t = \sigma^2$. Justify your choice of estimators.

2. (Section 8.1.2)
   In model (8.1.12) show that the minimization of $\Sigma_{t=1}^{T} [z_t(\lambda) - \mathbf{x}_t'\boldsymbol{\beta}]^2$ with respect to λ and $\boldsymbol{\beta}$ yields inconsistent estimates.

3. (Section 8.1.3)
   Prove the consistency of the estimator of $\boldsymbol{\alpha}$ obtained by minimizing $(\mathbf{y} - \mathbf{f})'[\mathbf{I} - \mathbf{V}(\mathbf{V}'\mathbf{V})^{-1}\mathbf{V}'](\mathbf{y} - \mathbf{f})$ and derive its asymptotic variance-covariance matrix. Show that the matrix is smaller (in the matrix sense) than $\mathbf{V}_\mathbf{M}$ given in (8.1.33).

4. (Section 8.1.3)
   In the model defined by (8.1.36) and (8.1.37), consider the following two-stage estimation method: In the first stage, regress z_t on x_t and define

$\hat{z}_t = \hat{\pi} x_t$, where $\hat{\pi}$ is the least squares estimator; in the second stage, regress y_t on $(\hat{z}_t)^2$ to obtain the least squares estimator of α. Show that the resulting estimator of α is inconsistent. (This method may be regarded as an application of Theil's interpretation—Section 7.3.6—to a nonlinear model.)

5. (Section 8.1.3)
In the model defined by (8.1.36) and (8.1.37), show that the consistency of MNL2S and NLLI requires (8.1.39).

6. (Section 8.1.3)
In the model defined by (8.1.36) and (8.1.37), assume $\pi = 1, x_t = 1$ for all t, $Vu_t = Vv_t = 1$, and $\text{Cov}(u_t, v_t) = c$. Evaluate the asymptotic variances, denoted V_1, V_2, V_3, and V_4, of the SNL2S, BNL2S, MNL2S, and NLLI estimators of α and show $V_1 \geqq V_2 \geqq V_3 \geqq V_4$ for every $|c| < 1$.

7. (Section 8.2.3)
Consider the following two-equation model (Goldfeld and Quandt, 1968):

$$\log y_{1t} = \gamma_1 \log y_{2t} + \beta_1 + \beta_2 x_t + u_{1t},$$

$$y_{2t} = \gamma_2 y_{1t} + \beta_3 x_t + u_{2t},$$

where $\gamma_1 > 0$ and $\gamma_2 < 0$. Show that there are two solutions of y_{1t} and y_{2t} for a given value of (u_{1t}, u_{2t}). Show also that (u_{1t}, u_{2t}) cannot be normally distributed.

8. (Section 8.2.3)
Consider the following model (Phillips, 1982):

$$\log y_{1t} + \alpha_1 x_t = u_{1t},$$

$$y_{2t} + \alpha_2 y_{1t} = u_{2t}.$$

Derive the conditions on u_{1t} and u_{2t} that make NLFI consistent. Use (8.2.14).

9 Qualitative Response Models

9.1 Introduction

Qualitative response models (henceforth to be abbreviated as QR models) are regression models in which dependent (or endogenous) variables take discrete values. These models have numerous applications in economics because many behavioral responses are qualitative in nature: A consumer decides whether to buy a car or not; a commuter chooses a particular mode of transportation from several available ones; a worker decides whether to take a job offer or not; and so on. A long list of empirical examples of QR models can be found in my recent survey (Amemiya, 1981).

Qualitative response models, also known as *quantal, categorical,* or *discrete* models, have been used in biometric applications longer than they have been used in economics. Biometricians use the models to study, for example, the effect of an insecticide on the survival or death of an insect, or the effect of a drug on a patient. The kind of QR model used by biometricians is usually the simplest kind—univariate binary (or dichotomous) dependent variable (survival or death) and a single independent variable (dosage).

Economists (and sociologists to a certain extent), on the other hand, must deal with more complex models, such as models in which a single dependent variable takes more than two discrete values (multinomial models) or models that involve more than one discrete dependent variable (multivariate models), as well as considering a larger number of independent variables. The estimation of the parameters of these complex models requires more elaborate techniques, many of which have been recently developed by econometricians.

This chapter begins with a discussion of the simplest model—the model for a univariate binary dependent variable (Section 9.2), and then moves on to multinomial and multivariate models (Sections 9.3 and 9.4). The emphasis here is on the theory of estimation (and hypothesis testing to a lesser extent) and therefore complementary to Amemiya's survey mentioned earlier, which discussed many empirical examples and contained only fundamental results on the theory of statistical inference. We shall also discuss important topics omitted by the survey—choice-based sampling (Section 9.5), distribution-free methods (Section 9.6), and panel data QR models (Section 9.7).

9.2 Univariate Binary Models

9.2.1 Model Specification

A univariate binary QR model is defined by

$$P(y_i = 1) = F(\mathbf{x}_i'\boldsymbol{\beta}_0), \qquad i = 1, 2, \ldots, n, \tag{9.2.1}$$

where $\{y_i\}$ is a sequence of independent binary random variables taking the value 1 or 0, $\mathbf{x}_i$ is a K-vector of known constants, $\boldsymbol{\beta}_0$ is a K-vector of unknown parameters, and F is a certain known function.

It would be more general to specify the probability as $F(\mathbf{x}_i, \boldsymbol{\beta}_0)$, but the specification (9.2.1) is most common. As in the linear regression model, specifying the argument of F as $\mathbf{x}_i'\boldsymbol{\beta}_0$ is more general than it seems because the elements of $\mathbf{x}_i$ can be transformations of the original independent variables. To the extent we can approximate a general nonlinear function of the original independent variables by $\mathbf{x}_i'\boldsymbol{\beta}_0$, the choice of F is not critical as long as it is a distribution function. An arbitrary distribution function can be attained by choosing an appropriate function H in the specification $F[H(x_i, \beta_0)]$.

The functional forms of F most frequently used in application are the following:

Linear Probability Model

$$F(x) = x.$$

Probit Model

$$F(x) = \Phi(x) \equiv \int_{-\infty}^{x} \frac{1}{\sqrt{2\pi}} \exp\left[-(t^2/2)\right] dt.$$

Logit Model

$$F(x) = \Lambda(x) \equiv \frac{e^x}{1 + e^x}.$$

The linear probability model has an obvious defect in that F for this model is not a proper distribution function as it is not constrained to lie between 0 and 1. This defect can be corrected by defining $F = 1$ if $F(\mathbf{x}_i'\boldsymbol{\beta}_0) > 1$ and $F = 0$ if $F(\mathbf{x}_i'\boldsymbol{\beta}_0) < 0$, but the procedure produces unrealistic kinks at the truncation points. Nevertheless, it has frequently been used in econometric applications, especially during and before the 1960s, because of its computational simplicity.

The probit model, like many other statistical models using the normal distribution, may be justified by appealing to a central limit theorem. A major justification for the logit model, although there are other justifications (notably, its connection with discriminant analysis, which we shall discuss in Section 9.2.8), is that the logistic distribution function Λ is similar to a normal distribution function but has a much simpler form. The logistic distribution has zero mean and variance equal to $\pi^2/3$. The standardized logistic distribution $e^{\lambda x}/(1 + e^{\lambda x})$ with $\lambda = \pi/\sqrt{3}$ has slightly heavier tails than the standard normal distribution.

We shall consider two examples, one biometric and one econometric, of the model (9.2.1) to gain some insight into the problem of specifying the probability function.

EXAMPLE 9.2.1. Suppose that a dosage x_i (actually the logarithm of dosage is used as x_i in most studies) of an insecticide is given to the ith insect and we want to study how the probability of the ith insect dying is related to the dosage x_i. (In practice, individual insects are not identified, and a certain dosage x_t is given to each of n_t insects in group t. However, the present analysis is easier to understand if we proceed as if each insect could be identified). To formulate this model, it is useful to assume that each insect possesses its own tolerance against a particular insecticide and dies when the dosage level exceeds the tolerance. Suppose that the tolerance y_i^* of the ith insect is an independent drawing from a distribution identical for all insects. Moreover, if the tolerance is a result of many independent and individually inconsequential additive factors, we can reasonably assume $y_i^* \sim N(\mu, \sigma^2)$ because of the central limit theorem. Defining $y_i = 1$ if the ith insect dies and $y_i = 0$ otherwise, we have

$$P(y_i = 1) = P(y_i^* < x_i) = \Phi[(x_i - \mu)/\sigma], \tag{9.2.2}$$

giving rise to a probit model where $\beta_1 = -\mu/\sigma$ and $\beta_2 = 1/\sigma$. If, on the other hand, we assume that y_i^* has a logistic distribution with mean μ and variance σ^2, we get a logit model

$$P(y_i = 1) = \Lambda\left[\frac{\pi}{\sqrt{3}}\frac{x_i - \mu}{\sigma}\right]. \tag{9.2.3}$$

EXAMPLE 9.2.2 (Domencich and McFadden, 1975). Let us consider the decision of a person regarding whether he or she drives a car or travels by transit to work. We assume that the utility associated with each mode of transport is a function of the mode characteristics $\mathbf{z}$ (mainly the time and the cost incurred by the use of the mode) and the individual's socioeconomic characteristics $\mathbf{w}$, plus an additive error term ϵ. We define U_{i1} and U_{i0} as the ith person's indirect utilities associated with driving a car and traveling by transit, respectively. Then, assuming a linear function, we have

$$U_{i0} = \alpha_0 + \mathbf{z}_{i0}'\boldsymbol{\beta} + \mathbf{w}_i'\boldsymbol{\gamma}_0 + \epsilon_{i0} \tag{9.2.4}$$

and

$$U_{i1} = \alpha_1 + \mathbf{z}_{i1}'\boldsymbol{\beta} + \mathbf{w}_i'\boldsymbol{\gamma}_1 + \epsilon_{i1}. \tag{9.2.5}$$

The basic assumption is that the ith person drives a car if $U_{i1} > U_{i0}$ and travels by transit if $U_{i1} < U_{i0}$. (There is indecision if $U_{i1} = U_{i0}$, but this happens with zero probability if ϵ_{i1} and ϵ_{i0} are continuous random variables.) Thus, defining $y_i = 1$ if the ith person drives a car, we have

$$\begin{aligned} P(y_i = 1) &= P(U_{i1} > U_{i0}) && (9.2.6) \\ &= P[\epsilon_{i0} - \epsilon_{i1} < \alpha_1 - \alpha_0 + (\mathbf{z}_{i1} - \mathbf{z}_{i0})'\boldsymbol{\beta} + \mathbf{w}_i'(\boldsymbol{\gamma}_1 - \boldsymbol{\gamma}_0)] \\ &= F[(\alpha_1 - \alpha_0) + (\mathbf{z}_{i1} - \mathbf{z}_{i0})'\boldsymbol{\beta} + \mathbf{w}_i'(\boldsymbol{\gamma}_1 - \boldsymbol{\gamma}_0)], \end{aligned}$$

where F is the distribution function of $\epsilon_{i0} - \epsilon_{i1}$. Thus a probit (logit) model arises from assuming the normal (logistic) distribution for $\epsilon_{i0} - \epsilon_{i1}$.

9.2.2 Consistency and Asymptotic Normality of the Maximum Likelihood Estimator

To derive the asymptotic properties of the MLE, we make the following assumptions in the model (9.2.1).

ASSUMPTION 9.2.1. F has derivative f and second-order derivative f', and $0 < F(x) < 1$ and $f(x) > 0$ for every x.

ASSUMPTION 9.2.2. The parameter space B is an open bounded subset of the Euclidean K-space.

ASSUMPTION 9.2.3. $\{\mathbf{x}_i\}$ are uniformly bounded in i and $\lim_{n\to\infty} n^{-1}\Sigma_{i=1}^{n} \mathbf{x}_i\mathbf{x}_i'$ is a finite nonsingular matrix. Furthermore the empirical distribution of $\{\mathbf{x}_i\}$ converges to a distribution function.

Both probit and logit models satisfy Assumption 9.2.1. The boundedness of $\{\mathbf{x}_i\}$ is somewhat restrictive and could be removed. However, we assume this to make the proofs of consistency and asymptotic normality simpler. In this way we hope that the reader will understand the essentials without being hindered by too many technical details.

The logarithm of the likelihood function of the model (9.2.1) is given by

$$\log L = \sum_{i=1}^{n} y_i \log F(\mathbf{x}_i'\boldsymbol{\beta}) + \sum_{i=1}^{n} (1 - y_i) \log [1 - F(\mathbf{x}_i'\boldsymbol{\beta})]. \tag{9.2.7}$$

Therefore the MLE $\hat{\boldsymbol{\beta}}$ is a solution (if it exists) of

$$\frac{\partial \log L}{\partial \boldsymbol{\beta}} = \sum_{i=1}^{n} \frac{y_i - F_i}{F_i(1 - F_i)} f_i \mathbf{x}_i = 0, \tag{9.2.8}$$

where $F_i = F(\mathbf{x}_i'\boldsymbol{\beta})$ and $f_i = f(\mathbf{x}_i'\boldsymbol{\beta})$.

To prove the consistency of $\hat{\boldsymbol{\beta}}$, we must verify the assumptions of Theorem 4.1.2. Assumptions A and B are clearly satisfied. To verify C, we use Theorem 4.2.2. If we define $g_i(y, \boldsymbol{\beta}) = [y - F(\mathbf{x}_i'\boldsymbol{\beta}_0)] \log F(\mathbf{x}_i'\boldsymbol{\beta})$, $g_i(y, \boldsymbol{\beta})$ in a compact neighborhood of $\boldsymbol{\beta}_0$ satisfies all the conditions for $g_t(y, \boldsymbol{\theta})$ in the theorem because of Assumptions 9.2.1 and 9.2.3. Furthermore $\lim_{n\to\infty} n^{-1}\Sigma_{i=1}^{n} F_{i0} \log F_i$ exists because of Theorem 4.2.3. Therefore $n^{-1}\Sigma_{i=1}^{n} y_i \log F_i$ converges to $\lim_{n\to\infty} n^{-1}\Sigma_{i=1}^{n} F_{i0} \log F_i$, where $F_{i0} = F(\mathbf{x}_i'\boldsymbol{\beta}_0)$, in probability uniformly in $\boldsymbol{\beta} \in N(\boldsymbol{\beta}_0)$, an open neighborhood of $\boldsymbol{\beta}_0$. A similar result can be obtained for the second term of the right-hand side of (9.2.7). Therefore

$$Q(\boldsymbol{\beta}) \equiv \operatorname{plim} n^{-1} \log L \tag{9.2.9}$$

$$= \lim n^{-1} \sum_{i=1}^{n} F_{i0} \log F_i + \lim n^{-1} \sum_{i=1}^{n} (1 - F_{i0}) \log (1 - F_i),$$

where the convergence is uniform in $\boldsymbol{\beta} \in N(\boldsymbol{\beta}_0)$. Because our assumptions enable us to differentiate inside the limit operation in (9.2.9),[1] we obtain

$$\frac{\partial Q}{\partial \boldsymbol{\beta}} = \lim n^{-1} \sum_{i=1}^{n} \frac{F_{i0}}{F_i} f_i \mathbf{x}_i - \lim n^{-1} \sum_{i=1}^{n} \frac{1 - F_{i0}}{1 - F_i} f_i \mathbf{x}_i, \tag{9.2.10}$$

which vanishes at $\boldsymbol{\beta} = \boldsymbol{\beta}_0$. Furthermore, because

$$\left. \frac{\partial^2 Q}{\partial \boldsymbol{\beta} \partial \boldsymbol{\beta}'} \right|_{\boldsymbol{\beta}_0} = -\lim n^{-1} \sum_{i=1}^{n} \frac{f_{i0}^2}{F_{i0}(1 - F_{i0})} \mathbf{x}_i \mathbf{x}_i', \tag{9.2.11}$$

which is negative definite by our assumptions, Q attains a strict local maximum at $\boldsymbol{\beta} = \boldsymbol{\beta}_0$. Thus assumption C of Theorem 4.1.2. holds, and hence the consistency of $\hat{\boldsymbol{\beta}}$ has been proved.

A solution of (9.2.8) may not always exist (see Albert and Anderson, 1984).

For example, suppose that $\{x_i\}$ are scalars such that $x_i < 0$ for $i \leqq c$ for some integer c between 1 and n and $x_i > 0$ for $i > c$ and that $y_i = 0$ for $i \leqq c$ and $y_i = 1$ for $i > c$. Then $\log L$ does not attain a maximum for any finite value of β. If $\{\mathbf{x}_i\}$ are K-vectors, the same situation arises if $y = 0$ for the values of $\mathbf{x}_i$ lying within one side of a hyperplane in R^K and $y = 1$ for the values of $\mathbf{x}_i$ lying within the other side. However, the possibility of no solution of (9.2.8) does not affect the consistency proof because the probability of no solution approaches 0 as n goes to ∞ as shown in Theorem 4.1.2.

Next we shall prove asymptotic normality using Theorem 4.2.4, which means that assumptions A, B, and C of Theorem 4.1.3 and Eq. (4.2.22) need to be verified. Differentiating (9.2.8) with respect to $\boldsymbol{\beta}$ yields

$$\frac{\partial^2 \log L}{\partial\boldsymbol{\beta}\partial\boldsymbol{\beta}'} = -\sum_{i=1}^{n}\left[\frac{y_i - F_i}{F_i(1-F_i)}\right]^2 f_i^2\mathbf{x}_i\mathbf{x}_i' + \sum_{i=1}^{n}\left[\frac{y_i - F_i}{F_i(1-F_i)}\right] f_i'\mathbf{x}_i\mathbf{x}_i'. \tag{9.2.12}$$

Thus assumption A of Theorem 4.1.3 is clearly satisfied. We can verify that Assumptions 9.2.1 and 9.2.3 imply assumption B of Theorem 4.1.3 by using Theorems 4.1.5 and 4.2.2. Next, we have from (9.2.8)

$$\frac{1}{\sqrt{n}}\frac{\partial \log L}{\partial\boldsymbol{\beta}}\bigg|_{\boldsymbol{\beta}_0} = \frac{1}{\sqrt{n}}\sum_{i=1}^{n}\frac{y_i - F_{i0}}{F_{i0}(1-F_{i0})} f_{i0}\mathbf{x}_i. \tag{9.2.13}$$

The asymptotic normality of (9.2.13) readily follows from Theorem 3.3.5 (Liapounov CLT) because each term in the summation is independent with bounded second and third absolute moments because of Assumptions 9.2.1, 9.2.2, and 9.3.3. Thus assumption C of Theorem 4.1.3 is satisfied and we obtain

$$\frac{1}{\sqrt{n}}\frac{\partial \log L}{\partial\boldsymbol{\beta}}\bigg|_{\boldsymbol{\beta}_0} \rightarrow N(\mathbf{0}, \mathbf{A}), \tag{9.2.14}$$

where

$$\mathbf{A} = \lim_{n\to\infty}\frac{1}{n}\sum_{i=1}^{n}\frac{f_{i0}^2}{F_{i0}(1-F_{i0})}\mathbf{x}_i\mathbf{x}_i'. \tag{9.2.15}$$

Finally, we obtain from (9.2.12)

$$\lim_{n\to\infty}\frac{1}{n}E\frac{\partial^2 \log L}{\partial\boldsymbol{\beta}\partial\boldsymbol{\beta}'}\bigg|_{\boldsymbol{\beta}_0} = -\mathbf{A}, \tag{9.2.16}$$

verifying (4.2.22). Therefore

$$\sqrt{n}(\hat{\boldsymbol{\beta}} - \boldsymbol{\beta}_0) \rightarrow N(\mathbf{0}, \mathbf{A}^{-1}). \tag{9.2.17}$$

For a proof of consistency and asymptotic normality under more general assumptions in the logit model, see the article by Gourieroux and Monfort (1981).

9.2.3 Global Concavity of the Likelihood Function in the Logit and Probit Models

Global concavity means that $\partial^2 \log L/\partial\boldsymbol{\beta}\partial\boldsymbol{\beta}'$ is a negative definite matrix for $\boldsymbol{\beta} \in \text{B}$. Because we have by a Taylor expansion

$$\log L(\boldsymbol{\beta}) = \log L(\hat{\boldsymbol{\beta}}) + \left.\frac{\partial \log L}{\partial \boldsymbol{\beta}'}\right|_{\hat{\boldsymbol{\beta}}} (\boldsymbol{\beta} - \hat{\boldsymbol{\beta}}) \tag{9.2.18}$$

$$+ \frac{1}{2} (\boldsymbol{\beta} - \hat{\boldsymbol{\beta}})' \left.\frac{\partial^2 \log L}{\partial\boldsymbol{\beta}\partial\boldsymbol{\beta}'}\right|_{\boldsymbol{\beta}^*} (\boldsymbol{\beta} - \hat{\boldsymbol{\beta}}).$$

where $\boldsymbol{\beta}^*$ lies between $\boldsymbol{\beta}$ and $\hat{\boldsymbol{\beta}}$, global concavity implies that $\log L(\hat{\boldsymbol{\beta}}) > \log L(\boldsymbol{\beta})$ for $\boldsymbol{\beta} \neq \hat{\boldsymbol{\beta}}$ if $\hat{\boldsymbol{\beta}}$ is a solution of (9.2.8). We shall prove global concavity for logit and probit models.

For the logit model we have

$$\frac{\partial \Lambda}{\partial x} = \Lambda(1 - \Lambda) \quad \text{and} \quad \frac{\partial^2 \Lambda}{\partial x^2} = (1 - 2\Lambda)\frac{\partial \Lambda}{\partial x}. \tag{9.2.19}$$

Inserting (9.2.19) into (9.2.12) with $F = \Lambda$ yields

$$\frac{\partial^2 \log L}{\partial\boldsymbol{\beta}\partial\boldsymbol{\beta}'} = -\sum_{i=1}^{n} \Lambda_i(1 - \Lambda_i)\mathbf{x}_i\mathbf{x}_i', \tag{9.2.20}$$

where $\Lambda_i = \Lambda(\mathbf{x}_i'\boldsymbol{\beta})$. Thus the global concavity follows from Assumption 9.2.3.

A proof of global concavity for the probit model is a little more complicated. Putting $F_i = \Phi_i$, $f_i = \phi_i$, and $f_i' = -\mathbf{x}_i'\boldsymbol{\beta}\phi_i$, where ϕ is the density function of $N(0, 1)$, into (9.2.12) yields

$$\frac{\partial^2 \log L}{\partial\boldsymbol{\beta}\partial\boldsymbol{\beta}'} = -\sum_{i=1}^{n} \phi_i\Phi_i^{-2}(1 - \Phi_i)^{-2}[(y_i - 2y_i\Phi_i + \Phi_i^2)\phi_i \tag{9.2.21}$$

$$+ (y_i - \Phi_i)\Phi_i(1 - \Phi_i)\mathbf{x}_i'\boldsymbol{\beta}]\mathbf{x}_i\mathbf{x}_i'.$$

Thus we need to show the positivity of

$$g_y(x) \equiv (y - 2y\Phi + \Phi^2)\phi + (y - \Phi)\Phi(1 - \Phi)x$$

for $y=1$ and 0. First, consider the case $y=1$. Because $g_1(x) = (1-\Phi)^2(\phi + \Phi x)$, we need to show $\phi + \Phi x > 0$. The inequality is clearly satisfied if $x \geqq 0$, so assume $x < 0$. But this is equivalent to showing

$$\phi > (1-\Phi)x \quad \text{for} \quad x > 0, \tag{9.2.22}$$

which follows from the identity (see Feller, 1961, p. 166)

$$x^{-1} \exp(-x^2/2) = \int_x^\infty (1 + y^{-2}) \exp(-y^2/2)\, dy. \tag{9.2.23}$$

Next, if $y = 0$, we have $g_0(x) = \Phi^2[\phi - (1-\Phi)x]$, which is clearly positive if $x \leqq 0$ and is positive if $x > 0$ because of (9.2.22). Thus we proved global concavity for the probit case.

9.2.4 Iterative Methods for Obtaining the Maximum Likelihood Estimator

The iterative methods we discussed in Section 4.4 can be used to calculate a root of Eq. (9.2.8). For the logit and probit models, iteration is simple because of the global concavity proved in the preceding section. Here we shall only discuss the method-of-scoring iteration and give it an interesting interpretation.

As we noted in Section 4.4, the method-of-scoring iteration is defined by

$$\hat{\boldsymbol{\beta}}_2 = \hat{\boldsymbol{\beta}}_1 - \left\{ \left[E \frac{\partial^2 \log L}{\partial \boldsymbol{\beta} \partial \boldsymbol{\beta}'} \right]_{\hat{\boldsymbol{\beta}}_1} \right\}^{-1} \left. \frac{\partial \log L}{\partial \boldsymbol{\beta}} \right|_{\hat{\boldsymbol{\beta}}_1}, \tag{9.2.24}$$

where $\hat{\boldsymbol{\beta}}_1$ is an initial estimator of $\boldsymbol{\beta}_0$ and $\hat{\boldsymbol{\beta}}_2$ is the second-round estimator. The iteration is to be repeated until a sequence of estimators thus obtained converges. Using (9.2.8) and (9.2.12), we can write (9.2.24) as

$$\hat{\boldsymbol{\beta}}_2 = \left[\sum_{i=1}^n \frac{\hat{f}_i^2}{\hat{F}_i(1-\hat{F}_i)} \mathbf{x}_i \mathbf{x}_i' \right]^{-1} \sum_{i=1}^n \frac{\hat{f}_i}{\hat{F}_i(1-\hat{F}_i)} \mathbf{x}_i [y_i - \hat{F}_i + \hat{f}_i \mathbf{x}_i' \hat{\boldsymbol{\beta}}_1], \tag{9.2.25}$$

where we have defined $\hat{F}_i = F(\mathbf{x}_i'\hat{\boldsymbol{\beta}}_1)$ and $\hat{f}_i = f(\mathbf{x}_i'\hat{\boldsymbol{\beta}}_1)$.

An interesting interpretation of the iteration (9.2.25) is possible. From (9.2.1) we obtain

$$y_i = F(\mathbf{x}_i'\boldsymbol{\beta}_0) + u_i, \tag{9.2.26}$$

where $Eu_i = 0$ and $Vu_i = F(\mathbf{x}_i'\boldsymbol{\beta}_0)[1 - F(\mathbf{x}_i'\boldsymbol{\beta}_0)]$. This is a heteroscedastic nonlinear regression model. Expanding $F(\mathbf{x}_i'\boldsymbol{\beta}_0)$ in a Taylor series around $\boldsymbol{\beta}_0 = \hat{\boldsymbol{\beta}}_1$

and rearranging terms, we obtain

$$y_i - \hat{F}_i + \hat{f}_i \mathbf{x}_i' \hat{\boldsymbol{\beta}}_1 \cong \hat{f}_i \mathbf{x}_i' \boldsymbol{\beta}_0 + u_i. \tag{9.2.27}$$

Thus $\hat{\boldsymbol{\beta}}_2$ defined in (9.2.25) can be interpreted as the weighted least squares (WLS) estimator of $\boldsymbol{\beta}_0$ applied to (9.2.27) with Vu_i estimated by $\hat{F}_i(1 - \hat{F}_i)$. For this reason the method-of-scoring iteration in the QR model is sometimes referred to as the *nonlinear weighted least squares* (NLWLS) *iteration* (Walker and Duncan, 1967).

9.2.5 Berkson's Minimum Chi-Square Method

There are many variations of the minimum chi-square (MIN χ^2) method, one of which is Berkson's method. For example, the feasible generalized least squares (FGLS) estimator defined in Section 6.2 is a MIN χ^2 estimator. Another example is the Barankin-Gurland estimator mentioned in Section 4.2.4. A common feature of these estimators is that the minimand evaluated at the estimator is asymptotically distributed as chi-square, from which the name is derived.

The MIN χ^2 method in the context of the QR model was first proposed by Berkson (1944) for the logit model but can be used for any QR model. It is useful only when there are many observations on the dependent variable y having the same value of the vector of independent variables $\mathbf{x}$ (sometimes referred to as "many observations per cell") so that $F(\mathbf{x}'\boldsymbol{\beta}_0)$ for the specific value of $\mathbf{x}$ can be accurately estimated by the relative frequency of y being equal to 1.

To explain the method in detail, we need to define new symbols. Suppose that the vector $\mathbf{x}_i$ takes T distinct vector values $\mathbf{x}_{(1)}, \mathbf{x}_{(2)}, \ldots, \mathbf{x}_{(T)}$; and classify integers $(1, 2, \ldots, n)$ into T disjoint sets $I_1, I_2, \ldots, I_T$ by the rule: $i \in I_t$ if $\mathbf{x}_i = \mathbf{x}_{(t)}$. Define $P_{(t)} = P(y_i = 1)$ if $i \in I_t$. In addition, define n_t as the number of integers contained in I_t, $r_t = \Sigma_{i \in I_t} y_i$, and $\hat{P}_{(t)} = r_t/n_t$. Note that $\{\hat{P}_{(t)}\}$ constitute the sufficient statistics of the model. In the following discussion we shall write $\mathbf{x}_{(t)}$, $P_{(t)}$, and $\hat{P}_{(t)}$ as $\mathbf{x}_t$, P_t, and $\hat{P}_t$ if there is no ambiguity.

From (9.2.1) we have

$$P_t = F(\mathbf{x}_t' \boldsymbol{\beta}_0), \qquad t = 1, 2, \ldots, T. \tag{9.2.28}$$

If F is one-to-one (which is implied by Assumption 9.2.1), we can invert the relationship in (9.2.28) to obtain

$$F^{-1}(P_t) = \mathbf{x}_t' \boldsymbol{\beta}_0, \tag{9.2.29}$$

where F^{-1} denotes the inverse function of F. Expanding $F^{-1}(\hat{P}_t)$ in a Taylor series around P_t (which is possible under Assumption 9.2.1), we obtain

$$F^{-1}(\hat{P}_t) = \mathbf{x}_t'\boldsymbol{\beta}_0 + \left.\frac{\partial F^{-1}}{\partial P_t}\right|_{P_t^*} (\hat{P}_t - P_t) \tag{9.2.30}$$

$$= \mathbf{x}_t'\boldsymbol{\beta}_0 + \frac{1}{f[F^{-1}(P_t^*)]} (\hat{P}_t - P_t)$$

$$\equiv \mathbf{x}_t'\boldsymbol{\beta}_0 + v_t + w_t,$$

where P_t^* lies between $\hat{P}_t$ and P_t,

$$v_t = \frac{1}{f[F^{-1}(P_t)]} (\hat{P}_t - P_t),$$

and

$$w_t = \left(\frac{1}{f[F^{-1}(P_t^*)]} - \frac{1}{f[F^{-1}(P_t)]} \right) (\hat{P}_t - P_t).$$

The fact that v_t and w_t depend on n has been suppressed.

Because

$$Vv_t \equiv \sigma_t^2 = \frac{P_t(1-P_t)}{n_t f^2[F^{-1}(P_t)]} \tag{9.2.31}$$

and because w_t is $O(n_t^{-1})$ and hence can be ignored for large n_t (as we shall show rigorously later), (9.2.30) approximately defines a heteroscedastic linear regression model. The MIN χ^2 estimator, denoted $\tilde{\boldsymbol{\beta}}$, is defined as the WLS estimator applied to (9.2.30) ignoring w_t. We can estimate σ_t^2 by $\hat{\sigma}_t^2$ obtained by substituting $\hat{P}_t$ for P_t in (9.2.31). Thus

$$\tilde{\beta} = \left(\sum_{t=1}^{T} \hat{\sigma}_t^{-2} \mathbf{x}_t \mathbf{x}_t' \right)^{-1} \sum_{t=1}^{T} \hat{\sigma}_t^{-2} \mathbf{x}_t F^{-1}(\hat{P}_t). \tag{9.2.32}$$

We shall prove the consistency and asymptotic normality of $\tilde{\boldsymbol{\beta}}$ (as n goes to ∞ with T fixed) under Assumptions 9.2.1, 9.2.3, and the following additional assumption:

Assumption 9.2.4. $\lim_{n\to\infty} (n_t/n) = c_t \neq 0$ for every $t = 1, 2, \ldots, T$, where T is a fixed integer.

We assume statement 9.2.4 to simplify the analysis. However, if $c_t = 0$ for some t, we can act as if the observations corresponding to that t did not exist and impose Assumptions 9.2.3 and 9.2.4 on the remaining observations.

Inserting (9.2.30) into (9.2.32) and rearranging terms yield

$$\sqrt{n}(\tilde{\boldsymbol{\beta}} - \boldsymbol{\beta}_0) = \left(\frac{1}{n}\sum_{t=1}^{T} \hat{\sigma}_t^{-2}\mathbf{x}_t\mathbf{x}_t'\right)^{-1} \frac{1}{\sqrt{n}}\sum_{t=1}^{T} \hat{\sigma}_t^{-2}\mathbf{x}_t(v_t + w_t). \tag{9.2.33}$$

Because T is fixed, we have by Theorem 3.2.6

$$\operatorname*{plim}_{n\to\infty} \frac{1}{n}\sum_{t=1}^{T} \hat{\sigma}_t^{-2}\mathbf{x}_t\mathbf{x}_t' = \sum_{t=1}^{T} \bar{\sigma}_t^{-2}\mathbf{x}_t\mathbf{x}_t', \tag{9.2.34}$$

where $\bar{\sigma}_t^{-2} = c_t f^2[F^{-1}(P_t)]/[P_t(1-P_t)]$. Also, using Theorem 3.2.7, we obtain

$$\begin{aligned} \frac{1}{\sqrt{n}}\sum_{t=1}^{T} \hat{\sigma}_t^{-2}\mathbf{x}_t(v_t + w_t) &= \sum_{t=1}^{T} \frac{1}{\sqrt{n}}(\hat{\sigma}_t^{-1})\,\hat{\sigma}_t^{-1}\sigma_t\mathbf{x}_t \\ &\quad \times(\sigma_t^{-1}v_t + \sigma_t^{-1}w_t) \\ &\overset{\text{LD}}{=} \sum_{t=1}^{T} \bar{\sigma}_t^{-1}\mathbf{x}_t\sigma_t^{-1}v_t, \end{aligned} \tag{9.2.35}$$

because $\operatorname{plim} n^{-1/2}\hat{\sigma}_t^{-1} = \bar{\sigma}_t^{-1}$, $\operatorname{plim} \hat{\sigma}_t^{-1}\sigma_t = 1$, and $\operatorname{plim} \sigma_t^{-1}w_t = 0$. But, because $\{v_t\}$ are independent, the vector $(\sigma_1^{-1}v_1, \sigma_2^{-1}v_2, \ldots, \sigma_T^{-1}v_T)$ converges to $N(\mathbf{0}, \mathbf{I}_T)$. Therefore

$$\sum_{t=1}^{T} \bar{\sigma}_t^{-1}\mathbf{x}_t\sigma_t^{-1}v_t \to N\left(\mathbf{0}, \sum_{t=1}^{T} \bar{\sigma}_t^{-2}\mathbf{x}_t\mathbf{x}_t'\right). \tag{9.2.36}$$

Finally, we obtain from (9.2.33) through (9.2.36) and Theorem 3.2.7

$$\sqrt{n}(\tilde{\boldsymbol{\beta}} - \boldsymbol{\beta}_0) \to N\left[\mathbf{0}, \left(\sum_{t=1}^{T} \bar{\sigma}_t^{-2}\mathbf{x}_t\mathbf{x}_t'\right)^{-1}\right]. \tag{9.2.37}$$

Because $\mathbf{A}$ defined in (9.2.15) is equal to $\Sigma_{t=1}^{T} \bar{\sigma}_t^{-2}\mathbf{x}_t\mathbf{x}_t'$ under Assumption 9.2.4, (9.2.17) and (9.2.37) show that the MIN χ^2 estimator has the same asymptotic distribution as the MLE.[2] The MIN χ^2 estimator is simpler to compute than the MLE because the former is explicitly defined as in (9.2.32), whereas the latter requires iteration. However, the MIN χ^2 method requires a large number of observations in each cell. If the model contains several independent variables, this may be impossible to obtain. In the next subsection we shall compare the two estimators in greater detail.

In the probit model, $F^{-1}(\hat{P}_t) = \Phi^{-1}(\hat{P}_t)$. Although Φ^{-1} does not have an explicit form, it can be easily evaluated numerically. The function $\Phi^{-1}(\cdot)$ is called the probit transformation. In the logit model we can explicitly write

$$\Lambda^{-1}(\hat{P}_t) = \log [\hat{P}_t/(1 - \hat{P}_t)], \tag{9.2.38}$$

which is called the logit transformation or the logarithm of the odds ratio.

Cox (1970, p. 33) mentioned the following modification of (9.2.38):

$$\Lambda_c^{-1}(\hat{P}_t) = \log \{[\hat{P}_t + (2n_t)^{-1}]/[1 - \hat{P}_t + (2n_t)^{-1}]\}. \tag{9.2.39}$$

This modification has two advantages over (9.2.38): (1) The transformation (9.2.39) can always be defined whereas (9.2.38) cannot be defined if $\hat{P}_t = 0$ or 1. (Nevertheless, it is not advisable to use Cox's modification when n_t is small.) (2) It can be shown that $E\Lambda_c^{-1}(\hat{P}_t) - \Lambda^{-1}(P_t)$ is of the order of n_t^{-2}, whereas $E\Lambda^{-1}(\hat{P}_t) - \Lambda^{-1}(P_t)$ is of the order of n_t^{-1}.

In the preceding passages we have proved the consistency and the asymptotic normality of Berkson's MIN χ^2 estimator assuming $\mathbf{x}_i = \mathbf{x}_t$ for $i \in I_t$. However, a situation may occur in practice where a researcher must proceed as if $\mathbf{x}_i = \mathbf{x}_t$ for $i \in I_t$ even if $\mathbf{x}_i \neq \mathbf{x}_t$ because individual observations $\mathbf{x}_i$ are not available and only their group mean $\mathbf{x}_t \equiv n_t^{-1}\Sigma_{i\in I_t}\mathbf{x}_i$ is available. (Such an example will be given in Example 9.3.1.) In this case the MIN χ^2 estimator is generally inconsistent. McFadden and Reid (1975) addressed this issue and, under the assumption of normality of x_t, evaluated the asymptotic bias of the MIN χ^2 estimator and proposed a modification of the MIN χ^2 estimator that is consistent.

9.2.6 Comparison of the Maximum Likelihood Estimator and the Minimum Chi-Square Estimator

In a simple model where the vector $\mathbf{x}_t$ consists of 1 and a single independent variable and where T is small, the exact mean and variance of MLE and the MIN χ^2 estimator can be computed by a direct method. Berkson (1955, 1957) did so for the logit and the probit model, respectively, and found the exact mean squared error of the MIN χ^2 estimator to be smaller in all the examples considered.

Amemiya (1980b) obtained the formulae for the bias to the order of n^{-1} and the mean squared error to the order of n^{-2} of MLE and MIN χ^2 in a general logit model.[3] The method employed in this study is as follows: Using (9.2.19) and the sampling scheme described in Section 9.2.5, the normal equation (9.2.8) is reduced to

$$\sum_{t=1}^{T} n_t[\hat{P}_t - \Lambda(\mathbf{x}_t'\boldsymbol{\beta})]\mathbf{x}_t = \mathbf{0}. \tag{9.2.40}$$

We can regard (9.2.40) as defining the MLE $\hat{\boldsymbol{\beta}}$ implicitly as a function of $\hat{P}_1, \hat{P}_2, \ldots, \hat{P}_T$, say, $\hat{\boldsymbol{\beta}} = \mathbf{g}(\hat{P}_1, \hat{P}_2, \ldots, \hat{P}_T)$. Expanding $\mathbf{g}$ in a Taylor series around $P_1, P_2, \ldots, P_T$ and noting that $\mathbf{g}(P_1, P_2, \ldots, P_T) = \boldsymbol{\beta}_0$, we obtain

$$\hat{\boldsymbol{\beta}} - \boldsymbol{\beta}_0 \cong \sum_t \mathbf{g}_t u_t + \frac{1}{2} \sum_t \sum_s \mathbf{g}_{ts} u_t u_s + \frac{1}{6} \sum_t \sum_s \sum_r \mathbf{g}_{tsr} u_t u_s u_r, \tag{9.2.41}$$

where $u_t = \hat{P}_t - P_t$ and $\mathbf{g}_t$, $\mathbf{g}_{ts}$, and $\mathbf{g}_{tsr}$ denote the first-, second-, and third-order partial derivatives of $\mathbf{g}$ evaluated at $(P_1, P_2, \ldots, P_T)$, respectively. The bias of the MLE to the order of n^{-1} is obtained by taking the expectation of the first two terms of the right-hand side of (9.2.41). The mean squared error of the MLE to the order of n^{-2} is obtained by calculating the mean squared error of the right-hand side of (9.2.41), ignoring the terms of a smaller order than n^{-2}. We need not consider higher terms in the Taylor expansion because Eu_t^k for $k \geqq 5$ are at most of the order of n_t^{-3}. A Taylor expansion for the MIN χ^2 estimator $\tilde{\boldsymbol{\beta}}$ is obtained by expanding the right-hand side of (9.2.32) around P_t.

Using these formulae, Amemiya calculated the approximate mean squared errors of MLE and the MIN χ^2 estimator in several examples, both artificial and empirical, and found the MIN χ^2 estimator to have a smaller mean squared error than MLE in all the examples considered. However, the difference between the two mean squared error matrices can be shown to be neither positive definite nor negative definite (Ghosh and Sinha, 1981). In fact, Davis (1984) showed examples in which the MLE has a smaller mean squared error to the order of n^{-2} and offered an intuitive argument that showed that the greater T, the more likely MLE is to have a smaller mean squared error.

Amemiya also derived the formulae for the n^{-2}-order mean squared errors of the bias-corrected MLE and the bias-corrected MIN χ^2 estimator and showed that the former is smaller. The bias-corrected MLE is defined as $\hat{\boldsymbol{\beta}} - \mathbf{B}(\hat{\boldsymbol{\beta}})$, where $\mathbf{B}$ is the bias to the order of n^{-1}, and similarly for MIN χ^2. This result is consistent with the second-order efficiency of MLE in the exponential family proved by Ghosh and Subramanyam (1974), as mentioned in Section 4.2.4. The actual magnitude of the difference of the n^{-2}-order mean squared errors of the bias-corrected MLE and MIN χ^2 in Amemiya's examples was always found to be extremely small. Davis did not report the corresponding results for her examples.

Smith, Savin, and Robertson (1984) conducted a Monte Carlo study of a logit model with one independent variable and found that although in point estimation MIN χ^2 did better than MLE, as in the studies of Berkson and Amemiya, the convergence of the distribution of the MIN χ^2 estimator to a normal distribution was sometimes disturbingly slow, being unsatisfactory in one instance even at $n = 480$.

For further discussion of this topic, see the article by Berkson (1980) and the comments following the article.

9.2.7 Tests of Hypotheses

To test a hypothesis on a single parameter, we can perform a standard normal test using the asymptotic normality of either MLE or the MIN χ^2 estimator. A linear hypothesis can be tested using general methods discussed in Section 4.5.1. The problem of choosing a model among several alternatives can be solved either by the Akaike Information Criterion (Section 4.5.2) or by Cox's test of nonnested hypotheses (Section 4.5.3). For other criteria for choosing models, see the article by Amemiya (1981).

Here we shall discuss only a chi-square test based on Berkson's MIN χ^2 estimator as this is not a special case of the tests discussed in Section 4.5. The test statistic is the weighted sum of squared residuals (WSSR) from Eq. (9.2.30) defined by

$$\text{WSSR} = \sum_{t=1}^{T} \hat{\sigma}_t^{-2}[F^{-1}(\hat{P}_t) - \mathbf{x}_t'\tilde{\boldsymbol{\beta}}]^2. \tag{9.2.42}$$

In the normal heteroscedastic regression model $\mathbf{y} \sim N(\mathbf{X}\boldsymbol{\beta}, \mathbf{D})$ with known $\mathbf{D}$, $(\mathbf{y} - \mathbf{X}\hat{\boldsymbol{\beta}}_G)'\mathbf{D}^{-1}(\mathbf{y} - \mathbf{X}\hat{\boldsymbol{\beta}}_G)$ is distributed as χ^2_{T-K}. From this fact we can deduce that WSSR defined in (9.2.42) is asymptotically distributed as χ^2_{T-K}.

We can use this fact to choose between the unconstrained model $P_t = F(\mathbf{x}_t'\boldsymbol{\beta}_0)$ and the constrained model $P_t = F(\mathbf{x}_{1t}'\boldsymbol{\beta}_{10})$, where $\mathbf{x}_{1t}$ and $\boldsymbol{\beta}_{10}$ are the first $K - q$ elements of $\mathbf{x}_t$ and $\boldsymbol{\beta}_0$, respectively. Let WSSR_u and WSSR_c be the values of (9.2.42) derived from the unconstrained and the constrained models, respectively. Then we should choose the unconstrained model if and only if

$$\text{WSSR}_c - \text{WSSR}_u > \chi^2_{q,\alpha}, \tag{9.2.43}$$

where $\chi^2_{q,\alpha}$ denotes the α% critical value of χ^2_q. Li (1977) has given examples of the use of this test with real data.

To choose among nonnested models, we can use the following variation of the Akaike Information Criterion:

$$\text{AIC} = \tfrac{1}{2}\,\text{WSSR} + K. \tag{9.2.44}$$

This may be justified on the grounds that in the normal heteroscedastic regression model mentioned earlier, $(\mathbf{y} - \mathbf{X}\hat{\boldsymbol{\beta}}_G)'\mathbf{D}^{-1}(\mathbf{y} - \mathbf{X}\hat{\boldsymbol{\beta}}_G)$ is equal to $-2 \log L$ aside from a constant term.

Instead of (9.2.42) we can also use

$$\sum_{t=1}^{T} n_t[\hat{P}_t(1 - \hat{P}_t)]^{-1}[\hat{P}_t - F(\mathbf{x}_t'\tilde{\boldsymbol{\beta}})]^2, \tag{9.2.45}$$

because this is asymptotically equivalent to (9.2.42).

9.2.8 Discriminant Analysis

The purpose of discriminant analysis is to measure the characteristics of an individual or an object and, on the basis of the measurements, to classify the individual or the object into one of two possible groups. For example, accept or reject a college applicant on the basis of examination scores, or determine whether a particular skull belongs to a man or an anthropoid on the basis of its measurements.

We can state the problem statistically as follows: Supposing that the vector of random variables $\mathbf{x}^*$ is generated according to either a density g_1 or g_0, we are to classify a given observation on $\mathbf{x}^*$, denoted $\mathbf{x}_i^*$, into the group characterized by either g_1 or g_0. It is useful to define $y_i = 1$ if $\mathbf{x}_i^*$ is generated by g_1 and $y_i = 0$ if it is generated by g_0. We are to predict y_i on the basis of $\mathbf{x}_i^*$. The essential information needed for the prediction is the conditional probability $P(y_i = 1|\mathbf{x}_i^*)$. We shall ignore the problem of prediction given the conditional probability and address the question of how to specify and estimate the conditional probability.[4]

By Bayes's rule we have

$$P(y_i = 1|\mathbf{x}_i^*) = \frac{g_1(\mathbf{x}_i^*)q_1}{g_1(\mathbf{x}_i^*)q_1 + g_0(\mathbf{x}_i^*)q_0}, \tag{9.2.46}$$

where q_1 and q_0 denote the marginal probabilities $P(y_i = 1)$ and $P(y_i = 0)$, respectively. We shall evaluate (9.2.46), assuming that g_1 and g_0 are the densities of $N(\boldsymbol{\mu}_1, \boldsymbol{\Sigma}_1)$ and $N(\boldsymbol{\mu}_0, \boldsymbol{\Sigma}_0)$, respectively. We state this assumption formally as

$$\mathbf{x}_i^*|(y_i = 1) \sim N(\boldsymbol{\mu}_1, \boldsymbol{\Sigma}_1) \tag{9.2.47}$$

$$\mathbf{x}_i^*|(y_i = 0) \sim N(\boldsymbol{\mu}_0, \boldsymbol{\Sigma}_0).$$

This is the most commonly used form of discriminant analysis, sometimes referred to as *normal discriminant analysis.*

Under (9.2.47), (9.2.46) reduces to the following quadratic logit model:

$$P(y_i = 1|\mathbf{x}_i^*) = \Lambda(\beta_{(1)} + \boldsymbol{\beta}_{(2)}'\mathbf{x}_i^* + \mathbf{x}_i^{*\prime}\mathbf{A}\mathbf{x}_i^*), \tag{9.2.48}$$

where

$$\beta_{(1)} = \frac{1}{2}\boldsymbol{\mu}_0'\boldsymbol{\Sigma}_0^{-1}\boldsymbol{\mu}_0 - \frac{1}{2}\boldsymbol{\mu}_1'\boldsymbol{\Sigma}_1^{-1}\boldsymbol{\mu}_1 + \log q_1 - \log q_0 \tag{9.2.49}$$

$$- \frac{1}{2}\log|\boldsymbol{\Sigma}_1| + \frac{1}{2}\log|\boldsymbol{\Sigma}_0|,$$

$$\boldsymbol{\beta}_{(2)} = \boldsymbol{\Sigma}_1^{-1}\boldsymbol{\mu}_1 - \boldsymbol{\Sigma}_0^{-1}\boldsymbol{\mu}_0, \tag{9.2.50}$$

and

$$\mathbf{A} = \frac{1}{2}(\boldsymbol{\Sigma}_0^{-1} - \boldsymbol{\Sigma}_1^{-1}). \tag{9.2.51}$$

In the special case $\boldsymbol{\Sigma}_1 = \boldsymbol{\Sigma}_0$, which is often assumed in econometric applications, we have $\mathbf{A} = \mathbf{0}$; therefore (9.2.48) further reduces to a linear logit model:

$$P(y_i = 1|\mathbf{x}_i^*) = \Lambda(\mathbf{x}_i'\boldsymbol{\beta}), \tag{9.2.52}$$

where we have written $\beta_{(1)} + \boldsymbol{\beta}_{(2)}'\mathbf{x}_i^* = \mathbf{x}_i'\boldsymbol{\beta}$ to conform with the notation of Section 9.2.1.

Let us consider the ML estimation of the parameters $\boldsymbol{\mu}_1, \boldsymbol{\mu}_0, \boldsymbol{\Sigma}_1, \boldsymbol{\Sigma}_0, q_1$, and q_0 based on observations $(y_i, \mathbf{x}_i^*)$, $i = 1, 2, \ldots, n$. The determination of q_1 and q_0 varies with authors. We shall adopt the approach of Warner (1963) and treat q_1 and q_0 as unknown parameters to estimate. The likelihood function can be written as

$$L = \prod_{i=1}^{n} [g_1(\mathbf{x}_i^*)q_1]^{y_i}[g_0(\mathbf{x}_i^*)q_0]^{1-y_i}. \tag{9.2.53}$$

Equating the derivatives of $\log L$ to 0 yields the following ML estimators:

$$\hat{q}_1 = \frac{n_1}{n}, \tag{9.2.54}$$

where $n_1 = \Sigma_{i=1}^n y_i$,

$$\hat{q}_0 = \frac{n_0}{n}, \tag{9.2.55}$$

where $n_0 = n - n_1$,

$$\hat{\mu}_1 = \frac{1}{n_1} \sum_{i=1}^{n} y_i \mathbf{x}_i^*, \tag{9.2.56}$$

$$\hat{\mu}_0 = \frac{1}{n_0} \sum_{i=1}^{n} (1 - y_i) \mathbf{x}_i^*, \tag{9.2.57}$$

$$\hat{\mathbf{\Sigma}}_1 = \frac{1}{n_1} \sum_{i=1}^{n} y_i (\mathbf{x}_i^* - \hat{\mu}_1)(\mathbf{x}_i^* - \hat{\mu}_i)', \tag{9.2.58}$$

and

$$\hat{\mathbf{\Sigma}}_0 = \frac{1}{n_0} \sum_{i=1}^{n} (1 - y_i)(\mathbf{x}_i^* - \hat{\mu}_0)(\mathbf{x}_i^* - \hat{\mu}_0)'. \tag{9.2.59}$$

If $\mathbf{\Sigma}_1 = \mathbf{\Sigma}_0 (\equiv \mathbf{\Sigma})$ as is often assumed, (9.2.58) and (9.2.59) should be replaced by

$$\hat{\mathbf{\Sigma}} = \frac{1}{n} \left[\sum_{i=1}^{n} y_i (\mathbf{x}_i^* - \hat{\mu}_1)(\mathbf{x}_i^* - \hat{\mu}_1)' + \sum_{i=1}^{n} (1 - y_i)(\mathbf{x}_i^* - \hat{\mu}_0)(\mathbf{x}_i^* - \hat{\mu}_0)' \right]. \tag{9.2.60}$$

The ML estimators of $\beta_{(1)}$, $\boldsymbol{\beta}_{(2)}$, and $\mathbf{A}$ are obtained by inserting these estimates into the right-hand side of (9.2.49), (9.2.50), and (9.2.51).

Discriminant analysis is frequently used in transport modal choice analysis. See, for example, articles by Warner (1962) and McGillivray (1972).

We call the model defined by (9.2.47) with $\mathbf{\Sigma}_1 = \mathbf{\Sigma}_0$ and by (9.2.52) the discriminant analysis (DA) model and call the estimator of $\boldsymbol{\beta} \equiv (\beta_{(1)}, \boldsymbol{\beta}'_{(2)})'$ obtained by inserting (9.2.56), (9.2.57), and (9.2.60) into (9.2.49) and (9.2.50) with $\mathbf{\Sigma}_1 = \mathbf{\Sigma}_0$ the DA estimator, denoted $\hat{\boldsymbol{\beta}}_{DA}$. In contrast, if we assume only (9.2.52) and not (9.2.47), we have a logit model. We denote the logit MLE of $\boldsymbol{\beta}$ by $\hat{\boldsymbol{\beta}}_{\Lambda}$. In the remainder of this section we shall compare these two estimators.

The relative performance of the two estimators will critically depend on the assumed true distribution for $\mathbf{x}_i^*$. If (9.2.47) with $\mathbf{\Sigma}_1 = \mathbf{\Sigma}_0$ is assumed in addition to (9.2.52), the DA estimator is the genuine MLE and therefore should be asymptotically more efficient than the logit MLE. However, if (9.2.47) is not assumed, the DA estimator loses its consistency in general, whereas the logit MLE retains its consistency. Thus we would expect the logit MLE to be more robust.

Efron (1975) assumed the DA model to be the correct model and studied the loss of efficiency that results if $\boldsymbol{\beta}$ is estimated by the logit MLE. He used the asymptotic mean of the *error rate* as a measure of the inefficiency of an estimator. Conditional on a given estimator $\hat{\boldsymbol{\beta}}$ (be it $\hat{\boldsymbol{\beta}}_{\mathrm{DA}}$ or $\hat{\boldsymbol{\beta}}_{\Lambda}$), the error rate is defined by

$$\begin{aligned}\text{Error Rate} &= P[\mathbf{x}'\hat{\boldsymbol{\beta}} \geqq 0|\mathbf{x} \sim N(\boldsymbol{\mu}_0, \boldsymbol{\Sigma})]q_0 \\ &\quad + P[\mathbf{x}'\hat{\boldsymbol{\beta}} < 0|\mathbf{x} \sim N(\boldsymbol{\mu}_1, \boldsymbol{\Sigma})]q_1 \\ &= q_0\Phi[(\hat{\boldsymbol{\beta}}'\boldsymbol{\Sigma}\hat{\boldsymbol{\beta}})^{-1/2}\boldsymbol{\mu}_0'\hat{\boldsymbol{\beta}}] + q_1\Phi[-(\hat{\boldsymbol{\beta}}'\boldsymbol{\Sigma}\hat{\boldsymbol{\beta}})^{-1/2}\boldsymbol{\mu}_1'\hat{\boldsymbol{\beta}}].\end{aligned} \tag{9.2.61}$$

Efron derived the asymptotic mean of (9.2.61) for each of the cases $\hat{\boldsymbol{\beta}} = \hat{\boldsymbol{\beta}}_{\mathrm{DA}}$ and $\hat{\boldsymbol{\beta}} = \hat{\boldsymbol{\beta}}_{\Lambda}$, using the asymptotic distributions of the two estimators. Defining the relative efficiency of the logit ML estimator as the ratio of the asymptotic mean of the error rate of the DA estimator to that of the logit ML estimator, Efron found that the efficiency ranges between 40 and 90% for the various experimental parameter values he chose.

Press and Wilson (1978) compared the classification derived from the two estimators in two real data examples in which many of the independent variables are binary and therefore clearly violate the DA assumption (9.2.47). Their results indicated a surprisingly good performance by DA (only slightly worse than the logit MLE) in terms of the percentage of correct classification both for the sample observations and for the validation set.

Amemiya and Powell (1983), motivated by the studies of Efron, Press, and Wilson, considered a simple model with characteristics similar to the two examples of Press and Wilson and analyzed it using the asymptotic techniques analogous to those of Efron. They compared the two estimators in a logit model with two binary independent variables. The criteria they used were the asymptotic mean of the *probability of correct classification* (PCC) (that is, one minus the error rate) and the asymptotic mean squared error. They found that in terms of the PCC criterion, the DA estimator does very well—only slightly worse than the logit MLE, thus confirming the results of Press and Wilson. For all the experimental parameter values they considered, the lowest efficiency of the DA estimator in terms of the PCC criterion was 97%. The DA estimator performed quite well in terms of the mean squared error criterion as well, although it did not do as well as it did in terms of the PCC criterion and it did poorly for some parameter values. Although the DA estimator is inconsistent in the model they considered, the degree of inconsistency (the difference between the probability limit and the true value) was surprisingly small in a majority of the cases. Thus normal discriminant analysis seems more robust against nonnormality than we would intuitively expect.

We should point out, however, that their study was confined to the case of binary independent variables; the DA estimator may not be robust against a different type of nonnormality. McFadden (1976a) illustrated a rather significant asymptotic bias of a DA estimator in a model in which the marginal distribution of the independent variable is normal. [Note that when we spoke of normality we referred to each of the two conditional distributions given in (9.2.47). The marginal distribution of $\mathbf{x}^*$ is not normal in the DA model but, rather, is a mixture of normals.] Lachenbruch, Sneeringer, and Revo (1973) also reported a poor performance of the DA estimator in certain nonnormal models.

9.2.9 Aggregate Prediction

We shall consider the problem of predicting the aggregate proportion $r \equiv n^{-1}\Sigma_{i=1}^{n} y_i$ in the QR model (9.2.1). This is often an important practical problem for a policymaker. For example, in the transport choice model of Example 9.2.2, a policymaker would like to know the proportion of people in a community who use the transit when a new fare and the other values of the independent variables $\mathbf{x}$ prevail. It is assumed that $\boldsymbol{\beta}$ (suppressing the subscript 0) has been estimated from the past sample. Moreover, to simplify the analysis, we shall assume for the time being that the estimated value of $\boldsymbol{\beta}$ is equal to the true value.

The prediction of r should be done on the basis of the conditional distribution of r given $\{\mathbf{x}_i\}$. When n is large, the following asymptotic distribution is accurate:

$$r \stackrel{A}{\sim} N\left[n^{-1} \sum_{i=1}^{n} F_i,\ n^{-2} \sum_{i=1}^{n} F_i(1 - F_i)\right]. \tag{9.2.62}$$

Once we calculate the asymptotic mean and variance, we have all the necessary information for predicting r.

If we actually observe every $\mathbf{x}_i$, $i = 1, 2, \ldots, n$, we can calculate the mean and variance for (9.2.62) straightforwardly. However, because it is more realistic to assume that we cannot observe every $\mathbf{x}_i$, we shall consider the problem of how to estimate the mean and variance for (9.2.62) in that situation. For that purpose we assume that $\{\mathbf{x}_i\}$ are i.i.d. random variables with the common K-variate distribution function G. Then the asymptotic mean and variance of r can be estimated by $EF(\mathbf{x}'\boldsymbol{\beta})$ and $n^{-1}EF(1 - F)$, respectively, where E is the expectation taken with respect to G.

Westin (1974) studied the evaluation of EF when $F = \Lambda$ (logistic distribution) and $\mathbf{x} \sim N(\boldsymbol{\mu}_x, \boldsymbol{\Sigma}_x)$. He noted that the density of $p \equiv \Lambda(\mathbf{x}'\boldsymbol{\beta})$ is given by

$$f(p) = \frac{1}{\sqrt{2\pi}\sigma} \frac{1}{p(1-p)} \exp\left\{-\frac{1}{2\sigma^2}\left[\log\left(\frac{p}{1-p}\right) - \mu\right]^2\right\}, \quad (9.2.63)$$

where $\mu = \boldsymbol{\mu}_x'\boldsymbol{\beta}$ and $\sigma^2 = \boldsymbol{\beta}'\boldsymbol{\Sigma}_x\boldsymbol{\beta}$. Because the mean of this density does not have a closed form expression, we must evaluate $\int pf(p)\,dp$ numerically for given values of μ and σ^2.

McFadden and Reid (1975) showed that if $F = \Phi$ (standard normal distribution) and $\mathbf{x} \sim N(\boldsymbol{\mu}_x, \boldsymbol{\Sigma}_x)$ as before, we have

$$E\Phi(\mathbf{x}'\boldsymbol{\beta}) = \Phi[(1 + \sigma^2)^{-1/2}\mu]. \quad (9.2.64)$$

Thus the evaluation of EF is much simpler than in the logit case.

Neither Westin nor McFadden and Reid considered the evaluation of the asymptotic variance of r, which constitutes an important piece of information for the purpose of prediction.

Another deficiency of these studies is that the variability due to the estimation of $\boldsymbol{\beta}$ is totally ignored. We shall suggest a partially Bayesian way to deal with this problem.[5] Given an estimate $\hat{\boldsymbol{\beta}}$ of $\boldsymbol{\beta}$, we treat $\boldsymbol{\beta}$ as a random variable with the distribution $N(\hat{\boldsymbol{\beta}}, \boldsymbol{\Sigma}_\beta)$. An estimate of the asymptotic covariance matrix of the estimator $\hat{\boldsymbol{\beta}}$ can be used for $\boldsymbol{\Sigma}_\beta$. We now regard (9.2.62) as the asymptotic distribution of r conditionally on $\{\mathbf{x}_i\}$ and $\boldsymbol{\beta}$. The distribution of r conditionally on $\{\mathbf{x}_i\}$ but not on $\boldsymbol{\beta}$ is therefore given by

$$r \overset{A}{\sim} N\left[E_\beta n^{-1} \sum_{i=1}^{n} F_i,\ E_\beta n^{-2} \sum_{i=1}^{n} F_i(1 - F_i) + V_\beta n^{-1} \sum_{i=1}^{n} F_i\right]. \quad (9.2.65)$$

Finally, if the total observations on $\{\mathbf{x}_i\}$ are not available and $\{\mathbf{x}_i\}$ can be regarded as i.i.d. random variables, we can approximate (9.2.65) by

$$r \overset{A}{\sim} N[E_x E_\beta F,\ n^{-1}E_x E_\beta F(1 - F) + E_x V_\beta F]. \quad (9.2.66)$$

9.3 Multinomial Models

9.3.1 Statistical Inference

In this section we shall define a general multinomial QR model and shall discuss maximum likelihood and minimum chi-square estimation of this model, along with the associated test statistics. In the subsequent sections we shall discuss various types of the multinomial QR model and the specific problems that arise with them.

Assuming that the dependent variable y_i takes $m_i + 1$ values 0, 1, 2, . . . , m_i, we define a general multinomial QR model as

$$P(y_i = j) = F_{ij}(\mathbf{x}^*, \theta), \qquad i = 1, 2, \ldots, n \quad \text{and} \qquad (9.3.1)$$
$$j = 1, 2, \ldots, m_i,$$

where $\mathbf{x}^*$ and θ are vectors of independent variables and parameters, respectively. (Strictly speaking, we should write j as j_i, but we shall suppress the subscript i.) We sometimes write (9.3.1) simply as $P_{ij} = F_{ij}$. We shall allow the possibility that not all the independent variables and parameters are included in the argument of every F_{ij}. Note that $P(y_i = 0)(\equiv F_{i0})$ need not be specified because it must be equal to one minus the sum of the m_i probabilities defined in (9.3.1).

It is important to let m_i depend on i because in many applications individuals face different choice sets. For example, in transport modal choice analysis, traveling by train is not included in the choice set of those who live outside of its service area.

To define the maximum likelihood estimator of θ in the model (9.3.1) it is useful to define $\Sigma_{i=1}^{n}(m_i + 1)$ binary variables

$$y_{ij} = 1 \quad \text{if} \quad y_i = j \qquad (9.3.2)$$
$$= 0 \quad \text{if} \quad y_i \neq j, \qquad i = 1, 2, \ldots, n \quad \text{and}$$
$$j = 0, 1, \ldots, m_i.$$

Then we can write the log likelihood function as

$$\log L = \sum_{i=1}^{n} \sum_{j=0}^{m_i} y_{ij} \log F_{ij}, \qquad (9.3.3)$$

which is a natural generalization of (9.2.7). The MLE $\hat{\theta}$ of θ is defined as a solution of the normal equation $\partial \log L/\partial\theta = \mathbf{0}$.

Many of the results about the MLE in the binary case hold for the model (9.3.1) as well. A reasonable set of sufficient conditions for its consistency and asymptotic normality can be found using the relevant theorems of Chapter 4, as we have done for the binary case. The equivalence of the method of scoring and the NLWLS (NLGLS to be exact) iteration can also be shown. However, we shall demonstrate these things under a slightly less general model than (9.3.1). We assume[6]

$$P(y_i = j) = F_j(\mathbf{x}'_{i1}\boldsymbol{\beta}_1, \mathbf{x}'_{i2}\boldsymbol{\beta}_2, \ldots, \mathbf{x}'_{iH}\boldsymbol{\beta}_H), \tag{9.3.4}$$
$$i = 1, 2, \ldots, n \quad \text{and} \quad j = 1, 2, \ldots, m,$$

where H is a fixed integer. In most specific examples of the multinomial QR model we have $H = m$, but this need not be so for this analysis. Note that we have now assumed that m does not depend on i to simplify the analysis.

We restate Assumptions 9.2.1, 9.2.2, and 9.2.3 with obvious modifications as follows.

ASSUMPTION 9.3.1. F_{ij} has partial derivatives $f_{ij}^k \equiv \partial F_{ij}/\partial(\mathbf{x}'_{ik}\boldsymbol{\beta}_k)$ and partial second-order derivatives $f_{ij}^{kl} \equiv \partial f_{ij}^k/\partial(\mathbf{x}'_{il}\boldsymbol{\beta}_l)$ for every i, j, k, l, and $0 < F_{ij} < 1$ and $f_{ij}^k > 0$ for every i, j, and k.

ASSUMPTION 9.3.2. The parameter space B is an open bounded subset of a Euclidean space.

ASSUMPTION 9.3.3. $\{\mathbf{x}_{ih}\}$ are uniformly bounded in i for every h and $\lim_{n\to\infty} n^{-1}\Sigma_{i=1}^n \mathbf{x}_{ih}\mathbf{x}'_{ih}$ is a finite nonsingular matrix for every h. Furthermore, the empirical distribution function of $\{\mathbf{x}_{ih}\}$ converges to a distribution function.

Under these assumptions the MLE $\hat{\boldsymbol{\beta}}$ of $\boldsymbol{\beta} = (\boldsymbol{\beta}'_1, \boldsymbol{\beta}'_2, \ldots, \boldsymbol{\beta}'_H)'$ can be shown to be consistent and asymptotically normal. We shall derive its asymptotic covariance matrix.

Differentiating (9.3.3) with respect go $\boldsymbol{\beta}_k$, we obtain

$$\frac{\partial \log L}{\partial \boldsymbol{\beta}_k} = \sum_{i=1}^{n} \sum_{j=0}^{m} y_{ij} F_{ij}^{-1} f_{ij}^k \mathbf{x}_{ik}. \tag{9.3.5}$$

Differentiating (9.3.5) with respect to $\boldsymbol{\beta}'_l$ yields

$$\frac{\partial^2 \log L}{\partial \boldsymbol{\beta}_k \partial \boldsymbol{\beta}'_l} = -\sum_{i=1}^{n} \sum_{j=0}^{m} y_{ij} F_{ij}^{-2} f_{ij}^k f_{ij}^l \mathbf{x}_{ik}\mathbf{x}'_{il} + \sum_{i=1}^{n} \sum_{j=0}^{m} y_{ij} F_{ij}^{-1} f_{ij}^{kl} \mathbf{x}_{ik}\mathbf{x}'_{il}. \tag{9.3.6}$$

Taking the expectation and noting $\Sigma_{j=0}^m f_{ij}^{kl} = 0$, we obtain

$$-E\frac{\partial^2 \log L}{\partial \boldsymbol{\beta}_k \partial \boldsymbol{\beta}'_l} = \sum_{i=1}^{n} \sum_{j=0}^{m} F_{ij}^{-1} f_{ij}^k f_{ij}^l \mathbf{x}_{ik}\mathbf{x}'_{il} \equiv \mathbf{A}_{kl}. \tag{9.3.7}$$

Define $\mathbf{A} = \{\mathbf{A}_{kl}\}$. Then we can show under Assumptions 9.3.1, 9.3.2, and 9.3.3

$$\sqrt{n}(\hat{\boldsymbol{\beta}} - \boldsymbol{\beta}) \rightarrow N(0, \lim_{n\rightarrow\infty} n\mathbf{A}^{-1}). \tag{9.3.8}$$

To show the equivalence between the method-of-scoring and the NLWLS iteration (see Amemiya, 1976b), it is convenient to rewrite (9.3.5) and (9.3.7) using the following vector notation:

$$\mathbf{y}_i = (y_{i1}, y_{i2}, \ldots, y_{im})' \tag{9.3.9}$$

$$\mathbf{F}_i = (F_{i1}, F_{i2}, \ldots, F_{im})'$$

$$\mathbf{f}_i^k = (f_{i1}^k, f_{i2}^k, \ldots, f_{im}^k)'$$

$$\boldsymbol{\Lambda}_i = E(\mathbf{y}_i - \mathbf{F}_i)(\mathbf{y}_i - \mathbf{F}_i)' = \mathbf{D}(\mathbf{F}_i) - \mathbf{F}_i\mathbf{F}_i',$$

where $\mathbf{D}(\mathbf{F}_i)$ is the diagonal matrix the jth diagonal element of which is F_{ij}. Then, using the identities $\Sigma_{j=0}^m F_{ij} = 1$ and $\Sigma_{j=0}^m f_{ij}^k = 0$ and noting

$$\boldsymbol{\Lambda}_i^{-1} = \mathbf{D}^{-1}(\mathbf{F}_i) + F_{i0}^{-1}\mathbf{l}\mathbf{l}', \tag{9.3.10}$$

where $\mathbf{l}$ is an m-vector of ones, we obtain from (9.3.5) and (9.3.7)

$$\frac{\partial \log L}{\partial \boldsymbol{\beta}_k} = \sum_{i=1}^n \mathbf{x}_{ik}\mathbf{f}_i^{k\prime}\boldsymbol{\Lambda}_i^{-1}(\mathbf{y}_i - \mathbf{F}_i) \tag{9.3.11}$$

and

$$-E\frac{\partial^2 \log L}{\partial \boldsymbol{\beta}_k \partial \boldsymbol{\beta}_l'} = \sum_{i=1}^n \mathbf{x}_{ik}\mathbf{f}_i^{k\prime}\boldsymbol{\Lambda}_i^{-1}\mathbf{f}_i^l\mathbf{x}_{il}'. \tag{9.3.12}$$

Suppose $\bar{\boldsymbol{\beta}}$ is the initial estimate of $\boldsymbol{\beta}$, let $\bar{\mathbf{F}}_i$, $\bar{\mathbf{f}}_i^k$, and $\bar{\boldsymbol{\Lambda}}_i$ be, respectively, $\mathbf{F}_i$, $\mathbf{f}_i^k$, and $\boldsymbol{\Lambda}_i$ evaluated at $\bar{\boldsymbol{\beta}}$ and define

$$\bar{\mathbf{A}}_{kl} = \sum_{i=1}^n \mathbf{x}_{ik}\bar{\mathbf{f}}_i^{k\prime}\bar{\boldsymbol{\Lambda}}_i^{-1}\bar{\mathbf{f}}_i^l\mathbf{x}_{il}' \tag{9.3.13}$$

and

$$\bar{\mathbf{c}}_k = \sum_{i=1}^n \mathbf{x}_{ik}\bar{\mathbf{f}}_i^{k\prime}\bar{\boldsymbol{\Lambda}}_i^{-1}\sum_{h=1}^H \bar{\mathbf{f}}_i^h\mathbf{x}_{ih}'\bar{\boldsymbol{\beta}}_h + \sum_{i=1}^n \mathbf{x}_{ik}\bar{\mathbf{f}}_i^{k\prime}\bar{\boldsymbol{\Lambda}}_i^{-1}(\mathbf{y}_i - \bar{\mathbf{F}}_i). \tag{9.3.14}$$

Then the second-round estimator $\bar{\bar{\boldsymbol{\beta}}}$ obtained by the method-of-scoring iteration started from $\bar{\boldsymbol{\beta}}$ is given by

$$\bar{\bar{\boldsymbol{\beta}}} = \bar{\mathbf{A}}^{-1}\bar{\mathbf{c}}, \tag{9.3.15}$$

where $\bar{\mathbf{A}} = \{\bar{\mathbf{A}}_{kl}\}$ and $\bar{\mathbf{c}} = (\bar{\mathbf{c}}_1', \bar{\mathbf{c}}_2', \ldots, \bar{\mathbf{c}}_m')'$.

We can interpret (9.3.15) as an NLGLS iteration. From (9.3.4) we obtain

$$\mathbf{y}_i = \mathbf{F}_i + \mathbf{u}_i, \qquad i = 1, 2, \ldots, n, \tag{9.3.16}$$

where $E\mathbf{u}_i = \mathbf{0}$, $E\mathbf{u}_i\mathbf{u}_i' = \mathbf{\Lambda}_i$, and $E\mathbf{u}_i\mathbf{u}_j' = \mathbf{0}$ for $i \neq j$. Expanding $\mathbf{F}_i$ in Taylor series around $\mathbf{x}_{ih}'\bar{\boldsymbol{\beta}}_h$, $h = 1, 2, \ldots, H$, we obtain

$$\mathbf{y}_i - \bar{\mathbf{F}}_i + \sum_{h=1}^{H} \bar{\mathbf{f}}_i^h \mathbf{x}_{ih}'\bar{\boldsymbol{\beta}}_h \cong \sum_{h=1}^{H} \bar{\mathbf{f}}_i^h \mathbf{x}_{ih}'\boldsymbol{\beta}_h + \mathbf{u}_i, \tag{9.3.17}$$

$$i = 1, 2, \ldots, n.$$

The approximation (9.3.17) can be regarded as a linear regression model of mn observations with a nonscalar covariance matrix. If we estimate $\mathbf{\Lambda}_i$ by $\bar{\mathbf{\Lambda}}_i$ and apply FGLS to (9.3.17), the resulting estimator is precisely (9.3.15).

Next we shall derive the MIN χ^2 estimator of $\boldsymbol{\beta}$ in model (9.3.4), following Amemiya (1976b). As in Section 9.2.5, we assume that there are many observations with the same value of independent variables. Assuming that the vector of independent variables takes T distinct values, we can write (9.3.4) as

$$P_{tj} = F_j(\mathbf{x}_{t1}'\boldsymbol{\beta}_1, \mathbf{x}_{t2}'\boldsymbol{\beta}_2, \ldots, \mathbf{x}_{tH}'\boldsymbol{\beta}_H), \tag{9.3.18}$$

$$t = 1, 2, \ldots, T \quad \text{and} \quad j = 1, 2, \ldots, m.$$

To define the MIN χ^2 estimator of $\boldsymbol{\beta}$, we must be able to invert m equations in (9.3.18) for every t and solve them for H variables $\mathbf{x}_{t1}'\boldsymbol{\beta}_1, \mathbf{x}_{t2}'\boldsymbol{\beta}_2, \ldots, \mathbf{x}_{tH}'\boldsymbol{\beta}_H$. Thus for the moment, assume $H = m$. Assuming, furthermore, that the Jacobian does not vanish, we obtain

$$\mathbf{x}_{tk}'\boldsymbol{\beta}_k = G_k(P_{t1}, P_{t2}, \ldots, P_{tm}), \tag{9.3.19}$$

$$t = 1, 2, \ldots, T \quad \text{and} \quad k = 1, 2, \ldots, m.$$

As in Section 9.2.5 we define $r_{tj} = \Sigma_{i \in I_t} y_{ij}$, where I_t is the set of i for which $\mathbf{x}_{ih} = \mathbf{x}_{th}$ for all h, and $\hat{P}_{tj} = r_{tj}/n_t$, where n_t is the number of integers in I_t. Expanding $G_k(\hat{P}_{t1}, \hat{P}_{t2}, \ldots, \hat{P}_{tm})$ in Taylor series around $(P_{t1}, P_{t2}, \ldots, P_{tm})$ and using (9.3.19), we obtain

$$G_k(\hat{P}_{t1}, \hat{P}_{t2}, \ldots, \hat{P}_{tm}) \cong \mathbf{x}_{tk}'\boldsymbol{\beta}_k + \sum_{j=1}^{m} g_{tk}^j(\hat{P}_{tj} - F_{tj}), \tag{9.3.20}$$

$$t = 1, 2, \ldots, T \quad \text{and} \quad k = 1, 2, \ldots, m,$$

where $g_{tk}^j = \partial G_k/\partial P_{tj}$. Equation (9.3.20) is a generalization of (9.2.30), but here we write it as an approximate equation, ignoring an error term that corresponds to w_t in (9.2.30). Equation (9.3.20) is an approximate linear regression equation with a nonscalar covariance matrix that depends on $\mathbf{\Lambda}_t \equiv E(\hat{\mathbf{P}}_t - \mathbf{F}_t)(\hat{\mathbf{P}}_t - \mathbf{F}_t)' = n_t^{-1}[\mathbf{D}(\mathbf{F}_t) - \mathbf{F}_t\mathbf{F}_t']$, where $\hat{\mathbf{P}}_t = (\hat{P}_{t1}, \hat{P}_{t2}, \ldots, \hat{P}_{tm})'$ and $\mathbf{F}_t = (F_{t1}, F_{t2}, \ldots, F_{tm})'$. The MIN χ^2 estimator $\tilde{\boldsymbol{\beta}}$ of $\boldsymbol{\beta}$ is defined as FGLS applied to (9.3.20), using $\hat{\mathbf{\Lambda}}_t = n_t^{-1}[\mathbf{D}(\hat{\mathbf{P}}_t) - \hat{\mathbf{P}}_t\hat{\mathbf{P}}_t']$ as an estimator of $\mathbf{\Lambda}_t$. An example of the MIN χ^2 estimator will be given in Example 9.3.1 in Section 9.3.2.

The consistency and the asymptotic normality of $\tilde{\boldsymbol{\beta}}$ can be proved by using a method similar to the one employed in Section 9.2.5. Let $\mathbf{\Omega}^{-1}$ be the asymptotic covariance matrix of $\tilde{\boldsymbol{\beta}}$, that is, $\sqrt{n}(\tilde{\boldsymbol{\beta}} - \boldsymbol{\beta}) \rightarrow N(\mathbf{0}, \lim_{n\rightarrow\infty} n\mathbf{\Omega}^{-1})$. Then it can be deduced from (9.3.20) that the k,lth subblock of $\mathbf{\Omega}$ is given by

$$\mathbf{\Omega}_{kl} = \sum_t \mathbf{x}_{tk}\{\underline{\mathbf{G}}_t'\mathbf{\Lambda}_t\underline{\mathbf{G}}_t\}_{kl}^{-1}\mathbf{x}_{tl}', \tag{9.3.21}$$

where $\underline{\mathbf{G}}_t'$ is an $m \times m$ matrix the kth row of which is equal to $(g_{tk}^1, g_{tk}^2, \ldots, g_{tk}^m)$ and $\{\quad\}_{kl}^{-1}$ denotes the k,lth element of the inverse of the matrix inside $\{\quad\}$. Now, we obtain from (9.3.12)

$$\mathbf{A}_{kl} = \sum_t \mathbf{x}_{tk}\{\underline{\mathbf{F}}_t'\mathbf{\Lambda}_t^{-1}\underline{\mathbf{F}}_t\}_{kl}\mathbf{x}_{tl}', \tag{9.3.22}$$

where $\underline{\mathbf{F}}_t'$ is an $m \times m$ matrix the kth row of which is equal to $(f_{tk}^1, f_{tk}^2, \ldots, f_{tk}^m)$. Thus the asymptotic equivalence of MIN χ^2 and MLE follows from the identity $\underline{\mathbf{G}}_t^{-1} = \underline{\mathbf{F}}_t'$.

In the preceding discussion we assumed $H = m$. If $H < m$, we can still invert (9.3.18) and obtain

$$\mathbf{x}_{tk}'\boldsymbol{\beta}_k = G_k(P_{t1}, P_{t2}, \ldots, P_{tm}), \tag{9.3.23}$$

$$t = 1, 2, \ldots, T \quad \text{and} \quad k = 1, 2, \ldots, H,$$

but the choice of function G_k is not unique. Amemiya (1976b) has shown that the MIN χ^2 estimator is asymptotically efficient only when we choose the correct function G_k from the many possible ones. This fact diminishes the usefulness of the method. For this case Amemiya (1977c) proposed the following method, which always leads to an asymptotically efficient estimator.

Step 1. Use some G_k in (9.3.23) and define

$$\hat{\mu}_{tk} = G_k(\hat{P}_{t1}, \hat{P}_{t2}, \ldots, \hat{P}_{tm}).$$

Step 2. In (9.3.17) replace $\bar{\mathbf{F}}_i$ and $\bar{\mathbf{f}}_i^h$ by $\mathbf{F}_i$ and $\mathbf{f}_i^h$ evaluated at $\hat{\mu}_{tk}$ and replace $\mathbf{x}_{ih}'\bar{\boldsymbol{\beta}}_h$ by $\hat{\mu}_{tk}$.

Step 3. Apply FGLS on (9.3.17) using $\mathbf{\Lambda}_i$ evaluated at $\hat{\mu}_{tk}$.

We shall conclude this subsection by generalizing WSSR defined by (9.2.42) and (9.2.45) to the multinomial case.

We shall not write the analog of (9.2.42) explicitly because it would require cumbersome notation, although the idea is simple. Instead, we shall merely point out that it is of the form $(\mathbf{y} - \mathbf{X}\hat{\boldsymbol{\beta}}_G)'\hat{\boldsymbol{\Sigma}}^{-1}(\mathbf{y} - \mathbf{X}\hat{\boldsymbol{\beta}}_G)$ obtained from the regression equation (9.3.20). It is asymptotically distributed as chi-square with degrees of freedom equal to mT minus the number of regression parameters.

Next, consider the generalization of (9.2.45). Define the vector $\tilde{\mathbf{F}}_t = \mathbf{F}_t(\tilde{\boldsymbol{\beta}})$. Then, the analog of (9.2.45) is

$$\begin{aligned} \text{WSSR} &= \sum_{t=1}^{T} (\hat{\mathbf{P}}_t - \tilde{\mathbf{F}}_t)'\hat{\boldsymbol{\Lambda}}_t^{-1}(\hat{\mathbf{P}}_t - \tilde{\mathbf{F}}_t) \qquad (9.3.24) \\ &= \sum_{t=1}^{T} n_t(\hat{\mathbf{P}}_t - \tilde{\mathbf{F}}_t)'[\mathbf{D}(\hat{\mathbf{P}}_t)^{-1} + \hat{P}_{t0}^{-1}\mathbf{l}\mathbf{l}'](\hat{\mathbf{P}}_t - \tilde{\mathbf{F}}_t) \\ &= \sum_{t=1}^{T} n_t \sum_{j=0}^{m} \frac{(\hat{P}_{tj} - \tilde{F}_{tj})^2}{\hat{P}_{tj}}. \end{aligned}$$

It is asymptotically equivalent to the analog of (9.2.42).

9.3.2 Ordered Models

Multinomial QR models can be classified into ordered and unordered models. In this subsection we shall discuss ordered models, and in the remainder of Section 9.3 we shall discuss various types of unordered models.

A general definition of the ordered model is

DEFINITION 9.3.1. The ordered model is defined by

$$P(y = j|\mathbf{x}, \theta) = p(S_j)$$

for some probability measure p depending on $\mathbf{x}$ and θ and a finite sequence of successive intervals $\{S_j\}$ depending on $\mathbf{x}$ and θ such that $\cup_j S_j = R$, the real line.

A model is unordered if it is not ordered. In other words, in the ordered model the values that y takes correspond to a partition of the real line, whereas in the unordered model they correspond either to a nonsuccessive partition of the real line or to a partition of a higher-dimensional Euclidean space.

In most applications the ordered model takes the simpler form

$$P(y = j|\mathbf{x}, \boldsymbol{\alpha}, \boldsymbol{\beta}) = F(\alpha_{j+1} - \mathbf{x}'\boldsymbol{\beta}) - F(\alpha_j - \mathbf{x}'\boldsymbol{\beta}), \qquad (9.3.25)$$

$$j = 0, 1, \ldots, m, \qquad \alpha_0 = -\infty, \qquad \alpha_j \leq \alpha_{j+1}, \qquad \alpha_{m+1} = \infty,$$

for some distribution function F. If $F = \Phi$, (9.3.25) defines the ordered probit model; and if $F = \Lambda$, it defines the ordered logit model. Pratt (1981) showed that the log likelihood function of the model (9.3.25) based on observations $(y_i, \mathbf{x}_i)$, $i = 1, 2, \ldots, n$, on $(y, \mathbf{x})$ is globally concave if f, derivative of F, is positive and $\log f$ is concave.

The model (9.3.25) is motivated by considering an unobserved continuous random variable y^* that determines the outcome of y by the rule

$$y = j \quad \text{if and only if} \quad \alpha_j < y^* < \alpha_{j+1}, \qquad j = 0, 1, \ldots, m. \tag{9.3.26}$$

If the distribution function of $y^* - \mathbf{x}'\boldsymbol{\beta}$ is F, (9.3.26) implies (9.3.25).

In empirical applications of the ordered model, y^* corresponds to a certain interpretative concept. For example, in the study of the effect of an insecticide by Gurland, Lee, and Dahm (1960), y^* signifies the tolerance of an insect against the insecticide. Depending on the value of y^*, y takes three discrete values corresponding to the three states of an insect—dead, moribund, and alive. In the study by David and Legg (1975), y^* is the unobserved price of a house, and the observed values of y correspond to various ranges of the price of a house. In the study by Silberman and Talley (1974), y^* signifies the excess demand for banking in a particular location and y the number of chartered bank offices in the location. See also Example 9.4.1 in Section 9.4.1.

The use of the ordered model is less common in econometric applications than in biometric applications. This must be due to the fact that economic phenomena are complex and difficult to explain in terms of only a single unobserved index variable. We should be cautious in using an ordered model because if the true model is unordered, an ordered model can lead to serious biases in the estimation of the probabilities. On the other hand, the cost of using an unordered model when the true model is ordered is a loss of efficiency rather than consistency.

We shall conclude this subsection by giving an econometric example of an ordered model, which is also an interesting application of the MIN χ^2 method discussed in Section 9.3.1.

EXAMPLE 9.3.1 (Deacon and Shapiro, 1975). In this article Deacon and Shapiro analyzed the voting behavior of Californians in two recent referenda: Rapid Transit Initiative (November 1970) and Coastal Zone Conservation Act (November 1972). We shall take up only the former. Let ΔU_i be the difference between the utilities resulting from rapid transit and no rapid transit for the ith individual. Deacon and Shapiro assumed that ΔU_i is distributed logistically with mean μ_i—that is, $P(\Delta U_i < x) = \Lambda(x - \mu_i)$—and that the individual vote is determined by the rule:

$$\begin{aligned} &\text{Vote yes} && \text{if } \Delta U_i > \delta_i \\ &\text{Vote no} && \text{if } \Delta U_i < -\delta_i \\ &\text{Abstain} && \text{otherwise.} \end{aligned} \tag{9.3.27}$$

Writing $P_i(Y)$ and $P_i(N)$ for the probabilities that the ith individual votes yes and no, respectively, we have

$$P_i(Y) = \Lambda(\mu_i - \delta_i) \tag{9.3.28}$$

and

$$P_i(N) = \Lambda(-\mu_i - \delta_i). \tag{9.3.29}$$

Deacon and Shapiro assumed $\mu_i = \mathbf{x}_i'\boldsymbol{\beta}_1$ and $\delta_i = \mathbf{x}_i'\boldsymbol{\beta}_2$, where $\mathbf{x}_i$ is a vector of independent variables and some elements of $\boldsymbol{\beta}_1$ and $\boldsymbol{\beta}_2$ are *a priori* specified to be zeros. (Note that if $\delta_i = 0$, the model becomes a univariate binary logit model.)

The model (9.3.27) could be estimated by MLE if the individual votes were recorded and $\mathbf{x}_i$ were observable. But, obviously, they are not: We only know the proportion of yes votes and no votes in districts and observed average values of $\mathbf{x}_i$ or their proxies in each district. Thus we are forced to use a method suitable for the case of many observations per cell.[7] Deacon and Shapiro used data on 334 California cities. For this analysis it is necessary to invoke the assumption that $\mathbf{x}_i = \mathbf{x}_t$ for all $i \in I_t$, where I_t is the set of individuals living in the tth city. Then we obtain from (9.3.28) and (9.3.29)

$$\log \frac{P_t(Y)}{1 - P_t(Y)} = \mathbf{x}_t'(\boldsymbol{\beta}_1 - \boldsymbol{\beta}_2) \tag{9.3.30}$$

and

$$\log \frac{P_t(N)}{1 - P_t(N)} = -\mathbf{x}_t'(\boldsymbol{\beta}_1 + \boldsymbol{\beta}_2). \tag{9.3.31}$$

Let $\hat{P}_t(Y)$ and $\hat{P}_t(N)$ be the proportion of yes and no votes in the tth city. Then, expanding the left-hand side of (9.3.30) and (9.3.31) by Taylor series around $\hat{P}_t(Y)$ and $\hat{P}_t(N)$, respectively, we obtain the approximate regression equations

$$\log \frac{\hat{P}_t(Y)}{1 - \hat{P}_t(Y)} \cong \mathbf{x}_t'(\boldsymbol{\beta}_1 - \boldsymbol{\beta}_2) + \frac{1}{P_t(Y)[1 - P_t(Y)]} [\hat{P}_t(Y) - P_t(Y)] \tag{9.3.32}$$

and

$$\log \frac{\hat{P}_t(N)}{1-\hat{P}_t(N)} \cong -\mathbf{x}_t'(\boldsymbol{\beta}_1+\boldsymbol{\beta}_2) + \frac{1}{P_t(N)[1-P_t(N)]}[\hat{P}_t(N)-P_t(N)]. \tag{9.3.33}$$

Note that (9.3.32) and (9.3.33) constitute a special case of (9.3.20). The error terms of these two equations are heteroscedastic and, moreover, correlated with each other. The covariance between the error terms can be obtained from the result Cov $[\hat{P}_t(Y), \hat{P}_t(N)] = -n_t^{-1}P_t(Y)P_t(N)$. The MIN χ^2 estimates of $(\boldsymbol{\beta}_1-\boldsymbol{\beta}_2)$ and $-(\boldsymbol{\beta}_1+\boldsymbol{\beta}_2)$ are obtained by applying generalized least squares to (9.3.32) and (9.3.33), taking into account both heteroscedasticity and the correlation.[8]

9.3.3 Multinomial Logit Model

In this and the subsequent subsections we shall present various types of unordered multinomial QR models. The multinomial logit model is defined by

$$P_{ij} = \left[\sum_{k=0}^{m_i} \exp(\mathbf{x}_{ik}'\boldsymbol{\beta})\right]^{-1} \exp(\mathbf{x}_{ij}'\boldsymbol{\beta}), \tag{9.3.34}$$

$$i = 1, 2, \ldots, n \quad \text{and} \quad j = 0, 1, \ldots, m_i,$$

where we can assume $\mathbf{x}_{i0} = \mathbf{0}$ without loss of generality. The log likelihood function is given by

$$\log L = \sum_{i=1}^{n}\sum_{j=0}^{m_i} y_{ij} \log P_{ij}. \tag{9.3.35}$$

Following McFadden (1974), we shall show the global concavity of (9.3.35).

Differentiating (9.3.35) with respect to $\boldsymbol{\beta}$, we obtain

$$\frac{\partial \log L}{\partial \boldsymbol{\beta}} = \sum_i \sum_j \frac{y_{ij}}{P_{ij}} \frac{\partial P_{ij}}{\partial \boldsymbol{\beta}}, \tag{9.3.36}$$

where Σ_i and Σ_j denote $\Sigma_{i=1}^{n}$ and $\Sigma_{j=0}^{m_i}$, respectively. Differentiating (9.3.36) further yields

$$\frac{\partial^2 \log L}{\partial \boldsymbol{\beta} \partial \boldsymbol{\beta}'} = \sum_i \sum_j \frac{y_{ij}}{P_{ij}} \left[\frac{\partial^2 P_{ij}}{\partial \boldsymbol{\beta} \partial \boldsymbol{\beta}'} - \frac{1}{P_{ij}} \frac{\partial P_{ij}}{\partial \boldsymbol{\beta}} \frac{\partial P_{ij}}{\partial \boldsymbol{\beta}'}\right]. \tag{9.3.37}$$

Next, differentiating (9.3.34), we obtain after some manipulation

$$\frac{\partial P_{ij}}{\partial \boldsymbol{\beta}} = P_{ij}(\mathbf{x}_{ij} - \bar{\mathbf{x}}_i), \tag{9.3.38}$$

where $\bar{\mathbf{x}}_i = [\Sigma_k \exp(\mathbf{x}_{ik}'\boldsymbol{\beta})]^{-1}\Sigma_k \exp(\mathbf{x}_{ik}'\boldsymbol{\beta})\mathbf{x}_{ik}$, and

$$\frac{\partial^2 P_{ij}}{\partial \boldsymbol{\beta}\partial \boldsymbol{\beta}'} = P_{ij}(\mathbf{x}_{ij} - \bar{\mathbf{x}}_i)(\mathbf{x}_{ij} - \bar{\mathbf{x}}_i)' \tag{9.3.39}$$

$$- P_{ij}\left[\sum_k \exp(\mathbf{x}_{ik}'\boldsymbol{\beta})\right]^{-1} \sum_k \exp(\mathbf{x}_{ik}'\boldsymbol{\beta})\mathbf{x}_{ik}\mathbf{x}_{ik}' + P_{ij}\bar{\mathbf{x}}_i\bar{\mathbf{x}}_i'.$$

Inserting (9.3.38) and (9.3.39) into (9.3.37) yields

$$\frac{\partial^2 \log L}{\partial \boldsymbol{\beta}\partial \boldsymbol{\beta}'} = -\sum_i \sum_j P_{ij}(\mathbf{x}_{ij} - \bar{\mathbf{x}}_i)(\mathbf{x}_{ij} - \bar{\mathbf{x}}_i)', \tag{9.3.40}$$

which, interestingly, does not depend on y_{ij}. Because $P_{ij} > 0$ in this model, the matrix (9.3.40) is negative definite unless $(\mathbf{x}_{ij} - \bar{\mathbf{x}}_i)'\boldsymbol{\alpha} = 0$ for every i and j for some $\boldsymbol{\alpha} \neq \mathbf{0}$. Because such an event is extremely unlikely, we can conclude for all practical purposes that the log likelihood function is globally concave in the multinomial logit model.

We shall now discuss an important result of McFadden (1974), which shows how the multinomial logit model can be derived from utility maximization. Consider for simplicity an individual i whose utilities associated with three alternatives are given by

$$U_{ij} = \mu_{ij} + \epsilon_{ij}, \qquad j = 0, 1, \text{ and } 2, \tag{9.3.41}$$

where μ_{ij} is a nonstochastic function of explanatory variables and unknown parameters and ϵ_{ij} is an unobservable random variable. (In the following discussion, we shall write ϵ_j for ϵ_{ij} to simplify the notation.) Thus (9.3.41) is analogous to (9.2.4) and (9.2.5). As in Example 9.2.2, it is assumed that the individual chooses the alternative for which the associated utility is highest. McFadden proved that the multinomial logit model is derived from utility maximization if and only if $\{\epsilon_j\}$ are independent and the distribution function of ϵ_j is given by $\exp[-\exp(-\epsilon_j)]$. This is called the Type I extreme-value distribution, or log Weibull distribution, by Johnson and Kotz (1970, p. 272), who have given many more results about the distribution than are given here. Its density is given by $\exp(-\epsilon_j)\exp[-\exp(\epsilon_j)]$, which has a unique mode at 0 and a mean of approximately 0.577. We shall give only a proof of the *if* part.

Denoting the density given in the preceding paragraph by $f(\cdot)$, we can write the probablity the ith person chooses alternative j as (suppressing the subscript i from μ_{ij} as well as from ϵ_{ij})

$$
\begin{aligned}
P(y_i = 2) &= P(U_{i2} > U_{i1}, U_{i2} > U_{i0}) \qquad (9.3.42)\\
&= P(\epsilon_2 + \mu_2 - \mu_1 > \epsilon_1, \epsilon_2 + \mu_2 - \mu_0 > \epsilon_0)\\
&= \int_{-\infty}^{\infty} f(\epsilon_2) \left[\int_{-\infty}^{\epsilon_2+\mu_2-\mu_1} f(\epsilon_1)\, d\epsilon_1 \cdot \int_{-\infty}^{\epsilon_2+\mu_2-\mu_0} f(\epsilon_0)\, d\epsilon_0 \right] d\epsilon_2\\
&= \int_{-\infty}^{\infty} \exp(-\epsilon_2) \exp[-\exp(-\epsilon_2)]\\
&\quad \times \exp[-\exp(-\epsilon_2 - \mu_2 + \mu_1)]\\
&\quad \times \exp[-\exp(-\epsilon_2 - \mu_2 + \mu_0)]\, d\epsilon_2\\
&= \frac{\exp(\mu_{i2})}{\exp(\mu_{i0}) + \exp(\mu_{i1}) + \exp(\mu_{i2})}.
\end{aligned}
$$

Expression (9.3.42) is equal to P_{i2} given in (9.3.34) if we put $\mu_{i2} - \mu_{i0} = \mathbf{x}_{i2}'\boldsymbol{\beta}$ and $\mu_{i1} - \mu_{i0} = \mathbf{x}_{i1}'\boldsymbol{\beta}$. The expressions for P_{i0} and P_{i1} can be similarly derived.

EXAMPLE 9.3.2. As an application of the multinomial logit model, consider the following hypothetical model of transport modal choice. We assume that the utilities associated with three alternatives—car, bus, and train (corresponding to the subscripts 0, 1, and 2, respectively)—are given by (9.3.41). As in (9.2.4) and (9.2.5), we assume

$$\mu_{ij} = \alpha + \mathbf{z}_{ij}'\boldsymbol{\beta} + \mathbf{w}_i'\boldsymbol{\gamma}, \qquad (9.3.43)$$

where $\mathbf{z}_{ij}$ is a vector of the mode characteristics and $\mathbf{w}_i$ is a vector of the ith person's socioeconomic characteristics. It is assumed that α, $\boldsymbol{\beta}$, and $\boldsymbol{\gamma}$ are constant for all i and j. Then we obtain the multinomial logit model (9.3.34) with $m = 2$ if we put $\mathbf{x}_{i2} = \mathbf{z}_{i2} - \mathbf{z}_{i0}$ and $\mathbf{x}_{i1} = \mathbf{z}_{i1} - \mathbf{z}_{i0}$.

The fact that $\boldsymbol{\beta}$ is constant for all the modes makes this model useful in predicting the demand for a certain new mode that comes into existence. Suppose that an estimate $\hat{\boldsymbol{\beta}}$ of $\boldsymbol{\beta}$ has been obtained in the model with three modes (Example 9.3.2) and that the characteristics $\mathbf{z}_{i3}$ of a new mode (designated by subscript 3) have been ascertained from engineering calculations and a sample survey. Then the probability that the ith person will use the new mode (assuming that the new mode is accessible to the person) can be estimated by

$$P_{i3} = \frac{\exp(\mathbf{x}_{i3}'\hat{\boldsymbol{\beta}})}{1 + \exp(\mathbf{x}_{i1}'\hat{\boldsymbol{\beta}}) + \exp(\mathbf{x}_{i2}'\hat{\boldsymbol{\beta}}) + \exp(\mathbf{x}_{i3}'\hat{\boldsymbol{\beta}})} \tag{9.3.44}$$

where $\mathbf{x}_{i3} = \mathbf{z}_{i3} - \mathbf{z}_{i0}$.

We should point out a restrictive property of the multinomial logit model: The assumption of independence of $\{\epsilon_j\}$ implies that the alternatives are dissimilar. Using McFadden's famous example, suppose that the three alternatives in Example 9.3.2 consist of car, red bus, and blue bus, instead of car, bus, and train. In such a case, the independence between ϵ_1 and ϵ_2 is a clearly unreasonable assumption because a high (low) utility for red bus should generally imply a high (low) utility for a blue bus. The probability $P_0 = P(U_0 > U_1, U_0 > U_2)$ calculated under the independence assumption would underestimate the true probability in this case because the assumption ignores the fact that the event $U_0 > U_1$ makes the event $U_0 > U_2$ more likely.

Alternatively, note that in the multinomial logit model the relative probabilities between a pair of alternatives are specified ignoring the third alternative. For example, the relative probabilities between car and red bus are specified the same way regardless of whether the third alternative is blue bus or train. Mathematically, this fact is demonstrated by noting that (9.3.34) implies

$$P(y_i = j | y_i = j \quad \text{or} \quad k) = [\exp(\mathbf{x}_{ij}'\boldsymbol{\beta}) + \exp(\mathbf{x}_{ik}'\boldsymbol{\beta})]^{-1} \exp(\mathbf{x}_{ij}'\boldsymbol{\beta}). \tag{9.3.45}$$

McFadden has called this characteristic of the model *independence from irrelevant alternatives* (IIA).

The following is another example of the model.

EXAMPLE 9.3.3 (McFadden, 1976b). McFadden (1976b) used a multinomial logit model to analyze the selection of highway routes by the California Division of Highways in the San Francisco and Los Angeles Districts during the years 1958–1966. The ith project among $n = 65$ projects chooses one from m_i routes and the selection probability is hypothesized precisely as (9.3.34), where $\mathbf{x}_{ij}$ is interpreted as a vector of the attributes of route j in project i.

There is a subtle conceptual difference between this model and the model of Example 9.3.2. In the latter model, j signifies a certain common type of transport mode for all the individuals i. For example, $j = 0$ means car for all i. In the McFadden model, the jth route of the first project and the jth route of the second project have nothing substantial in common except that both are number j routes. However, this difference is not essential because in this type of model each alternative is completely characterized by its characteristics vector $\mathbf{x}$, and a common name such as car is just as meaningless as a number j in the operation of the model.

McFadden tested the IIA hypothesis by reestimating one of his models using the choice set that consists of the chosen route and one additional route randomly selected from m_i. The idea is that if this hypothesis is true, estimates obtained from a full set of alternatives should be close to estimates obtained by randomly eliminating some nonchosen alternatives. For each coefficient the difference between the two estimates was found to be less than its standard deviation, a finding indicating that the hypothesis is likely to be accepted. However, to be exact, we must test the equality of all the coefficients simultaneously.

Such a test, an application of Hausman's test (see Section 4.5.1), is developed with examples in the article by Hausman and McFadden (1984). They tested the IIA hypothesis in a trichotomous logit model for which the three alternatives are owning an electric dryer, a gas dryer, or no dryer. In one experiment, data on the households without a dryer were discarded to obtain a consistent but inefficient estimator, and in the other experiment, data on those owning electric dryers were discarded. In both experiments Hausman's test rejected the IIA hypothesis at less than 1% significance level. Alternative tests of the IIA hypothesis will be discussed in Section 9.3.5.

9.3.4 Multinomial Discriminant Analysis

The DA model of Section 9.2.8 can be generalized to yield a multinomial DA model defined by

$$\mathbf{x}_i^* | (y_i = j) \sim N(\boldsymbol{\mu}_j, \boldsymbol{\Sigma}_j) \tag{9.3.46}$$

and

$$P(y_i = j) = q_j \tag{9.3.47}$$

for $i = 1, 2, \ldots, n$ and $j = 0, 1, \ldots, m$. By Bayes's rule we obtain

$$P(y_i = j | \mathbf{x}_i^*) = \frac{g_j(\mathbf{x}_i^*) q_j}{\sum_{k=0}^{m} g_k(\mathbf{x}_i^*) q_k}, \tag{9.3.48}$$

where g_j is the density function of $N(\boldsymbol{\mu}_j, \boldsymbol{\Sigma}_j)$. Just as we obtained (9.2.48) from (9.2.46), we can obtain from (9.3.48)

$$\frac{P(y_i = j|\mathbf{x}_i^*)}{P(y_i = 0|\mathbf{x}_i^*)} = \Lambda(\beta_{j(1)} + \boldsymbol{\beta}_{j(2)}'\mathbf{x}_i^* + \mathbf{x}_i^{*\prime}\mathbf{A}\mathbf{x}_i^*), \tag{9.3.49}$$

where $\beta_{j(1)}, \boldsymbol{\beta}_{j(2)}$, and $\mathbf{A}$ are similar to (9.2.49), (9.2.50), and (9.2.51) except that the subscripts 1 and 0 should be changed to j and 0, respectively.

As before, the term $\mathbf{x}_i^{*\prime}\mathbf{A}\mathbf{x}_i^*$ drops out if all the $\boldsymbol{\Sigma}$'s are identical. If we write $\beta_{j(1)} + \boldsymbol{\beta}_{j(2)}'\mathbf{x}_i^* = \boldsymbol{\beta}_j'\mathbf{x}_i$, the DA model with identical variances can be written exactly in the form of (9.3.34), except for a modification of the subscripts of $\boldsymbol{\beta}$ and $\mathbf{x}$.

Examples of multinomial DA models are found in articles by Powers et al. (1978) and Uhler (1968), both of which are summarized by Amemiya (1981).

9.3.5 Nested Logit Model

In Section 9.3.3 we defined the multinomial logit model and pointed out its weakness when some of the alternatives are similar. In this section we shall discuss the nested (or nonindependent) logit model that alleviates that weakness to a certain extent. This model is attributed to McFadden (1977) and is developed in greater detail in a later article by McFadden (1981). We shall analyze a trichotomous model in detail and then generalize the results obtained for this trichotomous model to a general multinomial case.

Let us consider the red bus–blue bus model once more for the purpose of illustration. Let $U_j = \mu_j + \epsilon_j$, $j = 0$, 1, and 2, be the utilities associated with car, red bus, and blue bus. (To avoid unnecessary complication in notation, we have suppressed the subscript i.) We pointed out earlier that it is unreasonable to assume independence between ϵ_1 and ϵ_2, although ϵ_0 may be assumed independent of the other two. McFadden suggested the following bivariate distribution as a convenient way to take account of a correlation between ϵ_1 and ϵ_2:

$$F(\epsilon_1, \epsilon_2) = \exp\{-[\exp(-\rho^{-1}\epsilon_1) + \exp(-\rho^{-1}\epsilon_2)]^{\rho}\}, \tag{9.3.50}$$
$$0 < \rho \leqq 1.$$

Johnson and Kotz (1972, p. 256) called this distribution *Gumbel's Type B bivariate extreme-value distribution.* The correlation coefficient can be shown to be $1 - \rho^2$. If $\rho = 1$ (the case of independence), $F(\epsilon_1, \epsilon_2)$ becomes the product of two Type I extreme-value distributions—in other words, the multinomial logit model. As for ϵ_0, we assume $F(\epsilon_0) = \exp[-\exp(-\epsilon_0)]$ as in the multinomial logit model.

Under these assumptions we can show

$$P(y=0) = \frac{\exp(\mu_0)}{\exp(\mu_0) + [\exp(\rho^{-1}\mu_1) + \exp(\rho^{-1}\mu_2)]^\rho} \tag{9.3.51}$$

and

$$P(y=1|y\neq 0) = \frac{\exp(\rho^{-1}\mu_1)}{\exp(\rho^{-1}\mu_1) + \exp(\rho^{-1}\mu_2)}. \tag{9.3.52}$$

The other probabilities can be deduced from (9.3.51) and (9.3.52). Therefore these two equations define a nested logit model in the trichotomous case. By dividing the numerator and the denominator of (9.3.51) by $\exp(\mu_0)$ and those of (9.3.52) by $\exp(-\rho^{-1}\mu_1)$, we note that the probabilities depend on $\mu_2 - \mu_0$, $\mu_1 - \mu_0$, and ρ. We would normally specify $\mu_j = \mathbf{x}_j'\boldsymbol{\beta}$, $j = 0, 1, 2$. The estimation of $\boldsymbol{\beta}$ and ρ will be discussed for more general nested logit models later.

The form of these two probabilities is intuitively attractive. Equation (9.3.52) shows that the choice between the two similar alternatives is made according to a binary logit model, whereas (9.3.51) suggests that the choice between car and noncar is also like a logit model except that a certain kind of a weighted average of $\exp(\mu_1)$ and $\exp(\mu_2)$ is used.

To obtain (9.3.51), note that

$$\begin{aligned} P(y=0) &= P(U_0 > U_1, U_0 > U_2) \\ &= P(\mu_0 + \epsilon_0 > \mu_1 + \epsilon_1, \mu_0 + \epsilon_0 > \mu_2 + \epsilon_2) \\ &= \int_{-\infty}^{\infty} \left\{ \int_{-\infty}^{\epsilon_0+\mu_0-\mu_1} \left[\int_{-\infty}^{\epsilon_0+\mu_0-\mu_2} \exp(-\epsilon_0) \right.\right. \\ &\quad \left.\left. \times \exp[-\exp(-\epsilon_0)] f(\epsilon_1, \epsilon_2)\, d\epsilon_2 \right] d\epsilon_1 \right\} d\epsilon_0 \\ &= \int_{-\infty}^{\infty} \exp(-\epsilon_0) \exp[-\exp(-\epsilon_0)] \\ &\quad \times \exp(-\{\exp[-\rho^{-1}(\epsilon_0 + \mu_0 - \mu_1)] \\ &\quad + \exp[-\rho^{-1}(\epsilon_0 + \mu_0 - \mu_2)]\}^\rho)\, d\epsilon_0 \\ &= \int_{-\infty}^{\infty} \exp(-\epsilon_0) \exp[-\alpha \exp(-\epsilon_0)]\, d\epsilon_0 \\ &= \alpha^{-1}, \end{aligned} \tag{9.3.53}$$

where $\alpha = 1 + \exp(-\mu_0)[\exp(\rho^{-1}\mu_1) + \exp(\rho^{-1}\mu_2)]^\rho$.

To obtain (9.3.52), we first observe that

$$P(y=1|y\neq 0)=P(U_1>U_2|U_1>U_0 \quad \text{or} \quad U_2>U_0) \qquad (9.3.54)$$
$$=P(U_1>U_2),$$

where the last equality follows from our particular distributional assumptions. Next we obtain

$$P(U_1>U_2)=P(\mu_1+\epsilon_1>\mu_2+\epsilon_2) \qquad (9.3.55)$$
$$=\int_{-\infty}^{\infty}\left[\int_{-\infty}^{\epsilon_1+\mu_1-\mu_2} f(\epsilon_1,\epsilon_2)\,d\epsilon_2\right]d\epsilon_1$$
$$=\int_{-\infty}^{\infty}\exp(-\epsilon_1)\{1+\exp[-\rho^{-1}(\mu_1-\mu_2)]\}^{\rho-1}$$
$$\times\exp(-\exp(-\epsilon_1)$$
$$\times\{1+\exp[-\rho^{-1}(\mu_1-\mu_2)]\}^{\rho})\,d\epsilon_1$$
$$=\{1+\exp[-\rho^{-1}(\mu_1-\mu_2)]\}^{-1},$$

where in the third equality we used

$$\frac{\partial F(\epsilon_1,\epsilon_2)}{\partial\epsilon_1}=[\exp(-\rho^{-1}\epsilon_1)+\exp(-\rho^{-1}\epsilon_2)]^{\rho-1} \qquad (9.3.56)$$
$$\times\exp(-\rho^{-1}\epsilon_1)F(\epsilon_1,\epsilon_2).$$

The model defined by (9.3.51) and (9.3.52) is reduced to the multinomial logit model if $\rho=1$. Therefore the IIA hypothesis, which is equivalent to the hypothesis $\rho=1$, can be tested against the alternative hypothesis of the nested logit model by any one of the three asymptotic tests described in Section 4.5.1. Hausman and McFadden (1984) performed the three tests using the data on the households' holdings of dryers, which we discussed in Section 9.3.3. The utilities of owning the two types of dryers were assumed to be correlated with each other, and the utility of owning no dryer was assumed to be independent of the other utilities. As did Hausman's test, all three tests rejected the IIA hypothesis at less than 1% significance level. They also conducted a Monte Carlo analysis of Hausman's test and the three asymptotic tests in a hypothetical trichotomous nested logit model. Their findings were as follows: (1) Even with $n=1000$, the observed frequency of rejecting the null hypothesis using the Wald and Rao tests differed greatly from the nominal size, whereas it was better for the LRT. (2) The power of the Wald test after correcting for the size was best, with Hausman's test a close second.

Next, we shall generalize the trichotomous nested logit model defined by (9.3.51) and (9.3.52) to the general case of $m+1$ responses. Suppose that the $m+1$ integers $0, 1, \ldots, m$ can be naturally partitioned into S groups so that each group consists of similar alternatives. Write the partition as

$$(0, 1, 2, \ldots, m) = B_1 \cup B_2 \cup \ldots \cup B_S, \tag{9.3.57}$$

where $\cup$ denotes the union. Then McFadden suggested the joint distribution

$$F(\epsilon_0, \epsilon_1, \ldots, \epsilon_m) = \exp \left\{ -\sum_{s=1}^{S} a_s \left[\sum_{j \in B_s} \exp(-\rho_s^{-1}\epsilon_j) \right]^{\rho_s} \right\}. \tag{9.3.58}$$

Then it can be shown that

$$\sum_{j \in B_s} P_j = \frac{a_s \left[\sum_{j \in B_s} \exp(\rho_s^{-1}\mu_j) \right]^{\rho_s}}{\sum_{\tau=1}^{S} a_\tau \left[\sum_{j \in B_\tau} \exp(\rho_\tau^{-1}\mu_j) \right]^{\rho_\tau}}, \tag{9.3.59}$$

$$s = 1, 2, \ldots, S,$$

and

$$P(y = j | j \in B_s) = \frac{\exp(\rho_s^{-1}\mu_j)}{\sum_{k \in B_s} \exp(\rho_s^{-1}\mu_k)}, \qquad s = 1, 2, \ldots, S. \tag{9.3.60}$$

Note that (9.3.59) and (9.3.60) are generalizations of (9.3.51) and (9.3.52), respectively. Clearly, these probabilities define the model completely. As before, we can interpret

$$\left[\sum_{j \in B_\tau} \exp(\rho_\tau^{-1}\mu_j) \right]^{\rho_\tau}$$

as a kind of weighted average of $\exp(\mu_j)$ for $j \in B_\tau$.

The nested logit model defined by (9.3.59) and (9.3.60) can be estimated by MLE, but it also can be consistently estimated by a natural two-step method, which is computationally simpler. Suppose we specify $\mu_j = \mathbf{x}_j'\boldsymbol{\beta}$. First, the part of the likelihood function that is the product of the conditional probabilities of the form (9.3.60) is maximized to yield an estimate of $\rho_s^{-1}\boldsymbol{\beta}$. Second, this estimate is inserted into the right-hand side of (9.3.59), and the product of (9.3.59) over s and i (which is suppressed) is maximized to yield estimates of ρ's and a's (one of the a's can be arbitrarily set). The asymptotic covariance matrix of these elements is given in McFadden (1981).

In a large-scale nested logit model, the two-step method is especially useful because of the near infeasibility of MLE. Another merit of the two-step method is that it yields consistent estimates that can be used to start a Newton-Raphson iteration to compute MLE, as done by Hausman and McFadden.

We shall present two applications of the nested logit model.

EXAMPLE 9.3.4 (Small and Brownstone, 1982). Small and Brownstone applied a nested logit model to analyze trip timing. The dependent variable takes 12 values corresponding to different arrival times, and the authors experimented with various ways of "nesting" the 12 responses, for example, $B_1 = (1, 2, \ldots, 8)$ and $B_2 = (9, 10, 11, 12)$ or $B_1 = (1, 2, \ldots, 8)$, $B_2 = (9)$, and $B_3 = (10, 11, 12)$. All a's were assumed to be equal to 1, and various specifications of the ρ's were tried. Small and Brownstone found that the two-step estimator had much larger variances than the MLE and often yielded unreasonable values. Also, the computation of the asymptotic covariance matrix of the two-step estimator took as much time as the second-round estimator obtained in the Newton-Raphson iteration, even though the fully iterated Newton-Raphson iteration took six times as much time.

EXAMPLE 9.3.5 (McFadden, 1978). A person chooses a community to live in and a type of dwelling to live in. There are S communities; integers in B_s signify the types of dwellings available in community s. Set $a_s =$ a constant, $\rho_s =$ a constant, and $\mu_{cd} = \boldsymbol{\beta}'\mathbf{x}_{cd} + \boldsymbol{\alpha}'\mathbf{z}_c$. Then

$$P(\text{community } c \text{ is chosen}) = \frac{\left\{\sum_{d \in B_c} \exp\,[\rho^{-1}(\boldsymbol{\beta}'\mathbf{x}_{cd} + \boldsymbol{\alpha}'\mathbf{z}_c)]\right\}^{\rho}}{\sum_{c'} \left\{\sum_{d \in B_{c'}} \exp\,[\rho^{-1}(\boldsymbol{\beta}'\mathbf{x}_{c'd} + \boldsymbol{\alpha}'\mathbf{z}_{c'})]\right\}^{\rho}} \tag{9.3.61}$$

and

$$P(\text{dwelling } d \text{ is chosen} \mid c \text{ is chosen}) = \frac{\exp\,(\rho^{-1}\boldsymbol{\beta}'\mathbf{x}_{cd})}{\sum_{d' \in B_c} \exp\,(\rho^{-1}\boldsymbol{\beta}'\mathbf{x}_{cd'})}. \tag{9.3.62}$$

As in this example, a nested logit is useful when a set of utilities can be naturally classified into independent classes while nonzero correlation is allowed among utilities within each class.

9.3.6 Higher-Level Nested Logit Model

The nested logit model defined in the preceding section can be regarded as implying two levels of nesting because the responses are classified into S groups and each group is further classified into the individual elements. In this section we shall consider a three-level nested logit. A generalization to a higher level can be easily deduced from the three-level case.

Figure 9.1 shows examples of two-level and three-level nested logit models for the case of eight responses.

Following McFadden (1981), we can generalize (9.3.58) to the three-level case by defining

$$F(\epsilon_0, \epsilon_1, \ldots, \epsilon_m) = \exp\left(-\sum_u b_u \left\{\sum_{s\in C_u} a_s \left[\sum_{j\in B_s} \exp(-\rho_s^{-1}\epsilon_j)\right]^{\rho_s/\sigma_u}\right\}^{\sigma_u}\right). \tag{9.3.63}$$

Then (9.3.59) and (9.3.60) can be generalized to

$$P(y=j|s) = \frac{\exp(\mu_j/\rho_s)}{\sum_{k\in B_s} \exp(\mu_k/\rho_s)}, \tag{9.3.64}$$

$$\sum_{j\in B_s} P(y=j|u) = \frac{a_s\left[\sum_{j\in B_s} \exp(\mu_j/\rho_s)\right]^{\rho_s/\sigma_u}}{\sum_{\tau\in C_u} a_\tau \left[\sum_{j\in B_\tau} \exp(\mu_j/\rho_\tau)\right]^{\rho_\tau/\sigma_u}}, \tag{9.3.65}$$

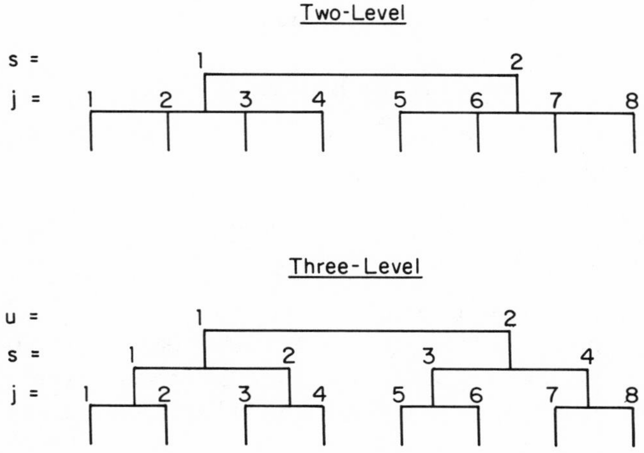

Figure 9.1 Two-level and three-level nested logit models

and

$$\sum_{j\in C_u} P(y=j) = \frac{b_u\left\{\sum_{\tau\in C_u} a_\tau\left[\sum_{j\in B_\tau}\exp(\mu_j/\rho_\tau)\right]^{\rho_\tau/\sigma_u}\right\}^{\sigma_u}}{\sum_w b_w\left\{\sum_{\tau\in C_w} a_\tau\left[\sum_{j\in B_\tau}\exp(\mu_j/\rho_\tau)\right]^{\rho_\tau/\sigma_w}\right\}^{\sigma_w}}. \tag{9.3.66}$$

A three-step estimation method can be defined in which, first, the parameters in (9.3.64) are estimated by maximizing the product of the terms of the form (9.3.64). Then these estimates are inserted into (9.3.65), and the product of the terms of the form (9.3.65) is maximized to yield the estimates of its parameters. Finally, (9.3.66) is maximized after inserting the estimates obtained by the first and second steps.

9.3.7 Generalized Extreme-Value Model

McFadden (1978) introduced the *generalized extreme-value* (GEV) *distribution* defined by

$$\begin{aligned} &F(\epsilon_1, \epsilon_2, \ldots, \epsilon_m) \\ &\quad = \exp\{-G[\exp(-\epsilon_1), \exp(-\epsilon_2), \ldots, \exp(-\epsilon_m)]\}, \end{aligned} \tag{9.3.67}$$

where G satisfies the conditions,

(i) $G(u_1, u_2, \ldots, u_m) \geqq 0, \quad u_1, u_2, \ldots, u_m \geqq 0.$

(ii) $G(\alpha u_1, \alpha u_2, \ldots, \alpha u_m) = \alpha G(u_1, u_2, \ldots, u_m).$

(iii) $\dfrac{\partial^k G}{\partial u_{i_1}\partial u_{i_2}\ldots\partial u_{i_k}} \geqq 0 \quad \text{if } k \text{ is odd}$

$\leqq 0 \quad \text{if } k \text{ is even}, \quad k = 1, 2, \ldots, m.$

If $U_j = \mu_j + \epsilon_j$ and the alternative with the highest utility is chosen as before, (9.3.67) implies the GEV model

$$P_j = \frac{\exp(\mu_j) G_j[\exp(\mu_1), \exp(\mu_2), \ldots, \exp(\mu_m)]}{G[\exp(\mu_1), \exp(\mu_2), \ldots, \exp(\mu_m)]}, \tag{9.3.68}$$

where G_j is the derivative of G with respect to its jth argument.

Both the nested logit model and the higher-level nested logit model discussed in the preceding sections are special cases of the GEV model. The only known application of the GEV model that is not a nested logit model is in a study by Small (1981).

The multinomial models presented in the subsequent subsections do not belong to the class of GEV models.

9.3.8 Universal Logit Model

In Section 9.2.1 we stated that for a binary QR model a given probability function $G(\mathbf{x}_i^*, \theta)$ can be approximated by $F[H(\mathbf{x}_i^*, \theta)]$ by choosing an appropriate $H(\mathbf{x}_i^*, \theta)$ for a given F. When F is chosen to be the logistic function Λ, such a model is called a *universal logit model.* A similar fact holds in the multinomial case as well. Consider the trichotomous case of Example 9.3.2. A universal logit model is defined by

$$P_{i2} = \frac{\exp(g_{i2})}{1 + \exp(g_{i1}) + \exp(g_{i2})}, \tag{9.3.69}$$

$$P_{i1} = \frac{\exp(g_{i1})}{1 + \exp(g_{i1}) + \exp(g_{i2})}, \tag{9.3.70}$$

and

$$P_{i0} = \frac{1}{1 + \exp(g_{i1}) + \exp(g_{i2})}, \tag{9.3.71}$$

where g_{i1} and g_{i2} are functions of *all* the explanatory variables of the model—$\mathbf{z}_{i0}$, $\mathbf{z}_{i1}$, $\mathbf{z}_{i2}$, and $\mathbf{w}_i$. Any arbitrary trichotomous model can be approximated by this model by choosing the functions g_{i1} and g_{i2} appropriately. As long as g_{i1} and g_{i2} depend on all the mode characteristics, the universal logit model does not satisfy the assumption of the independence from irrelevant alternatives. When the g's are linear in the explanatory variables with coefficients that generally vary with the alternatives, the model is reduced to a multinomial logit model sometimes used in applications (see Cox, 1966, p. 65), which differs from the one defined in Section 9.3.3.

9.3.9 Multinomial Probit Model

Let U_j, $j = 0, 1, 2, \ldots, m$, be the stochastic utility associated with the jth alternative for a particular individual. By the multinomial probit model, we mean the model in which $\{U_j\}$ are jointly normally distributed. Such a model was first proposed by Aitchison and Bennett (1970). This model has rarely been used in practice until recently because of its computational difficulty (except, of course, when $m = 1$, in which case the model is reduced to a binary probit model, which is discussed in Section 9.2). To illustrate the complexity of the problem, consider the case of $m = 2$. Then, to evaluate $P(y = 2)$, for example, we must calculate the multiple integral

$$P(y=2) = P(U_2 > U_1, U_2 > U_0) \tag{9.3.72}$$
$$= \int_{-\infty}^{\infty} \int_{-\infty}^{U_2} \int_{-\infty}^{U_2} f(U_0, U_1, U_2)\, dU_0\, dU_1\, dU_2,$$

where f is a trivariate normal density. The direct computation of such an integral is involved even for the case of $m = 3$.[9] Moreover, (9.3.72) must be evaluated at each step of an iterative method to maximize the likelihood function.

Hausman and Wise (1978) estimated a trichotomous probit model to explain the modal choice among driving own car, sharing rides, and riding a bus, for 557 workers in Washington, D.C. They specified the utilities by

$$U_{ij} = \beta_{i1} \log x_{1ij} + \beta_{i2} \log x_{2ij} + \beta_{i3} \frac{x_{3i}}{x_{4ij}} + \epsilon_{ij}, \tag{9.3.73}$$

where x_1, x_2, x_3, and x_4 represent in-vehicle time, out-of-vehicle time, income, and cost, respectively. They assume that $(\beta_{i1}, \beta_{i2}, \beta_{i3}, \epsilon_{ij})$ are independently (with each other) normally distributed with means $(\bar{\beta}_1, \bar{\beta}_2, \bar{\beta}_3, 0)$ and variances $(\sigma_1^2, \sigma_2^2, \sigma_3^2, 1)$. It is assumed that ϵ_{ij} are independent both through i and j and β's are independent through i; therefore correlation between U_{ij} and U_{ik} occurs because of the same β's appearing for all the alternatives. Hausman and Wise evaluated integrals of the form (9.3.72) using series expansion and noted that the method is feasible for a model with up to five alternatives.

Hausman and Wise also used two other models to analyze the same data: *Multinomial Logit* (derived from Eq. 9.3.73 by assuming that β's are nonstochastic and ϵ_{ij} are independently distributed as Type I extreme-value distribution) and *Independent Probit* (derived from the model defined in the preceding paragraph by putting $\sigma_1^2 = \sigma^2{}_2 = \sigma_3^2 = 0$). We shall call the original model *Nonindependent Probit.* The conclusions of Hausman and Wise are that (1) Logit and Independent Probit give similar results both in estimation and in the forecast of the probability of using a new mode; (2) Nonindependent Probit differs significantly from the other two models both in estimation and the forecast about the new mode; and (3) Nonindependent Probit fits best. The likelihood ratio test rejects Independent Probit in favor of Nonindependent Probit at the 7% significance level. These results appear promising for further development of the model.

Albright, Lerman, and Manski (1977) (see also Lerman and Manski, 1981) developed a computer program for calculating the ML estimator (by a gradient iterative method) of a multinomial probit model similar to, but slightly more general than, the model of Hausman and Wise. Their specification is

$$U_{ij} = \mathbf{x}_{ij}'\boldsymbol{\beta}_i + \epsilon_{ij}, \tag{9.3.74}$$

where $\boldsymbol{\beta}_i \sim N(\bar{\boldsymbol{\beta}}, \boldsymbol{\Sigma}_\beta)$ and $\boldsymbol{\epsilon}_i = (\epsilon_{i0}, \epsilon_{i1}, \ldots, \epsilon_{im}) \sim N(\mathbf{0}, \boldsymbol{\Sigma}_\epsilon)$. As in Hausman and Wise, $\boldsymbol{\beta}_i$ and $\boldsymbol{\epsilon}_i$ are assumed to be independent of each other and independent through i. A certain normalization is employed on the parameters to make them identifiable.

An interesting feature of their computer program is that it gives the user the option of calculating the probability in the form (9.3.72) at each step of the iteration either (1) by simulation or (2) by Clark's approximation (Clark, 1961), rather than by series expansion. The authors claim that their program can handle as many as ten alternatives. The simulation works as follows: Consider evaluating (9.3.72), for example. We artificially generate many observations on U_0, U_1, and U_2 according to f evaluated at particular parameter values and simply estimate the probability by the observed frequency. Clark's method is based on a normal approximation of the distribution of max (X, Y) when both X and Y are normally distributed. The exact mean and variance of max (X, Y), which can be evaluated easily, are used in the approximation. Albright, Lerman, and Manski performed a Monte Carlo study, which showed Clark's method to be quite accurate. However, several other authors have contradicted this conclusion, saying that Clark's approximation can be quite erratic in some cases (see, for example, Horowitz, Sparmann, and Daganzo, 1982).

Albright et al. applied their probit model to the same data that Hausman and Wise used, and they estimated the parameters of their model by Clark's method. Their model is more general than the model of Hausman and Wise, and their independent variables contained additional variables such as mode-specific dummies and the number of automobiles in the household. They also estimated an independent logit model. Their conclusions were as follows:

1. Their probit and logit estimates did not differ by much. (They compared the raw estimates rather than comparing $\partial P/\partial x$ for each independent variable.)
2. They could not obtain accurate estimates of $\boldsymbol{\Sigma}_\beta$ in their probit model.
3. Based on the Akaike Information Criterion (Section 4.5.2), an increase in log L in their probit model as compared to their logit model was not large enough to compensate for the loss in degrees of freedom.

4. The logit model took 4.5 seconds per iteration, whereas the probit model took 60–75 CPU seconds per iteration on an IBM 370 Model 158. Thus, though they demonstrated the feasibility of their probit model, the gain of using the probit model over the independent logit did not seem to justify the added cost for this particular data set.

The discrepancy between the conclusions of Hausman and Wise and those of Albright et al. is probably due to the fact that Hausman and Wise imposed certain zero specifications on the covariance matrix, an observation that suggests that covariance specification plays a crucial role in this type of model.

9.3.10 Sequential Probit and Logit Models

When the choice decision is made sequentially, the estimation of multinomial models can be reduced to the successive estimation of models with fewer responses, and this results in computational economy. We shall illustrate this with a three-response sequential probit model. Suppose an individual determines whether $y=2$ or $y\neq 2$ and then, given $y\neq 2$, determines whether $y=1$ or 0. Assuming that each choice is made according to a binary probit model, we can specify a sequential probit model by

$$P_2 = \Phi(\mathbf{x}_2'\boldsymbol{\beta}_2) \tag{9.3.75}$$

and

$$P_1 = [1-\Phi(\mathbf{x}_2'\boldsymbol{\beta}_2)]\Phi(\mathbf{x}_1'\boldsymbol{\beta}_1). \tag{9.3.76}$$

The likelihood function of this model can be maximized by maximizing the likelihood function of two binary probit models.

A sequential logit model can be analogously defined. Kahn and Morimune (1979) used such a model to explain the number of employment spells a worker experienced in 1966 by independent variables such as the number of grades completed, a health dummy, a marriage dummy, the number of children, a part-time employment dummy, and experience. The dependent variable y_i is assumed to take one of the four values (0, 1, 2, and 3) corresponding to the number of spells experienced by the ith worker, except that $y_i=3$ means "greater than or equal to 3 spells." Kahn and Morimune specified probabilities sequentially as

$$P(y_i=0) = \Lambda(\mathbf{x}_i'\boldsymbol{\beta}_0), \tag{9.3.77}$$

$$P(y_i=1|y_i\neq 0) = \Lambda(\mathbf{x}_i'\boldsymbol{\beta}_1), \tag{9.3.78}$$

and

$$P(y_i = 2 | y_i \neq 0, y_i \neq 1) = \Lambda(\mathbf{x}_i'\boldsymbol{\beta}_2). \tag{9.3.79}$$

Note that Kahn and Morimune could have used an ordered logit model with their data because we can conjecture that a continuous unobservable variable y_i^* (interpreted as a measure of the tendency for unemployment) exists that affects the discrete outcome. Specifying $y_i^* = \mathbf{x}_i'\boldsymbol{\beta} + \epsilon_i$ would lead to one of the ordered models discussed in Section 9.3.2.

9.4 Multivariate Models

9.4.1 Introduction

A multivariate QR model specifies the joint probability distribution of two or more discrete dependent variables. For example, suppose there are two binary dependent variables y_1 and y_2, each of which takes values 1 or 0. Their joint distribution can be described by Table 9.1, where $P_{jk} = P(y_1 = j, y_2 = k)$. The model is completed by specifying P_{11}, P_{10}, and P_{01} as functions of independent variables and unknown parameters. (P_{00} is determined as one minus the sum of the other three probabilities.)

A multivariate QR model is a special case of a multinomial QR model. For example, the model represented by Table 9.1 is equivalent to a multinomial model for a single discrete dependent variable that takes four values with probabilities P_{11}, P_{10}, P_{01}, and P_{00}. Therefore the theory of statistical inference discussed in regard to a multinomial model in Section 9.3.1 is valid for a multivariate model without modification.

In the subsequent sections we shall present various types of multivariate QR models and show in each model how the probabilities are specified to take account of the multivariate features of the model.

Before going into the discussion of various ways to specify multivariate QR models, we shall comment on an empirical article that is concerned with a

Table 9.1 Joint distribution of two binary random variables

	y_2	
y_1	1	0
1	P_{11}	P_{10}
0	P_{01}	P_{00}

multivariate model but in which its specific multivariate features are (perhaps justifiably) ignored. By doing this, we hope to shed some light on the distinction between a multivariate model and the other multinomial models.

EXAMPLE 9.4.1 (Silberman and Durden, 1976). Silberman and Durden analyzed how representatives voted on two bills (House bill and Substitute bill) concerning the minimum wage. The independent variables are the socioeconomic characteristics of a legislator's congressional district, namely, the campaign contribution of labor unions, the campaign contribution of small businesses, the percentage of persons earning less than $4000, the percentage of persons aged 16–21, and a dummy for the South. Denoting House bill and Substitute bill by H and S, the actual counts of votes on the bills are given in Table 9.2.

The zero count in the last cell explains why Silberman and Durden did not set up a multivariate QR model to analyze the data. Instead, they used an ordered probit model by ordering the three nonzero responses in the order of a representative's feeling in favor of the minimum wage as shown in Table 9.3. Assuming that y^* is normally distributed with mean linearly dependent on the independent variables, Silberman and Durden specified the probabilities as

$$P_{i0} = \Phi(\mathbf{x}_i'\boldsymbol{\beta}) \tag{9.4.1}$$

and

$$P_{i0} + P_{i1} = \Phi(\mathbf{x}_i'\boldsymbol{\beta} + \alpha), \tag{9.4.2}$$

where $\alpha > 0$.

An alternative specification that takes into consideration the multivariate nature of the problem and at the same time recognizes the zero count of the last cell may be developed in the form of a sequential probit model (Section 9.3.10) as follows:

$$P(\mathrm{H}_i = \mathrm{Yes}) = \Phi(\mathbf{x}_i'\boldsymbol{\beta}_1) \tag{9.4.3}$$

Table 9.2 Votes on House (H) and Substitute (S) bills

Vote for Substitute bill	Vote for House bill: Yes	Vote for House bill: No
Yes	75	119
No	205	0

Table 9.3 Index of feeling toward the minimum wage

y	S	H	y^* (feeling in favor of the minimum wage)
0	Yes	No	Weakest
1	Yes	Yes	Medium
2	No	Yes	Strongest

and

$$P(\mathrm{S}_i = \mathrm{No}|\mathrm{H}_i = \mathrm{Yes}) = \Phi(\mathbf{x}_i'\boldsymbol{\beta}_2). \tag{9.4.4}$$

The choice between these two models must be determined, first, from a theoretical standpoint based on an analysis of the legislator's behavior and, second, if the first consideration is not conclusive, from a statistical standpoint based on some measure of goodness of fit. Because the two models involve different numbers of parameters, adjustments for the degrees of freedom, such as the Akaike Information Criterion (Section 4.5.2), must be employed. The problem boils down to the question, Is the model defined by (9.4.3) and (9.4.4) sufficiently better than the model defined by (9.4.1) and (9.4.2) to compensate for a reduction in the degrees of freedom?

9.4.2 Multivariate Nested Logit Model

The model to be discussed in this subsection is identical to the nested logit model discussed in Section 9.3.5. We shall merely give an example of its use in a multivariate situation. We noted earlier that the nested logit model is useful whenever a set of alternatives can be classified into classes each of which contains similar alternatives. It is useful in a multivariate situation because the alternatives can be naturally classified according to the outcome of one of the variables. For example, in a 2×2 case such as in Table 9.1, the four alternatives can be classified according to whether $y_1 = 1$ or $y_1 = 0$. Using a parameterization similar to Example 9.3.5, we can specialize the nested logit model to a 2×2 multivariate model as follows:

$$\begin{aligned} P(y_1 = 1) = {} & a_1 \exp(\mathbf{z}_1'\boldsymbol{\gamma})[\exp(\rho_1^{-1}\mathbf{x}_{11}'\boldsymbol{\beta}) + \exp(\rho_1^{-1}\mathbf{x}_{10}'\boldsymbol{\beta})]^{\rho_1} \\ & \div \{a_1 \exp(\mathbf{z}_1'\boldsymbol{\gamma})[\exp(\rho_1^{-1}\mathbf{x}_{11}'\boldsymbol{\beta}) + \exp(\rho_1^{-1}\mathbf{x}_{10}'\boldsymbol{\beta})]^{\rho_1} \\ & + a_0 \exp(\mathbf{z}_0'\boldsymbol{\gamma})[\exp(\rho_0^{-1}\mathbf{x}_{01}'\boldsymbol{\beta}) + \exp(\rho_0^{-1}\mathbf{x}_{00}'\boldsymbol{\beta})]^{\rho_0}\}, \end{aligned} \tag{9.4.5}$$

$$P(y_2 = 1|y_1 = 1) = \frac{\exp(\rho_1^{-1}\mathbf{x}_{11}'\boldsymbol{\beta})}{\exp(\rho_1^{-1}\mathbf{x}_{11}'\boldsymbol{\beta}) + \exp(\rho_1^{-1}\mathbf{x}_{10}'\boldsymbol{\beta})}, \tag{9.4.6}$$

and

$$P(y_2 = 1|y_1 = 0) = \frac{\exp(\rho_0^{-1}\mathbf{x}_{01}'\boldsymbol{\beta})}{\exp(\rho_0^{-1}\mathbf{x}_{01}'\boldsymbol{\beta}) + \exp(\rho_0^{-1}\mathbf{x}_{00}'\boldsymbol{\beta})}. \tag{9.4.7}$$

The two-step estimation method discussed in Section 9.3.5 can be applied to this model.

9.4.3 Log-Linear Model

A log-linear model refers to a particular parameterization of a multivariate model. We shall discuss it in the context of the 2×2 model given in Table 9.1. For the moment we shall assume that there are no independent variables and that there is no constraint among the probabilities; therefore the model is completely characterized by specifying any three of the four probabilities appearing in Table 9.1. We shall call Table 9.1 the basic parameterization and shall consider two alternative parameterizations.

The first alternative parameterization is a logit model and is given in Table 9.4, where d is the normalization chosen to make the sum of probabilities equal to unity. The second alternative parameterization is called a log-linear model and is given in Table 9.5, where d, again, is a proper normalization, not necessarily equal to the d in Table 9.4.

The three models described in Tables 9.1, 9.4, and 9.5 are equivalent; they differ only in parameterization. Parameterizations in Tables 9.4 and 9.5 have the attractive feature that the conditional probabilities have a simple logistic form. For example, in Table 9.4 we have

$$P(y_1 = 1|y_2 = 1) = \frac{\exp(\mu_{11})}{\exp(\mu_{11}) + \exp(\mu_{01})} = \Lambda(\mu_{11} - \mu_{01}). \tag{9.4.8}$$

Note, however, that the parameterization in Table 9.5 has an additional attractive feature: $\alpha_{12} = 0$ if and only if y_1 and y_2 are independent. The role

Table 9.4 Bivariate logit model

	y_2	
y_1	1	0
1	$d^{-1}e^{\mu_{11}}$	$d^{-1}e^{\mu_{10}}$
0	$d^{-1}e^{\mu_{01}}$	$d^{-1}e^{\mu_{00}}$

Table 9.5 Log-linear model

	y_2	
y_1	1	0
1	$d^{-1}e^{\alpha_1+\alpha_2+\alpha_{12}}$	$d^{-1}e^{\alpha_1}$
0	$d^{-1}e^{\alpha_2}$	d^{-1}

of α_{12} also can be seen by the following equation that can be derived from Table 9.5:

$$P(y_1 = 1|y_2) = \Lambda(\alpha_1 + \alpha_{12}y_2). \tag{9.4.9}$$

The log-linear parameterization in Table 9.5 can also be defined by

$$P(y_1, y_2) \propto \exp(\alpha_1 y_1 + \alpha_2 y_2 + \alpha_{12} y_1 y_2), \tag{9.4.10}$$

where $\propto$ reads "is proportional to." This formulation can be generalized to a log-linear model of more than two binary random variables as follows (we shall write only the case of three variables):

$$P(y_1, y_2, y_3) \propto \exp(\alpha_1 y_1 + \alpha_2 y_2 + \alpha_3 y_3 + \alpha_{12} y_1 y_2 + \alpha_{13} y_1 y_3 + \alpha_{23} y_2 y_3 + \alpha_{123} y_1 y_2 y_3). \tag{9.4.11}$$

The first three terms in the exponential function are called the main effects. Terms involving the product of two variables are called second-order interaction terms, the product of three variables third-order interaction terms, and so on. Note that (9.4.11) involves seven parameters that can be put into a one-to-one correspondence with the seven probabilities that completely determine the distribution of y_1, y_2, and y_3. Such a model, without any constraint among the parameters, is called a *saturated* model. A saturated model for J binary variables involves $2^J - 1$ parameters. Researchers often use a constrained log-linear model, called an *unsaturated* model, which is obtained by setting some of the higher-order interaction terms to 0.

Example 9.4.2 is an illustration of a multivariate log-linear model.

EXAMPLE 9.4.2 (Goodman, 1972). Goodman sought to explain whether a soldier prefers a Northern camp to a Southern camp (y_0) by the race of the soldier (y_1), the region of his origin (y_2), and the present location of his camp (North or South) (y_3). Because each conditional probability has a logistic form, a log-linear model is especially suitable for analyzing a model of this sort. Generalizing (9.4.9), we can write a conditional probability as

$$P(y_0 = 1|y_1, y_2, y_3) = \Lambda(\alpha_0 + \alpha_{01}y_1 + \alpha_{02}y_2 + \alpha_{03}y_3 + \alpha_{012}y_1y_2 + \alpha_{013}y_1y_3 + \alpha_{023}y_2y_3 + \alpha_{0123}y_1y_2y_3). \quad (9.4.12)$$

Goodman looked at the asymptotic t value of the MLE of each α (the MLE divided by its asymptotic standard deviation) and tentatively concluded $\alpha_{012} = \alpha_{013} = \alpha_{0123} = 0$, called the null hypothesis. Then he proceeded to accept formally the null hypothesis as a result of the following testing procedure. Define $\hat{P}_t$, $t = 1, 2, \ldots, 16$, as the observed frequencies in the 16 cells created by all the possible joint outcomes of the four binary variables. (They can be interpreted as the unconstrained MLE's of the probabilities P_t.) Define $\hat{F}_t$ as the constrained MLE of P_t under the null hypothesis. Then we must reject the null hypothesis if and only if

$$n \sum_{t=1}^{16} \frac{(\hat{P}_t - \hat{F}_t)^2}{\hat{P}_t} > \chi^2_{3,\alpha}, \quad (9.4.13)$$

where n is the total number of soldiers in the sample and $\chi^2_{3,\alpha}$ is the α% critical value of χ^2_3. [Note that the left-hand side of (9.4.13) is analogous to (9.3.24).] Or, alternatively, we can use

$$2n \sum_{t=1}^{16} \hat{P}_t \log \frac{\hat{P}_t}{\hat{F}_t} > \chi^2_{3,\alpha}. \quad (9.4.14)$$

We shall indicate how to generalize a log-linear model to the case of discrete variables that take more than two values. This is done simply by using the binary variables defined in (9.3.2). We shall illustrate this idea by a simple example: Suppose there are two variables z and y_3 such that z takes the three values 0, 1, and 2 and y_3 takes the two values 0 and 1. Define two binary (0, 1) variables y_1 and y_2 by the rule: $y_1 = 1$ if $z = 1$ and $y_2 = 1$ if $z = 2$. Then we can specify $P(z, y_3)$ by specifying $P(y_1, y_2, y_3)$, which we can specify by a log-linear model as in (9.4.11). However, we should remember one small detail: Because in the present case $y_1y_2 = 0$ by definition, the two terms involving y_1y_2 in the right-hand side of (9.4.11) drop out.

In the preceding discussion we have touched upon only a small aspect of the log-linear model. There is a vast amount of work on this topic in the statistical literature. The interested reader should consult articles by Haberman (1978, 1979), Bishop, Feinberg, and Holland (1975), or the many references to Leo Goodman's articles cited therein.

Nerlove and Press (1973) proposed making the parameters of a log-linear model dependent on independent variables. Specifically, they proposed the main-effect parameters—α_1, α_2, and α_3 in (9.4.11)—to be linear combinations of independent variables. (However, there is no logical necessity to restrict this formulation to the main effects.)

Because in a log-linear model each conditional probability has a logit form as in (9.4.12), the following estimation procedure (which is simpler than MLE) can be used: Maximize the product of the conditional probabilities with respect to the parameters that appear therein. The remaining parameters must be estimated by maximizing the remaining part of the likelihood function. Amemiya (1975b) has given a sketch of a proof of the consistency of this estimator. We would expect that the estimator is, in general, not asymptotically as efficient as the MLE. However, Monte Carlo evidence, as reported by Guilkey and Schmidt (1979), suggests that the loss of efficiency may be minor.

9.4.4 Multivariate Probit Model

A multivariate probit model was first proposed by Ashford and Sowden (1970) and applied to a bivariate set of data. They supposed that a coal miner develops breathlessness ($y_1 = 1$) if his tolerance (y_1^*) is less than 0. Assuming that $y_1^* \sim N(-\boldsymbol{\beta}_1'\mathbf{x}, 1)$, where $\mathbf{x} = (1, \text{Age})'$, we have

$$P(y_1 = 1) = \Phi(\boldsymbol{\beta}_1'\mathbf{x}). \tag{9.4.15}$$

They also supposed that a coal miner develops wheeze ($y_2 = 1$) if his tolerance (y_2^*) against wheeze is less than 0 and that $y_2^* \sim N(-\boldsymbol{\beta}_2'\mathbf{x}, 1)$. Then we have

$$P(y_2 = 1) = \Phi(\boldsymbol{\beta}_2'\mathbf{x}). \tag{9.4.16}$$

Now that we have specified the marginal probabilities of y_1 and y_2, the multivariate model is completed by specifying the joint probability $P(y_1 = 1, y_2 = 1)$, which in turn is determined if the joint distribution of y_1^* and y_2^* is specified. Ashford and Sowden assumed that y_1^* and y_2^* are jointly normal with a correlation coefficient ρ. Thus

$$P(y_1 = 1, y_2 = 1) = F_\rho(\boldsymbol{\beta}_1'\mathbf{x}, \boldsymbol{\beta}_2'\mathbf{x}), \tag{9.4.17}$$

where F_ρ denotes the bivariate normal distribution function with zero means, unit variances, and correlation ρ.

The parameters $\boldsymbol{\beta}_1$, $\boldsymbol{\beta}_2$, and ρ can be estimated by MLE or MIN χ^2 (if there are many observations per cell for the latter method). Amemiya (1972) has given the MIN χ^2 estimation of this model.

Muthén (1979) estimated the following sociological model, which is equivalent to a bivariate probit model:

$$
\begin{aligned}
y_1 &= 1 \quad \text{if} \quad u_1 < \alpha_1 + \beta_1 \eta \\
y_2 &= 1 \quad \text{if} \quad u_2 < \alpha_2 + \beta_2 \eta \\
\eta &= \mathbf{x}'\gamma + v \\
u_1, u_2 &\sim N(0, 1), \qquad v \sim N(0, \sigma^2).
\end{aligned}
\tag{9.4.18}
$$

Here y_1 and y_2 represent responses of parents to questions about their attitudes toward their children, η is a latent (unobserved) variable signifying parents' sociological philosophy, and $\mathbf{x}$ is a vector of observable characteristics of parents. Muthén generalized this model to a multivariate model in which $\mathbf{y}$, $\mathbf{x}$, $\boldsymbol{\eta}$, $\mathbf{u}$, $\mathbf{v}$, and $\boldsymbol{\alpha}$ are all vectors following

$$
\begin{aligned}
\mathbf{y} &= \mathbf{l} \quad \text{if}\, \mathbf{u} < \boldsymbol{\alpha} + \boldsymbol{\Theta}\boldsymbol{\eta} \\
\mathbf{B}\boldsymbol{\eta} &= \boldsymbol{\Gamma}\mathbf{x} + \mathbf{v} \\
\mathbf{u} &\sim N(\mathbf{0}, \mathbf{I}), \qquad \mathbf{v} \sim N(\mathbf{0}, \boldsymbol{\Sigma}),
\end{aligned}
\tag{9.4.19}
$$

where $\mathbf{l}$ is a vector of ones, and discussed the problem of identification. In addition, Lee (1982a) has applied a model like (9.4.19) to a study of the relationship between health and wages.

It is instructive to note a fundamental difference between the multivariate probit model and the multivariate logit or log-linear models discussed earlier: in the multivariate probit model the marginal probabilities are first specified and then a joint probability consistent with the given marginal probabilities is found, whereas in the multivariate logit and log-linear models the joint probabilities or conditional probabilities are specified at the outset. The consequence of these different methods of specification is that marginal probabilities have a simple form (probit) in the multivariate probit model and the conditional probabilities have a simple form (logit) in the multivariate logit and log-linear models.

Because of this fundamental difference between a multivariate probit model and a multivariate logit model, it is an important practical problem for a researcher to compare the two types of models using some criterion of goodness of fit. Morimune (1979) compared the Ashford-Sowden bivariate probit model with the Nerlove-Press log-linear model empirically in a model in which the two binary dependent variables represent home ownership (y_1) and whether or not the house has more than five rooms (y_2). As criteria for comparison, Morimune used Cox's test (Section 4.5.3) and his own modification of it. He concluded that probit was preferred to logit by either test.

It is interesting to ask whether we could specify an Ashford-Sowden type bivariate logit model by assuming the logistic distribution for y_1^* and y_2^* in the Ashford-Sowden model. Although there is no "natural" bivariate logistic distribution the marginal distributions of which are logistic (unlike the normal case), Lee (1982b) found that Plackett's bivariate logistic distribution function (Plackett, 1965) yielded results similar to a bivariate probit model when applied to Ashford and Sowden's data and Morimune's data. Furthermore, it was computationally simpler.

Given two marginal distribution functions $F(x)$ and $G(y)$, Plackett's class of bivariate distributions $H(x, y)$ is defined by

$$\psi = \frac{H(1 - F - G + H)}{(F - H)(G - H)}, \tag{9.4.20}$$

for any fixed ψ in $(0, \infty)$.

Unfortunately, this method does not easily generalize to a higher-order multivariate distribution, where because of the computational burden of the probit model the logit analog of a multivariate probit model would be especially useful. Some progress in this direction has been made by Malik and Abraham (1973), who generalized Gumbel's bivariate logistic distribution (Gumbel, 1961) to a multivariate case.

9.5 Choice-Based Sampling

9.5.1 Introduction

Consider the multinominal QR model (9.3.1) or its special case (9.3.4). Up until now we have specified only the conditional probabilities of alternatives $j = 0, 1, \ldots, m$ given a vector of exogenous or independent variables $\mathbf{x}$ and have based our statistical inference on the conditional probabilities. Thus we have been justified in treating $\mathbf{x}$ as a vector of known constants just as in the classical linear regression model of Chapter 1. We shall now treat both j and $\mathbf{x}$ as random variables and consider different sampling schemes that specify how j and $\mathbf{x}$ are sampled.

First, we shall list a few basic symbols frequently used in the subsequent discussion:

$P(j\|\mathbf{x}, \boldsymbol{\beta})$ or $P(j)$	Conditional probability the jth alternative is chosen, given the exogenous variables $\mathbf{x}$

$P(j\|\mathbf{x}, \boldsymbol{\beta}_0)$ or $P_0(j)$	The above evaluated at the true value of $\boldsymbol{\beta}$
$f(\mathbf{x})$	True density of $\mathbf{x}$[10]
$g(\mathbf{x})$	Density according to which a researcher draws $\mathbf{x}$
$H(j)$	Probability according to which a researcher draws j

$Q(j) = Q(j|\boldsymbol{\beta}) = \int P(j|\mathbf{x}, \boldsymbol{\beta}) f(\mathbf{x})\, d\mathbf{x}$
$Q_0(j) = Q(j|\boldsymbol{\beta}_0) = \int P(j|\mathbf{x}, \boldsymbol{\beta}_0) f(\mathbf{x})\, d\mathbf{x}$

Let $i = 1, 2, \ldots, n$ be the individuals sampled according to some scheme. Then we can denote the alternative and the vector of the exogenous variables observed for the ith individual by j_i and $\mathbf{x}_i$, respectively.

We consider two types of sampling schemes called *exogenous sampling* and *endogenous sampling* (or choice-based sampling in the QR model). The first refers to sampling on the basis of exogenous variables, and the second refers to sampling on the basis of endogenous variables. The different sampling schemes are characterized by their likelihood functions. The likelihood function associated with exogenous sampling is given by[11]

$$L_e = \prod_{i=1}^{n} P(j_i|\mathbf{x}_i, \boldsymbol{\beta}) g(\mathbf{x}_i). \tag{9.5.1}$$

The likelihood function associated with choice-based sampling is given by

$$L_c = \prod_{i=1}^{n} P(j_i|\mathbf{x}_i, \boldsymbol{\beta}) f(\mathbf{x}_i) Q(j_i|\boldsymbol{\beta})^{-1} H(j_i) \tag{9.5.2}$$

if $Q(j|\boldsymbol{\beta}_0)$ is unknown and by

$$L_{c0} = \prod_{i=1}^{n} P(j_i|\mathbf{x}_i, \boldsymbol{\beta}) f(\mathbf{x}_i) Q(j_i|\boldsymbol{\beta}_0)^{-1} H(j_i) \tag{9.5.3}$$

if $Q(j|\boldsymbol{\beta}_0)$ is known. Note that if $g(\mathbf{x}) = f(\mathbf{x})$ and $H(j) = Q(j|\boldsymbol{\beta}_0)$, (9.5.1) and (9.5.3) both become

$$L^* = \prod_{i=1}^{n} P(j_i|\mathbf{x}_i, \boldsymbol{\beta}) f(\mathbf{x}_i), \tag{9.5.4}$$

which is the standard likelihood function associated with *random sampling*. This is precisely the likelihood function considered in the previous sections.

Although (9.5.2) may seem unfamiliar, it can be explained easily as follows. Consider drawing random variables j and $\mathbf{x}$ in the following order. We can first draw j with probability $H(j)$ and then, given j, we can draw $\mathbf{x}$ according to the conditional density $f(\mathbf{x}|j)$. Thus the joint probability is $f(\mathbf{x}|j)H(j)$, which by Bayes's rule is equal to $P(j|\mathbf{x})f(\mathbf{x})Q(j)^{-1}H(j)$.

This sampling scheme is different from a scheme in which the proportion of people choosing alternative j is *a priori* determined and fixed. This latter scheme may be a more realistic one. (Hsieh, Manski, and McFadden, 1983, have discussed this sampling scheme.) However, we shall adopt the definition of the preceding paragraphs (following Manski and Lerman, 1977) because in this way choice-based sampling contains random sampling as a special case $[Q(j) = H(j)]$ and because the two definitions lead to the same estimators with the same asymptotic properties.

Choice-based sampling is useful in a situation where exogenous sampling or random sampling would find only a very small number of people choosing a particular alternative. For example, suppose a small proportion of residents in a particular city use the bus for going to work. Then, to ensure that a certain number of bus riders are included in the sample, it would be much less expensive to interview people at a bus depot than to conduct a random survey of homes. Thus it is expected that random sampling augmented with choice-based sampling of rare alternatives would maximize the efficiency of estimation within the budgetary constraints of a researcher. Such augmentation can be analyzed in the framework of generalized choice-based sampling proposed by Cosslett (1981a) (to be discussed in Section 9.5.4).

In the subsequent subsections we shall discuss four articles: Manski and Lerman (1977), Cosslett (1981a), Cosslett (1981b), and Manski and McFadden (1981). These articles together cover the four different types of models, varying according to whether f is known and whether Q is known, and cover five estimators of $\boldsymbol{\beta}$—the *exogenous sampling maximum likelihood estimator* (ESMLE), the *random sampling maximum likelihood estimator* (RSMLE), the *choice-based sampling maximum likelihood estimator* (CBMLE), the *Manski-Lerman weighted maximum likelihood estimator* (WMLE), and the *Manski-McFadden estimator* (MME).

A comparison of RSMLE and CBMLE is important because within the framework of choice-based sampling a researcher controls $H(j)$, and the particular choice $H(j) = Q_0(j)$ yields random sampling. The choice of $H(j)$ is an important problem of sample design and, as we shall see later, $H(j) = Q_0(j)$ is not necessarily an optimal choice.

Table 9.6 indicates how the definitions of RSMLE and CBMLE vary with the four types of model; it also indicates in which article each case is discussed. Note that RSMLE = CBMLE if Q is known. ESMLE, which is not listed in

Table 9.6 Models, estimators, and cross references

f	Q	RSMLE	CBMLE	WMLE	MME
Known	Known		MM	MAL	—
		Max. L^* wrt $\boldsymbol{\beta}$ subject to $Q_0 = \int Pf\, d\mathbf{x}$	Max. L_{co} wrt $\boldsymbol{\beta}$ subject to $Q_0 = \int Pf\, d\mathbf{x}$		
Known	Unknown		MM	—	—
		Max. L^* wrt $\boldsymbol{\beta}$.	Max. L_c wrt. $\boldsymbol{\beta}$.		
Unknown	Known		C2 (see also Cosslett, 1978)	MAL	MM
		Max. L^* wrt $\boldsymbol{\beta}$ and f subject to $Q_0 = \int Pf\, d\mathbf{x}$.	Max. L_{co} wrt $\boldsymbol{\beta}$ and f subject to $Q_0 = \int Pf\, d\mathbf{x}$.		
Unknown	Unknown		C1 (also proves asymptotic efficiency)	—	—
		Max. L^* wrt $\boldsymbol{\beta}$.	Max. L_c wrt $\boldsymbol{\beta}$ and f.		

Note: RSMLE = random sampling maximum likelihood estimator; CBMLE = choice-based sampling maximum likelihood estimator; WMLE = Manski-Lerman weighted maximum likelihood estimator; MME = Manski-McFadden estimator.

MM = Manski and McFadden (1981); MAL = Manski and Lerman (1977); C2 = Cosslett (1981b); C1 = Cosslett (1981a).

Table 9.6, is the same as RSMLE except when f is unknown and Q is known. In that case ESMLE maximizes L_e with respect to $\boldsymbol{\beta}$ without constraints. RSMLE and CBMLE for the case of known Q will be referred to as the constrained RSMLE and the constrained CBMLE, respectively. For the case of unknown Q, we shall attach *unconstrained* to each estimator.

9.5.2 Results of Manski and Lerman

Manski and Lerman (1977) considered the choice-based sampling scheme represented by the likelihood function (9.5.3)—the case where Q is known—and proposed the estimator (WMLE), denoted $\hat{\boldsymbol{\beta}}_w$, which maximizes

$$S_n = \sum_{i=1}^{n} w(j_i) \log P(j_i|\mathbf{x}_i, \boldsymbol{\beta}), \tag{9.5.5}$$

where $w(j) = Q_0(j)/H(j)$. More precisely, $\hat{\boldsymbol{\beta}}_w$ is a solution of the normal equation

$$\frac{\partial S_n}{\partial \boldsymbol{\beta}} = \mathbf{0}. \tag{9.5.6}$$

It will become apparent that the weights $w(j)$ ensure the consistency of the estimator. If weights were not used, (9.5.5) would be reduced to the exogenous sampling likelihood function (9.5.1), and the resulting estimator to the usual MLE (the ESMLE), which can be shown to be inconsistent unless $H(j) = Q_0(j)$.

It should be noted that because WMLE does not depend on $f(\mathbf{x})$, it can be used regardless of whether or not f is known.

We shall prove the consistency of the WMLE $\hat{\boldsymbol{\beta}}_w$ in a somewhat different way from the authors' proof.[12] The basic theorems we shall use are Theorems 4.1.2 and 4.2.1. We need to make six assumptions.

Assumption 9.5.1. The parameter space B is an open subset of Euclidean space.

Assumption 9.5.2. $H(j) > 0$ for every $j = 0, 1, \ldots, m$.

Assumption 9.5.3. $\partial \log P(j|\mathbf{x}, \boldsymbol{\beta})/\partial \boldsymbol{\beta}$ exists and is continuous in an open neighborhood $N_1(\boldsymbol{\beta}_0)$ of $\boldsymbol{\beta}_0$ for every j and $\mathbf{x}$. (Note that this assumption requires $P(j|\mathbf{x}, \boldsymbol{\beta}) > 0$ in the neighborhood.)[13]

Assumption 9.5.4. $P(j|\mathbf{x}, \boldsymbol{\beta})$ is a measurable function of j and $\mathbf{x}$ for every $\boldsymbol{\beta} \in$ B.

Assumption 9.5.5. $\{j, \mathbf{x}\}$ are i.i.d. random variables.

Assumption 9.5.6. If $\boldsymbol{\beta} \neq \boldsymbol{\beta}_0$, $P[P(j|\mathbf{x}, \boldsymbol{\beta}) \neq P(j|\mathbf{x}, \boldsymbol{\beta}_0)] > 0$.

To prove the consistency of $\hat{\boldsymbol{\beta}}_w$, we first note that Assumptions 9.5.1, 9.5.2, and 9.5.3 imply conditions A and B of Theorem 4.1.2 for S_n defined in (9.5.5). Next, we check the uniform convergence part of condition C by putting $g(\mathbf{y}, \boldsymbol{\theta}) = \log P(j|\mathbf{x}, \boldsymbol{\beta}) - E \log P(j|\mathbf{x}, \boldsymbol{\beta})$ in Theorem 4.2.1. (Throughout Section 9.5, E always denotes the expectation taken under the assumption of choice-based sampling; that is, for any $g(j, \mathbf{x})$, $Eg(j, \mathbf{x}) = \int \Sigma_{j=0}^{m} g(j, \mathbf{x}) P(j|\mathbf{x}, \boldsymbol{\beta}_0) Q_0(j)^{-1} H(j) f(\mathbf{x})\, d\mathbf{x}$.) Because $0 < P(j|\mathbf{x}, \boldsymbol{\beta}) < 1$ for $\boldsymbol{\beta} \in \Psi$, where Ψ is some compact subset of $N_1(\boldsymbol{\beta}_0)$, by Assumption 9.5.3 we clearly have $E \sup_{\boldsymbol{\beta} \in \Psi} |\log P(j) - E \log P(j)| < \infty$. This fact, together with Assumptions 9.5.4 and 9.5.5, implies that all the conditions of Theorem 4.2.1 are fulfilled. Thus, to verify the remaining part of condition C, it only remains to show that $\lim_{n \to \infty} n^{-1} ES_n$ attains a strict local maximum at $\boldsymbol{\beta}_0$.

Using Assumption 9.5.5, we have

$$n^{-1}ES_n = \sum_{j=0}^{m} \int w(j)[\log P(j)]P_0(j)f(\mathbf{x})Q_0(j)^{-1}H(j)\, d\mathbf{x} \tag{9.5.7}$$
$$= \sum_{j=0}^{m} \int [\log P(j)]P_0(j)f(\mathbf{x})\, d\mathbf{x}$$
$$= E^* \log P(j),$$

where E in the left-hand side denotes the expectation taken according to the true choice-based sampling scheme, whereas E^* after the last equality denotes the expectation taken according to the hypothetical random sampling scheme. (That is, for any $g(j, \mathbf{x})$, $E^*g(j, \mathbf{x}) = \int \Sigma_{j=0}^{m} g(j, \mathbf{x})P(j|\mathbf{x}, \boldsymbol{\beta}_0)f(\mathbf{x})\, d\mathbf{x}$.) But, by Jensen's inequality (4.2.6) and Assumption 9.5.6, we have

$$E^* \log P(j|\mathbf{x}, \boldsymbol{\beta}) < E^* \log P(j|\mathbf{x}, \boldsymbol{\beta}_0) \quad \text{for} \quad \boldsymbol{\beta} \neq \boldsymbol{\beta}_0. \tag{9.5.8}$$

Thus the consistency of WMLE has been proved.

That the ESMLE is inconsistent under the present model can be shown as follows. Replacing $w(j)$ by 1 in the first equality of (9.5.7), we obtain

$$n^{-1}ES_n = \sum_{j=0}^{m} \int c_j[\log P(j)]P_0(j)f(\mathbf{x})\, d\mathbf{x}, \tag{9.5.9}$$

where $c_j = Q_0(j)^{-1}H(j)$. Evaluating the derivative of (9.5.9) with respect to $\boldsymbol{\beta}$ at $\boldsymbol{\beta}_0$ yields

$$\left.\frac{\partial n^{-1}ES_n}{\partial \boldsymbol{\beta}}\right|_{\boldsymbol{\beta}_0} = \left\{\frac{\partial}{\partial \boldsymbol{\beta}} \int \left[\sum_{j=0}^{m} c_j P(j|\mathbf{x}'\boldsymbol{\beta})\right] f(\mathbf{x})\, d\mathbf{x}\right\}_{\boldsymbol{\beta}_0}. \tag{9.5.10}$$

It is clear that we must generally have $c_j = 1$ for every j in order for (9.5.10) to be $\mathbf{0}$.[14]

The asymptotic normality of $\hat{\boldsymbol{\beta}}_w$ can be proved with suitable additional assumptions by using Theorem 4.1.3. We shall present merely an outline of the derivation and shall obtain the asymptotic covariance matrix. The necessary rigor can easily be supplied by the reader.

Differentiating (9.5.5) with respect to $\boldsymbol{\beta}$ yields

$$\frac{\partial S_n}{\partial \boldsymbol{\beta}} = \sum_{i=1}^{n} w(j_i) \frac{1}{P(j_i)} \frac{\partial P(j_i)}{\partial \boldsymbol{\beta}}. \tag{9.5.11}$$

Because (9.5.11) is a sum of i.i.d. random variables by Assumption 9.5.5, we can expect $n^{-1/2}(\partial S_n/\partial \boldsymbol{\beta})_{\boldsymbol{\beta}_0}$ to converge to a normal random variable under suitable assumptions. We can show

$$\frac{1}{\sqrt{n}} \frac{\partial S_n}{\partial \boldsymbol{\beta}}\bigg|_{\boldsymbol{\beta}_0} \rightarrow N(\mathbf{0}, \boldsymbol{\Lambda}), \tag{9.5.12}$$

where

$$\boldsymbol{\Lambda} = E[w(j)^2 \boldsymbol{\gamma}\boldsymbol{\gamma}'], \tag{9.5.13}$$

where $\boldsymbol{\gamma} = [\partial \log P(j)/\partial \boldsymbol{\beta}]_{\boldsymbol{\beta}_0}$. Differentiating (9.5.11) with respect to $\boldsymbol{\beta}'$ yields

$$\frac{\partial^2 S_n}{\partial \boldsymbol{\beta} \partial \boldsymbol{\beta}'} = -\sum_{i=1}^{n} w(j_i) \frac{1}{P(j_i)^2} \frac{\partial P(j_i)}{\partial \boldsymbol{\beta}} \frac{\partial P(j_i)}{\partial \boldsymbol{\beta}'} \tag{9.5.14}$$
$$+ \sum_{i=1}^{n} w(j_i) \frac{1}{P(j_i)} \frac{\partial^2 P(j_i)}{\partial \boldsymbol{\beta} \partial \boldsymbol{\beta}'}.$$

Using the fact that (9.5.14) is a sum of i.i.d. random variables, we can show

$$\operatorname*{plim}_{n\to\infty} \frac{1}{n} \frac{\partial^2 S_n}{\partial \boldsymbol{\beta} \partial \boldsymbol{\beta}'}\bigg|_{\boldsymbol{\beta}_0} = -Ew(j)\boldsymbol{\gamma}\boldsymbol{\gamma}' \tag{9.5.15}$$
$$\equiv \mathbf{A},$$

because

$$Ew(j) \frac{1}{P_0(j)} \frac{\partial^2 P(j)}{\partial \boldsymbol{\beta} \partial \boldsymbol{\beta}'}\bigg|_{\boldsymbol{\beta}_0} = \int \sum_{j=0}^{m} \frac{\partial^2 P(j)}{\partial \boldsymbol{\beta} \partial \boldsymbol{\beta}'}\bigg|_{\boldsymbol{\beta}_0} f(\mathbf{x})\, d\mathbf{x} \tag{9.5.16}$$
$$= \left[\frac{\partial^2}{\partial \boldsymbol{\beta} \partial \boldsymbol{\beta}'} \int \sum_{j=0}^{m} P(j) f(\mathbf{x})\, d\mathbf{x} \right]_{\boldsymbol{\beta}_0} = \mathbf{0}.$$

Therefore, from (9.5.12) and (9.5.15), we conclude

$$\sqrt{n}(\hat{\boldsymbol{\beta}}_w - \boldsymbol{\beta}_0) \rightarrow N(\mathbf{0}, \mathbf{A}^{-1}\boldsymbol{\Lambda}\,\mathbf{A}^{-1}). \tag{9.5.17}$$

As we noted earlier, a researcher controls $H(j)$ and therefore faces an interesting problem of finding an optimal design: What is the optimal choice of $H(j)$? We shall consider this problem here in the context of WMLE. Thus the question is, What choice of $H(j)$ will minimize $\mathbf{A}^{-1}\boldsymbol{\Lambda}\,\mathbf{A}^{-1}$?

First of all, we should point out that $H(j) = Q_0(j)$ is not necessarily the optimal choice. If it were, it would mean that random sampling is always preferred to choice-based sampling. The asymptotic covariance matrix of $\sqrt{n}(\hat{\boldsymbol{\beta}}_w - \boldsymbol{\beta}_0)$ when $H(j) = Q_0(j)$ is $(E^*\boldsymbol{\gamma}\boldsymbol{\gamma}')^{-1}$, where E^* denotes the expectation taken with respect to the probability distribution $P(j|\mathbf{x}, \boldsymbol{\beta}_0)f(\mathbf{x})$. Writing

$w(j)$ simply as w, the question is whether

$$(Ew\gamma\gamma')^{-1}Ew^2\gamma\gamma'(Ew\gamma\gamma')^{-1} > (E^*\gamma\gamma')^{-1}. \tag{9.5.18}$$

The answer is no, even though we do have

$$(Ew\gamma\gamma')^{-1}Ew^2\gamma\gamma'(Ew\gamma\gamma')^{-1} > (E\gamma\gamma')^{-1}, \tag{9.5.19}$$

which follows from the generalized Cauchy-Schwartz inequality $E\mathbf{yy}' > E\mathbf{yx}'(E\mathbf{xx}')^{-1}E\mathbf{xy}'$.

Let us consider an optimal choice of $H(j)$ by a numerical analysis using a simple logit model with a single scalar parameter. A more elaborate numerical analysis by Cosslett (1981b), which addressed this as well as some other questions, will be discussed in Section 9.5.5.

For this purpose it is useful to rewrite $\mathbf{\Lambda}$ and $\mathbf{A}$ as

$$\mathbf{\Lambda} = E^*w(j)\gamma\gamma' \tag{9.5.20}$$

and

$$\mathbf{A} = -E^*\gamma\gamma'. \tag{9.5.21}$$

Denoting the asymptotic variance of $\sqrt{n}(\hat{\beta}_w - \beta_0)$ in the scalar case by $V_w(H)$, we define the relative efficiency of $\hat{\beta}_w$ based on the design $H(j)$ by

$$\text{Eff}(H) = \frac{V_w(Q)}{V_w(H)} = \frac{E^*(\gamma^2)}{E^*[w(j)\gamma^2]}, \tag{9.5.22}$$

because γ is a scalar here.

We shall evaluate (9.5.22) and determine the optimal $H(j)$ that maximizes Eff(H) in a binary logit model:

$$P_0(1) = \Lambda(\beta_0 x),$$

where β_0 and x are scalars.

In this model the determination of the optimal value of $h \equiv H(1)$ is simple because we have

$$E^*w(j)\gamma^2 = \frac{a}{h} + \frac{b}{1-h}, \tag{9.5.23}$$

where

$$a = E_x\Lambda(\beta_0 x)E_x x^2 \exp(\beta_0 x)[1 + \exp(\beta_0 x)]^{-3} \tag{9.5.24}$$

and

$$b = E_x[1 - \Lambda(2\beta_0 x)]E_x x^2 \exp(2\beta_0 x)[1 + \exp(\beta_0 x)]^{-3}. \tag{9.5.25}$$

Because $a, b > 0$, (9.5.23) approaches ∞ as h approaches either 0 or 1 and attains a unique minimum at

$$h^* = \frac{a - \sqrt{ab}}{a - b} \quad \text{if} \quad a \neq b \tag{9.5.26}$$

$$= 0.5 \quad \text{if} \quad a = b.$$

We assume x is binary with probability distribution:

$$x = 1 \quad \text{with probability} \quad p$$

$$= 0 \quad \text{with probability} \quad 1 - p.$$

Then, inserting $\beta_0 = \log[(p + 2Q_0 - 1)/(p - 2Q_0 + 1)]$, where $Q_0 = Q_0(1)$, into the right-hand side of (9.5.22), Eff(H) becomes a function of p, Q_0, and h alone. In the last five columns of Table 9.7, the values of Eff(H) are shown for various values of p, Q_0, and h. For each combination of p and Q_0, the value of the optimal h, denoted h^*, is shown in the third column. For example, if $p = 0.9$ and $Q_0 = 0.75$, the optimal value of h is equal to 0.481. When h is set equal to this optimal value, the efficiency of WMLE is 1.387. The table shows that the efficiency gain of using choice-based sampling can be considerable and that $h = 0.5$ performs well for all the parameter values considered. It can be shown that if $Q_0 = 0.5$, then $h^* = 0.5$ for all the values of p.

In the foregoing discussion of WMLE, we have assumed $Q_0(j)$ to be known. However, it is more realistic to assume that $Q_0(j)$ needs to be estimated from a separate sample and such an estimate is used to define $w(j)$ in WMLE. Manski and Lerman did not discuss this problem except to note in a footnote

Table 9.7 Efficiency of WLME for various designs in a binary logit model

			h				
p	Q_0	h^*	h^*	0.75	0.5	0.25	0.1
0.9	0.75	0.481	1.387	1	1.385	1.08	0.531
0.9	0.25	0.519	1.387	1.08	1.385	1	0.470
0.9	0.1	0.579	3.548	3.068	3.462	2.25	1
0.5	0.7	0.337	1.626	0.852	1.471	1.563	1
0.5	0.3	0.663	1.626	1.563	1.471	0.852	0.36
0.1	0.525	0.378	1.087	0.625	1.026	1	0.585
0.1	0.475	0.622	1.087	1	1.026	0.625	0.270

that the modified WMLE using an estimate $\hat{Q}_0(j)$ is consistent as long as plim $\hat{Q}_0(j) = Q_0(j)$. To verify this statement we need merely observe that

$$\left| n^{-1} \sum_{i=1}^{n} [\hat{Q}_0(j_i) - Q_0(j_i)] H(j_i)^{-1} \log P(j_i|\mathbf{x}_i, \boldsymbol{\beta}) \right| \tag{9.5.27}$$

$$\leqq \max_j |\hat{Q}_0(j) - Q_0(j)| \cdot n^{-1} \sum_{i=1}^{n} |H(j_i)^{-1} \log P(j_i|\mathbf{x}_i, \boldsymbol{\beta})|.$$

The right-hand side of (9.5.27) converges to 0 in probability uniformly in $\boldsymbol{\beta}$ by Assumptions 9.5.2 and 9.5.3 and by the consistency of $\hat{Q}_0(j)$.

To show the asymptotic equivalence of the modified WMLE and the original WMLE, we need an assumption about the rate of convergence of $\hat{Q}_0(j)$. By examining (9.5.12), we see that for asymptotic equivalence we need

$$\text{plim}\ n^{-1/2} \sum_{i=1}^{n} [\hat{Q}_0(j_i) - Q_0(j_i)] H(j_i)^{-1} [\partial \log P(j_i)/\partial \boldsymbol{\beta}]_{\boldsymbol{\beta}_0} = \mathbf{0}. \tag{9.5.28}$$

Therefore we need

$$\hat{Q}_0(j) - Q_0(j) = o(n^{-1/2}). \tag{9.5.29}$$

If $\hat{Q}_0(j)$ is the proportion of people choosing alternative j in a separate sample of size n_1,

$$\hat{Q}_0(j) - Q_0(j) = O(n_1^{-1/2}). \tag{9.5.30}$$

Therefore asymptotic equivalence requires that n/n_1 should converge to 0. See Hsieh, Manski, and McFadden (1983) for the asymptotic distribution of the WMLE with Q estimated in the case where n/n_1 converges to a nonzero constant.

An application of WMLE in a model explaining family participation in the AFDC program can be found in the article by Hosek (1980).

9.5.3 Results of Manski and McFadden

Manski and McFadden (1981) presented a comprehensive summary of all the types of models and estimators under choice-based sampling, including the results of the other papers discussed elsewhere in Section 9.5. However, we shall discuss only those topics that are not dealt with in the other papers, namely, the consistency and the asymptotic normality of CBMLE in the cases where f is known and Q is either known or unknown and MME in the case where f is unknown and Q is known. Because the results presented here are straightforward, we shall only sketch the proof of consistency and asymptotic normality and shall not spell out all the conditions needed.

First, consider the case where both f and Q are known. CBMLE maximizes L_{c0} given in (9.5.3) subject to the condition

$$Q_0(j) = \int P(j|\mathbf{x}, \boldsymbol{\beta}) f(\mathbf{x})\, d\mathbf{x}, \qquad j = 1, 2, \ldots, m. \tag{9.5.31}$$

The condition corresponding to $j=0$ is redundant because $\Sigma_{j=0}^{m} P(j|\mathbf{x}, \boldsymbol{\beta}) = 1$, which will be implicitly observed throughout the following analysis. Ignoring the known components of L_{c0}, CBMLE is defined as maximizing $\Sigma_{i=1}^{n} \log P(j_i|\mathbf{x}_i, \boldsymbol{\beta})$ with respect to $\boldsymbol{\beta}$ subject to (9.5.31). Because the above maximand is the essential part of $\log L^*$ under random sampling, we have CBMLE = RSMLE in this case. However, the properties of the estimator must be derived under the assumption of choice-based sampling and are therefore different from the results of Section 9.3.

To prove consistency, we need merely note that consistency of the unconstrained CBMLE follows from the general result of Section 4.2.2 and that the probability limit of the constrained CBMLE should be the same as that of the unconstrained CBMLE if the constraint is true.

To prove asymptotic normality, it is convenient to rewrite the constraint (9.5.31) in the form of

$$\boldsymbol{\beta} = \mathbf{g}(\boldsymbol{\alpha}), \tag{9.5.32}$$

where $\boldsymbol{\alpha}$ is a $(k-m)$-vector, as we did in Section 4.5.1. Then, by a straightforward application of Theorem 4.2.4, we obtain

$$\sqrt{n}(\hat{\boldsymbol{\alpha}}_{\mathrm{ML}} - \boldsymbol{\alpha}_0) \rightarrow N[\mathbf{0}, (\mathbf{G}'E\gamma\gamma'\mathbf{G})^{-1}], \tag{9.5.33}$$

where $\mathbf{G} = [\partial\boldsymbol{\beta}/\partial\boldsymbol{\alpha}']_{\boldsymbol{\alpha}_0}$ and $\gamma = [\partial \log P(j)/\partial\boldsymbol{\beta}]_{\boldsymbol{\beta}_0}$. Therefore, using a Taylor series approximation,

$$\hat{\boldsymbol{\beta}}_{\mathrm{ML}} - \boldsymbol{\beta}_0 \cong \mathbf{G}(\hat{\boldsymbol{\alpha}}_{\mathrm{ML}} - \boldsymbol{\alpha}_0), \tag{9.5.34}$$

we obtain

$$\sqrt{n}(\hat{\boldsymbol{\beta}}_{\mathrm{ML}} - \boldsymbol{\beta}_0) \rightarrow N[\mathbf{0}, \mathbf{G}(\mathbf{G}'E\gamma\gamma'\mathbf{G})^{-1}\mathbf{G}']. \tag{9.5.35}$$

As we would expect, $\hat{\boldsymbol{\beta}}_{\mathrm{ML}}$ is asymptotically more efficient than WMLE $\hat{\boldsymbol{\beta}}_w$. In other words, we should have

$$\mathbf{G}(\mathbf{G}'E\gamma\gamma'\mathbf{G})^{-1}\mathbf{G}' \leqq (Ew\gamma\gamma')^{-1}Ew^2\gamma\gamma'(Ew\gamma\gamma')^{-1}, \tag{9.5.36}$$

for any w and $\mathbf{G}$. This inequality follows straightforwardly from (9.5.19).

Second, consider the case where f is known and Q is unknown. Here, CBMLE is defined as maximizing (9.5.2) without constraint. The estimator is consistent by the result of Section 4.2.2, and its asymptotic normally follows from Theorem 4.2.4. Thus

$$\sqrt{n}(\tilde{\beta}_{ML} - \beta_0) \rightarrow N[\mathbf{0}, (E\gamma\gamma' - E\delta\delta')^{-1}], \tag{9.5.37}$$

where $\delta = [\partial \log Q/\partial\beta]_{\beta_0}$. As we would expect, $\tilde{\beta}_{ML}$ is not as efficient as $\hat{\beta}_{ML}$ because

$$\mathbf{G}(\mathbf{G}'E\gamma\gamma'\mathbf{G})^{-1}\mathbf{G}' \leqq (E\gamma\gamma')^{-1} \leqq (E\gamma\gamma' - E\delta\delta')^{-1}. \tag{9.5.38}$$

Finally, consider the case where f is unknown and Q is known. We shall discuss CBMLE for this model in Section 9.5.5. Here, we shall consider the Manski-McFadden estimator (MME), which maximizes

$$\Psi = \prod_{i=1}^{n} \frac{P(j_i|\mathbf{x}_i, \beta)Q_0(j_i)^{-1}H(j_i)}{\sum_{j=0}^{m} P(j|\mathbf{x}_i, \beta)Q_0(j)^{-1}H(j)}. \tag{9.5.39}$$

The motivation for this estimator is the following: As we can see from (9.5.3), the joint probability of j and $\mathbf{x}$ under the present assumption is

$$h(j, \mathbf{x}) \equiv P(j|\mathbf{x}, \beta)f(\mathbf{x})Q_0(j)^{-1}H(j). \tag{9.5.40}$$

Therefore the conditional probability of j given $\mathbf{x}$ is

$$h(j|\mathbf{x}) \equiv \frac{h(j, \mathbf{x})}{\sum_{j=0}^{m} h(j, \mathbf{x})}, \tag{9.5.41}$$

which leads to the conditional likelihood function (9.5.39). The estimator is computationally attractive because the right-hand side of (9.5.39) does not depend on $f(\mathbf{x})$, which is assumed unknown and requires a nonstandard analysis of estimation, as we shall see in Sections 9.5.4 and 9.5.5.

To prove the consistency of the estimator, we observe that

$$\operatorname*{plim}_{n\rightarrow\infty} n^{-1} \log \Psi = E \log \frac{P(j)Q_0(j)^{-1}H(j)}{\sum_{j=0}^{m} P(j)Q_0(j)^{-1}H(j)} \tag{9.5.42}$$

$$= \int [E^{+} \log h(j|\mathbf{x})]\zeta(\mathbf{x})\, d\mathbf{x},$$

where $\zeta(\mathbf{x}) = \sum_{j=0}^{m} P_0(j)Q_0(j)^{-1}H_jf(\mathbf{x})$ and E^{+} is the expectation taken with respect to the true conditional probability $h_0(j|\mathbf{x})$. Equation (9.5.42) is maximized at $\boldsymbol{\beta}_0$ because $\zeta(\mathbf{x}) > 0$ and

$$E^+ \log h(j|\mathbf{x}) < E^+ \log h_0(j|\mathbf{x}), \tag{9.5.43}$$

which, like (9.5.8), is a consequence of Jensen's inequality (4.2.6).

By a straightforward application of Theorem 4.1.3, we can show

$$\sqrt{n}(\hat{\boldsymbol{\beta}}_{\text{MM}} - \boldsymbol{\beta}_0) \rightarrow N[\mathbf{0}, (E\boldsymbol{\gamma}\boldsymbol{\gamma}' - E\boldsymbol{\epsilon}\boldsymbol{\epsilon}')^{-1}], \tag{9.5.44}$$

where $\boldsymbol{\epsilon} = [\partial \log \Sigma_{j=0}^{m} P(j)Q_0(j)^{-1}H(j)/\partial\boldsymbol{\beta}]_{\boldsymbol{\beta}_0}$. The asymptotic covariance matrix in (9.5.44) is neither larger nor smaller (in matrix sense) than the asymptotic covariance matrix of WMLE given in (9.5.17).[15]

9.5.4 Results of Cosslett: Part I

Cosslett (1981a) proved the consistency and the asymptotic normality of CBMLE in the model where both f and Q are unknown and also proved that CBMLE asymptotically attains the Cramér-Rao lower bound. These results require much ingenuity and deep analysis because maximizing a likelihood function with respect to a density function f as well as parameters $\boldsymbol{\beta}$ creates a new and difficult problem that cannot be handled by the standard asymptotic theory of MLE. As Cosslett noted, his model does not even satisfy the conditions of Kiefer and Wolfowitz (1956) for consistency of MLE in the presence of infinitely many nuisance parameters.

Cosslett's sampling scheme is a generalization of the choice-based sampling we have hitherto considered.[16] His scheme, called *generalized choice-based sampling,* is defined as follows: Assume that the total sample of size n is divided into S subsamples, with n_s people (n_s is a fixed known number) in the sth subsample. A person in the sth subsample faces alternatives J_s, a subset of the total alternatives $(0, 1, 2, \ldots, m)$. He or she chooses alternative j with probability $Q(j)/\tilde{Q}(s)$, where $\tilde{Q}(s) = \Sigma_{j\in J_s} Q(j)$. Given j, he or she chooses a vector of exogenous variables $\mathbf{x}$ with a conditional density $f(\mathbf{x}|j)$.[17] Therefore the contribution of this typical person to the likelihood function is $\tilde{Q}(s)^{-1}Q(j)f(\mathbf{x}|j)$, which can be equivalently expressed as

$$\tilde{Q}(s)^{-1}P(j|\mathbf{x}, \boldsymbol{\beta})f(\mathbf{x}). \tag{9.5.45}$$

Taking the product of (9.5.45) over all the persons in the sth subsample (denoted by I_s) and then over all s, we obtain the likelihood function

$$\begin{aligned} L &= \prod_{s=1}^{S} \prod_{i\in I_s} \tilde{Q}(s)^{-1}P(j_i|\mathbf{x}_i, \boldsymbol{\beta})f(\mathbf{x}_i) \qquad (9.5.46) \\ &= \prod_{i=1}^{n} \tilde{Q}(s_i)^{-1}P(j_i|\mathbf{x}_i, \boldsymbol{\beta})f(\mathbf{x}_i). \end{aligned}$$

In the model under consideration, the $Q(j)$'s are unknown. Therefore we may wonder how, in subsample s, alternatives in J_s are sampled in such a way that the jth alternative is chosen with probability $\tilde{Q}(s)^{-1}Q(j)$. To this question Cosslett (1981b) gave an example of interviewing train riders at a train station, some of whom have traveled to the station by their own cars and some of whom have come by taxi. Thus this subsample consists of two alternatives, each of which is sampled according to the correct probability by random sampling conducted at the train station.

Cosslett's generalization of choice-based sampling is an attractive one, not only because it contains the simple choice-based sampling of the preceding sections as a special case (take $J_s = \{s\}$), but also because it contains an interesting special case of "enriched" samples.[18] That is, a researcher conducts random sampling, and if a particular alternative is chosen with a very low frequency, the sample is enriched by interviewing more of those who chose this particular alternative. Here we have, for example, $J_1 = (0, 1, 2, \ldots, m)$ and $J_2(0)$, if the 0th alternative is the one infrequently chosen.

Our presentation of Cosslett's results will not be rigorous, and we shall not spell out all the conditions needed for consistency, asymptotic normality, and asymptotic efficiency. However, we want to mention the following identification conditions as they are especially important.

ASSUMPTION 9.5.6. $\cup_{s=1}^{S} J_s = (0, 1, 2, \ldots, m)$.

ASSUMPTION 9.5.7. A subset M of integers $(1, 2, \ldots, S)$ such that $(\cup_{s\in M} J_s) \cap (\cup_{s\in \overline{M}} J_s) = \phi$, where $\overline{M}$ is the complement of M, cannot be found.

Note that if $S = 2$ and $m = 1$, for example, $J_1 = (0)$ and $J_2 = (1)$ violate Assumption 9.5.7, whereas $J_1 = (0)$ and $J_2 = (0, 1)$ satisfy it. Thus simple choice-based sampling violates this assumption. Cosslett noted that these assumptions are needed for the multinomial logit model but may not be needed for other QR models. Cosslett also gave an intuitive reason for these assumptions: If alternatives j and k are both contained in some subsample, then $Q(j)/Q(k)$ can be estimated consistently, and under Assumption 9.5.7 we have enough of these ratios to estimate all the $Q(j)$ separately. Thus Assumption 9.5.7 would not be needed in the case where $Q(j)$ are known.

Before embarking on a discussion of Cosslett's results, we must list a few more symbols as an addition to those listed in Section 9.5.1:

$$\tilde{P}(s) = \tilde{P}(s|\mathbf{x}, \beta) = \sum_{j\in J_s} P(j|\mathbf{x}, \beta)$$

$$\tilde{P}_0(s) = \tilde{P}(s|\mathbf{x}, \boldsymbol{\beta}_0) = \sum_{j \in J_s} P(j|\mathbf{x}, \boldsymbol{\beta}_0)$$

$$\tilde{Q}(s) = \sum_{j \in J_s} Q(j)$$

$$\tilde{Q}_0(s) = \sum_{j \in J_s} Q_0(j)$$

$$H(s) = n_s/n$$

From (9.5.46) we obtain

$$\log L = \sum_{i=1}^{n} \log P(j_i|\mathbf{x}_i, \boldsymbol{\beta}) + \sum_{i=1}^{n} \log f(\mathbf{x}_i) - \sum_{s=1}^{S} n_s \log \int \tilde{P}(s|\mathbf{x}, \boldsymbol{\beta}) f(\mathbf{x})\, d\mathbf{x}. \tag{9.5.47}$$

Our aim is to maximize (9.5.47) with respect to a parameter vector $\boldsymbol{\beta}$ and a function $f(\cdot)$. By observing (9.5.47) we can immediately see that we should put $f(\mathbf{x}) = 0$ for $\mathbf{x} \neq \mathbf{x}_i$, $i = 1, 2, \ldots, n$. Therefore our problem is reduced to the more manageable one of maximizing

$$\log L_1 = \sum_{i=1}^{n} \log P(j_i|\mathbf{x}_i, \boldsymbol{\beta}) + \sum_{i=1}^{n} \log w_i - \sum_{s=1}^{S} n_s \log \sum_{i=1}^{n} w_i \tilde{P}(s|\mathbf{x}_i, \boldsymbol{\beta}) \tag{9.5.48}$$

with respect to $\boldsymbol{\beta}$ and w_i, $i = 1, 2, \ldots, n$. Differentiating (9.5.48) with respect to w_i and setting the derivative equal to 0 yield

$$\frac{\partial \log L_1}{\partial w_i} = \frac{1}{w_i} - \sum_{s=1}^{S} \frac{n_s \tilde{P}(s|\mathbf{x}_i, \boldsymbol{\beta})}{\sum_{i=1}^{n} w_i \tilde{P}(s|\mathbf{x}_i, \boldsymbol{\beta})} = 0. \tag{9.5.49}$$

If we insert (9.5.49) into (9.5.48), we recognize that $\log L_1$ depends on w_i only through the S terms $\Sigma_{i=1}^{n} w_i \tilde{P}(s|\mathbf{x}_i, \boldsymbol{\beta})$, $s = 1, 2, \ldots, S$. Thus, if we define

$$\lambda_s(\boldsymbol{\beta}) = \frac{H(s)}{\sum_{i=1}^{n} w_i \tilde{P}(s|\mathbf{x}_i, \boldsymbol{\beta})}, \tag{9.5.50}$$

we can, after some manipulation, write $\log L_1$ as a function of $\boldsymbol{\beta}$ and $\{\lambda_s(\boldsymbol{\beta})\}$ as

$$\log L_1 = \sum_{i=1}^{n} \log P(j_i|\mathbf{x}_i, \boldsymbol{\beta}) - \sum_{i=1}^{n} \log \sum_{s=1}^{S} \lambda_s(\boldsymbol{\beta})\tilde{P}(s|\mathbf{x}_i, \boldsymbol{\beta}) \tag{9.5.51}$$

$$+ \sum_{s=1}^{S} n_s \log \lambda_s(\boldsymbol{\beta}) - \sum_{s=1}^{S} n_s \log n_s .$$

But maximizing (9.5.51) with respect to $\boldsymbol{\beta}$ and $\lambda_s(\boldsymbol{\beta})$, $s = 1\ 2, \ldots, S$, is equivalent to maximizing[19]

$$\Omega = \sum_{i=1}^{n} \log P(j_i|\mathbf{x}_i, \boldsymbol{\beta}) - \sum_{i=1}^{n} \log \sum_{s=1}^{S} \lambda_s \tilde{P}(s|\mathbf{x}_i, \boldsymbol{\beta}) + \sum_{s=1}^{S} n_s \log \lambda_s \tag{9.5.52}$$

with respect to $\boldsymbol{\beta}$ and λ_s, $s = 1, 2, \ldots, S$. This can be shown as follows. Inserting (9.5.50) into (9.5.49) yields

$$w_i = \frac{1}{n \sum_{s=1}^{S} \lambda_s(\boldsymbol{\beta})\tilde{P}(s|\mathbf{x}_i, \boldsymbol{\beta})}. \tag{9.5.53}$$

Multiplying both sides of (9.5.53) by $\tilde{P}(s|\mathbf{x}_i, \boldsymbol{\beta})$, summing over i, and using (9.5.50) yield

$$\frac{n_s}{\lambda_s(\boldsymbol{\beta})} = \sum_{i=1}^{n} \frac{\tilde{P}(s|\mathbf{x}_i, \boldsymbol{\beta})}{\sum_{s=1}^{S} \lambda_s(\boldsymbol{\beta})\tilde{P}(s|\mathbf{x}_i, \boldsymbol{\beta})}. \tag{9.5.54}$$

But setting the derivative of Ω with respect to λ_s equal to 0 yields

$$\frac{\partial \Omega}{\partial \lambda_s} = \frac{n_s}{\lambda_s} - \sum_{i=1}^{n} \frac{\tilde{P}(s|\mathbf{x}_i, \boldsymbol{\beta})}{\sum_{s=1}^{S} \lambda_s \tilde{P}(s|\mathbf{x}_i, \boldsymbol{\beta})} = 0. \tag{9.5.55}$$

Clearly, a solution of (9.5.55) is a solution of (9.5.54).

In the maximization of (9.5.52) with respect to $\boldsymbol{\beta}$ and $\{\lambda_s\}$, some normalization is necessary because $\Omega(\alpha\lambda_1, \alpha\lambda_2, \ldots, \alpha\lambda_S, \boldsymbol{\beta}) = \Omega(\lambda_1, \lambda_2, \ldots, \lambda_S, \boldsymbol{\beta})$. The particular normalization adopted by Cosslett is

$$\lambda_S = H(S). \tag{9.5.56}$$

Thus we define CBMLE of this model as the value of $\boldsymbol{\beta}$ that is obtained by maximizing Ω with respect to $\boldsymbol{\beta}$ and $\{\lambda_s\}$ subject to the normalization (9.5.56).

Although our aim is to estimate $\boldsymbol{\beta}$, it is of some interest to ask what the MLE of $\{\lambda_s\}$ is supposed to estimate. The probability limits of MLE $\hat{\beta}$ and $\{\hat{\lambda}_s\}$ can be obtained as the values that maximize $\text{plim}_{n\to\infty} n^{-1}\Omega$. We have

$$\begin{aligned}\underset{n\to\infty}{\text{plim}}\, n^{-1}\Omega &= E \log P(j_i|\mathbf{x}_i, \boldsymbol{\beta}) - E \log \sum_{s=1}^{S} \lambda_s \tilde{P}(s|\mathbf{x}_i, \boldsymbol{\beta}) \\ &\quad + \sum_{s=1}^{S} H(s) \log \lambda_s \\ &= \sum_{s=1}^{S} H(s) \int \sum_{j\in J_s} [\log P(j|\mathbf{x}, \boldsymbol{\beta})] \tilde{Q}_0(s)^{-1} P(j|\mathbf{x}, \boldsymbol{\beta}_0) f(\mathbf{x})\, d\mathbf{x} \\ &\quad - \sum_{s=1}^{S} H(s) \int \left[\log \sum_{s=1}^{S} \lambda_s \tilde{P}(s|\mathbf{x}, \boldsymbol{\beta})\right] \\ &\quad \times \tilde{Q}_0(s)^{-1} \tilde{P}(s|\mathbf{x}, \boldsymbol{\beta}_0) f(\mathbf{x})\, d\mathbf{x} \\ &\quad + \sum_{s=1}^{S} H(s) \log \lambda_s .\end{aligned} \tag{9.5.57}$$

Differentiating (9.5.57) with respect to λ_τ, $\tau = 1, 2, \ldots, S-1$, and $\boldsymbol{\beta}$ yields

$$\begin{aligned}\frac{\partial}{\partial \lambda_\tau} \text{plim}\, n^{-1}\Omega &= -\int \frac{\sum_{s=1}^{S} \tilde{Q}_0(s)^{-1} H(s) \tilde{P}(s|\mathbf{x}, \boldsymbol{\beta}_0)}{\sum_{s=1}^{S} \lambda_s \tilde{P}(s|\mathbf{x}, \boldsymbol{\beta})} \tilde{P}(\tau|\mathbf{x}, \boldsymbol{\beta}) f(\mathbf{x})\, d\mathbf{x} \\ &\quad + \frac{H(\tau)}{\lambda_\tau}, \qquad \tau = 1, 2, \ldots, S-1,\end{aligned} \tag{9.5.58}$$

and

$$\begin{aligned}&\frac{\partial}{\partial \boldsymbol{\beta}} \text{plim}\, n^{-1}\Omega \\ &= \sum_{s=1}^{S} H(s) \int \sum_{j\in J_s} \frac{1}{P(j|\mathbf{x}, \boldsymbol{\beta})} \frac{\partial P(j)}{\partial \boldsymbol{\beta}} \tilde{Q}_0(s)^{-1} P(j|\mathbf{x}, \boldsymbol{\beta}_0) f(\mathbf{x})\, d\mathbf{x} \\ &\quad - \sum_{s=1}^{S} H(s) \int \frac{1}{\sum_{s=1}^{S} \lambda_s \tilde{P}(s|\mathbf{x}, \boldsymbol{\beta})} \sum_{s=1}^{S} \lambda_s \frac{\partial \tilde{P}(s)}{\partial \boldsymbol{\beta}} \\ &\quad \times \tilde{Q}_0(s)^{-1} \tilde{P}(s|\mathbf{x}, \boldsymbol{\beta}_0) f(\mathbf{x})\, d\mathbf{x}.\end{aligned} \tag{9.5.59}$$

By studying (9.5.58) we see that the right-hand side vanishes if we put $\lambda_s =$

$\tilde{Q}_0(s)^{-1}H(s)\tilde{Q}_0(S)$ and $\boldsymbol{\beta} = \boldsymbol{\beta}_0$. Next, insert these same values into the right-hand side of (9.5.59). Then each term becomes

$$\sum_{s=1}^{S} \int \sum_{j \in J_s} \frac{\partial P(j)}{\partial \boldsymbol{\beta}} H(s)\tilde{Q}_0(s)^{-1} f(\mathbf{x})\, d\mathbf{x}$$

$$= \frac{\partial}{\partial \boldsymbol{\beta}} \sum_{s=1}^{S} \int \sum_{j \in J_s} P(j) H(s)\tilde{Q}_0(s)^{-1} f(\mathbf{x})\, d\mathbf{x} = \frac{\partial}{\partial \boldsymbol{\beta}} 1 = \mathbf{0}.$$

We conclude that

$$\operatorname{plim} \hat{\boldsymbol{\beta}} = \boldsymbol{\beta}_0 \tag{9.5.60}$$

and

$$\operatorname{plim} \hat{\lambda}_s = \frac{H(s)\tilde{Q}_0(S)}{\tilde{Q}_0(s)}. \tag{9.5.61}$$

It is interesting to note that if we replace λ_s that appears in the right-hand side of (9.5.52) by plim $\hat{\lambda}_s$ given in (9.5.61), Ω becomes identical to the logarithm of Ψ given in (9.5.39). This provides an alternative interpretation of the Manski-McFadden estimator.

The asymptotic normality of $\hat{\boldsymbol{\beta}}$ and $\{\hat{\lambda}_s\}$ can be proved by a straightforward, although cumbersome, application of Theorem 4.1.3. Although the same value of $\boldsymbol{\beta}$ maximizes log L given in (9.5.47) and Ω given in (9.5.52), Ω is, strictly speaking, not a log likelihood function. Therefore we must use Theorem 4.1.3, which gives the asymptotic normality of a general extremum estimator, rather than Theorem 4.2.4, which gives the asymptotic normality of MLE. Indeed, Cosslett showed that the asymptotic covariance matrix of $\hat{\boldsymbol{\alpha}} \equiv (\hat{\boldsymbol{\beta}}', \hat{\lambda}_1, \hat{\lambda}_2, \ldots, \hat{\lambda}_{S-1})'$ is given by a formula like that given in Theorem 4.1.3, which takes the form $\mathbf{A}^{-1}\mathbf{B}\mathbf{A}^{-1}$, rather than by $[-E\partial^2\Omega/\partial\boldsymbol{\alpha}\partial\boldsymbol{\alpha}']^{-1}$. However, Cosslett showed that the asymptotic covariance matrix of $\hat{\boldsymbol{\beta}}$ is equal to the first $K \times K$ block of $[-E\partial^2\Omega/\partial\boldsymbol{\alpha}\partial\boldsymbol{\alpha}']^{-1}$.

Cosslett showed that the asymptotic covariance matrix of $\hat{\boldsymbol{\beta}}$ attains the lower bound of the covariance matrix of any unbiased estimator of $\boldsymbol{\beta}$. This remarkable result is obtained by generalizing the Cramér-Rao lower bound (Theorem 1.3.1) to a likelihood function that depends on an unknown density function as in (9.5.47).

To present the gist of Cosslett's argument, we must first define the concept of differentiation of a functional with respect to a function. Let $F(f)$ be a mapping from a function to a real number (such a mapping is called a functional). Then we define

$$\left.\frac{\partial F}{\partial f}\right|_{\zeta} = \lim_{\epsilon \to 0} \frac{F(f+\epsilon\zeta) - F(f)}{\epsilon}, \tag{9.5.62}$$

where ζ is a function for which $F(f+\epsilon\zeta)$ can be defined. Let $\mathbf{t}_1$ (a K-vector) and t_2 (a scalar) be unbiased estimators of $\boldsymbol{\beta}$ and $\int f(\mathbf{x})\zeta(\mathbf{x})\, d\mathbf{x}$ for some function ζ such that $\int \zeta(\mathbf{x})\, d\mathbf{x} = 0$ and $\int \zeta(\mathbf{x})^2\, d\mathbf{x} = 1$. Then Cosslett showed that the $(2K+2)$-vector

$$\left[\mathbf{t}_1', t_2, \frac{\partial \log L}{\partial \boldsymbol{\beta}'}, \left.\frac{\partial \log L}{\partial f}\right|_{\zeta}\right]'$$

has covariance matrix of the form

$$\begin{bmatrix} \mathbf{C} & \mathbf{I} \\ \mathbf{I} & \mathbf{R}(\zeta) \end{bmatrix},$$

where $\mathbf{C}$ is the covariance matrix of $(\mathbf{t}_1', t_2)'$. Because this covariance matrix is positive definite, we have $\mathbf{C} > \mathbf{R}(\zeta)^{-1}$, as in Theorem 1.3.1. Finally, it is shown that the asymptotic covariance matrix of $\hat{\boldsymbol{\beta}}$ is equal to the first $K \times K$ block of $\max_\zeta \mathbf{R}(\zeta)^{-1}$.

Thus Cosslett seems justified in saying that $\hat{\boldsymbol{\beta}}$ is asymptotically efficient in the sense defined in Section 4.2.4. As we remarked in that section, this does not mean that $\hat{\boldsymbol{\beta}}$ has the smallest asymptotic covariance matrix among all consistent estimators. Whether the results of LeCam and Rao mentioned in Section 4.2.4 also apply to Cosslett's model remains to be shown.

9.5.5 Results of Cosslett: Part II

Cosslett (1981b) summarized results obtained elsewhere, especially from his earlier papers (Cosslett, 1978, 1981a). He also included a numerical evaluation of the asymptotic bias and variance of various estimators. We shall first discuss CBMLE of the generalized choice-based sample model with unknown f and known Q. Cosslett (1981b) merely stated the consistency, asymptotic normality, and asymptotic efficiency of the estimator, which are proved in Cosslett (1978). The discussion here will be brief because the results are analogous to those given in the previous subsection.

The log likelihood function we shall consider in this subsection is similar to (9.5.47) except that the last term is simplified because Q is now known. Thus

we have

$$\log L_2 = \sum_{i=1}^{n} \log P(j_i|\mathbf{x}_i, \boldsymbol{\beta}) + \sum_{i=1}^{n} \log f(\mathbf{x}_i) - \sum_{s=1}^{S} n_s \log \tilde{Q}_0(s), \tag{9.5.63}$$

which is to be maximized with respect to $\boldsymbol{\beta}$ and f subject to the constraints

$$\tilde{Q}_0(s) = \int \tilde{P}(s|\mathbf{x}, \boldsymbol{\beta}) f(\mathbf{x})\, d\mathbf{x}. \tag{9.5.64}$$

It is shown that this constrained maximization is equivalent to maximizing with respect to λ_j, $j = 0, 1, 2, \ldots, m$,

$$\Omega_1 = \sum_{i=1}^{n} \log \frac{P(j_i|\mathbf{x}_i, \boldsymbol{\beta})}{\sum_{j=0}^{m} \lambda_j P(j|\mathbf{x}_i, \boldsymbol{\beta})} \tag{9.5.65}$$

subject to the contraint $\Sigma_{j=0}^{m} \lambda_j Q_0(j) = 1$. Consistency, asymptotic normality, and asymptotic efficiency can be proved in much the same way as in the preceding subsection.

Next, we shall report Cosslett's numerical analysis, which is in the same spirit as that reported in Section 9.5.2 concerning the Manski-Lerman estimator. Cosslett compared RSMLE, CBMLE, WMLE, and MME in the simple choice-based sample model with f unknown and Q known.[20] Three binary QR models (logit, probit, and arctangent) were considered. In each model there is only one independent variable, which is assumed to be normally distributed. The asymptotic bias and the asymptotic variance of the estimators are evaluated for different values of $\boldsymbol{\beta}$ (two coefficients), $Q(1)$, $H(1)$, and the mean of the independent variable. The optimal design is also derived for each estimator. Cosslett concluded that (1) RSMLE can have a large asymptotic bias; (2) CBMLE is superior to WMLE and MME; (3) a comparison between WMLE and MME depends on parameters, especially $Q(1)$; (4) the choice of $H(1) = 0.5$ was generally quite good, leading to only a small loss of efficiency compared to the optimal design. (This last finding is consistent with the results of our numerical analysis reported in Section 9.5.2.)

9.6 Distribution-Free Methods

In this section we shall discuss two important articles by Manski (1975) and Cosslett (1983). Both articles are concerned with the distribution-free estimation of parameters in QR models—Manski for multinomial models and Cosslett for binary models. However, their approaches are different: Manski proposed a nonparametric method called *maximum score estimation* whereas Cosslett proposed *generalized maximum likelihood estimation* in which the likelihood function is maximized with respect to both F and $\boldsymbol{\beta}$ in the model (9.2.1). Both authors proved only consistency of their estimator but not asymptotic normality.

9.6.1 Maximum Score Estimator—A Binary Case

Manski (1975) considered a multinomial QR model, but here we shall define his estimator for a binary QR model and shall prove its consistency. Our proof will be different from Manski's proof.[21] We shall then indicate how to extend the proof to the case of a multinomial QR model in the next subsection.

Consider a binary QR model

$$P(y_i = 1) = F(\mathbf{x}_i'\boldsymbol{\beta}_0), \qquad i = 1, 2, \ldots, n, \tag{9.6.1}$$

and define the score function

$$S_n(\boldsymbol{\beta}) = \sum_{i=1}^{n} [y_i\chi(\mathbf{x}_i'\boldsymbol{\beta} \geqq 0) + (1 - y_i)\chi(\mathbf{x}_i'\boldsymbol{\beta} < 0)], \tag{9.6.2}$$

where

$$\begin{aligned} \chi(\mathrm{E}) &= 1 \qquad \text{if event E occurs} \\ &= 0 \qquad \text{otherwise.} \end{aligned} \tag{9.6.3}$$

Note that the score is the number of correct predictions we would make if we predicted y_i to be 1 whenever $\mathbf{x}_i'\boldsymbol{\beta} \geqq 0$. Manski's maximum score estimator $\hat{\boldsymbol{\beta}}_n$ is defined by

$$S_n(\hat{\boldsymbol{\beta}}_n) = \sup_{\boldsymbol{\beta} \in \mathrm{B}} S_n(\boldsymbol{\beta}), \tag{9.6.4}$$

where the parameter space B is taken as

$$\mathrm{B} = \{\boldsymbol{\beta} | \boldsymbol{\beta}'\boldsymbol{\beta} = 1\}. \tag{9.6.5}$$

Clearly, (9.6.5) implies no loss of generality because $S_n(c\boldsymbol{\beta}) = S_n(\boldsymbol{\beta})$ for any positive scalar c.

Because $S_n(\boldsymbol{\beta})$ is not continuous in $\boldsymbol{\beta}$, we cannot use Theorem 4.1.1 without a modification. However, an appropriate modification is possible by generalizing the concept of convergence in probability as follows:

DEFINITION 9.6.1. Let $(\Omega, \mathcal{A}, P)$ be a probability space. A sequence of not necessarily measurable functions $g_T(\omega)$ for $\omega \in \Omega$ is said to *converge* to 0 *in probability in the generalized sense* if for any $\epsilon > 0$ there exists $A_T \in \mathcal{A}$ such that

$$A_T \subset \{\omega | \quad |g_T(\omega)| < \epsilon\}$$

and $\lim_{T\to\infty} P(A_T) = 1$.

Using this definition, we can modify Theorem 4.1.1 as follows:

THEOREM 9.6.1. Make the following assumptions:

(A) The parameter space Θ is a compact subset of the Euclidean K-space (R^K).

(B) $Q_T(\mathbf{y}, \boldsymbol{\theta})$ is a measurable function of $\mathbf{y}$ for all $\boldsymbol{\theta} \in \Theta$.

(C) $T^{-1}Q_T(\boldsymbol{\theta})$ converges to a nonstochastic continuous function $Q(\boldsymbol{\theta})$ in probability uniformly in $\boldsymbol{\theta} \in \Theta$ as T goes to ∞, and $Q(\boldsymbol{\theta})$ attains a unique global maximum at $\boldsymbol{\theta}_0$.

Define $\hat{\boldsymbol{\theta}}_T$ as a value that satisfies

$$Q_T(\hat{\boldsymbol{\theta}}_T) = \max_{\boldsymbol{\theta} \in \Theta} Q_T(\boldsymbol{\theta}). \tag{9.6.6}$$

Then $\hat{\boldsymbol{\theta}}_T$ converges to $\boldsymbol{\theta}_0$ in probability in the generalized sense.

We shall now prove the consistency of the maximum score estimator with the convergence understood to be in the sense of Definition 9.6.1.

THEOREM 9.6.2. Assume the following:

(A) F is a distribution function such that $F(x) = 0.5$ if and only if $x = 0$.

(B) $\{\mathbf{x}_i\}$ are i.i.d. vector random variables with a joint density function $g(\mathbf{x})$ such that $g(\mathbf{x}) > 0$ for all $\mathbf{x}$.

Then any sequence $\{\hat{\boldsymbol{\beta}}_n\}$ satisfying (9.6.4) converges to $\boldsymbol{\beta}_0$ in probability in the generalized sense.

Proof. Let us verify the assumptions of Theorem 9.6.1. Assumptions A and B are clearly satisfied. The verification of assumption C will be done in five steps.

First, define for $\lambda > 0$

$$S_{\lambda n}(\boldsymbol{\beta}) = \sum_{i=1}^{n} [y_i \psi_\lambda(\mathbf{x}_i'\boldsymbol{\beta}) + (1 - y_i)\psi_\lambda(-\mathbf{x}_i'\boldsymbol{\beta})], \tag{9.6.7}$$

where

$$\begin{aligned} \psi_\lambda(x) &= 0 && \text{if} \quad x \leqq 0 \\ &= \lambda x && \text{if} \quad 0 < x < \lambda^{-1} \\ &= 1 && \text{if} \quad \lambda^{-1} \leqq x. \end{aligned} \tag{9.6.8}$$

Because each term of the summation in (9.6.7) minus its expected value satisfies all the conditions of Theorem 4.2.1 for a fixed positive λ, we can conclude that for any $\epsilon, \delta > 0$ there exists $n_1(\lambda)$, which may depend on λ, such that for all $n \geqq n_1(\lambda)$

$$P\left[\sup_{\boldsymbol{\beta} \in \mathbf{B}} |n^{-1}S_{\lambda n}(\boldsymbol{\beta}) - Q_\lambda(\boldsymbol{\beta})| > \frac{\epsilon}{3}\right] < \frac{\delta}{2}, \tag{9.6.9}$$

where

$$Q_\lambda(\boldsymbol{\beta}) = EF(\mathbf{x}'\boldsymbol{\beta}_0)\psi_\lambda(\mathbf{x}'\boldsymbol{\beta}) + E[1 - F(\mathbf{x}'\boldsymbol{\beta}_0)]\psi_\lambda(-\mathbf{x}'\boldsymbol{\beta}). \tag{9.6.10}$$

Second, we have

$$\begin{aligned} &\sup_{\boldsymbol{\beta}} |n^{-1}S_n(\boldsymbol{\beta}) - n^{-1}S_{\lambda n}(\boldsymbol{\beta})| \\ &\leqq \sup_{\boldsymbol{\beta}} \left| n^{-1} \sum_{i=1}^{n} \eta_\lambda(\mathbf{x}_i'\boldsymbol{\beta}) - E\eta_\lambda(\mathbf{x}'\boldsymbol{\beta}) \right| + \sup_{\boldsymbol{\beta}} E\eta_\lambda(\mathbf{x}'\boldsymbol{\beta}) \\ &\equiv A_1 + A_2, \end{aligned} \tag{9.6.11}$$

where

$$\begin{aligned} \eta_\lambda(x) &= 0 && \text{if} \quad \lambda^{-1} \leqq |x| \\ &= 1 + \lambda x && \text{if} \quad -\lambda^{-1} < x < 0 \\ &= 1 - \lambda x && \text{if} \quad 0 \leqq x < \lambda^{-1}. \end{aligned} \tag{9.6.12}$$

Applying Theorem 4.2.1 to A_1, we conclude that for any $\epsilon, \delta > 0$ there exists $n_2(\lambda)$, which may depend on λ, such that for all $n \geqq n_2(\lambda)$

$$P\left(A_1 > \frac{\epsilon}{6}\right) < \frac{\delta}{2}. \tag{9.6.13}$$

We have

$$A_2 \leqq \sup_{\beta} P[(\mathbf{x}'\beta)^2 < \lambda^{-2}]. \tag{9.6.14}$$

But, because the right-hand side of (9.6.14) converges to 0 as $\lambda \rightarrow \infty$ because of assumption B, we have for all $\lambda \geqq \lambda_1$

$$P\left(A_2 > \frac{\epsilon}{6}\right) = 0. \tag{9.6.15}$$

Therefore, from (9.6.11), (9.6.13), and (9.6.15), we conclude that for all $n \geqq n_2(\lambda)$ and for all $\lambda \geqq \lambda_1$

$$P\left[\sup_{\beta} |n^{-1}S_n(\beta) - n^{-1}S_{\lambda n}(\beta)| > \frac{\epsilon}{3}\right) < \frac{\delta}{2}. \tag{9.6.16}$$

Third, define

$$Q(\beta) = EF(\mathbf{x}'\beta_0) + \int_{\mathbf{x}'\beta<0} [1 - 2F(\mathbf{x}'\beta_0)]g(\mathbf{x})\, d\mathbf{x}. \tag{9.6.17}$$

Then we have

$$\sup_{\beta} |Q(\beta) - Q_\lambda(\beta)| \leqq \sup_{\beta} P[(\mathbf{x}'\beta)^2 < \lambda^{-2}]. \tag{9.6.18}$$

Therefore, using the same argument that led to (9.6.15), we conclude that for all $\lambda \geqq \lambda_1$

$$P\left[\sup_{\beta} |Q(\beta) - Q_\lambda(\beta)| > \frac{\epsilon}{3}\right] = 0. \tag{9.6.19}$$

Fourth, because

$$\begin{aligned} \sup_{\beta} |n^{-1}S_n(\beta) - Q(\beta)| \leqq & \sup_{\beta} |n^{-1}S_n(\beta) - n^{-1}S_{\lambda n}(\beta)| \\ & + \sup_{\beta} |n^{-1}S_{\lambda n}(\beta) - Q_\lambda(\beta)| \\ & + \sup_{\beta} |Q_\lambda(\beta) - Q(\beta)|, \end{aligned} \tag{9.6.20}$$

we conclude from (9.6.9), (9.6.16), and (9.6.19) that for any $\epsilon, \delta > 0$ we have for all $n \geqq \max[n_1(\lambda_1), n_2(\lambda_1)]$

$$P[\sup_{\beta} |n^{-1}S_n(\beta) - Q(\beta)| > \epsilon] < \delta. \tag{9.6.21}$$

Fifth and finally, it remains to show that $Q(\beta)$ defined in (9.6.17) attains a unique global maximum at β_0. This is equivalent to showing

$$\int_{\mathbf{x}'\beta_0<0} [1 - 2F(\mathbf{x}'\beta_0)]g(\mathbf{x})\, d\mathbf{x} \tag{9.6.2}$$

$$> \int_{\mathbf{x}'\beta<0} [1 - 2F(\mathbf{x}'\beta_0)]g(\mathbf{x})\, d\mathbf{x} \text{ if } \beta \neq \beta_0.$$

But, because $1 - 2F(\mathbf{x}'\beta_0) > 0$ in the region $\{\mathbf{x}|\mathbf{x}'\beta_0 < 0\}$ and $1 - 2F(\mathbf{x}'\beta_0) < 0$ in the region $\{\mathbf{x}|\mathbf{x}'\beta_0 > 0\}$ by assumption A, (9.6.22) follows immediately from assumption B.

9.6.2 Maximum Score Estimator—A Multinomial Case

The multinomial QR model considered by Manski has the following structure. The utility of the ith person when he or she chooses the jth alternative is given by

$$U_{ij} = \mathbf{x}_{ij}'\beta_0 + \epsilon_{ij}, \qquad i = 1, 2, \ldots, n, \qquad j = 0, 1, \ldots, m, \tag{9.6.23}$$

where we assume

ASSUMPTION 9.6.1. $\{\epsilon_{ij}\}$ are i.i.d. for both i and j.

ASSUMPTION 9.6.2. $(\mathbf{x}_{i0}', \mathbf{x}_{i1}', \ldots, \mathbf{x}_{im}')' \equiv \mathbf{x}_i$ is a sequence of $(m + 1)K$-dimensional i.i.d. random vectors, distributed independently of $\{\epsilon_{ij}\}$, with a joint density $g(\mathbf{x})$ such that $g(\mathbf{x}) > 0$ for all $\mathbf{x}$.

ASSUMPTION 9.6.3. The parameter space B is defined by $\mathrm{B} = \{\beta|\beta'\beta = 1\}$.

Each person chooses the alternative for which the utility is maximized. Therefore, if we represent the event of the ith person choosing the jth alternative by a binary random variable y_{ij}, we have

$$\begin{aligned} y_{ij} &= 1 \quad \text{if} \quad U_{ij} > U_{ik} \quad \text{for all} \quad k \neq j \\ &= 0 \quad \text{otherwise.} \end{aligned} \tag{9.6.24}$$

We need not worry about the possibility of a tie because of Assumption 9.6.2.

The maximum score estimator $\hat{\beta}_n$ is defined as the value of β that maximizes the score[22]

$$S_n(\boldsymbol{\beta}) = \sum_{i=1}^{n} \sum_{j=0}^{m} y_{ij}\chi(\mathbf{x}_{ij}'\boldsymbol{\beta} \geqq \mathbf{x}_{ik}'\boldsymbol{\beta} \quad \text{for all} \quad k \neq j) \tag{9.6.25}$$

subject to $\boldsymbol{\beta}'\boldsymbol{\beta} = 1$, where χ is defined in (9.6.3). We shall indicate how to generalize the consistency theorem to the present multinomial model.

As in the proof of Theorem 9.6.2, we must verify the assumptions of Theorem 9.6.1. Again, assumptions A and B are clearly satisfied. Assumption C can be verified in a manner very similar to the proof of Theorem 9.6.2. We merely note whatever changes are needed for the multinomial model.

We can generalize (9.6.7) as

$$S_{\lambda n}(\boldsymbol{\beta}) = \sum_{i=1}^{n} \sum_{j=0}^{m} y_{ij}\psi_\lambda[(\mathbf{x}_{ij} - \mathbf{x}_{i0})'\boldsymbol{\beta}, (\mathbf{x}_{ij} - \mathbf{x}_{i1})'\boldsymbol{\beta}, \ldots, \tag{9.6.26}$$
$$(\mathbf{x}_{ii} - \mathbf{x}_{i,j-1})'\boldsymbol{\beta}, (\mathbf{x}_{ij} - \mathbf{x}_{i,j+1})'\boldsymbol{\beta}, \ldots, (\mathbf{x}_{ij} - \mathbf{x}_{im})'\boldsymbol{\beta}],$$

where

$$\begin{aligned} \psi_\lambda(z_1, z_2, \ldots, z_m) &= 0 \qquad \text{if} \quad \min_i (z_i) \leqq 0 \\ &= 1 \qquad \text{if} \quad \min_i (z_i) > \lambda^{-1} \\ &= \lambda \min_i (z_i) \qquad \text{otherwise.} \end{aligned} \tag{9.6.27}$$

Then the first four steps of the proof of Theorem 9.6.2 generalize straightforwardly to the present case.

The fifth step is similar but involves a somewhat different approach. From (9.6.25) we obtain

$$\begin{aligned} Q(\boldsymbol{\beta}) &\equiv \operatorname*{plim}_{n\to\infty} n^{-1}S_n(\boldsymbol{\beta}) \\ &= E \sum_{j=0}^{m} P(y_j = 1|\mathbf{x}, \boldsymbol{\beta}_0)\chi(\mathbf{x}_j'\boldsymbol{\beta} \geqq \mathbf{x}_k'\boldsymbol{\beta} \qquad \text{for all} \quad k \neq j) \\ &= Eh(\mathbf{x}, \boldsymbol{\beta}), \end{aligned} \tag{9.6.28}$$

where $\{y_j\}$ and $\{\mathbf{x}_j\}$ are random variables from which i.i.d. observations $\{y_{ij}\}$ and $\{\mathbf{x}_{ij}\}$ are drawn and $\mathbf{x} = (\mathbf{x}_0', \mathbf{x}_1', \ldots, \mathbf{x}_m')'$. First, we want to show $h(\mathbf{x}, \boldsymbol{\beta})$ is uniquely maximized at $\boldsymbol{\beta}_0$. For this purpose consider maximizing

$$h^*(\mathbf{x}, \{A_j\}) = \sum_{j=0}^{m} P(y_j = 1|\mathbf{x}, \boldsymbol{\beta}_0)\chi(A_j) \tag{9.6.29}$$

for every $\mathbf{x}$ with respect to a nonoverlapping partition $\{A_j\}$ of the space of $\mathbf{x}$.

This is equivalent to the following question: Given a particular $\mathbf{x}_0$, to which region should we assign this point? Suppose

$$P(y_{j_0}=1|\mathbf{x}_0, \boldsymbol{\beta}_0) > P(y_j=1|\mathbf{x}_0, \boldsymbol{\beta}_0) \qquad \text{for all} \quad j \neq j_0. \tag{9.6.30}$$

Then it is clearly best to assign $\mathbf{x}_0$ to the region defined by

$$P(y_{j_0}=1|\mathbf{x}, \boldsymbol{\beta}_0) > P(y_j=1|\mathbf{x}, \boldsymbol{\beta}_0) \qquad \text{for all} \quad j \neq j_0. \tag{9.6.31}$$

Thus (9.6.29) is maximized by the partition $\{A_j^0\}$ defined by

$$A_j^0 = \{\mathbf{x}|\mathbf{x}_j'\boldsymbol{\beta}_0 \geqq \mathbf{x}_k'\boldsymbol{\beta}_0 \qquad \text{for} \quad k \neq j\}. \tag{9.6.32}$$

Clearly, this is also a solution to the more restricted problem of maximizing $h(\mathbf{x}, \boldsymbol{\beta})$. This maximum is unique because we always have a strict inequality in (9.6.30) because of our assumptions. Also our assumptions are such that if $h(\mathbf{x}, \boldsymbol{\beta})$ is uniquely maximized for every $\mathbf{x}$ at $\boldsymbol{\beta}_0$, then $Eh(\mathbf{x}, \boldsymbol{\beta})$ is uniquely maximized at $\boldsymbol{\beta}_0$. This completes the proof of the consistency of the maximum score estimator in the multonomial case. (Figure 9.2 illustrates the maximization of Eq. 9.6.29 for the case where $m=3$ and x is a scalar.)

The asymptotic distribution of the maximum score estimator has not yet been obtained. A major difficulty lies in the fact that the score function is not differentiable and hence Theorem 4.1.3, which is based on a Taylor expansion of the derivative of a maximand, cannot be used. The degree of difficulty for the maximum score estimator seems greater than that for the LAD estimator discussed in Section 4.6—the method of proving asymptotic normality for LAD does not work in the present case. In the binary case, maximizing (9.6.2)

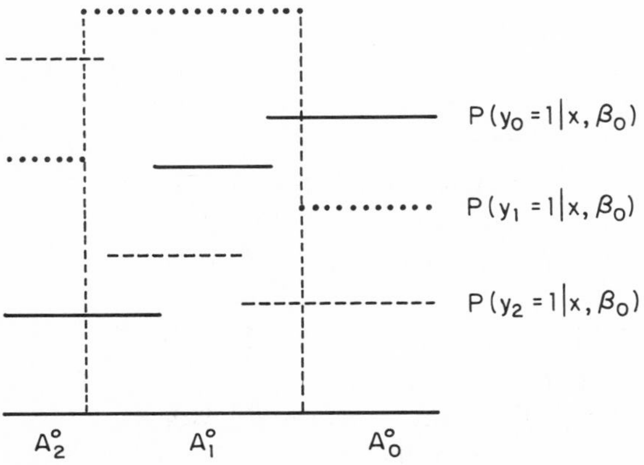

Figure 9.2 An optimal partition of the space of an independent variable

is equivalent to minimizing $\Sigma_{i=1}^{n}|y_i - \chi(\mathbf{x}_i'\boldsymbol{\beta} \geqq 0)|$. This shows both a similarity of the maximum score estimator to the LAD estimator and the additional difficulty brought about by the discontinuity of the χ function.

Manski (1975) reported results of a Monte Carlo study in which he compared the maximum score estimator with the logit MLE in a five-response multinomial logit model with four unknown parameters and 400 observations. The study demonstrated a fairly good performance by the maximum score estimator as well as its computational feasibility. The bias of the estimator is very small, whereas the root mean squared error is somewhere in the magnitude of double that of MLE. A comparison of the maximum score estimator and MLE under a model different from the one from which MLE is derived would be interesting.

9.6.3 Generalized Maximum Likelihood Estimator

Cosslett (1983) proposed maximizing the log likelihood function (9.2.7) of a binary QR model with respct to $\boldsymbol{\beta}$ and F, subject to the condition that F is a distribution function. The log likelihood function, denoted here as ψ, is

$$\psi(\boldsymbol{\beta}, F) = \sum_{i=1}^{n} \{y_i \log F(\mathbf{x}_i'\boldsymbol{\beta}) + (1 - y_i) \log [1 - F(\mathbf{x}_i'\boldsymbol{\beta})]\}. \quad (9.6.33)$$

The consistency proof of Kiefer and Wolfowitz (1956) applies to this kind of model. Cosslett showed how to compute MLE $\hat{\boldsymbol{\beta}}$ and $\hat{F}$ and derived conditions for the consistency of MLE, translating the general conditions of Kiefer and Wolfowitz into this particular model. The conditions Cosslett found, which are not reproduced here, are quite reasonable and likely to hold in most practical applications.

Clearly some kind of normalization is needed on $\boldsymbol{\beta}$ and F before we maximize (9.6.33). Cosslet adopted the following normalization: The constant term is 0 and the sum of squares of the remaining parameters is equal to 1. Note that the assumption of zero constant term is adopted in lieu of Manski's assumption $F(0) = 0.5$. We assume that the constant term has already been eliminated from the $\mathbf{x}_i'\boldsymbol{\beta}$ that appears in (9.6.33). Thus we can proceed, assuming $\boldsymbol{\beta}'\boldsymbol{\beta} = 1$.

The maximization of (9.6.33) is carried out in two stages. In the first stage we shall fix $\boldsymbol{\beta}$ and maximize $\psi(\boldsymbol{\beta}, F)$ with respect to F. Let the solution be $\hat{F}(\boldsymbol{\beta})$. Then in the second stage we shall maximize $\psi[\boldsymbol{\beta}, \hat{F}(\boldsymbol{\beta})]$ with respect to $\boldsymbol{\beta}$. Although the second stage presents a more difficult computational problem, we shall describe only the first stage because it is nonstandard and conceptually more difficult.

The first-stage maximization consists of several steps:

Step 1. Given $\boldsymbol{\beta}$, rank order $\{\mathbf{x}_i'\boldsymbol{\beta}\}$. Suppose $\mathbf{x}_{(1)}'\boldsymbol{\beta} < \mathbf{x}_{(2)}'\boldsymbol{\beta} < \ldots < \mathbf{x}_{(n)}'\boldsymbol{\beta}$, assuming there is no tie. Determine a sequence $(y_{(1)}, y_{(2)}, \ldots, y_{(n)})$ accordingly. Note that this is a sequence consisting only of ones and zeros.

Step 2. Partition this sequence into the smallest possible number of successive groups in such a way that each group consists of a nonincreasing sequence.

Step 3. Calculate the ratio of ones over the number of elements in each group. Let a sequence of ratios thus obtained be $(r_1, r_2, \ldots, r_K)$, assuming there are K groups. If this is a nondecreasing sequence, we are done. We define $F(\mathbf{x}_{(i)}'\boldsymbol{\beta}) = r_j$ if the (i)th observation is in the jth group.

Step 4. If, however, $r_j < r_{j-1}$ for some j, combine the jth and $(j-1)$th group and repeat step 3 until we obtain a nondecreasing sequence.

The preceding procedure can best be taught by example:

Example 1.

$y_{(i)}$	0 0	1 1 0	1 1
$\hat{F}(\mathbf{x}_{(i)}'\boldsymbol{\beta})$	0	$\frac{2}{3}$	1

In this example, there is no need for step 4.

Example 2.

$y_{(i)}$	0 0	1 1 0	1 0	1 1
$\hat{F}(\mathbf{x}_{(i)}'\boldsymbol{\beta})$	0	$\frac{2}{3}$	$\frac{1}{2}$	1

Here, the second and third group must be combined to yield

$y_{(i)}$	0 0	1 1 0 1 0	1 1
$\hat{F}(\mathbf{x}_{(i)}'\boldsymbol{\beta})$	0	$\frac{3}{5}$	1

Note that $\hat{F}$ is not unique over some parts of the domain. For example, between $\mathbf{x}_{(2)}'\boldsymbol{\beta}$ and $\mathbf{x}_{(3)}'\boldsymbol{\beta}$ in Example 1, $\hat{F}$ may take any value between 0 and $\frac{2}{3}$.

Asymptotic normality has not been proved for Cosslett's MLE $\hat{\boldsymbol{\beta}}$, nor for any model to which the consistency proof of Kiefer and Wolfowitz is applicable. This seems to be as difficult a problem as proving the asymptotic normality of Manski's maximum score estimator.

Cosslett's MLE may be regarded as a generalization of Manski's estimator because the latter searches only among one-jump step functions to maximize (9.6.33). However, this does not necessarily imply that Cosslett's estimator is superior. Ranking of estimators can be done according to various criteria. If the purpose is prediction, Manski's estimator is an attractive one because it maximizes the number of correct predictions.

9.7 Panel Data QR Models

Panel data consist of observations made on individuals over time. We shall consider models in which these observations are discrete. If observations are independent both over individuals and over time, a panel data QR model does not pose any new problem. It is just another QR model, possibly with more observations than usual. Special problems arise only when observations are assumed to be correlated over time. Serial correlation, or temporal correlation, is certainly more common than correlation among observations of different individuals or cross-section units. In this section we shall consider various panel data QR models with various ways of specifying serial correlation and shall study the problem of estimation in these models.

9.7.1 Models with Heterogeneity

We shall study the problem of specifying a panel data QR model by considering a concrete example of sequential labor force participation by married women, following the analysis of Heckman and Willis (1977). As is customary with a study of labor force participation, it is postulated that a person works if the offered wage exceeds the reservation wage (shadow price of time). The offered wage depends on the person's characteristics such as her education, training, intelligence, and motivation, as well as on local labor market conditions. The reservation wage depends on the person's assets, her husband's wage rate, prices of goods, interest rates, expected value of future wages and prices, and the number and age of her children. Let $y_{it} = 1$ if the ith person works at time t and $=0$ otherwise and let $\mathbf{x}_{it}$ be a vector of the observed independent variables (a subset of the variables listed above). Then for fixed t it seems reasonable to specify a binary QR model

$$P(y_{it} = 1) = F(\mathbf{x}_{it}'\boldsymbol{\beta}), \qquad i = 1, 2, \ldots, n, \tag{9.7.1}$$

where F is an appropriate distribution function.

However, with panel data, (9.7.1) is not enough because it specifies only a marginal probability for fixed t and leaves the joint probability $P(y_{i1}, y_{i2}, \ldots, y_{iT})$ unspecified. (We assume $\{y_{it}\}$ are independent over i.) The simplest way to specify a joint probablity is to assume independence and specify $P(y_{i1}, y_{i2}, \ldots, y_{iT}) = \Pi_{t=1}^{T} P(y_{it})$. Then we obtain the binary QR model studied in Section 9.2, the only difference being that we have nT observations here.

The independence assumption would imply $P(y_{it} = 1 | y_{i,t-1} = 1) = P(y_{it} = 1)$. In other words, once we observe $\mathbf{x}_{it}$, whether or not a woman worked in the previous year would offer no new information concerning her status this year. Surely, such a hypothesis could not be supported empirically.

There are two major reasons why we would expect $P(y_{it} = 1 | y_{i,t-1} = 1) \neq P(y_{it} = 1)$:

1. *Heterogeneity.* There are unobservable variables that affect people differently in regard to their tendency to work.[23]
2. *True State Dependence.* For each person, present status influences future status. For example, once you start doing something, it becomes habitual.

Heckman and Willis (1977) attempted to take account of only heterogeneity in their study. We shall consider how to model true state dependence in Section 9.7.2.

A straightforward approach to take account of heterogeneity is to specify

$$P(y_{it} = 1 | u_i) = F(\mathbf{x}_{it}'\boldsymbol{\beta} + u_i), \qquad (9.7.2)$$

$$i = 1, 2, \ldots, n, \qquad t = 1, 2, \ldots, T,$$

and assume $\{y_{it}\}$ are serially independent (that is, over t) conditional on u_i. Therefore we have (suppressing subscript i)

$$\begin{aligned} P(y_t = 1 | y_{t-1} = 1) - P(y_t = 1) \qquad (9.7.3) \\ = \frac{E[F(\mathbf{x}_t'\boldsymbol{\beta} + u)F(\mathbf{x}_{t-1}'\boldsymbol{\beta} + u)]}{EF(\mathbf{x}_{t-1}'\boldsymbol{\beta} + u)} - EF(\mathbf{x}_t'\boldsymbol{\beta} + u) \\ = \frac{\text{Cov}\,[F(\mathbf{x}_t'\boldsymbol{\beta} + u), F(\mathbf{x}_{t-1}'\boldsymbol{\beta} + u)]}{EF(\mathbf{x}_{t-1}'\boldsymbol{\beta} + u)}, \end{aligned}$$

which can be shown to be nonnegative. The joint probability of $\{y_{it}\}$, $t = 1, 2, \ldots, T$, is given by

$$\begin{aligned} P(y_{i1}, y_{i2}, \ldots, y_{iT}) \qquad (9.7.4) \\ = E_{u_i}\left\{\prod_{t=1}^{T} F(\mathbf{x}_{it}'\boldsymbol{\beta} + u_i)^{y_{it}}[1 - F(\mathbf{x}_{it}'\boldsymbol{\beta} + u_i)]^{1-y_{it}}\right\}. \end{aligned}$$

The likelihood function of the model is the product of (9.7.4) over all individuals $i = 1, 2, \ldots, n$. It is assumed that $\{u_i\}$ are i.i.d. over individuals.

The expectation occurring in (9.7.4) is computationally cumbersome in practice, except for the case where $F = \Phi$, the standard normal distribution function, and u_i is also normal. In this case, Butler and Moffitt (1982) pointed out that using the method of Gaussian quadrature, an evaluation of (9.7.4) for a model with, say, $n = 1500$ and $t = 10$ is within the capacity of most researchers having access to a high-speed computer. We shall come back to a generalization of model (9.7.4) in Section 9.7.2. But here we shall discuss a computationally simpler model in which (9.7.4) is expressed as a product and ratio of gamma functions.

Heckman and Willis proposed what they called a *beta-logistic model*, defined as[24]

$$P(y_{it} = 1|u_i) = u_i, \tag{9.7.5}$$

$$i = 1, 2, \ldots, n, \qquad t = 1, 2, \ldots, T,$$

where u_i is distributed according to the beta density

$$f_i(u_i) = \frac{\Gamma(a_i + b_i)}{\Gamma(a_i)\Gamma(b_i)} u_i^{a_i - 1} (1 - u_i)^{b_i - 1}, \tag{9.7.6}$$

$$0 \leqq u_i \leqq 1, \qquad a_i > 0, \qquad b_i > 0,$$

where $\Gamma(a) = \int_0^\infty x^{a-1} e^{-x}\, dx$. It is assumed that $\{y_{it}\}$ are serially independent conditional on u_i. (Independence over individuals is always assumed.)

The beta density has mean $(a+b)^{-1}a$ and variance $a(a+b)^{-2}(a+b+1)ab$ and can take various shapes: a bell shape if $a, b > 1$; monotonically increasing if $a > 1$ and $b < 1$; monotonically decreasing if $a < 1$ and $b > 1$; uniform if $a = b = 1$; and U shaped if $a, b < 1$.

We have (suppressing subscript i)

$$P(y_t = 1|y_{t-1} = 1) = \frac{P(y_t = 1, y_{t-1} = 1)}{P(y_{t-1} = 1)} = \frac{Eu^2}{Eu} \tag{9.7.7}$$

$$> Eu = P(y_t = 1),$$

where the inequality follows from $Vu > 0$.

Heckman and Willis postulated $a_i = \exp(\mathbf{x}_i'\boldsymbol{\alpha})$ and $b_i = \exp(\mathbf{x}_i'\boldsymbol{\beta})$, where $\mathbf{x}_i$ is a vector of time-independent characteristics of the ith individual. Thus, from (9.7.5), we have

$$P(y_{it} = 1) = \Lambda[\mathbf{x}_i'(\boldsymbol{\alpha} - \boldsymbol{\beta})]. \tag{9.7.8}$$

Equation (9.7.8) shows that if we consider only marginal probabilities we have a logit model; in this sense a beta-logistic model is a generalization of a logit model. By maximizing $\Pi_{i=1}^{n}\Pi_{t=1}^{T}\Lambda[\mathbf{x}_i'(\boldsymbol{\alpha}-\boldsymbol{\beta})]$ we can obtain a consistent estimate of $\boldsymbol{\alpha}-\boldsymbol{\beta}$. However, we can estimate each of $\boldsymbol{\alpha}$ and $\boldsymbol{\beta}$ consistently and also more efficiently by maximizing the full likelihood function. If the ith person worked s_i periods out of T, $i = 1, 2, \ldots, n$, the likelihood function of the beta-logistic model is given by

$$L = \prod_{i=1}^{n} E[u_i^{s_i}(1-u_i)^{T-s_i}] \tag{9.7.9}$$

$$= \prod_{i=1}^{n} \frac{\Gamma(a_i+b_i)}{\Gamma(a_i)\Gamma(b_i)} \cdot \frac{\Gamma(a_i+s_i)\Gamma(b_i+T-s_i)}{\Gamma(a_i+b_i+T)}.$$

An undesirable feature of the beta-logistic model (9.7.9) is that the independent variables $\mathbf{x}_i$ are time independent. Thus, in their empirical study of 1583 women observed over a five-year period, Heckman and Willis were forced to use the values of the independent variables at the first period as $\mathbf{x}_i$ even though some of the values changed with t.

9.7.2 Models with Heterogeneity and True State Dependence

In this subsection we shall develop a generalization of model (9.7.2) that can incorporate both heterogeneity and true state dependence.

Following Heckman (1981a), we assume that there is an unobservable continuous variable y_{it}^* that determines the outcome of a binary variable y_{it} by the rule

$$y_{it} = 1 \quad \text{if} \quad y_{it}^* > 0 \tag{9.7.10}$$

$$= 0 \quad \text{otherwise.}$$

In a very general model, y_{it}^* would depend on independent variables, lagged values of y_{it}^*, lagged values of y_{it}, and an error term that can be variously specified. We shall analyze a model that is simple enough to be computationally feasible and yet general enough to contain most of the interesting features of this type of model: Let

$$y_{it}^* = \mathbf{x}_{it}'\boldsymbol{\beta} + \gamma y_{i,t-1} + v_{it} \equiv \psi_{it} + v_{it}, \tag{9.7.11}$$

where for each i, v_{it} is serially correlated in general. We define *true state dependence* to mean $\gamma \neq 0$ and *heterogeneity* to mean serial correlation of $\{v_{it}\}$.

Model (9.7.2) results from (9.7.11) if we put $\gamma = 0$ and $v_{it} = u_i + \epsilon_{it}$, where $\{\epsilon_{it}\}$ are serially independent. Thus we see that model (9.7.2) is restrictive not only because it assumes no true state dependence but also because it assumes a special form of heterogeneity. This form of heterogeneity belongs to a so-called one-factor model and will be studied further in Section 9.7.3.

Here we shall assume that for each i, $\{v_{it}\}$ are serially correlated in a general way and derive the likelihood function of the model. Because $\{y_{it}\}$ are assumed to be independent over i, the likelihood function is the product of individual likelihood functions. Therefore we suppress i and consider the likelihood function of a typical individual.

Define T-vectors $\mathbf{y}$, $\boldsymbol{\psi}$, and $\mathbf{v}$ the tth elements of which are y_t, ψ_t, and v_t, respectively, and assume $\mathbf{v} \sim N(\mathbf{0}, \boldsymbol{\Sigma})$. Then the joint probability of $\mathbf{y}$ (hence, a typical individual likelihood function) conditional on y_0 can be concisely expressed as

$$P(\mathbf{y}) = F[\boldsymbol{\psi} * (2\mathbf{y} - \mathbf{l}); \boldsymbol{\Sigma} * (2\mathbf{y} - \mathbf{l})(2\mathbf{y} - \mathbf{l})'], \tag{9.7.12}$$

where $*$ denotes the Hadamard product (see Theorem 23 of Appendix 1), $\mathbf{l}$ is a T-vector of ones, and $F(\mathbf{x}; \boldsymbol{\Sigma})$ denotes the distribution function of $N(\mathbf{0}, \boldsymbol{\Sigma})$ evaluated at $\mathbf{x}$. Note that in deriving (9.7.12) we assumed that the conditional distribution of $\mathbf{v}$ given y_0 is $N(\mathbf{0}, \boldsymbol{\Sigma})$. This, however, may not be a reasonable assumption.

As with continuous variable panel data discussed in Section 6.6.3, the specification of the initial conditions y_{i0} (reintroducing subscript i) is an important problem in model (9.7.11), where T is typically small and N is large. The initial conditions y_{i0} can be treated in two ways. (We do assume they are observable. Treating them as N unknown parameters is not a good idea when N is large and T is small.)

1. Treat y_{i0} as known constants, 1 or 0. Then the likelihood function is as given in (9.7.12).

2. Assume that y_{i0} is a random variable with the probability distribution $P(y_{i0} = 1) = \Phi(\mathbf{x}_{i0}'\boldsymbol{\alpha})$, where $\boldsymbol{\alpha}$ is a vector of unknown parameters.

9.7.3 One-Factor Models

The individual likelihood function (9.7.12) involves a T-tuple normal integral, and therefore its estimation is computationally infeasible for large T (say, greater than 5). For this reason we shall consider in this subsection one-factor models that lead to a simplification of the likelihood function.

We assume

$$v_{it} = \alpha_t u_i + \epsilon_{it}, \tag{9.7.13}$$

where $\{\alpha_t\}$, $t = 1, 2, \ldots, T$, are unknown parameters, u_i and $\{\epsilon_{it}\}$ are normally distributed independent of each other, and $\{\epsilon_{it}\}$ are serially independent. We suppress subscript i as before and express (9.7.13) in obvious vector notation as

$$\mathbf{v} = \boldsymbol{\alpha} u + \boldsymbol{\epsilon}, \tag{9.7.14}$$

where $\mathbf{v}$, $\boldsymbol{\alpha}$, and $\boldsymbol{\epsilon}$ are T-vectors and u is a scalar. Then the joint probability of $\mathbf{y}$ can be written as

$$P(\mathbf{y}) = E_u F[\boldsymbol{\psi} * (2\mathbf{y} - \mathbf{l}); \mathbf{D} * (2\mathbf{y} - \mathbf{l})(2\mathbf{y} - \mathbf{l})'], \tag{9.7.15}$$

where $\boldsymbol{\psi}$ now includes $\boldsymbol{\alpha} u$ and $\mathbf{D} = E\boldsymbol{\epsilon}\boldsymbol{\epsilon}'$. Because $\mathbf{D}$ is a diagonal matrix, F in (9.7.15) can be factored as the product of T normal distribution functions. The estimation of this model, therefore, is no more difficult than the estimation of model (9.7.4).

For the case $T = 3$, model (9.7.14) contains a stationary first-order autoregressive model (see Section 5.2.1) as a special case. To see this, put $\boldsymbol{\alpha} = (1 - \rho^2)^{-1/2} (\rho, 1, \rho)'$, $Vu = \sigma^2$, and take the diagonal elements of $\mathbf{D}$ as σ^2, 0, and σ^2. Thus, if $T = 3$, the hypothesis of AR(1) can easily be tested within the more general model (9.7.14). Heckman (1981c) accepted the AR(1) hypothesis using the same data for female labor participation as used by Heckman and Willis (1977). If $T > 4$, model (9.7.13) can be stationary if and only if α_t is constant for all t. A verification of this is left as an exercise.

Consider a further simplification of (9.7.13) obtained by assuming $\alpha_t = 1$, $\{u_i\}$ are i.i.d. over i, and $\{\epsilon_{it}\}$ are i.i.d. both over i and t. This model differs from model (9.7.2) only in the presence of $y_{i,t-1}$ among the right-hand variables and is analogous to the Balestra-Nerlove model (Section 6.6.3) in the continuous variable case.

As in the Balestra-Nerlove model, $\{u_i\}$ may be regarded as unknown parameters to estimate. If both N and T go to ∞, $\boldsymbol{\beta}$, γ, and $\{u_i\}$ can be consistently estimated. An interesting question is whether we can estimate $\boldsymbol{\beta}$ and γ consistently when only N goes to ∞. Unlike the Balestra-Nerlove model, the answer to this question is generally negative for the model considered in this subsection. In a probit model, for example, the values of $\boldsymbol{\beta}$ and γ that maximize

$$L = \prod_{i=1}^{n} \prod_{t=1}^{T} \Phi(\psi_{it} + u_i)^{y_{it}}[1 - \Phi(\psi_{it} + u_i)]^{1-y_{it}}, \tag{9.7.16}$$

while treating $\{u_i\}$ as unknown constants, are not consistent. Heckman (1981b), in a small-scale Monte Carlo study for a probit model with $n = 100$ and $T = 8$, compared this estimator (with y_{i0} treated as given constants), called the transformation estimator, to the *random-effect probit MLE,* in which we maximize the expectation of (9.7.16) taken with respect to $\{u_i\}$, regarded as random variables, and specify the probability of y_{i0} under the specification 2 given at the end of Section 9.7.2.

Heckman concluded that (1) if $\gamma = 0$, the transformation estimator performed fairly well relative to the random-effect probit MLE; (2) if $\gamma \neq 0$, the random-effect probit MLE was better than the transformation estimator, the latter exhibiting a downward bias in γ as in the Balestra-Nerlove model (see Section 6.6.3).

Exercises

1. (Section 9.2.1)
In a Monte Carlo study, Goldfeld and Quandt (1972, Chapter 4) generated $\{y_i\}$ according to the model $P(y_i = 1) = \Phi(0.2 + 0.5x_{1i} + 2x_{2i})$ and, using the generated $\{y_i\}$ and given $\{x_{1i}, x_{2i}\}$, estimated the β's in the linear probability model $P(y_i = 1) = \beta_0 + \beta_1 x_{1i} + \beta_2 x_{2i}$. Their estimates were $\hat{\beta}_0 = 0.58$, $\hat{\beta}_1 = 0.1742$, and $\hat{\beta}_2 = 0.7451$. How do you convert these estimates into the estimates of the coefficients in the probit model?

2. (Section 9.2.2)
Consider a logit model $P(y_i = 1) = \Lambda(\beta_0 + \beta_1 x_i)$, where x_i is a binary variable taking values 0 and 1. This model can be also written as a linear probability model $P(y_i = 1) = \gamma_0 + \gamma_1 x_i$.
   a. Determine γ_0 and γ_1 as functions of β_0 and β_1.
   b. Show that the MLE of γ_0 and γ_1 are equal to the least squares estimates in the regression of y_i on x_i with an intercept.

3. (Section 9.2.3)
Show that global concavity is not invariant to a one-to-one transformation of the parameter space.

4. (Section 9.2.8)
In the model of Exercise 2, we are given the following data:

x	1	1	1	0	0	0	0	0	1	0	1
y	0	0	1	0	0	1	1	0	1	0	1.

Calculate the MLE and the DA estimates (with $\boldsymbol{\Sigma}_0 = \boldsymbol{\Sigma}_1$) of β_0 and β_1.

5. (Section 9.2.8)
The following data come from a hypothetical durable goods purchase study:

Case (t)	Constant	x_t	n_t	r_t	$\frac{r_t}{n_t}$	$\Phi^{-1}\left(\frac{r_t}{n_t}\right)$	$\phi\left[\Phi^{-1}\left(\frac{r_t}{n_t}\right)\right]$
1	1	5	25	12	0.4800	−0.0500	0.3984
2	1	7	26	16	0.6154	0.2930	0.3822
3	1	10	31	22	0.7097	0.5521	0.3426
4	1	15	27	21	0.7778	0.7645	0.2979

a. Compute the coefficient estimates $\hat{\beta}_0$ and $\hat{\beta}_1$ using the following models and estimators:
(1) Linear Probability Model—Least Squares
(2) Linear Probability Model—Weighted Least Squares
(3) Logit Minimum χ^2
(4) Probit Minimum χ^2
(5) Discriminant Analysis Estimator

b. For all estimators except (5), find the asymptotic variance-covariance matrix (evaluated at the respective coefficient estimates).

c. For all estimators, obtain estimates of the probabilities $\tilde{P}_t$ corresponding to each case t.

d. Rank the estimators according to each of the following criteria:

(1) $$\sum_t (\hat{P}_t - \tilde{P}_t)^2.$$

(2) $$\sum_t \frac{n_t}{\hat{P}_t(1-\hat{P}_t)} (\hat{P}_t - \tilde{P}_t)^2.$$

(3) $$\log L \equiv \sum_t [r_t \log \tilde{P}_t + (n_t - r_t) \log (1 - \tilde{P}_t)].$$

6. (Section 9.2.9)
It may be argued that in (9.2.62) the asymptotic variance of r should be the unconditional variance of r, which is $n^{-2}\Sigma_{i=1}^n F_i(1-F_i) + V(n^{-1}\Sigma_{i=1}^n F_i)$, where V is taken with respect to random variables $\{x_i\}$. What is the fallacy of this argument?

7. (Section 9.3.3)
In the multinomial logit model (9.3.34), assume $j = 0$, 1, and 2. For this model define the NLGLS iteration.

8. (Section 9.3.5)
Suppose $\{y_i\}$, $i = 1, 2, \ldots, n$, are independent random variables taking three values, 0, 1, and 2, according to the probability distribution defined by (9.3.51) and (9.3.52), where we assume $\mu_0 = 0$, $\mu_1 = \mathbf{x}_i'\boldsymbol{\beta}_1$, and $\mu_2 = \mathbf{x}_i'\boldsymbol{\beta}_2$. Indicate how we can consistently estimate $\boldsymbol{\beta}_1$, $\boldsymbol{\beta}_2$, and ρ using only a binary logit program.

9. (Section 9.3.5)
Write down (9.3.59) and (9.3.60) in the special case where $S = 2$, $B_1 = (1, 2)$, and $B_2 = (3, 4)$ and show for which values of the parameters the model is reduced to a four-response independent logit model.

10. (Section 9.3.5)
You are to analyze the decision of high school graduates as to whether or not they go to college and, if they go to college, which college they go to. For simplicity assume that each student considers only two possible colleges to go to. Suppose that for each person i, $i = 1, 2, \ldots, n$, we observe $\mathbf{z}_i$ (family income and levels of parents' education) and $\mathbf{x}_{ij}$ (the quality index and the cost of the jth school), $j = 1$ and 2. Also suppose that we observe for every person in the sample whether or not he or she went to college but observe a college choice only for those who went to college. Under these assumptions, define your own model and show how to estimate the parameters of the model (cf. Radner and Miller, 1970).

11. (Section 9.3.6)
Write down (9.3.64), (9.3.65), and (9.3.66) in the special case of Figure 9.1 (three-level), that is, $C_1 = (1, 2)$, $C_2 = (3, 4)$, $B_1 = (1, 2)$, $B_2 = (3, 4)$, $B_3 = (5, 6)$, and $B_4 = (7, 8)$.

12. (Section 9.3.10)
Suppose that y_i takes values 0, 1, and 2 with the probability distribution $P(y_i = 0) = \Lambda(\mathbf{x}_i'\boldsymbol{\beta}_0)$ and $P(y_i = 1 | y_i \neq 0) = \Lambda(\mathbf{x}_i'\boldsymbol{\beta}_1)$. Assuming that we have n_t independent observations on y_t with the same value $\mathbf{x}_t$ of the independent variables, $t = 1, 2, \ldots, T$, indicate how to calculate the MIN χ^2 estimates of $\boldsymbol{\beta}_0$ and $\boldsymbol{\beta}_1$.

13. (Section 9.4.3)
Consider two jointly distributed discrete random variables y and x such that y takes two values, 0 and 1, and x takes three values, 0, 1, and 2. The most general model (called the saturated model) is the model in which there is no constraint among the five probabilities that characterize the

joint distribution. Consider a specific model (called the null hypothesis model) in which

$$P(y=1|x)=[1+\exp(-\alpha-\beta x)]^{-1}$$

and the marginal distribution of x is unconstrained. Given n independent observations on (y, x), show how to test the null hypothesis against the saturated model. Write down explicitly the test statistic and the critical region you propose.

14. (Section 9.4.3)
Suppose the joint distribution of y_{1t} and y_{2t}, $t=1, 2, \ldots, T$, is given by the following table:

	y_{2t}	
y_{1t}	1	0
1	$d_t^{-1}\exp(\boldsymbol{\alpha}'\mathbf{x}_t+\boldsymbol{\beta}'\mathbf{z}_t)$	$d_t^{-1}\exp(\boldsymbol{\alpha}'\mathbf{x}_t)$
0	d_t^{-1}	d_t^{-1}

where $d_t=\exp(\boldsymbol{\alpha}'\mathbf{x}_t+\boldsymbol{\beta}'\mathbf{z}_t)+\exp(\boldsymbol{\alpha}'\mathbf{x}_t)+2$. Given n_t independent observations on (y_{1t}, y_{2t}), define the minimum chi-square estimates of the vectors $\boldsymbol{\alpha}$ and $\boldsymbol{\beta}$. Assume that $\mathbf{x}_t$ and $\mathbf{z}_t$ are vectors of known constants.

15. (Section 9.4.3)
Let y_j, $j=1, 2, \ldots, J$, be discrete random variables taking N_j values. Suppose the conditional probability $P(y_j|y_1, \ldots, y_{j-1}, y_{j+1}, \ldots, y_J)$ is given for every j and is positive. Then prove that there is at most one set of joint probabilities consistent with the given conditional probabilities (cf. Amemiya, 1975).

16. (Section 9.4.3)
Let y_1 and y_2 be binary variables taking the value 1 or 0. Show that if $P(y=1|y_2)=\Lambda(\mathbf{x}'\boldsymbol{\beta}_1+\beta_{12}y_2)$ and $P(y_2=1|y_1)=\Lambda(\mathbf{x}'\boldsymbol{\beta}_2+\beta_{21}y_1)$, then $\beta_{12}=\beta_{21}$.

17. (Section 9.5.2)
In the simple logit model defined in the paragraph after (9.5.22), the efficiency of the WMLE of β_0 using the optimal h^* depends only on p and Q_0. Prove $\text{Eff}[h^*(p, Q_0), p, Q_0]=\text{Eff}[h^*(p, 1-Q_0), p, 1-Q_0]$.

18. (Section 9.5.2)
In the same model described in Exercise 17, show that if $Q=0.5$, $h^*=0.5$.

19. (Section 9.5.3)
In the same model described in Exercise 17, show that the asymptotic variance of the MME of β_0 is the same as that of the WMLE.

20. (Section 9.5.3)
Show that (9.5.36) follows from (9.5.19).

21. (Section 9.6.3)
We are given the following data:

i	1	2	3	4	5
y_i	1	0	0	1	1
x_{1i}	−1	−1	0	0	1
x_{2i}	0	1	−1	1	0

a. Obtain the set of β values that maximize

$$S(\beta) = \sum_{i=1}^{5} [y_i\chi(\beta x_{1i} + x_{2i} \geqq 0) + (1 - y_i)\chi(\beta x_{1i} + x_{2i} < 0)],$$

where $\chi(\mathrm{E}) = 1$ if event E occurs, or is zero otherwise.

b. Obtain the set of β values that maximize

$$\psi(\beta, F) = \sum_{i=1}^{5} \{y_i \log F(\beta x_{1i} + x_{2i})$$
$$+ (1 - y_i) \log [1 - F(\beta x_{1i} + x_{2i})]\},$$

where F is also chosen to maximize ψ among all the possible distribution functions. (Note that I have adopted my own normalization, which may differ from Manski's or Cosslett's, so that the parameter space of β is the whole real line.)

22. (Section 9.6.3)
Cosslett (1983, p. 780) considered two sequences of y_i ordered according to the magnitude of $\mathbf{x}_i'\boldsymbol{\beta}$:

Sequence A:	1	0	1	0	1	1	1	1
Sequence B:	0	1	1	1	1	1	1	0

He showed that Sequence A yields a higher value of log L whereas Sequence B yields a higher score. Construct two sequences with nine observations each and an equal number of ones such that one sequence yields a higher value of log L and the other sequence yields a higher score. Your sequence should not contain any of Cosslett's sequences as a subset.

23. (Section 9.7.2)
Assume that $\boldsymbol{\beta} = \mathbf{0}$ and $\{v_{it}\}$ are i.i.d. across i in model (9.7.11) and derive the stationary probability distribution of $\{y_{it}\}$ for a particular i.

24. (Section 9.7.3)
Show that if $T > 4$, model (9.7.13) can be stationary if and only if α_t is constant for all t. Show that if $T = 4$ and $\alpha_t > 0$, then model (9.7.13) can be stationary if and only if α_t is constant for all t.

10 Tobit Models

10.1 Introduction

Tobit models refer to censored or truncated regression models in which the range of the dependent variable is constrained in some way. In economics, such a model was first suggested in a pioneering work by Tobin (1958). He analyzed household expenditure on durable goods using a regression model that specifically took account of the fact that the expediture (the dependent variable of his regression model) cannot be negative. Tobin called his model the model of *limited* dependent variables. It and its various generalizations are known popularly among economists as *Tobit models,* a phrase coined by Goldberger (1964), because of similarities to *probit models.* These models are also known as *censored* or *truncated* regression models. The model is called *truncated* if the observations outside a specified range are totally lost and *censored* if we can at least observe the exogenous variables. A more precise definition will be given later.

Censored and truncated regression models have been developed in other disciplines (notably, biometrics and engineering) more or less independently of their development in econometrics. Biometricians use the model to analyze the survival time of a patient. Censoring or truncation occurs when either a patient is still alive at the last observation date or he or she cannot be located. Similarly, engineers use the model to analyze the time to failure of material or of a machine or of a system. These models are called *survival* or *duration models.* Sociologists and economists have also used survival models to analyze the duration of such phenomena as unemployment, welfare receipt, employment in a particular job, residence in a particular region, marriage, and the period of time between births. Mathematically, survival models belong to the same general class of models as Tobit models; survival models and Tobit models share certain characteristics. However, because survival models possess special features, they will be discussed separately in Chapter 11.

Between 1958—when Tobin's article appeared—and 1970, the Tobit model was used infrequently in econometric applications, but since the early 1970s numerous applications ranging over a wide area of economics have appeared and continue to appear. This phenomenon is due to a recent increase in the availability of micro sample survey data, which the Tobit model analyzes well, and to a recent advance in computer technology that has made estimation of large-scale Tobit models feasible. At the same time, many generalizations of the Tobit model and various estimation methods for these models have been proposed. In fact, models and estimation methods are now so numerous and diverse that it is difficult for econometricians to keep track of all the existing models and estimation methods and maintain a clear notion of their relative merits. Thus it is now particularly useful to examine the current situation and prepare a unified summary and critical assessment of existing results.

We shall try to accomplish this objective by means of classifying the diverse Tobit models into five basic types. (Our review of the empirical literature suggests that roughly 95% of the econometric applications of Tobit models fall into one of these five types.) Although there are many ways to classify Tobit models, we have chosen to classify them according to the form of the likelihood function. This way seems to be the statistically most useful classification because a similarity in the likelihood function implies a similarity in the appropriate estimation and computation methods. It is interesting to note that two models that superficially seem to be very different from each other can be shown to belong to the same type when they are classified according to this scheme.

Sections 10.2 through 10.5 will deal with the standard Tobit model (or Type 1 Tobit), and Sections 10.6 through 10.10 will deal with the remaining four types of models. Basic estimation methods, which with a slight modification can be applied to any of the five types, will be discussed at great length in Section 10.4. More specialized estimation methods will be discussed in relevant passages throughout the chapter. Each model is illustrated with a few empirical examples.

We shall not discuss disequilibrium models except for a few basic models, which will be examined in Section 10.10.4. Some general references on disequilibrium models will be cited there. Nor shall we discuss the related topic of switching regression models. For a discussion of these topics, the reader should consult articles by Maddala (1980, 1983). We shall not discuss Tobit models for panel data (individuals observed through time), except to mention a few articles in relevant passages.

10.2 Standard Tobit Model (Type 1 Tobit Model)

Tobin (1958) noted that the observed relationship between household expenditures on a durable good and household incomes looks like Figure 10.1,

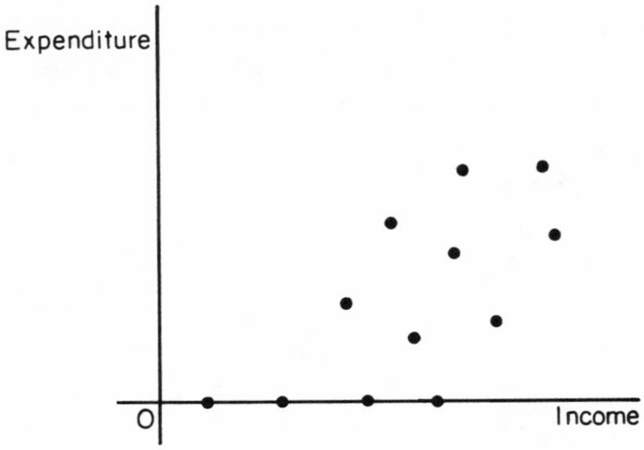

Figure 10.1 An example of censored data

where each dot represents an observation for a particular household. An important characteristic of the data is that there are several observations where the expenditure is 0. This feature destroys the linearity assumption so that the least squares method is clearly inappropriate. Should we fit a nonlinear relationship? First, we must determine a statistical model that can generate the kind of data depicted in Figure 10.1. In doing so the first fact we should recognize is that we cannot use any continuous density to explain the conditional distribution of expenditure given income because a continuous density is inconsistent with the fact that there are several observations at 0. We shall develop an elementary utility maximization model to explain the phenomenon in question.

Define the symbols needed for the utility maximization model as follows:

y a household's expenditure on a durable good
y_0 the price of the cheapest available durable good
z all the other expenditures
x income

A household is assumed to maximize utility $U(y, z)$ subject to the budget constraint $y + z \leqq x$ and the boundary constraint $y \geqq y_0$ or $y = 0$. Suppose y^* is the solution of the maximization subject to $y + z \leqq x$ but not the other constraint, and assume $y^* = \beta_1 + \beta_2 x + u$, where u may be interpreted as the collection of all the unobservable variables that affect the utility function. Then the solution to the original problem, denoted by y, can be defined by

$$\begin{aligned} y &= y^* && \text{if} \quad y^* > y_0 \\ &= 0 \quad \text{or} \quad y_0 && \text{if} \quad y^* \leqq y_0. \end{aligned} \tag{10.2.1}$$

If we assume that u is a random variable and that y_0 varies with households but is assumed known, this model will generate data like Figure 10.1. We can write the likelihood function for n independent observations from the model (10.2.1) as

$$L = \prod_0 F_i(y_{0i}) \prod_1 f_i(y_i), \tag{10.2.2}$$

where F_i and f_i are the distribution and density function, respectively, of y_i^*, Π_0 means the product over those i for which $y_i^* \leqq y_{0i}$, and Π_1 means the product over those i for which $y_i^* > y_{0i}$. Note that the actual value of y when $y^* \leqq y_0$ has no effect on the likelihood function. Therefore the second line of Eq. (10.2.1) may be changed to the statement "if $y^* \leqq y_0$, one merely observes that fact."

The model originally proposed by Tobin (1958) is essentially the same as the model given in the preceding paragraph except that he specifically assumed y^* to be normally distributed and assumed y_0 to be the same for all households. We define the *standard Tobit model* (or Type 1 Tobit) as follows:

$$y_i^* = \mathbf{x}_i'\boldsymbol{\beta} + u_i, \qquad i = 1, 2, \ldots, n, \tag{10.2.3}$$

$$\begin{aligned} y_i &= y_i^* \qquad \text{if} \quad y_i^* > 0 \\ &= 0 \qquad \text{if} \quad y_i^* \leqq 0, \end{aligned} \tag{10.2.4}$$

where $\{u_i\}$ are assumed to be i.i.d. drawings from $N(0, \sigma^2)$. It is assumed that $\{y_i\}$ and $\{\mathbf{x}_i\}$ are observed for $i = 1, 2, \ldots, n$ but $\{y_i^*\}$ are unobserved if $y_i^* \leqq 0$. Defining $\underline{\mathbf{X}}$ to be the $n \times K$ matrix the ith row of which is $\mathbf{x}_i'$, we assume that $\{\mathbf{x}_i\}$ are uniformly bounded and $\lim_{n\to\infty} n^{-1}\, \underline{\mathbf{X}}'\underline{\mathbf{X}}$ is positive definite. We also assume that the parameter space of $\boldsymbol{\beta}$ and σ^2 is compact. In the Tobit model we need to distinguish the vectors and matrices of positive observations from the vectors and matrices of all the observations; the latter appear with an underbar.

Note that $y_i^* > 0$ and $y_i^* \leqq 0$ in (10.2.4) may be changed to $y_i^* > y_0$ and $y_i^* \leqq y_0$ without essentially changing the model, whether y_0 is known or unknown, because y_0 can be absorbed into the constant term of the regression. If, however, y_{0i} changes with i and is known for every i, the model is slightly changed because the resulting model would be essentially equivalent to the model defined by (10.2.3) and (10.2.4), where one of the elements of $\boldsymbol{\beta}$ other than the constant term is known. The model where y_{0i} changes with i and is unknown is not generally estimable.

The likelihood function of the standard Tobit model is given by

$$L = \prod_0 [1 - \Phi(\mathbf{x}_i'\boldsymbol{\beta}/\sigma)] \prod_1 \sigma^{-1}\phi[(y_i - \mathbf{x}_i'\boldsymbol{\beta})/\sigma], \tag{10.2.5}$$

where Φ and ϕ are the distribution and density function, respectively, of the standard normal variable.

The Tobit model belongs to what is sometimes known as the *censored* regression model. In contrast, when we observe neither y_i nor $\mathbf{x}_i$ when $y_i^* \leqq 0$, the model is known as a *truncated* regression model. The likelihood function of the truncated version of the Tobit model can be written as

$$L = \prod_{1} \Phi(\mathbf{x}_i'\boldsymbol{\beta}/\sigma)^{-1}\sigma^{-1}\phi[(y_i - \mathbf{x}_i'\boldsymbol{\beta})/\sigma]. \tag{10.2.6}$$

Henceforth, the standard Tobit model refers to the model defined by (10.2.3) and (10.2.4), namely, a censored regression model, and the model the likelihood function of which is given by (10.2.6) will be called the *truncated standard Tobit model.*

10.3 Empirical Examples

Tobin (1958) obtained the maximum likelihood estimates of his model applied to data on 735 nonfarm households obtained from Surveys of Consumer Finances. The dependent variable of his estimated model was actually the ratio of total durable goods expenditure to disposable income and the independent variables were the age of the head of the household and the ratio of liquid assets to disposable income.

Since then, and especially since the early 1970s, numerous applications of the standard Tobit model have appeared in economic journals, encompassing a wide range of fields in economics. A brief list of recent representative references, with a description of the dependent variable (y) and the main independent variables ($\mathbf{x}$), is presented in Table 10.1. In all the references, except that by Kotlikoff, who uses a two-step estimation method to be discussed later, the method of estimation is maximum likelihood.

10.4 Properties of Estimators under Standard Assumptions

In this section we shall discuss the properties of various estimators of the Tobit model under the assumptions of the model. The estimators we shall consider are the probit maximum likelihood (ML), least squares (LS), Heckman's two-step least squares, nonlinear least squares (NLLS), nonlinear weighted least squares (NLWLS), and Tobit ML estimators.

Table 10.1 Applications of the standard Tobit model

Reference	y	$\mathbf{x}$
Adams (1980)	Inheritance	Income, marital status, number of children
Ashenfelter and Ham (1979)	Ratio of unemployed hours to employed hours	Years of schooling, working experience
Fair (1978)	Number of extramarital affairs	Sex, age, number of years married, number of children, education, occupation, degree of religiousness
Keeley et al. (1978)	Hours worked after a negative income tax program	Preprogram hours worked, change in the wage rate, family characteristics
Kotlikoff (1979)	Expected age of retirement	Ratio of social security benefits lost at time of full-time employment to full-time earnings
Reece (1979)	Charitable contributions	Price of contributions, income
Rosenzweig (1980)	Annual days worked	Wages of husbands and wives, education of husbands and wives, income
Stephenson and McDonald (1979)	Family earnings after a negative income tax program	Earnings before the program, husband's and wife's education, other family characteristics, unemployment rate, seasonal dummies
Wiggins (1981)	Annual marketing of new chemical entities	Research expenditure of the pharmaceutical industry, stringency of government regulatory standards
Witte (1980)	Number of arrests (or convictions) per month after release from prison	Accumulated work release funds, number of months after release until first job, wage rate after release, age, race, drug use

10.4.1 Probit Maximum Likelihood Estimator

The Tobit likelihood function (10.2.5) can be trivially rewritten as

$$L = \prod_0 [1 - \Phi(\mathbf{x}_i'\beta/\sigma)] \prod_1 \Phi(\mathbf{x}_i'\beta/\sigma) \tag{10.4.1}$$
$$\prod_1 \Phi(\mathbf{x}_i'\beta/\sigma)^{-1}\sigma^{-1}\phi[(y_i - \mathbf{x}_i'\beta)/\sigma].$$

Then the first two products of the right-hand side of (10.4.1) constitute the likelihood function of a probit model, and the last product is the likelihood function of the truncated Tobit model as given in (10.2.6). The probit ML estimator of $\alpha \equiv \beta/\sigma$, denoted $\hat{\alpha}$, is obtained by maximizing the logarithm of the first two products.

Note that we can only estimate the ratio β/σ by this method and not β or σ separately. Because the estimator ignores a part of the likelihood function that involves β and σ, it is not fully efficient. This loss of efficiency is not surprising when we realize that the estimator uses only the sign of y_i^*, ignoring its numerical value even when it is observed.

From the results of Section 9.2 we see that the probit MLE is consistent and follows

$$\hat{\alpha} - \alpha \stackrel{A}{=} (\underline{\mathbf{X}}'\underline{\mathbf{D}}_1\underline{\mathbf{X}})^{-1}\underline{\mathbf{X}}'\underline{\mathbf{D}}_1\underline{\mathbf{D}}_0^{-1}(\underline{\mathbf{w}} - E\underline{\mathbf{w}}), \tag{10.4.2}$$

where $\underline{\mathbf{D}}_0$ is the $n \times n$ diagonal matrix the ith element of which is $\phi(\mathbf{x}_i'\alpha)$, $\underline{\mathbf{D}}_1$ is the $n \times n$ diagonal matrix the ith element of which is $\Phi(\mathbf{x}_i'\alpha)^{-1}[1 - \Phi(\mathbf{x}_i'\alpha)]^{-1}\phi(\mathbf{x}_i'\alpha)^2$, and $\underline{\mathbf{w}}$ is the n-vector the ith element w_i of which is defined by

$$\begin{aligned} w_i &= 1 \quad \text{if} \quad y_i^* > 0 \\ &= 0 \quad \text{if} \quad y_i^* \leqq 0. \end{aligned} \tag{10.4.3}$$

Note that the ith element of $E\underline{\mathbf{w}}$ is equal to $\Phi(\mathbf{x}_i'\alpha)$. The symbol $\stackrel{A}{=}$ means that both sides have the same asymptotic distribution.[1] As shown in Section 9.2.2, $\hat{\alpha}$ is asymptotically normal with mean α and asymptotic variance-covariance matrix given by

$$V\hat{\alpha} = (\underline{\mathbf{X}}'\underline{\mathbf{D}}_1\underline{\mathbf{X}})^{-1}. \tag{10.4.4}$$

10.4.2 Least Squares Estimator

From Figure 10.1 it is clear that the least squares regression of expenditure on income using all the observations including zero expenditures yields biased estimates. Although it is not so clear from the figure, the least squares regression using only the positive expenditures also yields biased estimates. These facts can be mathematically demonstrated as follows.

First, consider the regression using only positive observations of y_i. We obtain from (10.2.3) and (10.2.4)

$$E(y_i|y_i > 0) = \mathbf{x}_i'\boldsymbol{\beta} + E(u_i|u_i > -\mathbf{x}_i'\boldsymbol{\beta}). \tag{10.4.5}$$

The last term of the right-hand side of (10.4.5) is generally nonzero (even without assuming u_i is normal). This implies the biasedness of the LS estimator using positive observation on y_i under more general models than the standard Tobit model. When we assume normality of u_i as in the Tobit model, (10.4.5) can be shown by straightforward integration to be

$$E(y_i|y_i > 0) = \mathbf{x}_i'\boldsymbol{\beta} + \sigma\lambda(\mathbf{x}_i'\boldsymbol{\beta}/\sigma), \tag{10.4.6}$$

where $\lambda(z) = \phi(z)/\Phi(z)$.[2] As shown later, this equation plays a key role in the derivation of Heckman's two-step, NLLS, and NLWLS estimators.

Equation (10.4.6) clearly indicates that the LS estimator of $\boldsymbol{\beta}$ is biased and inconsistent, but the direction and magnitude of the bias or inconsistency cannot be shown without further assumptions. Goldberger (1981) evaluated the asymptotic bias (the probability limit minus the true value) assuming that the elements of $\mathbf{x}_i$ (except the first element, which is assumed to be a constant) are normally distributed. More specifically, Goldberger rewrote (10.2.3) as

$$y_i^* = \beta_0 + \bar{\mathbf{x}}_i'\boldsymbol{\beta}_1 + u_i \tag{10.4.7}$$

and assumed $\bar{\mathbf{x}}_i \sim N(\mathbf{0}, \boldsymbol{\Sigma})$, distributed independently of u_i. (Here, the assumption of zero mean involves no loss of generality because a nonzero mean can be absorbed into β_0.) Under this assumption he obtained

$$\text{plim}\ \hat{\boldsymbol{\beta}}_1 = \frac{1-\gamma}{1-\rho^2\gamma}\boldsymbol{\beta}_1, \tag{10.4.8}$$

where $\gamma = \sigma_y^{-1}\lambda(\beta_0/\sigma_y)[\beta_0 + \sigma_y\lambda(\beta_0/\sigma_y)]$ and $\rho^2 = \sigma_y^{-2}\boldsymbol{\beta}_1'\boldsymbol{\Sigma}\boldsymbol{\beta}_1$, where $\sigma_y^2 = \sigma^2 + \boldsymbol{\beta}_1'\boldsymbol{\Sigma}\boldsymbol{\beta}_1$. It can be shown that $0 < \gamma < 1$ and $0 < \rho^2 < 1$; therefore (10.4.8) shows that $\hat{\boldsymbol{\beta}}_1$ shrinks $\boldsymbol{\beta}_1$ toward $\mathbf{0}$. It is remarkable that the degree of shrinkage is uniform in all the elements of $\boldsymbol{\beta}_1$. However, the result may not hold if $\bar{\mathbf{x}}_i$ is not normal; Goldberger gave a nonnormal example where $\boldsymbol{\beta}_1 = (1, 1)'$ and $\text{plim}\ \hat{\boldsymbol{\beta}}_1 = (1.111, 0.887)'$.

Consider the regression using all the observations of y_i, both positive and 0. To see that the least squares estimator is also biased in this case, we should look at the unconditional mean of y_i,

$$Ey_i = \Phi(\mathbf{x}_i'\boldsymbol{\beta}/\sigma)\mathbf{x}_i'\boldsymbol{\beta} + \sigma\phi(\mathbf{x}_i'\boldsymbol{\beta}/\sigma). \tag{10.4.9}$$

Writing (10.2.3) again as (10.4.7) and using the same assumptions as Goldberger, Greene (1981) showed

$$\text{plim}\, \tilde{\boldsymbol{\beta}}_1 = \Phi(\beta_0/\sigma_y)\boldsymbol{\beta}_1, \tag{10.4.10}$$

where $\tilde{\boldsymbol{\beta}}_1$ is the LS estimator of $\boldsymbol{\beta}_1$ in the regression of y_i on $\bar{\mathbf{x}}_i$ using all the observations. This result is more useful than (10.4.8) because it implies that $(n/n_1)\tilde{\boldsymbol{\beta}}_1$ is a consistent estimator of $\boldsymbol{\beta}_1$, where n_1 is the number of positive observations of y_i. A simple consistent estimator of β_0 can be similarly obtained. Greene (1983) gave the asymptotic variances of these estimators. Unfortunately, however, we cannot confidently use this estimator without knowing its properties when the true distribution of $\bar{\mathbf{x}}_i$ is not normal.[3]

10.4.3 Heckman's Two-Step Estimator

Heckman (1976a) proposed a two-step estimator in a two-equation generalization of the Tobit model, which we shall call the Type 3 Tobit model. But his estimator can also be used in the standard Tobit model, as well as in more complex Tobit models, with only a minor adjustment. We shall discuss the estimator in the context of the standard Tobit model because all the basic features of the method can be revealed in this model. However, we should keep in mind that since the method requires the computation of the probit MLE, which itself requires an iterative method, the computational advantage of the method over the Tobit MLE (which is more efficient) is not as great in the standard Tobit model as it is in more complex Tobit models.

To explain this estimator, it is useful to rewrite (10.4.6) as

$$y_i = \mathbf{x}_i'\boldsymbol{\beta} + \sigma\lambda(\mathbf{x}_i'\boldsymbol{\alpha}) + \epsilon_i, \qquad \text{for} \quad i \quad \text{such that} \quad y_i > 0, \tag{10.4.11}$$

where we have written $\boldsymbol{\alpha} \equiv \boldsymbol{\beta}/\sigma$ as before and $\epsilon_i = y_i - E(y_i|y_i > 0)$ so that $E\epsilon_i = 0$. The variance of ϵ_i is given by

$$V\epsilon_i = \sigma^2 - \sigma^2\mathbf{x}_i'\boldsymbol{\alpha}\lambda(\mathbf{x}_i'\boldsymbol{\alpha}) - \sigma^2\lambda(\mathbf{x}_i'\boldsymbol{\alpha})^2. \tag{10.4.12}$$

Thus (10.4.11) is a heteroscedastic nonlinear regression model with n_1 observations. The estimation method Heckman proposed consists of two steps:

Step 1. Estimate $\boldsymbol{\alpha}$ by the probit MLE (denoted $\hat{\boldsymbol{\alpha}}$) defined earlier.

Step 2. Regress y_i on $\mathbf{x}_i$ and $\lambda(\mathbf{x}_i'\hat{\boldsymbol{\alpha}})$ by least squares, using only the positive observations on y_i.

To facilitate further the discussion of Heckman's estimator, we can rewrite

(10.4.11) again as

$$y_i = \mathbf{x}_i'\boldsymbol{\beta} + \sigma\lambda(\mathbf{x}_i'\hat{\boldsymbol{\alpha}}) + \epsilon_i + \eta_i, \quad \text{for } i \text{ such that } y_i > 0, \tag{10.4.13}$$

where $\eta_i = \sigma[\lambda(\mathbf{x}_i'\boldsymbol{\alpha}) - \lambda(\mathbf{x}_i'\hat{\boldsymbol{\alpha}})]$. We can write (10.4.13) in vector notation as

$$\mathbf{y} = \mathbf{X}\boldsymbol{\beta} + \sigma\hat{\boldsymbol{\lambda}} + \boldsymbol{\epsilon} + \boldsymbol{\eta}, \tag{10.4.14}$$

where the vectors $\mathbf{y}$, $\hat{\boldsymbol{\lambda}}$, $\boldsymbol{\epsilon}$, and $\boldsymbol{\eta}$ have n_1 elements and matrix $\mathbf{X}$ has n_1 rows, corresponding to the positive observations of y_i. We can further rewrite (10.4.14) as

$$\mathbf{y} = \hat{\mathbf{Z}}\gamma + \boldsymbol{\epsilon} + \boldsymbol{\eta}, \tag{10.4.15}$$

where we have defined $\hat{\mathbf{Z}} = (\mathbf{X}, \hat{\boldsymbol{\lambda}})$ and $\gamma = (\boldsymbol{\beta}', \sigma)'$. Then Heckman's two-step estimator of γ is defined as

$$\hat{\gamma} = (\hat{\mathbf{Z}}'\hat{\mathbf{Z}})^{-1}\hat{\mathbf{Z}}'\mathbf{y}. \tag{10.4.16}$$

The consistency of $\hat{\gamma}$ follows easily from (10.4.15) and (10.4.16). We shall derive its asymptotic distribution for the sake of completeness, although the result is a special case of Heckman's result (Heckman, 1979). From (10.4.15) and (10.4.16) we have

$$\sqrt{n_1}(\hat{\gamma} - \gamma) = (n_1^{-1}\hat{\mathbf{Z}}'\hat{\mathbf{Z}})^{-1}(n_1^{-1/2}\hat{\mathbf{Z}}'\boldsymbol{\epsilon} + n_1^{-1/2}\hat{\mathbf{Z}}'\boldsymbol{\eta}). \tag{10.4.17}$$

Because the probit MLE $\hat{\boldsymbol{\alpha}}$ is consistent, we have

$$\operatorname*{plim}_{n_1\to\infty} n_1^{-1}\hat{\mathbf{Z}}'\hat{\mathbf{Z}} = \lim_{n_1\to\infty} n_1^{-1}\mathbf{Z}'\mathbf{Z}, \tag{10.4.18}$$

where $\mathbf{Z} = (\mathbf{X}, \boldsymbol{\lambda})$. Under the assumptions stated after (10.2.4), it can be shown that

$$n_1^{-1/2}\hat{\mathbf{Z}}'\boldsymbol{\epsilon} \to N(\mathbf{0}, \sigma^2 \lim n_1^{-1}\mathbf{Z}'\boldsymbol{\Sigma}\mathbf{Z}), \tag{10.4.19}$$

where $\sigma^2\boldsymbol{\Sigma} \equiv E\boldsymbol{\epsilon}\boldsymbol{\epsilon}'$ is the $n_1 \times n_1$ diagonal matrix the diagonal elements of which are $V\epsilon_i$ given in (10.4.12). We have by Taylor expansion of $\lambda(\mathbf{x}_i'\hat{\boldsymbol{\alpha}})$ around $\lambda(\mathbf{x}_i'\boldsymbol{\alpha})$

$$\boldsymbol{\eta} = -\sigma\frac{\partial\boldsymbol{\lambda}}{\partial\boldsymbol{\alpha}'}(\hat{\boldsymbol{\alpha}} - \boldsymbol{\alpha}) + O(n^{-1}). \tag{10.4.20}$$

Using (10.4.20) and (10.4.2), we can prove

$$n_1^{-1/2}\hat{\mathbf{Z}}'\boldsymbol{\eta} \to N[\mathbf{0}, \sigma^2\mathbf{Z}'(\mathbf{I} - \boldsymbol{\Sigma})\mathbf{X}(\underline{\mathbf{X}}'\underline{\mathbf{D}}_1\underline{\mathbf{X}})^{-1}\mathbf{X}'(\mathbf{I} - \boldsymbol{\Sigma})\mathbf{Z}], \tag{10.4.21}$$

where $\underline{\mathbf{D}}_1$ was defined after (10.4.2). Next, note that $\boldsymbol{\epsilon}$ and $\boldsymbol{\eta}$ are uncorrelated because $\boldsymbol{\eta}$ is asymptotically a linear function of $\underline{\mathbf{w}}$ on account of (10.4.2) and (10.4.20) and $\boldsymbol{\epsilon}$ and $\underline{\mathbf{w}}$ are uncorrelated. Therefore, from (10.4.17), (10.4.18), (10.4.19), and (10.4.21), we finally conclude that $\hat{\gamma}$ is asymptotically normal with mean γ and asymptotic variance-covariance matrix given by

$$V\hat{\gamma} = \sigma^2(\mathbf{Z}'\mathbf{Z})^{-1}\mathbf{Z}'[\boldsymbol{\Sigma} + (\mathbf{I} - \boldsymbol{\Sigma})\mathbf{X}(\underline{\mathbf{X}}'\underline{\mathbf{D}}_1\underline{\mathbf{X}})^{-1}\mathbf{X}'(\mathbf{I} - \boldsymbol{\Sigma})]\mathbf{Z}(\mathbf{Z}'\mathbf{Z})^{-1}. \tag{10.4.22}$$

Expression (10.4.22) may be consistently estimated either by replacing the unknown parameters by their consistent estimates or by $(\mathbf{Z}'\mathbf{Z})^{-1}\mathbf{Z}'\mathbf{A}\mathbf{Z}(\mathbf{Z}'\mathbf{Z})^{-1}$, where $\mathbf{A}$ is the diagonal matrix the ith diagonal element of which is $[y_i - \mathbf{x}_i'\hat{\boldsymbol{\beta}} - \hat{\sigma}\lambda(\mathbf{x}_i'\hat{\boldsymbol{\alpha}})]^2$, following the idea of White (1980).

Note that the second matrix within the square bracket in (10.4.22) arises because λ had to be estimated. If λ were known, we could apply least squares directly to (10.4.11) and the exact variance-covariance matrix would be $\sigma^2(\mathbf{Z}'\mathbf{Z})^{-1}\mathbf{Z}'\boldsymbol{\Sigma}\mathbf{Z}(\mathbf{Z}'\mathbf{Z})^{-1}$.

Heckman's two-step estimator uses the conditional mean of y_i given in (10.4.6). A similar procedure can also be applied to the unconditional mean of y_i given by (10.4.9).[4] That is to say, we can regress all the observations of y_i, including zeros, on $\Phi\mathbf{x}_i$ and ϕ after replacing the $\boldsymbol{\alpha}$ that appears in the argument of Φ and ϕ by the probit MLE $\hat{\boldsymbol{\alpha}}$. In the same way as we derived (10.4.11) and (10.4.13) from (10.4.6), we can derive the following two equations from (10.4.9):

$$y_i = \Phi(\mathbf{x}_i'\boldsymbol{\alpha})[\mathbf{x}_i'\boldsymbol{\beta} + \sigma\lambda(\mathbf{x}_i'\boldsymbol{\alpha})] + \delta_i \tag{10.4.23}$$

and

$$y_i = \Phi(\mathbf{x}_i'\hat{\boldsymbol{\alpha}})[\mathbf{x}_i'\boldsymbol{\beta} + \sigma\lambda(\mathbf{x}_i'\hat{\boldsymbol{\alpha}})] + \delta_i + \xi_i, \tag{10.4.24}$$

where $\delta_i = y_i - Ey_i$ and $\xi_i = [\Phi(\mathbf{x}_i'\boldsymbol{\alpha}) - \Phi(\mathbf{x}_i'\hat{\boldsymbol{\alpha}})]\mathbf{x}_i'\boldsymbol{\beta} + \sigma[\phi(\mathbf{x}_i'\boldsymbol{\alpha}) - \phi(\mathbf{x}_i'\hat{\boldsymbol{\alpha}})]$. A vector equation comparable to (10.4.15) is

$$\underline{\mathbf{y}} = \hat{\underline{\mathbf{D}}}\hat{\underline{\mathbf{Z}}}\gamma + \underline{\delta} + \underline{\xi}, \tag{10.4.25}$$

where $\hat{\underline{\mathbf{D}}}$ is the $n \times n$ diagonal matrix the ith element of which is $\Phi(\mathbf{x}_i'\hat{\boldsymbol{\alpha}})$. Note that the vectors and matrices appear with underbars because they consist of n elements or rows. The two-step estimator of γ based on all the observations, denoted $\tilde{\gamma}$, is defined as

$$\tilde{\gamma} = (\hat{\underline{\mathbf{Z}}}'\hat{\underline{\mathbf{D}}}^2\hat{\underline{\mathbf{Z}}})^{-1}\hat{\underline{\mathbf{Z}}}'\hat{\underline{\mathbf{D}}}\underline{\mathbf{y}}. \tag{10.4.26}$$

The estimator can easily be shown to be consistent. To derive its asymptotic distribution, we obtain from (10.4.25) and (10.4.26)

$$\sqrt{n}(\tilde{\gamma} - \gamma) = (n^{-1}\hat{\underline{\mathbf{Z}}}'\hat{\underline{\mathbf{D}}}^2\hat{\underline{\mathbf{Z}}})^{-1}(n^{-1/2}\hat{\underline{\mathbf{Z}}}'\hat{\underline{\mathbf{D}}}\underline{\delta} + n^{-1/2}\hat{\underline{\mathbf{Z}}}'\hat{\underline{\mathbf{D}}}\underline{\xi}). \tag{10.4.27}$$

Here, unlike the previous case, an interesting fact emerges: By expanding $\Phi(\mathbf{x}_i'\hat{\alpha})$ and $\phi(\mathbf{x}_i'\hat{\alpha})$ in Taylor series around $\mathbf{x}_i'\alpha$ we can show $\xi_i = O(n^{-1})$. Therefore

$$\text{plim } n^{-1/2}\hat{\underline{\mathbf{Z}}}'\hat{\underline{\mathbf{D}}}\underline{\xi} = \mathbf{0}. \tag{10.4.28}$$

Corresponding to (10.4.18), we have

$$\text{plim } n^{-1}\hat{\underline{\mathbf{Z}}}'\hat{\underline{\mathbf{D}}}^2\hat{\underline{\mathbf{Z}}} = \lim n^{-1}\underline{\mathbf{Z}}'\underline{\mathbf{D}}^2\underline{\mathbf{Z}}, \tag{10.4.29}$$

where $\underline{\mathbf{D}}$ is obtained from $\hat{\underline{\mathbf{D}}}$ by replacing $\hat{\alpha}$ with α. Corresponding to (10.4.19), we have

$$n^{-1/2}\hat{\underline{\mathbf{Z}}}'\hat{\underline{\mathbf{D}}}\underline{\delta} \rightarrow N(\mathbf{0}, \sigma^2 \lim n^{-1}\underline{\mathbf{Z}}'\underline{\mathbf{D}}^2\underline{\mathbf{\Omega}}\underline{\mathbf{Z}}), \tag{10.4.30}$$

where $\sigma^2\underline{\mathbf{\Omega}} \equiv E\underline{\delta}\underline{\delta}'$ is the $n \times n$ diagonal matrix the ith element of which is $\sigma^2\Phi(\mathbf{x}_i'\alpha)\{(\mathbf{x}_i'\alpha)^2 + \mathbf{x}_i'\alpha\lambda(\mathbf{x}_i'\alpha) + 1 - \Phi(\mathbf{x}_i'\alpha)[\mathbf{x}_i'\alpha + \lambda(\mathbf{x}_i'\alpha)]^2\}$. Therefore, from (10.4.27) through (10.4.30), we conclude that $\tilde{\gamma}$ is asymptotically normal with mean γ and asymptotic variance-covariance matrix given by[5]

$$V\tilde{\gamma} = \sigma^2(\underline{\mathbf{Z}}'\underline{\mathbf{D}}^2\underline{\mathbf{Z}})^{-1}\underline{\mathbf{Z}}'\underline{\mathbf{D}}^2\underline{\mathbf{\Omega}}\underline{\mathbf{Z}}(\underline{\mathbf{Z}}'\underline{\mathbf{D}}^2\underline{\mathbf{Z}})^{-1}. \tag{10.4.31}$$

Which of the two estimators $\hat{\gamma}$ and $\tilde{\gamma}$ is preferred? Unfortunately, the difference of the two matrices given by (10.4.22) and (10.4.31) is generally neither positive definite nor negative definite. Thus an answer to the preceding question depends on parameter values.

Both (10.4.15) and (10.4.25) represent heteroscedastic regression models. Therefore we can obtain asymptotically more efficient estimators by using weighted least squares (WLS) in the second step of the procedure for obtaining $\hat{\gamma}$ and $\tilde{\gamma}$. In doing so, we must use a consistent estimate of the asymptotic variance-covariance matrix of $\boldsymbol{\epsilon} + \boldsymbol{\eta}$ for the case of (10.4.15) and of $\underline{\delta} + \underline{\xi}$ for the case of (10.4.25). Because these matrices depend on γ, an initial consistent estimate of γ (say, $\hat{\gamma}$ or $\tilde{\gamma}$) is needed to obtain the WLS estimators. We call these WLS estimators $\hat{\gamma}_W$ and $\tilde{\gamma}_W$, respectively. It can be shown that they are consistent and asymptotically normal with asymptotic variance-covariance matrices given by

$$V\hat{\gamma}_W = \sigma^2\{\mathbf{Z}'[\mathbf{\Sigma} + (\mathbf{I} - \mathbf{\Sigma})\mathbf{X}(\underline{\mathbf{X}}'\underline{\mathbf{D}}_1\underline{\mathbf{X}})^{-1}\mathbf{X}'(\mathbf{I} - \mathbf{\Sigma})]^{-1}\mathbf{Z}\}^{-1} \tag{10.4.32}$$

and

$$V\hat{\gamma}_W = \sigma^2(\underline{\mathbf{Z}}'\underline{\mathbf{D}}^2\underline{\mathbf{\Omega}}^{-1}\underline{\mathbf{Z}})^{-1}. \tag{10.4.33}$$

Again, we cannot make a definite comparison between the two matrices.

10.4.4 Nonlinear Least Squares and Nonlinear Weighted Least Squares Estimators

In this subsection we shall consider four estimators: the NLLS and NLWLS estimators applied to (10.4.11), denoted $\hat{\gamma}_N$ and $\hat{\gamma}_{NW}$, respectively, and the NLLS and NLWLS estimators applied to (10.4.23), denoted $\tilde{\gamma}_N$ and $\tilde{\gamma}_{NW}$, respectively.

All these estimators are consistent and their asymptotic distributions can be obtained straightforwardly by noting that all the results of a linear regression model hold asymptotically for a nonlinear regression model if we treat the derivative of the nonlinear regression function with respect to the parameter vector as the regression matrix.[6] In this way we can verify the interesting fact that $\tilde{\gamma}_N$ and $\tilde{\gamma}_{NW}$ have the same asymptotic distributions as $\tilde{\gamma}$ and $\tilde{\gamma}_W$, respectively.[7] We can also show that $\hat{\gamma}_N$ and $\hat{\gamma}_{NW}$ are asymptotically normal with mean γ and with their respective asymptotic variance-covariance matrices given by

$$V\hat{\gamma}_N = \sigma^2(\mathbf{S}'\mathbf{S})^{-1}\mathbf{S}'\mathbf{\Sigma}\mathbf{S}(\mathbf{S}'\mathbf{S})^{-1} \tag{10.4.34}$$

and

$$V\hat{\gamma}_{NW} = \sigma^2(\mathbf{S}'\mathbf{\Sigma}^{-1}\mathbf{S})^{-1}, \tag{10.4.35}$$

where $\mathbf{S} = (\mathbf{\Sigma X}, \mathbf{D}_2\boldsymbol{\lambda})$, where $\mathbf{D}_2$ is the $n_1 \times n_1$ diagonal matrix the ith element of which is $1 + (\mathbf{x}_i'\boldsymbol{\alpha})^2 + \mathbf{x}_i'\boldsymbol{\alpha}\lambda(\mathbf{x}_i'\boldsymbol{\alpha})$. We cannot make a definite comparison either between (10.4.22) and (10.4.34) or between (10.4.32) and (10.4.35).

In the two-step methods defining $\hat{\gamma}$ and $\tilde{\gamma}$ and their generalizations $\hat{\gamma}_W$ and $\tilde{\gamma}_W$, we can naturally define an iteration procedure by repeating the two steps. For example, having obtained $\hat{\gamma}$, we can obtain a new estimate of $\boldsymbol{\alpha}$, insert it into the argument of λ, and apply least squares again to Eq. (10.4.11). The procedure is to be repeated until a sequence of estimates of $\boldsymbol{\alpha}$ thus obtained converges. In the iteration starting from $\hat{\gamma}_W$, we use the mth-round estimate of γ not only to evaluate λ but also to estimate the variance-covariance matrix of the error term for the purpose of obtaining the $(m+1)$st-round estimate. Iterations starting from $\tilde{\gamma}$ and $\tilde{\gamma}_W$ can be similarly defined but are probably not worthwhile because $\tilde{\gamma}$ and $\tilde{\gamma}_W$ are asymptotically equivalent to $\tilde{\gamma}_N$ and $\tilde{\gamma}_{NW}$, as we indicated earlier. The estimators $(\hat{\gamma}_N, \hat{\gamma}_{NW}, \tilde{\gamma}_N, \tilde{\gamma}_{NW})$ are clearly stationary values of the iterations starting from $(\hat{\gamma}, \hat{\gamma}_W, \tilde{\gamma}, \tilde{\gamma}_W)$. However, they may not necessarily be the converging values.

A simulation study by Wales and Woodland (1980) based on only one replication with sample sizes of 1000 and 5000 showed that $\hat{\gamma}_N$ is distinctly inferior to the MLE and is rather unsatisfactory.

10.4.5 Tobit Maximum Likelihood Estimator

The Tobit MLE maximizes the likelihood function (10.2.5). Under the assumptions given after (10.2.4), Amemiya (1973c) proved its consistency and asymptotic normality. If we define $\boldsymbol{\theta} = (\boldsymbol{\beta}', \sigma^2)'$, the asymptotic variance-covariance matrix of the Tobit MLE $\hat{\boldsymbol{\theta}}$ is given by

$$V\hat{\boldsymbol{\theta}} = \begin{bmatrix} \sum_{i=1}^{n} a_i \mathbf{x}_i \mathbf{x}_i' & \sum_{i=1}^{n} b_i \mathbf{x}_i \\ \sum_{i=1}^{n} b_i \mathbf{x}_i' & \sum_{i=1}^{n} c_i \end{bmatrix}^{-1}, \tag{10.4.36}$$

where

$$a_i = -\sigma^{-2}\{\mathbf{x}_i'\boldsymbol{\alpha}\phi_i - [\phi_i^2/(1-\Phi_i)] - \Phi_i\},$$

$$b_i = (1/2)\sigma^{-3}\{(\mathbf{x}_i'\boldsymbol{\alpha})^2\phi_i + \phi_i - [(\mathbf{x}_i'\boldsymbol{\alpha})\phi_i^2/(1-\Phi_i)]\}, \quad \text{and}$$

$$c_i = -(1/4)\sigma^{-4}\{(\mathbf{x}_i'\boldsymbol{\alpha})^3\phi_i + (\mathbf{x}_i'\boldsymbol{\alpha})\phi_i - [(\mathbf{x}_i'\boldsymbol{\alpha})\phi_i^2/(1-\Phi_i)] - 2\Phi_i\};$$

and ϕ_i and Φ_i stand for $\phi(\mathbf{x}_i'\boldsymbol{\alpha})$ and $\Phi(\mathbf{x}_i'\boldsymbol{\alpha})$, respectively.

The Tobit MLE must be computed iteratively. Olsen (1978) proved the global concavity of $\log L$ in the Tobit model in terms of the transformed parameters $\boldsymbol{\alpha} = \boldsymbol{\beta}/\sigma$ and $h = \sigma^{-1}$, a result that implies that a standard iterative method such as Newton-Raphson or the method of scoring always converges to the global maximum of $\log L$.[8] The $\log L$ in terms of the new parameters can be written as

$$\log L = \sum_0 \log [1 - \Phi(\mathbf{x}_i'\boldsymbol{\alpha})] + n_1 \log h - \frac{1}{2}\sum_1 (hy_i - \mathbf{x}_i'\boldsymbol{\alpha})^2, \tag{10.4.37}$$

from which Olsen obtained

$$\begin{bmatrix} \dfrac{\partial^2 \log L}{\partial\alpha\partial\alpha'} & \dfrac{\partial \log L}{\partial\alpha\partial h} \\ \dfrac{\partial^2 \log L}{\partial h\partial\alpha'} & \dfrac{\partial^2 \log L}{\partial h^2} \end{bmatrix} \tag{10.4.38}$$

$$= \begin{bmatrix} \sum_0 \dfrac{\phi_i}{1-\Phi_i}\left(\mathbf{x}_i'\alpha - \dfrac{\phi_i}{1-\Phi_i}\right)\mathbf{x}_i\mathbf{x}_i' & \mathbf{0} \\ \mathbf{0} & -\dfrac{n_1}{h^2} \end{bmatrix}$$

$$- \begin{bmatrix} \sum_1 \mathbf{x}_i\mathbf{x}_i' & -\sum_1 \mathbf{x}_i y_i \\ -\sum_1 y_i\mathbf{x}_i' & \sum_1 y_i^2 \end{bmatrix}.$$

Because $\mathbf{x}_i'\alpha - [1 - \Phi(\mathbf{x}_i'\alpha)]^{-1}\phi(\mathbf{x}_i'\alpha) < 0$, the right-hand side of (10.4.38) is the sum of two negative-definite matrices and hence is negative definite.

Even though convergence is assured by global concavity, it is a good idea to start an iteration with a good estimator because it will improve the speed of convergence. Tobin (1958) used a simple estimator based on a linear approximation of the reciprocal of Mills' ratio to start his iteration for obtaining the MLE. Although Amemiya (1973c) showed that Tobin's initial estimator is inconsistent, empirical researchers have found it to be a good starting value for iteration.

Amemiya (1973) proposed the following simple consistent estimator. We have

$$E(y_i^2|y_i > 0) = (\mathbf{x}_i'\beta)^2 + \sigma\mathbf{x}_i'\beta\lambda(\mathbf{x}_i'\alpha) + \sigma^2. \tag{10.4.39}$$

Combining (10.4.6) and (10.4.39) yields

$$E(y_i^2|y_i > 0) = \mathbf{x}_i'\beta E(y_i|y_i > 0) + \sigma^2, \tag{10.4.40}$$

which can be alternatively written as

$$y_i^2 = y_i\mathbf{x}_i'\beta + \sigma^2 + \zeta_i, \qquad \text{for } i \text{ such that } y_i > 0, \tag{10.4.41}$$

where $E(\zeta_i|y_i > 0) = 0$. Then consistent estimates of β and σ^2 are obtained by applying an instrumental variables method to (10.4.41) using $(\hat{y}_i\mathbf{x}_i', 1)$ as the instrumental variables, where $\hat{y}_i$ is the predictor of y_i obtained by regressing positive y_i on $\mathbf{x}_i$ and, perhaps, powers of $\mathbf{x}_i$. The asymptotic distribution of the estimator has been given by Amemiya (1973c). A simulation study by Wales and Woodland (1980) indicated that this estimator is rather inefficient.

10.4.6 The EM Algorithm

The EM algorithm is a general iterative method for obtaining the MLE; it was first proposed by Hartley (1958) and was generalized by Dempster, Laird, and Rubin (1977) to a form that is especially suited for censored regression models such as Tobit models. We shall first present the definition and the properties of the EM algorithm under a general setting and then apply it to the standard Tobit model. It can also be applied to general Tobit models.

We shall explain the EM algorithm in a general model where a vector of observable variables $\mathbf{z}$ is related to a vector of unobservable variables $\mathbf{y}^*$ in such a way that the value of $\mathbf{y}^*$ uniquely determines the value of $\mathbf{z}$ but not vice versa. In the Tobit model, $\{y_i^*\}$ defined in (10.2.3) constitute the elements of $\mathbf{y}^*$, and $\{y_i\}$ and $\{w_i\}$ defined in (10.2.4) and (10.4.3), respectively, constitute the elements of $\mathbf{z}$. Let the joint density or probability of $\mathbf{y}^*$ be $f(\mathbf{y}^*)$ and let the joint density or probability of $\mathbf{z}$ be $g(\mathbf{z})$. Also, define $k(\mathbf{y}^*|\mathbf{z}) = f(\mathbf{y}^*)/g(\mathbf{z})$. Note that $f(\mathbf{y}^*, \mathbf{z}) = f(\mathbf{z}|\mathbf{y}^*)f(\mathbf{y}^*) = f(\mathbf{y}^*)$ because $f(\mathbf{z}|\mathbf{y}^*) = 1$ inasmuch as $\mathbf{y}^*$ uniquely determines $\mathbf{z}$. We implicitly assume that f, g, and k depend on a vector of parameters $\boldsymbol{\theta}$. The purpose is to maximize

$$L(\boldsymbol{\theta}) \equiv n^{-1} \log g(\mathbf{z}) = n^{-1} \log f(\mathbf{y}^*) - n^{-1} \log k(\mathbf{y}^*|\mathbf{z}) \tag{10.4.42}$$

with respect to $\boldsymbol{\theta}$. Define

$$Q(\boldsymbol{\theta}|\boldsymbol{\theta}_1) = E[n^{-1} \log f(\mathbf{y}^*|\boldsymbol{\theta})|\mathbf{z}, \boldsymbol{\theta}_1], \tag{10.4.43}$$

where we are taking the expectation assuming $\boldsymbol{\theta}_1$ is the true parameter value and doing this conditional on $\mathbf{z}$. Then the EM algorithm purports to maximize $L(\boldsymbol{\theta})$ by maximizing $Q(\boldsymbol{\theta}|\boldsymbol{\theta}_1)$ with respect to $\boldsymbol{\theta}$ where $\boldsymbol{\theta}_1$ is given at each step of the iteration. The "E" of the name "EM" refers to the expectation taken in (10.4.43) and the "M" refers to the maximization of (10.4.43).

Consider the convergence properties of the EM algorithm. Define

$$H(\boldsymbol{\theta}|\boldsymbol{\theta}_1) = E[n^{-1} \log k(\mathbf{y}^*|\mathbf{z}, \boldsymbol{\theta})|\mathbf{z}, \boldsymbol{\theta}_1]. \tag{10.4.44}$$

Then we have from (10.4.42), (10.4.43), and (10.4.44) and the fact that $L(\boldsymbol{\theta}|\boldsymbol{\theta}_1) \equiv E[n^{-1} \log g(\mathbf{z})|\mathbf{z}, \boldsymbol{\theta}_1] = L(\boldsymbol{\theta})$

$$L(\boldsymbol{\theta}) = Q(\boldsymbol{\theta}|\boldsymbol{\theta}_1) - H(\boldsymbol{\theta}|\boldsymbol{\theta}_1). \tag{10.4.45}$$

But we have by Jensen's inequality (4.2.6)

$$H(\theta|\theta_1) < H(\theta_1|\theta_1) \qquad \text{for} \quad \theta \neq \theta_1. \tag{10.4.46}$$

Now, given θ_1, let $\mathbf{M}(\theta_1)$ maximize $Q(\theta|\theta_1)$ with respect to θ. Then we have

$$L(\mathbf{M}) = Q(\mathbf{M}|\theta_1) - H(\mathbf{M}|\theta_1). \tag{10.4.47}$$

But, because $Q(\mathbf{M}|\theta_1) \geqq Q(\theta|\theta_1)$ by definition and $H(\mathbf{M}|\theta_1) \leqq H(\theta_1|\theta_1)$ by (10.4.46), we have from (10.4.45) and (10.4.47)

$$L(\mathbf{M}) \geqq L(\theta_1). \tag{10.4.48}$$

Thus we have proved the desirable property that L always increases or stays constant at each step of the EM algorithm.

The preceding result implies that if L is bounded, then $\lim_{r\to\infty} L(\theta_r)$ exists. Let θ^* satisfy the equality $\lim_{r\to\infty} L(\theta_r) = L(\theta^*)$. ($\theta^*$ exists if the range of $L(\theta)$ is closed.) We shall show that if θ^* is a stationary point of the EM algorithm, then θ^* is a stationary point of L. For this we assume L is twice differentiable. Differentiating (10.4.45) with respect to θ and evaluating the derivative at $\theta = \theta_1$, we obtain

$$\left.\frac{\partial L}{\partial \theta}\right|_{\theta_1} = \left.\frac{\partial Q(\theta|\theta_1)}{\partial \theta}\right|_{\theta_1} - \left.\frac{\partial H(\theta|\theta_1)}{\partial \theta}\right|_{\theta_1}. \tag{10.4.49}$$

But the last term of the right-hand side of (10.4.49) is $\mathbf{0}$ because of (10.4.46). Therefore, if θ_1 is a stationary point of $Q(\theta|\theta_1)$, it is a stationary point of L.

Unfortunately, a local maximum of $Q(\theta|\theta_1)$ with respect to θ may not be a local maximum (let alone the global maximum) of $L(\theta)$ because the negative definiteness of $[\partial^2 Q(\theta|\theta_1)/\partial\theta\partial\theta']_{\theta_1}$ does not imply the negative definiteness of $[\partial^2 L/\partial\theta\partial\theta']_{\theta_1}$. However, this is true of any iterative method commonly used. See Wu (1983) for further discussion of the convergence properties of the EM algorithm.

Now consider an application of the algorithm to the Tobit model.[9] Define $\theta = (\beta', \sigma^2)$ as before. Then in the Tobit model we have

$$\log f(\mathbf{y}^*|\theta) = -\frac{n}{2}\log \sigma^2 - \frac{1}{2\sigma^2}\sum_{i=1}^{n}(y_i^* - \mathbf{x}_i'\beta)^2, \tag{10.4.50}$$

and, for a given estimate $\theta_1 = (\beta_1', \sigma_1^2)$, the EM algorithm maximizes with respect to $\boldsymbol{\beta}$ and σ^2

$$E[\log f(\mathbf{y}^*|\theta)|\mathbf{y}, \mathbf{w}, \theta_1] \tag{10.4.51}$$

$$= -\frac{n}{2}\log\sigma^2 - \frac{1}{2\sigma^2}\sum_1 (y_i - \mathbf{x}_i'\boldsymbol{\beta})^2 - \frac{1}{2\sigma^2}\sum_0 E[(y_i^* - \mathbf{x}_i'\boldsymbol{\beta})^2|w_i = 0, \theta_1]$$

$$= -\frac{n}{2}\log\sigma^2 - \frac{1}{2\sigma^2}\sum_1 (y_i - \mathbf{x}_i'\boldsymbol{\beta})^2 - \frac{1}{2\sigma^2}\sum_0 [E(y_i^*|w_i = 0, \theta_1) - \mathbf{x}_i'\boldsymbol{\beta}]^2$$

$$- \frac{1}{2\sigma^2}\sum_0 V(y_i^*|w_i = 0, \theta_1),$$

where

$$E(y_i^*|w_i = 0, \theta_1) = \mathbf{x}_i'\boldsymbol{\beta}_1 - \frac{\sigma_1\phi_{i1}}{1-\Phi_{i1}} \equiv y_i^0 \tag{10.4.52}$$

and

$$V(y_i^*|w_i = 0, \theta_1) = \sigma_1^2 + \mathbf{x}_i'\boldsymbol{\beta}_1\frac{\sigma_1\phi_{i1}}{1-\Phi_{i1}} - \left[\frac{\sigma_1\phi_{i1}}{1-\Phi_{i1}}\right]^2, \tag{10.4.53}$$

where $\phi_{i1} = \phi(\mathbf{x}_i'\boldsymbol{\beta}_1/\sigma_1)$ and $\Phi_{i1} = \Phi(\mathbf{x}_i'\boldsymbol{\beta}_1/\sigma_1)$.

From (10.4.51) it is clear that the second-round estimate of $\boldsymbol{\beta}$ in the EM algorithm, denoted $\boldsymbol{\beta}_2$, is obtained as follows: Assume without loss of generality that the first n_1 observations of y_i are positive and call the vector of those observations $\mathbf{y}$. Next, define an $(n - n_1)$-vector $\mathbf{y}^0$ the elements of which are the y_i^0 defined in (10.4.52). Then we have

$$\boldsymbol{\beta}_2 = (\underline{\mathbf{X}}'\underline{\mathbf{X}})^{-1}\underline{\mathbf{X}}'\begin{bmatrix}\mathbf{y}\\ \mathbf{y}^0\end{bmatrix}, \tag{10.4.54}$$

where $\underline{\mathbf{X}}$ was defined after (10.2.4). In other words, the EM algorithm amounts to predicting all the unobservable values of y_i^* by their conditional expectations and treating the predicted values as if they were the observed values. The second-round estimate of σ^2, denoted σ_2^2, is given by

$$\sigma_2^2 = n^{-1}\left[\sum_1 (y_i - \mathbf{x}_i'\boldsymbol{\beta}_2)^2 + \sum_0 (y_i^0 - \mathbf{x}_i'\boldsymbol{\beta}_2)^2 + \sum_0 V(y_i^*|w_i = 0, \theta_1)\right]. \tag{10.4.55}$$

We can directly show that the MLE $\hat{\theta}$ is the equilibrium solution of the iteration defined by (10.4.54) and (10.4.55). Partition $\underline{\mathbf{X}} = (\mathbf{X}', \mathbf{X}^{0\prime})'$ so that

$\mathbf{X}$ is multiplied by $\mathbf{y}$ and $\mathbf{X}^0$ by $\mathbf{y}^0$. Then inserting $\hat{\theta}$ into both sides of (10.4.54) yields, after collecting terms,

$$\mathbf{X}'\mathbf{X}\hat{\beta} = \mathbf{X}'\mathbf{y} - \mathbf{X}^{0\prime}\left[\frac{\hat{\sigma}\phi(\mathbf{x}_i'\hat{\beta}/\hat{\sigma})}{1 - \Phi(\mathbf{x}_i'\hat{\beta}/\hat{\sigma})}\right], \tag{10.4.56}$$

where the last bracket denotes an $(n - n_1)$-dimensional vector the typical element of which is given inside. Now, setting the derivative of log L with respect to $\boldsymbol{\beta}$ equal to $\mathbf{0}$ yields

$$-\sigma \sum_0 \frac{\phi_i}{1 - \Phi_i}\mathbf{x}_i + \sum_1 (y_i - \mathbf{x}_i'\boldsymbol{\beta})\mathbf{x}_i = \mathbf{0}. \tag{10.4.57}$$

But, clearly, (10.4.56) is equivalent to (10.4.57). Similarly, the normal equation for σ^2 can be shown to be equivalent to (10.4.55).

Schmee and Hahn (1979) performed a simulation study of the EM algorithm applied to a censored regression model (a survival model) defined by

$$\begin{aligned} y_i &= y_i^* \quad \text{if} \quad y_i^* \leqq c \\ &= c \quad \text{if} \quad y_i^* > c, \end{aligned}$$

where $y_i^* \sim N(\alpha + \beta x_i, \sigma^2)$. They generally obtained rapid convergence.

10.5 Properties of the Tobit Maximum Likelihood Estimator under Nonstandard Assumptions

In this section we shall discuss the properties of the Tobit MLE—the estimator that maximizes (10.2.5)—under various types of nonstandard assumptions: heteroscedasticity, serial correlation, and nonnormality. It will be shown that the Tobit MLE remains consistent under serial correlation but not under heteroscedasticity or nonnormality. The same is true of the other estimators considered earlier. This result contrasts with the classical regression model in which the least squares estimator (the MLE under the normality assumption) is generally consistent under all of the three types of nonstandard assumptions mentioned earlier.

Before proceeding with a rigorous argument, we shall give an intuitive explanation of the aforementioned result. By considering (10.4.11) we see that serial correlation of y_i should not affect the consistency of the NLLS estimator, whereas heteroscedasticity changes σ to σ_i and hence invalidates the estimation of the equation by least squares. If y_i^* is not normal, Eq. (10.4.11) itself is generally invalid, which leads to the inconsistency of the NLLS estimator.

Although the NLLS estimator is different from the ML estimator, we can expect a certain correspondence between the consistency properties of the two estimators.

10.5.1 Heteroscedasticity

Hurd (1979) evaluated the probability limit of the truncated Tobit MLE when a certain type of heteroscedasticity is present in two simple truncated Tobit models: (1) the i.i.d. case (that is, the case of the regressor consisting only of a constant term) and (2) the case of a constant term plus one independent variable. Recall that the truncated Tobit model is the one in which no information is available for those observations for which $y_i^* < 0$ and therefore the MLE maximizes (10.2.6) rather than (10.2.5).

In the i.i.d. case Hurd created heteroscedasticity by generating rn observations from $N(\mu, \sigma_1^2)$ and $(1-r)n$ observations from $N(\mu, \sigma_2^2)$. In each case he recorded only positive observations. Let y_i, $i = 1, 2, \ldots, n_1$, be the recorded observations. (Note $n_1 \leqq n$). We can show that the truncated Tobit MLE of μ and σ^2, denoted $\hat{\mu}$ and $\hat{\sigma}^2$, are defined by equating the first two population moments of y_i to their respective sample moments:

$$\hat{\mu} + \hat{\sigma}\lambda(\hat{\mu}/\hat{\sigma}) = n_1^{-1} \sum_{i=1}^{n_1} y_i \tag{10.5.1}$$

and

$$\hat{\mu}^2 + \hat{\sigma}\hat{\mu}\lambda(\hat{\mu}/\hat{\sigma}) + \hat{\sigma}^2 = n_1^{-1} \sum_{i=1}^{n_1} y_i^2 . \tag{10.5.2}$$

Taking the probability limit of both sides of (10.5.1) and (10.5.2) and expressing plim $n_1^{-1}\Sigma y_i$ and plim $n_1^{-1}\Sigma y_i^2$ as certain functions of the parameters μ, σ_1^2, σ_2^2, and r, we can define plim $\hat{\mu}$ and plim $\hat{\sigma}^2$ implicitly as functions of these parameters. Hurd evaluated the probability limits for various values of μ and σ_1 after having fixed $r = 0.5$ and $\sigma_2 = 1$. Hurd found large asymptotic biases in certain cases.

In the case of one independent variable, Hurd generated observations from $N(\alpha + \beta x_i, \sigma_i^2)$ after having generated x_i and $\log|\sigma_i|$ from bivariate $N(0, 0, V_1^2, V_2^2, \rho)$. For given values of α, β, V_1, V_2, and ρ, Hurd found the values of α, β, and σ^2 that maximize $E \log L$, where L is as given in (10.2.6). Those values are the probability limits of the MLE of α, β, and σ^2 under Hurd's model if the expectation of $\log L$ is taken using the same model. Again, Hurd found extremely large asymptotic biases in certain cases.

Arabmazar and Schmidt (1981) showed that the asymptotic biases of the censored Tobit MLE in the i.i.d. case are not as large as those obtained by Hurd.

10.5.2 Serial Correlation

Robinson (1982a) proved the strong consistency and the asymptotic normality of the Tobit MLE under very general assumptions about u_i (normality is presupposed) and obtained its asymptotic variance-covariance matrix, which is complicated and therefore not reproduced here. His assumptions are slightly stronger than the stationarity assumption but are weaker than the assumption that u_i possesses a continuous spectral density (see Section 5.1.3). His results are especially useful because the full MLE that takes account of even a simple type of serial correlation seems computationally intractable. The autocorrelations of u_i need not be estimated to compute the Tobit MLE but must be estimated to estimate its asymptotic variance-covariance matrix. The consistent estimator proposed by Robinson (1982b) may be used for that purpose.

10.5.3 Nonnormality

Goldberger (1983) considered an i.i.d. truncated sample model in which data are generated by a certain nonnormal distribution with mean μ and variance 1 and are recorded only when the value is smaller than a constant c. Let y represent the recorded random variable and let $\bar{y}$ be the sample mean. The researcher is to estimate μ by the MLE, assuming that the data are generated by $N(\mu, 1)$. As in Hurd's i.i.d. model, the MLE $\hat{\mu}$ is defined by equating the population mean of y to its sample mean:

$$\hat{\mu} - \lambda(c - \hat{\mu}) = \bar{y}. \tag{10.5.3}$$

Taking the probability limit of both sides of (10.5.3) under the true model and putting plim $\hat{\mu} = \mu^*$ yield

$$\mu^* - \lambda(c - \mu^*) = \mu - h(c - \mu), \tag{10.5.4}$$

where $h(c - \mu) = E(\mu - y | y < c)$, the expectation being taken using the true model. Defining $m = \mu^* - \mu$ and $\theta = c - \mu$, we can rewrite (10.5.4) as

$$m = \lambda(\theta - m) - h(\theta). \tag{10.5.5}$$

Goldberger calculated m as a function of θ when the data are generated by Student's t with various degrees of freedom, Laplace, and logistic distributions. The asymptotic bias was found to be especially great when the true distribution was Laplace. Goldberger also extended the analysis to the regression model with a constant term and one discrete independent variable. Arabmazar and Schmidt (1982) extended Goldberger's analysis to the case of an unknown variance and found that the asymptotic bias was further accentuated.

10.5.4 Tests for Normality

The fact that the Tobit MLE is generally inconsistent when the true distribution is nonnormal makes it important for a researcher to test whether the data are generated by a normal distribution. Nelson (1981) devised tests for normality in the i.i.d. censored sample model and the Tobit model. His tests are applications of the specification test of Hausman (1978) (see Section 4.5.1).

Nelson's i.i.d. censored model is defined by

$$\begin{aligned} y_i &= y_i^* && \text{if } y_i^* > 0 \\ &= 0 && \text{if } y_i^* \leqq 0, \qquad i = 1, 2, \ldots, n, \end{aligned}$$

where $y_i^* \sim N(\mu, \sigma^2)$ under the null hypothesis. Nelson considered the estimation of $P(y_i^* > 0)$. Its MLE is $\Phi(\hat{\mu}/\hat{\sigma})$, where $\hat{\mu}$ and $\hat{\sigma}$ are the MLE of the respective parameters. A consistent estimator is provided by n_1/n, where, as before, n_1 is the number of positive observations of y_i. Clearly, n_1/n is a consistent estimator of $P(y_i^* > 0)$ under any distribution, provided that it is i.i.d. The difference between the MLE and the consistent estimator is used as a test statistic in Hausman's test. Nelson derived the asymptotic variances of the two estimators under normality.

If we interpret what is being estimated by the two estimators as $\lim_{n\to\infty} n^{-1}\Sigma_{i=1}^{n} P(y_i^* > 0)$, Nelson's test can be interpreted as a test of the null hypothesis against a more general misspecification than just nonnormality. In fact, Nelson conducted a simulation study to evaluate the power of the test against a heteroscedastic alternative. The performance of the test was satisfactory but not especially encouraging.

In the Tobit model Nelson considered the estimation of $n^{-1}E\underline{\mathbf{X}}'\underline{\mathbf{y}} = n^{-1}\Sigma_{i=1}^{n}\mathbf{x}_i[\Phi(\mathbf{x}_i'\alpha)\mathbf{x}_i'\beta + \sigma\phi(\mathbf{x}_i'\alpha)]$. Its MLE is given by the right-hand side of this equation evaluated at the Tobit MLE, and its consistent estimator is provided by $n^{-1}\underline{\mathbf{X}}'\underline{\mathbf{y}}$. Hausman's test based on these two estimators will work because this consistent estimator is consistent under general distributional assumptions on $\underline{y}$. Nelson derived the asymptotic variance-covariance matrices of the two estimators.

Nelson was ingenious in that he considered certain functions of the original parameters for which estimators that are consistent under very general assumptions can easily be obtained. However, it would be better if a general consistent estimator for the original parameters themselves could be found. An example is Powell's least absolute deviations estimator, to be discussed in the next subsection.

Bera, Jarque, and Lee (1982) proposed using Rao's score test in testing for normality in the standard Tobit model where the error term follows the two-parameter Pearson family of distributions, which contains normal as a special case.

10.5.5 Powell's Least Absolute Deviations Estimator

Powell (1981, 1983) proposed the least absolute deviations (LAD) estimator (see Section 4.6) for censored and truncated regression models, proved its consistency under general distributions, and derived its asymptotic distribution. The intuitive appeal for the LAD estimator in a censored regression model arises from the simple fact that in the i.i.d. sample case the median (of which the LAD estimator is a generalization) is not affected by censoring (more strictly, left censoring below the mean), whereas the mean is. In a censored regression model the LAD estimator is defined as that which minimizes $\Sigma_{i=1}^{n}|y_i - \max(0, \mathbf{x}_i'\boldsymbol{\beta})|$. The motivation for the LAD estimator in a truncated regression model is less obvious. Powell defined the LAD estimator in the truncated case as that which minimizes $\Sigma_{i=1}^{n}|y_i - \max(2^{-1}y_i, \mathbf{x}_i'\boldsymbol{\beta})|$. In the censored case the limit distribution of $\sqrt{n}(\hat{\boldsymbol{\beta}} - \boldsymbol{\beta})$, where $\hat{\boldsymbol{\beta}}$ is the LAD estimator, is normal with zero mean and variance-covariance matrix $[4f(0)^2 \lim_{n\to\infty} n^{-1}\Sigma_{i=1}^{n}\chi(\mathbf{x}_i'\boldsymbol{\beta} > 0)\mathbf{x}_i\mathbf{x}_i']^{-1}$, where f is the density of the error term and χ is the indicator function taking on unity if $\mathbf{x}_i'\boldsymbol{\beta} > 0$ holds and 0 otherwise. In the truncated case the limit distribution of $\sqrt{n}(\hat{\boldsymbol{\beta}} - \boldsymbol{\beta})$ is normal with zero mean and variance-covariance matrix $2^{-1}\mathbf{A}^{-1}\mathbf{B}\mathbf{A}^{-1}$, where

$$\mathbf{A} = \lim_{n\to\infty} n^{-1} \sum_{i=1}^{n} \chi(\mathbf{x}_i'\boldsymbol{\beta} > 0)[f(0) - f(\mathbf{x}_i'\boldsymbol{\beta})]F(\mathbf{x}_i'\boldsymbol{\beta})^{-1}\mathbf{x}_i\mathbf{x}_i'$$

and

$$\mathbf{B} = \lim_{n\to\infty} n^{-1} \sum_{i=1}^{n} \chi(\mathbf{x}_i'\boldsymbol{\beta} > 0)[F(\mathbf{x}_i'\boldsymbol{\beta}) - F(0)]F(\mathbf{x}_i'\boldsymbol{\beta})^{-1}\mathbf{x}_i\mathbf{x}_i',$$

where F is the distribution function of the error term.

Powell's estimator is attractive because it is the only known estimator that is consistent under general nonnormal distributions. However, its main drawback is its computational difficulty. Paarsch (1984) conducted a Monte Carlo study to compare Powell's estimator, the Tobit MLE, and Heckman's two-step estimator in the standard Tobit model with one exogenous variable under situations where the error term is distributed as normal, exponential, and Cauchy. Paarsch found that when the sample size is small (50) and there is much censoring (50% of the sample), the minimum frequently occurred at the boundary of a wide region over which a grid search was performed. In large samples Powell's estimator appears to perform much better than Heckman's estimator under any of the three distributional assumptions and much better than the Tobit MLE when the errors are Cauchy.

Another problem with Powell's estimator is finding a good estimator of the asymptotic variance-covariance matrix that does not require the knowledge of the true distribution of the error. Powell (1983) proposed a consistent estimator.

Powell observed that his proof of the consistency and asymptotic normality of the LAD estimator generally holds even if the errors are heteroscedastic. This fact makes Powell's estimator even more attractive because the usual estimators are inconsistent under heteroscedastic errors, as noted earlier.

Another obvious way to handle nonnormality is to specify a nonnormal distribution for the u_i in (10.2.3) and use the MLE. See Amemiya and Boskin (1974), who used a lognormal distribution with upper truncation to analyze the duration of welfare dependency.

10.6 Generalized Tobit Models

As stated in Section 10.1, we can classify Tobit models into five common types according to similarities in the likelihood function. Type 1 is the standard Tobit model, which we have discussed in the preceding sections. In the following sections we shall define and discuss the remaining four types of Tobit models.

It is useful to characterize the likelihood function of each type of model schematically as in Table 10.2, where each y_j, $j = 1, 2$, and 3, is assumed to be distributed as $N(\mathbf{x}_j'\boldsymbol{\beta}_j, \sigma_j^2)$, and P denotes a probability or a density or a combination thereof. We are to take the product of each P over the observations that belong to a particular category determined by the sign of y_1. Thus, in Type 1 (standard Tobit model), $P(y_1 < 0) \cdot P(y_1)$ is an abbreviated notation for $\Pi_0 P(y_{1i}^* < 0) \cdot \Pi_1 f_{1i}(y_{1i})$, where f_{1i} is the density of $N(\mathbf{x}_{1i}'\boldsymbol{\beta}_1, \sigma_1^2)$. This

Table 10.2 Likelihood functions of the five types of Tobit models

Type	Likelihood function
1	$P(y_1 < 0) \cdot P(y_1)$
2	$P(y_1 < 0) \cdot P(y_1 > 0, y_2)$
3	$P(y_1 < 0) \cdot P(y_1, y_2)$
4	$P(y_1 < 0, y_3) \cdot P(y_1, y_2)$
5	$P(y_1 < 0, y_3) \cdot P(y_1 > 0, y_2)$

expression can be rewritten as (10.2.5) after dropping the unnecessary subscript 1.

Another way to characterize the five types is by the classification of the three dependent variables that appear in Table 10.3. In each type of model, the sign of y_1 determines one of the two possible categories for the observations, and a censored variable is observed in one category and unobserved in the other. Note that when y_1 is labeled C, it plays two roles: the role of the variable the sign of which determines categories and the role of a censored variable.

We allow for the possibility that there are constraints among the parameters of the model $(\boldsymbol{\beta}_j, \sigma_j^2)$, $j = 1, 2$, or 3. For example, constraints will occur if the original model is specified as a simultaneous equations model in terms of y_1, y_2, and y_3. Then the $\boldsymbol{\beta}$'s denote the reduced-form parameters.

We shall not discuss models in which there is more than one binary variable and, hence, models the likelihood function of which consists of more than two components. Such models are computationally more burdensome because they involve double or higher-order integration of joint normal densities. The only exception occurs in Section 10.10.6, which includes models that are

Table 10.3 Characterization of the five types of Tobit models

	Dependent variables		
Type	y_1	y_2	y_3
1	C	—	—
2	B	C	—
3	C	C	—
4	C	C	C
5	B	C	C

Note: C = censored; B = binary.

obvious generalizations of the Type 5 Tobit model. Neither shall we discuss a simultaneous equations Tobit model of Amemiya (1974b). The simplest two-equation case of this model is defined by $y_{1i} = \max(\gamma_1 y_{2i} + \mathbf{x}_{1i}'\boldsymbol{\beta}_1 + u_{1i}, 0)$ and $y_{2i} = \max(\gamma_2 y_{1i} + \mathbf{x}_{2i}'\boldsymbol{\beta}_2 + u_{2i}, 0)$, where (u_{1i}, u_{2i}) are bivariate normal and $\gamma_1\gamma_2 < 1$ must be assumed for the model to be logically consistent.[10] A schematic representation of the likelihood function of this two-equation model is

$$P(y_1, y_2) \cdot P(y_1 < 0, y_3) \cdot P(y_2 < 0, y_4) \cdot P(y_3 < 0, y_4 < 0)$$

with y's appropriately defined.

10.7 Type 2 Tobit Model: $P(y_1 < 0) \cdot P(y_1 > 0, y_2)$

10.7.1 Definition and Estimation

The Type 2 Tobit model is defined as follows:

$$\begin{aligned} y_{1i}^* &= \mathbf{x}_{1i}'\boldsymbol{\beta}_1 + u_{1i} \\ y_{2i}^* &= \mathbf{x}_{2i}'\boldsymbol{\beta}_2 + u_{2i} \\ y_{2i} &= y_{2i}^* \quad \text{if} \quad y_{1i}^* > 0 \\ &= 0 \quad \text{if} \quad y_{1i}^* \leqq 0, \qquad i = 1, 2, \ldots, n, \end{aligned} \tag{10.7.1}$$

where $\{u_{1i}, u_{2i}\}$ are i.i.d. drawings from a bivariate normal distribution with zero mean, variances σ_1^2 and σ_2^2, and covariance σ_{12}. It is assumed that only the sign of y_{1i}^* is observed and that y_{2i}^* is observed only when $y_{1i}^* > 0$. It is assumed that $\mathbf{x}_{1i}$ are observed for all i but that $\mathbf{x}_{2i}$ need not be observed for i such that $y_{1i}^* \leqq 0$. We may also define, as in (10.4.3),

$$\begin{aligned} w_{1i} &= 1 \quad \text{if} \quad y_{1i}^* > 0 \\ &= 0 \quad \text{if} \quad y_{1i}^* \leqq 0. \end{aligned} \tag{10.7.2}$$

Then $\{w_{1i}, y_{2i}\}$ constitute the observed sample of the model. It should be noted that, unlike the Type 1 Tobit, y_{2i} may take negative values.[11] As in (10.2.4), $y_{2i} = 0$ merely signifies the event $y_{1i}^* \leqq 0$.

The likelihood function of the model is given by

$$L = \prod_0 P(y_{1i}^* \leqq 0) \prod_1 f(y_{2i} | y_{1i}^* > 0) P(y_{1i}^* > 0), \tag{10.7.3}$$

where Π_0 and Π_1 stand for the product over those i for which $y_{2i} = 0$ and $y_{2i} \neq 0$, respectively, and $f(\cdot | y_{1i}^* > 0)$ stands for the conditional density of y_{2i}^* given $y_{1i}^* > 0$. Note the similarity between (10.4.1) and (10.7.3). As in Type 1

Tobit, we can obtain a consistent estimate of β_1/σ_1 by maximizing the probit part of (10.7.3).

$$\text{Probit } L = \prod_0 P(y_{1i}^* \leqq 0) \prod_1 P(y_{1i}^* > 0). \tag{10.7.4}$$

Also, (10.7.4) is a part of the likelihood function for every one of the five types of models; therefore a consistent estimate of β_1/σ_1 can be obtained by the probit MLE in each of these types of models.

We can rewrite (10.7.3) as

$$L = \prod_0 P(y_{1i}^* \leqq 0) \prod_1 \int_0^\infty f(y_{1i}^*, y_{2i})\, dy_{1i}^*, \tag{10.7.5}$$

where $f(\cdot, \cdot)$ denotes the joint density of y_{1i}^* and y_{2i}^*. We can write the joint density as the product of a conditional density and a marginal density, that is $f(y_{1i}^*, y_{2i}) = f(y_{1i}^*|y_{2i})f(y_{2i})$, and can determine a specific form for $f(y_{1i}^*|y_{2i})$ from the well-known fact that the conditional distribution of y_{1i}^* given $y_{2i}^* = y_{2i}$ is normal with mean $\mathbf{x}_{1i}'\beta_1 + \sigma_{12}\sigma_2^{-2}(y_{2i} - \mathbf{x}_{2i}'\beta_2)$ and variance $\sigma_1^2 - \sigma_{12}^2\sigma_2^{-2}$. Thus we can further rewrite (10.7.5) as

$$\begin{aligned} L = &\prod_0 [1 - \Phi(\mathbf{x}_{1i}'\beta_1\sigma_1^{-1})] \\ &\times \prod_1 \Phi\{[\mathbf{x}_{1i}'\beta_1\sigma_1^{-1} + \sigma_{12}\sigma_1^{-1}\sigma_2^{-2}(y_{2i} - \mathbf{x}_{2i}'\beta_2)] \\ &\times [1 - \sigma_{12}^2\sigma_1^{-2}\sigma_2^{-2}]^{-1/2}\}\sigma_2^{-1}\phi[\sigma_2^{-1}(y_{2i} - \mathbf{x}_{2i}'\beta_2)]. \end{aligned} \tag{10.7.6}$$

Note that L depends on σ_1 only through $\beta_1\sigma_1^{-1}$ and $\sigma_{12}\sigma_1^{-1}$; therefore, if there is no constraint on the parameters, we can put $\sigma_1 = 1$ without any loss of generality. Then the remaining parameters can be identified. If, however, there is at least one common element in β_1 and β_2, σ_1 can also be identified.

We shall show how Heckman's two-step estimator can be used in this model. To obtain an equation comparable to (10.4.11), we need to evaluate $E(y_{2i}^*|y_{1i}^* > 0)$. For this purpose we use

$$y_{2i}^* = \mathbf{x}_{2i}'\beta_2 + \sigma_{12}\sigma_1^{-2}(y_{1i}^* - \mathbf{x}_{1i}'\beta_1) + \zeta_{2i}, \tag{10.7.7}$$

where ζ_{2i} is normally distributed independently of y_{1i}^* with zero mean and variance $\sigma_2^2 - \sigma_{12}^2\sigma_1^{-2}$. Using (10.7.7), we can express $E(y_{2i}^*|y_{1i}^* > 0)$ as a simple linear function of $E(y_{1i}^*|y_{1i}^* > 0)$, which was already obtained in Section 10.4. Using (10.7.7), we can also derive $V(y_{2i}^*|y_{1i}^* > 0)$ easily. Thus we obtain

$$y_{2i} = \mathbf{x}_{2i}'\beta_2 + \sigma_{12}\sigma_1^{-1}\lambda(\mathbf{x}_{1i}'\alpha_1) + \epsilon_{2i}, \quad \text{for } i \text{ such that } y_{2i} \neq 0, \tag{10.7.8}$$

where $\boldsymbol{\alpha}_1 = \boldsymbol{\beta}_1 \sigma_1^{-1}$, $E\epsilon_{2i} = 0$, and

$$V\epsilon_{2i} = \sigma_2^2 - \sigma_{12}^2 \sigma_1^{-2} [\mathbf{x}_{1i}' \boldsymbol{\alpha}_1 \lambda(\mathbf{x}_{1i}' \boldsymbol{\alpha}_1) + \lambda(\mathbf{x}_{1i}' \boldsymbol{\alpha}_1)^2]. \tag{10.7.9}$$

As in the case of the Type 1 Tobit, Heckman's two-step estimator is the LS estimator applied to (10.7.8) after replacing $\boldsymbol{\alpha}_1$ with the probit MLE. The asymptotic distribution of the estimator can be obtained in a manner similar to that in Section 10.4.3 by defining η_{2i} in the same way as before. It was first derived by Heckman (1979).

The standard Tobit (Type 1) is a special case of Type 2 in which $y_{1i}^* = y_{2i}^*$. Therefore (10.7.8) and (10.7.9) will be reduced to (10.4.11) and (10.4.12) by putting $\mathbf{x}_{1i}' \boldsymbol{\beta}_1 = \mathbf{x}_{2i}' \boldsymbol{\beta}_2$ and $\sigma_1^2 = \sigma_2^2 = \sigma_{12}$.

A generalization of the two-step method applied to (10.4.23) can easily be defined for this model but will not be discussed.

Note that the consistency of Heckman's estimator does not require the joint normality of y_1^* and y_2^* provided that y_1^* is normal and that Eq. (10.7.7) holds with ζ_2 independently distributed of y_1^* but not necessarily normal (Olsen, 1980). For then (10.7.8) would still be valid. As pointed out by Lee (1982c), the asymptotic variance-covariance matrix of Heckman's estimator can be consistently estimated under these less restrictive assumptions by using White's estimator analogous to the one mentioned after Eq. (10.4.22). Note that White's estimator does not require (10.7.9) to be valid.

10.7.2 A Special Case of Independence

Dudley and Montmarquette (1976) analyzed whether or not the United States gives foreign aid to a particular country and, if it does, how much foreign aid it gives using a special case of the model (10.7.1), where the independence of u_{1i} and u_{2i} is assumed. In their model the sign of y_{1i}^* determines whether aid is given to the ith country, and y_{2i}^* determines the actual amount of aid. They used the probit MLE to estimate $\boldsymbol{\beta}_1$ (assuming $\sigma_1 = 1$) and the least squares regression of y_{2i} on x_{2i} to estimate $\boldsymbol{\beta}_2$. The LS estimator of $\boldsymbol{\beta}_2$ is consistent in their model because of the assumed independence between u_{1i} and u_{2i}. This makes their model computationally advantageous. However, it seems unrealistic to assume that the potential amount of aid, y_2^*, is independent of the variable that determines whether or not aid is given, y_1^*. This model is the opposite extreme of the Tobit model, which can be regarded as a special case of Type 2 model where there is total dependence between y_1^* and y_2^*, in the whole spectrum of models (with correlation between y_1^* and y_2^* varying from -1 to $+1$) contained in Type 2.

Because of the computational advantage mentioned earlier this "independence" model and its variations were frequently used in econometric applications in the 1960s and early 1970s. In many of these studies, authors made the additional linear probability assumption: $P(y_{1i}^* > 0) = \mathbf{x}_{1i}'\boldsymbol{\beta}_1$, which enabled them to estimate $\boldsymbol{\beta}_1$ (as well as $\boldsymbol{\beta}_2$) consistently by the least squares method. For examples of these studies, see the articles by Huang (1964) and Wu (1965).

10.7.3 Gronau's Model

Gronau (1973) assumed that the offered wage W^o is given to each housewife independently of hours worked (H), rather than as a schedule $W^o(H)$. Given W^o, a housewife maximizes her utility function $U(C, X)$ subject to $X = W^oH + V$ and $C + H = T$, where C is time spent at home for childcare, X represents all other goods, T is total available time, and V is other income. Thus a housewife does not work if

$$\left[\frac{\partial U}{\partial C}\left(\frac{\partial U}{\partial X}\right)^{-1}\right]_{H=0} > W^o \tag{10.7.10}$$

and works if the inequality in (10.7.10) is reversed. If she works, the hours of work H and the actual wage rate W must be such that

$$\frac{\partial U}{\partial C}\left(\frac{\partial U}{\partial X}\right)^{-1} = W.$$

Gronau called the left-hand side of (10.7.10) the housewife's value of time or, more commonly, the reservation wage, denoted W^r.[12]

Assuming that both W^o and W^r can be written as linear combinations of independent variables plus error terms, his model may be statistically described as follows:

$$\begin{aligned} W_i^o &= \mathbf{x}_{2i}'\boldsymbol{\beta}_2 + u_{2i} \qquad\qquad (10.7.11)\\ W_i^r &= \mathbf{z}_i'\boldsymbol{\alpha} + v_i \\ W_i &= W_i^o \qquad \text{if} \quad W_i^o > W_i^r \\ &= 0 \qquad\ \ \text{if} \quad W_i^o \leqq W_i^r, \qquad i = 1, 2, \ldots, n, \end{aligned}$$

where (u_{2i}, v_i) are i.i.d. drawings from a bivariate normal distribution with zero mean, variances σ_u^2 and σ_v^2, and covariance σ_{uv}. Thus the model can be written in the form of (10.7.1) by putting $W_i^o - W_i^r = y_{1i}^*$ and $W_i^o = y_{2i}^*$. Note that H (hours worked) is not explained by this statistical model although it is determined by Gronau's theoretical model. A statistical model explaining H as well as W was developed by Heckman (1974) and will be discussed in Section 10.8.2.

Because the model (10.7.11) can be transformed into the form (10.7.1) in such a way that the parameters of (10.7.11) can be determined from the parameters of (10.7.1), all the parameters of the model are identifiable except $V(W_i^o - W_i^r)$, which can be set equal to 1 without loss of generality. If, however, at least one element of $\mathbf{x}_{2i}$ is not included in $\mathbf{z}_i$, all the parameters are identifiable.[13] They can be estimated by the MLE or Heckman's two-step estimator by procedures described in Section 10.7.1. We can also use the probit MLE (the first step of Heckman's two-step) to estimate a certain subset of the parameters.[14]

10.7.4 Other Applications of the Type 2 Tobit Model

Nelson (1977) noted that a Type 2 Tobit model arises if y_0 in (10.2.1) is assumed to be a random variable with its mean equal to a linear combination of independent variables. He reestimated Gronau's model by the MLE.

In the study of Westin and Gillen (1978), y_2^* represents the parking cost with $\mathbf{x}_2$ including zonal dummies, wage rate (as a proxy for value of walking time), and the square of wage rate. A researcher observes $y_2^* = y_2$ if $y_2^* < C$ where C represents transit cost, which itself is a function of independent variables plus an error term.

10.8 Type 3 Tobit Model: $P(y_1 < 0) \cdot P(y_1, y_2)$

10.8.1 Definition and Estimation

The Type 3 Tobit model is defined as follows:

$$
\begin{aligned}
y_{1i}^* &= \mathbf{x}_{1i}'\boldsymbol{\beta}_1 + u_{1i} \qquad (10.8.1)\\
y_{2i}^* &= \mathbf{x}_{2i}'\boldsymbol{\beta}_2 + u_{2i} \\
y_{1i} &= y_{1i}^* \quad \text{if} \quad y_{1i}^* > 0 \\
&= 0 \quad \text{if} \quad y_{1i}^* \leqq 0 \\
y_{2i} &= y_{2i}^* \quad \text{if} \quad y_{1i}^* > 0 \\
&= 0 \quad \text{if} \quad y_{1i}^* \leqq 0, \qquad i = 1, 2, \ldots, n,
\end{aligned}
$$

where $\{u_{1i}, u_{2i}\}$ are i.i.d. drawings from a bivariate normal distribution with zero mean, variances σ_1^2 and σ_2^2, and covariance σ_{12}. Note that this model differs from Type 2 only in that in this model y_{1i}^* is also observed when it is positive.

Because the estimation of this model can be handled in a manner similar to the handling of Type 2, we shall discuss it only briefly. Instead, in the following we shall give a detailed discussion of the estimation of Heckman's model (1974), which constitutes the structural equations version of the model (10.8.1).

The likelihood function of the model (10.8.1) can be written as

$$L = \prod_0 P(y_{1i}^* \leqq 0) \prod_1 f(y_{1i}, y_{2i}), \tag{10.8.2}$$

where $f(\cdot, \cdot)$ is the joint density of y_{1i}^* and y_{2i}^*. Because y_{1i}^* is observed when it is positive, all the parameters of the model are identifiable, including σ_1^2.

Heckman's two-step estimator was originally proposed by Heckman (1976a) for this model. Here we shall obtain two conditional expectation equations, (10.4.11) and (10.7.8), for y_1 and y_2, respectively. [Add subscript 1 to all the variables and the parameters in (10.4.11) to conform to the notation of this section.] In the first step of the method, $\boldsymbol{\alpha}_1 = \boldsymbol{\beta}_1 \sigma_1^{-1}$ is estimated by the probit MLE $\hat{\boldsymbol{\alpha}}_1$. In the second step, least squares is applied separately to (10.4.11) and (10.7.8) after replacing $\boldsymbol{\alpha}_1$ by $\hat{\boldsymbol{\alpha}}_1$. The asymptotic variance-covariance matrix of the resulting estimates of $(\boldsymbol{\beta}_1, \sigma_1)$ is given in (10.4.22) and that for $(\boldsymbol{\beta}_2, \sigma_{12}\sigma_1^{-1})$ can be similarly obtained. The latter is given by Heckman (1979). A consistent estimate of σ_2 can be obtained using the residuals of Eq. (10.7.8). As Heckman (1976a) suggested and as was noted in Section 10.4.3, a more efficient WLS can be used for each equation in the second step of the method. An even more efficient GLS can be applied simultaneously to the two equations. However, even GLS is not fully efficient compared to MLE, and the added computational burden of MLE may be sufficiently compensated for by the gain in efficiency. A two-step method based on unconditional means of y_1 and y_2, which is a generalization of the method discussed in Section 10.4.3, can also be used for this model.

Wales and Woodland (1980) compared the LS estimator, Heckman's two-step estimator, probit MLE, conditional MLE (using only those who worked), MLE, and another inconsistent estimator in a Type 3 Tobit model in a simulation study with one replication (sample size 1000 and 5000). The particular model they used is the labor supply model of Heckman (1974), which will be discussed in the next subsection.[15] The LS estimator was found to be poor, and all three ML estimators were found to perform well. Heckman's two-step estimator was ranked somewhere between LS and MLE.

10.8.2 Heckman's Model

Heckman's model (Heckman, 1974) differs from Gronau's model (10.7.11) in that Heckman included the determination of hours worked (H) in his model.[16] Like Gronau, Heckman assumes that the offered wage W^o is given independently of H; therefore Heckman's W^o equation is the same as Gronau's:

$$W_i^o = \mathbf{x}_{2i}'\boldsymbol{\beta}_2 + u_{2i}. \tag{10.8.3}$$

Heckman defined $W^r = (\partial U/\partial C)/(\partial U/\partial X)$ and specified[17]

$$W_i^r = \gamma H_i + \mathbf{z}_i'\boldsymbol{\alpha} + v_i. \tag{10.8.4}$$

It is assumed that the ith individual works if

$$W_i^r(H_i = 0) \equiv \mathbf{z}_i'\boldsymbol{\alpha} + v_i < W_i^o \tag{10.8.5}$$

and then the wage W_i and hours worked H_i are determined by solving (10.8.3) and (10.8.4) simultaneously after putting $W_i^o = W_i^r = W_i$. Thus we can define Heckman's model as

$$W_i = \mathbf{x}_{2i}'\boldsymbol{\beta}_2 + u_{2i} \tag{10.8.6}$$

and

$$W_i = \gamma H_i + \mathbf{z}_i'\boldsymbol{\alpha} + v_i \tag{10.8.7}$$

for those i for which desired hours of work

$$H_i^* \equiv \mathbf{x}_{1i}'\boldsymbol{\beta}_1 + u_{1i} > 0, \tag{10.8.8}$$

where $\mathbf{x}_{1i}'\boldsymbol{\beta}_1 = \gamma^{-1}(\mathbf{x}_{2i}'\boldsymbol{\beta}_2 - \mathbf{z}_i'\boldsymbol{\alpha})$ and $u_{1i} = \gamma^{-1}(u_{2i} - v_i)$. Note that (10.8.5) and (10.8.8) are equivalent because $\gamma > 0$.

Call (10.8.6) and (10.8.7) the structural equations; then (10.8.6) and the identity part of (10.8.8) constitute the reduced-form equations. The reduced-form equations of Heckman's model can be shown to correspond to the Type 3 Tobit model (10.8.1) if we put $H^* = y_1^*$, $H = y_1$, $W^o = y_2^*$, and $W = y_2$.

We have already discussed the estimation of the reduced-form parameters in the context of the model (10.8.1), but we have not discussed the estimation of the structural parameters. Heckman (1974) estimated the structural parameters by MLE. In the next two subsections we shall discuss three alternative methods of estimating the structural parameters.

10.8.3 Two-Step Estimator of Heckman

Heckman (1976a) proposed the two-step estimator of the reduced-form parameters (which we discussed in Section 10.8.1); but he also reestimated the labor supply model of Heckman (1974) using the structural equations version. Because (10.8.6) is a reduced-form as well as a structural equation, the estimation of $\boldsymbol{\beta}_2$ is done in the same way as discussed in Section 10.8.1, namely, by applying least squares to the regression equation for $E(W_i|H_i^* > 0)$ after estimating the argument of λ (the hazard rate) by probit MLE. So we shall discuss only the estimation of (10.8.7), which we can rewrite as

$$H_i = \gamma^{-1} W_i - \mathbf{z}_i' \boldsymbol{\alpha} \gamma^{-1} - \gamma^{-1} v_i. \tag{10.8.9}$$

By subtracting $E(v_i|H_i^* > 0)$ from v_i and adding the same, we can rewrite (10.8.9) further as

$$H_i = \gamma^{-1} W_i - \mathbf{z}_i' \boldsymbol{\alpha} \gamma^{-1} - \sigma_{1v} \sigma_1^{-1} \gamma^{-1} \lambda(\mathbf{x}_{1i}' \boldsymbol{\beta}_1 / \sigma_1) - \gamma^{-1} \epsilon_i, \tag{10.8.10}$$

where $\sigma_{1v} = \text{Cov}\ (u_{1i}, v_i)$, $\sigma_1^2 = V u_{1i}$, and $\epsilon_i = v_i - E(v_i|H_i^* > 0)$. Then the consistent estimates of γ^{-1}, $\boldsymbol{\alpha}\gamma^{-1}$, and $\sigma_{1v}\sigma_1^{-1}\gamma^{-1}$ are obtained by the least squares regression applied to (10.8.10) after replacing $\boldsymbol{\beta}_1/\sigma_1$ by its probit MLE and W_i by $\hat{W}_i$, the least squares predictor of W_i obtained by applying Heckman's two-step estimator to (10.8.6). The asymptotic variance-covariance matrix of this estimator can be deduced from the results in the article by Heckman (1978), who considered the estimation of a more general model (which we shall discuss in the section on Type 5 Tobit models).

Actually, there is no apparent reason why we must first solve (10.8.7) for H_i and proceed as indicated earlier. Heckman could just as easily have subtracted and added $E(v_i|H_i^* > 0)$ to (10.8.7) itself and proceeded similarly. This method would yield alternative consistent estimates. Inferring from the well-known fact that the two-stage least squares estimates of the standard simultaneous equations model yield asymptotically equivalent estimates regardless of which normalization is chosen, the Heckman two-step method applied to (10.8.7) and (10.8.9) should also yield asymptotically equivalent estimates of γ and $\boldsymbol{\alpha}$.

Lee, Maddala, and Trost (1980) extended Heckman's simultaneous equations two-step estimator and its WLS version (taking account of the heteroscedasticity) to more general simultaneous equations Tobit models and obtained their asymptotic variance-covariance matrices.

10.8.4 Amemiya's Least Squares and Generalized Least Squares Estimators

Amemiya (1978c, 1979) proposed a general method of obtaining the estimates of the structural parameters from given reduced-form parameter estimates in general Tobit-type models and derived the asymptotic distribution. Suppose that a structural equation and the corresponding reduced-form equations are given by

$$\mathbf{y} = \mathbf{Y}\gamma + \mathbf{X}_1\boldsymbol{\beta} + \mathbf{u} \tag{10.8.11}$$

$$[\mathbf{y}, \mathbf{Y}] = \mathbf{X}[\boldsymbol{\pi}, \boldsymbol{\Pi}] + \mathbf{V},$$

where $\mathbf{X}_1$ is a subset of $\mathbf{X}$. Then the structural parameters γ and $\boldsymbol{\beta}$ are related to the reduced-form parameters $\boldsymbol{\pi}$ and $\boldsymbol{\Pi}$ in the following way:

$$\boldsymbol{\pi} = \boldsymbol{\Pi}\gamma + \mathbf{J}\boldsymbol{\beta}, \tag{10.8.12}$$

where $\mathbf{J}$ is a known matrix consisting of only ones and zeros. If, for example, $\mathbf{X}_1$ constitutes the first K_1 columns of $\mathbf{X}$ $(K = K_1 + K_2)$, then we have $\mathbf{J} = (\mathbf{I}, \mathbf{0})'$, where $\mathbf{I}$ is the identity matrix of size K_1 and $\mathbf{0}$ is the $K_2 \times K_1$ matrix of zeros. It is assumed that $\boldsymbol{\pi}$, γ, and $\boldsymbol{\beta}$ are vectors and $\boldsymbol{\Pi}$ and $\mathbf{J}$ are matrices of conformable sizes. Equation (10.8.12) holds for Heckman's model and more general simultaneous equations Tobit models, as well as for the standard simultaneous equations model (see Section 7.3.6).

Now suppose certain estimates $\hat{\boldsymbol{\pi}}$ and $\hat{\boldsymbol{\Pi}}$ of the reduced-form parameters are given. Then, using them, we can rewrite (10.8.12) as

$$\hat{\boldsymbol{\pi}} = \hat{\boldsymbol{\Pi}}\gamma + \mathbf{J}\boldsymbol{\beta} + (\hat{\boldsymbol{\pi}} - \boldsymbol{\pi}) - (\hat{\boldsymbol{\Pi}} - \boldsymbol{\Pi})\gamma. \tag{10.8.13}$$

Amemiya proposed applying LS and GLS estimation to (10.8.13). From Amemiya's result (Amemiya, 1978c), we can infer that Amemiya's GLS applied to Heckman's model yields more efficient estimates than Heckman's simultaneous equations two-step estimator discussed earlier. Amemiya (1983b) showed the superiority of the Amemiya GLS estimator to the WLS version of the Lee-Maddala-Trost estimator in a general simultaneous equations Tobit model.

10.8.5 Other Examples of Type 3 Tobit Models

Roberts, Maddala, and Enholm (1978) estimated two types of simultaneous equations Tobit models to explain how utility rates are determined. One of their models has a reduced form that is essentially Type 3 Tobit; the other is a simple extension of Type 3.

The structural equations of their first model are

$$y_{2i}^* = \mathbf{x}_{2i}'\boldsymbol{\beta}_2 + u_{2i} \tag{10.8.14}$$

and

$$y_{3i}^* = \gamma y_{2i}^* + \mathbf{x}_{3i}'\boldsymbol{\beta}_3 + u_{3i}, \tag{10.8.15}$$

where y_{2i}^* is the rate requested by the ith utility firm, y_{3i}^* is the rate granted for the ith firm, $\mathbf{x}_{2i}$ includes the embedded cost of capital and the last rate granted minus the current rate being earned, and $\mathbf{x}_{3i}$ includes only the last variable mentioned. It is assumed that y_{2i}^* and y_{3i}^* are observed only if

$$y_{1i}^* \equiv \mathbf{z}_i'\boldsymbol{\alpha} + v_i > 0, \tag{10.8.16}$$

where $\mathbf{z}_i$ include the earnings characteristics of the ith firm. (Vv_i is assumed to be unity.) The variable y_i^* may be regarded as an index affecting a firm'decision as to whether or not it requests a rate increase. The model (10.8.14) and (10.8.15) can be labeled as $P(y_1 < 0) \cdot P(y_1 > 0, y_2, y_3)$ in our shorthand notation and therefore is a simple generalization of Type 3. The estimation method of Roberts, Maddala, and Enholm is that of Lee, Maddala, and Trost (1980) and can be described as follows:

Step 1. Estimate $\boldsymbol{\alpha}$ by the probit MLE.

Step 2. Estimate $\boldsymbol{\beta}_2$ by Heckman's two-step method.

Step 3. Replace y_{2i}^* in the right-hand side of (10.8.15) by $\hat{y}_{2i}^*$ obtained in step 2 and estimate γ and $\boldsymbol{\beta}_3$ by the least squares applied to (10.8.15) after adding the hazard rate term $E(u_{3i}|y_{1i}^* > 0)$.

The second model of Roberts, Maddala, and Enholm is the same as the first model except that (10.8.16) is replaced by

$$y_{2i}^* > R_i, \tag{10.8.17}$$

where R_i refers to the current rate being earned, an independent variable. Thus this model is essentially Type 3. (It would be exactly Type 3 if $R_i = 0$.) The estimation method is as follows:

Step 1. Estimate $\boldsymbol{\beta}_2$ by the Tobit MLE.

Step 2. Repeat step 3 described in the preceding paragraph.

Nakamura, Nakamura, and Cullen (1979) estimated essentially the same model as Heckman (1974) using Canadian data on married women. They used the WLS version of Heckman's simultaneous equations two-step estimators, that is, they applied WLS to (10.8.10).

Hausman and Wise (1976, 1977, 1979) used Type 3 and its generalizations to analyze the labor supply of participants in the negative income tax (NIT) experiments. Their models are truncated models because they used observations on only those persons who participated in the experiments. The first model of Hausman and Wise (1977) is a minor variation of the standard Tobit model, where earnings Y follow

$$Y_i = Y_i^* \quad \text{if} \quad Y_i^* < L_i, \qquad Y_i^* \sim N(\mathbf{x}_i'\boldsymbol{\beta}, \sigma^2), \tag{10.8.18}$$

where L_i is a (known) poverty level that qualifies the ith person to participate in the NIT program. It varies systematically with family size. The model is estimated by LS and MLE. (The LS estimates were always found to be smaller in absolute value, confirming Greene's result given in Section 10.4.2.) In the second model of Hausman and Wise (1977), earnings are split into wage and hours as $Y = W \cdot H$, leading to the same equations as those of Heckman (Eqs. 10.8.6 and 10.8.7) except that the conditioning event is

$$\log W_i + \log H_i < \log L_i \tag{10.8.19}$$

instead of (10.8.8). Thus this model is a simple extension of Type 3 and belongs to the same class of models as the first model of Roberts, Maddala, and Enholm (1978), which we discussed earlier, except for the fact that the model of Hausman and Wise is truncated. The model of Hausman and Wise (1979) is also of this type. The model presented in their 1976 article is an extension of (10.8.18), where earnings observations are split into the preexperiment (subscript 1) and experiment (subscript 2) periods as

$$Y_{1i} = Y_{1i}^* \quad \text{and} \quad Y_{2i} = Y_{2i}^* \quad \text{if} \quad Y_{1i}^* < L_i. \tag{10.8.20}$$

Thus the model is essentially Type 3, except for a minor variation due to the fact that L_i varies with i.

10.9 Type 4 Tobit Model: $P(y_1 < 0, y_3) \cdot P(y_1, y_2)$

10.9.1 Definition and Estimation

The Type 4 Tobit model is defined as follows:

$$\begin{aligned}
y_{1i}^* &= \mathbf{x}_{1i}'\boldsymbol{\beta}_1 + u_{1i} \qquad (10.9.1)\\
y_{2i}^* &= \mathbf{x}_{2i}'\boldsymbol{\beta}_2 + u_{2i}\\
y_{3i}^* &= \mathbf{x}_{3i}'\boldsymbol{\beta}_3 + u_{3i}\\
y_{1i} &= y_{1i}^* \quad \text{if} \quad y_{1i}^* > 0\\
&= 0 \quad \text{if} \quad y_{1i}^* \leqq 0\\
y_{2i} &= y_{2i}^* \quad \text{if} \quad y_{1i}^* > 0\\
&= 0 \quad \text{if} \quad y_{1i}^* \leqq 0\\
y_{3i} &= y_{3i}^* \quad \text{if} \quad y_{1i}^* \leqq 0\\
&= 0 \quad \text{if} \quad y_{1i}^* > 0, \qquad i = 1, 2, \ldots, n,
\end{aligned}$$

where $\{u_{1i}, u_{2i}, u_{3i}\}$ are i.i.d. drawings from a trivariate normal distribution.

This model differs from Type 3 defined by (10.8.1) only by the addition of y_{3i}^*, which is observed only if $y_{1i}^* \leqq 0$. The estimation of this model is not significantly different from that of Type 3. The likelihood function can be written as

$$L = \prod_0 \int_{-\infty}^{0} f_3(y_{1i}^*, y_{3i})\, dy_{1i}^* \prod_1 f_2(y_{1i}, y_{2i}), \qquad (10.9.2)$$

where $f_3(\cdot\,,\cdot)$ is the joint density of y_{1i}^* and y_{3i}^* and $f_2(\cdot\,,\cdot)$ is the joint density of y_{1i}^* and y_{2i}^*. Heckman's two-step method for this model is similar to the method for the preceding model. However, we must deal with three conditional expectation equations in the present model. The equation for y_{3i} will be slightly different from the other two because the variable is nonzero when y_{1i}^* is nonpositive. We obtain

$$E(y_{3i}|y_{1i}^* \leqq 0) = \mathbf{x}_{3i}'\boldsymbol{\beta}_3 - \sigma_{13}\sigma_1^{-1}\lambda(-\mathbf{x}_{1i}'\boldsymbol{\beta}_1/\sigma_1). \qquad (10.9.3)$$

We shall discuss three examples of the Type 4 Tobit model in the following subsections: the model of Kenny et al. (1979); the model of Nelson and Olson (1978); and the model of Tomes (1981). In the first two models the y^* equations are written as simultaneous equations, like Heckman's model (1974), for which the reduced-form equations take the form of (10.9.1). Tomes' model has a slight twist. The estimation of the structural parameters of such models can be handled in much the same way as the estimation of Heckman's model (1974), that is, by either Heckman's simultaneous equations two-step method (and its Lee-Maddala-Trost extension) or by Amemiya's LS and GLS, both of which were discussed in Section 10.8.

In fact, these two estimation methods can easily accommodate the following very general simultaneous equations Tobit model:

$$\mathbf{\Gamma}'\mathbf{y}_i^* = \mathbf{B}'\mathbf{x}_i + \mathbf{u}_i, \qquad i = 1, 2, \ldots, n, \tag{10.9.4}$$

where the elements of the vector $\mathbf{y}_i^*$ contain the following three classes of variables: (1) always completely observable, (2) sometimes completely observable and sometimes observed to lie in intervals, and (3) always observed to lie in intervals. Note that the variable classified as *C* in Table 10.3 belongs to class 2 and the variable classified as *B* belongs to class 3. The models of Heckman (1974), Kenny et al. (1979), and Nelson and Olson (1978), as well as a few more models discussed under Type 5, such as that of Heckman (1978), are all special cases of the model (10.9.4).

10.9.2 Model of Kenny, Lee, Maddala, and Trost

Kenny et al. (1979) tried to explain earnings differentials between those who went to college and those who did not. We shall explain their model using the variables appearing in (10.9.1). In their model, y_1^* refers to the desired years of college education, y_2^* to the earnings of those who go to college, and y_3^* to the earnings of those who do not go to college. A small degree of simultaneity is introduced into the model by letting y_1^* appear in the right-hand side of the y_2^* equation. Kenny and his coauthors used the MLE. They noted that the MLE iterations did not converge when started from the LS estimates but did converge very fast when started from Heckman's two-step estimates (simultaneous equations version).

10.9.3 Model of Nelson and Olson

The empirical model actually estimated by Nelson and Olson (1978) is more general than Type 4 and is a general simultaneous equations Tobit model (10.9.4). The Nelson-Olson empirical model involves four elements of the vector $\mathbf{y}^*$:

y_1^* Time spent on vocational school training, completely observed if $y_1^* > 0$, and otherwise observed to lie in the interval $(-\infty, 0]$

y_2^* Time spent on college education, observed to lie in one of the three intervals $(-\infty, 0]$, $(0, 1]$, and $(1, \infty)$

y_3^* Wage, always completely observed

y_4^* Hours worked, always completely observed

These variables are related to each other by simultaneous equations. However, they merely estimate each reduced-form equation seperately by various appropriate methods and obtain the estimates of the structural parameters from the estimates of the reduced-form parameters in an arbitrary way.

The model that Nelson and Olson analyzed theoretically in more detail is the two-equation model:

$$y_{1i}^* = \gamma_1 y_{2i} + \mathbf{x}_{1i}'\boldsymbol{\alpha}_1 + v_{1i} \tag{10.9.5}$$

and

$$y_{2i} = \gamma_2 y_{1i}^* + \mathbf{x}_{2i}'\boldsymbol{\alpha}_2 + v_{2i}, \tag{10.9.6}$$

where y_{2i} is always observed and y_{1i}^* is observed to be y_{1i} if $y_{1i}^* > 0$. This model may be used, for example, if we are interested in explaining only y_1^* and y_3^* in the Nelson-Olson empirical model. The likelihood function of this model may be characterized by $P(y_1 < 0, y_2) \cdot P(y_1, y_2)$, and therefore, the model is a special case of Type 4.

Nelson and Olson proposed estimating the structural parameters of this model by the following sequential method:

Step 1. Estimate the parameters of the reduced-form equation for y_1^* by the Tobit MLE and those of the reduced-form equation for y_2 by LS.

Step 2. Replace y_{2i} in the right-hand side of (10.9.5) by its LS predictor obtained in step 1 and estimate the parameters of (10.9.5) by the Tobit MLE.

Step 3. Replace y_{1i}^* in the right-hand side of (10.9.6) by its predictor obtained in step 1 and estimate the parameters of (10.9.6) by LS.

Amemiya (1979) obtained the asymptotic variance-covariance matrix of the Nelson-Olson estimator and showed that the Amemiya GLS (see Section 10.8.4) based on the same reduced-form estimates is asymptotically more efficient.

10.9.4 Model of Tomes

Tomes (1981) studied a simultaneous relationship between inheritance and the recipient's income. Although it is not stated explicitly, Tomes' model can be defined by

$$y_{1i}^* = \gamma_1 y_{2i} + \mathbf{x}_{1i}'\boldsymbol{\beta}_1 + u_{1i}, \tag{10.9.7}$$

$$y_{2i} = \gamma_2 y_{1i} + \mathbf{x}_{2i}'\boldsymbol{\beta}_2 + u_{2i}, \tag{10.9.8}$$

and

$$y_{1i} = y_{1i}^* \quad \text{if} \quad y_{1i}^* > 0 \tag{10.9.9}$$
$$= 0 \quad \text{if} \quad y_{1i}^* \leqq 0,$$

where y_{1i}^* is the potential inheritance, y_{1i} is the actual inheritance, and y_{2i} is the recipient's income. Note that this model differs from Nelson's model defined by (10.9.5) and (10.9.6) only in that y_{1i}, not y_{1i}^*, appears in the right-hand side of (10.9.8). Assuming $\gamma_1\gamma_2 < 1$ for the logical consistency of the model (as in Amemiya, 1974b, mentioned in Section 10.6), we can rewrite (10.9.7) as

$$y_{1i}^* = (1 - \gamma_1\gamma_2)^{-1}[\gamma_1(\mathbf{x}_{2i}'\boldsymbol{\beta}_2 + u_{2i}) + \mathbf{x}_{1i}'\boldsymbol{\beta}_1 + u_{1i}] \tag{10.9.10}$$

and (10.9.8) as

$$y_{2i} = y_{2i}^{(1)} \equiv (1 - \gamma_1\gamma_2)^{-1}[\gamma_2(\mathbf{x}_{1i}'\boldsymbol{\beta}_1 + u_{1i}) + \mathbf{x}_{2i}'\boldsymbol{\beta}_2 + u_{2i}] \tag{10.9.11}$$
$$\text{if} \quad y_{1i}^* > 0,$$
$$= y_{2i}^{(0)} \equiv \mathbf{x}_{2i}'\boldsymbol{\beta}_2 + u_{2i} \qquad \text{if} \quad y_{1i}^* \leqq 0.$$

Thus the likelihood function of the model is

$$L = \prod_0 \int_{-\infty}^0 f(y_{1i}^*, y_{2i}^{(0)})\, dy_{1i}^* \prod_1 f(y_{1i}, y_{2i}^{(1)}), \tag{10.9.12}$$

which is the same as (10.9.2).

10.10 Type 5 Tobit Model: $P(y_1 < 0, y_3) \cdot P(y_1 > 0, y_2)$

10.10.1 Definition and Estimation

The Type 5 Tobit model is obtained from the Type 4 model (10.9.1) by omitting the equation for y_{1i}. We merely observe the sign of y_{1i}^*. Thus the model is defined by

$$y_{1i}^* = \mathbf{x}_{1i}'\boldsymbol{\beta}_1 + u_{1i} \tag{10.10.1}$$
$$y_{2i}^* = \mathbf{x}_{2i}'\boldsymbol{\beta}_2 + u_{2i}$$
$$y_{3i}^* = \mathbf{x}_{3i}'\boldsymbol{\beta}_3 + u_{3i}$$
$$y_{2i} = y_{2i}^* \quad \text{if} \quad y_{1i}^* > 0$$
$$= 0 \quad \text{if} \quad y_{1i}^* \leqq 0$$
$$y_{3i} = y_{3i}^* \quad \text{if} \quad y_{1i}^* \leqq 0$$
$$= 0 \quad \text{if} \quad y_{1i}^* > 0, \qquad i = 1, 2, \ldots, n,$$

where $\{u_{1i}, u_{2i}, u_{3i}\}$ are i.i.d. drawings from a trivariate normal distribution.

The likelihood function of the model is

$$L = \prod_0 \int_{-\infty}^{0} f_3(y_{1i}^*, y_{3i})\, dy_{1i}^* \prod_{\bar{0}} \int_0^{\infty} f_2(y_{1i}^*, y_{2i})\, dy_{1i}^* \tag{10.10.2}$$

where f_3 and f_2 are as defined in (10.9.2). Because this model is somewhat simpler than Type 4, the estimation methods discussed in the preceding section apply to this model *a fortiori*. Hence, we shall go immediately into the discussion of applications.

10.10.2 Model of Lee

In the model of Lee (1978), y_{2i}^* represents the logarithm of the wage rate of the ith worker in case he or she joins the union and y_{3i}^* represents the same in case he or she does not join the union. Whether or not the worker joins the union is determined by the sign of the variable

$$y_{1i}^* = y_{2i}^* - y_{3i}^* + \mathbf{z}_i'\boldsymbol{\alpha} + v_i. \tag{10.10.3}$$

Because we observe only y_{2i}^* if the worker joins the union and y_{3i}^* if the worker does not, the logarithm of the observed wage, denoted y_i, is defined by

$$\begin{aligned} y_i &= y_{2i}^* \quad \text{if} \quad y_{1i}^* > 0 \\ &= y_{3i}^* \quad \text{if} \quad y_{1i}^* \leqq 0. \end{aligned} \tag{10.10.4}$$

Lee assumed that $\mathbf{x}_2$ and $\mathbf{x}_3$ (the independent variables in the y_2^* and y_3^* equations) include the individual characteristics of firms and workers such as regional location, city size, education, experience, race, sex, and health, whereas $\mathbf{z}$ includes certain other individual characteristics and variables that represent the monetary and nonmonetary costs of becoming a union member. Because y_1^* is unobserved except for the sign, the variance of y_1^* can be assumed to be unity without loss of generality.

Lee estimated his model by Heckman's two-step method applied separately to the y_2^* and y_3^* equations. In Lee's model simultaneity exists only in the y_1^* equation and hence is ignored in the application of Heckman's two-step method. Amemiya's LS or GLS, which accounts for the simultaneity, will, of course, work for this model as well, and the latter will yield more efficient estimates—although, of course, not as fully efficient as the MLE.

10.10.3 Type 5 Model of Heckman

The Type 5 model of Heckman (1978) is a simultaneous equations model consisting of two equations

$$y_{1i}^* = \gamma_1 y_{2i} + \mathbf{x}_{1i}'\boldsymbol{\beta}_1 + \delta_1 w_i + u_{1i} \tag{10.10.5}$$

and

$$y_{2i} = \gamma_2 y_{1i}^* + \mathbf{x}_{2i}'\boldsymbol{\beta}_2 + \delta_2 w_i + u_{2i}, \tag{10.10.6}$$

where we observe y_{2i}, $\mathbf{x}_{1i}$, $\mathbf{x}_{2i}$, and w_i defined by

$$\begin{aligned} w_i &= 1 \quad \text{if} \quad y_{1i}^* > 0 \\ &= 0 \quad \text{if} \quad y_{1i}^* \leqq 0. \end{aligned} \tag{10.10.7}$$

There are no empirical results in the 1978 article, but the same model was estimated by Heckman (1976b); in this application y_{2i}^* represents the average income of black people in the ith state, y_{1i}^* the unobservable sentiment toward blacks in the ith state, and $w_i = 1$ if an antidiscrimination law is instituted in the ith state.

When we solve (10.10.5) and (10.10.6) for y_{1i}^*, the solution should not depend upon w_i, for that would clearly lead to logical inconsistencies. Therefore we must assume

$$\gamma_1\delta_2 + \delta_1 = 0 \tag{10.10.8}$$

for Heckman's model to be logically consistent. Using the constraint (10.10.8), we can write the reduced-form equations (although strictly speaking not reduced-form because of the presence of w_i) of the model as

$$y_{1i}^* = \mathbf{x}_i'\boldsymbol{\pi}_1 + v_{1i} \tag{10.10.9}$$

and

$$y_{2i} = \delta_2 w_i + \mathbf{x}_i'\boldsymbol{\pi}_2 + v_{2i}, \tag{10.10.10}$$

where we can assume $Vv_{1i} = 1$ without loss of generality. Thus Heckman's model is a special case of Type 5 with just a constant shift between y_2^* and y_3^* (that is, $y_{2i}^* = \mathbf{x}_i'\boldsymbol{\pi}_2 + v_{2i}$ and $y_{3i}^* = \delta_2 + \mathbf{x}_i'\boldsymbol{\pi}_2 + v_{2i}$). Moreover, if $\delta_2 = 0$, it is a special case of Type 5 where $y_2^* = y_3^*$.

Let us compare Heckman's reduced-form model defined by (10.10.9) and (10.10.10) with Lee's model. Equation (10.10.9) is essentially the same as (10.10.3) of Lee's model. Equation (10.10.4) of Lee's model can be rewritten as

$$y_i = w_i(\mathbf{x}_{2i}'\boldsymbol{\beta}_2 + u_{2i}) + (1 - w_i)(\mathbf{x}_{3i}'\boldsymbol{\beta}_3 + u_{3i}) \tag{10.10.11}$$
$$= \mathbf{x}_{3i}'\boldsymbol{\beta}_3 + u_{3i} + w_i(\mathbf{x}_{2i}'\boldsymbol{\beta}_2 + u_{2i} - \mathbf{x}_{3i}'\boldsymbol{\beta}_3 - u_{3i}).$$

By comparing (10.10.10) and (10.10.11), we readily see that Heckman's reduced-form model is a special case of Lee's model in which the coefficient multiplied by w_i is a constant.

Heckman proposed a sequential method of estimation for the structural parameters, which can be regarded as an extension of Heckman's simultaneous equations two-step estimation discussed in Section 10.8.3. His method consists of the following steps:

Step 1. Estimate $\boldsymbol{\pi}_1$ by applying the probit MLE to (10.10.9). Denote the estimator $\hat{\boldsymbol{\pi}}_1$ and define $\hat{F}_i = F(\mathbf{x}_i'\hat{\boldsymbol{\pi}}_1)$.

Step 2. Insert (10.10.9) into (10.10.6), replace $\boldsymbol{\pi}_1$ with $\hat{\boldsymbol{\pi}}_1$ and w_i with $\hat{F}_i$, and then estimate γ_2, $\boldsymbol{\beta}_2$, and δ_2 by least squares applied to (10.10.6).

Step 3. Solve (10.10.5) for y_{2i}, eliminate y_{1i}^* by (10.10.9), and then apply least squares to the resulting equation after replacing $\boldsymbol{\pi}_1$ by $\hat{\boldsymbol{\pi}}_1$ and w_i by $\hat{F}_i$ to estimate γ_1^{-1}, $\gamma_1^{-1}\boldsymbol{\beta}_1$, and $\gamma_1^{-1}\delta_1$.

Amemiya (1978c) derived the asymptotic variance-covariance matrix of Heckman's estimator defined in the preceding paragraph and showed that Amemiya's GLS (defined in Section 10.8.4) applied to the model yields an asymptotically more efficient estimator in the special case of $\delta_1 = \delta_2 = 0$. As pointed out by Lee (1981), however, Amemiya's GLS can also be applied to the model with nonzero δ's as follows:

Step 1. Estimate $\boldsymbol{\pi}_1$ by the probit MLE $\hat{\boldsymbol{\pi}}_1$ applied to (10.10.9).

Step 2. Estimate δ_2 and $\boldsymbol{\pi}_2$ by applying the instrumental variables method to (10.10.10), using $\hat{F}_i$ as the instrument for w_i. Denote these estimators as $\hat{\delta}_2$ and $\hat{\boldsymbol{\pi}}_2$.

Step 3. Derive the estimates of the structural parameters γ_1, $\boldsymbol{\beta}_1$, δ_1, γ_2, $\boldsymbol{\beta}_2$, and δ_2 from $\hat{\boldsymbol{\pi}}_1$, $\hat{\boldsymbol{\pi}}_2$, and $\hat{\delta}_2$, using the relationship between the reduced-form parameters and the structural parameters as well as the constraint (10.10.8) in the manner described in Section 10.8.4.

The resulting estimator can be shown to be asymptotically more efficient than Heckman's estimator.

10.10.4 Disequilibrium Models

Disequilibrium models constitute an extensive area of research, about which numerous papers have been written. Some of the early econometric models have been surveyed by Maddala and Nelson (1974). A more extensive and up-to-date survey has been given by Quandt (1982). See, also, the article by Hartley (1976a) for a connection between a disequilibrium model and the standard Tobit model. Here we shall mention two basic models first discussed in the pioneering work of Fair and Jaffee (1972).

The simplest disequilibrium model of Fair and Jaffee is a special case of the Type 5 model (10.10.1), in which y_{2i}^* is the quantity demanded in the ith period, y_{3i}^* is the quantity supplied in the ith period, and $y_{1i}^* = y_{3i}^* - y_{2i}^*$. Thus the actual quantity sold, which a researcher observes, is the minimum of supply and demand. The fact that the variance-covariance matrix of (y_1^*, y_2^*, y_3^*) is only of rank 2 because of the linear relationship above does not essentially change the nature of the model because the likelihood function (10.10.2) involves only bivariate densities.

In another model Fair and Jaffee added the price equation to the model of the preceding paragraphs as

$$y_{4i} = \gamma(y_{2i}^* - y_{3i}^*), \tag{10.10.12}$$

where y_{4i} denotes a change in the price at the ith period. The likelihood function of this model can be written as[18]

$$L = \prod_0 \int_{-\infty}^{0} f_3(y_{1i}^*, y_{3i}|y_{4i}) f(y_{4i})\, dy_{1i}^* \tag{10.10.13}$$

$$\times \prod_1 \int_0^{\infty} f_2(y_{1i}^*, y_{2i}|y_{4i}) f(y_{4i})\, dy_{1i}^*.$$

The form of the likelihood function does not change if we add a normal error term to the right-hand side of (10.10.12). In either case the model may be schematically characterized by

$$P(y_1 < 0, y_3, y_4) \cdot P(y_1 > 0, y_2, y_4), \tag{10.10.14}$$

which is a simple generalization of the Type 5 model.

10.10.5 Multivariate Generalizations

By a multivariate generalization of Type 5, we mean a model in which $\mathbf{y}_{2i}^*$ and $\mathbf{y}_{3i}^*$ in (10.10.1) are vectors, whereas y_{1i}^* is a scalar variable the sign of which is observed as before. Therefore the Fair-Jaffee model with likelihood function characterized by (10.10.14) is an example of this type of model.

In Lee's model (1977) the $\mathbf{y}_{2i}^*$ equation is split into two equations

$$C_{2i}^* = \mathbf{x}_{2i}^{*\prime}\beta_2 + u_2 \tag{10.10.15}$$

and

$$T_{2i}^* = \mathbf{z}_{2i}'\boldsymbol{\alpha}_2 + v_2, \tag{10.10.16}$$

where C_{2i}^* and T_{2i}^* denote the cost and the time incurred by the ith person traveling by a private mode of transportation, and, similarly, the cost and the time of traveling by a public mode are specified as

$$C_{3i}^* = \mathbf{x}_{3i}'\boldsymbol{\beta}_3 + u_3 \tag{10.10.17}$$

and

$$T_{3i}^* = \mathbf{z}_{3i}'\boldsymbol{\alpha}_3 + v_3. \tag{10.10.18}$$

Lee assumed that C_{2i}^* and T_{2i}^* are observed if the ith person uses a private mode and C_{3i}^* and T_{3i}^* are observed if he or she uses a public mode. A private mode is used if $y_{1i}^* > 0$, where y_{1i}^* is given by

$$y_{1i}^* = \mathbf{s}_i'\boldsymbol{\delta}_1 + \delta_2 T_{2i}^* + \delta_3 T_{3i}^* + \delta_4 (C_{3i}^* - C_{2i}^*) + \epsilon_i. \tag{10.10.19}$$

Lee estimated his model by the following sequential procedure:

Step 1. Apply the probit MLE to (10.10.19) after replacing the starred variables with their respective right-hand sides.

Step 2. Apply LS to each of the four equations (10.10.15) through (10.10.18) after adding to the right-hand side of each the estimated hazard from step 1.

Step 3. Predict the dependent variables of the four equations (10.10.15) through (10.10.18), using the estimates obtained in step 2; insert the predictors into (10.10.19) and apply the probit MLE again.

Step 4. Calculate the MLE by iteration, starting from the estimates obtained at the end of the step 3.

Willis and Rosen (1979) studied earnings differentials between those who went to college and those who did not, using a more elaborate model than that of Kenny et al. (1979), which was discussed in Section 10.9.2. In the model of Kenny et al., y_{1i}^* (the desired years of college education, the sign of which determines whether an individual attends college) is specified not to depend directly on y_{2i}^* and y_{3i}^* (the earnings of the college-goer and the non-college-goer, respectively). The first inclination of a researcher might be to hypothesize $y_{1i}^* = y_{2i}^* - y_{3i}^*$. However, this would be an oversimplification because the decision to go to college should depend on the difference in expected lifetime earnings rather than in current earnings.

Willis and Rosen solved this problem by developing a theory of the maximization of discounted, expected lifetime earnings, which led to the following model:

$$I_{2i}^* = \mathbf{x}_{2i}'\boldsymbol{\beta}_2 + u_2, \tag{10.10.20}$$

$$G_{2i}^* = \mathbf{z}_{2i}'\boldsymbol{\alpha}_2 + v_2, \tag{10.10.21}$$

$$I_{3i}^* = \mathbf{x}_{3i}'\boldsymbol{\beta}_3 + u_3, \tag{10.10.22}$$

$$G_{3i}^* = \mathbf{z}_{3i}'\boldsymbol{\alpha}_3 + v_3, \tag{10.10.23}$$

and

$$R_i = \mathbf{s}_i'\gamma + \epsilon_i, \qquad i = 1, 2, \ldots, n \tag{10.10.24}$$

where I_{2i}^* and G_{2i}^* denote the initial earnings (in logarithm) and the growth rate of earnings for the college-goer, I_{3i}^* and G_{3i}^* denote the same for the non-college-goer, and R_i denotes the discount rate. It is assumed that the ith person goes to college if $y_{1i}^* > 0$ where

$$y_{1i}^* = I_{2i}^* - I_{3i}^* + \delta_0 + \delta_1 G_{2i}^* + \delta_2 G_{3i}^* + \delta_3 R_i \tag{10.10.25}$$

and that the variables with subscript 2 are observed if $y_{1i}^* > 0$, those with subscript 3 are observed if $y_{1i}^* \leqq 0$, and R_i is never observed. Thus the model is formally identical to Lee's model (1977). Willis and Rosen used an estimation method identical to that of Lee, given earlier in this subsection.

Borjas and Rosen (1980) used the same model as Willis and Rosen to study the earnings differential between those who changed jobs and those who did not within a certain period of observation.

10.10.6 Multinomial Generalizations

In all the models we have considered so far in Section 10.10, the sign of y_{1i}^* determined two basic categories of observations, such as union members versus nonunion members, states with an antidiscrimination law versus those without, or college-goers versus non-college-goers. By a multinomial generalization of Type 5, we mean a model in which observations are classified into more than two categories. We shall devote most of this subsection to a discussion of the article by Duncan (1980).

Duncan presented a model of joint determination of the location of a firm and its input–output vectors. A firm chooses the location for which profits are maximized, and only the input–output vector for the chosen location is observed. Let $s_i(k)$ be the profit of the ith firm when it chooses location k, $i = 1, 2, \ldots, n$ and $k = 1, 2, \ldots, K$, and let $\mathbf{y}_i(k)$ be the input–output vector for the ith firm at the kth location. To simplify the analysis, we shall subsequently assume $y_i(k)$ is a scalar, for a generalization to the vector case is straightforward. It is assumed that

$$s_i(k) = \mathbf{x}_{ik}^{(1)\prime}\boldsymbol{\beta} + u_{ik} \tag{10.10.26}$$

and

$$y_i(k) = \mathbf{x}_{ik}^{(2)\prime}\boldsymbol{\beta} + v_{ik}, \tag{10.10.27}$$

where $\mathbf{x}_{ik}^{(1)}$ and $\mathbf{x}_{ik}^{(2)}$ are vector functions of the input-output prices and economic theory dictates that the same $\boldsymbol{\beta}$ appears in both equations.[19] It is assumed that $(u_{i1}, u_{i2}, \ldots, u_{iK}, v_{i1}, v_{i2}, \ldots, v_{iK})$ are i.i.d. drawings from a $2K$-variate normal distribution. Suppose $s_i(k_i) > s_i(j)$ for any $j \neq k_i$. Then a researcher observes $y_i(k_i)$ but does not observe $y_i(j)$ for $j \neq k_i$.

For the following discussion, it is useful to define K binary variables for each i by

$$\begin{aligned} w_i(k) &= 1 \quad \text{if } i\text{th firm chooses } k\text{th location} \\ &= 0 \quad \text{otherwise} \end{aligned} \tag{10.10.28}$$

and define the vector $\mathbf{w}_i = [w_i(1), w_i(2), \ldots, w_i(K)]'$. Also define $P_{ik} = P[w_i(k) = 1]$ and the vector $\mathbf{P}_i = (P_{i1}, P_{i2}, \ldots, P_{iK})'$.

There are many ways to write the likelihood function of the model, but perhaps the most illuminating way is to write it as

$$L = \prod_i f[y_i(k_i)|w_i(k_i) = 1]P_{ik_i}, \tag{10.10.29}$$

where k_i is the actual location the ith firm was observed to choose.

The estimation method proposed by Duncan can be outlined as follows:

Step 1. Estimate the $\boldsymbol{\beta}$ that characterize f in (10.10.29) by nonlinear WLS.

Step 2. Estimate the $\boldsymbol{\beta}$ that characterize P in (10.10.29) by the multinomial probit MLE using the nonlinear WLS iteration.

Step 3. Choose the optimum linear combination of the two estimates of $\boldsymbol{\beta}$ obtained in steps 1 and 2.

To describe step 1 explicitly, we must evaluate $\mu_i \equiv E[y_i(k_i)|w_i(k_i) = 1]$ and $\sigma_i^2 = V[y_i(k_i)|w_i(k_i) = 1]$ as functions of $\boldsymbol{\beta}$ and the variances and covariances of the error terms of Eqs. (10.10.26) and (10.10.27). These conditional moments can be obtained as follows. Define $z_i(j) = s_i(k_i) - s_i(j)$ and the $(K-1)$-vector $\mathbf{z}_i = [z_i(1), \ldots, z_i(k_i - 1), z_i(k_i + 1), \ldots, z_i(K)]'$. To simplify the notation, write $\mathbf{z}_i$ as $\mathbf{z}$, omitting the subscript. Similarly, write $y_i(k_i)$ as y. Also, define $\mathbf{R} = E(y - Ey)(\mathbf{z} - E\mathbf{z})'[E(\mathbf{z} - E\mathbf{z})(\mathbf{z} - E\mathbf{z})']^{-1}$ and $Q = Vy - \mathbf{R}E(\mathbf{z} - E\mathbf{z})(y - Ey)$. Then we obtain[20]

$$\mu_i = E(y|\mathbf{z} > \mathbf{0}) = Ey + \mathbf{R}E(\mathbf{z}|\mathbf{z} > \mathbf{0}) - \mathbf{R}E\mathbf{z} \tag{10.10.30}$$

and

$$\sigma_i^2 = V(y|\mathbf{z} > \mathbf{0}) = \mathbf{R}V(\mathbf{z}|\mathbf{z} > \mathbf{0})\mathbf{R}' + Q. \quad (10.10.31)$$

The conditional moments of $\mathbf{z}$ appearing in (10.10.30) and (10.10.31) can be found in the articles by Amemiya (1974b, p. 1002) and Duncan (1980, p. 850). Finally, we can describe the nonlinear WLS iteration of step 1 as follows: Estimate σ_i^2 by inserting the initial estimates (for example, those obtained by minimizing $[y_i(k_i) - \mu_i]^2$) of the parameters into the right-hand side of (10.10.31)—call it $\hat{\sigma}_i^2$. Minimize

$$\sum_i \hat{\sigma}_i^{-2}[y_i(k_i) - \mu_i]^2 \quad (10.10.32)$$

with respect to the parameters that appear in the right-hand side of (10.10.30). Use these estimates to evaluate the right-hand side of (10.10.31) again to get another estimate of σ_i^2. Repeat the process to yield new estimates of $\boldsymbol{\beta}$.

Now consider step 2. Define

$$\boldsymbol{\Sigma}_i \equiv E(\mathbf{w}_i - \mathbf{P}_i)(\mathbf{w}_i - \mathbf{P}_i)' = \mathbf{D}_i - \mathbf{P}_i\mathbf{P}_i', \quad (10.10.33)$$

where $\mathbf{D}_i$ is the $K \times K$ diagonal matrix the kth diagonal element of which is P_{ik}. To perform the nonlinear WLS iteration, first, estimate $\boldsymbol{\Sigma}_i$ by inserting the initial estimates of the parameters into the right-hand side of (10.10.33) (denote the estimate thus obtained as $\hat{\boldsymbol{\Sigma}}_i$); second, minimize

$$\sum_i (\mathbf{w}_i - \mathbf{P}_i)'\hat{\boldsymbol{\Sigma}}_i^{-}(\mathbf{w}_i - \mathbf{P}_i), \quad (10.10.34)$$

where the minus sign in the superscript denotes a generalized inverse, with respect to the parameters that characterize $\mathbf{P}_i$, and repeat the process until the estimates converge. A generalized inverse $\mathbf{A}^-$ of $\mathbf{A}$ is any matrix that satisfies $\mathbf{A}\mathbf{A}^-\mathbf{A} = \mathbf{A}$ (Rao, 1973, p. 24). A generalized inverse $\boldsymbol{\Sigma}_i^-$ is obtained from the matrix $\mathbf{D}_i^{-1} - P_{ik}^{-1}\mathbf{l}\mathbf{l}'$, where $\mathbf{l}$ is a vector of ones, by replacing its kth column and row by a zero vector. It is not unique because we may choose any k.

Finally, regarding step 3, if we denote the two estimates of $\boldsymbol{\beta}$ obtained by steps 1 and 2 by $\hat{\boldsymbol{\beta}}_1$ and $\hat{\boldsymbol{\beta}}_2$, respectively, and their respective asymptotic variance-covariance matrices by $\mathbf{V}_1$ and $\mathbf{V}_2$, the optimal linear combination of the two estimates is given by $(\mathbf{V}_1^{-1} + \mathbf{V}_2^{-1})^{-1}\mathbf{V}_1^{-1}\hat{\boldsymbol{\beta}}_1 + (\mathbf{V}_1^{-1} + \mathbf{V}_2^{-1})^{-1}\mathbf{V}_2^{-1}\hat{\boldsymbol{\beta}}_2$. This final estimator is asymptotically not fully efficient, however. To see this, suppose the regression coefficients of (10.10.26) and (10.10.27) differ: Call them $\boldsymbol{\beta}_2$ and $\boldsymbol{\beta}_1$, say. Then, by a result of Amemiya (1976b), we know that $\hat{\boldsymbol{\beta}}_2$ is an asymptotically efficient estimator of $\boldsymbol{\beta}_2$. However, as we have indicated in Section 10.4.4, $\hat{\boldsymbol{\beta}}_1$ is not asymptotically efficient. So a weighted average of the two could not be asymptotically efficient.

Dubin and McFadden (1984) used a model similar to that of Duncan in their study of the joint determination of the choice of electric appliances and the consumption of electricity. In their model, $s_i(k)$ may be interpreted as the utility of the ith family when they use the kth portfolio of appliances, and $y_i(k)$ as the consumption of electricity for the ith person holding the kth portfolio. The estimation method is essentially similar to Duncan's method. The main difference is that Dubin and McFadden assumed that the error terms of (10.10.26) and (10.10.27) are distributed with Type I extreme-value distribution and hence that the P part of (10.10.29) is multinomial logit.

Exercises

1. (Section 10.4.3)
   Verify (10.4.19).

2. (Section 10.4.3)
   Verify (10.4.28).

3. (Section 10.4.3)
   Consider $V\hat{\gamma}_W$ and $V\tilde{\gamma}_W$ given in (10.4.32) and (10.4.33). As stated in the text, the difference of the two matrices is neither positive definite nor negative definite. Show that the first part of $V\hat{\gamma}_W$, namely, $\sigma^2(\mathbf{Z}'\Sigma^{-1}\mathbf{Z})^{-1}$, is smaller than $V\tilde{\gamma}_W$ in the matrix sense.

4. (Section 10.4.5)
   In the standard Tobit model (10.2.3), assume that $\sigma^2 = 1$, β is a scalar and the only unknown parameter, and $\{x_i\}$ are i.i.d. binary random variables taking 1 with probability p and 0 with probability $1-p$. Derive the formulae of $p \cdot \text{AV}[\sqrt{n}(\hat{\beta}-\beta)]$ for $\hat{\beta}$ = Probit MLE, Tobit MLE, Heckman's LS, and NLLS. Evaluate them for $\beta = 0$, 1, and 2.

5. (Section 10.4.6)
   Consider the following model:

$$
\begin{aligned}
y_i &= 1 \quad \text{if} \quad y_i^* \geqq 0 \\
&= 0 \quad \text{if} \quad y_i^* < 0, \qquad i = 1, 2, \ldots, n,
\end{aligned}
$$

   where $\{y_i^*\}$ are independent $N(\mathbf{x}_i'\boldsymbol{\beta}, 1)$. It is assumed that $\{y_i\}$ are observed but $\{y_i^*\}$ are not. Write a step-by-step instruction of the EM algorithm to obtain the MLE of $\boldsymbol{\beta}$ and show that the MLE is an equilibrium solution of the iteration.

6. (Section 10.6)
Consider the following model:

$$y_{1i}^* = \mathbf{x}_{1i}'\boldsymbol{\beta}_1 + u_{1i}$$

$$y_{2i}^* = \mathbf{x}_{2i}'\boldsymbol{\beta}_2 + u_{2i}$$

$$\begin{aligned} y_{1i} &= y_{1i}^* && \text{if} \quad y_{2i}^* > 0 \\ &= 0 && \text{if} \quad y_{2i}^* \leqq 0 \\ y_{2i} &= 1 && \text{if} \quad y_{2i}^* > 0 \\ &= 0 && \text{if} \quad y_{2i}^* \leqq 0, \qquad i = 1, 2, \ldots, n, \end{aligned}$$

where (u_{1i}, u_{2i}) are i.i.d. with the continuous density $f(\,\cdot\,,\,\cdot\,)$. Denote the marginal density of u_{1i} by $f_1(\,\cdot\,)$ and that of u_{2i} by $f_2(\,\cdot\,)$.

a. Assuming that y_{1i}, y_{2i}^*, $\mathbf{x}_{1i}$ and $\mathbf{x}_{2i}$ are observed for $i = 1, 2, \ldots, n$, express the likelihood function in terms of f, f_1, and f_2.

b. Assuming that y_{1i}, y_{2i}, $\mathbf{x}_{1i}$, and $\mathbf{x}_{2i}$ are observed for all i, express the likelihood function in terms of f, f_1 and f_2.

7. (Section 10.6)
Consider the following model:

$$y_i^* = \alpha z_i + u_i$$

$$z_i^* = \beta y_i + v_i$$

$$\begin{aligned} y_i &= 1 && \text{if} \quad y_i^* \geqq 0 \\ &= 0 && \text{if} \quad y_i^* < 0 \\ z_i &= 1 && \text{if} \quad z_i^* \geqq 0 \\ &= 0 && \text{if} \quad z_i^* < 0, \end{aligned}$$

where u_i and v_i are jointly normal with zero means and nonzero covariance. Assume that y^*, z^*, u, and v are unobservable and y and z are observable. Show that the model makes sense (that is, y and z are uniquely determined as functions of u and v) if and only if $\alpha\beta = 0$.

8. (Section 10.6)
In the model of Exercise 7, assume that $\beta = 0$ and that we have n i.i.d. observations on (y_i, z_i), $i = 1, 2, \ldots, n$. Write the likelihood function of α. You may write the joint density of (u, v) as simply $f(u, v)$ without explicitly writing the bivariate normal density.

9. (Section 10.6)
Suppose y_i^* and z_i^*, $i = 1, 2, \ldots, n$, are i.i.d. and jointly normally distributed with nonzero correlation. For each i, we observe (1) only y_i^*, (2) only z_i^*, or (3) neither, according to the following scheme:

(1) Observe $y_i^* = y_i$ and do not observe z_i^* if $y_i^* \geqq z_i^* \geqq 0$.

(2) Observe $z_i^* = z_i$ and do not observe y_i if $z_i^* > y_i^* \geqq 0$.

(3) Do not observe either if $y_i^* < 0$ or $z_i^* < 0$.

Write down the likelihood function of the model. You may write the joint normal density simply as $f(\cdot, \cdot)$.

10. Section (10.7.1)
Write the likelihood function of the following two models (cf. Cragg, 1971).

a. $(y_1^*, y_2^*) \sim$ Bivariate $N(\mathbf{x}_1'\boldsymbol{\beta}_1, \mathbf{x}_2'\boldsymbol{\beta}_2, 1, \sigma_2^2, \sigma_{12})$

$$\begin{aligned} y_2 &= y_2^* \quad &&\text{if} \quad y_1^* > 0 \quad \text{and} \quad y_2^* > 0 \\ &= 0 &&\text{otherwise.} \end{aligned}$$

We observe only y_2.

b. $(y_1^*, y_2^*) \sim$ Bivariate $N(\mathbf{x}_1'\boldsymbol{\beta}_1, \mathbf{x}_2'\boldsymbol{\beta}_2, 1, \sigma_2^2, \sigma_{12})$ with y_2^* truncated so that $y_2^* > 0$

$$\begin{aligned} y_2 &= y_2^* \quad &&\text{if} \quad y_1^* > 0 \\ &= 0 &&\text{if} \quad y_1^* \leqq 0 \end{aligned}$$

We observe only y_2.

11. (Section 10.9.4)
In Tomes' model defined by (10.9.7) through (10.9.9), consider the following estimation method: *Step 1.* Regress y_{2i} on $\mathbf{x}_{1i}$ and $\mathbf{x}_{2i}$ and obtain the least squares predictor $\hat{y}_{2i}$. *Step 2.* Substitute $\hat{y}_{2i}$ for y_{2i} in (10.9.7) and apply the Tobit MLE to Eqs. (10.9.7) and (10.9.9). Will this method yield consistent estimates of γ_1 and $\boldsymbol{\beta}_1$?

12. (Section 10.10)
Suppose the joint distribution of a binary variable w and a continuous variable y is determined by $P(w = 1 | y) = \Lambda(\gamma_1 y)$ and $f(y|w) = N(\gamma_2 w, \sigma^2)$. Show that we must assume $\sigma^2 \gamma_1 = \gamma_2$ for logical consistency.

13. (Section 10.10.1)
In model (10.10.1), Type 5 Tobit, define an observed variable y_i by

$$\begin{aligned} y_i &= y_{2i}^* && \text{if} \quad y_{1i}^* > 0 \\ &= y_{3i}^* && \text{if} \quad y_{1i}^* \leqq 0 \end{aligned}$$

and assume that a researcher does not observe whether $y_{1i}^* > 0$ or $\leqq 0$; that is, the sample separation is unknown. Write the likelihood function of this model.

14. (Section 10.10.4)
Let $(y_{1i}^*, y_{2i}^*, y_{3i}^*)$ be a three-dimensional vector of continuous random variables that are independent across $i = 1, 2, \ldots, n$ but may be correlated among themselves for each i. These random variables are unobserved; instead, we observe z_i and y_i defined as follows

$$\begin{aligned} z_i &= y_{2i}^* && \text{if} \quad y_{1i}^* > 0 \\ &= y_{3i}^* && \text{if} \quad y_{1i}^* \leqq 0. \end{aligned}$$

$$\begin{aligned} y_i &= \begin{cases} 0 & \text{with probability } \lambda \\ 1 & \text{with probability } 1 - \lambda \end{cases} && \text{if } y_{1i}^* > 0 \\ &= \ 0 && \text{if } y_{1i}^* \leqq 0. \end{aligned}$$

Write down the likelihood function. Use the following symbols:

$$\begin{aligned} & f_{2i}(y_{1i}^*, y_{2i}^*) && \text{joint density of} \quad y_{1i}^* \quad \text{and} \quad y_{2i}^* \\ & f_{3i}(y_{1i}^*, y_{3i}^*) && \text{joint density of} \quad y_{1i}^* \quad \text{and} \quad y_{3i}^*. \end{aligned}$$

15. (Section 10.10.4)
Consider a regression model: $y_{1i}^* = \mathbf{x}_{1i}'\boldsymbol{\beta}_1 + u_{1i}$ and $y_{2i}^* = \mathbf{x}_{2i}'\boldsymbol{\beta}_2 + u_{2i}$, where the observable random variable y_i is defined by $y_i = y_{1i}^*$ with probability λ and $y_i = y_{2i}^*$ with probability $1 - \lambda$. This is called a *switching regression model.* Write down the likelihood function of the model, assuming that (u_{1i}, u_{2i}) are i.i.d. with joint density $f(\cdot\,,\cdot)$.

16. (Section 10.10.6)
Show $\boldsymbol{\Sigma}_i \boldsymbol{\Sigma}_i^- \boldsymbol{\Sigma}_i = \boldsymbol{\Sigma}_i$ where $\boldsymbol{\Sigma}_i$ is given in (10.10.33) and $\boldsymbol{\Sigma}_i^-$ is given after (10.10.34). Let $\mathbf{w}_i^*$ and $\mathbf{P}_i^*$ be the vectors obtained by eliminating the kth element from $\mathbf{w}_i$ and $\mathbf{P}_i$, where k can be arbitrary, and let $\boldsymbol{\Sigma}_i^*$ be the variance-covariance matrix of $\mathbf{w}_i^*$. Then show $(\mathbf{w}_i - \mathbf{P}_i)'\boldsymbol{\Sigma}_i^-(\mathbf{w}_i - \mathbf{P}_i) = (\mathbf{w}_i^* - \mathbf{P}_i^*)'(\boldsymbol{\Sigma}_i^*)^{-1}(\mathbf{w}_i^* - \mathbf{P}_i^*)$.

11 Markov Chain and Duration Models

We can use the term *time series models* in a broad sense to mean statistical models that specify how the distribution of random variables observed over time depends on their past observations. Thus defined, Markov chain models and duration models, as well as the models discussed in Chapter 5, are special cases of time series models. However, time series models in a narrow sense refer to the models of Chapter 5, in which random variables take on continuous values and are observed at discrete times. Thus we may characterize the models of Chapter 5 as continuous-state, discrete-time models. Continuous-state, continuous-time models also constitute an important class of models, although we have not discussed them. In contrast, *Markov chain models* (or, more simply, *Markov models*) may be characterized as discrete-state, discrete-time models, and *duration models* (or, *survival models*) as discrete-state, continuous-time models. In this chapter we shall take up these two models in turn.

The reader who wishes to pursue either of these topics in greater detail than is presented here should consult the textbooks by Bartholomew (1982) for Markov models and by Kalbfleisch and Prentice (1980) or Miller (1981) for duration models. For recent results on duration models with econometric applications, see Heckman and Singer (1984b).

11.1 Markov Chain Models

11.1.1 Basic Theory

Define a sequence of binary random variables

$$\begin{aligned} y_j^i(t) &= 1 \quad \text{if} \quad i\text{th person is in state } j \text{ at time } t \\ &= 0 \quad \text{otherwise,} \\ i &= 1, 2, \ldots, N, \qquad t = 1, 2, \ldots, T, \\ j &= 1, 2, \ldots, M. \end{aligned} \tag{11.1.1}$$

Markov chain models specify the probability distribution of $y_j^i(t)$ as a function of $y_k^i(s)$, $k = 1, 2, \ldots, M$ and $s = t-1, t-2, \ldots$, as well as (possibly) of exogenous variables.

Markov chain models can be regarded as generalizations of qualitative response models. As noted in Section 9.7, Markov chain models reduce to QR models if $y_j^i(t)$ are independent over t. In fact, we have already discussed one type of Markov models in Section 9.7.2.

Models where the distribution of $y_j^i(t)$ depends on $y_k^i(t-1)$ but not on $y_k^i(t-2)$, $y_k^i(t-3)$, . . . are called *first-order Markov models.* We shall primarily discuss such models, although higher-order Markov models will also be discussed briefly.

First-order Markov models are completely characterized if we specify the *transition probabilities* defined by

$$P_{jk}^i(t) = \text{Prob [}i\text{th person is in state } k \text{ at time } t \text{ given that he was in state } j \text{ at time } t-1] \tag{11.1.2}$$

and the distribution of $y_j^i(0)$, the initial conditions.

The following symbols will be needed for our discussion:

$$\mathbf{y}^i(t) = M\text{-vector the } j\text{th element of which is } y_j^i(t) \tag{11.1.3}$$

$$n_j(t) = \sum_{i=1}^{N} y_j^i(t)$$

$$n_{jk}(t) = \sum_{i=1}^{N} y_j^i(t-1)y_k^i(t)$$

$$n_{jk}^i = \sum_{t=1}^{T} y_j^i(t-1)y_k^i(t)$$

$$n_{jk} = \sum_{t=1}^{T} n_{jk}(t) = \sum_{i=1}^{N} n_{jk}^i$$

$$\mathbf{P}^i(t) = \{P_{jk}^i(t)\}, \qquad \text{an } M \times M \text{ matrix}$$

$$p_j^i(t) = \text{Prob[}i\text{th person is in state } j \text{ at time } t]$$

$$\mathbf{p}^i(t) = M\text{-vector the } j\text{th element of which is } p_j^i(t).$$

The matrix $\mathbf{P}^i(t)$ is called a *Markov matrix.* It has the following properties: (1) Every element of $\mathbf{P}^i(t)$ is nonnegative. (2) The sum of each row is unity. (In other words, if $\mathbf{l}$ is an M-vector of ones, then $\mathbf{P}^i(t)\mathbf{l} = \mathbf{l}$.)

If $y_j^i(0)$ is a binary random variable taking the value of 1 with probability

$p_j^i(0)$, the likelihood function of the first-order Markov model can be written as

$$L = \prod_t \prod_i \prod_k \prod_j P_{jk}^i(t)^{y_j^i(t-1)y_k^i(t)} \cdot \prod_i \prod_j p_j^i(0)^{y_j^i(0)}, \tag{11.1.4}$$

where t ranges from 1 to T, i ranges from 1 to N, and k and j range from 1 to M unless otherwise noted. If the initial values $y_j^i(0)$ are assumed to be known constants, the last product term of the right-hand side of (11.1.4) should be dropped.

Clearly, all the parameters $P_{jk}^i(t)$ and $p_j^i(0)$ cannot be estimated consistently. Therefore they are generally specified as functions of a parameter vector θ, where the number of elements in θ is either fixed or goes to ∞ at a sufficiently slow rate (compared to the sample size). Later we shall discuss various ways to parameterize the transition probabilities $P_{jk}^i(t)$.

A Markov model where $P_{jk}^i(t) = P_{jk}^i$ for all t is called the *stationary* Markov model. If $P_{jk}^i(t) = P_{jk}(t)$ for all i, the model is called *homogeneous.* (Its antonym is *heterogeneous.*) A parameterization similar to the one used in QR models is to specify $P_{jk}^i(t) = F_{jk}[\mathbf{x}^i(t)'\boldsymbol{\beta}]$ for some functions F_{jk} such that $\Sigma_{k=1}^M F_{jk} = 1$. Examples will be given in Sections 11.1.3 and 11.1.4. The case where $y_j^i(t)$ are independent over t (the case of pure QR models) is a special case of the first-order Markov model obtained by setting $P_{jk}^i(t) = P_{j'k}^i(t)$ for all j and j' for each i and t.

For QR models we defined the nonlinear regression models: (9.2.26) for the binary case and (9.3.16) for the multinomial case. A similar representation for the first-order Markov model can be written as

$$E[\mathbf{y}^i(t)|\mathbf{y}^i(t-1), \mathbf{y}^i(t-2), \ldots] = \mathbf{P}^i(t)'\mathbf{y}^i(t-1) \tag{11.1.5}$$

or

$$\mathbf{y}^i(t) = \mathbf{P}^i(t)'\mathbf{y}^i(t-1) + \mathbf{u}^i(t). \tag{11.1.6}$$

Because these M equations are linearly dependent (their sum is 1), we eliminate the Mth equation and write the remaining $M-1$ equations as

$$\bar{\mathbf{y}}^i(t) = \bar{\mathbf{P}}^i(t)'\mathbf{y}^i(t-1) + \bar{\mathbf{u}}^i(t). \tag{11.1.7}$$

Conditional on $\mathbf{y}^i(t-1), \mathbf{y}^i(t-2), \ldots$, we have $E\bar{\mathbf{u}}^i(t) = \mathbf{0}$ and $V\bar{\mathbf{u}}^i(t) = \mathbf{D}(\boldsymbol{\mu}) - \boldsymbol{\mu}\boldsymbol{\mu}'$, where $\boldsymbol{\mu} = \bar{\mathbf{P}}^i(t)'\mathbf{y}^i(t-1)$ and $\mathbf{D}(\boldsymbol{\mu})$ is the diagonal matrix with the elements of $\boldsymbol{\mu}$ in the diagonal. Strictly speaking, the analog of (9.3.16) is (11.1.7) rather than (11.1.6) because in (9.3.16) a redundant equation has been eliminated.

As in QR models, the NLGLS estimator of the parameters that characterize $\bar{\mathbf{P}}^i(t)$, derived from (11.1.7), yields asymptotically efficient estimates. The presence of $\mathbf{y}^i(t-1)$ in the right-hand side of the equation does not cause any problem asymptotically. This is analogous to the fact that the properties of the least squares estimator in the classical regression model (Model 1) hold asymptotically for the autoregressive models discussed in Chapter 5. We shall discuss the NLWLS estimator in greater detail in Section 11.1.3. There we shall consider a two-state Markov model in which $\mathbf{P}^i(t)$ depends on exogenous variables in a specific way.

As in QR models, minimum chi-square estimation is possible for Markov models in certain cases. We shall discuss these cases in Section 11.1.3.

Taking the expectation of both sides of (11.1.5) yields

$$\mathbf{p}^i(t) = \mathbf{P}^i(t)'\mathbf{p}^i(t-1). \tag{11.1.8}$$

It is instructive to rewrite the likelihood function (11.1.4) as a function of $P^i_{jk}(t)$ and $\mathbf{p}^i(t)$ as follows. Because

$$\prod_j P^i_{jk}(t)^{y^i_j(t-1)y^i_k(t)} = \prod_j \left[\frac{P^i_{jk}(t)}{p^i_k(t)}\right]^{y^i_j(t-1)y^i_k(t)} \cdot p^i_k(t)^{y^i_k(t)}, \tag{11.1.9}$$

we can write (11.1.4) alternatively as

$$\begin{aligned} L &= \prod_t \prod_i \prod_k \prod_j \left[\frac{P^i_{jk}(t)}{p^i_k(t)}\right]^{y^i_j(t-1)y^i_k(t)} \cdot \prod_{t=0}^{T} \prod_i \prod_j p^i_j(t)^{y^i_j(t)} \qquad (11.1.10) \\ &\equiv L_1 \cdot L_2. \end{aligned}$$

If we specify $P^i_{jk}(t)$ and $p^i_j(0)$ to be functions of a parameter vector $\boldsymbol{\theta}$, then by (11.1.8) L_2 is also a function of $\boldsymbol{\theta}$. The partial likelihood function $L_2(\boldsymbol{\theta})$ has the same form as the likelihood function of a QR model, and maximizing it will yield consistent but generally asymptotically inefficient estimates of $\boldsymbol{\theta}$.

As we noted earlier, if $y^i_j(t)$ are independent over t, the rows of the matrix $\mathbf{P}^i(t)$ are identical. Then, using (11.1.8), we readily see $P^i_{jk}(t) = p^i_k(t)$. Therefore $L = L_2$, implying that the likelihood function of a Markov model is reduced to the likelihood function of a QR model.

Because $p^i_j(t)$ is generally a complicated function of the transition probabilities, maximizing L_2 cannot be recommended as a practical estimation method. However, there is an exception (aside from the independence case mentioned earlier), that is, the case when $p^i_j(0)$ are equilibrium probabilities.

The notion of equilibrium probability is an important concept for stationary Markov models. Consider a typical individual and therefore drop the superscript i from Eq. (11.1.8). Under the stationarity assumption we have

$$\mathbf{p}(t) = \mathbf{P}'\mathbf{p}(t-1). \tag{11.1.11}$$

By repeated substitution we obtain from (11.1.11)

$$\mathbf{p}(t) = (\mathbf{P}')^t\mathbf{p}(0). \tag{11.1.12}$$

if $\lim_{t\to\infty} (\mathbf{P}')^t$ exists, then

$$\mathbf{p}(\infty) = (\mathbf{P}')^\infty\mathbf{p}(0). \tag{11.1.13}$$

We call the elements of $\mathbf{p}(\infty)$ *equilibrium probabilities.* They exist if every element of $\mathbf{P}$ is positive.

It is easy to prove (Bellman, 1970, p. 269) that if every element of $\mathbf{P}$ is positive, the largest (in absolute value or modulus) characteristic root of $\mathbf{P}$ is unity and is unique. Therefore, by Theorem 1 of Appendix 1, there exist a matrix $\mathbf{H}$ and a Jordan canonical form $\mathbf{D}$ such that $\mathbf{P}' = \mathbf{HDH}^{-1}$. Therefore we obtain

$$(\mathbf{P}')^\infty = \mathbf{HD}^\infty\mathbf{H}^{-1} = \mathbf{HJH}^{-1}, \tag{11.1.14}$$

where $\mathbf{J}$ is the $M \times M$ matrix consisting of 1 in the northwestern corner and 0 elsewhere. Equilibrium probabilities, if they exist, must satisfy

$$\mathbf{p}(\infty) = \mathbf{P}'\mathbf{p}(\infty), \tag{11.1.15}$$

which implies that the first column of $\mathbf{H}$ is $\mathbf{p}(\infty)$ and hence the first row of $\mathbf{H}^{-1}$ is the transpose of the M-vector of unity denoted $\mathbf{l}$. Therefore, from (11.1.14),

$$(\mathbf{P}')^\infty = \mathbf{p}(\infty)\mathbf{l}'. \tag{11.1.16}$$

Inserting (11.1.16) into (11.1.13) yields the identity $\mathbf{p}(\infty) = \mathbf{p}(\infty)\mathbf{l}'\mathbf{p}(0) = \mathbf{p}(\infty)$ for any value of $\mathbf{p}(0)$. If $\mathbf{p}(\infty)$ exists, it can be determined by solving (11.1.15) subject to the constraint $\mathbf{l}'\mathbf{p}(\infty) = 1$. Because the rank of $\mathbf{I} - \mathbf{P}'$ is $M-1$ under the assumption, the $\mathbf{p}(\infty)$ thus determined is unique.

If $p_j^i(0) = p_j^i(\infty)$, L_2 reduces to

$$L_2^* = \prod_i \prod_j p_j^i(\infty)^{\Sigma_{t=0}^T y_j^i(t)}, \tag{11.1.17}$$

which is the likelihood function of a standard multinomial QR model. Even if $p_j^i(0) \neq p_j^i(\infty)$, maximizing L_2^* yields a consistent estimate as T goes to infinity. We shall show this in a simple case in Section 11.1.3.

Now consider the simplest case of homogeneous and stationary Markov models characterized by

$$P_{jk}^{i}(t) = P_{jk} \quad \text{for all} \quad i \quad \text{and} \quad t. \tag{11.1.18}$$

The likelihood function (11.1.4) conditional on $y_j^i(0)$ is reduced to

$$L = \prod_k \prod_j P_{jk}{}^{n_{jk}}. \tag{11.1.19}$$

It is to be maximized subject to M constraints $\Sigma_{k=1}^{M} P_{jk} = 1, j = 1, 2, \ldots, M$. Consider the Lagrangian

$$S = \sum_k \sum_j n_{jk} \log P_{jk} - \sum_j \lambda_j \left(\sum_k P_{jk} - 1 \right). \tag{11.1.20}$$

Setting the derivative of S with respect to P_{jk} equal to 0 yields

$$n_{jk} = \lambda_j P_{jk}. \tag{11.1.21}$$

Summing both sides of (11.1.21) over k and using the constraints, we obtain the MLE

$$\hat{P}_{jk} = n_{jk} \Big/ \sum_k n_{jk}. \tag{11.1.22}$$

See Anderson and Goodman (1957) for the asymptotic properties of the MLE (11.1.22).

Anderson and Goodman also discussed the test of various hypotheses in the homogeneous stationary Markov model. Suppose we want to test the null hypothesis that P_{jk} is equal to a certain (nonzero) specified value P_{jk}^{*} for $k = 1, 2, \ldots, M$ and for a particular j. Then, using a derivation similar to (9.3.24), we can show

$$S_j \equiv \left(\sum_{k=1}^{M} n_{jk} \right) \sum_{k=1}^{M} \frac{(\hat{P}_{jk} - P_{jk}^{*})^2}{P_{jk}^{*}} \overset{A}{\sim} \chi_{M-1}^2, \tag{11.1.23}$$

where $\hat{P}_{jk}$ is the MLE. Furthermore, if P_{jk}^{*} is given for $j = 1, 2, \ldots, M$ as well as k, we can use the test statistic $\Sigma_{j=1}^{M} S_j$, which is asymptotically distributed as chi-square with $M(M-1)$ degrees of freedom. Next, suppose we want to test (11.1.18) itself against a homogeneous but nonstationary model characterized by $P_{jk}^{i}(t) = P_{jk}(t)$. This can be tested by the likelihood ratio test statistic with the following distribution:

$$-2 \log \prod_t \prod_j \prod_k [\hat{P}_{jk} / \hat{P}_{jk}(t)]^{n_{jk}(t)} \sim \chi_{(T-1)M(M-1)}^2, \tag{11.1.24}$$

where $\hat{P}_{jk}(t) = n_{jk}(t) / \Sigma_{k=1}^{M} n_{jk}(t)$.

In the same article Anderson and Goodman also discussed a test of the first-order assumption against a second-order Markov chain.

11.1.2 Empirical Examples of Markov Models without Exogenous Variables

In this subsection we shall discuss several empirical articles, in which Markov chain models without exogenous variables are estimated, for the purpose of illustrating some of the theoretical points discussed in the preceding subsection. We shall also consider certain new theoretical problems that are likely to be encountered in practice.

Suppose we assume a homogeneous stationary first-order Markov model and estimate the Markov matrix (the matrix of transition probabilities) by the MLE $\hat{P}_{jk}$ given by (11.1.22). Let $P_{jk}^{(2)}$ be a transition probability of lag two; that is, $P_{jk}^{(2)}$ denotes the probability a person is in state k at time t given that he or she was in state j at time $t-2$. If we define $n_{jk}^{(2)}(t) = \Sigma_{i=1}^{N} y_j^i(t-2)y_k^i(t)$ and $n_{jk}^{(2)} = \Sigma_{t=2}^{T} n_{jk}^{(2)}(t)$, a consistent estimate of $P_{jk}^{(2)}$ is also given by $\hat{P}_{jk}^{(2)} = n_{jk}^{(2)}/\Sigma_{k=1}^{M} n_{jk}^{(2)}$. Now, if our assumption is correct, we should have approximately

$$\hat{\mathbf{P}}^{(2)} \cong \hat{\mathbf{P}}^2, \tag{11.1.25}$$

where $\hat{\mathbf{P}}^2 = \hat{\mathbf{P}}\hat{\mathbf{P}}$. Many studies of the mobility of people among classes of income, social status, or occupation have shown the invalidity of the approximate equality (11.1.25). There is a tendency for the diagonal elements of $\hat{\mathbf{P}}^{(2)}$ to be larger than those of $\hat{\mathbf{P}}^2$ (see, for example, Bartholomew, 1982, Chapter 2). This phenomenon may be attributable to a number of reasons. Two empirical articles have addressed this issue: McCall (1971) explained it by population heterogeneity, whereas Shorrocks (1976) attributed the phenomenon in his data to a violation of the first-order assumption itself.

McCall (1971) analyzed a Markov chain model of income mobility, where the dependent variable is classified into three states: low income, high income, and unknown. McCall estimated a model for each age-sex-race combination so that he did not need to include the exogenous variables that represent these characteristics. Using the *mover-stayer model* (initially proposed by Blumen, Kogan, and McCarthy, 1955, and theoretically developed by Goodman, 1961), McCall postulated that a proportion S_j of people, $j = 1$, 2, and 3, stay in state j throughout the sample period and the remaining population follows a nonstationary first-order Markov model. Let $V_{jk}(t)$ be the probability a mover is in state k at time t given that he or she was in state j at time $t-1$. Then the transition probabilities of a given individual, unidentified to be either a stayer or a mover, are given by

$$P_{jj}(t) = S_j + (1 - S_j)V_{jj}(t) \quad \text{and} \tag{11.1.26}$$

$$P_{jk}(t) = (1 - S_j)V_{jk}(t) \quad \text{if} \quad j \neq k.$$

McCall assumed that $V_{jk}(t)$ depends on t (nonstationarity) because of economic growth, but he got around the nonstationarity problem simply by estimating $V_{jk}(t)$ for each t separately. He used the simplest among several methods studied by Goodman (1961). Stayers in state j are identified as people who remained in state j throughout the sample periods. Once each individual is identified to be either a stayer or a mover, S_j and $V_{jk}(t)$ can be estimated in a straightforward manner. This method is good only when there are many periods. If the number of periods is small (in McCall's data $T = 10$), this method will produce bias (even if n is large) because a proportion of those who stayed in a single state throughout the sample periods may actually be movers. After obtaining estimates of $V_{jk}(t)$, McCall regressed them on a variable representing economic growth to see how economic growth influences income mobility.

For a stationary Markov model, Goodman discussed several estimates of S_j and V_{jk} that are consistent (as n goes to infinity) even if T is small (provided $T > 1$). We shall mention only one simple consistent estimator. By defining matrices $\mathbf{V} = \{V_{jk}\}$, $\mathbf{P} = \{P_{jk}\}$, and a diagonal matrix $\mathbf{S} = \mathbf{D}(S_j)$, we can write (11.1.26) as

$$\mathbf{P} = \mathbf{S} + (\mathbf{I} - \mathbf{S})\mathbf{V}. \tag{11.1.27}$$

The matrix of transition probabilities of lag two is given by

$$\mathbf{P}^{(2)} = \mathbf{S} + (\mathbf{I} - \mathbf{S})\mathbf{V}^2. \tag{11.1.28}$$

Now, $\mathbf{P}$ and $\mathbf{P}^{(2)}$ can be consistently estimated by the MLE mentioned earlier. Inserting the MLE into the left-hand side of (11.1.27) and (11.1.28) gives us $2M(M-1)$ equations. But since there are only M^2 parameters to estimate in $\mathbf{S}$ and $\mathbf{V}$, solving M^2 equations out of the $2M(M-1)$ equations for $\mathbf{S}$ and $\mathbf{V}$ will yield consistent estimates.

The empirical phenomenon mentioned earlier can be explained by the mover–stayer model as follows: From (11.1.27) and (11.1.28) we obtain after some manipulation

$$\begin{aligned}\mathbf{P}^{(2)} - \mathbf{P}^2 &= \mathbf{S} + (\mathbf{I} - \mathbf{S})\mathbf{V}^2 - [\mathbf{S} + (\mathbf{I} - \mathbf{S})\mathbf{V}][\mathbf{S} + (\mathbf{I} - \mathbf{S})\mathbf{V}] \\ &= (\mathbf{I} - \mathbf{S})(\mathbf{I} - \mathbf{V})\mathbf{S}(\mathbf{I} - \mathbf{V}).\end{aligned} \tag{11.1.29}$$

Therefore the diagonal elements of $\mathbf{P}^{(2)} - \mathbf{P}^2$ are positive if the diagonal elements of $(\mathbf{I} - \mathbf{V})\mathbf{S}(\mathbf{I} - \mathbf{V})$ are positive. But the jth diagonal element of $(\mathbf{I} - \mathbf{V})\mathbf{S}(\mathbf{I} - \mathbf{V})$ is equal to

$$S_j(1-V_{jj})^2+\sum_{\substack{k=1\\k\neq j}}^{M} S_k V_{jk} V_{kj},$$

which is positive.

Shorrocks (1976) accounted for the invalidity of (11.1.25) in a study of income mobility by postulating a second-order Markov model. Depending on the initial conditions and the values of the parameters, a second-order Markov model can lead to a situation where the diagonal elements of $\mathbf{P}^{(2)}$ are larger than the corresponding elements of $\mathbf{P}^2$.

The likelihood function of a second-order Markov model conditional on the initial values $y_j^i(-1)$ and $y_j^i(0)$ is given by

$$L=\prod_t \prod_i \prod_j \prod_k \prod_l P_{jkl}^i(t)^{y_j^i(t-2)y_k^i(t-1)y_l^i(t)}, \tag{11.1.30}$$

where $P_{jkl}^i(t)$ is the probability the ith person is in state l at time t given that he or she was in state j at time $t-2$ and in state k at time $t-1$. If homogeneity and stationarity are assumed, then $P_{jkl}^i(t)=P_{jkl}$. Even then the model contains $M^2(M-1)$ parameters to estimate. Shorrocks grouped income into five classes ($M=5$), thus implying 100 parameters. By assuming the Champernowne process (Champernowne, 1953), where income mobility at each time change is restricted to the three possibilities—staying in the same class or moving up or down to an adjacent income class, he reduced the number of parameters to six, which he estimated by ML. We can see this as follows: Let $\eta, \xi=-1, 0, 1$ represent the three possible movements. Then the Champernowne process is characterized by $P_{\eta\xi}$, the probability a person moves by ξ from $t-1$ to t given that he or she moved by η from $t-2$ to $t-1$. Notice that the model is reduced to a first-order Markov chain with $M=3$.

For the purpose of illustrating the usefulness of equilibrium probabilities in an empirical problem and of introducing the problem of entry and exit, let us consider a model presented by Adelman (1958). Adelman analyzed the size distribution of firms in the steel industry in the United States using the data for the periods 1929–1939 and 1945–1956 (excluding the war years). Firms are grouped into six size classes according to the dollar values of the firms' total assets. In addition, state 0 is affixed to represent the state of being out of the industry. Adelman assumed a homogeneous stationary first-order model.

Movements into and from state 0 are called *exit* and *entry,* and they create a special problem because the number of firms in state 0 at any particular time is not observable. In our notation it means that $\Sigma_{l=0}^{6} n_{0l}$ is not observable, and hence, MLE $\hat{P}_{0k}=n_{0k}/\Sigma_l n_{0l}$ cannot be evaluated. Adelman circumvented the problem by setting $\Sigma_{l=0}^{6} n_{0l} = 100{,}000$ arbitrarily. We shall see that although changing $\Sigma_{l=0}^{6} n_{0l}$ changes the estimates of the transition probabilities, it does not affect the equilibrium relative size distribution of firms (except relative to size 0).

Let $\mathbf{p} \equiv \mathbf{p}(\infty)$ be a vector of equilibrium probabilities. Then, as was shown earlier, $\mathbf{p}$ can be obtained by solving

$$\begin{bmatrix} [\mathbf{I} - \hat{\mathbf{P}}']^* \\ \mathbf{1}' \end{bmatrix} \mathbf{p} = \begin{bmatrix} \mathbf{0} \\ 1 \end{bmatrix}, \tag{11.1.31}$$

where * means eliminating the first row of the matrix. Now, consider p_j/p_k for $j, k \neq 0$, where p_j and p_k are solved from (11.1.31) by Cramer's rule. Because $\Sigma_{l=0}^{6} n_{0l}$ affects only the first column of $[\mathbf{I} - \hat{\mathbf{P}}']^*$ proportionally, it does not affect p_j/p_k.

Duncan and Lin (1972) criticized Adelman's model, saying that it is unrealistic to suppose a homogeneous pool of firms in state 0 because a firm that once goes out of business is not likely to come back. Duncan and Lin solved the problem by treating entry and exit separately. Exit is assumed to be an *absorbing state.* Suppose $j = 1$ is an absorbing state, then $P_{11} = 1$ and $P_{1k} = 0$ for $k = 2, 3, \ldots, M$. Entry into state k—$m_k(t)$ firms at time t, $k = 2, 3, \ldots, M$—is assumed to follow a Poisson distribution:

$$F_k(t) = \mu_k(t)^{m_k(t)} e^{-\mu_k(t)} [m_k(t)!]^{-1}. \tag{11.1.32}$$

Then P_{jk} and μ_k are estimated by maximizing the likelihood function

$$L^* = L \cdot \sum_{t=1}^{T} \sum_{k=2}^{M} F_k(t), \tag{11.1.33}$$

where L is as given in (11.1.4). This model is applied to data on five classes of banks according to the ratio of farm loans to total loans. Maximum likelihood estimates are obtained, and a test of stationarity is performed following the Anderson-Goodman methodology.

11.1.3 Two-State Models with Exogenous Variables

We shall consider a two-state Markov model with exogenous variables, which accounts for the heterogeneity and nonstationarity of the data. This model is closely related to the models considered in Section 9.7.2. We shall also discuss an example of the model, attributed to Boskin and Nold (1975), to illustrate several important points.

This model is similar to a univariate binary QR model. To make the subsequent discussion comparable to the discussion of Chapter 9, assume that $j = 0$ or 1 rather than 1 or 2. Let $y_{it} = 1$ if the ith person is in state 1 at time t and $y_{it} = 0$ otherwise. (Note that y_{it} is the same as the $y_1^i(t)$ we wrote earlier.) The model then can be written as

$$P(y_{it} = 1 | y_{i,t-1}) = F(\boldsymbol{\beta}'\mathbf{x}_{it} + \boldsymbol{\alpha}'\mathbf{x}_{it} y_{i,t-1}), \tag{11.1.34}$$

where F is a certain distribution function. Note that (11.1.34) is equivalent to

$$P_{01}^i(t) = F(\boldsymbol{\beta}'\mathbf{x}_{it}) \tag{11.1.35}$$
$$P_{11}^i(t) = F[(\boldsymbol{\alpha} + \boldsymbol{\beta})'\mathbf{x}_{it}].$$

Writing the model as (11.1.34) rather than as (11.1.35) makes clearer the similarity of this model to a QR model. The model defined by (9.7.11) is a special case of (11.1.34) if $\{v_{it}\}$ in (9.7.11) are i.i.d.

Using (11.1.4), we can write the likelihood function of the model conditional on y_{i0} as

$$L = \prod_i \prod_t P_{11}^i(t)^{y_{i,t-1}y_{it}} P_{10}^i(t)^{y_{i,t-1}(1-y_{it})} \tag{11.1.36}$$
$$\times P_{01}^i(t)^{(1-y_{i,t-1})y_{it}} P_{00}^i(t)^{(1-y_{i,t-1})(1-y_{it})}.$$

However, the similarity to a QR model becomes clearer if we write it alternatively as

$$L = \prod_i \prod_t F_{it}^{y_{it}}[1 - F_{it}]^{1-y_{it}}, \tag{11.1.37}$$

where $F_{it} = F(\boldsymbol{\beta}'\mathbf{x}_{it} + \boldsymbol{\alpha}'\mathbf{x}_{it} y_{i,t-1})$.

Because we can treat (i, t) as a single index, model (11.1.34) differs from a binary QR model only by the presence of $y_{i,t-1}$ in the argument of F. But, as mentioned earlier, its presence causes no more difficulty than it does in the continuous-variable autoregressive model; we can treat $y_{i,t-1}$ as if it were an exogenous variable so far as the asymptotic results are concerned. Thus, from (9.2.17) we can conclude that the MLE of $\boldsymbol{\gamma} = (\boldsymbol{\beta}', \boldsymbol{\alpha}')'$ follows

$$\sqrt{NT}\,(\hat{\boldsymbol{\gamma}} - \boldsymbol{\gamma}) \rightarrow N\left\{\mathbf{0}, \left[\operatorname{plim} \frac{1}{NT} \sum_i \sum_t \frac{f_{it}^2}{F_{it}(1 - F_{it})} \mathbf{w}_{it}\mathbf{w}_{it}'\right]^{-1}\right\}, \tag{11.1.38}$$

where f_{it} is the derivative of F_{it} and

$$\mathbf{w}_{it} = \begin{bmatrix} \mathbf{x}_{it} \\ \mathbf{x}_{it} y_{i,t-1} \end{bmatrix}.$$

The equivalence of the NLWLS iteration to the method of scoring also holds for this model.

Similarly, the minimum chi-square estimator can also be defined for this model as in Section 9.2.5. It is applicable when there are many observations of y_{it} with the same value of $\mathbf{x}_{it}$. Although a more general grouping can be handled by the subsequent analysis, we assume $\mathbf{x}_{it} = \mathbf{x}_t$ for every i, so that y_{it}, $i = 1, 2, \ldots, N$, are associated with the same vector $\mathbf{x}_t$.

Define

$$\hat{P}_t^0 = \frac{\sum_{i=1}^{N} y_{it}(1 - y_{i,t-1})}{\sum_{i=1}^{N} (1 - y_{i,t-1})} \tag{11.1.39}$$

and

$$\hat{P}_t^1 = \frac{\sum_{i=1}^{N} y_{it} y_{i,t-1}}{\sum_{i=1}^{N} y_{i,t-1}}. \tag{11.1.40}$$

Then we have

$$F^{-1}(\hat{P}_t^0) = \boldsymbol{\beta}'\mathbf{x}_t + \xi_t, \qquad t = 1, 2, \ldots, T \tag{11.1.41}$$

and

$$F^{-1}(\hat{P}_t^1) = (\boldsymbol{\alpha} + \boldsymbol{\beta})'\mathbf{x}_t + \eta_t, \qquad t = 1, 2, \ldots, T. \tag{11.1.42}$$

The error terms ξ_t and η_t approximately have zero means, and their respective conditional variances given $y_{i,t-1}$, $i = 1, 2, \ldots, N$, are approximately

$$V(\xi_t) = \frac{P_t^0(1 - P_t^0)}{f^2[F^{-1}(P_t^0)] \sum_{i=1}^{N} (1 - y_{i,t-1})} \tag{11.1.43}$$

and

$$V(\eta_t) = \frac{P_t^1(1 - P_t^1)}{f^2[F^{-1}(P_t^1)] \sum_{i=1}^{N} y_{i,t-1}}, \tag{11.1.44}$$

where $P_t^0 = P_{01}^i(t)$ and $P_t^1 = P_{11}^i(t)$. The MIN χ^2 estimator of γ is the weighted least squares estimator applied simultaneously to the heteroscedastic regression equations (11.1.41) and (11.1.42). As in QR models, this estimator has the same asymptotic distribution as the MLE given in (11.1.38), provided that N goes to ∞ for a fixed T.

To illustrate further the specific features of the two-state Markov model, we shall examine a model presented by Boskin and Nold (1975). In this model, $j=1$ represents the state of an individual being on welfare and $j=0$ the state of the individual being off welfare. Boskin and Nold postulated

$$P_{10}^{i}(t)=\Lambda(\boldsymbol{\alpha}'\mathbf{x}_i)\equiv A_i \tag{11.1.45}$$

$$P_{01}^{i}(t)=\Lambda(\boldsymbol{\beta}'\mathbf{x}_i)\equiv B_i,$$

where $\Lambda(x)=(1+e^{-x})^{-1}$, a logistic distribution. The model can be equivalently defined by

$$P(y_{it}=1|y_{i,t-1})=\Lambda[\boldsymbol{\beta}'\mathbf{x}_i-(\boldsymbol{\alpha}+\boldsymbol{\beta})'\mathbf{x}_i y_{i,t-1}]. \tag{11.1.46}$$

Thus we see that the Boskin-Nold model is a special case of (11.1.34).

Note that the exogenous variables in the Boskin-Nold model do not depend on t, a condition indicating that their model is heterogeneous but stationary. The exogenous variables are dummy variables characterizing the economic and demographic characteristics of the individuals. The model is applied to data on 440 households (all of which were on welfare initially) during a 60-month period (thus t denotes a month).

Because of stationarity the likelihood function (11.1.36) can be simplified for this model as

$$L=\prod_i A_i^{n_{10}^i}(1-A_i)^{n_{11}^i}B_i^{n_{01}^i}(1-B_i)^{n_{00}^i}. \tag{11.1.47}$$

It is interesting to evaluate the equilibrium probability—the probability that a given individual is on welfare after a sufficiently long time has elapsed since the initial time. By considering a particular individual and therefore omitting the subscript i, the Markov matrix of the Boskin-Nold model can be written as

$$\mathbf{P}'=\begin{bmatrix}1-A & B\\ A & 1-B\end{bmatrix}. \tag{11.1.48}$$

Solving (11.1.15) together with the constraint $\mathbf{l}'\mathbf{p}(\infty)=1$ yields

$$\mathbf{p}(\infty)'=\left[\frac{B}{A+B},\frac{A}{A+B}\right]. \tag{11.1.49}$$

The first component of the vector signifies the equilibrium probability that the person is on welfare. It increases proportionally with the transition probability P_{01} ($\equiv B$).

It is instructive to derive the characteristic roots and vectors of $\mathbf{P}'$ given in (11.1.48). Solving the determinantal equation

$$\det \begin{bmatrix} 1-A-\lambda & B \\ A & 1-B-\lambda \end{bmatrix} = 0$$

yields the characteristic roots $\lambda_1 = 1$ and $\lambda_2 = 1 - A - B$. Solving

$$\begin{bmatrix} -A & B \\ A & -B \end{bmatrix} \mathbf{h}_1 = \begin{bmatrix} 0 \\ 0 \end{bmatrix}$$

yields (the solution is not unique) the first characteristic vector $\mathbf{h}_1 = (B, A)'$. Solving

$$\begin{bmatrix} B & B \\ A & A \end{bmatrix} \mathbf{h}_2 = \begin{bmatrix} 0 \\ 0 \end{bmatrix}$$

yields the second characteristic vector $\mathbf{h}_2 = (-1, 1)'$. Therefore

$$\mathbf{H} = \begin{bmatrix} B & -1 \\ A & 1 \end{bmatrix} \quad \text{and} \quad \mathbf{H}^{-1} = \frac{1}{A+B} \begin{bmatrix} 1 & 1 \\ -A & B \end{bmatrix}.$$

Using these results, we obtain

$$\begin{aligned} (\mathbf{P}')^{\infty} &= \lim_{t \to \infty} \mathbf{H} \begin{bmatrix} 1^t & 0 \\ 0 & (1-A-B)^t \end{bmatrix} \mathbf{H}^{-1} \\ &= \mathbf{H} \begin{bmatrix} 1 & 0 \\ 0 & 0 \end{bmatrix} \mathbf{H}^{-1} \\ &= \begin{bmatrix} \dfrac{B}{A+B} & \dfrac{B}{A+B} \\ \dfrac{A}{A+B} & \dfrac{A}{A+B} \end{bmatrix}, \end{aligned} \tag{11.1.50}$$

which, of course, could have been obtained directly from (11.1.16) and (11.1.49).

Although the asymptotic variance-covariance matrix of the MLE $\hat{\alpha}$ and $\hat{\beta}$ in the Boskin-Nold model can be derived from (11.1.38), we can derive it directly using the likelihood function (11.1.47). We shall do so only for $\hat{\alpha}$ because the derivation for $\hat{\beta}$ is similar. We shall assume $T \to \infty$, for this assumption enables us to obtain a simple formula.

We need to consider only the part of (11.1.47) that involves A_i; its logarithm is

$$\log L = \sum_i n_{10}^i \log A_i + \sum_i n_{11}^i \log (1 - A_i). \tag{11.1.51}$$

Differentiating (11.1.51) with respect to $\boldsymbol{\alpha}$, we obtain

$$\frac{\partial \log L}{\partial \boldsymbol{\alpha}} = \sum_i \frac{n_{10}^i}{A_i} \frac{\partial A_i}{\partial \boldsymbol{\alpha}} - \sum_i \frac{n_{11}^i}{1 - A_i} \frac{\partial A_i}{\partial \boldsymbol{\alpha}} \tag{11.1.52}$$

and

$$\frac{\partial^2 \log L}{\partial \boldsymbol{\alpha} \partial \boldsymbol{\alpha}'} = - \sum_i \left[\frac{n_{10}^i}{A_i^2} + \frac{n_{11}^i}{(1 - A_i)^2} \right] \frac{\partial A_i}{\partial \boldsymbol{\alpha}} \frac{\partial A_i}{\partial \boldsymbol{\alpha}'} + \sum_i \left[\frac{n_{10}^i}{A_i} - \frac{n_{11}^i}{1 - A_i} \right] \frac{\partial^2 A_i}{\partial \boldsymbol{\alpha} \partial \boldsymbol{\alpha}'}. \tag{11.1.53}$$

To take the expectation of (11.1.53), we need to evaluate En_{10}^i and En_{11}^i. We have

$$\begin{aligned} En_{10}^i &= E \sum_{t=1}^{T} y_1^i(t-1) y_0^i(t) \\ &= \left[\sum_{t=0}^{T-1} p_1^i(t) \right] P_{10}^i \\ &= (1, 0) \left[\sum_{t=0}^{T-1} (\mathbf{P}')^t \right] \mathbf{p}(0) P_{10}^i. \end{aligned} \tag{11.1.54}$$

If we define $\mathbf{D}$ to be the 2×2 diagonal matrix consisting of the characteristic roots of $\mathbf{P}'$, we have from (11.1.50)

$$\begin{aligned} \sum_{t=0}^{T-1} (\mathbf{P}')^t &= \mathbf{H} \left[\sum_{t=0}^{T-1} \mathbf{D}^t \right] \mathbf{H}^{-1} \\ &\cong \frac{T}{A+B} \begin{bmatrix} B & B \\ A & A \end{bmatrix}, \end{aligned} \tag{11.1.55}$$

where the approximation is valid for large T. Inserting (11.1.55) into (11.1.54) yields

$$En_{10}^i \cong \frac{T A_i B_i}{A_i + B_i}. \tag{11.1.56}$$

Similarly,

$$En_{11}^{i} \cong \frac{T(1-A_i)B_i}{A_i+B_i}. \tag{11.1.57}$$

From (11.1.53), (11.1.56), and (11.1.57) we obtain

$$-E\frac{\partial^2 \log L}{\partial\boldsymbol{\alpha}\partial\boldsymbol{\alpha}'} = T\sum_i \frac{A_i(1-A_i)B_i}{A_i+B_i}\mathbf{x}_i\mathbf{x}_i'. \tag{11.1.58}$$

Hence,[1]

$$\text{AV}(\hat{\boldsymbol{\alpha}}) = \left[T\sum_i \frac{A_i(1-A_i)B_i}{A_i+B_i}\mathbf{x}_i\mathbf{x}_i'\right]^{-1}. \tag{11.1.59}$$

Similarly,

$$\text{AV}(\hat{\boldsymbol{\beta}}) = \left[T\sum_i \frac{B_i(1-B_i)A_i}{A_i+B_i}\mathbf{x}_i\mathbf{x}_i\right]^{-1}. \tag{11.1.60}$$

Next, let us consider the consistency of the estimator of $\boldsymbol{\alpha}$ and $\boldsymbol{\beta}$ obtained by maximizing L_2^* defined in (11.1.17). Using (11.1.50), we can write the logarithm of (11.1.17) in the Boskin-Nold model as

$$\log L_2^* = \sum_i \left[\sum_{t=0}^{T} y_1^i(t)\right] \log\left[B_i/(A_i+B_i)\right] \tag{11.1.61}$$

$$+ \sum_i \left[\sum_{t=0}^{T} y_0^i(t)\right] \log\left[A_i/(A_i+B_i)\right].$$

Defining $\mathbf{y}^i(t) = [y_1^i(t), y_0^i(t)]'$, we have

$$\operatorname*{plim}_{T\to\infty} \frac{1}{T}\sum_{t=0}^{T} \mathbf{y}^i(t) = \operatorname*{plim}_{T\to\infty} \frac{1}{T}\sum_{t=0}^{T} (\mathbf{P}')^t\mathbf{y}^i(0) \tag{11.1.62}$$

$$= \frac{1}{A_{i0}+B_{i0}}\begin{bmatrix} B_{i0} \\ A_{i0} \end{bmatrix},$$

where the subscript 0 denotes the true value. Therefore we obtain

$$\operatorname*{plim}_{\substack{N\to\infty \\ T\to\infty}} \frac{1}{NT}\log L_2^* \tag{11.1.63}$$

$$= \lim_{N\to\infty} \frac{1}{N}\sum_{i=1}^{N}\left[\frac{B_{i0}}{A_{i0}+B_{i0}}\log\left(\frac{B_i}{A_i+B_i}\right) + \frac{A_{i0}}{A_{i0}+B_{i0}}\log\left(\frac{A_i}{A_i+B_i}\right)\right],$$

from which we can conclude the consistency of the estimator.

We can now introduce in the context of the Boskin-Nold model an important concept in the Markov model called *duration*. Let t_1 be the number of months a particular individual stays on welfare starting from the beginning of the sample period. It is called the duration of the first spell of welfare. Its probability is defined as the probability that the individual stays on welfare up to time t_1 and then moves off welfare at time t_1. Therefore

$$P(t_1) = (1 - A)^{t_1 - 1} A. \tag{11.1.64}$$

The *mean duration* can be evaluated as

$$\begin{aligned} Et_1 &= \sum_{\tau=1}^{\infty} \tau (1 - A)^{\tau - 1} A = A \sum_{\tau=1}^{\infty} \frac{\partial}{\partial r} r^{\tau} \\ &= A \frac{\partial}{\partial r} \sum_{\tau=1}^{\infty} r^{\tau} = A \frac{\partial}{\partial r} \frac{r}{1 - r} \\ &= \frac{A}{(1 - r)^2} = \frac{1}{A}, \end{aligned} \tag{11.1.65}$$

where $r = 1 - A$. In words, this equation says that the mean duration on welfare is the inverse of the probability of moving off welfare.

Suppose the ith person experiences H welfare spells of duration $t_1^i, t_2^i, \ldots, t_H^i$ and K off-welfare spells of duration $s_1^i, s_2^i, \ldots, s_K^i$. If we generalize the Boskin-Nold model and let the ith person's transition probabilities A_i and B_i vary with spells (but stay constant during each spell), the likelihood function can be written as

$$L = \prod_i \left\{ \prod_{h=1}^{H} [1 - A_i(h)]^{t_h^i - 1} A_i(h) \prod_{k=1}^{K} [1 - B_i(k)]^{s_k^i - 1} B_i(k) \right\}. \tag{11.1.66}$$

Equation (11.1.66) collapses to (11.1.47) if A_i and B_i do not depend on h and k and therefore is of intermediate generality between (11.1.36) and (11.1.47). Expressing the likelihood function in terms of duration is especially useful in the continuous-time Markov model, which we shall study in Section 11.2.

11.1.4 Multistate Models with Exogenous Variables

Theoretically, not much need be said about this model beyond what we have discussed in Section 11.1.1 for the general case and in Section 11.1.3 for the two-state case. The likelihood function can be derived from (11.1.4) by specifying $P_{jk}^i(t)$ as a function of exogenous variables and parameters. The equivalence of the NLWLS to the method of scoring iteration was discussed for the general case in Section 11.1.1, and the minimum chi-square estimator defined for the two-state case in Section 11.1.3 can be straightforwardly generalized to the multistate case. Therefore it should be sufficient to discuss an empirical article by Toikka (1976) as an illustration of the NLWLS (which in his case is a linear WLS estimator because of his linear probability specification).

Toikka's model is a three-state Markov model of labor market decisions in which the three states (corresponding to $j = 1, 2$, and 3) are the state of being employed, the state of being in the labor force (actively looking for a job) and unemployed, and the state of being out of the labor force.

The exogenous variables used by Toikka consist of average (over individuals) income, average wage rate, and seasonal dummies, all of which depend on time (months) but not on individuals. Thus Toikka's model is a homogeneous and nonstationary Markov model. Moreover, Toikka assumed that transition probabilities depend linearly on the exogenous variables.[2] Thus, in his model, Eq. (11.1.7) can be written as

$$\bar{\mathbf{y}}^i(t)' = [\mathbf{y}^i(t-1)' \otimes \mathbf{x}_t']\mathbf{\Pi} + \bar{\mathbf{u}}^i(t)', \tag{11.1.67}$$

which is a multivariate heteroscedastic linear regression equation. As we indicated in Section 11.1.1, the generalized least squares estimator of $\mathbf{\Pi}$ is asymptotically efficient.

Let $\mathbf{Y}_t$ be the $N \times M$ matrix the ith row of which is $\mathbf{y}^i(t)'$ and let $\bar{\mathbf{Y}}_t$ be the $N \times (M-1)$ matrix consisting of the first $M-1$ columns of $\mathbf{Y}_t$. Define $\bar{\mathbf{U}}_t$ similarly. Then we can write (11.1.67) as

$$\begin{bmatrix} \bar{\mathbf{Y}}_1 \\ \bar{\mathbf{Y}}_2 \\ \cdot \\ \cdot \\ \cdot \\ \bar{\mathbf{Y}}_T \end{bmatrix} = \begin{bmatrix} \mathbf{Y}_0 \otimes \mathbf{x}_1' \\ \mathbf{Y}_1 \otimes \mathbf{x}_2' \\ \cdot \\ \cdot \\ \cdot \\ \mathbf{Y}_{T-1} \otimes \mathbf{x}_T' \end{bmatrix} \mathbf{\Pi} + \begin{bmatrix} \bar{\mathbf{U}}_1 \\ \bar{\mathbf{U}}_2 \\ \cdot \\ \cdot \\ \cdot \\ \bar{\mathbf{U}}_T \end{bmatrix}. \tag{11.1.68}$$

The LS estimator $\hat{\mathbf{\Pi}}$ is therefore given by

$$\hat{\mathbf{\Pi}} = \left[\sum_{t=1}^{T} (\mathbf{Y}_{t-1}'\mathbf{Y}_{t-1} \otimes \mathbf{x}_t\mathbf{x}_t') \right]^{-1} \sum_{t=1}^{T} (\mathbf{Y}_{t-1}'\bar{\mathbf{Y}}_t \otimes \mathbf{x}_t). \tag{11.1.69}$$

To define the FGLS estimator of $\mathbf{\Pi}$, write (11.1.68) as $\mathbf{Y} = \mathbf{X\Pi} + \mathbf{U}$ and write the columns of $\mathbf{Y}$, $\mathbf{\Pi}$, and $\mathbf{U}$ explicitly as $\mathbf{Y} = [\mathbf{y}_1, \mathbf{y}_2, \ldots, \mathbf{y}_G]$, $\mathbf{\Pi} = [\boldsymbol{\pi}_1, \boldsymbol{\pi}_2, \ldots, \boldsymbol{\pi}_G]$, and $\mathbf{U} = [\mathbf{u}_1, \mathbf{u}_2, \ldots, \mathbf{u}_G]$, where $G = M - 1$. Also define $\mathbf{y} = (\mathbf{y}_1', \mathbf{y}_2', \ldots, \mathbf{y}_G')'$, $\boldsymbol{\pi} = (\boldsymbol{\pi}_1', \boldsymbol{\pi}_2', \ldots, \boldsymbol{\pi}_G')'$, and $\mathbf{u} = (\mathbf{u}_1', \mathbf{u}_2', \ldots, \mathbf{u}_G')'$. Then (11.1.68) can be written as

$$\mathbf{y} = \mathbf{X}\boldsymbol{\pi} + \mathbf{u}. \tag{11.1.70}$$

The FGLS estimator of $\boldsymbol{\pi}$ is $(\mathbf{X}'\hat{\boldsymbol{\Omega}}^{-1}\mathbf{X})^{-1}\mathbf{X}'\hat{\boldsymbol{\Omega}}^{-1}\mathbf{y}$, where $\hat{\boldsymbol{\Omega}}$ is a consistent estimator of $\boldsymbol{\Omega} = E\mathbf{uu}'$. Here, $\boldsymbol{\Omega}$ has the following form:

$$\boldsymbol{\Omega} = \begin{bmatrix} \mathbf{D}_{11} & \mathbf{D}_{12} & \cdots & \mathbf{D}_{1G} \\ \mathbf{D}_{21} & \mathbf{D}_{22} & & \mathbf{D}_{2G} \\ \cdot & & & \cdot \\ \cdot & & & \cdot \\ \cdot & & & \cdot \\ \mathbf{D}_{G1} & & & \mathbf{D}_{GG} \end{bmatrix}, \tag{11.1.71}$$

where each $\mathbf{D}_{jk}$ is a diagonal matrix of size NT. If each $\mathbf{D}_{jk}$ were a constant times the identity matrix, (11.1.70) would be Zellner's seemingly unrelated regression model (see Section 6.4), and therefore the LS estimator would be asymptotically efficient. In fact, however, the diagonal elements of $\mathbf{D}_{jk}$ are not constant.

Toikka's estimator of $\boldsymbol{\Pi}$, denoted $\tilde{\boldsymbol{\Pi}}$, is defined by

$$\tilde{\boldsymbol{\Pi}} = \left[\sum_{t=1}^{T} (\mathbf{I} \otimes \mathbf{x}_t\mathbf{x}_t')\right]^{-1} \sum_{t=1}^{T} [(\mathbf{Y}_{t-1}'\mathbf{Y}_{t-1})^{-1}\mathbf{Y}_{t-1}'\overline{\mathbf{Y}}_t \otimes \mathbf{x}_t]. \tag{11.1.72}$$

Because $(\mathbf{Y}_{t-1}'\mathbf{Y}_{t-1})^{-1}\mathbf{Y}_{t-1}'\overline{\mathbf{Y}}_t$ is the first $M-1$ columns of the unconstrained MLE of the Markov matrix $\mathbf{P}(t)$, Toikka's estimator can be interpreted as the LS estimator in the regression of $\hat{\mathbf{P}}(t)$ on $\mathbf{x}_t$. Although this idea may seem intuitively appealing, Toikka's estimator is asymptotically neither more nor less efficient than $\hat{\boldsymbol{\Pi}}$. Alternatively, Toikka's estimator can be interpreted as premultiplying (11.1.68) by the block-diagonal matrix

$$\begin{bmatrix} (\mathbf{Y}_0'\mathbf{Y}_0)^{-1}\mathbf{Y}_0' & & & & \\ & (\mathbf{Y}_1'\mathbf{Y}_1)^{-1}\mathbf{Y}_1' & & & \\ & & \cdot & & \\ & & & \cdot & \\ & & & & \cdot \\ & & & & (\mathbf{Y}_{T-1}'\mathbf{Y}_{T-1})^{-1}\mathbf{Y}_{T-1}' \end{bmatrix}$$

and then applying least squares. If, instead, generalized least squares were applied in the last stage, the resulting estimator of $\boldsymbol{\Pi}$ would be identical with the GLS estimator of $\boldsymbol{\Pi}$ derived from (11.1.68).

11.1.5 Estimation Using Aggregate Data

Up to now we have assumed that a complete history of each individual, $y_j^i(t)$ for every i, t, and j, is observed. In this subsection we shall assume that only the aggregate data $n_j(t) \equiv \Sigma_{i=1}^N y_j^i(t)$ are available. We shall first discuss LS and GLS estimators and then we shall discuss MLE briefly.

Suppose the Markov matrix $\mathbf{P}^i(t)$ is constant across i, so that $\mathbf{P}^i(t) = \mathbf{P}(t)$. Summing both sides of (11.1.7) over i yields

$$\sum_i \overline{\mathbf{y}}^i(t) = \overline{\mathbf{P}}(t)' \sum_i \mathbf{y}^i(t-1) + \sum_i \overline{\mathbf{u}}^i(t). \tag{11.1.73}$$

The conditional covariance matrix of the error term is given by

$$V\left[\sum_i \overline{\mathbf{u}}^i(t) \middle| \sum_i \mathbf{y}^i(t-1)\right] = \sum_i [\mathbf{D}(\boldsymbol{\mu}_i) - \boldsymbol{\mu}_i\boldsymbol{\mu}_i'], \tag{11.1.74}$$

where $\boldsymbol{\mu}_i = \overline{\mathbf{P}}(t)'\mathbf{y}^i(t-1)$. Depending on whether $\overline{\mathbf{P}}(t)$ depends on unknown parameters linearly or nonlinearly, (11.1.73) defines a multivariate heteroscedastic linear or nonlinear regression model. The parameters can be estimated by either LS or GLS (NLLS or NLGLS in the nonlinear case), and it should be straightforward to prove their consistency and asymptotic normality as NT goes to ∞.

The simplest case occurs when $\mathbf{P}^i(t)$ is constant across both i and t, so that $\mathbf{P}^i(t) = \mathbf{P}$. If, moreover, $\overline{\mathbf{P}}$ is unconstrained with $M(M-1)$ free parameters, (11.1.73) becomes a multivariate linear regression model. We can apply either a LS or a GLS method, the latter being asymptotically more efficient, as was explained in Section 11.1.4. See the article by Telser (1963) for an application of the LS estimator to an analysis of the market shares of three major cigarette brands in the period 1925–1943.

If $\mathbf{P}(t)$ varies with t, the ensuing model is generally nonlinear in parameters, except in Toikka's model. As we can see from (11.1.68), the estimation on the basis of aggregate data is possible by LS or GLS in Toikka's model, using the equation obtained by summing the rows of each $\mathbf{Y}_t$. A discussion of models where the elements of $\mathbf{P}(t)$ are nonlinear functions of exogenous variables and parameters can be found in an article by MacRae (1977). MacRae also discussed maximum likelihood estimation and the estimation based on incomplete sample.

In the remainder of this subsection, we shall again consider a two-state Markov model (see Section 11.1.3). We shall present some of the results we have mentioned so far in more precise terms and shall derive the likelihood function.

Using the same notation as that given in Section 11.1.3, we define $r_t = \Sigma_{i=1}^N y_{it}$. The conditional mean and variance of r_t given r_{t-1} are given by

$$Er_t = \sum_{i=1}^N F_{it} = P_t^1 r_{t-1} + P_t^0(N - r_{t-1}) \tag{11.1.75}$$

and

$$Vr_t = \sum_{i=1}^{N} F_{it}(1 - F_{it}) = P_t^1(1 - P_t^1)r_{t-1} + P_t^0(1 - P_t^0)(N - r_{t-1}). \tag{11.1.76}$$

The NLWLS estimation of γ is defined as that which minimizes

$$\sum_{t=1}^{T} \frac{\left(r_t - \sum_{i=1}^{N} F_{it}\right)^2}{\hat{V}r_t}, \tag{11.1.77}$$

where $\hat{V}r_t$ is obtained by estimating P_t^1 and P_t^0 by $F(\hat{\boldsymbol{\beta}}'\mathbf{x}_t + \hat{\boldsymbol{\alpha}}'\mathbf{x}_t)$ and $F(\hat{\boldsymbol{\beta}}'\mathbf{x}_t)$, respectively, where $\hat{\boldsymbol{\alpha}}$ and $\hat{\boldsymbol{\beta}}$ are consistent estimates obtained, for example, by minimizing $\Sigma_{t=1}^{T}(r_t - \Sigma_{i=1}^{N} F_{it})^2$. Alternatively we can minimize

$$\sum_{t=1}^{T} \frac{\left(r_t - \sum_{i=1}^{N} F_{it}\right)^2}{Vr_t} + \sum_{t=1}^{T} \log \sum_{i=1}^{N} F_{it}(1 - F_{it}), \tag{11.1.78}$$

which will asymptotically give the same estimator.[3] Let $\tilde{\gamma}$ be the estimator obtained by minimizing either (11.1.77) or (11.1.78). Then we have

$$\sqrt{NT}(\tilde{\gamma} - \gamma) \rightarrow N\left(\mathbf{0}, \left[\operatorname{plim} \frac{1}{NT} \sum_{t=1}^{T} \frac{\sum_{i=1}^{N} \frac{\partial F_{it}}{\partial \gamma} \sum_{i=1}^{N} \frac{\partial F_{it}}{\partial \gamma'}}{\sum_{i=1}^{N} F_{it}(1 - F_{it})}\right]^{-1}\right). \tag{11.1.79}$$

The asymptotic variance-covariance matrix of $\tilde{\gamma}$ can be shown to be larger (in matrix sense) than that of $\hat{\gamma}$ given in (11.1.38) as follows: The inverse of the latter can be also written as

$$\operatorname{plim} \frac{1}{NT} \sum_{t=1}^{T} \sum_{i=1}^{N} \frac{1}{F_{it}(1 - F_{it})} \frac{\partial F_{it}}{\partial \gamma} \frac{\partial F_{it}}{\partial \gamma'}. \tag{11.1.80}$$

Put $\mathbf{z}_{it} = [F_{it}(1 - F_{it})]^{-1/2} \partial F_{it}/\partial \gamma$ and $a_{it} = [F_{it}(1 - F_{it})]^{1/2}$. Then the desired inequality follows from

$$\sum_{i=1}^{N} \mathbf{z}_{it}\mathbf{z}_{it}' \geqq \frac{\sum_{i=1}^{N} a_{it}\mathbf{z}_{it} \sum_{i=1}^{N} a_{it}\mathbf{z}_{it}'}{\sum_{i=1}^{N} a_{it}^2}. \tag{11.1.81}$$

Finally, we can define the MLE, which maximizes the joint probability of r_t and r_{t-1}, $t = 1, 2, \ldots, T$. The joint probability can be shown to be

$$\prod_{t=1}^{T} \sum_{l=\max[r_t - r_{t-1}, 0]}^{\min[N - r_{t-1}, r_t]} \left[\binom{r_{t-1}}{r_t - l} (P_t^1)^{r_t - l} (1 - P_t^1)^{r_{t-1} - r_t + l} \right. \tag{11.1.82}$$

$$\left. \times \binom{N - r_{t-1}}{l} (P_t^0)^l (1 - P_t^0)^{N - r_{t-1} - l} \right].$$

The maximization of (11.1.82) is probably too difficult to make this estimator of any practical value. Thus we must use the NLLS or NLWLS estimator if only aggregate observations are available, even though the MLE is asymptotically more efficient, as we can conclude from the study of Barankin and Gurland (1951).

11.2 Duration Models

11.2.1 Stationary Models — Basic Theory

We shall first explain a continuous-time Markov model as the limit of a discrete-time Markov model where the time distance between two adjacent time periods approaches 0. Paralleling (11.1.2), we define

$$\lambda_{jk}^i(t)\, \Delta t = \text{Prob}[i\text{th person is in state } k \text{ at time } t + \Delta t \tag{11.2.1}$$
$$\text{given that he or she was in state } j \text{ at time } t].$$

In Sections 11.2.1 through 11.2.4 we shall deal only with stationary (possibly heterogeneous) models so that we have $\lambda_{jk}^i(t) = \lambda_{jk}^i$ for all t.

Let us consider a particular individual and omit the subscript i to simplify the notation. Suppose this person stayed in state j in period $(0, t)$ and then moved to state k in period $(t, t + \Delta t)$. Then, assuming $t/\Delta t$ is an integer, the probability of this event (called A) is

$$P(\text{A}) = (1 - \lambda_j\, \Delta t)^{t/\Delta t} \lambda_{jk}\, \Delta t, \tag{11.2.2}$$

where $\lambda_j = (\Sigma_{k=1}^M \lambda_{jk}) - \lambda_{jj}$ determines the probability of exiting j. But using the well-known identity $\lim_{n \to \infty} (1 - n^{-1})^n = e^{-1}$, we obtain for small Δt

$$P(\text{A}) = \exp(-\lambda_j t) \lambda_{jk}\, \Delta t. \tag{11.2.3}$$

Because Δt does not depend on unknown parameters, we can drop it and regard $\exp(-\lambda_j t)\lambda_{jk}$ as the contribution of this event to the likelihood function. The complete likelihood function of the model is obtained by first taking the product of these terms over all the recorded events of an individual and then over all the individuals in the sample. Because of (11.2.3), a stationary model is also referred to as an *exponential model.*

Suppose $M = 3$ and a particular individual's event history is as follows: This person stays in state 1 in period $(0, t_1)$, moves to state 2 at time t_1 and stays there until time $t_1 + t_2$, moves to state 3 at time $t_1 + t_2$ and stays there until $t_1 + t_2 + t_3$, at which point this person is observed to move back to state 1. (The observation is terminated after we have seen him or her move to state 1.) Then this person's likelihood function is given by

$$L = \exp(-\lambda_1 t_1)\lambda_{12} \exp(-\lambda_2 t_2)\lambda_{23} \exp(-\lambda_3 t_3)\lambda_{31}. \tag{11.2.4}$$

If we change this scenario slightly and assume that we observe this person to leave state 3 at time $t_1 + t_2 + t_3$ but do not know where he or she went, we should change λ_{31} to λ_3 in (11.2.4). Furthermore, if we terminate our observation at time $t_1 + t_2 + t_3$ without knowing whether he or she continues to stay in state 3 or not, we should drop λ_{31} altogether from (11.2.4). In this last case we say "*censoring* (more exactly, *right-censoring*) occurs at time $t_1 + t_2 + t_3$."

Let us consider the simple case of $M = 2$. In this case we have $\lambda_1 = \lambda_{12}$ and $\lambda_2 = \lambda_{21}$. (We are still considering a particular individual and therefore have suppressed the subscript i.) To have a concrete idea, let us suppose that state 1 signifies unemployment and state 2, employment. The event history of an individual may consist of unemployment spells and employment spells. (If the observation is censored from the right, the last spell is incomplete.) The individual's likelihood function can be written as the product of two terms—the probability of unemployment spells and the probability of employment spells. We shall now concentrate on unemployment spells. Suppose our typical individual experienced r completed unemployment spells of duration $t_1, t_2, \ldots, t_r$ during the observation period. Then the contribution of these r spells to the likelihood function is given by

$$L = \lambda^r e^{-\lambda T}, \tag{11.2.5}$$

where we have defined $T = \Sigma_{j=1}^r t_j$ and have written λ for λ_1. The individual's complete likelihood function is (11.2.5) times the corresponding part for the employment spells.

We now wish to consider closely the likelihood function of one complete spell: $e^{-\lambda t}\lambda$. At the beginning of this section, we derived it by a limit operation, but, here, we shall give it a somewhat different (although essentially the same) interpretation. We can interpret $e^{-\lambda t}$ as $P(T > t)$ where T is a random variable that signifies the duration of an unemployment spell. Therefore the distribution function $F(\cdot)$ of T is given by

$$F(t) = 1 - P(T > t) = 1 - e^{-\lambda t}. \tag{11.2.6}$$

Differentiating (11.2.6) we obtain the density function $f(\cdot)$ of T:

$$f(t) = \lambda e^{-\lambda t}. \tag{11.2.7}$$

Thus we have interpreted $e^{-\lambda t}\lambda$ as the density of the observed duration of an unemployment spell.

From (11.2.6) and (11.2.7) we have

$$\lambda = \frac{f(t)}{1 - F(t)}. \tag{11.2.8}$$

The meaning of λ becomes clear when we note

$$\begin{aligned} \lambda\, \Delta t &= \frac{f(t)\, \Delta t}{1 - F(t)} \\ &= \text{Prob [leaves unemployment in } (t, t + \Delta t) | \text{has not left unemployment in } (0, t)]. \end{aligned} \tag{11.2.9}$$

We call λ the *hazard rate.* The term originates in survival analysis, where the state in question is "life" rather than unemployment.

Still concentrating on the unemployment duration, let us suppose that we observe one completed unemployment spell of duration t_i for the ith individual, $i = 1, 2, \ldots, N$. Then, defining $f^i(t_i) = \lambda^i \exp(-\lambda^i t_i)$, we can write the likelihood function as

$$L = \prod_{i=1}^{N} f^i(t_i), \tag{11.2.10}$$

which is a standard likelihood function of a model involving continuous random variables. Suppose, however, that individuals $i = 1, 2, \ldots, n$ complete their unemployment spells of duration t_i but individuals $i = n + 1, \ldots, N$ are right-censored at time t_i^*. Then the likelihood function is given by

$$L = \prod_{i=1}^{n} f^i(t_i) \prod_{i=n+1}^{N} [1 - F^i(t_i^*)], \tag{11.2.11}$$

which is a mixture of densities and probabilities just like the likelihood function of a standard Tobit model. Thus we see that a duration model with right-censoring is similar to a standard Tobit model.

11.2.2 Number of Completed Spells

The likelihood function (11.2.5) depends on the observed durations $t_1, t_2, \ldots, t_r$ only through r and T. In other words, r and T constitute the sufficient statistics. This is a property of a stationary model. We shall show an alternative way of deriving the equivalent likelihood function.

We shall first derive the probability of observing two completed spells in total unemployment time T, denoted $P(2, T)$. The assumption that there are two completed unemployment spells implies that the third spell is incomplete (its duration may be exactly 0). Denoting the duration of the three spells by t_1, t_2, and t_3, we have

$$
\begin{aligned}
P(2, T) &= P(0 \leqq t_1 < T, 0 < t_2 \leqq T - t_1, t_3 \geqq T - t_1 - t_2) \qquad (11.2.12) \\
&= \int_0^T f(z_1) \left\{ \int_0^{T-z_1} f(z_2) \left[\int_{T-z_1-z_2}^{\infty} f(z_3)\, dz_3 \right] dz_2 \right\} dz_1 \\
&= \int_0^T \lambda \exp(-\lambda z_1) \\
&\quad \times \left(\int_0^{T-z_1} \lambda \exp(-\lambda z_2) \{\exp[-\lambda(T - z_1 - z_2)]\}\, dz_2 \right) dz_1 \\
&= \frac{(\lambda T)^2 e^{-\lambda T}}{2}.
\end{aligned}
$$

It is easy to deduce from the derivation in (11.2.12) that the probability of observing r completed spells in total time T is given by

$$
P(r,T) = \frac{(\lambda T)^r e^{-\lambda T}}{r!}, \qquad (11.2.13)
$$

which is a Poisson distribution. This is equivalent to (11.2.5) because T^r and $r!$ do not depend on the unknown parameters.

We can now put back the subscript i in the right-hand side of (11.2.5) and take the product over i to obtain the likelihood function of all the individuals:

$$
L = \prod_{i=1}^{N} \lambda_i^{r_i} \exp(-\lambda_i T_i). \qquad (11.2.14)
$$

Assuming that λ_i depends on a vector of the ith individual's characteristics $\mathbf{x}_i$, we can specify

$$
\lambda_i = \exp(\alpha + \boldsymbol{\beta}'\mathbf{x}_i), \qquad (11.2.15)
$$

where the scalar α and the vector $\boldsymbol{\beta}$ are unknown parameters. We shall derive the ML estimators of these parameters.[4] In the following discussion it will become apparent why we have separated the constant term α from the other regression coefficients.

The log likelihood function is given by

$$\log L = \sum_i r_i(\alpha + \boldsymbol{\beta}'\mathbf{x}_i) - \sum_i T_i \exp(\alpha + \boldsymbol{\beta}'\mathbf{x}_i). \tag{11.2.16}$$

The ML estimators $\hat{\alpha}$ and $\hat{\boldsymbol{\beta}}$ are the solutions of the normal equations:

$$\frac{\partial \log L}{\partial \alpha} = \sum_i r_i - e^{\alpha} \sum_i T_i \exp(\boldsymbol{\beta}'\mathbf{x}_i) = 0 \tag{11.2.17}$$

and

$$\frac{\partial \log L}{\partial \boldsymbol{\beta}} = \sum_i r_i \mathbf{x}_i - e^{\alpha} \sum_i T_i \exp(\boldsymbol{\beta}'\mathbf{x}_i)\mathbf{x}_i = \mathbf{0}. \tag{11.2.18}$$

Solving (11.2.17) for e^{α} and inserting it into (11.2.18) yield

$$\sum_i r_i \mathbf{x}_i - \frac{\sum_i r_i \sum_i T_i \exp(\boldsymbol{\beta}'\mathbf{x}_i)\mathbf{x}_i}{\sum_i T_i \exp(\boldsymbol{\beta}'\mathbf{x}_i)} = \mathbf{0}. \tag{11.2.19}$$

Thus $\hat{\boldsymbol{\beta}}$ can be obtained from (11.2.19) by the method given in the following paragraph. Inserting $\hat{\boldsymbol{\beta}}$ into (11.2.17) yields an explicit solution for $\hat{\alpha}$.

The following method of obtaining $\hat{\boldsymbol{\beta}}$ was proposed by Holford (1980). Define

$$L_1 = \prod_i \left[\frac{T_i \exp(\boldsymbol{\beta}'\mathbf{x}_i)}{\sum_i T_i \exp(\boldsymbol{\beta}'\mathbf{x}_i)} \right]^{r_i}. \tag{11.2.20}$$

Therefore, we have

$$\begin{aligned} \log L_1 = {} & \sum_i r_i \log T_i + \sum_i r_i \boldsymbol{\beta}'\mathbf{x}_i \\ & - \left(\sum_i r_i\right) \log \sum_i T_i \exp(\boldsymbol{\beta}'\mathbf{x}_i). \end{aligned} \tag{11.2.21}$$

Setting the derivative of (11.2.21) with respect to $\boldsymbol{\beta}$ equal to $\mathbf{0}$ yields

$$\frac{\partial \log L_1}{\partial \boldsymbol{\beta}} = \sum_i r_i \mathbf{x}_i - \frac{\sum_i r_i \sum_i T_i \exp(\boldsymbol{\beta}'\mathbf{x}_i)\mathbf{x}_i}{\sum_i T_i \exp(\boldsymbol{\beta}'\mathbf{x}_i)} = \mathbf{0}, \tag{11.2.22}$$

which is identical to (11.2.19). Note that L_1 is the likelihood function of a multinomial logit model (9.3.34). To see this, pretend that the i in (11.2.20) refers to the ith alternative and r_i people chose the ith alternative. This is a model where the exogenous variables depend only on the characteristics of the alternatives and not on those of the individuals. Thus the maximization of L_1 and hence the solution of (11.2.19) can be accomplished by a standard multinomial logit routine.

We can write L_1 as a part of the likelihood function L as follows:

$$L = L_1 \cdot L_2 \cdot \frac{\left(\sum_i r_i\right)!}{\prod_i T_i^{r_i}}, \tag{11.2.23}$$

where

$$L_2 = \frac{\exp\left[-\sum_i T_i \exp(\alpha+\boldsymbol{\beta}'\mathbf{x}_i)\right]\left[\sum_i T_i \exp(\alpha+\boldsymbol{\beta}'\mathbf{x}_i)\right]^{\Sigma_i r_i}}{\left(\sum_i r_i\right)!}. \tag{11.2.24}$$

Note that L_2 is a Poisson distribution. Setting $\partial \log L_2/\partial\alpha = 0$ yields (11.2.17). We can describe the calculation of the MLE as follows: First, maximize L_1 with respect to $\boldsymbol{\beta}$; second, insert $\hat{\boldsymbol{\beta}}$ into L_2 and maximize it with respect to α.

11.2.3 Durations as Dependent Variables of a Regression Equation

Suppose that each individual experiences one complete spell. Then the likelihood function is

$$L = \prod_{i=1}^{N} \lambda_i \exp(-\lambda_i t_i). \tag{11.2.25}$$

The case of a person having more than one complete spell can be handled by behaving as if these spells belonged to different individuals. Assume as before

$$\lambda_i = \exp(\boldsymbol{\beta}'\mathbf{x}_i). \tag{11.2.26}$$

But, here, we have absorbed the constant term α into $\boldsymbol{\beta}$ as there is no need to separate it out.

We shall derive the asymptotic covariance matrix of the MLE $\hat{\boldsymbol{\beta}}$. We have

$$\frac{\partial^2 \log L}{\partial\boldsymbol{\beta}\partial\boldsymbol{\beta}'} = -\sum_i t_i \exp(\boldsymbol{\beta}'\mathbf{x}_i)\mathbf{x}_i\mathbf{x}_i'. \tag{11.2.27}$$

But we have

$$Et_i = \int_0^\infty z\lambda_i \exp(-\lambda_i z)\, dz = \frac{1}{\lambda_i}, \tag{11.2.28}$$

which is the continuous-time analog of (11.1.65). Therefore we have

$$E \frac{\partial^2 \log L}{\partial \boldsymbol{\beta} \partial \boldsymbol{\beta}'} = -\sum_i \mathbf{x}_i \mathbf{x}_i'. \tag{11.2.29}$$

Therefore, by Theorem 4.2.4, $\hat{\boldsymbol{\beta}}$ is asymptotically normal with asymptotic covariance matrix

$$V\hat{\boldsymbol{\beta}} = \left(\sum_i \mathbf{x}_i \mathbf{x}_i'\right)^{-1}. \tag{11.2.30}$$

Now, suppose we use $\log t_i$ as the dependent variable of a linear regression equation. For this purpose we need the mean and variance of $\log t_i$. We have[5]

$$\begin{aligned} E \log t_i &= \lambda_i \int_0^\infty (\log z) \exp(-\lambda_i z)\, dz \\ &= -c - \log \lambda_i, \end{aligned} \tag{11.2.31}$$

where $c \cong 0.577$ is Euler's constant, and

$$\begin{aligned} E(\log t_i)^2 &= \lambda_i \int_0^\infty (\log z)^2 \exp(-\lambda_i z)\, dz \\ &= \frac{\pi^2}{6} + (c + \log \lambda_i)^2. \end{aligned} \tag{11.2.32}$$

Therefore we have

$$V \log t_i = \frac{\pi^2}{6}. \tag{11.2.33}$$

We can write (11.2.31) and (11.2.33) as a linear regression

$$\log t_i + c = -\boldsymbol{\beta}' \mathbf{x}_i + u_i, \tag{11.2.34}$$

where $Eu_i = 0$ and $Vu_i = \pi^2/6$. Because $\{u_i\}$ are independent, (11.2.34) defines a classical regression model, which we called Model 1 in Chapter 1. Therefore the exact covariance matrix of the LS estimator $\hat{\boldsymbol{\beta}}_{LS}$ is given by

$$V\hat{\boldsymbol{\beta}}_{\text{LS}} = \frac{\pi^2}{6} \left(\sum_i \mathbf{x}_i \mathbf{x}_i'\right)^{-1}. \tag{11.2.35}$$

Comparing (11.2.35) with (11.2.30), we see exactly how much efficiency we lose by this method.

Alternatively, we can define a nonlinear regression model using t_i itself as the dependent variable. From (11.2.28) we have

$$t_i = \exp(-\boldsymbol{\beta}'\mathbf{x}_i) + v_i, \tag{11.2.36}$$

where $Ev_i = 0$. We have by integration by parts

$$Et_i^2 = \int_0^\infty z^2 \lambda_i \exp(-\lambda_i z)\, dz = \frac{2}{\lambda_i^2}. \tag{11.2.37}$$

Therefore we have

$$Vv_i = \exp(-2\boldsymbol{\beta}'\mathbf{x}_i). \tag{11.2.38}$$

This shows that (11.2.26) defines a heteroscedastic nonlinear regression model. The asymptotic normality of the NLWLS estimator $\hat{\boldsymbol{\beta}}_{\text{WLS}}$ can be proved under general assumptions using the results of Sections 4.3.3 and 6.5.3. Its asymptotic covariance matrix can be deduced from (4.3.21) and (6.1.4) and is given by

$$V\hat{\boldsymbol{\beta}}_{\text{WLS}} = \left[\sum_i \exp(2\boldsymbol{\beta}'\mathbf{x}_i)\frac{\partial f_i}{\partial \boldsymbol{\beta}}\frac{\partial f_i}{\partial \boldsymbol{\beta}'}\right]^{-1} = \left(\sum_i \mathbf{x}_i\mathbf{x}_i'\right)^{-1}. \tag{11.2.39}$$

Therefore the NLWLS estimator is asymptotically efficient. In practice Vv_i will be estimated by replacing $\boldsymbol{\beta}$ by some consistent estimator of $\boldsymbol{\beta}$, such as $\hat{\boldsymbol{\beta}}_{\text{LS}}$ defined earlier, which converges to $\boldsymbol{\beta}$ at the speed of $\sqrt{n}$. The NLWLS estimator using the estimated Vv_i has the same asymptotic distribution.

The foregoing analysis was based on the assumption that t_i is the duration of a *completed* spell of the ith individual. If some of the spells are right-censored and not completed, the regression method cannot easily handle them. However, maximum likelihood estimation can take account of right-censoring, as we indicated in Section 11.2.1.

11.2.4 Discrete Observations

In the analysis presented in the preceding three subsections, we assumed that an individual is continuously observed and his or her complete event history during the sample period is provided. However, in many practical situations a researcher may be able to observe the state of an individual only at discrete times. If the observations occur at irregular time intervals, it is probably more reasonable to assume a continuous-time Markov model rather than a discrete-time model.

We shall derive the likelihood function based on discrete observations in the case of $M = 2$. The underlying model is the same stationary (or exponential) model we have so far considered. We define

$$P^i_{jk}(t) = \text{Prob [}i\text{th person is in state } k \text{ at time } t \tag{11.2.40}$$
$$\text{given that he or she was in state } j \text{ at time 0].}$$

Note that this definition differs slightly from the definition (11.1.2) of the same symbol used in the Markov chain model. We shall use the definition (11.2.1) with the stationarity assumption $\lambda^i_{jk}(t) = \lambda^i_{jk}$ for all t.

As before, we shall concentrate on a particular individual and suppress the superscript i. When Δt is sufficiently small, we have approximately

$$P_{12}(t + \Delta t) = P_{11}(t)\lambda_{12}\,\Delta t + P_{12}(t)(1 - \lambda_{21}\,\Delta t). \tag{11.2.41}$$

Dividing (11.2.41) by Δt and letting Δt go to 0 yield

$$\frac{dP_{12}}{dt} = P_{11}\lambda_{12} - P_{12}\lambda_{21}. \tag{11.2.42}$$

Performing an analogous operation on P_{11}, P_{21}, and P_{22}, we obtain the linear vector differential equation

$$\begin{bmatrix} \frac{dP_{11}}{dt} & \frac{dP_{21}}{dt} \\ \frac{dP_{12}}{dt} & \frac{dP_{22}}{dt} \end{bmatrix} = \begin{bmatrix} -\lambda_{12} & \lambda_{21} \\ \lambda_{12} & -\lambda_{21} \end{bmatrix} \begin{bmatrix} P_{11} & P_{21} \\ P_{12} & P_{22} \end{bmatrix}, \tag{11.2.43}$$

$$\text{or} \quad \frac{d\mathbf{P}'}{dt} = \mathbf{\Lambda P}'.$$

A solution of (11.2.43) can be shown to be[6]

$$\mathbf{P}' = \mathbf{H}\, e^{\mathbf{D}t}\mathbf{H}^{-1}, \tag{11.2.44}$$

where the columns $\mathbf{H}$ are characteristic vectors of $\mathbf{\Lambda}$, $\mathbf{D}$ is the diagonal matrix consisting of the characteristic roots of $\mathbf{\Lambda}$, and $e^{\mathbf{D}t}$ is the diagonal matrix consisting of $\exp(d_j t)$, d_j being the elements of $\mathbf{D}$.

We shall derive $\mathbf{D}$ and $\mathbf{H}$. Solving the determinantal equation

$$|\mathbf{\Lambda} - d\mathbf{I}| = 0 \tag{11.2.45}$$

yields the two characteristic roots $d_1 = 0$ and $d_2 = -(\lambda_{12} + \lambda_{21})$. Therefore we have

$$\mathbf{D} = \begin{bmatrix} 0 & 0 \\ 0 & -(\lambda_{12} + \lambda_{21}) \end{bmatrix}. \tag{11.2.46}$$

Let $\mathbf{h}_1$ be the first column of $\mathbf{H}$ (the characteristic vector corresponding to the zero root). Then it should satisfy $\mathbf{\Lambda h}_1 = \mathbf{0}$, which yields a solution (which is not unique) $\mathbf{h}_1 = (\lambda_{21}, \lambda_{12})'$. Next, the second column $\mathbf{h}_2$ of $\mathbf{H}$ should satisfy $[\mathbf{\Lambda} + (\lambda_{12} + \lambda_{21})\mathbf{I}]\mathbf{h}_2 = \mathbf{0}$, which yields a solution $\mathbf{h}_2 = (-1, 1)'$. Combining the two vectors, we obtain

$$\mathbf{H} = \begin{bmatrix} \lambda_{21} & -1 \\ \lambda_{12} & 1 \end{bmatrix}. \tag{11.2.47}$$

Finally, inserting (11.2.46) and (11.2.47) into (11.2.44) yields the following expressions for the elements of $\mathbf{P}'$ (putting back the superscript i):

$$P^i_{11}(t) = 1 - \gamma_i + \gamma_i \exp(-\delta_i t) \tag{11.2.48}$$

$$P^i_{12}(t) = \gamma_i - \gamma_i \exp(-\delta_i t)$$

$$P^i_{21}(t) = 1 - \gamma_i - (1 - \gamma_i) \exp(-\delta_i t)$$

$$P^i_{22}(t) = \gamma_i + (1 - \gamma_i) \exp(-\delta_i t),$$

where $\gamma_i = \lambda^i_{12}/(\lambda^i_{12} + \lambda^i_{21})$ and $\delta_i = \lambda^i_{12} + \lambda^i_{21}$. Suppose we observe the ith individual in state j_i at time 0 and in state k_i at time t_i, $i = 1, 2, \ldots, N$. Then the likelihood function is given by

$$L = \prod_{i=1}^{N} P^i_{j_i k_i}(t_i). \tag{11.2.49}$$

11.2.5 Nonstationary Models

So far we have assumed $\lambda^i_{jk}(t) = \lambda^i_{jk}$ for all t (constant hazard rate). Now we shall remove this assumption. Such models are called *nonstationary* or *semi-Markov*.

Suppose a typical individual stayed in state j in period $(0, t)$ and then moved to state k in period $(t, t + \Delta t)$. We call this event A and derive its probability $P(\text{A})$, generalizing (11.2.2) and (11.2.3). Defining $m = t/\Delta t$ and using $\log(1 - \epsilon) \cong -\epsilon$ for small ϵ, we obtain for sufficiently large m

$$P(A) = \left\{\left[\prod_{l=1}^{m}\left[1 - \lambda_j\left(\frac{lt}{m}\right)\frac{t}{m}\right]\right\} \lambda_{jk}(t)\frac{t}{m} \tag{11.2.50}$$
$$= \left\{\exp\left[-\int_0^t \lambda_j(z)\,dz\right]\right\} \lambda_{jk}(t)\frac{t}{m}.$$

The likelihood function of this individual is the last expression in (11.2.50) except for t/m.

Let us obtain the likelihood function of the same event history we considered in the discussion preceding (11.2.4). The likelihood function now becomes

$$L = \exp\left[-\int_0^{t_1} \lambda_1(z)\,dz\right]\lambda_{12}(t_1) \tag{11.2.51}$$
$$\times \exp\left[-\int_{t_1}^{t_1+t_2} \lambda_2(z)\,dz\right]\lambda_{23}(t_1+t_2)$$
$$\times \exp\left[-\int_{t_1+t_2}^{t_1+t_2+t_3} \lambda_3(z)\,dz\right]\lambda_{31}(t_1+t_2+t_3).$$

As in (11.2.4), λ_{31} should be changed to λ_3 if the individual is only observed to leave state 3, and λ_{31} should be dropped if right-censoring occurs at that time.

We shall concentrate on the transition from state 1 to state 2 and write $\lambda_{12}(t)$ simply as $\lambda(t)$, as we did earlier. The distribution function of duration under a nonstationary model is given by

$$F(t) = 1 - \exp\left[-\int_0^t \lambda(z)\,dz\right], \tag{11.2.52}$$

which is reduced to (11.2.6) if $\lambda(t) = \lambda$. The density function is given by

$$f(t) = \lambda(t)\exp\left[-\int_0^t \lambda(z)\,dz\right]. \tag{11.2.53}$$

The likelihood function again can be written in the form of (11.2.10) or (11.2.11), depending on whether right-censoring is absent or present.

Thus we see that there is no problem in writing down the likelihood function. The problem, of course, is how to estimate the parameters. Suppose we specify $\lambda^i(t)$ generally as

$$\lambda^i(t) = g(\mathbf{x}_{it}, \boldsymbol{\beta}). \tag{11.2.54}$$

To evaluate $\int_0^t \lambda^i(z)\,dz$, which appears in the likelihood function, a researcher must specify $\mathbf{x}_{it}$ precisely as a continuous function of t—not an easy thing to do in practice. We shall discuss several empirical articles and shall see how these articles deal with the problem of nonstationarity, as well as with other problems that may arise in empirical work.

Model of Tuma. Tuma (1976) analyzed the duration of employment at a particular job. The ith individual's hazard rate at time t is specified as

$$\lambda^i(t) = \boldsymbol{\beta}'\mathbf{x}_i + \alpha_1 t + \alpha_2 t^2, \tag{11.2.55}$$

where $\mathbf{x}_i$ is a vector of socioeconomic characteristics of the ith individual.[7] The parameter values are assumed to be such that the hazard rate is nonnegative over a relevant range of t. Because of the simple form of the hazard rate, it can easily be integrated to yield

$$\int_0^t \lambda^i(z)\,dz = \boldsymbol{\beta}'\mathbf{x}_i t + \frac{\alpha_1}{2}t^2 + \frac{\alpha_2}{3}t^3. \tag{11.2.56}$$

Some people terminate their employment during the sample period, but some remain in their jobs at the end of the sample period (right-censoring). Therefore Tuma's likelihood function is precisely in the form of (11.2.11).

Model of Tuma, Hannan, and Groeneveld. Tuma, Hannan, and Groeneveld (1979) studied the duration of marriage. They handled nonstationarity by dividing the sample period into four subperiods and assuming that the hazard rate remains constant within each subperiod but varies across different subperiods. More specifically, they specified

$$\lambda^i(t) = \boldsymbol{\beta}_p'\mathbf{x}_i \quad \text{for} \quad t \in T_p, \qquad p = 1, 2, 3, 4, \tag{11.2.57}$$

where T_p is the pth subperiod. This kind of a discrete change in the hazard rate creates no real problem. Suppose that the event history of an individual consists of a single completed spell of duration t and that during this period a constant hazard rate $\lambda(1)$ holds from time 0 to time τ and another constant rate $\lambda(2)$ holds from time τ to time t. Then this individual's likelihood function is given by

$$L = e^{-\lambda(1)\tau}e^{-\lambda(2)(t-\tau)}\lambda(2). \tag{11.2.58}$$

Model of Lancaster. Lancaster (1979) was concerned with unemployment duration and questioned the assumption of a constant hazard rate. Although a simple search theory may indicate an increasing hazard rate, it is not clear from economic theory alone whether we should expect a constant, decreasing, or increasing hazard rate for unemployment spells. Lancaster used a Weibull distribution, which leads to a nonconstant hazard rate. The Weibull distribution is defined by

$$F(t) = 1 - \exp(-\lambda t^{\alpha}). \tag{11.2.59}$$

If $\alpha = 1$, (11.2.59) is reduced to the exponential distribution considered in the preceding subsections. Its density is given by

$$f(t) = \lambda \alpha t^{\alpha-1} \exp(-\lambda t^{\alpha}) \tag{11.2.60}$$

and its hazard rate by

$$\lambda(t) = \frac{f(t)}{1 - F(t)} = \lambda \alpha t^{\alpha-1}. \tag{11.2.61}$$

Whether α is greater than 1 or not determines whether the hazard rate is increasing or not, as is shown in the following correspondence:

$$\alpha > 1 \leftrightarrow \frac{\partial \lambda}{\partial t} > 0 \quad \text{(increasing hazard rate)} \tag{11.2.62}$$

$$\alpha = 1 \leftrightarrow \frac{\partial \lambda}{\partial t} = 0 \quad \text{(constant hazard rate)}$$

$$\alpha < 1 \leftrightarrow \frac{\partial \lambda}{\partial t} < 0 \quad \text{(decreasing hazard rate).}$$

Lancaster specified the ith person's hazard rate as

$$\lambda^i(t) = \alpha t^{\alpha-1} \exp(\boldsymbol{\beta}'\mathbf{x}_i), \tag{11.2.63}$$

where $\mathbf{x}_i$ is a vector of the ith person's characteristics. His ML estimate of α turned out to be 0.77, a result indicating a decreasing hazard rate. However, Lancaster reported an interesting finding: His estimate of α increases as he included more exogenous variables in the model. This result indicates that the decreasing hazard rate implied by his first estimate was at least partly due to the heterogeneity caused by the initially omitted exogenous variables rather than true duration dependence.

Because it may not be possible to include all the relevant exogenous variables, Lancaster considered an alternative specification for the hazard rate

$$\mu^i(t) = v_i \lambda^i(t), \tag{11.2.64}$$

where $\lambda^i(t)$ is as given in (11.2.63) and v_i is an unobservable random variable independently and identically distributed as Gamma$(1, \sigma^2)$. The random variable v_i may be regarded as a proxy for all the unobservable exogenous variables. By (11.2.52) we have (suppressing i)

$$F(t|v) = 1 - \exp[-v\Lambda(t)], \tag{11.2.65}$$

where $\Lambda(t) = \int_0^t \lambda(z)\,dz$. Taking the expectation of (11.2.65) yields

$$F^*(t) \equiv E_v F(t|v) = 1 - [1 + \sigma^2\Lambda(t)]^{-\sigma^{-2}}. \tag{11.2.66}$$

Therefore, using (11.2.8), we obtain

$$\begin{aligned} \lambda^*(t) &= \lambda(t)[1 + \sigma^2\Lambda(t)]^{-1} \\ &= \lambda(t)[1 - F^*(t)]^{\sigma^2}. \end{aligned} \tag{11.2.67}$$

Because $[1 - F^*(t)]^{\sigma^2}$ is a decreasing function of t, (11.2.67) shows that the heterogeneity adds a tendency for a decreasing hazard rate. Under this new model (with σ^2 as an additional unknown parameter), Lancaster finds the MLE of α to be 0.9. Thus he argues that a decreasing hazard rate in his model is caused more by heterogeneity than true duration dependence.

Model of Heckman and Borjas. In their article, which is also concerned with unemployment duration, Heckman and Borjas (1980) introduced another source of variability of λ in addition to the Weibull specification and heterogeneity. In their model, λ also varies with spells. Let l denote the lth unemployment spell the ith individual experiences. Then Heckman and Borjas specify the hazard rate as

$$\lambda^{il}(t) = \alpha t^{\alpha-1} \exp(\boldsymbol{\beta}_l' \mathbf{x}_{il} + v_i), \tag{11.2.68}$$

where v_i is unobservable and therefore should be integrated out to obtain the marginal distribution function of duration.[8]

Model of Flinn and Heckman. In a study of unemployment duration, Flinn and Heckman (1982) generalized (11.2.68) further as

$$\lambda^{il}(t) = \exp\left[\boldsymbol{\beta}_l' \mathbf{x}_{il}(t) + c_l v_i + \gamma_1 \frac{t^{\lambda_1} - 1}{\lambda_1} + \gamma_2 \frac{t^{\lambda_2} - 1}{\lambda_2}\right]. \tag{11.2.69}$$

The function $(t^\lambda - 1)/\lambda$ is the Box-Cox transformation (see Section 8.1.2) and approaches $\log t$ as λ approaches 0. Therefore putting $\lambda_1 = 0$ and $\gamma_2 = 0$ in (11.2.69) reduces it to a Weibull model. Note that $\mathbf{x}_{il}$ is assumed to depend on t in (11.2.69). Flinn and Heckman assumed that changes in $\mathbf{x}_{il}(t)$ occurred only at the beginning of a month and that the levels were constant throughout the month. The authors devised an efficient computation algorithm for handling the heterogeneity correlated across spells and the exogenous variables varying with time.

11.2.6 Problem of Left-Censoring

In this subsection we shall consider the problem of left-censoring in models for unemployment duration. When every individual is observed at the start of his or her unemployment spell, there is no problem of left-censoring. Often, however, an individual is observed to be in an unemployment spell at the start of the sample period. This complicates the estimation.

Suppose that an unemployment spell of a particular individual starts at time $-s$, the individual is interviewed at time 0, and the spell terminates at t. (To simplify the analysis, we assume that right-censoring at time t does not occur.) The treatment of left-censoring varies according to the following three cases: (1) s is observed but t is not observed, (2) both s and t are observed, and (3) t is observed but s is not observed. For each case we shall derive the relevant likelihood function.

The first case corresponds to the situation analyzed by Nickell (1979), although his is a Markov chain model. Assuming that the underlying distribution of the duration is $F(\cdot)$ and its density $f(\cdot)$, we can derive the density $g(s)$. Denoting the state of "being unemployed" by U, we have for sufficiently small Δs

$$\begin{aligned} g(s)\,\Delta s &= P[U \text{ started in } (-s-\Delta s, -s) \mid U \text{ at } 0] \qquad (11.2.70)\\ &= \frac{P[U \text{ at } 0 \mid U \text{ started in } (-s-\Delta s, -s)]P[U \text{ started in } (-s-\Delta s, -s)]}{\displaystyle\int_0^\infty (\text{Numerator})\, ds}\\ &= \frac{P[U \text{ at } 0 \mid U \text{ started in } (-s-\Delta s, -s)]\,\Delta s}{\displaystyle\int_0^\infty (\text{Numerator})\, ds}\\ &= \frac{[1-F(s)]\,\Delta s}{\displaystyle\int_0^\infty [1-F(s)]\, ds} = \frac{[1-F(s)]\,\Delta s}{ES}, \end{aligned}$$

where $ES = \int_0^\infty sf(s)\, ds$. In (11.2.70) the third equality follows from the assumption that $P[U$ started in $(-s-\Delta s, -s)]$ does not depend on s (the assumption of constant entry rate), and the last equality follows from integration by parts. By eliminating Δs from both sides of (11.2.70), we obtain

$$g(s) = \frac{1 - F(s)}{ES}. \tag{11.2.71}$$

In the second case we should derive the joint density $g(s,t) = g(t|s)g(s)$. The density $g(s)$ has been derived, but we still need to derive $g(t|s)$. Let X denote total unemployment duration. First evaluate

$$\begin{aligned} P(X > s + t | X > s) &= \frac{P(X > s + t, X > s)}{P(X > s)} \\ &= \frac{P(X > s + t)}{P(X > s)} \\ &= \frac{1 - F(s + t)}{1 - F(s)}. \end{aligned} \tag{11.2.72}$$

If we denote the distribution function of $g(t|s)$ by $G(t|s)$, (11.2.72) implies

$$G(t|s) = \frac{F(s + t)}{1 - F(s)}. \tag{11.2.73}$$

Therefore, differentiating (11.2.73) with respect to t, we obtain

$$g(t|s) = \frac{f(s + t)}{1 - F(s)}. \tag{11.2.74}$$

Finally, from (11.2.71) and (11.2.74), we obtain

$$g(s,t) = \frac{f(s + t)}{ES}. \tag{11.2.75}$$

This situation holds for Lancaster (1979), as he observed both s and t. However, Lancaster used the conditional density (11.2.74) rather than the joint density (11.2.75) because he felt uncertain about the assumption of constant entry rate.

Finally, in the third case we need $g(t)$. This can be obtained by integrating $g(s,t)$ with respect to s as follows:

$$\begin{aligned} g(t) &= \frac{1}{ES} \int_0^\infty f(s + t)\, ds \\ &= \frac{1 - F(t)}{ES}. \end{aligned} \tag{11.2.76}$$

See Flinn and Heckman (1982) for an alternative derivation of $g(t)$.

11.2.7 Cox's Partial Maximum Likelihood Estimator

Cox (1972) considered a hazard rate of the form

$$\lambda^i(t) = \lambda(t) \exp(\boldsymbol{\beta}'\mathbf{x}_i), \tag{11.2.77}$$

which generalizes (11.2.63). This model is often referred to as a *proportional hazards model.* Cox proposed a *partial MLE* (PMLE) obtained by maximizing a part of the likelihood function. We shall first derive the whole likelihood function and then write it as a product of the part Cox proposed to maximize and the remainder.

Cox allowed for right-censoring. Let t_i, $i = 1, 2, \ldots, n$, be completed durations and let t_i, $i = n+1, n+2, \ldots, N$, be censored durations. We assume for simplicity $\{t_i\}$ are distinct.[9] Then the likelihood function has the form (11.2.11): specifically,

$$\begin{aligned} L = \prod_{i=1}^{n} \exp(\boldsymbol{\beta}'\mathbf{x}_i)\lambda(t_i) \exp[-\exp(\boldsymbol{\beta}'\mathbf{x}_i)\Lambda(t_i)] \\ \times \prod_{i=n+1}^{N} \exp[-\exp(\boldsymbol{\beta}'\mathbf{x}_i)\Lambda(t_i)], \end{aligned} \tag{11.2.78}$$

where $\Lambda(t) = \int_0^t \lambda(z)\, dz$. Combining the exp functions that appear in both terms and rewriting the combined term further, we obtain

$$\begin{aligned} L &= \prod_{i=1}^{n} \exp(\boldsymbol{\beta}'\mathbf{x}_i)\lambda(t_i) \cdot \exp\left[-\sum_{i=1}^{N} \exp(\boldsymbol{\beta}'\mathbf{x}_i) \int_0^{t_i} \lambda(z)\, dz\right] \\ &= \prod_{i=1}^{n} \exp(\boldsymbol{\beta}'\mathbf{x}_i)\lambda(t_i) \cdot \exp\left\{-\int_0^{\infty} \left[\sum_{h\in R(t)} \exp(\boldsymbol{\beta}'\mathbf{x}_h)\right] \lambda(t)\, dt\right\}, \end{aligned} \tag{11.2.79}$$

where $R(t) = \{i \mid t_i \geqq t\}$. To understand the second equality in (11.2.79), note that $\sum_{h\in R(t)} \exp(\boldsymbol{\beta}'\mathbf{x}_h)$ is a step function described in Figure 11.1.

Cox's PMLE $\hat{\boldsymbol{\beta}}_p$ maximizes

$$L_1 = \prod_{i=1}^{n} \frac{\exp(\boldsymbol{\beta}'\mathbf{x}_i)}{\sum_{h\in R(t_i)} \exp(\boldsymbol{\beta}'\mathbf{x}_h)}. \tag{11.2.80}$$

It is a part of L because we can write L as

$$L = L_1 L_2, \tag{11.2.81}$$

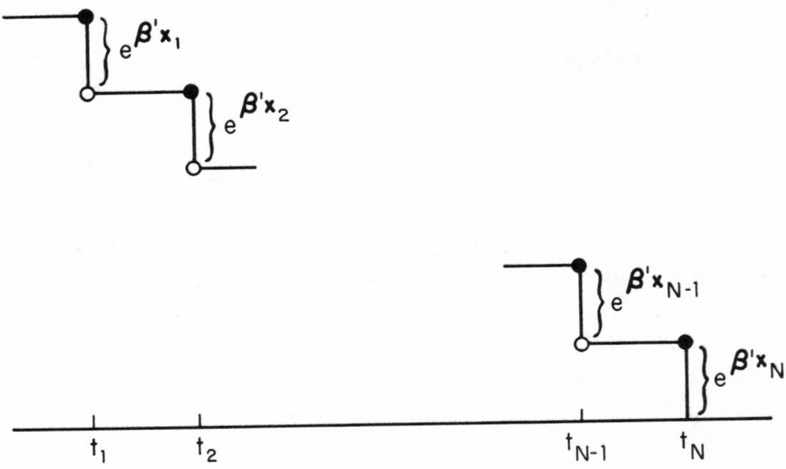

Figure 11.1 $\Sigma_{h \in R(t)} \exp(\boldsymbol{\beta}'\mathbf{x}_h)$ as a function of t

where

$$L_2 = \prod_{i=1}^{n} \left[\sum_{h \in R(t_i)} \exp(\boldsymbol{\beta}'\mathbf{x}_h)\lambda(t_i) \right] \times \exp\left\{ - \int_0^\infty \left[\sum_{h \in R(t)} \exp(\boldsymbol{\beta}'\mathbf{x}_h) \right] \lambda(t)\, dt \right\}. \tag{11.2.82}$$

Because L_1 does not depend on $\lambda(t)$, Cox's method enables us to estimate $\boldsymbol{\beta}$ without specifying $\lambda(t)$. Cox (1975) suggested and Tsiatis (1981) proved that under general conditions the PMLE is consistent and asymptotically normal with the asymptotic covariance matrix given by

$$V\hat{\boldsymbol{\beta}}_p = -\left[E \frac{\partial^2 \log L_1}{\partial \boldsymbol{\beta} \partial \boldsymbol{\beta}'} \right]^{-1}. \tag{11.2.83}$$

This result is remarkable considering that L_1 is not even a conditional likelihood function in the usual sense.[10]

However, L_1 and L_2 do have intuitive meanings. We shall consider their meanings in a simple example. Suppose $N = 2$ and t_1 is a completed duration (say, the first person dies at time t_1) and t_2 a censored duration (the second person lives at least until time t_2), with $t_2 > t_1$. Then we have

$$L = \lambda^1(t_1) \exp\left[- \int_0^{t_1} \lambda^1(z)\, dz \right] \exp\left[- \int_0^{t_2} \lambda^2(z)\, dz \right]. \tag{11.2.84}$$

We can write (11.2.84) as

$$L = L_1 L_{21} L_{22} L_{23}, \tag{11.2.85}$$

where

$$L_1 = \frac{\lambda^1(t_1)}{\lambda^1(t_1) + \lambda^2(t_1)}, \tag{11.2.86}$$

$$L_{21} = \lambda^1(t_1) + \lambda^2(t_1), \tag{11.2.87}$$

$$L_{22} = \exp\left[-\int_0^{t_1} \lambda^1(z)\,dz\right] \exp\left[-\int_0^{t_1} \lambda^2(z)\,dz\right], \tag{11.2.88}$$

and

$$L_{23} = \exp\left[-\int_{t_1}^{t_2} \lambda^2(z)\,dz\right]. \tag{11.2.89}$$

These four components of L can be interpreted as follows:

$L_1 = P(\#1$ dies at $t_1|$both #1 and #2 live until t_1 and either #1 or #2 dies at $t_1)$

$L_{21} = P($either #1 or #2 dies at $t_1|$both #1 and #2 live until $t_1)$

$L_{22} = P($both #1 and #2 live until $t_1)$

$L_{23} = P(\#2$ lives at least until $t_2|\#2$ lives until $t_1)$.

Note that $L_{21}L_{22}L_{23}$ corresponds to L_2 of (11.2.82).

Kalbfleisch and Prentice (1973) gave an alternative interpretation of Cox's partial likelihood function. First, consider the case of no censoring. Let $t_1 < t_2 < \ldots < t_N$ be an ordered sequence of durations. Then by successive integrations we obtain

$$\begin{aligned} &P(t_1 < t_2 < \ldots < t_N) \\ &= \int_0^\infty \int_{t_1}^\infty \ldots \int_{t_{N-1}}^\infty \prod_{i=1}^N \lambda(t_i) \exp(\boldsymbol{\beta}'\mathbf{x}_i) \\ &\quad \times \exp\left[-\exp(\boldsymbol{\beta}'\mathbf{x}_i) \int_0^{t_i} \lambda(z)\,dz\right] dt_N\, dt_{N-1} \ldots dt_1 \\ &= \int_0^\infty \int_{t_1}^\infty \ldots \int_{t_{N-2}}^\infty \prod_{i=1}^{N-2} \lambda(t_i) \exp(\boldsymbol{\beta}'\mathbf{x}_i) \\ &\quad \times \exp\left[-\exp(\boldsymbol{\beta}'\mathbf{x}_i) \int_0^{t_i} \lambda(z)\,dz\right] \\ &\quad \times \lambda(t_{N-1}) \exp(\boldsymbol{\beta}'\mathbf{x}_{N-1}) \end{aligned} \tag{11.2.90}$$

$$\times \exp\left\{-[\exp(\boldsymbol{\beta}'\mathbf{x}_{N-1}) + \exp(\boldsymbol{\beta}'\mathbf{x}_N)] \int_0^{t_{N-1}} \lambda(z)\, dz\right\}$$

$$\times dt_{N-1}\, dt_{N-2} \ldots dt_1$$

$$= \int_0^\infty \int_{t_1}^\infty \ldots \int_{t_{N-3}}^\infty \prod_{i=1}^{N-2} \lambda(t_i) \exp(\boldsymbol{\beta}'\mathbf{x}_i)$$

$$\times \exp\left[-\exp(\boldsymbol{\beta}'\mathbf{x}_i) \int_0^{t_i} \lambda(z)\, dz\right]$$

$$\times \frac{\exp(\boldsymbol{\beta}'\mathbf{x}_{N-1})}{\exp(\boldsymbol{\beta}'\mathbf{x}_{N-1}) + \exp(\boldsymbol{\beta}'\mathbf{x}_N)}$$

$$\times \exp\left\{-[\exp(\boldsymbol{\beta}'\mathbf{x}_{N-1}) + \exp(\boldsymbol{\beta}'\mathbf{x}_N)] \int_0^{t_{N-2}} \lambda(z)\, dz\right\}$$

$$\times dt_{N-2}\, dt_{N-3} \ldots dt_1$$

$$= \exp(\boldsymbol{\beta}'\mathbf{x}_N) \exp(\boldsymbol{\beta}'\mathbf{x}_{N-1}) \cdots \exp(\boldsymbol{\beta}'\mathbf{x}_1)$$

$$\div \{\exp(\boldsymbol{\beta}'\mathbf{x}_N)[\exp(\boldsymbol{\beta}'\mathbf{x}_N) + \exp(\boldsymbol{\beta}'\mathbf{x}_{N-1})]$$

$$\cdots [\exp(\boldsymbol{\beta}'\mathbf{x}_N) + \exp(\boldsymbol{\beta}'\mathbf{x}_{N-1}) + \ldots + \exp(\boldsymbol{\beta}'\mathbf{x}_1)]\},$$

Next, suppose that completed durations are ordered as $t_1 < t_2 < \ldots < t_n$ and in the interval $[t_i, t_{i+1})$, $i = 1, 2, \ldots, n$ (with the understanding $t_{n+1} = \infty$), we observe censored durations $t_{i1}, t_{i2}, \ldots, t_{iq_i}$. Then we have

$$P(t_1 < t_2 < \ldots < t_n, t_i \leqq t_{i1}, t_{i2}, \ldots, t_{iq_i} \text{ for all } i) \tag{11.2.91}$$

$$= \int_0^\infty \int_{t_1}^\infty \ldots \int_{t_{n-1}}^\infty P(t_i \leqq t_{i1}, t_{i2}, \ldots, t_{iq_i} \text{ for all } i | t_1, t_2, \ldots, t_n)$$

$$\times f^1(t_1) f^2(t_2) \ldots f^n(t_n)\, dt_n\, dt_{n-1} \ldots dt_1$$

$$= \int_0^\infty \int_{t_1}^\infty \ldots \int_{t_{n-1}}^\infty \prod_{i=1}^{n} \lambda(t_i) \exp(\boldsymbol{\beta}'\mathbf{x}_i)$$

$$\times \exp\left\{-\left[\exp(\boldsymbol{\beta}'\mathbf{x}_i) + \sum_{j=1}^{q_i} (\exp \boldsymbol{\beta}'\mathbf{x}_{ij})\right] \int_0^{t_i} \lambda(z)\, dz\right\}$$

$$\times dt_n\, dt_{n-1} \ldots dt_1$$

$$= \exp(\boldsymbol{\beta}'\mathbf{x}_n) \exp(\boldsymbol{\beta}'\mathbf{x}_{n-1}) \cdots \exp(\boldsymbol{\beta}'\mathbf{x}_1)$$

$$\div \{[\exp(\boldsymbol{\beta}'\mathbf{x}_n) + c_n][\exp(\boldsymbol{\beta}'\mathbf{x}_n) + \exp(\boldsymbol{\beta}'\mathbf{x}_{n-1}) + c_n + c_{n-1}]$$

$$\cdots [\exp(\boldsymbol{\beta}'\mathbf{x}_n) + \ldots + \exp(\boldsymbol{\beta}'\mathbf{x}_1) + c_n + \ldots + c_1]\},$$

where $c_i = \sum_{j=1}^{q_i} \exp(\boldsymbol{\beta}'\mathbf{x}_{ij})$.

Because the parameter vector $\boldsymbol{\beta}$ appears in both L_1 and L_2, we expect Cox's PMLE to be asymptotically less efficient than the full MLE in general. This is indeed the case. We shall compare the asymptotic covariance matrix of the two estimators in the special case of a stationary model where the $\lambda(t)$ that appears in the right-hand side of (11.2.77) is a constant. Furthermore, we shall suppose there is no censoring. In this special case, Cox's model is identical to the model considered in Section 11.2.3. Therefore the asymptotic covariance matrix of the MLE $\hat{\boldsymbol{\beta}}$ can be derived from (11.2.30) by noting that the $\boldsymbol{\beta}$ of the present section can be regarded as the vector consisting of all but the last element of the $\boldsymbol{\beta}$ of Section 11.2.3. Hence, by Theorem 13 of Appendix 1, we obtain

$$V\hat{\boldsymbol{\beta}} = \left[\sum_{i=1}^{N} (\mathbf{x}_i - \bar{\mathbf{x}})(\mathbf{x}_i - \bar{\mathbf{x}})' \right]^{-1}. \tag{11.2.92}$$

The asymptotic covariance matrix of Cox's PMLE can be derived from (11.2.83) as

$$\begin{aligned} V\hat{\boldsymbol{\beta}}_p = -\Bigg\{ E \sum_{i=1}^{N} & \left[\sum_h \exp(\boldsymbol{\beta}'\mathbf{x}_h) \right]^{-2} \\ & \times \Bigg[\sum_h \mathbf{x}_h \mathbf{x}_h' \exp(\boldsymbol{\beta}'\mathbf{x}_h) \sum_h \exp(\boldsymbol{\beta}'\mathbf{x}_h) \\ & - \sum_h \mathbf{x}_h \exp(\boldsymbol{\beta}'\mathbf{x}_h) \sum_h \mathbf{x}_h' \exp(\boldsymbol{\beta}'\mathbf{x}_h) \Bigg] \Bigg\}^{-1}, \end{aligned} \tag{11.2.93}$$

where Σ_h denotes $\Sigma_{h \in R(t_i)}$ and E denotes the expectation taken with respect to random variables t_i that appear in $R(t_i)$.

This expectation is rather cumbersome to derive in general cases. Therefore, we shall make a further simplification and assume β is a scalar and equal to 0. Under this simplifying assumption, we can show that the PMLE is asymptotically efficient. (Although this is not a very interesting case, we have considered this case because this is the only case where the asymptotic variance of the PMLE can be derived without lengthy derivations while still enabling the reader to understand essentially what kind of operation is involved in the expectation that appears in (11.2.93). For a comparison of the two estimates in more general cases, a few relevant references will be given at the end.) Under this simplification (11.2.93) is reduced to

$$V\hat{\beta}_p = -\left\{ E \sum_{i=1}^{N} \left[\frac{\sum_h x_h^2}{\sum_h 1} - \left(\frac{\sum_h x_h}{\sum_h 1} \right)^2 \right] \right\}^{-1}. \tag{11.2.94}$$

We shall first evaluate (11.2.94) for the case $N = 3$ and then for the case of general N. If $t_1 < t_2 < t_3$, we have

$$\sum_{i=1}^{3} \left[\frac{\sum_h x_h^2}{\sum_h 1} \right] = \frac{x_1^2 + x_2^2 + x_3^2}{3} + \frac{x_2^2 + x_3^2}{2} + \frac{x_3^2}{1}. \tag{11.2.95}$$

If we change the rank order of (t_1, t_2, t_3), the right-hand side of (11.2.95) will change correspondingly. But, under our stationarity (constant λ) and homogeneity ($\beta = 0$) assumptions, each one of six possible rank orderings can happen with an equal probability. Therefore we obtain

$$E \sum_{i=1}^{3} \left[\frac{\sum_h x_h^2}{\sum_h 1} \right] = \sum_{i=1}^{3} x_i^2 . \tag{11.2.96}$$

Similarly, if $t_1 < t_2 < t_3$, we have

$$\sum_{i=1}^{3} \left[\frac{\sum_h x_h}{\sum_h 1} \right]^2 = \left[\frac{x_1 + x_2 + x_3}{3} \right]^2 + \left[\frac{x_2 + x_3}{2} \right]^2 + \left[\frac{x_3}{1} \right]^2 . \tag{11.2.97}$$

By using an argument similar to that above, we obtain

$$E \sum_{i=1}^{3} \left[\frac{\sum_h x_h}{\sum_h 1} \right]^2 = \frac{1}{3} \left(\frac{1}{3} + \frac{1}{2} + 1 \right) \sum_{i=1}^{3} x_i^2 + \frac{1}{6} \left(\frac{2}{2^2} + \frac{6}{3^2} \right) \sum_{i=1}^{2} \sum_{j=i+1}^{3} 2x_i x_j . \tag{11.2.98}$$

Generalizing (11.2.96) and (11.2.98) to a general N, we obtain

$$E \sum_{i=1}^{N} \left[\frac{\sum_h x_h^2}{\sum_h 1} \right] = \sum_{i=1}^{N} x_i^2 \tag{11.2.99}$$

and

$$E \sum_{i=1}^{N} \left[\frac{\sum_h x_h}{\sum_h 1} \right]^2 = \frac{1}{N} \sum_{k=1}^{N} \frac{1}{k} \sum_{i=1}^{N} x_i^2 + \frac{1}{N(N-1)} \sum_{k=2}^{N} \frac{k-1}{k} \sum_{i=1}^{N-1} \sum_{j=i+1}^{N} 2x_i x_j . \tag{11.2.100}$$

The coefficient on $\Sigma_{i=1}^{N-1}\Sigma_{j=i+1}^{N}2x_ix_j$ can be derived as follows: There are $N!$ permutations of N integers $1, 2, \ldots, N$, each of which happens with an equal probability. Let P_k be the number of permutations in which a given pair of integers, say, 1 and 2, appear in the last k positions. Then $P_k = \binom{k}{2}2[(N-2)!]$. Therefore the desired coefficient is given by $(N!)^{-1}\Sigma_{k=2}^{N}\{\binom{k}{2}2[(N-2)!]/k^2\}$.

Finally, from (11.2.94), (11.2.99), and (11.2.100), we conclude

$$V\hat{\beta}_p = \left[\frac{1}{N-1}\sum_{k=2}^{N}\frac{k-1}{k}\sum_{i=1}^{N}(x_i-\bar{x})^2\right]^{-1}. \tag{11.2.101}$$

Compare (11.2.101) with $V\hat{\beta}$ given in (11.2.92). Because

$$1-\frac{\log N}{N-1} < \frac{1}{N-1}\sum_{k=2}^{N}\frac{k-1}{k} < 1, \tag{11.2.102}$$

we see that Cox's PMLE is asymptotically efficient in this special case.

Kalbfleisch (1974) evaluated the asymptotic relative efficiency of the PMLE also for nonzero β in a model that is otherwise the same as the one we have just considered. He used a Taylor expansion of (11.2.93) around $\beta = 0$. Kay (1970) extended Kalbfleisch's results to a case where $\boldsymbol{\beta}$ is a two-dimensional vector. Han (1983), using a convenient representation of the asymptotic relative efficiency of the PMLE obtained by Efron (1977), evaluated it for Weibull as well as exponential models with any number of dimensions of the $\boldsymbol{\beta}$ vector and with or without censoring. Cox's estimator is found to have a high asymptotic relative efficiency in most of the cases considered by these authors. However, it would be useful to study the performance of Cox's estimator in realistic situations, which are likely to occur in econometric applications.

Exercises

1. (Section 11.1.1)
   Using (11.1.5), express the unconditional mean and variance of $y^i(2)$ as a function of the mean and variance of $y^i(0)$.

2. (Section 11.1.1)
   Write L and L_2 defined in (11.1.10) explicitly in the special case where $P_{jk}^i(t) = P_{jk}$, $M = 2$, and $T = 2$.

3. (Section 11.1.1)
   Find an example of a matrix that is not necessarily positive but for which a unique vector of equilibrium probabilities exists.

4. (Section 11.1.1)
Prove the statement following (11.1.15).

5. (Section 11.1.1)
Verify statement (11.1.23).

6. (Section 11.1.3)
Derive the asymptotic variance-covariance matrix of the MLE of α in the Boskin-Nold model using (11.1.38).

7. (Section 11.1.3)
The mean duration is derived in (11.1.65). Using a similar technique, derive Vt_1.

8. (Section 11.1.5)
Let the Markov matrix of a two-state (1 or 0) stationary homogeneous first-order Markov chain model be

$$\begin{bmatrix} P_{11} & P_{10} \\ P_{01} & P_{00} \end{bmatrix} = \begin{bmatrix} 1-A & A \\ \frac{1}{5} & \frac{4}{5} \end{bmatrix},$$

where A is the only unknown parameter of the model. Define the following symbols:

n_{jk} Number of people who were in state j at time 0 and are in state k at time 1
$n_{j\cdot}$ Number of people who were in state j at time 0
$n_{\cdot j}$ Number of people who are in state j at time 1

We are to treat $n_{j\cdot}$ as given constants and n_{jk} and $n_{\cdot j}$ as random variables.
a. Supposing $n_{1\cdot} = 10$, $n_{0\cdot} = 5$, $n_{\cdot 1} = 8$, and $n_{\cdot 0} = 7$, compute the least squares estimate of A based on Eq. (11.1.73). Also, compute an estimate of its variance conditional on $n_{j\cdot}$.
b. Supposing $n_{11} = 7$ and $n_{01} = 1$ in addition to the data given in a, compute the MLE of A and an estimate of its variance conditional on $n_{j\cdot}$.

9. (Section 11.1.5)
Prove that minimizing (11.1.78) yields the asymptotically same estimator as minimizing (11.1.77).

10. (Section 11.1.5)
Write down the aggregate likelihood function (11.1.82) explicitly in the following special case: $T = 1$, $N = 5$, $r_0 = 3$, and $r_1 = 2$.

11. (Section 11.2.5)
Verify (11.2.50).

12. (Section 11.2.5)
Consider a particular individual. Suppose his hazard rate of moving from state 1 to state 2 is $\alpha_1 t + \beta_1 k$, where t is the duration in state 1 and k denotes the kth spell in state 1. The hazard rate of moving from state 2 to 1 is $\alpha_2 t + \beta_2 k$, where t is the duration in state 2 and k denotes the kth spell in state 2. Suppose he was found in state 1 at time 0. This is his first spell in state 1. (He may have stayed in state 1 prior to time 0.) Then he moved to state 2 at time t_1, completed his first spell in state 2, moved back to state 1 at time t_2, and stayed in state 1 at least until time t_3. Write down his contribution to the likelihood function. Assume $\alpha_1, \alpha_2 > 0$.

13. (Section 11.2.5)
Consider a homogeneous nonstationary duration model with the hazard rate

$$\lambda(t) = \alpha t, \qquad \alpha > 0.$$

Supposing we observe n completed spells of duration $t_1, t_2, \ldots, t_n$ and $N - n$ censored spells of duration $t_{n+1}, t_{n+2}, \ldots, t_N$, derive the MLE of α and its asymptotic variance.

14. (Section 11.2.5)
Let $F(t|\lambda) = 1 - e^{-\lambda t}$ where λ is a random variable distributed with density $g(\cdot)$. Define $\lambda(t) = f(t)/[1 - F(t)]$, where $F(t) = E_\lambda F(t|\lambda)$ and $f(t) = \partial F/\partial t$. Show $\partial\lambda(t)/\partial t < 0$ (cf. Flinn and Heckman, 1982).

Appendix 1
Useful Theorems in Matrix Analysis

The theorems listed in this appendix are the ones especially useful in econometrics. All matrices are assumed to be real. Proofs for many of these theorems can be found in Bellman (1970).

1. For any square matrix $\mathbf{A}$, with distinct characteristic roots, there exists a nonsingular matrix $\mathbf{P}$ such that $\mathbf{PAP}^{-1} = \mathbf{\Lambda}$, where $\mathbf{\Lambda}$ is a diagonal matrix with the characteristic roots of $\mathbf{A}$ in the diagonal. If the characteristic roots are not distinct, $\mathbf{\Lambda}$ takes the *Jordan canonical form* (see Bellman, p. 198).

2. The determinant of a matrix is the product of its characteristic roots.

3. For any symmetric matrix $\mathbf{A}$, there exists an orthogonal matrix $\mathbf{H}$ such that $\mathbf{H}'\mathbf{H} = \mathbf{I}$ and $\mathbf{H}'\mathbf{AH} = \mathbf{\Lambda}$, where $\mathbf{\Lambda}$ is a diagonal matrix with the *characteristic roots* (which are real) of $\mathbf{A}$ in the diagonal. The ith column of $\mathbf{H}$ is called the *characteristic vector* of $\mathbf{A}$ corresponding to the characteristic root of $\mathbf{A}$ that is the ith diagonal element of $\mathbf{\Lambda}$.

4. For a symmetric matrix $\mathbf{A}$, the following statements are equivalent:

   (i) $\mathbf{A}$ is a positive definite. (Write $\mathbf{A} > \mathbf{0}$.)
   (ii) $\mathbf{x}'\mathbf{Ax}$ is positive for any nonzero vector $\mathbf{x}$.
   (iii) Principal minors of $\mathbf{A}$ are all positive.
   (iv) Characteristic roots of $\mathbf{A}$ are all positive.

The above is true if we change the word *positive* to *nonnegative*.

5. For any matrices $\mathbf{A}$ and $\mathbf{B}$, the nonzero characteristic roots of $\mathbf{AB}$ and $\mathbf{BA}$ are the same, whenever both $\mathbf{AB}$ and $\mathbf{BA}$ are defined.

6. $\text{tr}\, \mathbf{AB} = \text{tr}\, \mathbf{BA}$.

7. For any square matrix $\mathbf{A}$, $\text{tr}\, \mathbf{A}$ is equal to the sum of its characteristic roots.

8. Let $\mathbf{A}$, $\mathbf{B}$ be symmetric matrices of the same size. A necessary and

sufficient condition that there exists an orthogonal matrix $\mathbf{H}$ such that both $\mathbf{H}'\mathbf{A}\mathbf{H}$ and $\mathbf{H}'\mathbf{B}\mathbf{H}$ are diagonal is that $\mathbf{AB} = \mathbf{BA}$.

9. Any nonnegative (semipositive) definite matrix $\mathbf{A}$ can be written as $\mathbf{A} = \mathbf{TT}'$, where $\mathbf{T}$ is a lower triangular matrix with nonnegative diagonal elements.

10. Let $\lambda_1, \lambda_2, \ldots, \lambda_n$ be the characteristic roots of a symmetric matrix $\mathbf{A}$ in descending order (λ_1 being the largest). Then

$$\lambda_1 = \max_{\mathbf{x}} \frac{\mathbf{x}'\mathbf{A}\mathbf{x}}{\mathbf{x}'\mathbf{x}} \left(= \frac{\mathbf{x}_1'\mathbf{A}\mathbf{x}_1}{\mathbf{x}_1'\mathbf{x}_1} \right),$$

$$\lambda_2 = \max_{\mathbf{x}'\mathbf{x}_1=0} \frac{\mathbf{x}'\mathbf{A}\mathbf{x}}{\mathbf{x}'\mathbf{x}} \left(= \frac{\mathbf{x}_2'\mathbf{A}\mathbf{x}_2}{\mathbf{x}_2'\mathbf{x}_2} \right),$$

$$\lambda_3 = \max_{\substack{\mathbf{x}'\mathbf{x}_1=0 \\ \mathbf{x}'\mathbf{x}_2=0}} \frac{\mathbf{x}'\mathbf{A}\mathbf{x}}{\mathbf{x}'\mathbf{x}}, \quad \text{and so on.}$$

11. Let $\mathbf{A}$ and $\mathbf{B}$ be symmetric matrices ($n \times n$) with $\mathbf{B}$ nonnegative definite. Then $\mu_i(\mathbf{A} + \mathbf{B}) \geqq \lambda_i(\mathbf{A})$, $i, = 1, 2, \ldots, n$, where λ's and μ's are the characteristic roots in descending order. The strict inequality holds if $\mathbf{B}$ is positive definite.

12. $$\det \begin{bmatrix} \mathbf{A} & \mathbf{B} \\ \mathbf{C} & \mathbf{D} \end{bmatrix} = |\mathbf{D}| \cdot |\mathbf{A} - \mathbf{B}\mathbf{D}^{-1}\mathbf{C}| \quad \text{if} \quad |\mathbf{D}| \neq 0.$$

13. $$\begin{bmatrix} \mathbf{A} & \mathbf{B} \\ \mathbf{C} & \mathbf{D} \end{bmatrix}^{-1} = \begin{bmatrix} \mathbf{E}^{-1} & -\mathbf{E}^{-1}\mathbf{B}\mathbf{D}^{-1} \\ -\mathbf{D}^{-1}\mathbf{C}\mathbf{E}^{-1} & \mathbf{F}^{-1} \end{bmatrix}$$

where $\mathbf{E} = \mathbf{A} - \mathbf{B}\mathbf{D}^{-1}\mathbf{C}$, $\mathbf{F} = \mathbf{D} - \mathbf{C}\mathbf{A}^{-1}\mathbf{B}$, $\mathbf{E}^{-1} = \mathbf{A}^{-1} + \mathbf{A}^{-1}\mathbf{B}\mathbf{F}^{-1}\mathbf{C}\mathbf{A}^{-1}$, and $\mathbf{F}^{-1} = \mathbf{D}^{-1} + \mathbf{D}^{-1}\mathbf{C}\mathbf{E}^{-1}\mathbf{B}\mathbf{D}^{-1}$.

14. Let $\mathbf{A}$ be an $n \times r$ matrix of rank r. A matrix of the form $\mathbf{P} = \mathbf{A}(\mathbf{A}'\mathbf{A})^{-1}\mathbf{A}'$ is called a projection matrix and is of special importance in statistics.

(i) $\mathbf{P} = \mathbf{P}' = \mathbf{P}^2$ (Hence, $\mathbf{P}$ is symmetric and *idempotent*.)
(ii) rank $(\mathbf{P}) = r$.
(iii) Characteristic roots of $\mathbf{P}$ consist of r ones and $n - r$ zeros.
(iv) If $\mathbf{x} = \mathbf{A}\mathbf{c}$ for some vector $\mathbf{c}$, then $\mathbf{P}\mathbf{x} = \mathbf{x}$. (Hence the word *projection*.)
(v) $\mathbf{M} = \mathbf{I} - \mathbf{A}(\mathbf{A}'\mathbf{A})^{-1}\mathbf{A}'$ is also idempotent, with rank $n - r$, its characteristic roots consisting of $n - r$ ones and r zeros, and if $\mathbf{x} = \mathbf{A}\mathbf{c}$, then $\mathbf{M}\mathbf{x} = \mathbf{0}$.

(vi) $\mathbf{P}$ can be written as $\mathbf{G}'\mathbf{G}$, where $\mathbf{G}\mathbf{G}' = \mathbf{I}$, or as $\mathbf{v}_1\mathbf{v}_1' + \mathbf{v}_2\mathbf{v}_2' + \ldots + \mathbf{v}_r\mathbf{v}_r'$, where $\mathbf{v}_i$ is a vector and $r = \text{rank}\,(\mathbf{P})$.

15. Let $\mathbf{A}$ be an $n \times r$ matrix of rank r. Partition $\mathbf{A}$ as $\mathbf{A} = (\mathbf{A}_1, \mathbf{A}_2)$ such that $\mathbf{A}_1$ is $n \times r_1$ and $\mathbf{A}_2$ is $n \times r_2$. If we define $\overline{\mathbf{A}}_2 = [\mathbf{I} - \mathbf{A}_1(\mathbf{A}_1'\mathbf{A}_1)^{-1}\mathbf{A}_1']\mathbf{A}_2$, then we have $\mathbf{A}(\mathbf{A}'\mathbf{A})^{-1}\mathbf{A}' = \mathbf{A}_1(\mathbf{A}_1'\mathbf{A}_1)^{-1}\mathbf{A}_1' + \overline{\mathbf{A}}_2(\overline{\mathbf{A}}_2'\overline{\mathbf{A}}_2)^{-1}\overline{\mathbf{A}}_2'$.

16. If $\mathbf{A}$ is positive definite and $\mathbf{B}$ is symmetric, there exists a nonsingular matrix $\mathbf{C}$ such that $\mathbf{C}'\mathbf{A}\mathbf{C} = \mathbf{I}$, $\mathbf{C}'\mathbf{B}\mathbf{C} = \mathbf{D}$, where $\mathbf{D}$ is diagonal and the diagonal elements of $\mathbf{D}$ are the roots of $|\mathbf{B} - \lambda\mathbf{A}| = 0$.

17. Let $\mathbf{A}$ and $\mathbf{B}$ be symmetric nonsingular matrices of the same size. Then $\mathbf{A} \geqq \mathbf{B} \geqq \mathbf{0}$ implies $\mathbf{B}^{-1} \geqq \mathbf{A}^{-1}$.

18. Let $\mathbf{A}$ be any nonsingular matrix. The characteristic roots of $\mathbf{A}^{-1}$ are the reciprocals of the characteristic roots of $\mathbf{A}$.

19. Let $\mathbf{A}$ and $\mathbf{B}$ be nonsingular matrices of the same size such that $\mathbf{A} + \mathbf{B}$ and $\mathbf{A}^{-1} + \mathbf{B}^{-1}$ are nonsingular. Then

(i) $(\mathbf{A} + \mathbf{B})^{-1} = \mathbf{A}^{-1}(\mathbf{A}^{-1} + \mathbf{B}^{-1})^{-1}\mathbf{B}^{-1}$
(ii) $\mathbf{A}^{-1} - (\mathbf{A} + \mathbf{B})^{-1} = \mathbf{A}^{-1}(\mathbf{A}^{-1} + \mathbf{B}^{-1})^{-1}\mathbf{A}^{-1}$.

20. Let $\mathbf{X}$ be a matrix with a full column rank. Then

$$(\mathbf{I} + \mathbf{X}\mathbf{X}')^{-1} = \mathbf{I} - \mathbf{X}(\mathbf{I} + \mathbf{X}'\mathbf{X})^{-1}\mathbf{X}'.$$

21. *Rules for Matrix Differentiation.* ξ is an element of $\mathbf{X}$. Every other symbol is a matrix. $\| \quad \|$ denotes the absolute value of the determinant.

(i) $\dfrac{d}{d\xi}\,\text{tr}\,\mathbf{X}\mathbf{Y} = \text{tr}\,\dfrac{d\mathbf{X}}{d\xi}\mathbf{Y}$

(ii) $\dfrac{d}{d\xi}\log\|\mathbf{X}\| = \text{tr}\,\mathbf{X}^{-1}\dfrac{d\mathbf{X}}{d\xi}$

(iii) $\dfrac{d}{d\mathbf{A}}\log\|\mathbf{A}\| = (\mathbf{A}')^{-1}$

(iv) $\dfrac{d}{d\xi}\mathbf{X}^{-1} = -\mathbf{X}^{-1}\dfrac{d\mathbf{X}}{d\xi}\mathbf{X}^{-1}$

(v) $\dfrac{d}{d\xi}\,\text{tr}\,\mathbf{X}^{-1}\mathbf{Y} = -\text{tr}\left(\mathbf{X}^{-1}\dfrac{d\mathbf{X}}{d\xi}\mathbf{X}^{-1}\mathbf{Y}\right)$

(vi) $\dfrac{d}{d\mathbf{A}}\,\text{tr}\,\mathbf{A}^{-1}\mathbf{B} = -\mathbf{A}^{-1}\mathbf{B}\mathbf{A}^{-1}$

$$\text{(vii)} \quad \frac{d}{d\mathbf{A}} \operatorname{tr} \mathbf{AB} = \mathbf{B}'$$

$$\text{(viii)} \quad \frac{d}{d\mathbf{A}} \operatorname{tr} \mathbf{ABA}'\mathbf{C} = \mathbf{CAB} + \mathbf{C}'\mathbf{AB}'$$

$$\text{(ix)} \quad \frac{d}{d\mathbf{A}} \operatorname{tr} \mathbf{A}'\mathbf{BAC} = \mathbf{B}'\mathbf{AC}' + \mathbf{BAC}$$

22. *Kronecker Products.* Let $\mathbf{A} = \{a_{ij}\}$ be a $K \times L$ matrix and let $\mathbf{B}$ be a $M \times N$ matrix. Then the Kronecker product $\mathbf{A} \otimes \mathbf{B}$ is a $KM \times LN$ matrix defined by

$$\mathbf{A} \otimes \mathbf{B} = \begin{bmatrix} a_{11}\mathbf{B} & a_{12}\mathbf{B} & \cdot & \cdot & a_{1L}\mathbf{B} \\ a_{21}\mathbf{B} & a_{22}\mathbf{B} & \cdot & \cdot & a_{2L}\mathbf{B} \\ \cdot & \cdot & & & \cdot \\ \cdot & \cdot & & & \cdot \\ a_{K1}\mathbf{B} & a_{K2}\mathbf{B} & \cdot & \cdot & a_{KL}\mathbf{B} \end{bmatrix}.$$

(i) $(\mathbf{A} \otimes \mathbf{B})(\mathbf{C} \otimes \mathbf{D}) = \mathbf{AC} \otimes \mathbf{BD}$ if $\mathbf{AC}$ and $\mathbf{BD}$ can be defined.
(ii) $\operatorname{tr} (\mathbf{A} \otimes \mathbf{B}) = \operatorname{tr} \mathbf{A} \cdot \operatorname{tr} \mathbf{B}$ if $\mathbf{A}$ and $\mathbf{B}$ are square.
(iii) Let $\mathbf{A}$ be a $K \times K$ matrix with characteristic roots $\lambda_1, \lambda_2, \ldots, \lambda_K$ and let $\mathbf{B}$ be a $M \times M$ matrix with characteristic roots $\mu_1, \mu_2, \ldots, \mu_M$. Then the KM characteristic roots of $\mathbf{A} \otimes \mathbf{B}$ are $\lambda_i \mu_j$, $i = 1, 2, \ldots, K$, $j = 1, 2, \ldots, M$.
(iv) Let $\mathbf{A}$ and $\mathbf{B}$ be as in (iii). Then

$$|\mathbf{A} \otimes \mathbf{B}| = |\mathbf{A}|^M \cdot |\mathbf{B}|^K.$$

(v) Let $\mathbf{A}$, $\mathbf{B}$, and $\mathbf{C}$ be matrices of appropriate sizes such that $\mathbf{ABC}$ can be defined. Suppose $\mathbf{A}$ has L columns and write the L columns as $\mathbf{A} = (\mathbf{A}_1, \mathbf{A}_2, \ldots, \mathbf{A}_L)$. Define $\operatorname{vec}(\mathbf{A}) = (\mathbf{A}_1', \mathbf{A}_2', \ldots, \mathbf{A}_L')'$. Then

$$\operatorname{vec}(\mathbf{ABC}) = (\mathbf{C}' \otimes \mathbf{A}) \operatorname{vec}(\mathbf{B}).$$

23. *Hadamard Products.* (Minc and Marcus, 1964, p. 120.) Let $\mathbf{A} = \{a_{ij})$ and $\mathbf{B} = \{b_{ij}\}$ be matrices of the same size. Then the Hadamard product $\mathbf{A} * \mathbf{B}$ is defined by $\mathbf{A} * \mathbf{B} = \{a_{ij} b_{ij}\}$.

(i) Let $\mathbf{A}$ and $\mathbf{B}$ be both $n \times n$. Then $\mathbf{A} * \mathbf{B} = \mathbf{S}'(\mathbf{A} \otimes \mathbf{B})\mathbf{S}$, where $\mathbf{S}$ is the $n^2 \times n$ matrix the ith column of which has 1 in its $[(i-1)n + i]$th position and 0 elsewhere.

Appendix 2
Distribution Theory

The theorems listed in this appendix, as well as many other results concerning the distribution of a univariate continuous random variable, can be found in Johnson and Kotz (1970a,b). "Rao" stands for Rao (1973) and "Plackett" for Plackett (1960).

1. *Chi-Square Distribution.* (Rao, p. 166.) Let an n-component random vector $\mathbf{z}$ be distributed as $N(\mathbf{0}, \mathbf{I})$. Then the distribution of $\mathbf{z}'\mathbf{z}$ is called the chi-square distribution with n degrees of freedom. Symbolically we write $\mathbf{z}'\mathbf{z} \sim \chi_n^2$. Its density is given by

$$f(x) = 2^{-n/2}\Gamma(n/2)e^{-x/2}x^{-n/2-1},$$

where $\Gamma(p) = \int_0^\infty \lambda^{p-1}e^{-\lambda}\,d\lambda$ is called a gamma function. Its mean is n and its variance $2n$.

2. (Rao, p. 186). Let $\mathbf{z} \sim N(\mathbf{0}, \mathbf{I})$ and let $\mathbf{A}$ be a symmetric and idempotent matrix with rank n. Then $\mathbf{z}'\mathbf{A}\mathbf{z} \sim \chi_n^2$.

3. *Student's t Distribution.* (Rao, p. 170.) If $z \sim N(0, 1)$ and $w \sim \chi_n^2$ and if z and w are independent, $n^{1/2}zw^{-1/2}$ has the Student's t distribution with n degrees of freedom, for which the density is given by

$$f(x) = \left[\sqrt{n}\beta\left(\frac{1}{2}, \frac{n}{2}\right)\right]^{-1}\left(1 + \frac{x^2}{n}\right)^{-(n+1)/2},$$

where

$$\beta(\gamma, \delta) = \frac{\Gamma(\gamma)\Gamma(\delta)}{\Gamma(\gamma + \delta)}, \quad \text{beta function.}$$

Symbolically we write

$$\left(\frac{n}{w}\right)^{1/2} z \sim S_n.$$

4. *F Distribution.* (Rao, p. 167.) If $w_1 \sim \chi^2_{n_1}$ and $w_2 \sim \chi^2_{n_2}$ and if w_1 and w_2 are independent, $n_1^{-1} w_1 n_2 w_2^{-1}$ has the F distribution with n_1 and n_2 degrees of freedom, for which the density is given by

$$f(x) = \frac{(n_1/n_2)^{n_1/2} x^{n_1/2-1}}{\beta[(n_1/2),(n_2/2)](1 + n_1 x/n_2)^{(n_1+n_2)/2}}$$

Symbolically we write

$$\frac{w_1/n_1}{w_2/n_2} \sim F(n_1, n_2).$$

5. (Plackett, p. 24.) Let $\mathbf{z} \sim N(\mathbf{0}, \mathbf{I})$. Let $\mathbf{A}$ and $\mathbf{B}$ be symmetric matrices. Then $\mathbf{z}'\mathbf{A}\mathbf{z}$ is independent of $\mathbf{z}'\mathbf{B}\mathbf{z}$ if and only if $\mathbf{AB} = \mathbf{0}$.

6. (Plackett, p. 30.) Let $\mathbf{z} \sim N(\mathbf{0}, \mathbf{I})$. Then $\mathbf{c}'\mathbf{z}$ and $\mathbf{z}'\mathbf{A}\mathbf{z}$ are independent if and only if $\mathbf{Ac} = \mathbf{0}$.

7. (Plackett, p. 30.) Let $\mathbf{z} \sim N(\mathbf{0}, \mathbf{I})$ and let $\mathbf{A}$ be a symmetric matrix. Then $\mathbf{z}'\mathbf{A}\mathbf{z}/\mathbf{z}'\mathbf{z}$ and $\mathbf{z}'\mathbf{z}$ are independent.

Notes

1. Classical Least Squares Theory

1. This statement is true only when x_i^* is a scalar. If y, x_1, and x_2 are scalar dichotomous random variables, we have $E(y|x_1, x_2) = \beta_0 + \beta_1 x_1 + \beta_2 x_2 + \beta_3 x_1 x_2$, where the β's are appropriately defined.

2. The $\boldsymbol{\beta}$ that appears in (1.2.1) denotes the domain of the function S and hence, strictly speaking, should be distinguished from the parameter $\boldsymbol{\beta}$, which is unknown and yet can be regarded as fixed in value. To be precise, therefore, we should use two different symbols; however, we shall use the same symbol to avoid complicating the notation, so the reader must judge from the context which of the two meanings the symbol conveys.

3. Again, the warning of note 2 is in order here. The $\boldsymbol{\beta}$ and σ^2 that appear in the likelihood function represent the domain of the function whereas those that appear in Model 1 are unknown fixed values of the parameters—so-called true values.

4. The Cramér-Rao lower bound is discussed, for example, by Cox and Hinkley (1974), Bickel and Doksum (1977), Rao (1973), and Zacks (1971), roughly in ascending order of sophistication.

5. Good references for Bayesian statistics are Zellner (1971) and Box and Tiao (1973). For a quick review, Lindley (1972) is useful.

6. Even in this situation some people prefer using the t test. The procedure is also asymptotically correct, but there is no theoretical reason for the t test to be superior to the standard normal test in nonnormal cases. The same remark applies to the F test discussed later. See Pearson and Please (1975) for a discussion of the properties of the t and F tests in nonnormal cases. See White and MacDonald (1980) for tests of nonnormality using the least squares residuals.

7. Chow (1960) considered the case where $T_2 < K^*$ and indicated how the subsequent analysis can be modified to incorporate this case.

8. This formula can easily be generalized to the situation where there are n regimes ($n > 2$). Simply combine n equations like (1.5.25) and (1.5.27) and calculate the sum of squared residuals from each equation. Then the numerator chi-square has $(n-1)K^*$ degrees of freedom and the denominator chi-square has $\Sigma_{i=1}^{n} T_i - nK^*$ degrees of freedom.

9. These two tests can easily be generalized to the case of n regimes mentioned in note 8.

10. If we have cross-section data, p refers to a cross-section unit not included in the sample.
11. Theorem 1.6.1 is true even if we let $\mathbf{C}$ depend on $\mathbf{x}_p$. Then the two theorems are equivalent because any $\mathbf{d}$ satisfying (1.6.5) can be written as $\mathbf{C}\mathbf{x}_p$ for some $\mathbf{C}$ such that $\mathbf{C}'\mathbf{X} = \mathbf{I}$.

2. Recent Developments in Regression Analysis

1. A much more detailed account of this topic can be found in Amemiya (1980a).
2. We use the term *estimator* here, but all the definitions and the results of this subsection remain the same if we interpret $\mathbf{d}$ as any decision function mapping Y into Θ.
3. We assume that the losses do not depend on the parameters of the models. Otherwise, the choice of models and the estimation of the parameters cannot be sequentially analyzed, which would immensely complicate the problem. However, we do not claim that our assumption is realistic. We adopt this simplification for the purpose of illustrating certain basic ideas.
4. For ways to get around this problem, see, for example, Akaike (1976) and Schwartz (1978).
5. See Thisted (1976) for an excellent survey of this topic, as well as for some original results. More recent surveys are given by Draper and Van Nostrand (1979) and Judge and Bock (1983).
6. The matrix $\mathbf{H}_1\mathbf{\Lambda}_1^{-1}\mathbf{H}_1'$ is sometimes referred to as the Moore-Penrose generalized inverse of $\mathbf{X}'\mathbf{X}$ and is denoted by $(\mathbf{X}'\mathbf{X})^+$. See Rao (1973, p. 24) for more discussion of generalized inverses.
7. This question was originally posed and solved by Silvey (1969).
8. Although Sclove considers the random coefficients model and the prediction (rather than estimation) of the regression vector, there is no essential difference between his approach and the Bayesian estimation.
9. What follows simplifies the derivation of Sclove et al. (1972).
10. See Section 4.6.1. In Chapter 3 we shall discuss large sample theory and make the meaning of the term *asymptotically* more precise. For the time being, the reader should simply interpret it to mean "approximately when T is large."
11. See the definition of probability limit in Chapter 3. Loosely speaking, the statement means that when T is large, s is close to s_0 with probability close to 1.

3. Large Sample Theory

1. Representative textbooks are, in a roughly increasing order of difficulty, Hoel (1971); Freund (1971); Mood, Graybill, and Boes (1974); Cox and Hinkley (1974), and Bickel and Doksum (1977).
2. For a more complete study of the subject, the reader should consult Chung (1974) or Loève (1977), the latter being more advanced than the former. Rao (1973), which is

an excellent advanced textbook in mathematical statistics, also gives a concise review of the theory of probability and random variables.

3. If a set function satisfies only (i) and (iii) of Definition 3.1.2, it is called a *measure*. In this case the triplet defined in Definition 3.1.3 is called a *measure space*. Thus the theory of probability is a special case of measure theory. (A standard textbook for measure theory is Halmos, 1950.)

4. If we have a measure space, then a function that satisfies the condition of Definition 3.1.4 is called a *measurable function*. Thus a random variable is a function measurable with respect to the probability measure.

5. Lebesgue measure can be defined also for certain non-Borel sets. The Lebesgue measure defined only for Borel sets is called *Borel measure*.

6. For Y to be a random variable, h must satisfy the condition $\{\omega | h[X(\omega)] < y\} \in \mathcal{A}$ for every y. Such a function is said to be *Borel-measurable*. A continuous function except for a countable number of discontinuities is Borel-measurable.

7. The following is a simple example in which the Riemann-Stieltjes integral does not exist. Suppose $F(x) = 0$ for $a \leqq x \leqq c$ and $F(x) = 1$ for $c < x \leqq b$ and suppose $h(x) = F(x)$. Then, depending on the point x^* we choose in an interval that contains c, S_n is equal to either 1 or 0. This is a weakness of the Riemann-Stieltjes integral. In this example the *Lebesgue-Stieltjes integral* exists and is equal to 0. However, we will not go into this matter further. The reader may consult references cited in Note 2 to Chapter 3.

8. Sometimes we also say X_n converges to X *almost everywhere* or *with probability one*. Convergence in probability and convergence almost surely are sometimes referred to as *weak convergence* and *strong convergence*, respectively.

9. Between M and a.s., we cannot establish a definite logical relationship without further assumptions.

10. The law of large numbers implied by Theorem 3.2.1 (Chebyshev) can be slightly generalized so as to do away with the requirement of a finite variance. Let $\{X_t\}$ be independent and suppose $E|X_t|^{1+\delta} < M$ for some $\delta > 0$ and some $M < \infty$. Then $\bar{X}_n - E\bar{X}_n \xrightarrow{P} 0$. This is called *Markov's law of large numbers*.

11. The *principal logarithm* of a complex number $re^{i\theta}$ is defined as $\log r + i\theta$.

12. It seems that for most practical purposes the weak consistency of an estimator is all that a researcher would need, and it is not certain how much more practical benefit would result from proving strong consistency in addition.

13. Lai, Robbins, and Wei (1978) proved that if $\{u_t\}$ are assumed to be independent in Model 1 and if the conditions of Theorem 3.5.1 are met, the least squares estimator is strongly consistent. Furthermore, the homoscedasticity assumption can be relaxed, provided the variances of $\{u_t\}$ are uniformly bounded from above.

4. Asymptotic Properties of Extremum Estimators

1. In the proof of Theorem 4.1.1, continuity of $Q_T(\theta)$ is used only to imply continuity of $Q(\theta)$ and to make certain the measurability of $\hat{\theta}_T$. Therefore we can modify this

theorem in such a way that we assume continuity of $Q(\theta)$ but not of $Q_T(\theta)$ and define convergence in probability in a more general way that does not require measurability of $\hat{\theta}_T$. This is done in Theorem 9.6.1.

Also note that the proof of Theorem 4.1.1 can easily be modified to show that if the convergence in the sense of (i) holds in assumption C, $\hat{\theta}_T$ converges to θ_0 almost surely.

2. Strictly speaking, (4.1.10) is defined only for those T's for which Θ_T is nonempty. However, the probability that Θ_T is nonempty approaches 1 as T goes to infinity because of Assumption C of Theorem 4.1.2. As an aside, Jennrich (1969) proved that θ^* is a measurable function.

3. This proof is patterned after the proof of a similar theorem by Jennrich (1969).

4. Note that if $\mathbf{z}_T$ is merely defined as a random variable with mean $\mu(\theta)$ and variance-covariance matrix $\Sigma(\theta)$, the minimization of the quadratic form does not even yield a consistent estimator of θ.

5. The term *second-order efficiency* is sometimes used to denote a related but different concept (see Pfanzagl, 1973).

6. If the error term is multiplicative as in $Q = \beta_1 K^{\beta_2} L^{\beta_3} e^u$, the log transformation reduces it to a linear regression model. See Bodkin and Klein (1967) for the estimation of both models.

7. The methods of proof used in this section and Section 4.3.3 are similar to those of Jennrich (1969).

8. Because a function continuous on a compact set is uniformly continuous, we can assume without loss of generality that $f_t(\beta)$ is uniformly continuous in $\beta \in N$.

9. The nonsingularity is not needed here but is assumed as it will be needed later.

10. Note that in the special case where the constraint $\mathbf{h}(\beta) = \mathbf{0}$ is linear and can be written as $\mathbf{Q}'\beta = \mathbf{c}$, (4.5.21) is similar to (4.3.32). We cannot unequivocally determine whether the chi-square approximation of the distribution of (4.5.21) is better or worse than the F approximation of the distribution of (4.3.32).

11. If the sample is (1, 2, 3), 2 is the unique median. If the sample is (1, 2, 3, 4), any point in the closed interval [2, 3] may be defined as a median. The definition (4.6.3) picks 2 as the median. If $f(x) > 0$ in the neighborhood of $x = M$, this ambiguity vanishes as the sample size approaches infinity.

12. The second term of the right-hand side of (4.6.10) does not affect the minimization but is added so that plim $T^{-1}S_T$ can be evaluated without assuming the existence of the first absolute moment of Y_t. This idea originates in Huber (1965).

13. Alternative methods of proof of asymptotic normality can be found in Bassett and Koenker (1978) and in Amemiya (1982a).

5. Time Series Analysis

1. We are using the approximation sign $\cong$ to mean that most elements of the matrices of both sides are equal.

2. The subscript p denotes the order of the autoregression. The size of the matrix should be inferred from the context.

3. Almon (1965) suggested an alternative method of computing $\boldsymbol{\beta}$ based on Lagrangian interpolation polynomials. Cooper (1972) stated that although the method discussed in the text is easier to understand, Almon's method is computationally superior.

6. Generalized Least Squares Theory

1. If rank $(\mathbf{H}_2'\mathbf{X}) = K$, $\boldsymbol{\beta}$ is uniquely determined by (6.1.2).

2. Farebrother (1980) presented the relevant tables for the case in which there is no intercept.

3. Breusch (1978) and Godfrey (1978) showed that Durbin's test is identical to Rao's score test (see Section 4.5.1). See also Breusch and Pagan (1980) for the Lagrange multiplier test closely related to Durbin's test.

4. In the special case in which $N = 2$ and $\boldsymbol{\beta}$ changes with i (so that we must estimate both $\boldsymbol{\beta}_1$ and $\boldsymbol{\beta}_2$), statistic (6.5.9) is a simple transformation of the F statistic (1.5.44). In this case (1.5.44) is preferred because the distribution given there is exact.

5. It is not essential to use the unbiased estimators $\tilde{\sigma}_i^2$ here. If $\hat{\sigma}_i^2$ are used, the distribution of $\hat{\gamma}$ is only trivially modified.

6. In either FGLS or MLE we can replace $\hat{\boldsymbol{\beta}}_1$ by $\tilde{\boldsymbol{\beta}}_1$ without affecting the asymptotic distribution.

7. Hildreth and Houck suggested another estimator $(\mathbf{Z}'\dot{\mathbf{M}}\mathbf{Z})^{-1}\mathbf{Z}'\hat{\mathbf{u}}^2$, which is the instrumental variables estimator applied to (6.5.23) using $\mathbf{Z}$ as the instrumental variables. Using inequality (6.5.29), we can show that this estimator is also asymptotically less efficient than $\hat{\boldsymbol{\alpha}}_3$. See Hsiao (1975) for an interesting derivation of the two estimators of Hildreth and Houck from the MINQUE principle of Rao (1970). Froehlich (1973) suggested FGLS applied to (6.5.23). By the same inequality, the estimator can be shown to be asymptotically less efficient than $\hat{\boldsymbol{\alpha}}_3$. Froehlich reported a Monte Carlo study that compared the FGLS subject to the nonnegativity of the variances with several other estimators. A further Monte Carlo study has been reported by Dent and Hildreth (1977).

8. The symbol $\mathbf{l}$ here denotes an NT-vector of ones. The subscripts will be omitted whenever the size of $\mathbf{l}$ is obvious from the context. The same is true for the identity matrix.

9. For the consistency of $\hat{\beta}_{Q0}$ we need both N and T to go to ∞. For further discussion, see Anderson and Hsiao (1981, 1982).

10. The presence of the vector $\mathbf{f}$ in a variance term would cause a problem in the derivation of the asymptotic results if T were allowed to go to ∞, but in the Lillard-Weiss model, as in most of econometric panel-data studies, T is small and N is large.

7. Linear Simultaneous Equations Models

1. More general constraints on the elements of $\boldsymbol{\Gamma}$ and $\mathbf{B}$ have been discussed by Fisher (1966) and Hsiao (1983).

2. For alternative definitions of identification, see Hsiao (1983).

3. Identification of the structural parameters may be possible because of constraints on the variance-covariance matrix of the errors (see Fisher, 1966, or Hsiao, 1983).

4. For an alternative derivation, see Koopmans and Hood (1953).

5. Basmann (1957) independently proposed the same estimator and called it the *generalized classical linear estimator.*

6. Exact distributions and densities are expressed as twofold or threefold infinite series and therefore are difficult to work with. For this reason approximations based on various asymptotic expansions have been proposed. They are mainly classified into two types: one based on a Taylor expansion of the logarithm of the characteristic function, as in Anderson and Sawa (1973), and one that is a direct expansion of the probability, as in Anderson (1974).

7. An instrumental variables estimator satisfying conditions (i) and (ii) but not (iii) is consistent and could be asymptotically more efficient than 2SLS.

8. Nonlinear Simultaneous Equations Models

1. A slightly more general model defined by $f_t(y_t, \mathbf{Y}_t, \mathbf{X}_{it}, \boldsymbol{\alpha}_0) = u_t$ will be considered in Section 8.1.2.

2. Tsurumi (1970) estimated a CES production function by first linearizing the function around certain initial estimates of the parameters and then proceeding as if he had the model nonlinear only in variables. Thus his method was in effect a Gauss-Newton iteration for obtaining NL2S. However, Tsurumi did not discuss the statistical properties of the estimator he used. Applications of models nonlinear only in variables can be found in Strickland and Weiss (1976) and Rice and Smith (1977).

3. The subscript 0 indicating the true value is henceforth suppressed to simplify the notation.

4. Goldfeld and Quandt (1968) considered a two-equation model nonlinear only in variables that yields two solutions of dependent variables for a given vector value of the error terms. For this model they conducted a Monte Carlo study of how the performance of various estimators is affected by different mechanisms of choosing a unique solution.

5. This lemma, stated slightly differently, is originally attributed to Stein (1973). Amemiya (1977a) independently rediscovered the lemma. The proof can be found in an article by Amemiya (1982b).

9. Qualitative Response Models

1. If $\lim_{\Delta\to 0} [g_n(x+\Delta) - g_n(x)]/\Delta = dg_n/dx$ uniformly in n, $d(\lim_{n\to\infty} g_n)/dx = \lim_{n\to\infty} dg_n/dx$. See, for example, Apostol (1974, p. 221) for a proof.

2. The asymptotic efficiency of Berkson's MIN χ^2 estimator can also be proved as a corollary of the Barankin and Gurland theorem quoted in Section 4.2.4. See Taylor (1953).

3. There is a slight error in the formula for the mean squared error of MLE, which has been corrected by Amemiya (1984b).

4. See Anderson (1958, Ch. 6) for a thorough discussion of discriminant analysis.

5. Certain areas of statistics are more amenable to Bayesian analysis than to classical analysis. The simultaneous determination of prediction and estimation is one of them.

6. To simplify the notation we shall omit the subscript 0 that denotes the true value. The reader should be able to understand from the context whether a symbol denotes the true value of a parameter or the domain of the parameter space.

7. The possible inconsistency due to this approximation was briefly discussed at the end of Section 9.2.5.

8. Deacon and Shapiro actually used (9.3.32) and the equation obtained by summing (9.3.32) and (9.3.33). The resulting estimates of $\boldsymbol{\beta}_1$ and $\boldsymbol{\beta}_2$ are the same as those obtained by the method described in the text.

9. The triple integral in (9.3.72) can be reduced to a double integral by a certain transformation. In general, we must evaluate m-tuple integrals for $m + 1$ responses.

10. We assume that a component of the vector $\mathbf{x}$ is either discrete or continuous, so that f is actually the density and the probability combined (density with respect to some measure). Thus the integration with respect to $\mathbf{x}$ that will appear later should be regarded as the integral and summation combined (the Lebesgue-Stieltjes integral with respect to the appropriate measure).

11. Because $g(\mathbf{x}_i)$ is known, it can be ignored in the maximization of L_e. However, we retained it to remind the reader of the sampling scheme. In (9.5.2), $H(j_i)$ is retained for the same reason.

12. The main difference between the two proofs is that we define $\hat{\boldsymbol{\beta}}_w$ as a solution of (9.5.6) whereas Manski and Lerman define it as the value of $\boldsymbol{\beta}$ that attains the global maximum of (9.5.5) over a compact parameter space containing the true value.

13. The following analysis can be modified to allow for the possibility that for j and $\mathbf{x}$, $P(j|\mathbf{x}, \boldsymbol{\beta}) = 0$ for all $\boldsymbol{\beta}$. Such a case arises when certain alternatives are unavailable for a certain individual. See Manski and McFadden (1983, footnote 23, p. 13).

14. Manski and Lerman quote an interesting result attributed to McFadden, which states that in a multinomial logit model with alternative-specific intercepts—that is, the model in which α in (9.3.43) varies with j as in (9.2.4) and (9.2.5), the inconsistency is confined to the parameters $\{\alpha_j\}$.

15. In the simple logit model considered after (9.5.22), it can be shown that the asymptotic variances of MME and WMLE are identical, so that Table 9.7 applies to MME as well.

16. Cosslett's sampling scheme can be generalized further to yield a general *stratified sampling* (see Manski and McFadden, 1983, p. 28).

17. This interpretation does not contradict the fact that in actual decisions the determination of $\mathbf{x}$ precedes that of j.

18. There is a subtle difference. In the simple choice-based sampling defined earlier, a person choosing alternative j is sampled with probability $H(j)$, whereas in the gener-

alized choice-based sampling the number of people in the subsample s is fixed and not random.

19. It is interesting to note that maximizing Ω with respect to $\boldsymbol{\beta}$ and λ_s is equivalent to maximizing Ψ defined in (9.5.39) with respect to $\boldsymbol{\beta}$ and $Q_0(j)$. Manski and McFadden (1983, p. 24) suggested this version of MME without realizing its equivalence to CBMLE.

20. Cosslett defined WMLE and MME using the actual proportions of people choosing j instead of $H(j)$.

21. Manski's proof is not complete because in the fourth line from the bottom on page 218 of his article, double limit operations are interchanged without verifying the necessary conditions. It seems that we would have to make more assumptions than made by Manski in order for the necessary conditions to hold. A correct proof for the binary case can be found in Manski (1985).

22. Manski (1975) considered a more general score function than that defined here.

23. The heterogeneity problem is also known as the mover–stayer problem in the literature of Markov chain models. Among the first to discuss the problem were Blumen, Kogan, and McCarthy (1955), who found that individuals who changed occupations most frequently in the past were more likely to change in the future.

24. The $\{u_i\}$ in (9.7.5) are not i.i.d., unlike the $\{u_i\}$ in (9.7.2).

10. Tobit Models

1. More precisely, $\overset{A}{=}$ means in this particular case that both sides of the equation multiplied by $\sqrt{n}$ have the same limit distribution.

2. $\lambda(\cdot)$ is known as the hazard rate and its reciprocal is known as Mills's ratio. Tobin (1958) has given a figure that shows that $\lambda(z)$ can be closely approximated by a linear function of z for $-1 < z < 5$. Johnson and Kotz (1970a, p. 278f.) gave various expansions of Mills' ratio.

3. Chung and Goldberger (1984) generalized the results of Goldberger (1981) and Greene (1981) to the case where y^* and $\bar{\mathbf{x}}$ are not necessarily jointly normal but $E(\bar{\mathbf{x}}|y^*)$ is linear in y^*.

4. This was suggested by Wales and Woodland (1980).

5. See Stapleton and Young (1984).

6. See Section 4.3.5. Hartley (1976b) proved the asymptotic normality of $\hat{\gamma}_N$ and $\hat{\gamma}_{NW}$ and that they are asymptotically not as efficient as the MLE.

7. The asymptotic equivalence of $\tilde{\gamma}_N$ and $\tilde{\gamma}$ was proved by Stapleton and Young (1984).

8. Amemiya (1973c) showed that the Tobit likelihood function is not globally concave with respect to the original parameters $\boldsymbol{\beta}$ and σ^2.

9. For an alternative account, see Hartley (1976c).

10. An inequality constraint like this is often necessary in simultaneous equations models involving binary or truncated variables. For an interesting unified approach to this problem, see Gourieroux, Laffont, and Monfort (1980).

11. See Cragg (1971) for models that ensure the nonnegativity of y_2 as well as of y_1.

12. For a more elaborate derivation of the reservation wage model based on search theory, see Gronau (1974).

13. Gronau specified that the independent variables in the W^r equation include a woman's age and education, family income, number of children, and her husband's age and education, whereas the independent variables in the W^o equation include only a woman's age and education. However, Gronau readily admitted to the arbitrariness of the specification and the possibility that all the variables are included in both.

14. Gronau assumed the independence between u_2 and v and used an estimator different from those mentioned here. Amemiya (1984a) pointed out an error in Gronau's procedure. The independence between u_2 and v is unnecessary if we use either the MLE or Heckman's two-step estimator.

15. Although Heckman's model (1974) is a simultaneous equations model, the two-step estimator of Heckman studied by Wales and Woodland is essentially a reduced-form estimator, which we have discussed in this subsection, rather than the structural equations version we shall discuss in the next subsection.

16. For a panel data generalization of Heckman's model, see Heckman and MaCurdy (1980).

17. Actually, Heckman used log W^r and log W^o. The independent variables $\mathbf{x}_2$ include husband's wage, asset income, prices, and individual characteristics and $\mathbf{z}$ includes housewife's schooling and experience.

18. A more explicit expression for the likelihood function was obtained by Amemiya (1974a), who pointed out the incorrectness of the likelihood function originally given by Fair and Jaffee.

19. Equation (10.10.26) is the maximized profit function and (10.10.27) is an input demand or output supply function obtained by differentiating (10.10.26) with respect to the own input or output price (Hotelling's lemma). For convenience only one input or output has been assumed; so, strictly speaking, $x_{ik}^{(1)}$ and $x_{ik}^{(2)}$ are scalars.

20. These two equations correspond to the two equations in a proposition of Duncan (1980, p. 851). It seems that Duncan inadvertently omitted the last term from (10.10.30).

11. Markov Chain and Duration Models

1. Note that this result can be obtained from (11.1.38) using the Boskin-Nold assumptions as well as the assumption that T goes to ∞. The result (11.1.38) is valid even if T does not go to ∞ provided that NT goes to ∞. If we assumed $\mathbf{p}(0) = \mathbf{p}(\infty)$, the approximate equality in (11.1.55) would be exact and hence (11.1.59) would be valid without assuming $T \rightarrow \infty$ provided that $NT \rightarrow \infty$.

2. Actually, Toikka is interested only in three out of the six transition probabilities, and he lets those three depend linearly on exogenous variables. However, for the simplicity of analysis, we shall proceed in our discussion as if all the six transition probabilities depended linearly on exogenous variables.

3. Note that minimizing (11.1.78) is equivalent to maximizing the pseudo likelihood function under the assumption that r_t is normally distributed.

4. The likelihood function (11.2.14) pertains only to unemployment spells. When we also observe employment spells, (11.2.14) should be multiplied by a similar expression for employment spells. When there is no common unknown parameter in both parts of the likelihood function, each part can be separately maximized.

5. See Gradshteyn and Ryzhik (1965, p. 576).

6. See Bellman (1970, Chapter 10).

7. Here we have simplified Tuma's model slightly to bring out the essential points.

8. To integrate out v, we must specify its distribution as Lancaster did. A wrong distribution would introduce a specification bias. Heckman and Singer (1982, 1984a) discussed an interesting procedure of treating the distribution of v as unknown and maximizing the likelihood function with respect to that distribution as well as the other unknown parameters of the model.

9. See Kalbfleisch and Prentice (1980) for a procedure for modifying the following analysis in the case of ties.

10. Let $L(\mathbf{y}, \theta)$ be a joint density function (or a likelihood function if it is considered as a function of θ) of a vector of random variables $\mathbf{y}$. If $\mathbf{y}$ is transformed into $(\mathbf{v}, \mathbf{w})$ by a transformation not dependent on θ, the conditional density $L(\mathbf{v}|\mathbf{w}, \theta)$ is called a conditional likelihood function.

References

Abramowitz, M., and I. A. Segun. 1965. *Handbook of Mathematical Functions.* New York: Dover Publishing.

Adams, J. D. 1980. "Personal Wealth Transfers." *Quarterly Journal of Economics* 95:159–179.

Adelman, I. G. 1958. "A Stochastic Analysis of the Size Distribution of Firms." *Journal of the American Statistical Association* 53:893–904.

Aigner, D. J., T. Amemiya, and D. J. Poirier. 1976. "On the Estimation of Production Frontiers: Maximum Likelihood Estimation of the Parameters of a Discontinuous Density Function." *International Economic Review* 17:377–396.

Aigner, D. J., and G. G. Judge. 1977. "Application of Pre-Test and Stein Estimators to Economic Data." *Econometrica* 45:1279–1288.

Aitchison, J., and J. Bennett. 1970. "Polychotomous Quantal Response by Maximum Indicant." *Biometrika* 57:253–262.

Akahira, M. 1983. "Asymptotic Deficiency of the Jackknife Estimator." *The Australian Journal of Statistics* 25:123–129.

Akaike, H. 1973. "Information Theory and an Extension of the Maximum Likelihood Principle," in B. N. Petrov and F. Csaki, eds., *Second International Symposium on Information Theory,* pp. 267–281. Budapest: Akademiai Kiado.

——— 1976. "On Entropy Maximization Principle." Paper presented at the Symposium on Applications of Statistics, Dayton, Ohio.

Albert, A., and J. A. Anderson. 1984. "On the Existence of Maximum Likelihood Estimates in Logistic Regression Models." *Biometrika* 71:1–10.

Albright, R. L., S. R. Lerman, and C. F. Manski. 1977. "Report on the Development of an Estimation Program for the Multinomial Probit Model." Mimeographed paper prepared for the Federal Highway Administration.

Almon, S. 1965. "The Distributed Lag between Capital Appropriations and Expenditures." *Econometrica* 33:178–196.

Amemiya, T. 1966. "On the Use of Principal Components of Independent Variables in Two-Stage Least-Squares Estimation." *International Economic Review* 7:283–303.

——— 1967. "A Note on the Estimation of Balestra-Nerlove Models." Technical Report no. 4, Institute for Mathematical Studies in the Social Sciences, Stanford University, Calif.

——— 1971. "The Estimation of the Variances in a Variance-Components Model." *International Economic Review* 12:1–13.

——— 1972. "Bivariate Probit Analysis: Minimum Chi-Square Methods." *Journal of the American Statistical Association* 69:940–944.

——— 1973a. "Generalized Least Squares with an Estimated Autocovariance Matrix." *Econometrica* 41:723–732.

——— 1973b. "Regression Analysis When the Variance of the Dependent Variable Is Proportional to the Square of Its Expectation." *Journal of the American Statistical Association* 68:928–934.

——— 1973c. "Regression Analysis When the Dependent Variable Is Truncated Normal." *Econometrica* 41:997–1016.

——— 1974a. "A Note on a Fair and Jaffee Model." *Econometrica* 42:759–762.

——— 1974b. "Multivariate Regression and Simultaneous Equation Models When the Dependent Variables Are Truncated Normal." *Econometrica* 42:999–1012.

——— 1974c. "The Nonlinear Two-Stage Least-Squares Estimator." *Journal of Econometrics* 2:105–110.

——— 1975a. "The Nonlinear Limited-Information Maximum-Likelihood Estimator and the Modified Nonlinear Two-Stage Least-Squares Estimator." *Journal of Econometrics* 3:375–386.

——— 1975b. "Qualitative Response Models." *Annals of Economic and Social Measurement* 4:363–372.

——— 1976a. "Estimation in Nonlinear Simultaneous Equation Models." Paper presented at and published by Institut National de la Statistique et des Etudes Economiques, Paris. Published in French: E. Malinvaud, ed., *Cahiers du sêminaire d'econometrie,* no. 19, 1978.

——— 1976b. "The Maximum Likelihood, the Minimum Chi-Square and the Nonlinear Weighted Least-Squares in the General Qualitative Response Model." *Journal of the American Statistical Association* 71:347–351.

——— 1977a. "The Maximum Likelihood and the Nonlinear Three-Stage Least Squares Estimator in the General Nonlinear Simultaneous Equation Model." *Econometrica* 45:955–968.

——— 1977b. "A Note on a Heteroscedastic Model." *Journal of Econometrics* 6:365–370.

——— 1977c. "The Modified Second-Round Estimator in the General Qualitative Response Model." *Journal of Econometrics.* 5:295–299.

——— 1978a. "Corrigenda: A Note on a Heteroscedastic Model." *Journal of Econometrics* 8:265.

——— 1978b. "A Note on a Random Coefficients Model." *International Economic Review* 19:793–796.

——— 1978c. "The Estimation of a Simultaneous Equation Generalized Probit Model." *Econometrica* 46:1193–1205.

——— 1979. "The Estimation of a Simultaneous-Equation Tobit Model." *International Economic Review* 20:169–181.
——— 1980a. "Selection of Regressors." *International Economic Review* 21:331–345.
——— 1980b. "The n^{-2}-order Mean Squared Errors of the Maximum Likelihood and the Minimum Logit Chi-Square Estimator." *Annals of Statistics* 8:488–505.
——— 1981. "Qualitative Response Models: A Survey." *Journal of Economic Literature* 19:1483–1536.
——— 1982a. "Two Stage Least Absolute Deviations Estimators." *Econometrica* 50:689–711.
——— 1982b. "Correction to a Lemma." *Econometrica* 50:1325–1328.
——— 1983a. "Non-Linear Regression Models," in Z. Griliches and M. D. Intrilligator, eds., *Handbook of Econometrics,* 1:333–389. Amsterdam: North-Holland Publishing.
——— 1983b. "A Comparison of the Amemiya GLS and the Lee-Maddala-Trost G2SLS in a Simultaneous-Equations Tobit Model." *Journal of Econometrics* 23:295–300.
——— 1983c. "Partially Generalized Least Squares and Two-Stage Least Squares Estimators." *Journal of Econometrics.* 23:275–283.
——— 1984a. "Tobit Models: A Survey." *Journal of Econometrics* 24:3–61.
——— 1984b. "Correction." *Annals of Statistics* 12:783.
Amemiya, T., and M. Boskin. 1974. "Regression Analysis When the Dependent Variable Is Truncated Lognormal, with an Application to the Determinants of the Duration of Welfare Dependency." *International Economic Review* 15:485–496.
Amemiya, T., and W. A. Fuller. 1967. "A Comparative Study of Alternative Estimators in a Distributed-Lag Model." *Econometrica* 35:509–529.
Amemiya, T., and T. E. MaCurdy. 1983. "Instrumental Variable Estimation of an Error Components Model." Technical Report no. 414, Institute for Mathematical Studies in the Social Sciences, Stanford University, Calif. (Forthcoming in *Econometrica.*)
Amemiya, T., and K. Morimune. 1974. "Selecting the Optimal Order of Polynomial in the Almon Distributed Lag." *Review of Economics and Statistics* 56:378–386.
Amemiya, T., and J. L. Powell. 1981. "A Comparison of the Box-Cox Maximum Likelihood Estimator and the Non-Linear Two-Stage Least Squares Estimator." *Journal of Econometrics* 17:351–381.
——— 1983. "A Comparison of the Logit Model and Normal Discriminant Analysis When the Independent Variables Are Binary," in S. Karlin, T. Amemiya, and L. A. Goodman, eds., *Studies in Econometric, Time Series, and Multivariate Statistics,* pp.3–30. New York: Academic Press.
Anderson, T. W. 1958. *Introduction to Multivariate Statistical Analysis.* New York: John Wiley & Sons.

——— 1969. "Statistical Inference for Covariance Matrices with Linear Structure," in P. R. Krishnaiah, ed., *Proceedings of the Second International Symposium on Multivariate Analysis,* pp. 55–66. New York: Academic Press.

——— 1971. *The Statistical Analysis of Time Series.* New York: John Wiley and Sons.

——— 1974."An Asymptotic Expansion of the Distribution of the Limited Information Maximum Likelihood Estimate of a Coefficient in a Simultaneous Equation System." *Journal of the American Statistical Association* 60:565–573.

——— 1982. "Some Recent Developments of the Distributions of Single-Equation Estimators," in W. Hildenbrand, ed., *Advances in Econometrics* pp. 109–122. Cambridge: Cambridge Univerity Press.

Anderson, T. W., and L. A. Goodman. 1957. "Statistical Inference about Markov Chains." *Annals of Mathematical Statistics* 28:89–110.

Anderson, T. W., and C. Hsiao. 1981. "Estimation of Dynamic Models with Error Components." *Journal of the American Statistical Association* 76:598–606.

——— 1982. "Formulation and Estimation of Dynamic Models Using Panel Data." *Journal of Econometrics* 18:47–82.

Anderson, T. W., and H. Rubin. 1949. "Estimator of the Parameters of a Single Equation in a Complete System of Stochastic Equations." *Annals of Mathematical Statistics* 20:46–63.

Anderson, T. W., and T. Sawa. 1973. "Distributions of Estimates of Coefficients of a Single Equation in a Simultaneous System and Their Asymptotic Expansions." *Econometrica* 41:683–714.

Andrews, D. F. 1974. "A Robust Method for Multiple Linear Regression." *Technometrics* 16:523–531.

Andrews, D. F., P. J. Bickel, F. R. Hampel, P. J. Huber, W. H. Rogers, and J. W. Tukey. 1972. *Robust Estimates of Location.* Princeton: Princeton University Press.

Anscombe, F. J. (1961). "Examination of Residuals," in J. Neyman, ed., *Proceedings of the Fourth Berkeley Symposium on Mathematical Statistics and Probability,* 1:1–36. Berkeley: University of California Press.

Apostol, T. M. 1974. *Mathematical Analysis,* 2nd ed. Reading, Mass.: Addison-Wesley.

Arabmazar, A., and P. Schmidt. 1981. "Further Evidence on the Robustness of the Tobit Estimator to Heteroscedasticity." *Journal of Econometrics* 17:253–258.

——— 1982. "An Investigation of the Robustness of the Tobit Estimator to Non-Normality." *Econometrica* 50:1055–1063.

Arrow, K. J., H. B. Chenery, B. S. Minhas, and R. M. Solow. 1961. "Capital-Labor Substitution and Economic Efficiency." *Review of Economics and Statistics* 43:225–250.

Ashenfelter, O., and J. Ham. 1979. "Education, Unemployment, and Earnings." *Journal of Political Economy* 87:S99–S116.

Ashford, J. R., and R. R. Sowden. 1970. "Multivariate Probit Analysis." *Biometrics* 26:535–546.

Baldwin, R. E. 1971. "Determinants of the Commodity Structure of U.S. Trade." *American Economic Review* 61:126–146.

Balestra, P., and M. Nerlove. 1966. "Pooling Cross-Section and Time Series Data in the Estimation of a Dynamic Model: The Demand for Natural Gas." *Econometrica* 34:585–612.

Baltagi, B. H. 1981. "Pooling: An Experimental Study of Alternative Testing and Estimation Procedures in a Two-Way Error Component Model." *Journal of Econometrics* 17:21–49.

Baranchik, A. J. 1970. "A Family of Minimax Estimators of the Mean of a Multivariate Normal Distribution." *Annals of Mathematical Statistics* 41:642–645.

Barankin, E. W., and J. Gurland. 1951. "On Asymptotically Normal Efficient Estimators: I." *University of California Publications in Statistics* 1:86–130.

Bartholomew, D. J. 1982. *Stochastic Models for Social Processes,* 3rd ed. New York: John Wiley & Sons.

Basmann, R. L. 1957. "A Generalized Classical Method of Linear Estimation of Coefficients in a Structural Equation." *Econometrica* 25:77–83.

Bassett, G., Jr., and R. Koenker. 1978. "Asymptotic Theory of Least Absolute Error Regression." *Journal of the American Statistical Association* 73:618–622.

Beach, C. M., and J. G. MacKinnon. 1978. "A Maximum Likelihood Procedure for Regression with Auto-correlated Errors," *Econometrica* 46:51–58.

Bellman, R. 1970. *Introduction to Matrix Analysis,* 2d ed. New York: McGraw-Hill.

Belsley, D. A. 1979. "On the Computational Competitiveness of Full-Information Maximum-Likelihood and Three-Stage Least-Squares in the Estimation of Nonlinear Simultaneous-Equations Models." *Journal of Econometrics* 9:315–342.

Benus, J., J. Kmenta, and H. Shapiro. 1976. "The Dynamics of Household Budget Allocation to Food Expenditures." *Review of Economics and Statistics* 58:129–138.

Bera, A. K., C. M. Jarque, and L. F. Lee. 1982. "Testing for the Normality Assumption in Limited Dependent Variable Models." Mimeographed paper, Department of Economics, University of Minnesota.

Berger, J. O. 1975. "Minimax Estimation of Location Vectors for a Wide Class of Densities." *Annals of Statistics* 3:1318–1328.

——— 1976. "Admissible Minimax Estimation of a Multivariate Normal Mean with Arbitrary Quadratic Loss." *Annals of Statistics* 4:223–226.

Berkson, J. 1944. "Application of the Logistic Function to Bio-Assay." *Journal of the American Statistical Association* 39:357–365.

——— 1955. "Maximum Likelihood and Minimum χ^2 Estimates of the Logistic Function." *Journal of the American Statistical Association* 50:130–162.

——— 1957. "Tables for Use in Estimating the Normal Distribution Function by Normit Analysis." *Biometrika* 44:411–435.

——— 1980. "Minimum Chi-Square, Not Maximum Likelihood!" *Annals of Statistics* 8:457–487.

Berndt, E. R., B. H. Hall, R. E. Hall, and J. A. Hausman. 1974. "Estimation and Inference in Nonlinear Structural Models." *Annals of Economic and Social Measurement* 3:653–666.

Berndt, E. R., and N. E. Savin. 1977. "Conflict among Criteria for Testing Hypotheses in the Multivariate Linear Regression Model." *Econometrica* 45:1263–1278.

Berzeg, K. 1979. "The Error Components Model: Conditions for the Existence of the Maximum Likelihood Estimates." *Journal of Econometrics* 10:99–102.

Bhattacharya, P. K. 1966. "Estimating the Mean of a Multivariate Normal Population with General Quadratic Loss Function." *Annals of Mathematical Statistics* 32:1819–1824.

Bhattacharya, R. N., and R. R. Rao. 1976. *Normal Approximation and Asymptotic Expansions.* New York: John Wiley & Sons.

Bianchi, C., and G. Calzolari. 1980. "The One-Period Forecast Error in Nonlinear Econometric Models." *International Economic Review* 21:201–208.

Bickel, P. J. 1975. "One-Step Huber Estimation in the Linear Model." *Journal of the American Statistical Association* 70:428–433.

——— 1978. "Using Residuals Robustly, I: Tests for Heteroscedasticity, Nonlinearity and Nonadditivity." *Annals of Statistics* 6:266–291.

Bickel, P. J., and K. A. Doksum. 1977. *Mathematical Statistics: Basic Ideas and Selected Topics.* San Francisco: Holden-Day.

Bishop, Y. M. M., S. E. Fienberg, and P. W. Holland. 1975. *Discrete Multivariate Analysis, Theory and Practice.* Cambridge, Mass.: MIT Press.

Blattberg, R., and T. Sargent. 1971. "Regression with Non-Gaussian Stable Disturbances: Some Sampling Results." *Econometrica* 39:501–510.

Blumen, I., M. Kogan, and P. J. McCarthy. 1955. *The Industrial Mobility of Labor as a Probability Process.* Ithaca, N.Y.: Cornell University Press.

Bock, M. E. 1975. "Minimax Estimators of the Mean of a Multivariate Distribution." *Annals of Statistics* 3:209–218.

Bodkin, R. G., and L. R. Klein. 1967. "Nonlinear Estimation of Aggregate Production Functions." *Review of Economics and Statistics* 49:28–44.

Borjas, G. J., and S. Rosen. 1980. "Income Prospects and Job Mobility of Young Men." *Research in Labor Economics* 3:159–181.

Boskin, M. J., and F. C. Nold. 1975. "A Markov Model of Turnover in Aid to Families with Dependent Children." *Journal of Human Resources* 10:476–481.

Box, G. E. P., and D. R. Cox. 1964. "An Analysis of Transformations." *Journal of the Royal Statistical Society* ser. B, 26:211–252 (with discussion).

Box, G. E. P., and G. M. Jenkins. 1976. *Time Series Analysis: Forecasting and Control,* rev. ed. San Francisco: Holden-Day.

Box, G. E. P., and G. C. Tiao. 1973. *Bayesian Inference in Statistical Analysis.* Reading, Mass.: Addison-Wesley.

Breusch, T. S. 1978. "Testing for Autocorrelation in Dynamic Linear Models." *Australian Economic Papers* 17:334–335.

Breusch, T. S., and A. R. Pagan. 1979. "A Simple Test for Heteroscedasticity and Random Coefficient Variation." *Econometrica* 47:1287–1294.

——— 1980. "The Lagrange Multiplier Test and Its Applications to Model Specification in Econometrics." *Review of Economic Studies* 47:239–253.

Brillinger, D. R. 1975. *Time Series: Data Analysis and Theory.* New York: Holt, Rinehart, and Winston.

Brook, R. J. 1976. "On the Use of a Regret Function to Set Significance Points in Prior Tests of Estimation." *Journal of the American Statistical Association* 71:126–131.

Brown, B. W. 1983. "The Identification Problem in Systems Nonlinear in the Variables." *Econometrica* 51:175–196.

Brown, B. W., and R. S. Mariano. 1982. "Residual-Based Stochastic Prediction in a Nonlinear Simultaneous System." Analysis Center, The Wharton School, University of Pennsylvania.

Brown, M., and D. Heien. 1972. "The S-Branch Utility Tree: A Generalization of the Linear Expenditure System." *Econometrica* 40:737–747.

Brown, P., and C. Payne. 1975. "Election Night Forecasting." *Journal of the Royal Statistical Society* ser. A, 138:463–498 (with discussion).

Brown, R. L., J. Durbin, and J. M. Evans. 1975. "Techniques for Testing the Constancy of Regression Relationships over Time." *Journal of the Royal Statistical Society* ser. B, 37:149–192 (with discussion).

Brown, W. G., and B. R. Beattie. 1975. "Improving Estimates of Economic Parameters by Use of Ridge Regression with Production Function Applications." *American Journal of Agricultural Economics* 57:21–32.

Brundy, J. M., and D. W. Jorgenson. 1974. "Consistent and Efficient Estimation of Systems of Simultaneous Equations by Means of Instrumental Variables," in P. Zarembka, ed., *Frontiers in Econometrics,* pp. 215–244. New York: Academic Press.

Buse, A. 1982. "Tests for Additive Heteroscedasticity: Some Monte Carlo Results." Research Paper no. 82-13, Department of Economics, University of Alberta.

Butler, J. S., and R. Moffitt. 1982. "A Computationally Efficient Quadrature Procedure for the One-Factor Multinomial Probit Model." *Econometrica* 50:761–764.

Carroll, R. J., and D. Ruppert. 1982a. "Robust Estimation in Heteroscedastic Linear Models." *Annals of Statistics* 10:429–441.

——— 1982b. "A Comparison between Maximum Likelihood and Generalized Least Squares in a Heteroscedastic Linear Model." *Journal of the American Statistical Association* 77:878–882.

Chamberlain, G. 1982. "Multivariate Regression Models for Panel Data." *Journal of Econometrics* 18:5–46.

Chamberlain, G., and Z. Griliches. 1975. "Unobservables with a Variance-Components Structure: Ability, Schooling and the Economic Success of Brothers." *International Economic Review* 16:422–429.

Champernowne, D. G. 1953. "A Model of Income Distribution." *Economic Journal* 63:318–351.

Charatsis, E. G. 1971. "A Computer Program for Estimation of the Constant Elasticity of Substitution Production Function." *Applied Statistics* 20:286–296.

Chow, G. C. 1960. "Tests for Equality between Sets of Coefficients in Two Linear Regressions." *Econometrica* 28:591–605.

——— 1968. "Two Methods of Computing Full-Information Maximum Likelihood Estimates in Simultaneous Stochastic Equations." *International Economic Review* 9:100–112.

——— 1973. "On the Computation of Full-Information Maximum Likelihood Estimates for Nonlinear Equation Systems." *Review of Economics and Statistics* 55:104–109.

Chow, G. C., and R. C. Fair. 1973. "Maximum Likelihood Estimation of Linear Equation Systems with Auto-Regressive Residuals." *Annals of Economic and Social Measurement* 2:17–28.

Christ, C. F. 1966. *Econometric Models and Methods.* New York: John Wiley & Sons.

Christensen, L. R., D. W. Jorgenson, and L. J. Lau. 1975. "Transcendental Logarithmic Utility Functions." *American Economic Review* 65:367–383.

Chung, C. F., and A. S. Goldberger. 1984. "Proportional Projections in Limited Dependent Variable Models." *Econometrica* 52:531–534.

Chung, K. L. 1974. *A Course in Probability Theory,* 2d ed. New York: Academic Press.

Clark, C. 1961. "The Greatest of a Finite Set of Random Variables." *Operations Research* 9:145–162.

Cochrane, D., and G. H. Orcutt. 1949. "Application of Least Squares Regression to Relationships Containing Autocorrelated Error Terms." *Journal of the American Statistical Association* 44:32–61.

Cooley, T. F., and E. C. Prescott. 1976. "Estimation in the Presence of Stochastic Parameter Variation." *Econometrica* 44:167–184.

Cooper, J. P. 1972. "Two Approaches to Polynomial Distributed Lags Estimation: An Expository Note and Comment." *The American Statistician* 26:32–35.

Cosslett, S. R. 1978. "Efficient Estimation of Discrete-Choice Models from Choice-Based Samples." Workshop in Transportation Economics, University of California, Berkeley.

——— 1981a. "Maximum Likelihood Estimator for Choice-Based Samples." *Econometrica* 49:1289–1316.

——— 1981b. 'Efficient Estimation of Discrete-Choice Models," in C. F. Manski and D. McFadden, eds., *Structural Analysis of Discrete Data with Econometric Applications,* pp. 51–111. Cambridge, Mass.: MIT Press.

——— 1983. "Distribution-Free Maximum Likelihood Estimator of the Binary Choice Model." *Econometrica* 51:765–782.

Cox, D. R. 1961. "Tests of Separate Families of Hypotheses," in J. Neyman, ed., *Proceedings of the Fourth Berkeley Symposium on Mathematical Statistics and Probability,* 1:105–123. Berkeley: University of California Press.

——— 1962. "Further Results on Tests of Separate Families of Hypotheses." *Journal of the Royal Statistical Society* ser. B, 24:406–424.

——— 1966. "Some Procedures Connected with the Logistic Qualitative Response Curve," in F. N. David, ed., *Research Papers in Statistics,* pp. 55–71. New York: John Wiley & Sons.

——— 1970. *Analysis of Binary Data.* London: Methuen.

——— 1972. "Regression Models and Life Tables." *Journal of the Royal Statistical Society* ser. B, 34:187–220 (with discussion).

——— 1975. "Partial Likelihood." *Biometrika* 62:269–276.

Cox, D. R., and D. V. Hinkley. 1974. *Theoretical Statistics.* London: Chapman and Hall.

Cragg, J. G. 1971. "Some Statistical Models for Limited Dependent Variables with Application to the Demand for Durable Goods." *Econometrica* 39:829–844.

Cramér, H. 1946. *Mathematical Methods of Statistics.* Princeton: Princeton University Press.

Crowder, M. J. 1980. "On the Asymptotic Properties of Least-Squares Estimators in Autoregression." *Annals of Statistics* 8:132–146.

Dagenais, M. G. 1978. "The Computation of FIML Estimates as Iterative Generalized Least Squares Estimates in Linear and Nonlinear Simultaneous Equations Models." *Econometrica* 46:1351–1362.

David, J. M., and W. E. Legg. 1975. "An Application of Multivariate Probit Analysis to the Demand for Housing: A Contribution to the Improvement of the Predictive Performance of Demand Theory, Preliminary Results." *American Statistical Association Proceedings of the Business and Economics and Statistics Section,* pp. 295–300.

Davidson, W. C. 1959. "Variable Metric Method for Minimization." Atomic Energy Commission, Research Development Report ANL-5990, Washington, D.C.

Davis, L. 1984. "Comments on a Paper by T. Amemiya on Estimation in a Dichotomous Logit Regression Model." *Annals of Statistics* 12:778–782.

Deacon, R., and P. Shapiro. 1975. "Private Preference for Collective Goods Revealed through Voting and Referenda." *American Economic Review* 65:943–955.

Dempster, A. P., N. M. Laird, and D. B. Rubin. 1977. "Maximum Likelihood from Incomplete Data via the EM Algorithm." *Journal of the Royal Statistical Society* ser. B, 39:1–38 (with discussion).

Dempster, A. P., M. Schatzoff, and N. Wermuth. 1977. "A Simulation Study of Alternatives to Ordinary Least Squares." *Journal of the American Statistical Association* 72:77–111 (with discussion).

Dent, W. T., and C. Hildreth. 1977. "Maximum Likelihood Estimation in Random Coefficient Models." *Journal of the American Statistical Association* 72:69–72.

Dhrymes, P. J. 1971. *Distributed Lags: Problems of Estimation and Formulation.* San Francisco: Holden-Day.

Diewert, W. E. 1974. "Applications of Duality Theory," in M. D. Intrilligator and D. A. Kendrick, eds., *Frontiers of Quantitative Economics,* 2:106–171. Amsterdam: North-Holland Publishing.

Domencich, T. A., and D. McFadden. 1975. *Urban Travel Demand.* Amsterdam: North-Holland Publishing.

Doob, J. L. 1953. *Stochastic Processes.* New York: John Wiley & Sons.

Draper, N. R., and D. R. Cox. 1969. "On Distributions and Their Transformation to Normality." *Journal of the Royal Statistical Society* ser. B, 31:472–476.

Draper, N. R., and H. Smith. 1981. *Applied Regression Analysis,* 2d ed. New York: John Wiley & Sons.

Draper, N. R., and R. C. Van Nostrand. 1979. "Ridge Regression and James-Stein Estimation: Review and Comments." *Technometrics* 21:451–466.

Dubin, J. A., and D. McFadden. 1984. "An Econometric Analysis of Residential Electric Appliance Holdings and Consumption." *Econometrica* 52:345–362.

Dudley, L., and C. Montmarquette. 1976. "A Model of the Supply of Bilateral Foreign Aid." *American Economic Review* 66:132–142.

Duncan, G. M. 1980. "Formulation and Statistical Analysis of the Mixed, Continuous/Discrete Dependent Variable Model in Classical Production Theory." *Econometrica* 48:839–852.

Duncan, G. T., and L. G. Lin. 1972. "Inference for Markov Chains Having Stochastic Entry and Exit." *Journal of the American Statistical Association* 67:761–767.

Durbin, J. 1960. "Estimation of Parameters in Time-Series Regression Models." *Journal of the Royal Statistical Society* ser. B, 22:139–153.

——— 1963. "Maximum-Likelihood Estimation of the Parameters of a System of Simultaneous Regression Equations." Paper presented at the Copenhagen Meeting of the Econometric Society.

——— 1970. "Testing for Serial Correlation in Least-Squares Regression When Some of the Regressors Are Lagged Dependent." *Econometrica* 38:410–421.

Durbin, J., and G. S. Watson. 1950. "Testing for Serial Correlation in Least Squares Regression, I." *Biometrika* 37:409–428.

——— 1951. "Testing for Serial Correlation in Least Squares Regression, II." *Biometrika* 38:159–178.

——— 1971. "Testing for Serial Correlation in Least Squares Regression, III." *Biometrika* 58:1–19.

Efron, B. 1975. "The Efficiency of Logistic Regression Compared to Normal Discriminant Analysis." *Journal of the American Statistical Association* 70:892–898.

——— 1977. "The Efficiency of Cox's Likelihood Function for Censored Data." *Journal of the American Statistical Association* 72:557–565.

——— 1982. *The Jackknife, the Bootstrap, and Other Resampling Plans.* Philadelphia: Society for Industrial and Applied Mathematics.

Efron, B., and C. Morris. 1972. "Limiting the Risk of Bayes and Empirical Bayes Estimators—Part II: The Empirical Bayes Case." *Journal of the American Statistical Association* 67:130–139.

——— 1973. "Stein's Estimation Rule and Its Competitors—An Empirical Bayes Approach." *Journal of the American Statistical Association* 68:117–130.

——— 1975. "Data Analysis Using Stein's Estimator and Its Generalizations." *Journal of the American Statistical Association* 70:311–319.

——— 1976. "Families of Minimax Estimators of the Mean of a Multivariate Normal Distribution." *Annals of Statistics* 4:11–21.

Ehrlich, I. 1977. "Capital Punishment and Deterrence: Some Further Thoughts and Additional Evidence." *Journal of Political Economy* 85:741–788.

Eicker, F. 1963. "Asymptotic Normality and Consistency of the Least Squares Estimators for Families of Linear Regressions." *Annals of Mathematical Statistics* 34:447–456.

Eisenpress, H., and J. Greenstadt. 1966. "The Estimation of Nonlinear Econometric Systems." *Econometrica* 34:851–861.

Engle, R. F. 1984. "Wald, Likelihood Ratio, and Lagrange Multiplier Tests in Econometrics," in Z. Griliches and M. D. Intrilligator, eds., *Handbook of Econometrics,* 2:775–826. Amsterdam: North-Holland Publishing.

Fair, R. C. 1974. "On the Robust Estimation of Econometric Models." *Annals of Economic and Social Measurement* 3:667–677.

——— 1976. *A Model of Macroeconomic Activity.* Vol. 2, *The Empirical Model.* Cambridge, Mass.: Ballinger.

——— 1978. "A Theory of Extramarital Affairs." *Journal of Political Economy* 86:45–61.

Fair, R. C., and D. M. Jaffee. 1972. "Methods of Estimation for Markets in Disequilibrium." *Econometrica* 40:497–514.

Fair, R. C., and W. R. Parke. 1980. "Full-Information Estimates of a Nonlinear Macroeconometric Model." *Journal of Econometrics* 13:269–291.

Farebrother, R. W. 1975. "Minimax Regret Significance Points for a Preliminary Test in Regression Analysis." *Econometrica* 43:1005–1006.

——— 1980. "The Durbin-Watson Test for Serial Correlation When There Is No Intercept in the Regression." *Econometrica* 48:1553–1563.

Feller, W. 1961. *An Introduction to Probability Theory and Its Applications,* vol. I, 2d ed. New York: John Wiley & Sons.

Ferguson, T. S. 1958. "A Method of Generating Best Asymptotically Normal Estimates with Application to the Estimation of Bacterial Densities." *Annals of Mathematical Statistics* 29:1046–1062.

Fisher, F. M. 1966. *The Identification Problem in Econometrics.* New York: McGraw-Hill.

——— 1970. "A Correspondence Principle for Simultaneous Equation Models." *Econometrica* 38:73–92.

Fletcher, R., and M. J. D. Powell. 1963. "A Rapidly Convergent Descent Method for Minimization." *Computer Journal* 6:163–168.

Flinn, C. J., and J. J. Heckman. 1982. "Models for the Analysis of Labor Force Dynamics." *Advances in Econometrics* 1:35–95.

Fomby, T. B., R. C. Hill, and S. R. Johnson. 1978. "An Optimal Property of Principal Components in the Context of Restricted Least Squares." *Journal of the American Statistical Association* 73:191–193.

Forsythe, A. B. 1972. "Robust Estimation of Straight Line Regression Coefficients by Minimizing *p*-th Power Deviations." *Technometrics* 14:159–166.

Freund, J. F. 1971. *Mathematical Statistics,* 2d ed. Englewood Cliffs, N.J.: Prentice-Hall.

Froehlich, B. R. 1973. "Some Estimates for a Random Coefficient Regression Model." *Journal of the American Statistical Association.* 68:329–335.

Fuller, W. A. 1976. *Introduction to Statistical Time Series.* New York: John Wiley & Sons.

——— 1977. "Some Properties of a Modification of the Limited Information Estimator." *Econometrica* 45:939–953.

Fuller, W. A., and G. E. Battese. 1974. "Estimation of Linear Models with Crossed-Error Structure." *Journal of Econometrics* 2:67–78.

Gallant, A. R. 1975a. "Nonlinear Regression." *The American Statistician* 29:73–81.

——— 1975b. "Testing a Subset of the Parameters of a Nonlinear Regression Model." *Journal of the American Statistical Association* 70:927–932.

——— 1977. "Three-Stage Least-Squares Estimation for a System of Simultaneous, Nonlinear, Implicit Equations." *Journal of Econometrics* 5:71–88.

Gallant, A. R., and A. Holly. 1980. "Statistical Inference in an Implicit, Nonlinear, Simultaneous Equation Model in the Context of Maximum Likelihood Estimation." *Econometrica* 48:697–720.

Gallant, A. R., and D. W. Jorgenson. 1979. "Statistical Inference for a System of Simultaneous, Nonlinear, Implicit Equations in the Context of Instrumental Variable Estimation." *Journal of Econometrics* 11:275–302.

Gastwirth, J. L. 1966. "On Robust Procedures." *Journal of the American Statistical Association* 65:946–973.

Gaver, K. M., and M. S. Geisel. 1974. "Discriminating Among Alternative Models: Bayesian and Non-Bayesian Methods," in P. Zarembka, ed., *Frontiers in Econometrics.* pp. 49–80. New York: Academic Press.

Ghosh, J. K., and B. K. Sinha. 1981. "A Necessary and Sufficient Condition for Second Order Admissibility with Applications to Berkson's Bioassay Problem." *Annals of Statistics* 9:1334–1338.

Ghosh, J. K., and K. Subramanyam. 1974. "Second-Order Efficiency of Maximum Likelihood Estimators." *Sankhya* ser. A, 36:325–358.

Gnedenko, B. V., and A. N. Kolmogorov. 1954. *Limit Distributions for Sums of Independent Random Variables.* Reading, Mass.: Addison-Wesley.

Godfrey, L. G. 1978. "Testing Against General Autoregressive and Moving Average Error Models When the Regressors Include Lagged Dependent Variables." *Econometrica* 46:1293–1302.

Goldberg, S. 1958. *Introduction to Difference Equations.* New York: John Wiley & Sons.

Goldberger, A. S. 1964. *Econometric Theory.* New York: John Wiley & Sons.

——— 1981. "Linear Regression After Selection." *Journal of Econometrics* 15:357–366.

——— 1983. "Abnormal Selection Bias," in S. Karlin, T. Amemiya, and L. A. Goodman, eds., *Studies in Econometrics, Time Series, and Multivariate Statistics,* pp. 67–84. New York: Academic Press.

Goldfeld, S. M., and R. E. Quandt. 1965. "Some Tests for Homoscedasticity." *Journal of the American Statistical Association* 60:539–547.

——— 1968. "Nonlinear Simultaneous Equations: Estimation and Prediction." *International Economic Review* 9:113–136.

——— 1972. *Nonlinear Methods in Econometrics.* Amsterdam: North-Holland Publishing.

——— 1978. "Asymptotic Tests for the Constancy of Regressions in the Heteroscedastic Case." Research Memorandum no. 229, Econometric Research Program, Princeton University.

Goldfeld, S. M., R. E. Quandt, and H. F. Trotter. 1966. "Maximization by Quadratic Hill-Climbing." *Econometrica* 34:541–551.

Goodman, L. A. 1961. "Statistical Methods for the 'Mover-Stayer' Model." *Journal of the American Statistical Association* 56:841–868.

——— 1972. "A Modified Multiple Regression Approach to the Analysis of Dichotomous Variables." *American Sociological Review* 37:28–46.

Gourieroux, C., J. J. Laffont, and A. Monfort. 1980. "Coherency Conditions in Simultaneous Linear Equation Models with Endogenous Switching Regimes." *Econometrica* 48:675–695.

Gourieroux, C., and A. Monfort. 1981. "Asymptotic Properties of the Maximum Likelihood Estimator in Dichotomous Logit Models." *Journal of Econometrics* 17:83–97.

Gradshteyn, I. S., and I. M. Ryzhik. 1965. *Table of Integrals, Series, and Products.* New York: Academic Press.

Granger, C. W. J., and P. Newbold. 1977. *Forecasting Economic Time Series.* New York: Academic Press.

Greene, W. H. 1981. "On the Asymptotic Bias of the Ordinary Least Squares Estimator of the Tobit Model." *Econometrica* 49:505–513.

——— 1983. "Estimation of Limited Dependent Variable Models by Ordinary Least Squares and the Method of Moments." *Journal of Econometrics* 21:195–212.

Grenander, U., and G. Szego. 1958. *Toeplitz Forms and Their Applications.* Berkeley: University of California Press.

Griliches, Z. 1967. "Distributed Lags: A Survey." *Econometrica* 35:16–49.

Gronau, R. 1973. "The Effects of Children on the Housewife's Value of Time." *Journal of Political Economy* 81:S168–S199.

——— 1974. "Wage Comparisons—a Selectivity Bias." *Journal of Political Economy* 82:1119–1143.

Guilkey, D. K., and P. Schmidt. 1979. "Some Small Sample Properties of Estimators and Test Statistics in the Multivariate Logit Model." *Journal of Econometrics* 10:33–42.

Gumbel, E. J. 1961. "Bivariate Logistic Distributions." *Journal of the American Statistical Association* 56:335–349.

Gunst, R. F., and R. L. Mason. 1977. "Biased Estimation in Regression: An Evaluation Using Mean Squared Error." *Journal of the American Statistical Association* 72:616–628.

Gurland, J., I. Lee, and P. A. Dahm. 1960. "Polychotomous Quantal Response in Biological Asssay." *Biometrics* 16:382–398.

Haberman, S. J. 1978. *Analysis of Qualitative Data.* Vol. 1, *Introductory Topics.* New York: Academic Press.

——— 1979. *Analysis of Qualitative Data.* Vol. 2, *New Developments.* New York: Academic Press.

Haessel, W. 1976. "Demand for Agricultural Commodities in Ghana: An Application of Nonlinear Two-Stage Least Squares with Prior Information." *American Journal of Agricultural Economics* 58:341–345.

Halmos, D. R. 1950. *Measure Theory.* Princeton: D. Van Nostrand.

Hammerstrom, T. 1981. "Asymptotically Optimal Tests for Heteroscedasticity in the General Linear Model." *Annals of Statistics* 9:368–380.

Han, A. K. 1983. "Asymptotic Efficiency of the Partial Likelihood Estimator in the Proportional Hazard Model." Technical Report no. 412, Institute for Mathematical Studies in the Social Sciences, Stanford University, Calif.

Hartley, H. O. 1958. "Maximum Likelihood Estimation from Incomplete Data." *Biometrics* 14:174–194.

——— 1961. "The Modified Gauss-Newton Method for the Fitting of Non-Linear Regression Functions by Least Squares." *Technometrics* 3:269–280.

Hartley, M. J. 1976a. "The Estimation of Markets in Disequilibrium: The Fixed Supply Case." *International Economic Review* 17:687–699.

——— 1976b. "Estimation of the Tobit Model by Nonlinear Least Squares Methods." Discussion Paper no. 373, State University of New York, Buffalo.

——— 1976c. "The Tobit and Probit Models: Maximum Likelihood Estimation by Ordinary Least Squares." Discussion Paper no. 374, State University of New York, Buffalo.

Harvey, A. C. 1976. "Estimating Regression Models with Multiplicative Heteroscedasticity." *Econometrica* 44:461–465.

——— 1978. "The Estimation of Time-Varying Parameters from Panel Data." *Annales de l'insee* 30–31:203–226.

——— 1981a. *The Econometric Analysis of Time Series.* Oxford: Philip Allan Publishers.

——— 1981b. *Time Series Models.* Oxford: Philip Allan Publishers.

Hatanaka, M. 1974. "An Efficient Two-Step Estimator for the Dynamic Adjustment Model with Autoregressive Errors." *Journal of Econometrics* 2:199–220.

——— 1978. "On the Efficient Estimation Methods for the Macro-Economic Models Nonlinear in Variables." *Journal of Econometrics* 8:323–356.

Hause, J. C. 1980. "The Fine Structure of Earnings and On-the-Job Training Hypothesis." *Econometrica* 48:1013–1029.

Hausman, J. A. 1975. "An Instrumental Variable Approach to Full Information Estimators for Linear and Certain Nonlinear Econometric Models." *Econometrica* 43:727–738.

——— 1978. "Specification Tests in Econometrics." *Econometrica* 46:1251–1272.

Hausman, J. A., and D. McFadden. 1984. "Specification Tests for the Multinomial Logit Model." *Econometrica* 52:1219–1240.

Hausman, J. A., and W. E. Taylor. 1981. "Panel Data and Unobservable Individual Effects." *Econometrica* 49:1377–1398.

Hausman, J. A., and D. A. Wise. 1976. "The Evaluation of Results from Truncated Samples: The New Jersey Income Maintenance Experiment." *Annals of Economic and Social Measurement* 5:421–445.

——— 1977. "Social Experimentation, Truncated Distributions, and Efficient Estimation." *Econometrica* 45:919–938.

——— 1978. "A Conditional Probit Model for Qualitative Choice: Discrete Decisions Recognizing Interdependence and Heterogeneous Preferences." *Econometrica* 46:403–426.

——— 1979. "Attrition Bias in Experimental and Panel Data: The Gary Income Maintenance Experiment." *Econometrica* 47:455–473.

Heckman, J. J. 1974. "Shadow Prices, Market Wages, and Labor Supply." *Econometrica* 42:679–693.

——— 1976a. "The Common Structure of Statistical Models of Truncation, Sample Selection and Limited Dependent Variables and a Simple Estimator for Such Models." *Annals of Economic and Social Measurement* 5:475–492.

——— 1976b. "Simultaneous Equations Models with Continuous and Discrete Endogenous Variables and Structural Shifts," in S. M. Goldfeld and R. E. Quandt, eds., *Studies in Nonlinear Estimation,* pp. 235–272. Cambridge, Mass.: Ballinger Publishing.

——— 1978. "Dummy Endogenous Variables in a Simultaneous Equation System." *Econometrica* 46:931–960.

——— 1979. "Sample Selection Bias as a Specification Error." *Econometrica* 47:153–161.

——— 1981a. "Statistical Models for Discrete Panel Data," in C. F. Manski and D. McFadden, eds., *Structural Analysis of Discrete Data with Econometric Applications,* pp. 114–178. Cambridge, Mass.: MIT Press.

——— 1981b. "The Incidental Parameters Problem and the Problem of Initial Conditions in Estimating a Discrete Time—Discrete Data Stochastic Process," in C. F. Manski and D. McFadden, eds., *Structural Analysis of Discrete Data with Econometric Applications,* pp. 179–195. Cambridge, Mass.: MIT Press.

——— 1981c. "Heterogeneity and State Dependence," in S. Rosen, ed., *Studies in Labor Markets,* pp. 91–139. Cambridge, Mass.: National Bureau of Economic Reseach.

Heckman, J. J., and G. J. Borjas. 1980. "Does Unemployment Cause Future Unemployment? Definitions, Questions and Answers from a Continuous Time Model of Heterogeneity and State Dependence." *Economica* 47:247–283.

Heckman, J. J., and T. E. MaCurdy. 1980. "A Life Cycle Model of Female Labor Supply." *Review of Economic Studies* 47:47–74.

Heckman, J. J., and S. Polachek. 1974. "Empirical Evidence on the Functional Form of the Earnings-Schooling Relationship." *Journal of the American Statistical Association* 69:350–354.

Heckman, J. J., and B. Singer. 1982. "The Identification Problem in Econometric Models for Duration Data," in W. Hildenbrand, ed., *Advances in Econometrics,* pp. 39–77. Cambridge: Cambridge University Press.

——— 1984a. "A Method for Minimizing the Impact of Distributional Assumptions in Econometric Models for Duration Data." *Econometrica* 52:271–320.

——— 1984b. "Econometric Duration Analysis." *Journal of Econometrics* 24:63–132.

Heckman, J. J., and R. J. Willis. 1977. "A Beta-Logistic Model for the Analysis of Sequential Labor Force Participation by Married Women." *Journal of Political Economy* 85:27–58.

Hettmansperger, T. P., and J. W. McKean. 1977. "A Robust Alternative Based on Ranks to Least Squares in Analyzing Linear Models." *Technometrics* 19:275–284.

Hildreth, C., and J. P. Houck. 1968. "Some Estimators for a Linear Model with Random Coefficients." *Journal of the American Statistical Association* 63:584–595.

Hill, R. W., and P. W. Holland. 1977. "Two Robust Alternatives to Least-Squares Regression." *Journal of the American Statistical Association* 72:1041–1067.

Hinkley, D. V. 1971. "Inference in Two-Phase Regression." *Journal of the American Statistical Association* 66:736–743.

——— 1975. "On Power Transformations to Symmetry." *Biometrika* 62:101–112.

Hoadley, B. 1971. "Asymptotic Properties of Maximum Likelihood Estimators for the Independent Not Identically Distributed Case." *Annals of Mathematical Statistics* 42:1977–1991.

Hodges, J. L., and E. L. Lehmann. 1950. "Some Problems in Minimax Point Estimation." *Annals of Mathematical Statistics* 21:182–197.

——— 1963. "Estimates of Location Based on Rank Tests." *Annals of Mathematical Statistics* 34:598–611.

Hoel, P. G. 1971. *Introduction to Mathematical Statistics,* 4th ed. New York: John Wiley & Sons.

Hoerl, A. E., and R. W. Kennard. 1970a. "Ridge Regression: Biased Estimation for Nonorthogonal Problems." *Technometrics* 12:55–67.

——— 1970b. "Ridge Regression: Applications to Nonorthogonal Problems." *Technometrics* 12:69–82.

Hoerl, A. E., R. W. Kennard, and K. F. Baldwin. 1975. "Ridge Regression: Some Simulations." *Communications in Statistics* 4:105–123.

Hogg, R. V. 1974. "Adaptive Robust Procedures: A Partial Review and Some Suggestions for Future Applications and Theory." *Journal of the American Statistical Association* 69:909–923.

Holford, T. R. 1980. "The Analysis of Rates and of Survivorship Using Log-Linear Models." *Biometrics* 36:299–305.

Horowitz, J. L., J. M. Sparmann, and C. F. Daganzo. 1982. "An Investigation of the Accuracy of the Clark Approximation for the Multinomial Probit Model." *Transportation Science* 16:382–401.

Hosek, J. R. 1980. "Determinants of Family Participation in the AFDC-Unemployed Fathers Program." *Review of Economics and Statistics* 62:466–470.

Howe, H., R. A. Pollack, and T. J. Wales. 1979. "Theory and Time Series Estimation of the Quadratic Expenditure System." *Econometrica* 47:1231–1248.

Hsiao, C. 1974. "Statistical Inference for a Model with Both Random Cross-Sectional and Time Effects." *International Economic Review* 15:12–30.

——— 1975. "Some Estimation Methods for a Random Coefficient Model." *Econometrica* 43:305–325.

——— 1983. "Identification," in Z. Griliches and M. D. Intrilligator, eds., *Handbook of Econometrics* 1:223–283. Amsterdam: North-Holland Publishing.

Hsieh, D., C. F. Manski, and D. McFadden. 1983. "Estimation of Response Probabilities from Augmented Retrospective Observations." Mimeographed Paper, Department of Economics, Massachusetts Institute of Technology, Cambridge, Mass.

Huang, D. S. 1964. "Discrete Stock Adjustment: The Case of Demand for Automobiles." *International Economic Review* 5:46–62.

Huber, P. J. 1964. "Robust Estimation of a Location Parameter." *Annals of Mathematical Statistics* 35:73–101.

——— 1965. "The Behavior of Maximum Likelihood Estimates under Nonstandard Conditions," in J. Neyman, ed., *Proceedings of the Fifth Berkeley Symposium,* 1:221–233. Berkeley: University of California Press.

——— 1972. "Robust Statistics: A Review." *Annals of Mathematical Statistics* 43:1041–1067.

——— 1977. *Robust Statistical Procedures.* Philadelphia: Society for Industrial and Applied Mathematics.

——— 1981. *Robust Statistics.* New York: John Wiley & Sons.

Hurd, M. 1979. "Estimation in Truncated Samples When There Is Heteroscedasticity." *Journal of Econometrics* 11:247–258.

Imhof, J. P. 1961. "Computing the Distribution of Quadratic Forms in Normal Variables." *Biometrika* 48:419–426.

Jaeckel, L. A. 1972. "Estimating Regression Coefficients by Minimizing the Dispersion of the Residuals." *Annals of Mathematical Statistics* 43:1449–1458.

James, W., and C. Stein. 1961. "Estimation with Quadratic Loss," in J. Neyman, ed., *Proceedings of the Fourth Berkeley Symposium on Mathematical Statistics and Probability,* 1:361–379. Berkeley: University of California Press.

Jennrich, R. I. 1969. "Asymptotic Properties of Non-Linear Least Squares Estimators." *The Annals of Mathematical Statistics* 40:633–643.

Jobson, J. D., and W. A. Fuller. 1980. "Least Squares Estimation When the Covariance Matrix and Parameter Vector Are Functionally Related." *Journal of the American Statistical Association* 75:176–181.

Johnson, N. L., and S. Kotz. 1970a. *Continuous Univariate Distributions—1.* Boston: Houghton Mifflin.

——— 1970b. *Continuous Univariate Distributions—2.* Boston: Houghton Mifflin.

——— 1972. *Distributions in Statistics: Continuous Multivariate Distributions.* New York: John Wiley & Sons.

Johnston, J. 1972. *Econometric Methods.* 2d ed. New York: McGraw-Hill.

Joreskog, K. G., and D. Sorbom. 1976. *LISREL III Estimation of Structural Equation Systems by Maximum Likelihood Methods.* Chicago: National Educational Resources.

Jorgenson, D. W., and J. Laffont. 1974. "Efficient Estimation of Nonlinear Simultaneous Equations with Additive Disturbances." *Annals of Economic and Social Measurement* 3:615–640.

Jorgenson, D. W., and L. J. Lau. 1975. "The Structure of Consumer Preferences." *Annals of Economic and Social Measurement* 4:49–101.

——— 1978. "Testing the Integrability of Consumer Demand Functions, United States, 1947–1971." Mimeographed paper.

Judge, G. G., and M. E. Bock, 1983. "Biased Estimation," in Z. Griliches and M. D. Intrilligator, eds., *Handbook of Econometrics,* 1:599–649. Amsterdam: North-Holland Publishing.

Kahn, L. M., and K. Morimune. 1979. "Unions and Employment Stability: A Sequential Logit Approach." *International Economic Review* 20:217–236.

Kakwani, N. C. 1967. "The Unbiasedness of Zellner's Seemingly Unrelated Regression Equations Estimators." *Journal of the American Statistical Association* 62:141–142.

Kalbfleisch, J. D. 1974. "Some Efficiency Calculations for Survival Distributions." *Biometrika* 61:31–38.

Kalbfleisch, J. D., and R. L. Prentice. 1973. "Marginal Likelihoods Based On Cox's Regression and Life Models." *Biometrika* 60:267–278.

——— 1980. *The Statistical Analysis of Failure Time Data.* New York: John Wiley & Sons.

Kariya, T. 1981. "Bounds for the Covariance Matrices of Zellner's Estimator in the SUR Model and the 2SAE in a Heteroscedastic Model." *Journal of the American Statistical Asssociation* 76:975–979.

Kay, R. 1979. "Some Further Asymptotic Efficiency Calculations for Survival Data Regression Models." *Biometrika* 66:91–96.

Keeley, M. C., P. K. Robins, R. G. Spiegelman, and R. W. West. 1978. "The Estimation of Labor Supply Models Using Experimental Data." *American Economic Review* 68:873–887.

Kelejian, H. H. 1971. "Two-Stage Least Squares and Econometric Systems Linear in Parameters but Nonlinear in the Endogenous Variables." *Journal of the American Statistical Association* 66:373–374.

——— 1974. "Efficient Instrumental Variable Estimation of Large Scale Nonlinear Econometric Models." Mimeographed paper.

Kelejian, H. H., and S. W. Stephan. 1983. "Inference in Random Coefficient Panel Data Models: A Correction and Clarification of the Literature." *International Economic Review* 24:249–254.

Kendall, M. G., and A. Stuart. 1979. *The Advanced Theory of Statistics,* 4th ed., vol. 2. New York: Charles Griffin and Co.

Kenny, L. W., L. F. Lee, G. S. Maddala, and R. P. Trost. 1979. "Returns to College Education: An Investigation of Self-Selection Bias Based on the Project Talent Data." *International Economic Review* 20:775–789.

Kiefer, J., and J. Wolfowitz. 1956. "Consistency of the Maximum Likelihood Estimator in the Presence of Infinitely Many Incidental Parameters." *Annals of Mathematical Statistics* 27:887–906.

Koenker, R. 1981a. "Robust Methods in Econometrics." Bell Laboratories Economics Discussion Paper no. 228.

——— 1981b. "A Note on Studentizing a Test for Heteroscedasticity." *Journal of Econometrics* 17:107–112.

Koenker, R., and G. Bassett, Jr. 1978. "Regression Quantiles." *Econometrica* 46:33–50.

——— 1982. "Robust Tests for Heteroscedasticity Based on Regression Quantiles." *Econometrica* 50:43–61.

Koopmans, T. C., and W. C. Hood. 1953. "The Estimation of Simultaneous Linear Economic Relationships," in W. C. Hood and T. C. Koopmans, eds., *Studies in Econometric Method,* pp. 112–199. New York: John Wiley & Sons.

Kotlikoff, L. J. 1979. "Testing the Theory of Social Security and Life Cycle Accumulation." *American Economic Review* 69:396–410.

Koyck, L. M. 1954. *Distributed Lags and Investment Analysis.* Amsterdam: North-Holland Publishing.

Lachenbruch, P. A., C. Sneeringer, and L. T. Revo. 1973. "Robustness of the Linear and Quadratic Discriminant Function to Certain Types of Nonnormality." *Communications in Statistics* 1:39–56.

Lai, T. L., H. Robbins, and C. Z. Wei. 1978. "Strong Consistency of Least Squares Estimates in Multiple Regression." *Proceedings of the National Academy of Sciences* 75:3034–3036.

Lancaster, T. 1979. "Econometric Methods for the Duration of Unemployment." *Econometrica* 47:939–956.

LeCam, L. 1953. "On Some Asymptotic Properties of Maximum Likelihood Estimates and Related Bayes Estimates." *University of California Publications in Statistics* 1:277–330.

Lee, L. F. 1977. "Estimation of a Modal Choice Model for the Work Journey with Incomplete Observations." Mimeographed paper, Department of Economics, University of Minnesota.

——— 1978. "Unionism and Wage Rates: A Simultaneous Equations Model with Qualitative and Limited Dependent Variables." *International Economic Review* 19:415–433.

——— 1981. "Simultaneous Equations Models with Discrete and Censored Variables," in C. F. Manski and D. McFadden, eds., *Structural Analysis of Discrete Data with Econometric Applications,* pp. 346–364. Cambridge, Mass.: MIT Press.

——— 1982a. "Health and Wage: A Simultaneous Equation Model with Multiple Discrete Indicators." *International Economic Review* 23:199–221.

——— 1982b. "A Bivariate Logit Model." Mimeographed paper, Center for Econometrics and Decision Sciences, University of Florida.

——— 1982c. "Some Approaches to the Correction of Selectivity Bias." *Review of Economic Studies* 49:355–372.

Lee, L. F., G. S. Maddala, and R. P. Trost. 1980. "Asymptotic Covariance Matrices of Two-Stage Probit and Two-Stage Tobit Methods for Simultaneous Equations Models with Selectivity." *Econometrica* 48:491–503.

Lerman, S. R., and C. F. Manski. 1981. "On the Use of Simulated Frequencies to Approximate Choice Probabilities," in C. F. Manski and D. McFadden, eds., *Structural Analysis of Discrete Data with Econometric Applications,* pp. 305–319. Cambridge, Mass.: MIT Press.

Li, M. M. 1977. "A Logit Model of Homeownership." *Econometrica* 45:1081–1098.

Lillard, L. A., and Y. Weiss. 1979. "Components of Variation in Panel Earnings Data: American Scientists 1960–70." *Econometrica* 47:437–454.

Lillard, L. A., and R. Willis. 1978. "Dynamic Aspects of Earnings Mobility." *Econometrica* 46:985–1012.

Lindley, D. V. 1972. *Bayesian Statistics, A Review.* Philadephia: Society for Industrial and Applied Mathematics.

Loève, M. 1977. *Probability Theory,* 4th ed. Princeton: D. Van Nostrand.

McCall, J. J. 1971. "A Markovian Model of Income Dynamics." *Journal of the American Statistical Association* 66:439–447.

McFadden, D. 1974. "Conditional Logit Analysis of Qualitative Choice Behavior," in P. Zarembka, ed., *Frontiers in Econometrics,* pp. 105–142. New York: Academic Press.

——— 1976a. "A Comment on Discriminant Analysis 'versus' Logit Analysis." *Annals of Economic and Social Measurement* 5:511–524.

——— 1976b. "The Revealed Preferences of a Government Bureaucracy: Empirical Evidence." *Bell Journal of Economics* 7:55–72.

——— 1977. "Quantitative Methods for Analyzing Travel Behavior of Individuals: Some Recent Developments." Cowles Foundation Discussion Paper no. 474.

——— 1978. "Modelling the Choice of Residential Location," in A. Karlqvist et al., eds., *Spatial Interaction Theory and Planning Models,* pp. 75–96. Amsterdam: North-Holland Publishing.

——— 1981. "Econometric Models of Probabilistic Choice," in C. F. Manski and D. McFadden, eds., *Structural Analysis of Discrete Data with Econometric Applications,* pp. 198–272. Cambridge, Mass.: MIT Press.

McFadden, D., and F. Reid. 1975. "Aggregate Travel Demand Forecasting from Disaggregated Behavior Models." Transportation Research Board, *Record,* no. 534, Washington, D. C.

McGillivray, R. G. 1972. "Binary Choice of Urban Transport Mode in the San Francisco Bay Region." *Econometrica* 40:827–848.

McKean, J. W., and T. P. Hettmansperger. 1976. "Tests of Hypothesis in the General Linear Model Based on Ranks." *Communications in Statistics* A,1:693–709.

MacRae, E. 1977. "Estimation of Time-Varying Markov Process with Aggregate Data." *Econometrica* 45:183–198.

MaCurdy, T. E. 1980. "An Intertemporal Analysis of Taxation and Work Disincentives." Working Papers in Economics no. E-80-4, The Hoover Institution, Stanford University, Calif.

——— 1982. "The Use of Time Series Processes to Model the Error Structure of Earnings in a Longitudinal Data Analysis." *Journal of Econometrics.* 18:83–114.

Maddala, G. S. 1971. "The Use of Variance Components Models in Pooling Cross Section and Time Series Data." *Econometrica* 39:341–358.

——— 1980. "Disequilibrium, Self-Selection and Switching Models." Social Science Working Paper 303, California Institute of Technology.

——— 1983. *Limited-Dependent and Qualitative Variables in Econometrics.* Cambridge: Cambridge University Press.

Maddala, G. S., and F. D. Nelson. 1974. "Maximum Likelihood Methods for Models of Markets in Disequilibrium." *Econometrica* 42:1013–1030.

Malik, H. J., and B. Abraham. 1973. "Multivariate Logistic Distributions." *Annals of Statistics* 1:588–590.

Malinvaud, E. 1961. "Estimation et prévision dans les modèles Économiques autorégressifs." *Revue de l'institut international de statistique* 29:1–32.

——— 1980. *Statistical Methods of Econometrics,* 3d rev. ed. Amsterdam: North-Holland Publishing.

Mallows, C. L. 1964. "Choosing Variables in a Linear Regression: A Graphical Aid." Paper presented at the Central Region Meeting of the Institute of Mathematical Statistics, Manhattan, Kansas.

Mandelbrot, B. 1963. "New Methods in Statistical Economics." *Journal of Political Economy* 71:421–440.

Mann, H. B., and A. Wald. 1943. "On Stochastic Limit and Order Relationships." *Annals of Mathematical Statistics* 14:217–226.

Manski, C. F. 1975. "The Maximum Score Estimation of the Stochastic Utility Model of Choice." *Journal of Econometrics* 3:205–228.

——— 1985. "Semiparametric Analysis of Discrete Response: Asymptotic Properties of the Maximum Score Estimator." *Journal of Econometrics* 27:313–333.

Manski, C. F., and S. R. Lerman. 1977. "The Estimation of Choice Probabilities from Choice-Based Samples." *Econometrica* 45:1977–1988.

Manski, C. F., and D. McFadden. 1981. "Alternative Estimators and Sample Designs for Discrete Choice Analysis," in C. F. Manski and D. McFadden, eds., *Structural Analysis of Discrete Data with Econometric Applications,* pp. 2–50. Cambridge, Mass.: MIT Press.

Marcus, M., and H. Minc. 1964. *A Survey of Matrix Theory and Matrix Inequalities.* Boston: Prindle, Weber & Schmidt.

Mariano, R. S. 1982. "Analytical Small-Sample Distribution Theory in Econometrics: The Simultaneous-Equations Case." *International Economic Review* 23:503–533.

Mariano, R. S., and B. W. Brown. 1983. "Asymptotic Behavior of Predictors in a Nonlinear Simultaneous System." *International Economic Review* 24:523–536.

Marquardt, D. W. 1963. "An Algorithm for the Estimation of Non-Linear Parameters." *Society for Industrial and Applied Mathematics Journal* 11:431–441.

Mayer, T. 1975. "Selecting Economic Hypotheses by Goodness of Fit." *Economic Journal* 85:877–883.

Miller, R. G., Jr. 1981. *Survival Analysis.* New York: John Wiley & Sons.

Mizon, G. E. 1977. "Inferential Procedures in Nonlinear Models: An Application in a UK Industrial Cross Section Study of Factor Substitution and Returns to Scale." *Econometrica* 45:1221–1242.

Mood, A. M., F. A. Graybill, and D. C. Boes. 1974. *Introduction to the Theory of Statistics,* 3d ed. New York: McGraw-Hill.

Morimune, K. 1979. "Comparisons of Normal and Logistic Models in the Bivariate Dichotomous Analysis." *Econometrica* 47:957–976.

Mosteller, F. 1946. "On Some Useful 'Inefficient' Statistics." *Annals of Mathematical Statistics* 17:377–408.

Muthén, B. 1979. "A Structural Probit Model with Latent Variables." *Journal of the American Statistical Association* 74:807–811.

Nagar, A. L., and S. N. Sahay. 1978. "The Bias and Mean Squared Error of Forecasts from Partially Restricted Reduced Form." *Journal of Econometrics* 7:227–243.

Nakamura, M., A. Nakamura, and D. Cullen. 1979. "Job Opportunities, the Offered Wage, and the Labor Supply of Married Women." *American Economic Review* 69:787–805.

Nelder, J. A., and R. W. M. Wedderburn. 1972. "Generalized Linear Models." *Journal of the Royal Statistical Society* ser. B, 135:370–384.

Nelson, F. D. 1977. "Censored Regression Models with Unobserved, Stochastic Censoring Thresholds." *Journal of Econometrics* 6:309–327.

——— 1981. "A Test for Misspecification in the Censored Normal Model." *Econometrica* 49:1317–1329.

Nelson, F. D., and L. Olson. 1978. "Specification and Estimation of a Simultaneous-Equation Model with Limited Dependent Variables." *International Economic Review* 19:695–709.

Nerlove, M. 1958. *Distributed Lags and Demand Analysis for Agricultural and Other Commodities.* Washington, D.C.: U.S. Department of Agriculture.

——— 1971. "Further Evidence on the Estimation of Dynamic Relations from a Time Series of Cross Sections." *Econometrica* 39:359–382.

Nerlove, M., D. M. Grether, and J. L. Carvalho. 1979. *Analysis of Economic Time Series: A Synthesis.* New York: Academic Press.

Nerlove, M., and S. J. Press. 1973. "Univariate and Multivariate Log-Linear and Logistic Models." RAND Corporation Paper R-1306-EDA/NIH, Santa Monica, Calif.

Neyman, J., and E. L. Scott. 1948. "Consistent Estimates Based on Partially Consistent Observations." *Econometrica* 16:1–32.

Nickell, S. 1979. "Estimating the Probability of Leaving Unemployment." *Econometrica* 47:1249–1266.

Norden, R. H. 1972. "A Survey of Maximum Likelihood Estimation." *International Statistical Revue* 40:329–354.

——— 1973. "A Survey of Maximum Likelihood Estimation, Part 2." *International Statistical Revue* 41:39–58.

Oberhofer, W., and J. Kmenta. 1974. "A General Procedure for Obtaining Maximum Likelihood Estimates in Generalized Regression Models." *Econometrica* 42:579–590.

Olsen, R. J. 1978. "Note on the Uniqueness of the Maximum Likelihood Estimator for the Tobit Model." *Econometrica* 46:1211–1215.

——— 1980. "A Least Squares Correction for Selectivity Bias." *Econometrica* 48:1815–1820.

Paarsch, H. J. 1984. "A Monte Carlo Comparison of Estimators for Censored Regression Models." *Journal of Econometrics* 24:197–213.

Parke, W. R. 1982. "An Algorithm for FIML and 3SLS Estimation of Large Nonlinear Models." *Econometrica* 50:81–95.

Pearson, E. S., and N. W. Please. 1975. "Relation between the Shape of Population Distribution and the Robustness of Four Simple Statistical Tests." *Biometrika* 62:223–241.

Pesaran, M. H. 1982. "Comparison of Local Power of Alternative Tests of Non-Nested Regression Models." *Econometrica* 50:1287–1305.

Pfanzagl, J. 1973. "Asymptotic Expansions Related to Minimum Contrast Estimators." *Annals of Statistics* 1:993–1026.

Phillips, P. C. B. 1977. "Approximations to Some Finite Sample Distributions Associated with a First-Order Stochastic Difference Equation." *Econometrica* 45:463–485.

——— 1982. "On the Consistency of Nonlinear FIML." *Econometrica* 50:1307–1324.

——— 1983. "Exact Small Sample Theory in the Simultaneous Equations Model," in Z. Griliches and M. D. Intrilligator, eds., *Handbook of Econometrics,* 2:449–516. Amsterdam: North-Holland Publishing.

Pierce, D. A. 1971. "Least Squares Estimation in the Regression Model with Autoregressive-Moving Average Errors." *Biometrika* 58:299–312.

Plackett, R. L. 1960. *Principles of Regression Analysis.* London: Oxford University Press.

——— 1965. "A Class of Bivariate Distributions." *Journal of American Statistical Association* 60:516–522.

Poirier, D. J. 1978. "The Use of the Box-Cox Transformation in Limited Dependent Variable Models." *Journal of the American Statistical Association* 73:284–287.

Powell, J. L. 1981. "Least Absolute Deviations Estimation for Censored and Truncated Regression Models." Technical Report no. 356, Institute for Mathematical Studies in the Social Sciences, Stanford University, Calif.

——— 1983. "Asymptotic Normality of the Censored and Truncated Least Absolute Deviations Estimators." Technical Report no. 395, Institute for Mathematical Studies in the Social Sciences, Stanford University, Calif.

Powell, M. J. D. 1964. "An Efficient Method for Finding the Minimum of a Function of Several Variables without Calculating Derivatives." *Computer Journal* 7:115–162.

Powers, J. A., L. C. Marsh, R. R. Huckfeldt, and C. L. Johnson. 1978. "A Comparison of Logit, Probit and Discriminant Analysis in Predicting Family Size." *American Statistical Association Proceedings of the Social Statistics Section,* pp. 693–697.

Prais, S. J., and H. S. Houthakker. 1955. *The Analysis of Family Budgets.* Cambridge: Cambridge University Press.

Pratt, J. W. 1981. "Concavity of the Log Likelihood." *Journal of the American Statistical Association* 76:103–106.

Press, S. J., and S. Wilson. 1978. "Choosing Between Logistic Regression and Discriminant Analysis." *Journal of the American Statistical Association* 73:699–705.

Quandt, R. E. 1958. "The Estimation of the Parameters of a Linear Regression System Obeying Two Separate Regimes." *Journal of the American Statistical Association* 53:873–880.

——— 1982. "Econometric Disequilibrium Models." *Econometric Reviews* 1:1–63.

——— 1983. "Computational Problems and Methods," in Z. Griliches and M. D. Intrilligator, eds., *Handbook of Econometrics,* 1:699–764. Amsterdam: North-Holland Publishing.

Quandt, R. E., and J. B. Ramsey. 1978. "Estimating Mixtures of Normal Distributions and Switching Regressions." *Journal of the American Statistical Association* 73:730–738.

Radner, R., and L. S. Miller. 1970. "Demand and Supply in U. S. Higher Education: A Progress Report." *American Economic Review—Papers and Proceedings* 60:326–334.

Rao, C. R. 1947. "Large Sample Tests of Statistical Hypotheses Concerning Several Parameters with Applications to Problems of Estimation." *Proceedings of the Cambridge Philosophical Society* 44:50–57.

——— 1965. "The Theory of Least Squares When the Parameters Are Stochastic and Its Applications to the Analysis of Growth Curves." *Biometrika* 52:447–458.

——— 1970. "Estimation of Heteroscedastic Variances in a Linear Model." *Journal of the American Statistical Association* 65:161–172.

——— 1973. *Linear Statistical Inference and Its Applications,* 2d ed. New York: John Wiley & Sons.

Reece, W. S. 1979. "Charitable Contributions: The New Evidence on Household Behavior." *American Economic Review* 69:142–151.

Rice, P., and V. K. Smith. 1977. "An Econometric Model of the Petroleum Industry." *Journal of Econometrics* 6:263–288.

Roberts, R. B., G. S. Maddala, and G. Enholm. 1978. "Determinants of the Requested Rate of Return and the Rate of Return Granted in a Formal Regulatory Process." *Bell Journal of Economics* 9:611–621.

Robinson, P. M. 1982a. "On the Asymptotic Properties of Estimators of Models Containing Limited Dependent Variables." *Econometrica* 50:27–41.

——— 1982b. "Analysis of Time Series from Mixed Distributions." *Annals of Statistics* 10:915–925.

Rosenberg, B. 1973. "The Analysis of a Cross Section of Time Series by Stochastically Convergent Parameter Regression." *Annals of Economic and Social Measurement* 2:399–428.

Rosenzweig, M. R. 1980. "Neoclassical Theory and the Optimizing Peasant: An Econometric Analysis of Market Family Labor Supply in a Developing Country." *Quarterly Journal of Economics* 94:31–55.

Royden, H. L. 1968. *Real Analysis,* 2d ed. New York: Macmillan.

Ruppert, D., and R. J. Carroll. 1980. "Trimmed Least Squares Estimation in the Linear Model." *Journal of the American Statistical Association* 75:828–838.

Sant, D. T. 1978. "Partially Restricted Reduced Forms: Asymptotic Relative Efficiency." *International Economic Review* 19:739–747.

Sargent, T. J. 1978. "Estimation of Dynamic Labor Schedules under Rational Expectations." *Journal of Political Economy* 86:1009–1044.

Sawa, T., and T. Hiromatsu. 1973. "Minimax Regret Significance Points for a Preliminary Test in Regression Analysis." *Econometrica* 41:1093–1101.

Scheffé, H. 1959. *The Analysis of Variance.* New York: John Wiley & Sons.

Schlossmacher, E. J. 1973. "An Iterative Technique for Absolute Deviation Curve Fitting." *Journal of the American Statistical Association* 68:857–865.

Schmee, J., and G. J. Hahn. 1979. "A Simple Method for Regression Analysis with Censored Data." *Technometrics* 21:417–432.

Schmidt, P., and R. Sickles. 1977. "Some Further Evidence on the Use of the Chow Test under Heteroscedasticity." *Econometrica* 45:1293–1298.

Schwarz, G. 1978. "Estimating the Dimension of a Model." *Annals of Statistics* 6:461–464.

Sclove, S. L. 1973. "Least Squares Problems with Random Regression Coefficients." Technical Report no. 87, Institute for Mathematical Studies in the Social Sciences, Stanford University, Calif.

Sclove, S. L., C. L. Morris, and R. Radhakrishnan. 1972. "Non-Optimality of Preliminary-Test Estimators for the Mean of a Multivariate Normal Distribution." *Annals of Mathematical Statistics* 43:1481–1490.

Shiller, R. J. 1978. "Rational Expectations and the Dynamic Structure of Macroeconomic Models." *Journal of Monetary Economics* 4:1–44.

Shorrocks, A. F. 1976. "Income Mobility and the Markov Assumption." *Economic Journal* 86:566–578.

Silberman, J. I., and G. C. Durden. 1976. "Determining Legislative Preferences on the Minimum Wage: An Economic Approach." *Journal of Political Economy* 84:317–329.

Silberman, J. I., and W. K. Talley. 1974. "*N*-Chotomous Dependent Variables: An Application to Regulatory Decision-Making." *American Statistical Association Proceedings of the Business and Economic Statistics Section,* pp. 573–576.

Silvey, S. D. 1959. "The Lagrangian Multiplier Test." *Annals of Mathematical Statistics* 30:389–407.

——— 1969. "Multicollinearity and Imprecise Estimation." *Journal of the Royal Society* ser. B, 31:539–552.

Small, K. A. 1981. "Ordered Logit: A Discrete Choice Model with Proximate Covariance Among Alternatives." Research Memorandum no. 292, Econometric Research Program, Princeton University.

Small, K. A., and D. Brownstone. 1982. "Efficient Estimation of Nested Logit Models: An Application to Trip Timing." Research Memorandum no. 296, Econometric Research Program, Princeton University.

Smith, K. C., N. E. Savin, and J. L. Robertson. 1984. "A Monte Carlo Comparison of Maximum Likelihood and Minimum Chi-Square Sampling Distributions in Logit Analysis." *Biometrics* 40:471–482.

Spitzer, J. J. 1976. "The Demand for Money, the Liquidity Trap, and Functional Forms." *International Economic Review* 17:220–227.

——— 1978. "A Monte Carlo Investigation of the Box-Cox Transformation in Small Samples." *Journal of the American Statistical Association* 73:488–495.

Srivastava, V. K., and T. D. Dwivedi. 1979. "Estimation of Seemingly Unrelated Regression Equations: A Brief Survey." *Journal of Econometrics* 10:15–32.

Stapleton, D. C., and D. J. Young. 1984. "Censored Normal Regression with Measurement Error on the Dependent Variable." *Econometrica* 52:737–760.

Stein, C. 1973. "Estimation of the Mean of a Multivariate Normal Distribution." Technical Report no. 48, Department of Statistics, Stanford University, Calif.

Stephenson, S. P., and J. F. McDonald. 1979. "Disaggregation of Income Maintenance Impacts on Family Earnings." *Review of Economics and Statistics* 61:354–360.

Stigler, S. M. 1973. "Simon Newcomb, Percy Daniell, and the History of Robust Estimation, 1885–1920." *Journal of the American Statistical Association* 68:872–879.

——— 1977. "Do Robust Estimators Work with Real Data?" *Annals of Statistics* 5:1055–1098.

Strawderman, W. E. 1978. "Minimax Adaptive Generalized Ridge Regression Estimators." *Journal of the American Statistical Association* 73:623–627.

Strickland, A. D., and L. W. Weiss. 1976. "Advertising, Concentration, and Price-Cost Margins." *Journal of Political Economy* 84:1109–1121.

Strotz, R. H. 1960. "Interdependence as a Specification Error." *Econometrica* 28:428–442.

Swamy, P. A. V. B. 1970. "Efficient Inference in a Random Coefficient Regression Model." *Econometrica* 38:311–323.

——— 1980. "A Comparison of Estimators for Undersized Samples." *Journal of Econometrics* 14:161–181.

Swamy, P. A. V. B., and J. S. Mehta. 1977. "Estimation of Linear Models with Time and Cross-Sectionally Varying Parameters." *Journal of the American Statistical Association* 72:890–891.

Taylor, W. E. 1978. "The Heteroscedastic Linear Model: Exact Finite Sample Results." *Econometrica* 46:663–676.

——— 1980. "Small Sample Considerations in Estimation from Panel Data." *Journal of Econometrics* 13:203–223.

——— 1981. "On the Efficiency of the Cochrane-Orcutt Estimator." *Journal of Econometrics* 17:67–82.

——— 1983. "On the Relevance of Finite Sample Distribution Theory." *Econometric Reviews* 2:1–39.

Taylor, W. F. 1953. "Distance Functions and Regular Best Asymptotically Normal Estimates." *Annals of Mathematical Statistics* 24:85–92.

Telser, L. G. 1963. "Least-Squares Estimates of Transition Probabilities," in C. Christ, ed., *Measurement in Economics,* pp. 270–292. Stanford, Calif.: Stanford University Press.

Theil, H. 1953. "Repeated Least-Squares Applied to Complete Equation Systems." Mimeographed paper. The Hague: Central Planning Bureau.

——— 1961. *Economic Forecasts and Policy,* 2d ed. Amsterdam: North-Holland Publishing.

——— 1971. *Principles of Econometrics.* New York: John Wiley & Sons.

Theil, H., and A. S. Goldberger. 1961. "On Pure and Mixed Statistical Estimation in Economics." *International Economic Review* 2:65–78.

Thisted, R. A. 1976. "Ridge Regression, Minimax Estimation, and Empirical Bayes Method." Technical Report no. 28, Division of Biostatistics, Stanford University, Calif.

Tobin, J. 1958. "Estimation of Relationships for Limited Dependent Variables." *Econometrica* 26:24–36.

Toikka, R. S. 1976. "A Markovian Model of Labor Market Decisions by Workers." *American Economic Review* 66:821–834.

Tomes, N. 1981. "The Family, Inheritance, and the Intergenerational Transmission of Inequality." *Journal of Political Economy* 89:928–958.

Toyoda, T. 1974. "Use of the Chow Test Under Heteroscedasticity." *Econometrica* 42:601–608.

Tsiatis, A. A. 1981. "A Large Sample Study of Cox's Regression Model." *The Annals of Statistics* 9:93–108.

Tsurumi, H. 1970. "Nonlinear Two-Stage Least Squares Estimation of CES Production Functions Applied to the Canadian Manufacturing Industries." *Review of Economics and Statistics* 52:200–207.

Tuma, N. B. 1976. "Rewards, Resources, and the Rate of Mobility: A Nonstationary Multivariate Stochastic Model." *American Sociological Review* 41:338–360.

Tuma, N. B., M. T. Hannan, and L. P. Groeneveld. 1979. "Dynamic Analysis of Event Histories." *Journal of Sociology* 84:820–854.

Uhler, R. S. 1968. "The Demand for Housing: An Inverse Probability Approach." *Review of Economics and Statistics* 50:129–134.

Vinod, H. D. 1978. "A Ridge Estimator Whose MSE Dominates OLS." *International Economic Review* 19:727–737.

Wald, A. 1943. "Tests of Statistical Hypotheses Concerning Several Parameters When

the Number of Observations Is Large." *Transactions of the American Mathematical Society* 54:426–482.
——— 1949. "Note on the Consistency of the Maximum Likelihood Estimate." *Annals of Mathematical Statistics* 60:595–601.
Wales, T. J., and A. D. Woodland. 1980. "Sample Selectivity and the Estimation of Labor Supply Functions." *International Economic Review* 21:437–468.
Walker, S. H., and D. B. Duncan. 1967. "Estimation of the Probability of an Event as a Function of Several Independent Variables." *Biometrika* 54:167–179.
Wallace, T. D., and A. Hussain. 1969. "The Use of Error Components Models in Combining Cross-Section with Time Series Data." *Econometrica* 37:55–72.
Wallis, K. F. 1980. "Econometric Implications of the Rational Expectations Hypothesis." *Econometrica* 48:49–73.
Warner, S. L. 1962. *Stochastic Choice of Mode in Urban Travel—A Study in Binary Choice.* Evanston, Ill.: Northwestern University Press.
——— 1963. "Multivariate Regression of Dummy Variates Under Normality Assumptions." *Journal of the American Statistical Association* 58:1054–1063.
Watson, G. S. 1955. "Serial Correlation in Regression Analysis, I." *Biometrika* 42:327–341.
Welch, B. L. 1938. "The Significance of the Difference between Two Means When the Population Variances Are Unequal." *Biometrika* 29:350–362.
Westin, R. B. 1974. "Predictions from Binary Choice Models." *Journal of Econometrics* 2:1–16.
Westin, R. B., and P. W. Gillen. 1978. "Parking Location and Transit Demand." *Journal of Econometrics* 8:75–101.
White, H. 1980a. "A Heteroskedasticity-Consistent Covariance Matrix Estimator and a Direct Test for Heteroskedasticity." *Econometrica* 48:817–838.
——— 1980b. "Nonlinear Regression on Cross-Section Data." *Econometrica* 48:721–746.
——— 1982. "Instrumental Variables Regression with Independent Observations." *Econometrica* 50:483–499.
———, ed. 1983. "Non-Nested Models." *Journal of Econometrics* 21:1–160.
White, H., and G. M. MacDonald. 1980. "Some Large Sample Tests for Nonnormality in the Linear Regression Model." *Journal of the American Statistical Association* 75:16–28.
White, K. J. 1972. "Estimation of the Liquidity Trap with a Generalized Functional Form." *Econometrica* 40:193–199.
Whittle, P. 1983. *Prediction and Regulation.* Minneapolis: University of Minnesota Press.
Wiggins, S. N. 1981. "Product Quality Regulation and New Drug Introductions: Some New Evidence from the 1970's." *Review of Economics and Statistics* 63:615–619.
Willis, R. J., and S. Rosen. 1979. "Education and Self-Selection." *Journal of Political Economy* 87:S7–S36.

Witte, A. D. 1980. "Estimating the Economic Model of Crime with Individual Data." *Quarterly Journal of Economics* 94:57–84.

Wu, C. F. J. 1983. "On the Convergence Properties of the EM Algorithm." *Annals of Statistics* 11:95–103.

Wu, D. M. 1965. "An Empirical Analysis of Household Durable Goods Expenditure." *Econometrica* 33:761–780.

Zacks, S. 1971. *Theory of Statistical Inference.* New York: John Wiley & Sons.

Zarembka, P. 1968. "Functional Form in the Demand for Money." *Journal of the American Statistical Association* 63:502–511.

Zellner, A. 1962. "An Efficient Method of Estimating Seemingly Unrelated Regressions and Tests for Aggregation Bias." *Journal of the American Statistical Association* 57:348–368.

——— 1971. *An Introduction to Bayesian Inference in Econometrics.* New York: John Wiley & Sons.

Zellner, A., D. S. Huang, and L. C. Chau. 1965. "Further Analysis of the Short-Run Consumption Function with Emphasis on the Role of Liquid Assets." *Econometrica* 40:193–199.

Zellner, A., and H. Theil. 1962. "Three-Stage Least Squares: Simultaneous Estimation of Simultaneous Equations." *Econometrica* 30:54–78.

Name Index

Abraham, B., 319
Abramovitz, M., 193
Adams, J. D., 365
Adelman, I. G., 420
Aigner, D. J., 67, 69, 123
Aitchison, J., 307
Akahira, M., 136
Akaike, H., 52, 146, 147, 466
Albert, A., 271
Albright, R. L., 309, 310
Almon, S., 178, 469
Amemiya, T., 40, 52, 123, 146, 147, 161, 178, 179, 189, 195, 199, 202, 203, 204, 205, 206, 211, 215, 217, 218, 222, 245, 246, 248, 249, 251, 254, 257, 258, 259, 264, 269, 278, 285, 286, 295, 296, 298, 299, 300, 302, 303, 304, 305, 306, 321, 322, 328, 408, 465, 468, 470, 471, 472
Anderson, J. A., 271
Anderson, T. W., 10, 159, 172, 173, 174, 180, 183, 187, 216, 221, 235, 238, 239, 240, 417, 469, 470, 471
Andrews, D. F., 72, 73, 75
Anscombe, F. J., 203
Apostol, T. M., 470
Arabmazer, A., 380, 381
Arrow, K. J., 128
Ashenfelter, O., 365
Ashford, J. R., 317, 319

Baldwin, K. F., 64, 69
Balestra, P., 211, 213, 214, 215
Baltagi, B. H., 211
Baranchik, A. J., 63
Barankin, E. W., 125, 433, 470
Bartholomew, D. J., 412, 418
Basmann, R. L., 239, 470
Bassett, G., 77, 78, 154, 468
Battese, G. E., 211, 212
Beach, C. M., 176, 190
Beattie, B. R., 67
Bellman, R., 416, 459, 474
Belsley, D. A., 264
Bennett, J., 307
Benus, J., 252
Bera, A. K., 382
Berger, J. O., 65
Berkson, J., 275, 278, 280
Berndt, E. R., 138, 145
Berzeg, K., 214
Bhattacharya, P. J., 65
Bhattacharya, R. K., 92
Bianchi, C., 262, 263
Bickel, P. J., 71, 72, 73, 75, 154, 203, 465, 466
Bishop, Y. M. M., 316
Blattberg, R., 77
Blumen, I., 418, 472
Bock, M. E., 69, 466
Bodkin, R. G., 141, 468
Boes, D. C., 466
Borjas, G. J., 405, 406
Boskin, M. J., 383, 421, 424
Box, G. E. P., 172, 249, 250, 465
Breusch, T. S., 145, 206–207, 469
Brillinger, D. R., 159
Brook, R. J., 54
Brown, B. W., 256, 263
Brown, M., 128
Brown, R. L., 222
Brown, W. G., 67
Brownstone, D., 304
Brundy, J. M., 242
Buse, A., 206
Butler, J. S., 350

Calzolari, G., 262, 263
Carroll, R. J., 78, 154, 202
Carvalho, J. L., 159, 178
Chamberlain, G., 199, 217
Champernowne, D. G., 420
Charatsis, E. G., 141

Chau, L. C., 246
Chenery, H. B., 128
Chow, G. C., 234, 264, 465
Christ, C. F., 228
Christensen, L. R., 128
Chung, K. L., 90, 466, 472
Clark, C., 309
Cochrane, D., 189–190
Cooley, T. F., 222
Cooper, J. M., 469
Cosslett, S. R., 321, 322, 326, 331, 332, 334, 336, 337, 338, 339, 346, 358, 471, 472
Cox, D. R., 147, 249, 250, 251, 278, 307, 449, 450, 465, 466
Cragg, J. G., 410, 472
Cramér, H., 93, 118
Crowder, J. M., 178
Cullen, D., 395

Daganzo, C. F., 309
Dagenais, M. G., 264
Dahm, P. A., 293
David, J. M., 293
Davidson, W. C., 138
Davis, L., 279
Deacon, R., 293, 294, 471
Dempster, A. P., 66, 375
Dent, W. T., 469
Dhrymes, P. J., 178
Diewert, W. E., 128
Doksum, K. A., 71, 465, 466
Domencich, T. A., 269
Doob, J. L., 159
Draper, N. R., 137, 251, 466
Dubin, J. A., 408
Dudley, L., 387
Duncan, D. B., 275
Duncan, G. M., 405, 406, 407, 408, 473
Duncan, G. T., 421
Durbin, J., 191, 192, 193, 194, 196, 222, 224, 225, 233
Durden, G. C., 312
Dwivedi, T. D., 198

Efron, B., 62, 63, 64, 67, 135, 283, 284, 455
Ehrlich, I., 252
Eicker, F., 199
Eisenpress, H., 264
Engle, R. F., 142
Enholm, G., 394, 395
Evans, J. M., 222

Fair, R. C., 78, 264, 265, 365, 403, 473
Farebrother, N. W., 53, 469
Feinberg, S. E., 316
Feller, W., 274
Ferguson, T. S., 125
Fisher, F. M., 229, 256, 469, 470
Fisher, R. A., 16
Fletcher, R., 138
Flinn, C. J., 446, 448, 457
Fomby, T. B., 59
Forsythe, A. B., 77
Freund, J. F., 466
Froehlich, B. R., 469
Fuller, W. A., 159, 161, 178, 195, 202, 211, 212, 238, 239

Gallant, A. R., 113, 136, 137, 141, 145, 257, 262
Gastwirth, J. L., 74
Gaver, K. M., 49
Geisel, M. S., 49
Ghosh, J. K., 125, 279
Gillen, P. W., 389
Gnedenko, B. V., 90
Godfrey, L. G., 469
Goldberg, S., 166
Goldberger, A. S., 25, 360, 367, 380, 381, 472
Goldfeld, S. M., 37, 38, 137, 138, 204, 206, 207, 256, 266, 354, 470
Goodman, L. A., 315, 316, 417, 418, 419
Gourieroux, C., 273, 472
Gradshteyn, I. S., 474
Granger, C. W. J., 159
Graybill, F. A., 466
Greene, W. H., 368, 472
Greenstadt, J., 264
Grenander, U., 161
Grether, D. M., 159, 178
Griliches, Z., 178, 217
Groeneveld, L. P., 444
Gronau, R., 388, 473
Guilkey, D. K., 317
Gumbel, E. J., 319
Gunst, R. F., 66
Gurland, J., 124, 293, 433, 470

Haberman, S. J., 316
Haessel, W., 258
Hahn, G. J., 378
Hall, B. H., 138
Hall, R. E., 138

Halmos, D. R., 467
Ham, J., 365
Hammerstrom, T., 203
Hampel, F. R., 72, 73, 75
Han, A. K., 455
Hannan, M. T., 444
Hartley, H. O., 140, 141
Hartley, M. J., 375, 403, 472
Harvey, A. C., 159, 172, 189, 222, 242
Hatanaka, M., 178, 265
Hause, J. C., 217
Hausman, J. A., 138, 145, 217, 218, 233, 299, 302, 304, 308, 309, 310, 381, 395
Heckman, J. J., 252, 348, 349, 350, 351, 353, 354, 368, 369, 387, 389, 390, 391, 392, 395, 396, 397, 401, 402, 412, 446, 448, 457, 473, 474
Heien, D., 128
Hettmansperger, T. P., 79
Hildreth, C., 204, 469
Hill, R. C., 59
Hill, R. W., 75, 77
Hinkley, D. V., 222, 251, 465, 466
Hiromatsu, T., 53–54
Hoadley, B., 117
Hodges, J. L., 61, 74, 79, 124
Hoel, P. G., 466
Hoerl, A. E., 56, 60, 64
Hogg, R. J., 72, 74
Holford, T. R., 437
Holland, P. W., 75, 77, 316
Holly, A., 145, 262
Hood, W. C., 470
Horowitz, J. L., 309
Hosek, J. R., 328
Houck, J. P., 204, 469
Houthakker, H. S., 198, 203
Howe, H., 128
Hsiao, C., 216, 218, 220, 221, 469, 470
Hsieh, D., 321, 328
Huang, D. S., 246, 388
Huber, P. J., 71, 72, 73, 75, 105, 468
Huckfeldt, R. R., 300
Hurd, M., 379
Hussain, A., 210

Imhoff, J. P., 173, 192

Jaeckel, L. A., 78, 79
Jaffee, D. M., 403, 473
James, W., 56, 61–62
Jarque, C. M., 382
Jenkins, G. M., 172
Jennrich, R. I., 107, 117, 468
Jobson, J. D., 202
Johnson, C. L., 300
Johnson, N. L., 62, 296, 300, 463, 472
Johnson, S. R., 59
Johnston, J., 238
Joreskog, K. G., 217
Jorgenson, D. W., 128, 242, 257, 258, 262
Judge, G. G., 67, 69, 466

Kahn, L. M., 310, 311
Kakwani, N. C., 198
Kalbfleisch, J. D., 412, 451, 455, 474
Kariya, T., 198, 202
Kay, R., 455
Keeley, M. C., 365
Kelejian, H. H., 218, 219, 220, 246, 249
Kendall, M. G., 36
Kennard, R. W., 56, 60, 64
Kenny, L. W., 396, 397, 404
Kiefer, J., 331, 346, 347
Klein, L. R., 141, 468
Kmenta, J., 186, 252
Koenker, R., 72, 77, 78, 154, 207, 468
Kogan, M., 418, 472
Kolmogorov, A. N., 90
Koopmans, T. C., 470
Kotlikoff, L. J., 364, 365
Kotz, S., 62, 296, 300, 463, 472
Koyck, L. M., 178

Lachenbruch, P. A., 285
Laffont, J., 257, 472
Lai, T. L., 467
Laird, N. M., 375
Lancaster, T., 444, 445, 446, 448, 474
Lau, L. J., 128, 258, 262
LeCam, L., 124, 337
Lee, L. F., 293, 318, 319, 382, 387, 392, 394, 396, 397, 400, 402, 403, 404, 405
Legg, W. E., 293
Lehmann, E. L., 61, 74, 79
Lermann, S. R., 309, 310, 321, 322, 327, 471
Li, M. M., 280
Lillard, L. A., 216
Lin, L. G., 421
Lindley, D. V., 465
Loeve, M., 466

McCall, J. J., 418, 419
McCarthy, P. J., 418, 472
MacDonald, G. M., 465
McDonald, J. F., 365
McFadden, D., 269, 278, 285, 286, 295, 296, 298, 299, 300, 302, 303, 304, 305, 306, 321, 322, 328, 408, 471, 472
McGillivray, R. G., 283
McKean, J. W., 79
MacKinnon, J. G., 176, 190
MacRae, E., 431
MaCurdy, T. E., 217, 218, 257, 473
Maddala, G. S., 213, 214, 216, 361, 392, 394, 395, 396, 397, 402, 404
Malik, H. J., 319
Malinvaud, E., 225, 228
Mallows, C. L., 52
Mandelbrot, B., 71
Mann, H. B., 87, 88, 89
Manski, C. F., 309, 310, 321, 322, 327, 328, 339, 343, 346, 471, 472
Marcus, M., 462
Mariano, R. S., 238, 263
Marquardt, D. W., 140
Marsh, L. C., 300
Mason, R. L., 66
Mayer, T., 51
Mehta, J. S., 218, 221
Miller, L. S., 356
Miller, R. G., 412
Minc, H., 462
Minhas, B. S., 128
Mizon, G. E., 128, 141, 145
Moffitt, R., 350
Monfort, A., 273, 472
Montmarquette, C., 387
Mood, A. M., 466
Morimune, K., 179, 310, 311, 318, 319
Morris, C. L., 62, 63, 64, 66, 67, 68, 466
Mosteller, F., 74
Muthén, B., 318

Nagar, A. L., 242
Nakamura, A., 395
Nakamura, M., 395
Nelder, J. A., 203
Nelson, F. D., 381, 382, 389, 396, 397, 398, 402
Nerlove, M., 159, 178, 211, 213, 214, 215, 216, 317
Newbold, P., 159
Neyman, J., 120, 155
Nickell, S., 447
Nold, F. C., 421, 424
Norden, R. H., 118

Oberhofer, W., 186
Olsen, R. J., 373, 387, 396, 397, 398
Orcutt, G. H., 189-190

Paarsch, H. J., 383
Pagan, A. R., 145, 206-207, 469
Parke, W. R., 264, 265
Payne, C., 67
Pearson, E. S., 465
Pesaran, M. H., 148
Pfanzagl, J., 135, 468
Phillips, P. C. B., 173, 238, 260, 266
Plackett, R. L., 192, 319, 463, 464
Please, W. W., 465
Poirier, D. J., 123, 251
Polachek, S., 252
Powell, J. L., 251, 252, 284, 382, 383
Powell, M. J. D., 138, 141
Powers, J. A., 300
Prais, S. J., 198, 203
Pratt, J. W., 293
Prentice, R. L., 412, 451, 474
Prescott, E. C., 222
Press, S. J., 284, 317

Quandt, R. E., 37, 38, 120, 137, 138, 141, 204, 206, 207, 222, 256, 266, 354, 403, 470

Radhankrishnan, R., 67, 68, 466
Radner, R., 356
Ramsey, J. B., 120
Rao, C. R., 58, 87, 89, 90, 91, 92, 93, 94, 116, 118, 124, 138, 142, 183, 337, 407, 463, 464, 465, 466, 469
Reece, W. S., 365
Reid, F., 278, 286
Revo, L. T., 285
Rice, P., 470
Robbins, H., 467
Robins, P. K., 365
Robinson, P. M., 380
Roberts, R. B., 394, 395
Robertson, J. L., 280
Rogers, W. H., 72, 73, 75

Rosen, S., 404, 405
Rosenberg, B., 222
Rosenzweig, M. R., 365
Royden, H. L., 19, 117
Rubin, D. B., 375
Rubin, H., 235
Ruppert, D., 78, 154, 202
Ryzhik, I. M., 474

Sahay, S. N., 242
Sant, D. T., 242
Sargent, T. J., 77, 141
Savin, N. E., 145, 280
Sawa, T., 53–54, 240, 470
Schatzoff, M., 66
Scheffe, H., 30
Schlossmacher, E. J., 78
Schmee, J., 378
Schmidt, P., 37, 317, 319, 380, 381
Schwartz, G., 79, 466
Sclove, S. L., 60, 64, 67, 68, 466
Scott, E. L., 120, 155
Segun, I. A., 193
Shapiro, H., 252
Shapiro, P., 293, 294, 471
Shiller, R. J., 178
Shorrocks, A. F., 418, 420
Sickles, R., 37
Silberman, J. I., 293, 312
Silvey, S. D., 142, 466
Singer, B., 412, 474
Sinha, B. K., 279
Small, K. A., 304, 306
Smith, H., 137
Smith, K. C., 280
Smith, V. K., 470
Sneeringer, C., 285
Solow, R. M., 128
Sorbom, D., 217
Sowden, R. R., 317
Sparmann, J. M., 309
Spiegelman, R. G., 365
Spitzer, J. J., 252
Srivastava, V. K., 198
Stapleton, D. C., 472
Stein, C., 56, 61–62, 470
Stephan, S. W., 218, 219, 220
Stephenson, S. P., 365
Stigler, S. M., 71, 75
Strawderman, W. E., 65
Strickland, A. D., 470
Strotz, R. H., 229
Stuart, A., 36
Subramanyam, K., 125, 279
Swamy, P. A. V. B., 218, 221, 242
Szego, G., 161

Talley, W. K., 293
Taylor, W. E., 189, 201, 213, 217, 218, 238, 239
Taylor, W. F., 125, 470
Telser, L. G., 431
Theil, H., 6, 24, 25, 49, 236, 239, 241
Thisted, R. A., 64, 66, 466
Tiao, G. C., 465
Tobin, J., 360, 361, 363, 364, 374, 472
Toikka, R. S., 429, 430, 473
Tomes, N., 396, 398
Toyoda, T., 37
Trost, R. P., 392, 394, 396, 397, 404
Trotter, H. F., 138
Tsiatis, A. A., 450
Tsurumi, H., 470
Tukey, J. W., 72, 73, 75
Tuma, N. B., 444, 474

Uhler, R. S., 300

Van Nostrand, R. C., 466
Vinod, H. D., 67

Wald, A., 28, 87, 88, 89, 118, 142
Wales, T. J., 128, 373, 375, 390, 472, 473
Walker, S. H., 275
Wallace, T. D., 210
Wallis, K. F., 178
Warner, S. L., 282, 283
Watson, G. S., 191, 192, 193, 194, 225
Wedderburn, R. W. M., 203
Wei, C. Z., 467
Weiss, Y., 216, 470
Welch, B. L., 36
Wermuth, N., 66
West, R. W., 365
Westin, R. B., 285, 286, 389
White, H., 117, 148, 199, 200, 370, 465
White, K. J., 252
Whittle, P., 159, 167, 171, 177
Wiggins, S. N., 365

Willis, R. J., 216, 348, 349, 350, 351, 353, 404, 405
Wilson, S., 284
Wise, D. A., 308, 309, 310, 395
Witte, A. D., 365
Wolfowitz, J., 331, 346, 347
Woodland, A. D., 373, 375, 390, 472, 473
Wu, C. F. J., 375
Wu, D., 388

Young, D. J., 472

Zacks, S., 46, 138, 465
Zarembka, P., 251, 252
Zellner, A., 24, 49, 197, 241, 246, 465

Subject Index

Absorbing state, 421
Admissible, 47, 48
Akaike Information Criterion (AIC): as solution to general model selection problem, 146-147; as solution to problem of selecting regressors, 52; in choosing optimal significance level, 54-55; in qualitative response model, 280-281, 313
Almon lag model, 178-179
Almost sure convergence, 86
Almost surely uniform convergence, 106
α-trimmed mean, 71, 73, 78
Amemiya's least squares and generalized least squares, 393
Asymptotic bias, 95
Asymptotic distribution, 92
Asymptotic efficiency, 123-125
Asymptotic expectation: definition, 94; relationship with limit of expectation and probability limit, 93-95
Asymptotic *F*-test, 37, 38
Asymptotic likelihood ratio test, 37-38
Asymptotic mean. *See* Asymptotic expectation
Asymptotically normal, 92
Asymptotically unbiased, 95
Autocovariance: definition, 160; derivation in first-order autoregressive (AR(1)) model, 163; derivation in second-order autoregressive (AR(2)) model, 165-166; spectral density as Fourier transform of, 160. *See also* Autocovariance matrix
Autocovariance matrix: characteristic roots, 161, 169; general form, 160; in first-order autoregressive (AR(1)) model, 163-164; in second-order autoregressive (AR(2)) model, 166-167; in *p*th order autoregressive (AR(p)) model, 167; relationship between that of moving-average model and that of autoregressive model, 171-172
Autoregressive integrated moving-average (ARIMA) process, 172
Autoregressive model
First-order (AR(1)): asymptotic normality of least squares estimator in, 174-175; autocovariance matrix of, 163-164; consistency of least squares estimator in, 173-174; definition, 162; maximum likelihood estimators of parameters, 175-176; optimal predictor in, 177; spectral density of, 164
*p*th order (AR(p)): autocovariance matrix of, 167; definition, 167; least squares estimators of parameters, 172-173; moving-average representation of, 167-168; properites of, 167-170
Second-order (AR(2)): autocovariance matrix of, 165-167; definition, 164
Autoregressive model with moving-average residuals (ARMA(p,q)): definition, 170; optimal predictor in, 177; spectral density of, 170

Balestra-Nerlove model, 215-216
Bayes estimator: generalized, 48; in classical linear regression model, 24-26; proper, 47, 48
Bayes's rule, 24, 48, 321
Bayesian statistics, 23-24, 47, 48-49, 456
Behrens-Fisher problem, 36
Berkson's minimum chi-square (MIN χ^2) estimator
In binary qualitative response model: asymptotic distribution of, 276-277; chi-square tests based on, 280-281; comparison with maximum likelihood estimator, 278-279; definition, 276; inconsistency of, 278
In first-order Markov model, 415

Berkson's minimum chi-square (MIN χ^2) estimator *(continued)*
In multinomial qualitative response model: asymptotic distribution of, 291; definition, 290-291; in the Deacon-Shapiro model, 294-295
In two-state Markov model with exogenous variables, 423-424
Best asymptotically normal (BAN) estimators, 124-125
Best linear predictor, 3
Best linear unbiased estimator (BLUE): constrained least squares as, 21, 23; least squares as, 4, 11-13
Best nonlinear three-stage least squares (BNL3S) estimator: comparison with nonlinear full information (NLFI) maximum likelihood estimator, 259, 261; computation of, 258; definition, 257-258
Best nonlinear two-stage least squares (BNL2S) estimator: asymptotic inferiority to NLLI maximum likelihood estimator, 252, 254–255; computation of, 249; definition, 248
Best predictor, 3, 39
Best unbiased estimator, 13, 17-20
Beta-logistic model, 350-351
Better (Best) estimator, 8-11, 40
Bootstrap method, 135
Borel field, 83
Borel measurable, 84, 467
Borel sets, 83
Box-Cox maximum likelihood estimator, 250-252
Box-Cox transformation: applications, 141, 252; definition, 249; nonlinear two-stage least squares (N2LS) estimator in, 250

Categorical models. *See* Qualitative response models
Cauchy distribution, 70, 94, 383
Cauchy-Schwartz inequality: applications, 98, 130; generalized, 326
Censored regression models, 360, 364. *See also* Tobit models
Censoring in duration models: left-, 447-448; right-, 434
Central limit theorems (CLT): for *K*-dependent sequence, 175; Liapounov's, 92; Lindeberg-Feller's, 92; Lindeberg-Levy's, 91
Champernowne process, 420
Characteristic function, 91, 149
Characteristic root, 459
Characteristic vector, 459
Chebyshev's inequality, 86-87
Chi-square distribution, 463
Choice-based sampling, 320, 325-327, 331-332, 338
Choice-based sampling maximum likelihood estimator (CBMLE): relationship with random sampling maximum likelihood estimator (RSMLE), 321-322; case where the density *f* of the independent variables is known and the selection probability *Q* is known, 329; case where *f* is known and *Q* is unknown, 330; case where *f* is unknown and *Q* is known, 337-338; case where *f* is unknown and *Q* is unknown, 333-337
Manski-Lerman weighted maximum likelihood estimator (WMLE): asymptotic normality of, 324-325; consistency of, 323-324; definition, 322-323; modification of, 327-328
Manski-McFadden estimator (MME): alternative interpretation of, 336; asymptotic normality of, 331; consistency of, 330-331; definition, 330
Clark's approximation, 309
Classical linear regression model: assumption of normality, 13, 27; definition, 2; with linear constraints, 20-26; with stochastic constraints, 23-26
Cochrane-Orcutt transformation, 189-190
Concentrated likelihood function, 125-127
Conditional likelihood function: definition, 474; in Nerlove-Press model, 317; in nested logit model, 303
Conditional mean squared prediction error, 11, 39, 40
Conjugate gradient method, 141
Consistency, 95
Constrained least squares (CLS) estimator: as best linear unbiased estimator (BLUE), 23; definition, 21-22; in Almon lag model, 179; relationship with Bayes estimator under stochastic constraints, 25-26

Convergence, modes of: almost sure, 86; almost surely uniform, 106; in distribution, 85; in mean square, 85; in probability, 85; in probability in the generalized sense, 340; in probability uniformly, 106; in probability semi-uniformly, 106; logical relationship among, 86; theorems concerning, 86-89
Covariance estimator. *See* Transformation estimator
Covariance matrix of error terms, 185, 186
Cox's partial maximum likelihood estimator (PMLE): as maximization of the joint density of order statistics, 451-452; asymptotic distribution of, 450, 453-455; definition, 449; intuitive motivation of, 450-451
Cox's test: definition, 147-148; in multivariate qualitative response model, 319
Cramér-Rao lower bound: applicability asymptotically, 123-124; for regression coefficients, 17-19; for residual variance, 18, 19-20; general theorem on, 14-17; generalization of, 336-337
Cumulants, 91

Decision theory. *See* Statistical decision theory
Dependent variables. *See* Endogenous variables
Determinant as a criterion for ranking estimators, 10-11
DFP iteration: definition, 138; in nonlinear simultaneous equations model, 264
Diffuse natural conjugate, 49
Discrete models. *See* Qualitative response models
Discriminant analysis: in binary qualitative response model, 281, 282-285; in multinominal qualitative response model, 299-300
Disequilibrium models, 361, 402-403
Distributed lag models: Almon, 178-179; definition, 177-178; geometric, 178
Disturbance. *See* Error term
Dummy variable regression. *See* Transformation estimator
Duration, 428, 434-435
Duration dependence, 445-446. *See also* State dependence
Duration models
  Nonstationary (semi-Markov): applications, 444-447; definition, 442; heterogeneity in, 445-446; left-censoring in, 447-448; proportional hazards form of, 449-455
  Stationary: definition, 433-434; duration as dependent variable of regression in, 438-440; maximum likelihood estimates of parameters of, 437-438; relationship to standard Tobit model, 435; relationship with Poisson distribution, 436; right-censoring in, 434; when observations are discrete, 440-442
Durbin's test: definition, 196-197; equivalence with Rao's score test, 469
Durbin-Watson test: asymptotic distribution of test statistic, 191; definition, 191; exact distribution of test statistic, 191-193; lower and upper bounds for, 193-194; when lagged endogenous variables are present, 195-196

Edgeworth expansion, 93, 135, 173
Efficient. *See* Better (Best) estimator
EM algorithm: definition and convergence properties, 375-376; in Tobit model, 376-378
Empirical Bayes method, 60-61
Empirical distribution function, 118, 135
Endogenous sampling. *See* Choice-based sampling
Endogenous variables, 2
Enriched samples, 332
Equilibrium probabilities: definition, 415-416; in Boskin-Nold model, 424-425
Error components model
  Three-error components model (3ECM): asymptotic properties of LS and GLS in, 209; definition, 208; definition and properties of transformation estimator in, 209-211; estimation of variances in, 211
  Two-error components model (2ECM): as between-group and within-group regression equations, 212-213; definition, 211-212; definition of GLS estimator in, 213; definition of transformation estimator in, 212; maximum likelihood estimation of,

Error components model *(continued)*
213-214; with endogenous regressors, 217-218; with serially correlated error, 216-217
See also Balestra-Nerlove model
Error rate, 284
Error term: additive versus multiplicative, 128, 468; assumptions on density function of, 152; constant variance (homoscedasticity) 2, 127; normality, 2-3, 13, 129; serial correlation, 128; serial independence, 2-3, 13
Estimable, 58
Exogenous sampling, 320
Exogenous sampling maximum likelihood estimator (ESMLE): definition, 321-322; inconsistency in choice-based sampling model, 324
Exogenous variables, 2
Exponential family density, 124-125, 203, 279
Extremum estimators: asymptotic normality of, 105, 111-112, 114; consistency of, 106-111, 114; definition, 105

F-distribution, 464
F-test, 28-31, 32-35, 38, 136-137, 184
Feasible generalized least squares (FGLS) estimator, 186
In linear regression model with heteroscedasticity: as a BAN estimator, in case of general parametric heteroscedasticity, 202-203; definition, in case of constant variance in subset of sample, 200; definition, in case of unrestricted heteroscedasticity, 199; definition, when variance is a linear function of regressors, 206; exact distribution, in case of constant variance in subset of sample, 201-202
In linear regression model with serial correlation: asymptotic deviation from GLS in case of lagged endogenous variables, 194-195; asymptotic equivalence with GLS, 189; Cochrane-Orcutt transformation as procedure for calculating, 189-190; efficiency relative to least squares, 189
In Markov model when only aggregate data are available, 431
In seemingly unrelated regression (SUR) model, 198
In Toikka's three-state Markov model, 429-430
In three-error components model, 211
In two-error components model, 212, 213
Iterated, 186
See also Generalized least squares (GLS) estimator
Fixed effects estimator. *See* Transformation estimator
Fourier transform, 160
Full information maximum likelihood (FIML) estimator: asymptotic equivalence with 3SLS estimator, 242; asymptotic normality, 233-234; consistency, 231-233; definition, 231-232; instrumental variables interpretation of, 233-234

Gauss-Markov theorem, 11. *See also* Best linear unbiased estimator
Gauss-Newton method: definition, 139, 140; for obtaining BNL3S estimator, 261; for obtaining NL2S estimator, 470; Hartley's algorithm, 140-141; Marquardt's algorithm, 140; second round estimator, 139-140, 141
Generalized Bayes estimator, 48
Generalized classical linear estimator. *See* Two-stage least squares (2SLS) estimator
Generalized extreme value (GEV) distribution, 306
Generalized extreme value (GEV) model, 306-307
Generalized least squares (GLS) estimator: as best linear unbiased estimator (BLUE), 182; definition, in case of known, positive definite covariance matrix, 181-182; definition, in case of singular covariance matrix, 185; examples of equivalence with least squares, 182-184; in linear regression model with unknown covariance matrix, 197, 199; in three-error components model, 210-211; in two-error components model, 212-213. *See also* Feasible generalized least squares (FGLS) estimator; Partially generalized least squares (PGLS) estimator
Generalized maximum likelihood estimator, 339, 346-348
Generalized ridge estimators, 61-66
Generalized two-stage least squares (G2SLS) estimator, 240-241

Generalized Wald test: definition, 145; in nonlinear simultaneous equations model, 261-262
Geometric lag model, 178
Goldfeld-Quandt estimator, 204-205, 206
Goldfeld-Quandt peak test for homoscedasticity, 207
Goodness of fit. *See* R^2
Gumbel's type B bivariate extreme value distribution, 300

Hadamard product, 462
Hausman's specification test: as test for independence of irrelevant alternatives (IIA), 299, 302; as test for normality in Tobit model, 381; asymptotic properties of, 145-146; in nonlinear simultaneous equations model, 265
Hazard rate: in duration model, 435; in Tobit model, 472
Heckman's two-step estimator: in standard Tobit model, 367-372; in Type 2 Tobit model, 386-387; in Type 3 Tobit model, 390, 392-393; in Type 4 Tobit model, 396; in Type 5 Tobit model, 402
Heterogeneity: in duration model, 445, 446-447; in Markov model, 414; in panel data qualitative response model, 349, 350-353. *See also* Mover-stayer model
Heteroscedasticity: constant variance in a subset of the sample, 200-202; definition, 198; general parametric, 202-203; in standard Tobit model, 378, 379-380; tests for, 200, 201, 203, 206-207; unrestricted, 198-200; variance as an exponential function of the regressors, 207; variance as a linear function of regressors, 204-207
Hildreth-Houck estimator in a heteroscedastic regression model: definition, 204, 205, 206; modifications, 205-206, 469
Hölder's inequality, 19
Homoscedasticity, 2

Idempotent, 460
Identification: in a linear simultaneous equations model, 230; in a nonlinear simultaneous equations model, 256
Incidental parameters. *See* Nuisance parameters
Independence of irrelevant alternatives (IIA): as characteristic of multinomial logit model, 298-299; nested multinomial logit model as correction for, 300, 302; tests for, 299, 302
Independent variables. *See* Exogenous variables
Information matrix, 16
Initial conditions: in Balestra-Nerlove model, 215, 216; in first-order autoregressive (AR(1)) model, 163; in Markov chain model, 413-414; in panel data qualitative response model, 352, 353-354; in two-error components model with serially correlated error, 216, 217
Instrumental variables (IV) estimator: definition, 11-12; FIML estimator as, 223-224; G2SLS estimator as, 241; in two-error components model with endogenous regressors, 217-218; two-stage least squares as asymptotically best, 239-240
Iterative methods. *See* EM algorithm; Gauss-Newton method; Method of scoring; Newton-Raphson method

Jackknife estimator, 135-136
Jackknife method, 135-136
Jensen's inequality, 116
Jordan canonical form, 459

Khinchine's weak law of large numbers (WLLN), 102
Kolmogorov laws of large numbers (LLN), 90
Koyck lag model, 178
Kronecker product, 462

L estimators, 73-74, 77-78
L_p estimators, 72, 73, 77
Lag operator, 162
Lagrange multiplier test. *See* Score test
Lagrangian interpolation polynomial, 469
Laplace distribution, 70
Laws of large numbers (LLN): Khinchine's, 102; Kolmogorov's number 1 and number 2, 90; Markov's, 467; strong, 90; weak, 90
Least absolute deviations (LAD) estimator: in classical regression model, 152-154; in standard Tobit model, 382-383. *See also* Median
Least squares (LS) estimator
In autoregressive model: asymptotic

Least squares (LS) estimator *(continued)*
normality in first-order case, 174-175; asymptotic normality in *p*th order case, 173; consistency in first-order case, 173-174; small sample properties, 173
In classical linear regression model: as best linear unbiased estimator (BLUE), 11-13; as best unbiased estimator under normality of error terms, 17-20; asymptotic normality of, 96-98, 99; consistency of, 95-96; definition, 4-5; equivalence under normality of, with maximum likelihood estimator (MLE), 13; geometric interpretation of, 5-6; mean and variance of, 7-8; of a linear combination of regression parameters, 7, 58; of a subset of regression parameters, 6-7; unbiased alternative to estimate of variance of error terms, 8
In duration model with one completed spell per individual, 439
In geometric lag model, 178
In linear regression model with general covariance matrix of error terms: asymptotic normality in case of known covariance matrix, 185; asymptotic normality in case of serial correlation, 187-188; consistency, 184-185; covariance matrix, 182; examples of equivalence with GLS, 183-184; inconsistency in presence of lagged endogenous variables and serial correlation, 194; relative efficiency as compared with GLS, 182-183
In Markov model when only aggregate data are available, 431
In standard Tobit model: biasedness when all observations used, 367-368; biasedness when positive observations used, 367
In Toikka's three-state Markov model, 429, 430
See also Constrained least squares (CLS) estimator; Generalized least squares (GLS) estimator.
Least squares predictor, 39-40
Least squares residuals, 5, 21, 32-33
Lebesgue convergence theorem, 117
Lebesgue measure, 83, 106, 113, 124, 467
Lebesgue-Stieltjes integral, 467
Liapounov central limit theorem (CLT), 90-91, 92
Likelihood function. *See* Concentrated likelihood function; Conditional likelihood function; Maximum likelihood estimator (MLE)
Likelihood ratio test
As test for homoscedasticity, 201
In nonlinear regression model, 144, 145
Under general parametric hypotheses: asymptotic distribution of, 142-144; definition, 142; small sample properties of, 145
Under linear hypotheses on a linear model: definition, 28-32, 32-34, 38; relationship with Wald test and score test, 144-145
Limit distribution, 85, 92
Limited dependent variables model. *See* Tobit model
Limited information maximum likelihood (LIML) estimator: asymptotic distribution, 237-238; asymptotic equivalence with 2SLS estimator, 236, 238; definition, 235-236; exact distribution, 238-239; Fuller's modification, 238
Limited information model, 234-235
Linear regression model, with general covariance matrix of error terms, 184
Linear simultaneous equations model, 228-229
Lindeberg-Feller central limit theorem (CLT), 90-91, 92
Lindeberg-Levy central limit theorem (CLT), 90-92
Linear constraints: as testable hypotheses, 27; form of, 20; stochastic, 23-24
Logistic distribution: Gumbel's bivariate, 319; Plackett's bivariate, 319; relationship with normal distribution, 269
Logit model
Binary: definition, 268-269; global concavity of likelihood function, 273
Multinomial: as result of utility-maximizing behavior, 296-297; definition, 295; global concavity of likelihood function, 295-296; independence of irrelevant alternatives (IIA) in, 298

Logit model *(continued)*
Multivariate: definition, 314; fundamental difference between multivariate probit model and, 318
Multivariate nested, 313-314
Nested: definition, 300-302, 303; estimation, 303-304; multiple-level forms, 305-306
Ordered, 292-293
Sequential, 310
Universal, 307
Logit transformation, 278
Log-linear model: definition, 314, 315; estimation of, 317; saturated, 315; unsaturated, 315
Log Weibull distribution, 296

M estimators, 72-73, 75-77, 105. *See also* Extremum estimators
Mallow's criterion: definition, 52; optimal critical value of *F*-test implied by, 55
Markov chain model: definition, 412-413; duration in, 428; estimation of, when only aggregate data are available, 430-433; homogeneous, 414; hypotheses tests in, 417; maximum likelihood estimates of parameters, 417, 422; minimum chi-square (MIN χ^2) estimates of parameters of, 415, 423-424; mover-stayer model, 418; multi-state (Toikka's model), 428-430; nonlinear generalized least squares estimates of parameters, 414-415; second-order model, 420; stationary, 414; two-state (Boskin-Nold model), 421-428
Markov matrix, 413
Markov's law of large numbers (LLN), 467
Maximum likelihood estimator (MLE): asymptotic efficiency, 123-124; asymptotic normality, 120-121; consistency, 115-116, 118; definition, 115; in autoregressive moving average model (ARMA (p,q)) model, 172; in Balestra-Nerlove model, 216; in binary qualitative response model, 271-273, 274-275, 278-279; in Boskin-Nold model, 425-427; in classical linear regression model, 13-14, 17-19, 21, 37-38, 118-119, 121-123; in duration model, 437-439; in first-order autoregressive (AR(1)) model, 175-176; in homogeneous and stationary first-order Markov model, 417; in Hsiao's random coefficients model, 220-221; in linear regression model with general parametric heteroscedasticity, 202-203; in linear regression model with serial correlation, 190-191; in Markov model when only aggregate data are available, 433; in multinomial qualitative response model, 287, 288-289; in two-error components model, 213-214; in two-state Markov model with exogenous variables, 422, 424; inconsistency in certain models, 120; iterative methods for obtaining, 137-139; second-order efficiency, 124-125, 279; under constraints on the parameters, 142. *See also* Box-Cox maximum likelihood estimator; Choice-based sampling; Cox's partial maximum likelihood estimator (PMLE); Exogenous sampling maximum likelihood estimator; Full information maximum likelihood (FIML) estimator; Generalized maximum likelihood estimator in qualitative response model; Limited information maximum likelihood (LIML) estimator; Nonlinear full information (NLFI) maximum likelihood estimator; Nonlinear limited information (NLLI) maximum likelihood estimator; Probit maximum likelihood estimator; Random-effect probit maximum likelihood estimator; Random sampling maximum likelihood estimator (RSMLE); Tobit maximum likelihood estimator
Maximum score estimator: consistency, 340-343, 344-345; definition, 339, 343-344; relationship with generalized maximum likelihood estimator, 347-348
Mean squared error, 8, 40
Measurable function, 467
Measure, 467
Measure space, 467
Median
Population, 148
Sample: asymptotic normality, 149-151; asymptotic variance under normal, Laplace, and Cauchy distributions, 70-71; consistency, 150; definition, 70, 73, 149. *See also* Least absolute deviations (LAD) estimator

Method of scoring: conditions for equivalence with Gauss-Newton method, 203; definition, 138; equivalence with nonlinear weighted least squares (NLWLS) iteration, 274-275, 289-290; in random coefficients model, 221; when variance is linear function of regressors, 206
Mills' ratio, 472
Minimax estimator, 47, 48
Minimax regret, 47
Minimini principle, 51
Minimum chi-square (MIN χ^2) method, 275. *See also* Berkson's minimum chi-square (MIN χ^2) estimator
MINQUE, 469
Mixed estimator under stochastic constraints, 25
Mixture of normal distributions, 72, 77, 119-120
Model selection problem, 146
Modified nonlinear two-stage least squares (MN2LS) estimator: definition, 254; inconsistency when normality fails to hold, 255
Moore-Penrose generalized inverse, 112, 466
Mover-stayer model, 418-419
Moving-average (MA) models: autocovariance matrix of, 171; first-order (MA(1)), 171-172; spectral density of, 170-171
Multicollinearity, 56, 59

Newton-Raphson method: applications, 141; as method of calculating FIML estimator, 234; definition, 137; DFP iteration, 138; for obtaining NLFI maximum likelihood estimator, 264; method of scoring as means of finding MLE, 138; quadratic hill-climbing, 138; second-round estimator, 137, 139
Nonlinear full information (NLFI) maximum likelihood estimator: asymptotic properties, 259, 261; definition, 259; inconsistency when error terms are not normal, 259-260; iterative method, 260-261
Nonlinear generalized least squares (NLGLS) estimator: in first-order Markov model, 415; in Markov model when only aggregate data are available, 431. *See also* Nonlinear weighted least squares (NLWLS) estimator
Nonlinear least squares (NLLS) estimator: asymptotic normality of, 132-134; consistency of, 129-130; definition, 127-129; equivalence of, with MLE under normality, 129; in Markov model when only aggregate data are available, 431, 433; in standard Tobit model, 372-373, 378; inconsistency in nonlinear simultaneous equations model, 245; under general parametric constraints, 144; under linear constraints, 136-137
Nonlinear limited information (NLLI) maximum likelihood estimator: asymptotic covariance matrix of, 254; definition, 252-254; inconsistency of, when normality fails to hold, 255; iterative methods for solving for, 254
Nonlinear regression model, 127-128
Nonlinear simultaneous equations models: full information case, 255-256; limited information case, 252-253
Nonlinear three-stage least squares (NL3S) estimator: asymptotic normality of, 257; consistency of, 257; definition (Amemiya), 257; definition (Jorgenson and Laffont), 257. *See also* Best nonlinear three-stage least squares (BNL3S) estimator
Nonlinear two-stage least squares (NL2S) estimator: asymptotic normality, 247-248; consistency, 246-247; definition, 246, 250; in case of Box-Cox transformation, 250, 251-252. *See also* Best nonlinear two-stage least squares (BNL2S) estimator; Modified nonlinear two-stage least squares (MNL2S) estimator
Nonlinear weighted least squares (NLWLS) estimator: in binary qualitative response model, 274-275; in duration model with one completed spell per individual, 440; in Markov model when only aggregate data are available, 432, 433; in multinomial qualitative response model, 289-290; in multi-state Markov model with exogenous variables, 428-429; in standard Tobit model, 372-373, 472; in two-state Markov model with exogenous variables, 423. *See also* Method of scoring
Nonnested models, 147-148
Nonnormality: in standard Tobit model, 378, 380-382, 383; robust estimation under, 70-71

Normal discriminant analysis. *See* Discriminant analysis
Nuisance parameters, 120

Odds ratio: in Bayesian solution to selection-of-regressors problem, 48-49; in binary logit model, 278
One-factor model in panel data qualitative response model: definition, 352-353; random-effect probit maximum likelihood estimator in, 354; transformation estimator in, 353-354
Optimal significance level, 52-55
Order condition of identifiability, 230-231
Order relationship, 90-91
Overidentification, 231

Panel data qualitative response model: definition, 348; heterogeneity, 349-353; one-factor, 352-354; specification of initial conditions, 352, 353-354; true state dependence, 349, 351-353
Parke's derivative free algorithm, 264
Partially generalized least squares (PGLS) estimator, 199-200
Posterior distribution, 24
Posterior probability, 48
Posterior risk, 47
Prediction
- In classical linear regression model: best linear predictor, 3; best predictor, 3, 39; conditional mean squared prediction error, 39, 40; least squares as best linear unbiased predictor, 39-40; unconditional mean squared prediction error, 40
- In nonlinear simultaneous equations model, 262-264
- In time series model, 177

Prediction criterion: definition, 51; optimal critical value of F-test implied by, 54, 55
Pre-test estimator, 67
Principal components, 58
Principal components estimator, 58-60
Probability measure, 82
Probability of correct classification (PCC), 284
Probability space, 82
Probit maximum likelihood estimator: in binary qualitative response model, 271, 273-274; in multinomial qualitative response model, 307-310; in multivariate qualitative response model, 317-318; in Tobit model, 366, 386. *See also* Probit model
Probit model
- Binary: definition, 268, 269; global concavity of likelihood function, 273-274
- Multinomial: definition, 307-308; independent versus nonindependent, 308; iterative methods for calculating estimators in, 309
- Multivariate: definition, 317, 318; fundamental difference between multinomial logit model and, 318
- Ordered, 292-293
- Sequential, 310

Probit transformation, 277
Projection matrix, 14
Proportional hazards model, 449-455

Quadratic hill-climbing, 138
Qualitative response models, 267
- Binary: definition, 268; hypotheses tests, 280-282; prediction of aggregate proportion, 285-286
- Multinomial: definition, 287; hypotheses tests, 291-292; ordered, 292-293; unordered, 292, 293
- Multivariate, 311

Quantal response models. *See* Qualitative response models

R estimators, 74, 78-79
R^2: definition, 6; test for equality with zero, 31; Theil's correction, 49-51, 54, 55; weakness, 46
Random coefficients models (RCM's): Hildreth-Houck and error components models as special cases of, 204, 218; Hsiao's model, 220-221; Kelejian and Stephan model, 218-220; Swamy-Mehta model, 221-222; Swamy's model, 221; varying parameter regression model, 222
Random-effect probit maximum likelihood estimator, 354
Random sampling maximum likelihood estimator (RSMLE), 321-322, 329
Random variables, 81, 83
Rank condition of identifiability, 230

Rao's score test. *See* Score test
Reduced form equations, 229
Regret, 47
Reverse least squares estimator, 42, 99-101
Ridge regression: generalized ridge estimators, 63-66; relationship with empirical Bayes method, 60–61; relationship with Stein-type estimators, 56; ridge estimators, 60-66; ridge trace method, 60
Riemann integal, 84
Riemann-Stieltjes integral, 84-85
Risk, 47
Robust estimation: concept of, 70-72; in regression case, 75-79; L estimator, 73-74, 77-78; L_p estimator, 73, 77; M estimator, 72-73, 75-77, 105; median, 70-71, 73, 148-151; R estimator, 74, 78-79; trimmed mean, 73, 78; Winsorized mean, 73. *See also* Least absolute deviations (LAD) estimator

Sample space, 81-82
Schwartz's criterion, 79
Score function, 339
Score test: as test for homoscedasticity, 206-207; asymptotic distribution in general case, 142, 144; asymptotic distribution in nonlinear simultaneous equations model, 145; definition, 142; equivalence with Durbin's test, 469; in linear model with linear constraint, 144-145; in nonlinear regression model with normality, 144; relationship with Lagrange multiplier test, 142
Second-order efficiency of maximum likelihood estimator, 125. *See also* Best asymptotically normal (BAN) estimator
Seemingly unrelated regression (SUR) model, 197-198
Selection of regressors: Bayesian solution, 48-49; selection among nested models, 45, 52-55; selection among nonnested models, 46-52
Separate families of hypotheses, 147
Serial correlation of error terms: as first-order autoregressive (AR(1)) process, 188-195; definition, 186; in linear regression model with lagged endogenous variables, 194-197; properties of least squares (LS) estimator in case of, 184-185, 187-188
σ-algebra, 82
Spectral density: conditions for existence and continuity, 169; definition, 160-161; of autoregressive moving average (ARMA (p,q)) process, 170; relationship between that of moving-average model and that of autoregressive model, 170-171; relationship with characteristic roots of autocovariance matrix, 161
Standard linear regression model. *See* Classical linear regression model
State dependence, 349, 351. *See also* Duration dependence
Stationary time series: as infinite sum of cycles with random coefficients, 161; definition (strictly), 159; definition (weakly), 159
Statistical decision theory, 46-48
Stein's estimator, 61-62
Stein's modified estimator, 63
Stein's positive rule estimator, 63
Stieltjes integral, 84-85, 467
Stochastic order relationship. *See* Order relationship
Stratified sampling, 471
Strictly stationary time series, 159
Strong convergence, 467. *See also* Almost sure convergence
Strong laws of large numbers (LLN), 90
Strongly consistent, 95
Structural change, tests for, 31-35, 36-38
Structural equations, 229
Student's *t* distribution, 463
Superefficient estimators, 124
Survival models. *See* Duration models
Switching regression model, 120, 411

t-test, 27-28, 34-35, 36-37, 136, 184, 465
Test for equality of variances, 35. *See also* Heteroscedasticity
Tests of general parametric hypotheses: generalized Wald statistic, 145; Hausman's specification test, 146-147; likelihood ratio test, 142-145; score test, 142, 144-145; Wald test, 142-145
Tests of linear hypotheses: *F*-test (likelihood ratio test), 28-31, 32-34, 184, 465; generalization of *F*-test to nonlinear model, 136-137; generalization of *t*-test to nonlinear model, 136; *t*-test, 27-28, 34-35,

Tests of linear hypotheses *(continued)* 36-37, 184, 465; tests for structural change, 31-35, 36-38
Theil's corrected R^2: appraisal of, 49-51, 55; optimal critical value of F-test implied by, 54
Three-stage least squares (3SLS) estimator, 241-242. *See also* Nonlinear three stage least squares (NL3S) estimator
Tobit maximum likelihood estimator: as an equilibrium solution of the EM algorithm, 376-378; asymptotic properties, 373; consistency under serial correlation, 380; definition, 373; global concavity of likelihood function, 373-374; inconsistency under heteroscedasticity, 379-380; inconsistency under nonnormality, 380-381
Tobit model: Amemiya's consistent estimator, 374-375; applications, 364, 365, 387-389, 391-392, 394-395, 397-399, 400-408; as result of utility maximizing behavior, 362; classifications, 383-384; consistency of estimators under serial correlation, 378-379, 380; definition, 360; disequilibrium models, 402-403; general simultaneous equations forms, 385, 392-393, 396-397; global concavity of likelihood function, 373-374; inconsistency of estimators, 378-381; tests for nonnormality, 381-382; Tobin's initial estimator, 373. *See also* Heckman's two-step estimator; Least absolute deviations (LAD) estimator; Least squares (LS) estimator; Nonlinear least squares (NLLS) estimator; Nonlinear weighted least squares (NLWLS) estimator; Probit maximum likelihood estimator; Tobit maximum likelihood estimator
Toeplitz form, 160
Trace, as a criterion for ranking estimators, 10, 11
Transformation estimator: in Balestra-Nerlove model, 215-216; in discrete case, 353-354; in Hsiao's random coefficients model, 220; in three-error components model, 209-211; in two-error components model, 212-213
Transition probabilities, 413
Truncated regression model, 360, 364. *See also* Tobit models
Two-stage least squares (2SLS) estimator: asymptotic distribution, 236-237; asymptotic equivalence with LIML estimator, 238; definition, 236; exact distribution, 238-239; interpretations, 239-240. *See also* Generalized two-stage least squares (G2SLS) estimator; Nonlinear two-stage least squares (N2SLS) estimator
Two-step method of estimation: in multivariate nested logit model, 303-304; in nested logit model, 314. *See also* Heckman's two-step estimator
Type I extreme value distribution, 296

Unconditional mean squared prediction error, 40
Underidentification, 231
Uniform convergence of a sequence of random variables: almost surely uniform, 106; in probability semi-uniformly, 106; in probability uniformly, 106
Uniformly smaller risk, 47

Wald's test: asymptotic distribution in nonlinear simultaneous equations model, 145; asymptotic distribution, 142, 144; definition, 142; in linear model with linear constraints, 144-145; in nonlinear regression model with normality, 144
Weak convergence, 467. *See also* Consistency; Convergence in probability
Weak laws of large numbers (LLN), 90
Weakly consistent, 95
Weakly stationary time series, 159
Weibull distribution, 445
Weighted least squares (WLS) estimator, 371-372. *See also* Feasible generalized least squares (FGLS) estimator; Generalized least squares (GLS) estimator; Nonlinear weighted least squares (NLWLS) estimator
Welch's method, 36-37
Winsorized mean, 73